T0408758

WORLD WAR II ENCYCLOPEDIA OF AIRCRAFT, TANKS & WARSHIPS

WORLD WAR II ENCYCLOPEDIA OF AIRCRAFT, TANKS & WARSHIPS

CHRIS MCNAB

amber
BOOKS

First published in 2025

Published by
Amber Books Ltd
United House
North Road
London N7 9DP
United Kingdom

www.amberbooks.co.uk
Facebook: amberbooks
YouTube: amberbooksltd
Instagram: amberbooksltd
X(Twitter): @amberbooks

ISBN: 978-1-83886-497-2

Project Editor: Michael Spilling
Designers: Lewis Hughes-Batley and Mark Batley
Design assistance: Cecilia Valsecchi
Picture Research: Terry Forshaw

Printed in China

Contents

Introduction

World War II created an arms race of ultimate consequence. Between 1939 and 1945, the warring nations not only focused their attention upon the mass production of armaments, they also sought out innovations that might give them the decisive edge on the global battlefield.

ABOVE:
USS *Intrepid* was one of 24 Essex-class aircraft carriers built for the US Navy during and after World War II. By the end of the war, the United States was the world's preeminent naval power, with more than a hundred carriers in service across four oceans.

NEW TECHNOLOGY

Just over two decades before Hitler's armies rolled across the borders of Poland, the guns fell silent on another global conflict. World War I has been described as history's first true industrial war, in which the volume and effects of advanced weaponry shaped battlefield outcomes as much as the individual warriors using it.

Certainly, the conflict is today recognised for its grim new efficiency in killing, courtesy of tools of violence such as belt-fed automatic machines guns, breech-loading artillery with hydro-pneumatic recoil systems, poison gas, lumbering tanks, big-gun dreadnought battleships, combat submarines and the first generations of aerial fighters and bombers. But in many ways, World War I remained an infantry conflict, one in which great volumes of men ultimately decided the struggle for terrain.

World War II was different. Certainly, much changed in the interwar years. Armoured vehicles became more lethal, faster and more reliable, tactically integrated with infantry, artillery and even (in the case of Germany) air support. Air forces were progressively replacing biplanes with faster, more destructive monoplane designs, not only fighters and bombers, but also new generations of ground-attack, transport and reconnaissance types. At sea, the experiments in aircraft carriers begun by the British in 1914 were overtaken, in the 1920s, by the first carriers purpose-designed from the keel up, and Germany's U-boat fleet expanded significantly. Artillery became more mobile and mechanized, and lightweight mortars made practical additions to infantry firepower.

MANOEUVRE WARFARE

Such changes alone, combined with the emerging mechanization and motorization of land warfare, meant that from the outset World War II looked dramatically different to the previous conflict. While acknowledging plenty of exceptions, World War II would primarily be a war of combined-arms manoeuvre. It also brought even greater expressions of attrition, an exponential growth of mass killing made possible by new technologies, such as long-range strategic bombing.

During the war, furthermore, the pace of advances in science, design and engineering accelerated ferociously, as each side attempted to take and seize the technological high ground. Not for nothing, for example, did the German Messerschmitt Me 109 and the British

Supermarine Spitfire each go through literally dozens of variants and sub-variants during the war years, in the effort of trying to stay one step ahead of their competitors.

This high-stakes technological competition, plus the embrace of mass-produced weapon types, is reflected in this book. Here we present many of the key aircraft, armoured fighting vehicles (AFVs), artillery pieces and warships of World War II. Their individual histories are extremely varied. Some were dismal failures, or indifferent solutions, while others changed the face of warfare and even history. Regardless, taken collectively, they represent the extraordinary inventiveness of humankind when faced with the threat of defeat or the possibilities of victory in an age of total war.

LEFT:
Mk IX Spitfires from No. 611 Squadron fly over southern England. The superlative Spitfire was produced in 19 separate marks and 52 sub-variants during World War II.

BELOW:
A column of Red Army ISU-152 self-propelled guns stand by the roadside in a Berlin suburb, 1945.

Aircraft

At no other time in history did science and technology make faster progress than in the years between 1939 and 1945, and in no area was that progress swifter and more dramatic than in the design of aircraft. The 1920s and 1930s saw military aviation gravitate away from relatively sluggish biplanes to high-performing monoplanes, offering heavier armament, greater speeds and longer ranges. The pace of development quickened during the war years, refining or producing such outstanding aircraft as the Supermarine Spitfire, Boeing B-17 Flying Fortress, North American P-51 Mustang, Focke-Wulf Fw 190 and dozens of other types. Combat aviation reshaped strategy as much as tactics, giving the warring nations the means to reach the enemy hundreds or even thousands of miles from home bases. A consequence was terrible new levels of civilian deaths from strategic bombing, and the termination of the war in the searing blasts of two atomic bombs dropped from Boeing B-29 Superfortresses.

DOOLITTLE RAID
USAAF B-25B bombers are tethered to the flight deck of USS *Hornet* (CV-8) while en route to launch positions for the famous 'Doolittle Raid' on Tokyo on 8 April 1942. The raid did little significant damage, but was a celebrated propaganda success for the United States.

Hawker Fury (1931)

TYPE • *Fighter* **COUNTRY** • *United Kingdom*

The delightful Hawker Fury fighter has its roots in the radial-engined Hoopoe prototype, which was produced by Hawker as a private-venture to meet Naval Specification N.21/26 and was subsequently tailored to the new Rolls-Royce Kestrel engine enclosed in a contoured nose.

SPECIFICATIONS (Fury Mk II)

DIMENSIONS:	Length: 8.15m (26ft 9in); Wingspan: 9.14m (30ft 0in); Height: 3.10m (10ft 2in)
WEIGHT:	1,637kg (3,609lb) loaded
POWERPLANT:	1 × 477kW (640hp) Rolls-Royce Kestrel VI engine
MAX SPEED:	359km/h (223mph)
RANGE:	435km (270 miles)
SERVICE CEILING:	8990m (29,500ft)
CREW:	1
ARMAMENT:	2 × 7.7mm (0.303in) Vickers forward-firing MGs

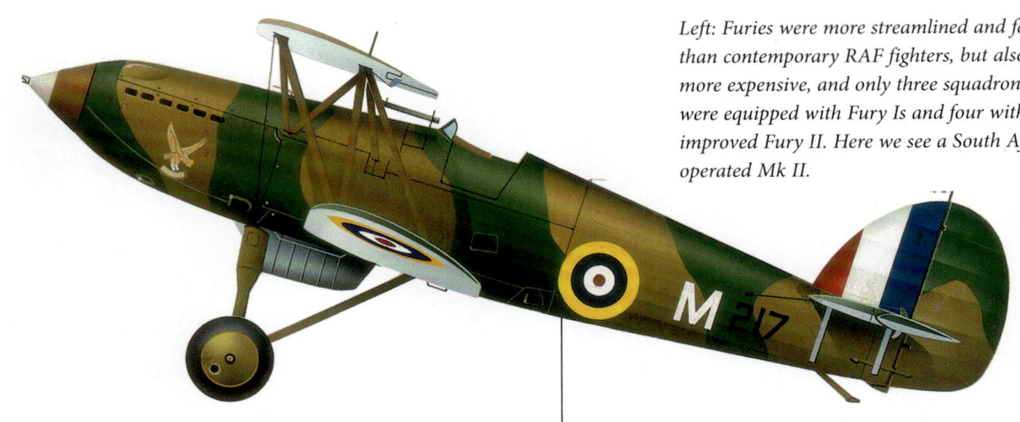

Left: Furies were more streamlined and faster than contemporary RAF fighters, but also more expensive, and only three squadrons were equipped with Fury Is and four with the improved Fury II. Here we see a South African-operated Mk II.

POWERPLANT
The Mk II was powered by a Rolls-Royce Kestrel VI engine that generated 477kW (640hp) and could take the aircraft to a speed of 359km/h (223mph).

MANOEUVRABILITY
The Fury's wing design had exceptional manoeuvrability, assisted by highly sensitive cockpit controls for the pilot.

FURY MK II
The Fury Mk II had a strong climb rate for the time; it could climb to 3,000m) (10,000ft) in 4 minutes 25 seconds.

DEVELOPMENT
The initial Hawker design exceeded by a good margin the requirements of Air Ministry Specification F.20/27, and in prototype form as the Hawker Hornet it was displayed at the 1929 Olympia Aero Show. Before commencing flight trials the Hornet was re-engined with a supercharged Kestrel and demonstrated such impressive performance that Specification 13/30 was written around it. The preliminary order for three development aircraft, designated the Fury, was followed by the first batch of 18 production aircraft.

FURY MK II
This Hawker Fury Mk II (K8238) belonged to the Central Flying School at Upavon, 1938. The Mk II was a re-engined variant of the experimental 'High Speed Fury' and was accepted as an interim fighter during the Hawker Hurricane's development period.

Junkers Ju 52 (1932)

TYPE • *Transport* **COUNTRY** • *Germany*

During the Aegean campaign and operations on the Eastern Front, the Ju 52/3m was often a 'sitting duck' and suffered unsustainable losses. However, the aircraft's reliability and ability to operate in all conditions ensured that it remained vital to the German war effort.

SPECIFICATIONS (Ju 52/3mg4e)

Dimensions:	Length: 19.90m (62ft 0in); Wingspan: 29.20m (95ft 10in); Height: 4.52m (14ft 10in)
Weight:	10,499kg (23,146lb) maximum take-off
Powerplant:	3 x 541kW (725hp) BMW 132A-3 9-cylinder radial engines
Max speed:	286km/h (178mph)
Range:	1,305km (811 miles)
Service ceiling:	5,900m (19,360ft)
Crew:	2/3; 17 passengers
Armament:	1 x 7.92mm (0.31in) MG 15 machine gun or 1 x 13mm (0.51in) MG 131 machine gun (dorsal)

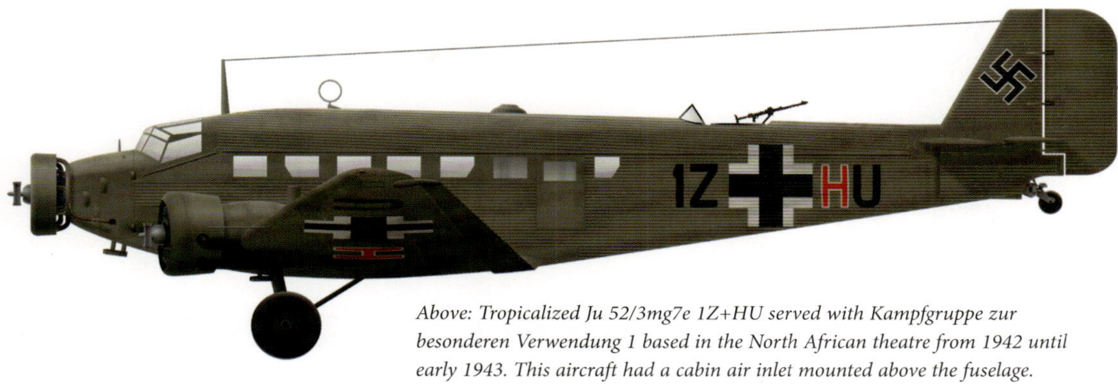

Above: Tropicalized Ju 52/3mg7e 1Z+HU served with Kampfgruppe zur besonderen Verwendung 1 based in the North African theatre from 1942 until early 1943. This aircraft had a cabin air inlet mounted above the fuselage.

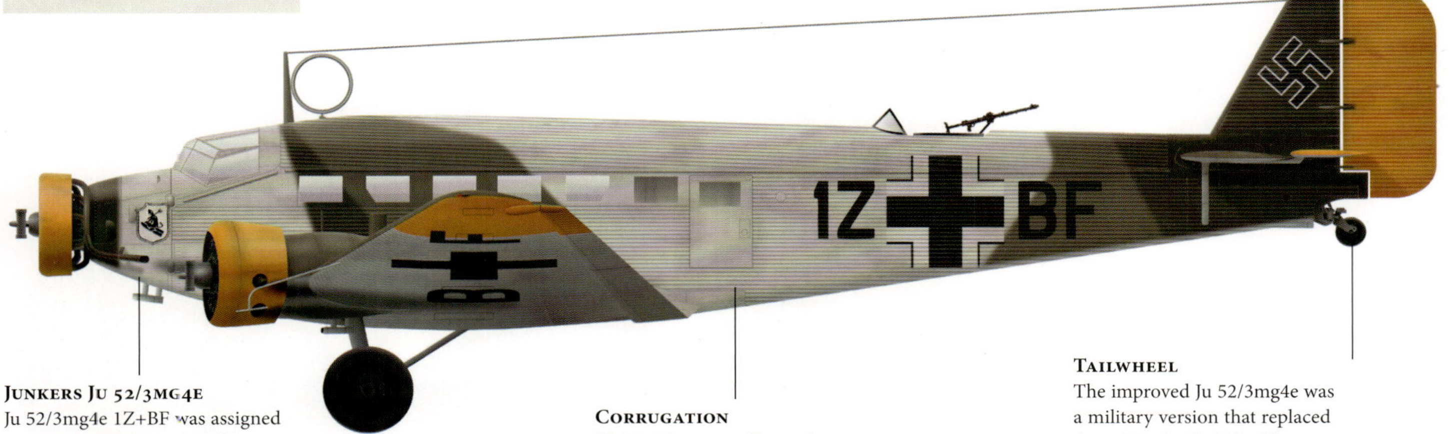

Junkers Ju 52/3mg4e
Ju 52/3mg4e 1Z+BF was assigned to the Stabsschwarm (Staff Flight) of IV./Kampfgruppe zur besonderen Verwendung 1, taking part in assault operations over Crete in spring 1941.

Corrugation
The Ju 52 was an all-metal aircraft, covered mainly with corrugated Duralumin skinning. The corrugation gave the aircraft immense strength while keeping the weight of the aircraft low.

Tailwheel
The improved Ju 52/3mg4e was a military version that replaced the original tail-skid with a tailwheel and featured some internal equipment changes compared with the Ju 52/3mg3e.

PRODUCTION DEMAND

Wherever the Luftwaffe was at war, the Ju 53/3m found itself in action and proved to be an exceptionally versatile design. Demand was so great that additional production lines were established at the Amiot factory in Colombes, France, from where aircraft began to be delivered from June 1942. Additional capacity was generated by PIRT in Budapest, where German-supplied components were used to build another 26 Ju 52/3m aircraft.

JUNKERS JU 52/3M
The most famous operational use of the Ju 52 was during the invasion of Crete in May 1941. Carrying 16 paratroopers at a time, the Ju 52 squadrons based in mainland Greece made repeated missions to drop over 10,000 paratroopers and then land thousands more troops on Crete's airfields. Nearly 150 Ju 52s were lost and as many damaged during the assault.

Polikarpov I-16 (1934)

TYPE • *Fighter* **COUNTRY** • *Soviet Union*

Given the pace of fighter development in the 1930s, it is all the more remarkable that the Soviet-designed I-16 was essentially the best fighter in the world for a period of six years. It only met its match once pitted against the Luftwaffe's Messerschmitt Bf 109E.

SPECIFICATIONS

Dimensions:	Length: 6.04m (19ft 10in); Wingspan: 8.88m (29ft 1in); Height: 3.25m (10ft 8in)
Weight:	1,475kg (3,252lb)
Powerplant:	M-62 radial piston engine, 820kW (1100hp)
Max speed:	490km/h (304mph) at 3,000m (9,845ft)
Range:	700km (435 miles)
Service ceiling:	9,700m (31,825ft)
Crew:	1
Armament:	2 × 7.62mm (0.3in) ShKAS machine guns; 2 × 20mm (0.79 in) ShVAK cannons; 6 × unguided RS-82 rockets or up to 500kg (1,102lb) of bombs

Above: The Republicans called the I-16 the 'Mosca' (fly) and the Nationalists called it the 'Rata' (rat). The Soviet-built Polikarpov was the first monoplane fighter with a retractable undercarriage.

Gun armament
Gun armament comprised four 7.62mm (0.3in) ShKAS machine guns, two synchronized in the forward fuselage and two in the wings; the wing machine guns were replaced on some aircraft by two 20mm (0.79in) ShVAK cannon.

Cockpit
The cramped cockpit was equipped with only rudimentary instruments. No radio or oxygen equipment was fitted, and there was no indicator for the undercarriage.

Tail surfaces
The tail surfaces were necessarily large to counter the lack of stability caused by the short rear fuselage. Despite the designers' best efforts, the I-16 had only limited stability longitudinally, but this instability brought great dividends in manoeuvrability at high speeds.

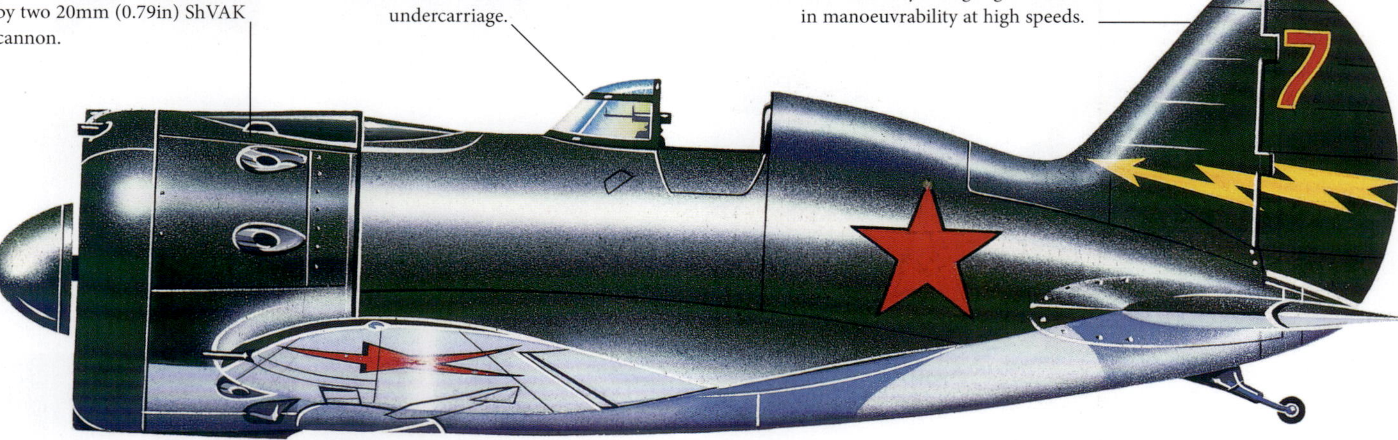

WING STRUCTURE
The I-16 had a metal two-spar wing structure, with trussed KhMA chrome molybdenum steel alloy centre-section spars and tubular outer spars. Wing ribs were made of dural and skinning was aluminium inboard and fabric outboard. The long ailerons were operated by rods and bell cranks. They could be drooped to act as flaps on landing.

READY FOR TAKE-OFF
The I-16 was a robust but basic aircraft to fly. For example, no fuel gauge was fitted in the cockpit; the pilot had to listen to the engine note to determine when fuel was low while keeping a close eye on his watch.

PZL P.11c (1934)

TYPE • *Fighter* COUNTRY • *Poland*

SPECIFICATIONS	
DIMENSIONS:	Length: 7.55m (24ft 9in); Height 2.85m (9ft 4in); Wingspan 10.72m (35ft 2in)
WEIGHT:	Loaded 1,650kg (3,638lb)
POWERPLANT:	418kW (560hp) Bristol Mercury VS2 radial
MAX SPEED:	375km/h (233mph)
RANGE:	550km (341 miles)
CEILING:	8,000m (26,246ft)
CREW:	1
ARMAMENT:	2 to 4 x 7.92mm (0.31in) machine guns, plus 50kg (110lb) bombload

The gull-winged monoplane fighters produced by the Polish *Panstowe Zaklady Lotnicze* (National Aviation Establishments) during the inter-war years were among the best in service with any air force, but they were outmoded by the time Germany invaded Poland in 1939.

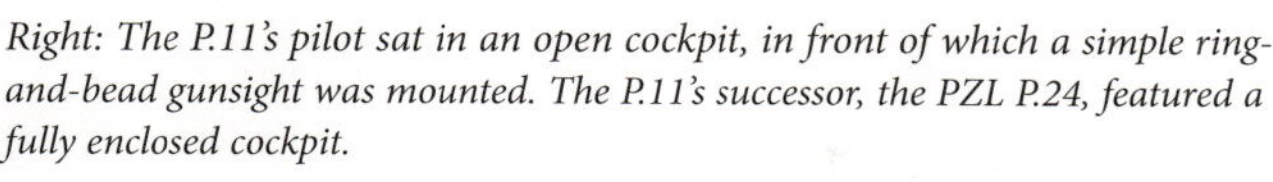

Right: The P.11's pilot sat in an open cockpit, in front of which a simple ring-and-bead gunsight was mounted. The P.11's successor, the PZL P.24, featured a fully enclosed cockpit.

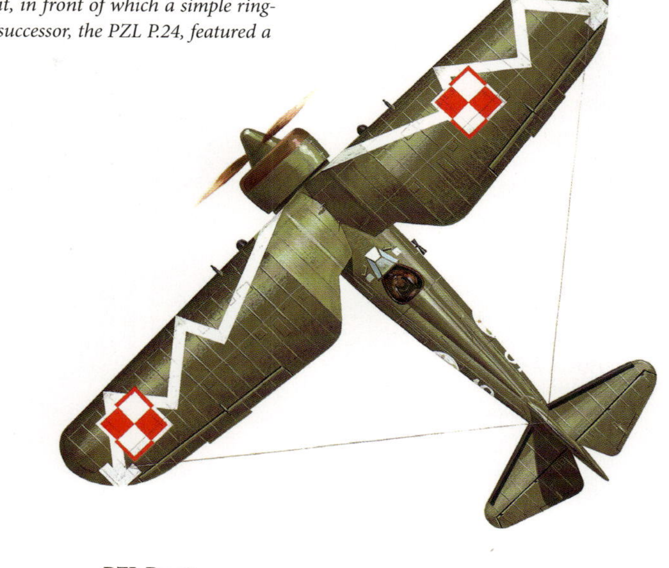

ENGINE
The P.11c was powered by the extremely reliable Bristol Mercury radial engine, which was also the powerplant chosen for aircraft like Britain's Gloster Gladiator biplane fighter.

GULL WING
The cut-out centre section of the P.11's gull wing gave the pilot a good view forward, further improved in the P.11c by lowering the engine mounting and repositioning the pilot farther to the rear.

PZL P.11C
This aircraft belonged to No. 122 Squadron, 2nd Air Regiment in Krakow in the late 1930s.

SUCCESSOR
The gull-winged PZL P.11 was a more powerful derivative of the PZL P.7, which equipped all first-line fighter squadrons of the Polish Air Force's 1st, 2nd, 3rd and 4th Air Regiments at the end of 1933 and was one of the best fighter aircraft of its day. Its successor, the PZL P.11, was basically a more powerful derivative which first flew in September 1931, with deliveries beginning in 1934.

POLISH P.11S IN FLIGHT
Most P.11s were powered by Bristol Mercury engines built under licence by Skoda. The definitive version of the fighter was the P.11c, of which 175 were built. They suffered heavy losses during the German invasion of Poland in September 1939 against superior German Bf 109 fighters.

Fiat CR.32 (1934)

TYPE • *Fighter* **COUNTRY** • *Italy*

SPECIFICATIONS

Dimensions:	Length: 7.45m (24ft 5in); Wingspan: 9.5m (31ft 2in); Height: 2.63m (8ft 7in)
Weight:	Empty: 1,325kg (2,921lb); Maximum take-off: 1,850kg (4,079lb)
Powerplant:	1 × 447kW (600hp) Fiat A.30 RA bis 12-cylinder Vee piston engine
Max speed:	375km/h (233mph)
Range:	680km (422 miles)
Service ceiling:	8,800m (28,870ft)
Crew:	1
Armament:	2 × 7.7mm (0.303in) fixed forward-firing Breda-SAFAT machine guns

The Italian Fiat CR.32 lays a claim to being the most important biplane fighter of the 1930s, certainly in terms of the number built (1,712) and arguably because of its combat influence during the Spanish Civil War.

Left: The CR.32 was built in large numbers and formed the backbone of the Regia Aeronautica fighter force in 1935–40. It also achieved widespread export sales.

Armament
Standard armament was a pair of 7.7mm (0.3in) Breda-SAFAT machine guns fitted on top of the engine cowling.

Construction
From the nose to the cockpit, and under the tail and on the back, the aircraft was constructed by aluminium and steel tubes covered by duraluminium. A fabric covering was used on the sides and the belly.

Powerplant
The powerplant was a single 447kW (600hp) Fiat A.30 RA bis 12-cylinder Vee piston engine, giving a top speed of 375km/h (233mph).

ROSATELLI DESIGN

The CR.32 stemmed from the CR.30, designed by chief engineer Rosatelli in 1931 as a single-seat fighter and bearing many of his hallmarks, such as W-form interplane bracing. The CR.30 offered a considerable leap in performance over the previous CR.1 and was ordered for the Regia Aeronautica. Rosatelli was not content to rest on his laurels and refined the Cr.30 to produce the CR.32.

CAPTURED CR.32
This Fiat CR.32 was captured intact by Republicans in 1937 and photographed at Los Alcanzares airfield during the Spanish Civil War. The CR.32 was used extensively in Spain, and its performance in this theatre lulled the Italian Air Ministry into the false belief that the fighter biplane was a viable weapon of future war.

Savoia-Marchetti SM.79 Sparviero (1934)

TYPE • *Bomber* **COUNTRY** • *Italy*

SPECIFICATIONS

Dimensions:	Length 15.62m (51ft 3in); Wingspan 21.20m (69ft 5.5in); Height 4.40m (14ft 5.25in)
Weight:	Empty 6,800kg (14,991lb); Maximum take-off 11,300kg (24,912lb)
Powerplant:	3 x 746kW (1,000hp) Piaggio P.XI RC 40 radial engines
Max Speed:	435km/h (270mph) at 3,650m (11,975ft)
Range:	1,900km (1,181 miles)
Service Ceiling:	6,500m (21,325ft)
Crew:	5/6
Armament:	3 x 12.7mm (0.5in) machine guns and 1 x 7.7mm (0.303in) machine gun; 2 x 450mm (17.7in) torpedoes or 1250kg (2756lb) of bombs

Of all the Italian bombers that served during World War II, the *Sparviero* (Sparrowhawk) was probably the best known and most effective. It was one of the finest anti-shipping aircraft of the war, not least because it could carry two torpedoes.

Right: On its upper wings, this SM.79 carried the insignia of fascist Italy, the 'fasces' – a bundle of rods around an axe, carried before a magistrate in ancient Rome as a symbol of authority.

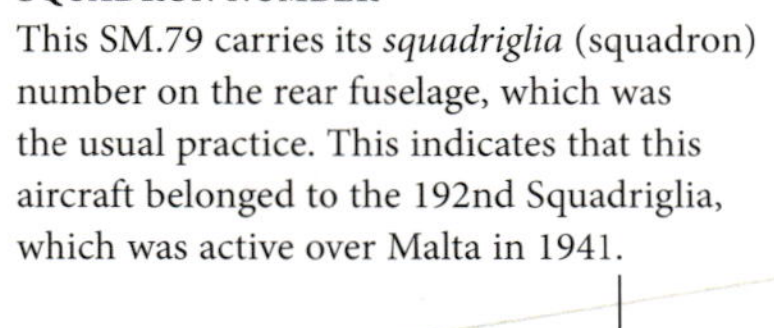

Squadron number
This SM.79 carries its *squadriglia* (squadron) number on the rear fuselage, which was the usual practice. This indicates that this aircraft belonged to the 192nd Squadriglia, which was active over Malta in 1941.

Rear MG
Defence of the upper rear of the aircraft was the responsibility of the flight engineer or radio operator, who used a 12.7mm (0.5in) gun on a flexible mount. The gun could be retracted and a panel put in place to cover the hole in the fuselage.

Bomb aimer
The ventral gondola contained the bomb aimer, who was equipped with a small wheel enabling him to make corrections to the aircraft's course by adjusting the rudder. The Italians were renowned for their extremely accurate high-level bombing.

MARITIME PREDATOR
When Italy entered World War II in June 1940, SM.79s accounted for well over half the Italian Air Force's total bomber strength. SM.79s saw continual action in the air campaign against Malta and in North Africa, becoming renowned for their high-level precision bombing, while the torpedo-bomber version was active against British shipping in the Aegean and the central Mediterranean.

MEDITERRANEAN OPERATIONS
Ground crew cheer an SM.79 as it taxis out from a coastal airstrip. Production of the aircraft, which was the military counterpart of an eight-seat civil airliner, began in October 1936 and was to have an uninterrupted run until June 1943, by which time 1,217 aircraft in total had been built.

Avia B.534 (1935)

TYPE • *Fighter* **COUNTRY** • *Czechoslovakia*

SPECIFICATIONS (B.534-IV)

DIMENSIONS:	Length: 8.2m (26ft 10in); Wingspan: 9.4m (30ft 10in); Height: 3.1m (10ft 2in)
WEIGHT:	Empty: 1,460kg (3,219lb); Maximum take-off: 2,120kg (4,674lb)
POWERPLANT:	1 × 634kW (850hp) Hispano-Suiza HS 12Ydrs inline piston engine
MAX SPEED:	394km/h (245mph)
RANGE:	580km (360 miles)
SERVICE CEILING:	10,600m (34,775ft)
CREW:	1
ARMAMENT:	4 × 7.7mm fixed forward-firing Model 30 machine guns in forward fuselage; underwing Pantof racks with provision for up to 6 × 20kg (44lb) bombs

In 1930 the Avia aircraft company at Prague-Letnany appointed Frantisek Novotny as its chief engineer. His first design was the B.34 fighter that was re-engined with a Hispano-Suiza 12Ydrs engine and eventually gelled into the B.534-I prototype.

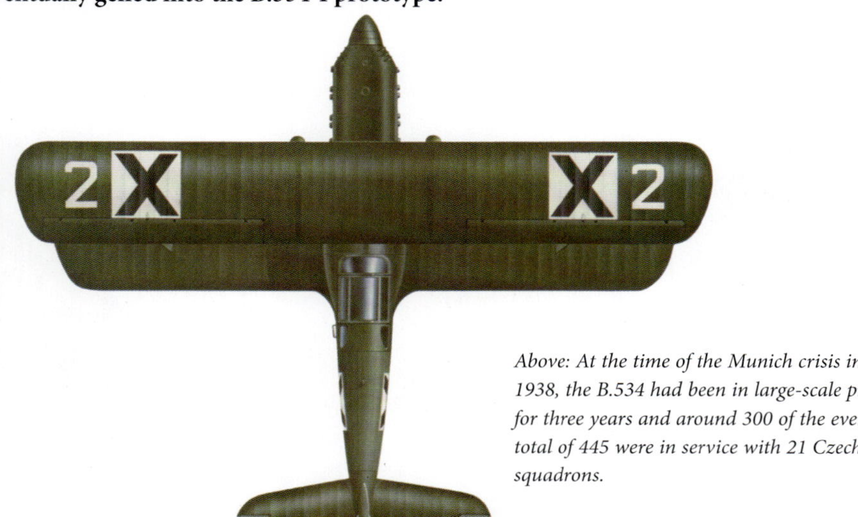

Above: At the time of the Munich crisis in September 1938, the B.534 had been in large-scale production for three years and around 300 of the eventual total of 445 were in service with 21 Czech fighter squadrons.

POWERPLANT
The aircraft was powered by a 634kW (850hp) Hispano-Suiza HS 12Ydrs inline piston engine.

FUSELAGE BLISTERS
The prominent fuselage blisters just beneath the cockpit on each side of the fuselage incorporated the thick breeches of the aircraft's machine guns.

WHEELS
The wheels were housed within streamlined spatted fairings. In winter conditions, these could be replaced with ski fittings.

VARIANTS
The first production model of this outstanding fighter was the B.534-I, which had a wooden screw to replace the metal unit of the prototype, an open cockpit and twin fuselage machine guns with two more carried in lower-wing fairings. The B.534-II carried all four machine guns in fuselage blisters, and also had underwing racks for light bombs. The B.534-III had mainwheel fairings and revised carburettor air intake, and the definitive B.536-IV had an enclosed cockpit and revised aft fuselage decking.

AVIA B.534-I
This stripped down B.534 shows the Hispano-Suiza HS 12Ydrs inline piston engine and the two-blade wooden prop in fine detail.

Savoia-Marchetti SM.81 Pipistrello (1935)

TYPE • *Bomber* **COUNTRY** • *Italy*

Developed in parallel with the SM.73 transport, with which it shared a basically common airframe, the *Pipistrello* (Bat) was a dual-role bomber and transport that first flew in 1934 and entered service in 1935.

SPECIFICATIONS

Dimensions:	Length: 17.80m (58ft 5in); Wingspan: 24m (78ft 9in); Height: 6m (19ft 8in)
Weight:	Maximum take-off: 10,055kg (22,167lb)
Powerplant:	3 × 499.5kW (670hp) Piaggio P.X RC.35 9-cylinder single-row radial engines or 3 × 485kW (650hp) Alfa Romeo 125 RC.35 or 126 RC.34 9-cylinder single-row radial engines or 3 × 485kW (650hp) Gnome-Rhône 14-K 14-cylinder 2-row radial engines
Max speed:	340km/h (211mph)
Range:	2,000km (1,243 miles)
Service ceiling:	7,000m (22,965ft)
Crew:	5–6
Armament:	2 × 7.7mm (0.303in) or 1 × 12.7mm (0.5in) machine guns in dorsal turret; 2 × 7.7mm (0.303in) machine guns in ventral turret; 1 × 7.7mm (0.303in) machine gun in beam positions; internal bombload of 2,000kg (4,409lb)

Above: An SM.81 in desert colour scheme. Note the large spats around the fixed undercarriage, to reduce drag.

Trimotor design
The SM.81's trimotor design gave it plenty of speed and power for its size. It had a maximum speed of 340km/h (211mph) and could climb to 3,000m (9,845ft) in 12 minutes.

Construction
The aircraft was built from a mixture of materials. The fuselage had a framework of steel tubes with a sheet metal-covered aft portion while the rest of the aircraft was largely fabric-covered wood.

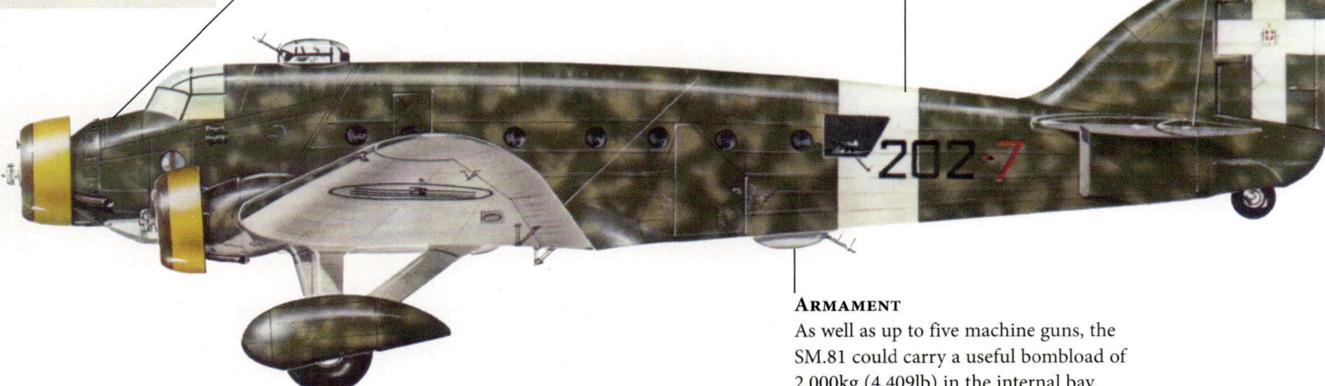

Armament
As well as up to five machine guns, the SM.81 could carry a useful bombload of 2,000kg (4,409lb) in the internal bay.

SERVICE
The SM.81 saw extensive service in the Italian conquest of Abyssinia in the mid-1930s and still proved moderately effective in the early part of the Spanish Civil War, but from the time of Italy's June 1940 entry into World War II was used increasingly in the dedicated transport role, although it did undertake night bombing raids in North Africa. The type survived the war in modest numbers and remained in Italian service to 1950.

BOMBING RAID
A Savoia-Marchetti SM.81 during a bombing raid. The distinctive black crosses on the tails are Saint Andrew's Cross, the insignia of the Spanish Nationalist Air Force during the Spanish Civil War. The planes in the background are FIAT CR.32s of the Italian XVI *Gruppo Autonomo Cucaracha.*

Supermarine Walrus (1935)

TYPE • *Seaplane* **COUNTRY** • *United Kingdom*

SPECIFICATIONS (Walrus Mk I)

DIMENSIONS:	Length: 11.46m (37ft 7in); Wingspan: 13.97m (45ft 10in); Height: 4.65m (15ft 3in)
WEIGHT:	8,050kg (3,651lb) maximum take-off
POWERPLANT:	1 × 560kW (750hp) Bristol Pegasus VI 9-cylinder air-cooled radial piston engine
MAX SPEED:	217km/h (135mph)
RANGE:	970km (600 miles)
CEILING:	5,600m (18,500ft)
CREW:	4
ARMAMENT:	1 × 7.7mm (0.303in) Vickers K machine gun flexibly mounted in nose position; 1 × 7.7mm (0.303in) Vickers K machine gun flexibly mounted in dorsal position; up to 450kg (600lb) bombload

Designed for use on warship catapults, the elderly but versatile Walrus flying boat ultimately made its greatest contribution to the Allied war effort as an Air–Sea Rescue aircraft, an aerial lifeline for downed pilots.

Right: Royal Navy Walrus flying boats of the 2nd Cruiser Squadron maintain a tight formation.

ENGINE NACELLE
A curious feature of the aircraft was that the entire engine nacelle assembly was angled three degrees to the right to counteract the torque of the propeller.

ADVANCED DESIGN
Despite its biplane configuration, the Walrus was quite an advanced aircraft for its era, being the first British military aircraft to combine the features of retractable undercarriage, a fully enclosed cockpit and a metal fuselage in the same airframe.

HULL
The hull was initially of anodized alloy construction although the Mk II version substituted this for an all-wood hull due to wartime shortages of light alloys.

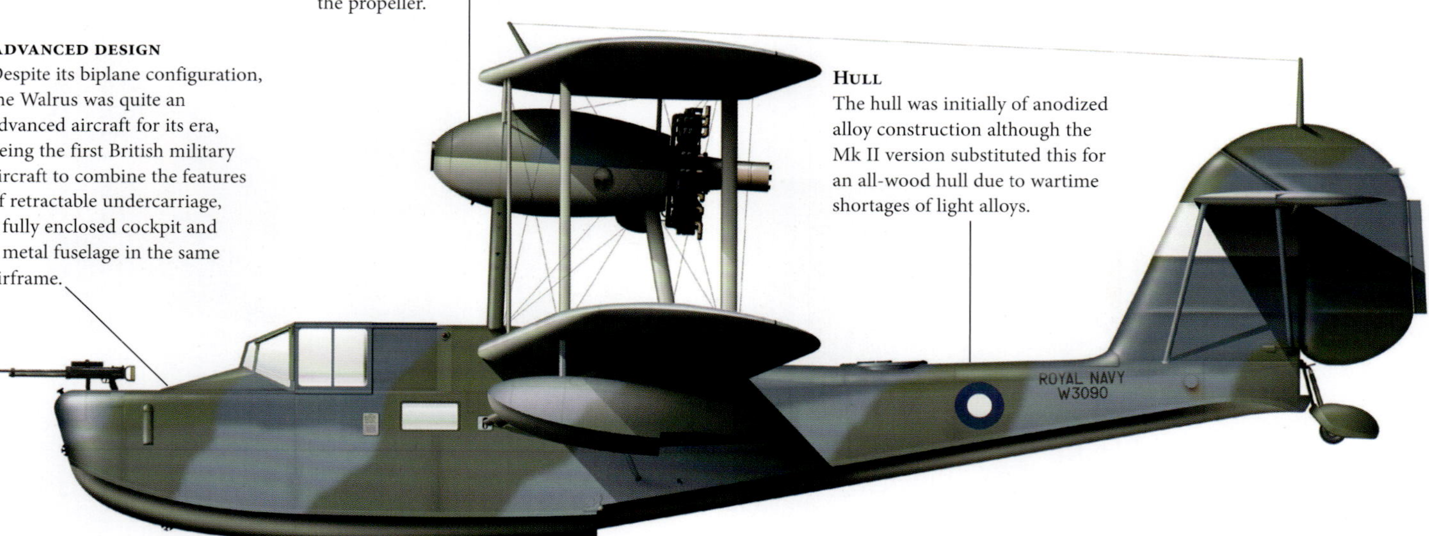

COMBAT ROLES

The primary task for Royal Navy Walruses assigned to cruisers and battleships was expected to be gunnery spotting in naval actions. However, the Walrus would perform this function only twice, at the battles of Cape Spartivento and Cape Matapan. The main tasks carried out by the Walrus from warships was patrolling for submarines and enemy shipping.

TAXIING WALRUS
This Supermarine Walrus (serial K5783) was deployed from His Majesty's New Zealand Ship (HMNZS) *Leander*, a light cruiser that operated in the Mediterreanean and the Pacific theatres.

Mitsubishi G3M 'Nell' (1935)

TYPE • *Bomber* **COUNTRY** • *Japan*

SPECIFICATIONS (G3M1)

DIMENSIONS:	Length: 16.45m (53ft 11.75in); Wingspan: 25.00m (82ft 0.25in); Height: 3.69m (12ft 1.25in)
WEIGHT:	7,642kg (16,848lb) loaded
POWERPLANT:	2 × 679kW (910hp) Mitsubishi Kinsei 3 radial piston engines
MAX SPEED:	348km/h (216mph) at 2,000m (6,560ft)
RANGE:	Unavailable
SERVICE CEILING:	7,480m (24,540ft)
CREW:	7
ARMAMENT:	3 × 7.7mm (0.303in) machine guns; 1 × 800kg (1,764lb) torpedo or equivalent bombload

Renowned for its ship-killing exploits in the early days of the conflict in the Pacific, the G3M was typical of the bomber-transports developed between the wars. For its time, it was one of the longest-ranged twin-engined medium bombers in the world.

Above: (Left) A G3M3, with its large dorsal turret mounting a 20mm (0.79in) cannon. (Right) A G3M2 Model 21.

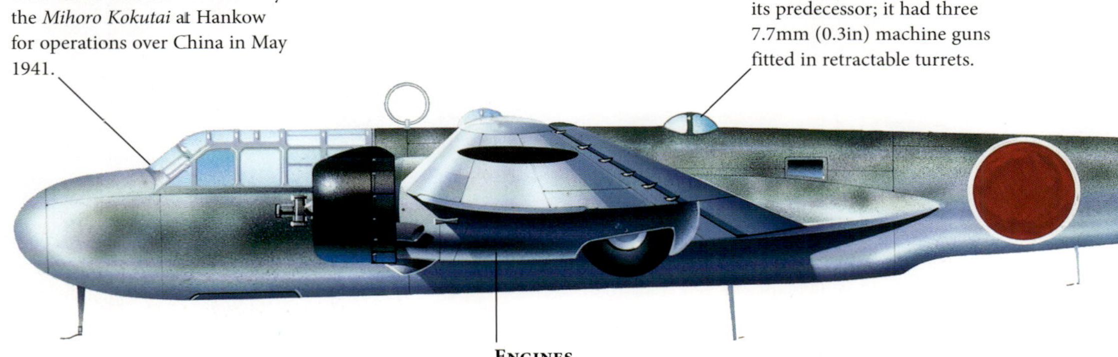

G3M2
This G3M2 aircraft was flown by the *Mihoro Kokutai* at Hankow for operations over China in May 1941.

DEFENSIVE ARMAMENT
The G3M2 Model 21's defensive armament was unchanged from its predecessor; it had three 7.7mm (0.3in) machine guns fitted in retractable turrets.

ENGINES
In the second major production derivative, the G3M2 Model 21, the Kinsei 3 engines of the G3M1 were replaced with 802kW (1075hp) Kinsei 41 or 42 radials.

9-SHI SPECIFICATION

The G3M began life in 1934 and was tailored to meet a requirement for a twin-engined, land-based naval bomber and transport. The forward-thinking 9-Shi specification was the brainchild of Admiral Isoroku Yamamoto, who was a proponent of long-range, land-based naval air power for use in an offensive capacity. The resulting aircraft employed a cantilever mid-wing monoplane configuration with retractable tailwheel undercarriage.

SHIP HUNTING IN THE PACIFIC

In World War II, the G3M made a name for itself with involvement in the raids against the British battleship HMS *Prince of Wales* and the battlecruiser HMS *Repulse* in December 1941, only days after the Japanese attack on Pearl Harbor.

Douglas C-47 Skytrain (1935)

TYPE • *Transport* COUNTRY • *United States*

SPECIFICATIONS	
DIMENSIONS:	Length: 19.43m (63ft 9in); Wingspan: 29.11m (95ft 6in); Height: 5.18m (17ft)
WEIGHT:	11,793kg (26,000lb) maximum take-off
POWERPLANT:	4 × Pratt & Whitney R-1830-92 14-cylinder radial piston engines, 895kW (1200hp)
MAX SPEED:	370km/h (230mph)
RANGE:	2,575km (1,600 miles)
CEILING:	7,315m (24,000ft)
CREW:	3
ARMAMENT:	None

Without question, the transport workhorse of the Allies in World War II was the Douglas C-47, the military version of the immortal DC-3, which had revolutionized commercial air transport in the second half of the 1930s.

Right: The C-47 pictured here is camouflaged in standard Troop Carrier Command scheme of olive drab upper surfaces and grey under surfaces, the two separated by an undulating line.

COCKPIT
While the C-47 captain occupies the usual left-hand seat, the co-pilot sits on the right, and is also responsible for the radios and throttles.

FUEL
The main fuel tanks (containing 795 litres/210 gallons) are located in the centre section forward of the wing spar. These are supplemented by two auxiliary tanks (760 litres/201 gallons) aft of the spar.

CABIN
The typical interior layout for trooping operations comprises a row of utility bucket seats fitted along each cabin wall. These can be removed for freighting work.

TRANSPORTER
The first C-47s began to equip the USAAF in 1941, initially in only small numbers. From 1942, however, production accelerated, and the C-47 served as the USAAF's standard transport and glider tug and as such took part in every US airborne operation during the war. General Dwight D. Eisenhower ranked the C-47 alongside the bazooka, jeep and atomic bomb as weapons that contributed most to the Allied victory.

SKYTRAIN OVER GIZA
A Douglas C-47 Skytrain flies over the pyramids of Giza in Egypt, 1944. The C-47's cabin could accommodate 28 fully equipped troops, or 14 passengers as a sleeper transport/ambulance.

Heinkel He 111 (1935)

TYPE • *Bomber* **COUNTRY** • *Germany*

The He 111 was a major part of the Luftwaffe's expansion in the 1930s. It was often described as 'the wolf in sheep's clothing' because it first masqueraded as a transport aircraft, but its duty was to provide the Luftwaffe with a fast medium bomber.

SPECIFICATIONS (He 111H-6)

Dimensions:	Length 16.40m (53ft 9.5in); Height 3.40m (11ft 1.5in); Wingspan 22.60m (74ft 1.33in)
Weight:	Empty 8,680kg (19,139lb); Maximum take-off 14,000kg (30,865lb)
Powerplant:	2 × 1,007kW (1,350hp) Junkers Jumo 211F inverted V-12 engines
Max Speed:	436km/h (271mph) at 6,000m (19,685ft)
Range:	1,950km (1,212 miles)
Ceiling:	6,700m (21,980ft)
Crew:	5
Armament:	1 × 20mm (0.79in) cannon; 1 × 13mm (0.51in) machine gun; 4 × 7.92mm (0.31in) machine guns plus a maximum bombload of 4,000kg (8,818lb)

Right: The upper wing surfaces of this Heinkel are painted in the standard Luftwaffe medium/dark green 'splinter' camouflage of the early-war years.

Wing shape
Early variants of the Heinkel He 111 had an elliptical wing; the He 111F was the first to feature a straight leading edge.

He 111P-2
The aircraft here is an He 111P-2, which conducted nocturnal raids against the United Kingdom in late 1940 and early 1941.

Armament
The He 111H-6 could carry a pair of 765kg (1687lb) LT F5b torpedoes, and was armed with six 7.92mm (0.31in) MG 15 machine guns and a forward-firing 20mm (0.79in) cannon.

BOMBER BACKBONE

In mid-1939 the He 111P variant made its appearance. Relatively few He 111Ps were completed before production switched to the He 111H, the variant which formed the backbone of the Luftwaffe's bomber force between 1940 and 1943, about 6,150 being built before production ended in 1944.

HE 111P
The He 111P version, which was powered by two 858kW (1,150hp) Daimler-Benz DB 601Aa engines, introduced a fully glazed asymmetric nose, with its offset ball turret, in place of the stepped-up cockpits of the earlier variants.

Messerschmitt Bf 109 (1935)

TYPE • *Fighter* **COUNTRY** • *Germany*

The classic Luftwaffe fighter of World War II, the Bf 109 served throughout the conflict in a series of increasingly capable variants. It was the mount for Germany's most celebrated aces, including Erich Hartmann, Gerhard Barkhorn and Hans-Joachim Marseille.

SPECIFICATIONS
Bf 109F-2/Trop

Dimensions:	Length: 8.94m (29ft 4in); Wingspan: 9.92m (32ft 6in); Height: 2.59m (8ft 6in)
Weight:	2,746kg (6,054lb)
Powerplant:	1 × 864kW (1,159hp) DB 601N 12-cylinder inverted-V engine
Max speed:	628km/h (390mph)
Range:	700km (435 miles)
Service ceiling:	11,600m (38,000ft)
Crew:	2
Armament:	1 × 15mm (0.59in) MG 151/15 cannon; 2 × 7.92mm (0.31in) MG 17 machine guns

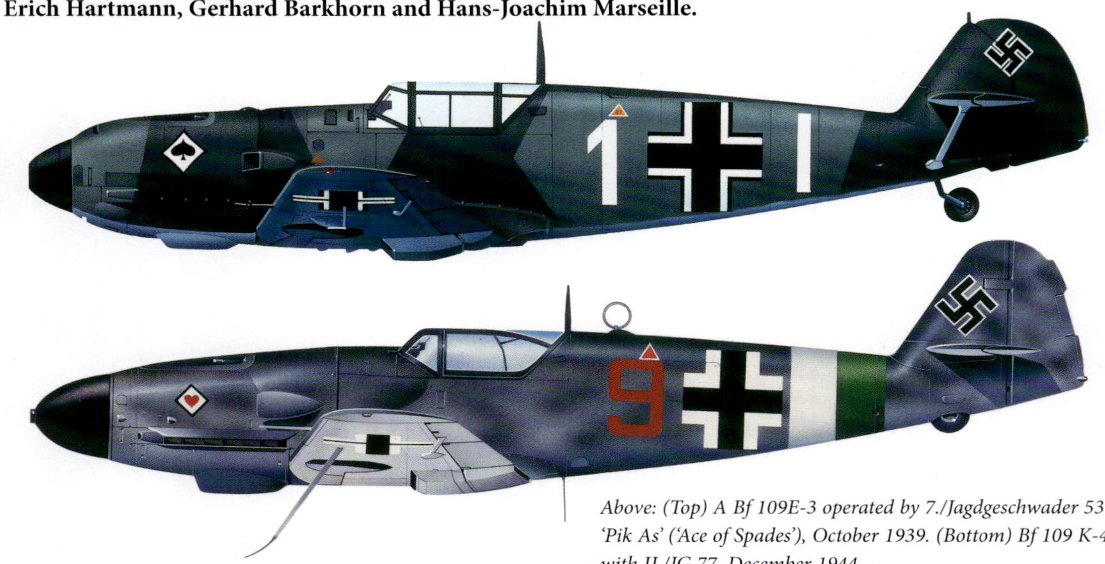

Above: (Top) A Bf 109E-3 operated by 7./Jagdgeschwader 53 'Pik As' ('Ace of Spades'), October 1939. (Bottom) Bf 109 K-4 with II./JG 77, December 1944.

Powerplant
Power was provided by the DB 601N engine, featuring piston heads with a higher compression ratio and higher-octane fuel.

Armament
The Bf 109F-2 was delivered alongside the F-1 and differed in its armament of MG 151/15 cannon in place of the MG FF/M.

Bf 109F-2/Trop
Desert camouflage scheme was applied to Bf 109F-2/Trop 'Red 4' of II./Jagdgeschwader 27, based at Sanyet, Egypt, in September 1942.

HIGH PERFORMER
By making continual improvements to the basic design, the Bf 109 remained viable right until the end of World War II. Despite the appearance of the more capable Fw 109, the Bf 109 remained the backbone of the Luftwaffe fighter arm. The Bf 109 remains associated, therefore, with the legendary aces of the *Jadgverband*. The top-scoring ace of all time, Erich Hartmann, achieved his 352 victories in the space of three and a half years, all at the controls of a Bf 109.

BF 109E
The Bf 109E was comparable to the Spitfire Mk I in speed and manoeuvrability. Its fuel-injected Daimler-Benz engine had the advantage of not cutting out when subjected to negative G-forces (unlike the Merlin) and its 20mm (0.79in) cannon packed a powerful punch.

Hawker Hurricane (1935)

TYPE • *Fighter* **COUNTRY** • *United Kingdom*

SPECIFICATIONS (Mk IA)

DIMENSIONS:	Length: 9.55m (31ft 4in); Wingspan: 12.19m (40ft 0in); Height: 4.07m (13ft 4.5in)
WEIGHT:	2,820kg (6218lb) loaded
POWERPLANT:	1 x 768kW (1030hp) Rolls-Royce Merlin II liquid-cooled V-12
MAX SPEED:	496km/h (308mph)
RANGE:	845km (525 miles)
SERVICE CEILING:	10,180m (33,400ft)
CREW:	1
ARMAMENT:	8 x 7.7mm (0.303in) Browning MGs

The Royal Air Force's first monoplane fighter began a dynasty of Hawker warplanes. The most successful British fighter during the Battle of Britain subsequently excelled in the ground-attack role in North Africa and the Far East.

Above, right: Throughout its career, the Hurricane retained a fabric-covered rear fuselage. Although antiquated, this proved easier to repair and contributed to survivability.

HURRICANE MK IA
This Hurricane Mk IA was of No. 85 Squadron, RAF Fighter Command, as seen in August 1940 during the height of the Battle of Britain.

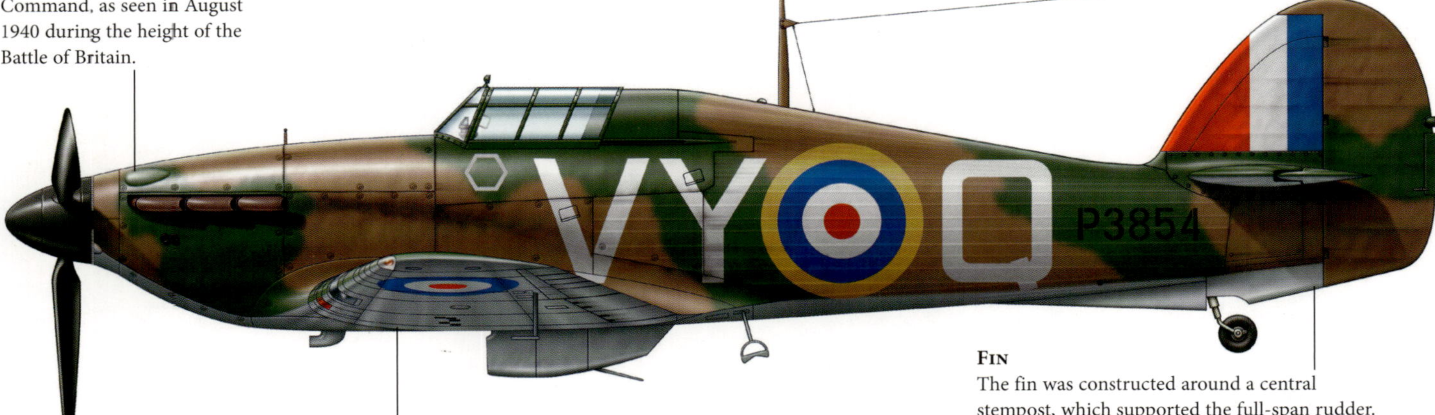

FIN
The fin was constructed around a central stempost, which supported the full-span rudder. The rudder had a small horn at the top and was fitted with a navigation light.

AIRFRAME IMPROVEMENT
During its production run, the Hurricane benefitted from changes including metal-skinned wings, an enlarged rudder and (on later Mk Is) a ventral underfin.

ANTI-TANK AIRCRAFT
A specialist anti-tank version was the Hurricane Mk IID, armed with 40mm (1.57in) cannon under the wings. A 'universal wing' was the primary feature of the Hurricane Mk IV; this could mount up to eight rocket projectiles or other external stores. Indeed, the Hurricane Mk IV was the first Allied aircraft to deploy air-to-ground rockets, a capability that did much to extend the operational utility of the basic airframe.

RCAF MK IIB
Loaded with a pair of 114kg (250lb) bombs under its wing, this Hawker Hurricane Mk IIB of No. 402 Squadron, RCAF, prepares for a cross-Channel sortie in 1941.

Junkers Ju 87 Stuka (1935)

TYPE • *Dive-bomber* **COUNTRY** • *Germany*

SPECIFICATIONS (Ju 87R-2)

Dimensions:	Length: 11.50m (37ft 8in); Wingspan: 13.8m (45ft 3in); Height: 4.01m (13ft 2in)
Weight:	5,100kg (11,240lb) maximum take-off
Powerplant:	1 × 883kW (1,200hp) Jumo 211Da in-line engine
Max speed:	410km/h (254mph)
Range:	960km (593 miles)
Service ceiling:	7,285m (23,900ft)
Crew:	2
Armament:	2 × 7.92mm (0.31in) MG 17 machine guns (forward firing); 1 × 7.92mm (0.31in) MG 15 machine gun (cockpit rear); 1 × 250kg (550lb) bomb; 2 × 300 litre (79 US gal) drop tanks

The Stuka is remembered as a symbol of the success of Nazi Germany's *Blitzkrieg* operations in 1939 and 1940. Although rapidly outclassed in its original dive-bomber role, the Ju 87 saw service with the Luftwaffe until the end of the war.

Above: Another of the long-range Ju 87R-2s, this example from 6./ Stukageschwader 2 'Immelmann' was based at Trimini, Libya, in 1941.

Junkers Ju 87R-2
3./Stukageschwader 5 flew this long-range Ju 87R-2, J9+LL, on the Eastern Front in March 1943. Based at Alakurtti near Murmansk, the aircraft received a winter coat of distemper.

Tailplane
To provide additional strength, the Ju 87B's two-spar tailplane was braced by two external struts, replaced on the improved Ju 87D by single aerodynamic struts. The elevators were used in conjunction with aerodynamic brakes to help pull out of a dive.

Gull wing
The very strong inverted gull wing was based on a two-spar structure with closely spaced ribs. The centre section was integral with the fuselage.

WING DESIGN

The Stuka's 'inverted-gull' wing permitted the fixed undercarriage to be kept short, reducing drag as much as possible. The wing featured large dive brakes, and had underwing pylons for two 250kg (551lb) or four 50kg (110lb) bombs. The Stuka could carry either a single 500kg (1,100lb) or 250kg (551lb) bomb on a cradle under the fuselage. The cradle ensured that the bomb swung clear of the propeller arc after it was released.

WINTER WARPLANES
Ju 87Ds wear temporary winter camouflage for operations on the Eastern Front in 1942. The aircraft are armed with AB 500 cluster bomb containers and centreline SC 250 bombs. The Eastern Front also saw heavy use of the Ju 87G, a specialist anti-tank aircraft, armed with a powerful pair of 37mm (1.45in) cannon under the wings.

Boeing B-17 Flying Fortress (1935)

TYPE • *Bomber* **COUNTRY** • *United States*

The B-17 was a mainstay of the US Eighth Air Force, ranging across occupied Europe as a daylight bomber and experiencing some of the hardest-fought air battles in history. The Flying Fortress also served widely in other theatres and in a variety of different roles.

SPECIFICATIONS (B-17G)

DIMENSIONS:	Length: 22.66m (74ft 4in); Wingspan: 31.62m (103ft 9in); Height 5.82m (19ft 1in)
WEIGHT:	29,710kg (65,000lb) loaded
POWERPLANT:	4 × 895kW (1,200hp) Wright radial engines
MAX SPEED:	462km/h (287mph)
RANGE:	3,219km (2,000 miles)
SERVICE CEILING:	10,850m (35,800ft)
CREW:	9–10
ARMAMENT:	2 × 12.7mm (0.5in) Browning trainable MGs in chin, dorsal, ventral and tail turrets; 1 × 12.7mm (0.5in) MG in two waist, cheek and single dorsal positions; up to 7,983kg (17,600lb) of bombs

Above: (Top) A B-17C was also the model for the RAF's Fortress Mk I. (Bottom) The B-17E introduced the definitive rear fuselage and redesigned vertical tail surfaces of the Flying Fortress family.

COCKPIT
Well laid out and spacious, the cockpit of the B-17 benefitted from Boeing's experience in airliner design. The pilot (and aircraft commander) sat on the right, with the co-pilot on the left.

TOP TURRET
The power-operated Sperry top turret was operated by the flight engineer, who was also responsible for fuel management and basic in-flight repairs.

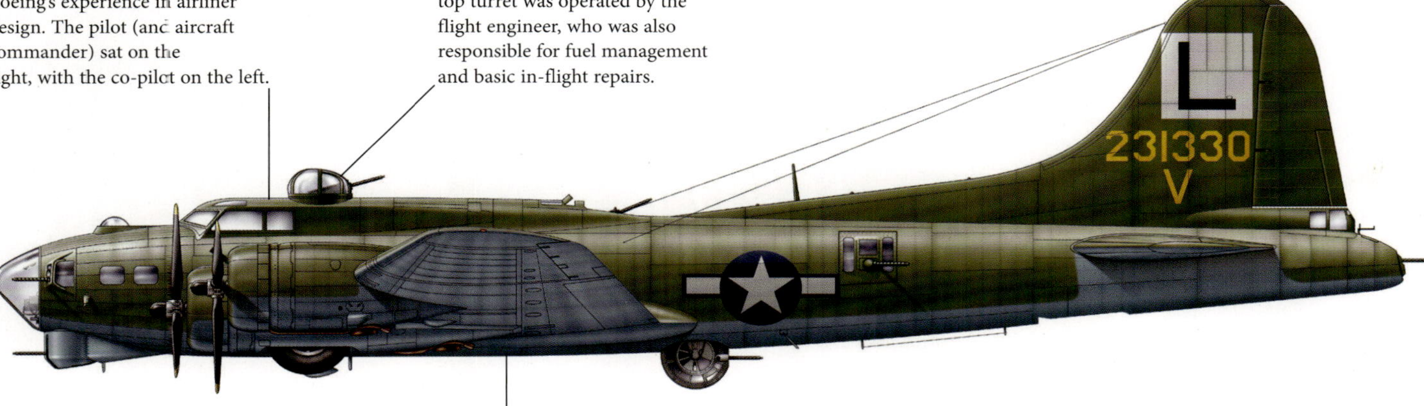

UPGRADES
The Flying Fortress was the iconic aircraft of the Eighth Air Force. As German defences improved, early models like the B-17E were found to lack defensive armament and armour plate. The B-17F and the B-17G were the main versions used in Europe by the Eighth Air Force from 1942 to 1945. The chin turret was introduced on late-model B-17Fs and was fitted to all production Gs. A new tail turret provided better visibility.

B-17G BOMBLOAD
Although the B-17G could in theory carry a bombload of up to 7,800kg (17,160lb), in practice a typical long-range load amounted to 2,000kg (4,400lb).

BOEING B-17B
When the B-17B entered service in 1939 (in the teeth of US Navy opposition), it was the fastest, highest-flying bomber in the world, ideal for the USAAC which was perfecting the art of daylight strategic bombing with large formations of aircraft with heavy defensive armament.

Mitsubishi A5M Claude (1936)

TYPE • *Fighter* **COUNTRY** • *Japan*

When it entered service at the beginning of 1937, the A5M 'Claude' represented a giant leap forwards in carrier-based fighters. Replacing antiquated biplane aircraft, it was the fastest naval fighter in the world and would remain so for almost two years.

SPECIFICATIONS (A5M4)

DIMENSIONS:	Length: 7.55m (24ft 9in); Wingspan: 11m (36ft 1in); Height: 3.2m (10ft 6in)
WEIGHT:	1,216kg (2,681lb)
POWERPLANT:	Nakajima Kotobuki 41 KAI 9-cylinder air-cooled radial engine, 585kW (785hp) at 3,000m (9,840ft)
MAX SPEED:	440km/h (273mph)
RANGE:	1,200km (746 miles)
CEILING:	9,800m (32,150ft)
CREW:	1
ARMAMENT:	2 × 7.7mm (0.303in) Type 89 machine guns

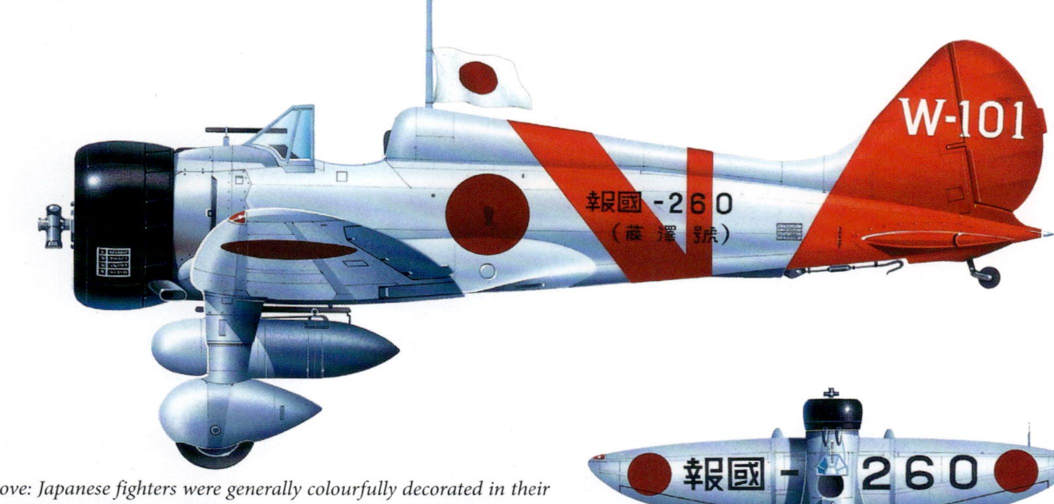

Above: Japanese fighters were generally colourfully decorated in their squadron markings. Many aircraft were funded by public subscription and carried the inscription 'Hokokugo' (patriotism).

ENGINE
The Nakajima Kotobuki 41 KAI nine-cylinder radial engine drove a three-bladed propeller. To improve forward visibility from the cockpit, an NACA (National Advisory Committee for Aeronautics) cowling with cooling flaps was fitted.

COCKPIT
Pilots of the 'Claude' had to face the elements; this was the last Japanese naval fighter to be fitted with an open cockpit. It did, however, have an exceptional field of view.

A5M2-KO, SUMMER 1938
This machine was based aboard *Kaga* (indicated by the 'K' on its fin) during operations off the coast of China, for which camouflage was adopted.

K-125

IMPORTANCE
It is impossible to overstate the importance of the A5M carrier-borne fighter in the development of Japanese industry and military capabilities in the mid-1930s. With this type, Japan moved from dependence on Western imports and thinking to an indigenous product that became its first carrier-borne monoplane fighter – one that was comparable with the best of its Western equivalents.

A5M2S IN FLIGHT, CHINA, 1938
The '3' prefix in the tailcode of these A5M2s signifies allocation to the 12th Kokutai, a large composite unit which saw much action in China during 1938.

Supermarine Spitfire (1936)

TYPE • *Fighter* **COUNTRY** • *United Kingdom*

SPECIFICATIONS (Spitfire Mk 1)

DIMENSIONS:	Length 9.12m (29ft 11in); Wingspan 11.23m (36ft 10in); Height 3.86m (12ft 8in)
WEIGHT:	Empty 2,049kg (4,517lb); Loaded 2,651kg (5,844lb)
POWERPLANT:	2 x Rolls-Royce Merlin II or III rated at 768kW (1,030hp) at 4,953m (16,250ft)
MAX SPEED:	557km/h (346mph)
RANGE:	1,014km (630 miles)
CEILING:	9,296m (30,500ft)
CREW:	1
ARMAMENT:	8 x Browning Mk II 7.7mm (0.303-in) machine guns

The pre-eminent British fighter of World War II was a thoroughbred with a racing lineage. A masterpiece of design from R.J. Mitchell, the Spitfire is remembered as one of the classic fighters of all time, seeing service in every theatre of combat from 1939 until 1945.

Right: The FR Mk XIVe was a late-war reconnaissance variant. Most Mk XIVes flew with 'clipped' wings to improve manoeuvrability at low altitude and had a 'teardrop' canopy for enhanced all-round visibility.

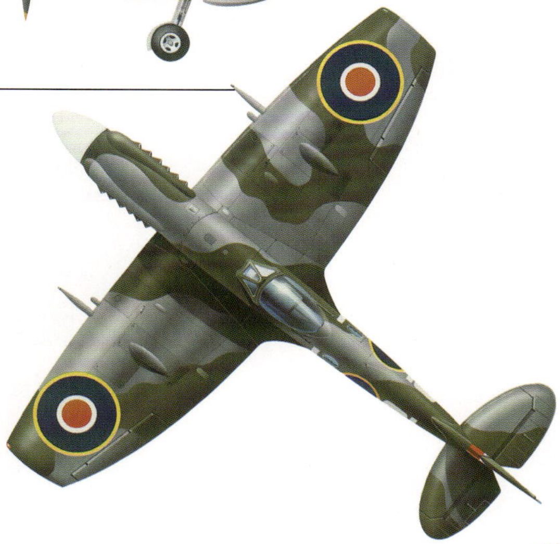

ARMAMENT
Fitted with the 'E' wing, the Mk XIVs were armed with two Hispano 20mm cannon in the outboard positions. The 'E' wing also had provision for a pair of Browning 12.7mm (0.5in) machine guns, but these were often removed.

CANOPY
The straight-topped canopy of the first Mk Is was replaced by the familiar 'blown' hood. This was done more to accommodate taller pilots than to improve visibility. (The variant here is the Mk IA.)

WINGS
Much of the success of the Spitfire was due to its thin and gracefully tapered wing. There was little room for larger weapons, however, and later marks gained bulges on the wing to allow for the ammunition drums of two or four Hispano cannon.

MK V SPITFIRE
The Mk V, which appeared in March 1941, was the second most numerous production Spitfire (after the Mk IX), accounting for 6,479 aircraft built. As RAF Fighter Command's standard fighter, the Mk V introduced the Merlin Mk 45. This was produced in a number of subvariants, including the Mk VB with cannon and machine-gun armament, and the Mk VC fighter-bomber with provision for external stores.

SPITFIRE MK XVI
Spitfire Mk IXs and XVIs became increasingly engaged in ground attack sorties after D-Day. Provided that the centreline underwing position was not occupied by a drop tank to increase range, the Mk IX/XVI had a 454kg (1,000lb) bombload.

Junkers Ju 88 (1936)

TYPE • *Heavy fighter* **COUNTRY** • *Germany*

SPECIFICATIONS (Ju 88A-11)

Dimensions:	Length: 14.4m (47ft 3in); Wingspan: 20m (65ft 7.5in); Height: 4.8m (15ft 8in)
Weight:	14,000kg (30,860lb) maximum take-off
Powerplant:	2 × 1,051kW (1,410hp) Junkers Jumo 211J-2 engines
Max speed:	470km/h (292mph)
Range:	2,700km (1,677 miles)
Service ceiling:	8,200m (26,900ft)
Crew:	4
Armament:	4 × 7.92mm (0.31in) MG 81J machine guns; 1 × 7.92mm (0.31in) MG 81Z twin machine gun; up to 1,400kg (3,100lb) bombload

One of the most versatile warplanes to see service in World War II, the Ju 88 excelled in roles as diverse as medium bomber, anti-shipping strike, close support and night-fighter. It was a mainstay of the Luftwaffe throughout the conflict.

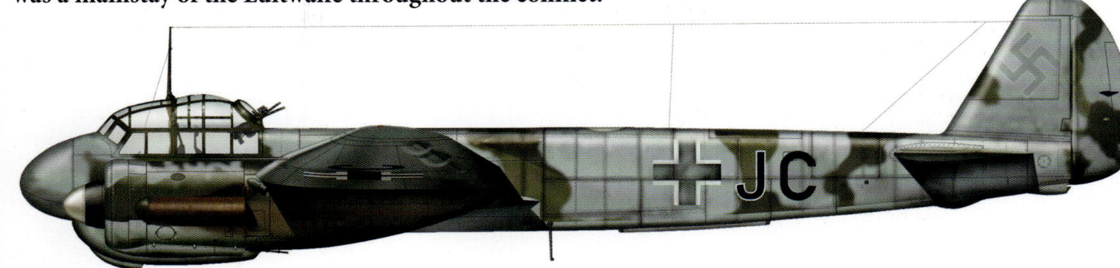

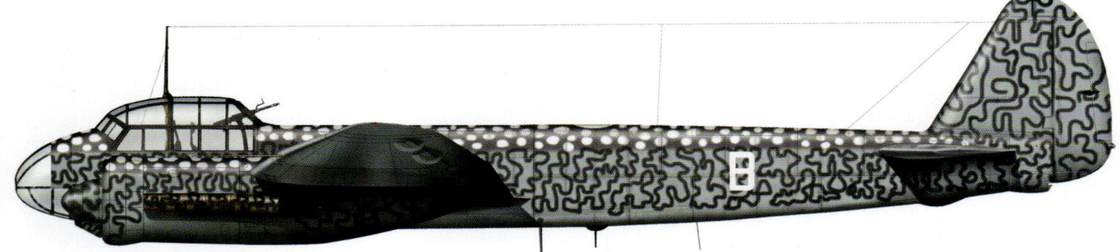

Above: (Top) A Ju 88C-6 used against Allied anti-submarine aircraft and as an escort fighter for the Focke-Wulf Fw 200 Condor maritime patrol aircraft. (Bottom) A Ju 88 in 'squiggle' camouflage, intended to provide protection for the aircraft parked on the ground and in the open.

Leading position
The bombardier had easy access to the glazed nose section, where a bombsight was located for conventional bombing. For dive-bombing, the pilot used a sight mounted in the cockpit, which swung to the side when not in use.

Rear MG
The flight engineer had the secondary task of operating the rearward-firing 7.92mm (0.31in) MG 15 machine gun in the rear of the glazed cabin.

Heavy weapons
The Ju 88 was fitted with four underwing racks, each of which could carry a 500kg (1,100lb) bomb. There were also two fuselage bays, with accommodation for a maximum of 28 50kg (110lb) SC50 bombs.

SERVICE

The prototype Ju 88 flew for the first time on 21 December 1936 and the first pre-series Ju 88A-0s were delivered to the Luftwaffe in August 1939. The Ju 88A was built in 17 different variants up to the Ju 88A-17, with progressively up-rated engines and enhanced defensive armament. The most widely used variant was the Ju 88A-4.

JU 88A-5, KG 54
The Ju 88A-4 version featured an increased wingspan and structural strengthening in order to carry greater loads. The powerplant was also to be upgraded to the Jumo 211F or 211J, but with these still not ready, production of the new version commenced with the A-1's engines, creating the interim Ju 88A-5 that saw widespread use in the Battle of Britain.

Messerschmitt Bf 110 (1936)

TYPE • *Heavy fighter* **COUNTRY** • *Germany*

SPECIFICATIONS

Dimensions:	Length: 13.05m (42ft 8in); Wingspan: 16.27m (53ft 4in); Height: 3.5m (11ft 6in)
Weight:	6,750kg (14,881lb) maximum take-off
Powerplant:	2 × 1,100kW (1,475hp) DB 605B 12-cylinder inverted-V engines
Max speed:	560km/h (349mph)
Range:	775km (482 miles)
Service ceiling:	10,900m (35,760ft)
Crew:	2–3
Armament:	2 × 20mm (0.79in) MG 151/20 cannon; 4 × 7.92mm (0.31in) MG 17 machine guns

Messerschmitt's Bf 110 was one of the Luftwaffe's great hopes at the start of World War II, but the twin-engined *Zerstörer* (destroyer) proved hopelessly vulnerable to single-engined fighter opposition during the Battle of Britain.

Above: The definitive night fighter was the Bf 110G-4, initially equipped with Lichtenstein C-1 (FuG 212) air interception (AI) radar; in this form, it was known as the Bf 110G-4a.

Radar
The Lichtenstein BC radar improved the chances of a Bf 110 detecting a bomber at night, but it reduced the aircraft's top speed by around 40km/h (25mph).

Crew
The Bf 110 was designed to carry a crew of three, comprising pilot, radio operator and gunner. In practice a crew of two was usually carried, the radio operator also acting as the gunner.

Messerschmitt Bf 110G-4b/R3
This Bf 110G-4b night fighter was flown by Wilhelm Johnen of 5./NJG 5, in April 1944. The aircraft strayed into Switzerland and was forced to land near Lake Constance, where Johnen and his crew were interned.

NEW ROLES
The Bf 110's performance during the Battle of Britain did not consign the aircraft to obsolescence. As the war progressed, it proved to be a solid fighting machine as a long-range fighter and fighter-bomber, as a bomber-destroyer and particularly as a night-fighter. It had become outclassed on daylight operations by late 1941, but when equipped with radar the Bf 110 night-fighters proved deadly against the RAF's bombers and made up 75 per cent of the night-fighter force by late 1942.

BF 110C, WESTERN DESERT
The availability of the 820kW (1,100hp) Daimler-Benz DB 601A engine with fuel injection provided the impetus to produce the Bf 110C series.

Consolidated Catalina (1936)

TYPE • *Seaplane* **COUNTRY** • *United States*

The exceptional flying boat of World War II, the 'Cat' was perhaps all the more remarkable since it had first been ordered for the US Navy back in 1933. It served with great success throughout World War II, and it became the most extensively built flying boat in aviation history.

SPECIFICATIONS (PBY-5)

Dimensions:	Length: 19.47m (63ft 10in); Wingspan: 31.7m (104ft); Height: 6.15m (25ft 1in)
Weight:	16,066kg (35,420lb)
Powerplant:	2 x Pratt & Whitney R1830-92 Twin Wasp radial piston engines, 895kW (1,200hp)
Max Speed:	288km/h (175mph)
Range:	4,030km (2,520 miles)
Ceiling:	4,000m (15,800ft)
Crew:	8
Armament:	3 x 7.62mm (0.3in) machine guns; 2 x 12.7mm (0.5in) machine guns; up to 1,814kg (4,000lb) of bombs or depth charges

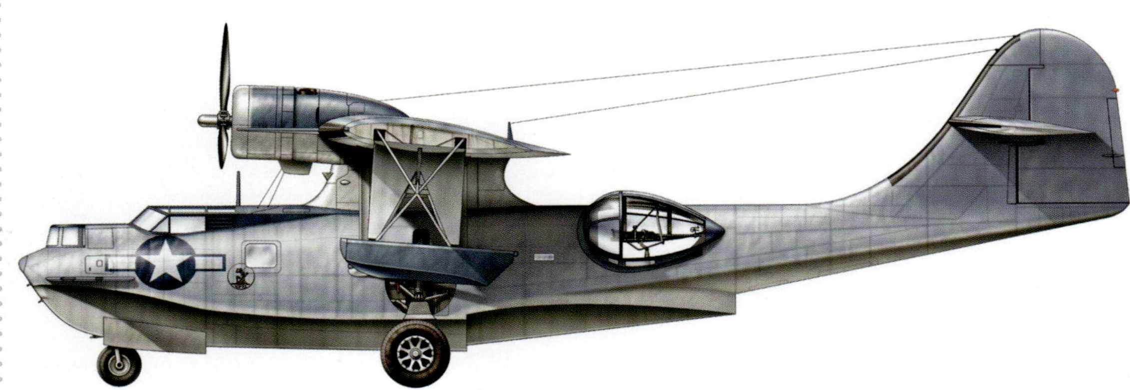

Above: The large observation blisters, first installed in the PBY-4, provided excellent visual coverage.

FLIGHT DECK
The pilot and co-pilot sat side by side on the flight deck and were provided with a roof escape hatch for emergencies.

ENGINE MOUNTS
The PBY's twin Pratt & Whitney Twin Wasp radial engines were mounted as high as possible to escape the effects of spray, which could be quite serious if the aircraft was taking off or alighting in a heavy swell.

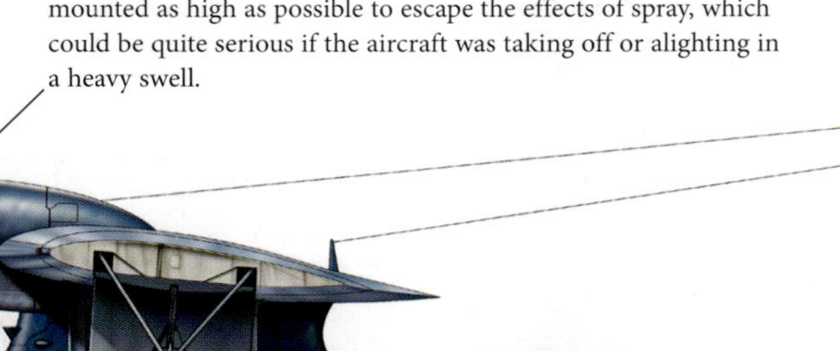

BEAM GUNS
The Catalina carried two 12.7mm (0.5in) machine guns in cupolas on each side of the fuselage. The waist gunners stood on a semi-circular platform, allowing them to traverse their guns over a wide arc.

AMPHIBIOUS
Following tests with a retractable tricycle wheel landing gear in the last PBY-4, the final 33 US Navy PBY-5s were completed in the amphibian form, as were 761 PBY-5A aircraft. Following early successful use of the PBY-5 by the RAF's Coastal Command in 1941 as the Catalina Mk I, large orders continued to be placed for the US Navy, additional production being undertaken by Canadian Vickers and Boeing of Canada.

PBY-5A IN FLIGHT
A Consolidated PBY-5A Catalina conducts an ocean patrol during 1942–43. More than 800 amphibious versions of the PBY-5 were built, mainly for the US Navy. The retractable tricycle landing gear meant it could be used for conventional runways.

Avro Anson (1936)

TYPE • *Multi-role* **COUNTRY** • *United Kingdom*

SPECIFICATIONS (GR Mk I)

Dimensions:	Length 12.88m (42ft 3in); Wingspan: 17.22m (56ft 6in); Height: 3.99m (13ft 1in)
Weight:	3,629kg (8,000lb) loaded
Powerplant:	2 × 261kW (350hp) Armstrong Siddeley Cheetah IX radial piston engines
Max speed:	303km/h (188mph)
Range:	1,271km (790 miles)
Service ceiling:	5,791m (19,000ft)
Crew:	3–4
Armament:	2 × 7.7mm (0.303in) MGs; provision to carry up to 163kg (360lb) of bombs

Although the Avro Anson was regarded as obsolescent as a combat aircraft soon into World War II, it nevertheless proved to be a useful and prolific multi-role type, particularly in reconnaissance, training, ferrying and logistics duties.

Above: No. 206 Squadron, RAF Coastal Command, received this Anson in 1937 and flew it over the North Sea until 1940 before passing the aeroplane to No. 1 Operational Training Unit. The machine crashed and was lost on 29 August 1940.

Turret
The Armstrong Whitworth-built turret was located on the Anson's dorsal section and was fitted with a single Lewis gun. The turret was turned manually.

Avro Anson GR Mk I
This Anson is seen in Coastal Command's standard finish and markings of the period immediately before World War II, namely an overall silver dope finish with yellow-outlined roundels, black serials and yellow squadron markings.

Landing gear
The Anson was the first RAF aircraft with retractable landing gear. The process of lowering or raising the gear, however, was performed in the cockpit via a manual hand crank.

NO. 48 SQN
No. 48 Sqn was the first RAF unit to receive the Avro Anson, with which it undertook coastal patrols until October 1941. Duties included convoy and anti-submarine flights and Armed Rover reconnaissance patrols. Shortly after receipt of the Lockheed Hudson, however, it moved to Gibraltar to cover the Torch landings in North Africa, and remained on the 'Rock' until February 1944, flying patrols over the western Mediterranean and Atlantic, occasionally tangling with Fw 200 Condors.

ANSON IN FLIGHT
An Avro Anson GR Mk I, flown by No. 217 Squadron RAF Coastal Command, in flight in 1937. This British twin-engined, multi-role aircraft went on to serve in a variety of roles for the Royal Air Force (RAF), Fleet Air Arm (FAA), Royal Canadian Air Force (RCAF) and numerous other air forces before, during and after World War II.

Tupolev SB-2 (1936)

TYPE • *Bomber* **COUNTRY** • *Soviet Union*

The Tupolev SB-2 was almost certainly the most capable light bomber in service anywhere in the world in the mid-1930s. It was the first aircraft of modern stressed-skin construction to be produced in the USSR, and in numerical terms was also the most important bomber of its day.

SPECIFICATIONS (SB-2bis)

Dimensions:	Length 12.57m (41ft 2.33in); Wingspan 20.33m (66ft 8.5in); Height 3.25m (10ft 8in)
Weight:	Empty 4,768kg (10,511lb); Maximum take-off 7,880kg (17,372lb)
Powerplant:	2 × 716kW (960hp) Klimov M-103 12-cylinder V-type
Max Speed:	450km/h (280mph) at 1,000m (3,281ft)
Range:	2,300km (1,429 miles)
Ceiling:	9,000m (29,530ft)
Crew:	3
Armament:	4 × 7.62mm (0.30in) machine guns; bombload of 600kg (1,323lb)

Right: The SB-2 was used operationally in Spain, where its crews held it in great esteem and gave it the nickname 'Katushka'. It was then considered to be invulnerable, as it was faster than most fighters then in service.

Crew positions
The aircraft attracted complaints about the high noise level, cramped crew compartments, hard undercarriage suspension and in particular about the front gunner's position. This could only be reached through a hatch under the fuselage, so he had no means of escape in the event of a belly landing or a ditching.

Performance
The SB-2's broad, high aspect ratio wing gave it a good altitude performance of nearly 9,150m (30,000ft). Russian crews nicknamed the bomber the 'Pterodactyl'.

Engines
Most production SB-2s were fitted with the Klimov M-103 engine, which drove new VISh variable-pitch propellers. In order to make full use of the engine's performance, a new engine cowling was produced without frontal radiators; these were replaced with new radiators placed under the engine nacelle.

DEVELOPMENT

The story of the SB-2 began in the early 1930s, when Andrei N. Tupolev built three prototype fast tactical bombers, designated ANT-40, ANT-40-1 and ANT-40-2. The latter proved the best variant. The type entered service in 1936, and 6,967 aircraft were built before production ended in 1941. Among the principal variants were the SB-2bis of 1938, with up-rated engines and greater fuel capacity, and the SB-2RK dive-bomber version of 1940.

FINNISH SB-2
The SB-2 seen here in October 1943 was actually a captured aircraft in service with the Finnish Air Force. By the time of the German invasion of Russia in 1941 the SB-2 was obsolescent in Soviet service, and heavy losses sustained in daylight attacks led to the aircraft being switched to night bombing.

Fairey Swordfish (1936)

TYPE • *Torpedo bomber* **COUNTRY** • *United Kingdom*

SPECIFICATIONS (Swordfish Mk I)

Dimensions:	Length 10.87m (35ft 8in); Wingspan 12.97m (42ft 6in); Height 3.76m (12ft 4in)
Weight:	Empty 2,132kg (4,700lb); Maximum take-off 4,196kg (9,250lb)
Powerplant:	514kW (690hp) Bristol Pegasus IIIM radial engine
Max Speed:	222km/h (138mph)
Range:	879km (546 miles)
Ceiling:	5,867m (19,250ft)
Crew:	2/3
Armament:	2 × 7.7mm (0.303in) machine guns, plus 1 × 457mm (18in) torpedo or 8 × 27.2kg (60lb) rocket projectiles

Affectionately known as the 'Stringbag', the Fairey Swordfish made a decisive contribution to the war, especially in the Mediterranean. Archaic in appearance even when it first flew, it was the Fleet Air Arm's premier torpedo bomber at the outbreak of hostilities.

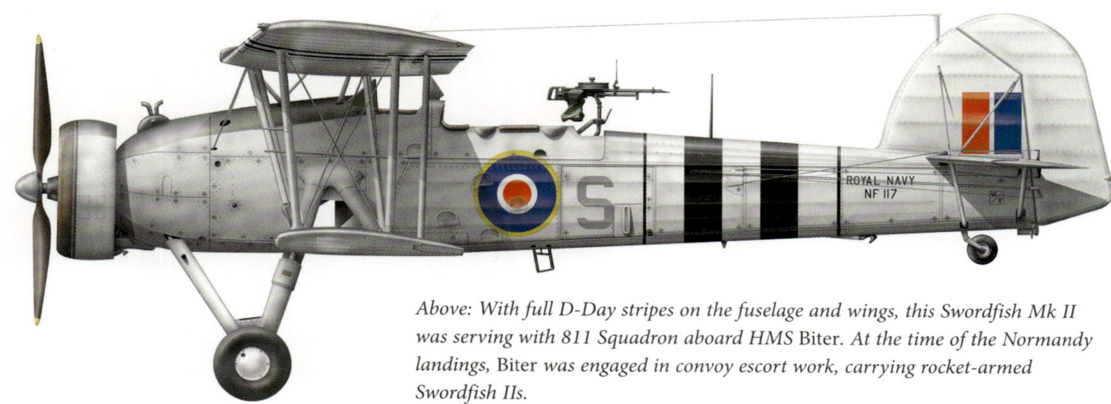

Above: With full D-Day stripes on the fuselage and wings, this Swordfish Mk II was serving with 811 Squadron aboard HMS Biter. *At the time of the Normandy landings,* Biter *was engaged in convoy escort work, carrying rocket-armed Swordfish IIs.*

Powerplant
Early production Mk IIs retained the Pegasus IIIM engine which delivered 514kW (690hp), but later examples were fitted with the more powerful 560kW (750hp) Pegasus XXX.

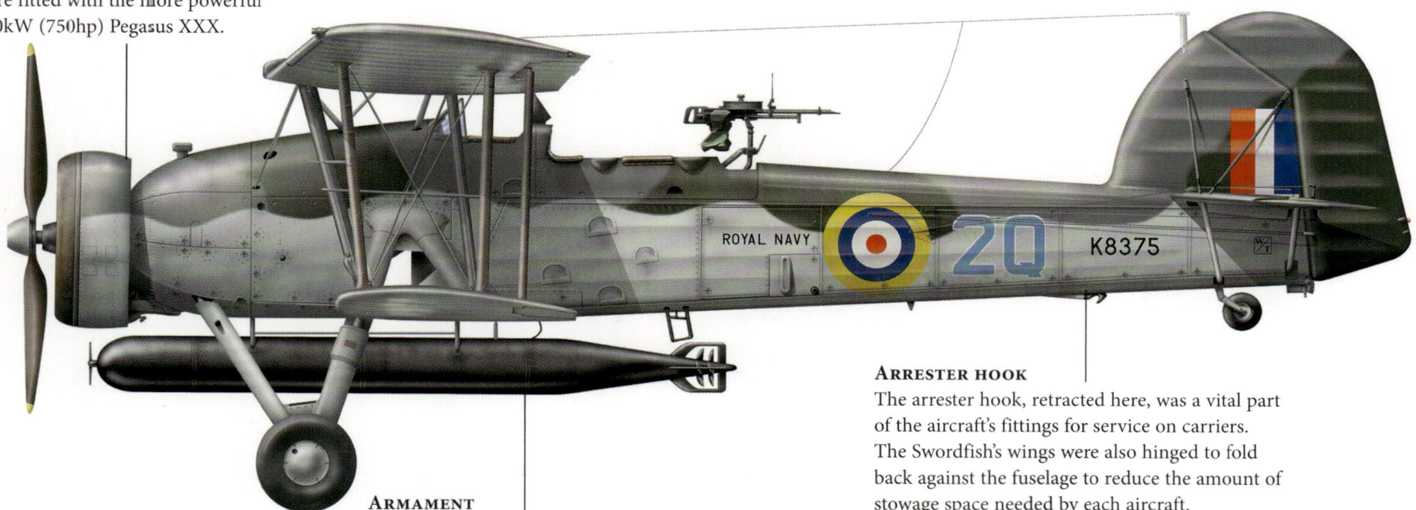

Arrester Hook
The arrester hook, retracted here, was a vital part of the aircraft's fittings for service on carriers. The Swordfish's wings were also hinged to fold back against the fuselage to reduce the amount of stowage space needed by each aircraft.

Armament
Primary armament of the Swordfish was the 457mm (18in) torpedo. In May 1941, this weapon crippled the mighty German battleship *Bismarck*, enabling warships to close in and finish her off.

TARANTO

In 1940 came the supreme triumph of the Swordfish – the memorable assault on the Italian fleet at anchor in Taranto harbour. The attack, made by 21 Swordfish on the night of 11 November 1940, was launched in two waves. The Italian Navy was dealt a shattering blow: three battleships were damaged severely; a cruiser and two destroyers had been hit; and two auxiliary vessels had been sunk.

CARRIER AIRCRAFT
Seen overflying the newly commissioned British aircraft carrier HMS *Ark Royal* in early 1939, this Swordfish Mk I is from No. 820 Squadron. The unit had become the first squadron to deploy aboard the carrier in January of that year.

Morane-Saulnier MS.406 (1937)

TYPE • *Fighter* **COUNTRY** • *France*

SPECIFICATIONS (MS.406 C.1)

Dimensions:	Length: 8.17m (26ft 9.33in); Wingspan: 10.62m (34ft 9.5in); Height: 3.25m (10ft 8in)
Weight:	2,471kg (5,448lb) loaded
Powerplant:	1 x 641kW (860hp) Hispano-Suiza 12Y-31 liquid-cooled V-12
Max speed:	490km/h (304mph)
Range:	750km (466 miles)
Service ceiling:	9,400m (30,840ft)
Crew:	1
Armament:	1 x 20mm (0.79in) HS-9 or HS-404 cannon; 2 x 7.5mm (0.295in) MAC1934 MGs

The MS.406 was France's first 'modern' monoplane fighter, but was in all major respects – except firepower and its ability to withstand battle damage– an indifferent warplane with little to commend it except ease of manufacture and availability.

Above: The MS.406 C.1 was numerically the most important French fighter in the campaign that led to France's defeat in May–June 1940. Production amounted to 1,077 aircraft, and the survivors were used mostly for training from 1941.

Nose cannon
In common with other fighter aircraft of European design, the MS.406 mounted a 20mm (0.79in) cannon between the engine blocks, firing through the propeller hub.

Antennae
The MS.406 had a rather curious antenna arrangement, with an aerial under the fuselage as well as one above. The one under the fuselage retracted automatically when the main undercarriage was lowered.

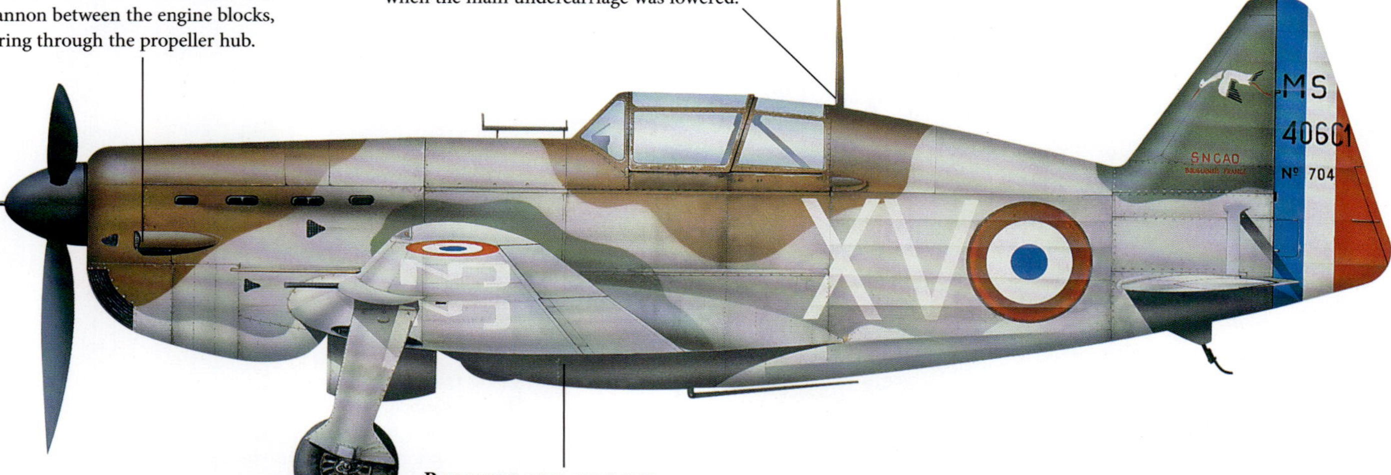

Radiator and coolant
A prominent radiator was mounted under the fuselage for cooling the engine. The coolant reservoir was mounted beneath the engine in the fuselage.

OUTFOUGHT

In terms of numbers, the MS.406 was the most important fighter in French service in September 1939. The MS.406 equipped 16 Groupes de Chasse and three Escadrilles in France and overseas, and 12 of the Groupes saw action against the Luftwaffe. The aircraft was very manoeuvrable and could withstand heavy battle damage, but it was outclassed by the Bf 109 and losses were heavy.

MS.406, 1939
An early MS.406 in flight in the pre-war months. The MS.406 was developed from the MS.405 monoplane fighter, which had a basic all-metal structure and a retractable main undercarriage, and which first flew on 8 August 1935.

Nakajima B5N (1937)

TYPE • *Torpedo bomber* **COUNTRY** • *Japan*

Used to devastating effect at Pearl Harbor the B5N *Tenzan* (called 'Kate' by the Allies) was an important weapon in the initial stages of the Pacific War. However, by the time its replacement, the B6N, had entered service the tide had turned against the Japanese.

SPECIFICATIONS (B5N2)

DIMENSIONS:	Length 10.30m (33ft 9.5in); Wingspan 15.51m (50ft 11in); Height 3.70m (12ft 1.33in)
WEIGHT:	Empty 2,279kg (5,025lb); Maximum take-off 4,108kg (9,056lb)
POWERPLANT:	746kW (1,000hp) Nakajima NK1B Sakae 11 14-cylinder rad
MAX SPEED:	378km/h (235mph) at 3,600m (11,811ft)
RANGE:	2,000km (1,243 miles)
CEILING:	8,260m (27,100ft)
CREW:	3
ARMAMENT:	1 × 7.7mm (0.303in) machine gun; 1 × 800kg (1,764lb) torpedo or up to 800kg (1,764lb) of bombs

Above: The B5N was tested in two versions, one with Fowler-type flaps, hydraulic flaps and hydraulic wing folding, and the other with plain flaps and manual wing folding. It was the latter version that was ordered into production.

VISIBILITY
The adoption of the 14-cylinder Sakae 11 engine in the B5N2, which had a relatively small diameter, meant that a smaller cowling could be fitted, improving the pilot's forward visibility – a vital factor in carrier operations – and also reducing drag.

COCKPIT
The B5N2 had a crew of three in a fully enclosed cockpit, comprising the pilot, an observer/navigator who also acted as bomb aimer and the radio operator, who also manned the trainable 7.7mm (0.3in) machine gun that was the aircraft's sole means of defence.

TAIL LETTERS
The 'AI' code letters on the tail of the B5N2 seen here indicate that it belongs to the *Akagi* Air Group, the *Akagi* being one of the carriers assigned to the attack on Pearl Harbor.

B5N2
Designed in 1936, the prototype B5N carrier attack bomber first flew in January 1937 and became operational as the B5N1 light bomber during the Sino–Japanese war. After its usefulness in that conflict was assessed, no major modifications were found necessary, but the need to improve the aircraft's performance was apparent. This led to a more powerful, definitive version, the B5N2.

B5N2S OVER TRUK
Two Nakajima B5N2 'Kates' make a pass over Truk lagoon in 1943. The B5N2 remained in production until 1943, by which time 1,149 examples of both variants had been built. Many B5Ns were later assigned to anti-submarine patrol work, after staggering losses sustained during the battle for the Philippines.

Bristol Blenheim Mk IV (1937)

TYPE • *Bomber* **COUNTRY** • *United Kingdom*

SPECIFICATIONS

Dimensions:	Length 12.98m (42ft 7in); Wingspan 17.70m (58ft 1in); Height 2.99m (9ft 10in)
Weight:	Empty 4,441kg (9,790lb); Maximum take-off 6,537kg (14,400lb)
Powerplant:	2 × 674kW (905hp) Bristol Mercury XV radial engines
Max Speed:	428km/h (266mph) at 3,595m (11,800ft)
Range:	2,340km (1,460 miles)
Ceiling:	6,705m (22,000ft)
Crew:	2
Armament:	5 × 7.7mm (0.303in) machine guns; internal bombload of 454kg (1,000lb)

Hailed at the time as the fastest light bomber in the world, the Blenheim was a fundamental part of the RAF's attack force, only to achieve disappointing results and heavy losses in combat during the early years of the war.

Above: The Mk V was the last Blenheim variant, its most distinctive modification being the interchangeable nose gun pack or bomb-aimer position.

Engines
The Blenheim's Bristol Mercury engines had a prominent intake projecting forward from the engine cowling. These were ram air intakes for the oil cooler.

Escape hatches
The gunner had an emergency exit hatch behind him in the roof of the fuselage. The pilot and navigator had sliding panels in the cockpit roof and an escape hatch in the floor of the nose section.

Tail surfaces
Only a small proportion of the Blenheim's vertical tail surfaces was fixed, the aircraft having a large full-height rudder controlled by cables running the length of the fuselage.

COMBAT PERFORMANCE

On the second day of the war, Blenheims of Nos 107 and 110 Squadrons from Marham, Norfolk, carried out the RAF's first offensive operation when they unsuccessfully attacked units of the German Navy in the Elbe estuary. The total inadequacy of the Blenheim's defensive armament became apparent in the battles of Norway and France, where they suffered appalling losses.

BOMBING UP
The ground crew of No. 40 Squadron RAF Bomber Command, RAF Wyton in Cambridgeshire, England, pull a trolley loaded with 114kg (250lb) general-purpose bombs to load onto a Blenheim Mk IV for a raid on 29 July 1940.

Gloster Gladiator (1937)

TYPE • *Fighter* **COUNTRY** • *United Kingdom*

Somewhat overrated and largely sentimentalized as a result of myth rather than actual achievement, the Gladiator stands in history as the RAF's last biplane interceptor. It served just prior to World War II, as the era of the classic monoplane fighter was dawning.

SPECIFICATIONS (Gladiator Mk I)

DIMENSIONS:	Length: 8.36m (27ft 5in); Wingspan 9.83m (32ft 3in); Height 3.53m (11ft 7in)
WEIGHT:	Empty 1,562kg (3,444lb); Maximum take-off 2,206kg (4,864lb)
POWERPLANT:	619kW (830hp) Bristol Mercury VIIIA 9-cylinder radial
MAX SPEED:	414km/h (257mph)
RANGE:	708km (440 miles)
SERVICE CEILING:	10,210m (33,500ft)
CREW:	1
ARMAMENT	4 x 7.7mm (0.303in) machine guns

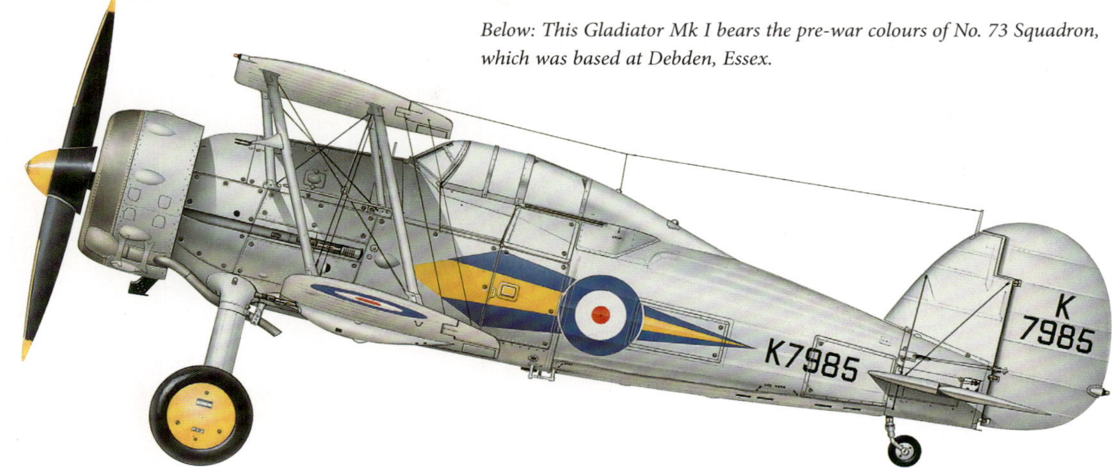

Below: This Gladiator Mk I bears the pre-war colours of No. 73 Squadron, which was based at Debden, Essex.

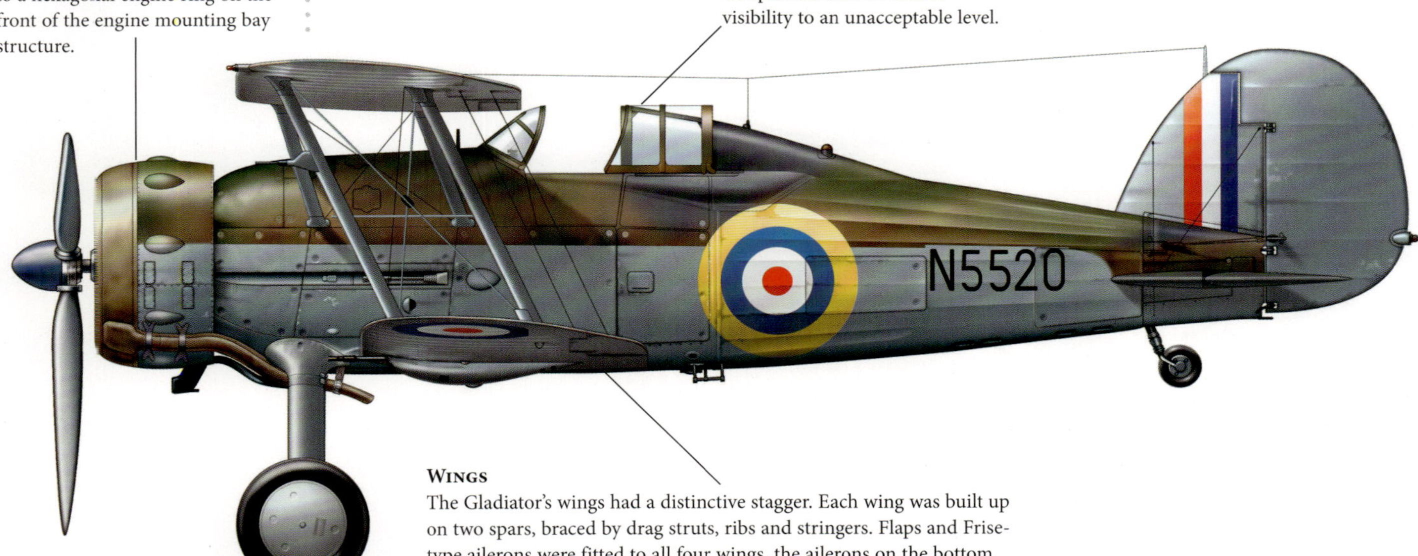

ENGINE MOUNT
The Gladiator's Bristol Mercury engine was secured by eight bolts to a hexagonal engine ring on the front of the engine mounting bay structure.

COCKPIT
For the first time, RAF fighter pilots had the benefit of a fully enclosed cockpit. Some diehards complained that it reduced visibility to an unacceptable level.

WINGS
The Gladiator's wings had a distinctive stagger. Each wing was built up on two spars, braced by drag struts, ribs and stringers. Flaps and Frise-type ailerons were fitted to all four wings, the ailerons on the bottom wings actuating those above by means of tie rods.

GAUNTLET SUCCESSOR

Designed as a more advanced successor to the open-cockpit Gauntlet fighter, the prototype Gladiator was flown in September 1934 and evaluated by the Air Ministry in the following year, the trials resulting in a production order for 23 machines, followed by further orders for 128 aircraft. First deliveries were made in February 1937.

K5200 PROTOTYPE
The K5200 prototype of the Gladiator, its prototype status indicated by the open cockpit. The Gloster Gladiator was the last British biplane fighter to enter service.

Fieseler Fi 156 Storch (1937)

TYPE • *Reconnaissance* **COUNTRY** • *Germany*

SPECIFICATIONS

DIMENSIONS:	Length: 9.9m (32ft 6in); Wingspan: 14.3m (46ft 11in); Height: 3.1m (10ft 2in)
WEIGHT:	Maximum take-off 1,260kg (2,778lb)
POWERPLANT:	1 × 180kW (240hp) Argus As 10 V-8 inverted air-cooled piston engine
MAX SPEED:	175km/h (109mph)
RANGE:	380km (240 miles)
SERVICE CEILING:	4,600m (15,090ft)
CREW:	2
ARMAMENT:	1 × 7.92mm (0.31in) MG 15 machine gun

Widely used by the Luftwaffe throughout the conflict, the Fieseler Fi 156 *Storch* ('Stork') set the trend for subsequent aircraft in its class, with a combination of excellent short take-off and landing (STOL) performance and an extensively glazed cockpit.

Left: An Fi 156 V4, the fourth Storch prototype (D-IFMR), prepares to make a take-off running from skis rather than its customary wheels.

DEFENCES
The Storch was given a single 7.9mm (0.3in) MG 15, firing through the rear canopy to fend off any fighters attacking from the rear.

PROPELLER
The second prototype Fi 156 was tested with a variable-pitch metal propeller, but all other Storch aircraft had a fixed-pitch wooden Schwarz propeller.

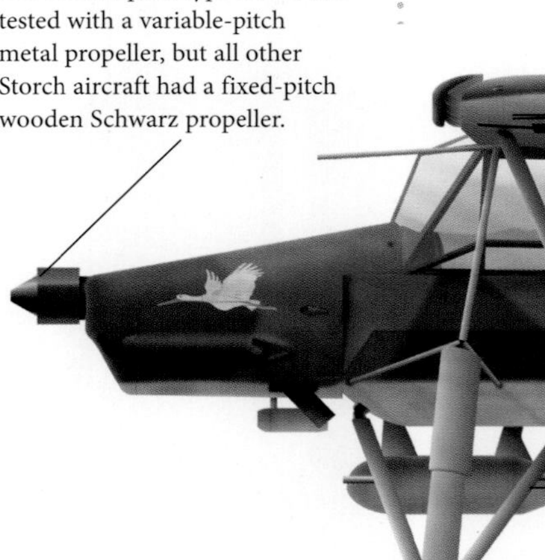

UNDERCARRIAGE
The Storch's STOL capability was enhanced by its strong undercarriage. The energy-absorbing oleos could easily withstand the high vertical sink-rate imposed by very steep approaches.

FAMOUS EXPLOITS
The Storch's wartime exploits in the hands of the Luftwaffe included the rescue of Italian leader Benito Mussolini from his imprisonment in a hotel high in the Apennine Mountains on 12 September 1943. Meanwhile, test pilot Hanna Reitsch flew into the ruins of Berlin on 26 April 1945 carrying General Ritter von Greim, who Hitler would appoint as the new – and final – commander of the Nazi-era Luftwaffe.

PARIS LANDING
Shortly after the fall of Paris to the German Blitzkrieg in 1940, this Storch landed in the Place de la Concorde, demonstrating its excellent STOL characteristics. The aircraft's STOL capability was the result of a wing equipped with high-lift devices, including a fixed slat that extended over the full span of the leading edge, while the trailing edge was equipped with slotted ailerons and, across its full length, slotted camber-changing flaps.

Ilyushin DB-3 (1937)

TYPE • *Bomber* **COUNTRY** • *Soviet Union*

SPECIFICATIONS

Dimensions:	Length: 14.22m (46ft 8in); Wingspan: 21.44m (70ft 4in); Height: 4.19m (13ft 9in)
Weight:	Maximum take-off 9,450kg (20,834lb)
Powerplant:	2 x 709kW (951hp) Nazarov 9-cylinder air cooled radial engines
Max Speed:	439km/h (273mph)
Range:	3,800km (2,400 miles)
Ceiling:	9,600m (31,500ft)
Crew:	3
Armament	1 x 7.62mm (0.3in) ShKAS machine gun flexibly mounted in nose; 1 x 7.62mm (0.3in) ShKAS machine gun in dorsal turret; 1 x 7.62mm (0.3in) ShKAS flexibly mounted in ventral hatch; up to 2,500kg (5,511lb) bombload

After demonstrating spectacular long-range capability in propaganda flights in the late 1930s, on 7 August 1941 the DB-3 set an important landmark in Soviet wartime history – it became the first Soviet aircraft to bomb Berlin.

Above: The DB-3TP floatplane was converted from a standard DB-3 with the addition of a pair of British-built floats. Tested at Sevastopol during 1938, the aircraft was found unsatisfactory and no production ensued.

Crew
The crew of three consisted of the pilot, navigator/front gunner with a 7.62mm (0.3in) ShKAS and the radio operator/rear gunner who was required to divide his time between the dorsal turret and a ventral gun position.

Black Sea fleet aircraft
An M-86-engined DB-3T of 2 MTAP serving with the Black Sea Fleet in the spring of 1941. Black Sea Fleet DB-3Ts were the first Soviet aircraft to bomb Berlin in August 1941.

Airframe
The aircraft featured new construction techniques that allowed for a light structure but it was difficult to build and production was slow – only 45 aircraft were built by two factories during 1937.

MODERN FEATURES
Developed from the all-wood TsKB-26, the first Soviet twin engine to be looped, the DB-3 was an all-metal long-range bomber that, although it could carry five times the bombload of Tupolev's SB-2, was only 24km/h (15mph) slower. It also boasted modern features such as self-sealing fuel tanks and a crew intercom system, both included as a result of Soviet aircraft experience over Spain.

BOMBING MISSION
With its engines turning in the background, the crew of an Ilyushin DB-3 bomber on the South-Western Front in May 1942 are briefed by a senior officer.

Vought SB2U Vindicator (1937)

TYPE • *Naval bomber* **COUNTRY** • *United States*

The first monoplane dive bomber in US Navy service, the SB2U Vindicator was still in use with Marine Corps units in 1943 and saw combat at the Battle of Midway as well as in French hands during the Battle of France.

SPECIFICATIONS (SB2U-3)

Dimensions:	Length: 10.36m (34ft); Wingspan: 12.77m (41ft 11in); Height: 4.34m (14ft 3in)
Weight:	Maximum take-off 4273kg (9421lb)
Powerplant:	1 × 615kW (825hp) Pratt & Whitney R-1535-02 Twin Wasp Junior 14-cylinder air-cooled radial piston engine
Max Speed:	391km/h (243mph)
Range:	1,800km (1,120 miles)
Ceiling:	7,200m (23,600ft)
Crew:	2
Armament:	1 × 12.7mm (0.5in) M2 Browning machine gun in starboard wing; 1 × 12.7mm (0.5in) M2 Browning machine gun flexibly mounted in rear cockpit; up to 453kg (1,000lb) bombload under fuselage

Above: This aircraft was assigned to Escadrille 10 of AB3 at Cuers in July 1940. Attrition of the French V-156s was high, the aircraft proving vulnerable to enemy fighters and ground fire. At the armistice, only eight aircraft survived of 40 originally ordered by the Aeronavale.

Canopy
The long greenhouse-style canopy was one of the key distinguishing features of the Vindicator. The canopy housed the aircraft's two-man crew, which consisted of a pilot and a gunner seated in tandem.

SB2U-1
Serving aboard USS *Ranger* with VS-41 in August 1941, immediately before the aircraft's withdrawal from front-line operations, this SB2U-1 was engaged in scouting missions over the Atlantic.

MIDWAY
In the US, the Vindicator had been replaced by the Dauntless on carriers by December 1941 but continued to be used by the US Navy as a training aircraft. Few Marine Corps units ever operated the SB2U and one of these, VMSB-231 consisting of both SB2U-3s and SBD-2 Dauntlesses, was formed on Midway Island on 1 March 1942 to defend the island in the event of a Japanese attack. During the subsequent Battle of Midway, the squadron lost 23 out of 30 aircraft over the course of 4–6 June.

VINDICATORS IN FORMATION
Vought SB2U-3 Vindicators of Marine Scouting Squadron One in flight on 7 June 1941. The Vindicator also attracted the attention of the French Aeronavale, who would be the first to take the aircraft into action.

Dornier Do 24 (1937)

TYPE • *Seaplane* **COUNTRY** • *Germany*

SPECIFICATIONS (Do 24K-2)

DIMENSIONS:	Length: 22.05m (72ft 4in); Wingspan: 27m (88ft 7in); Height: 5.75m (18ft 10in)
WEIGHT:	18,400kg (40,565lb) maximum take-off
POWERPLANT:	3 x 746kW (1,000hp) Wright R-1820-G102 engines
MAX SPEED:	330km/h (210mph)
RANGE:	2,900km (1,800 miles)
SERVICE CEILING:	7,500m (24,600ft)
CREW:	4 or 6
ARMAMENT:	N/A

The Dornier Do 24 was developed to meet a Dutch requirement in 1935 for a flying boat to use in the Dutch East Indies. Only small numbers were completed before Germany invaded and occupied the Netherlands in 1940 and took over production for themselves.

Above: This German Luftwaffe Do 24T-2 of the 7.Seenotstaffel/SBK XI flew in the Aegean area in 1942.

POWERPLANT
The Do 24K-2 differed from the Do 24K-1 in its powerplant of three 746kW (1,000hp) Wright R-1820-G102 engines.

DORNIER DO 24K-2
This Dutch-built Do 24K-2 was completed for the Luftwaffe for air-sea rescue duties.

LAYOUT
The Do 24 was equipped with a strut-mounted wing carrying three engines, and it combined all-metal construction with a shallow, broad-beamed hull and stabilizing sponsons.

GERMAN TAKEOVER
After the German invasion, three examples of the Do 24K-2 were transferred to Germany for evaluation. After successful testing in the air-sea rescue role, production was reinstated. Production amounted to 170 aircraft for Luftwaffe use, beginning with 11 Dutch-built Do 24N-1 aircraft that were completed to the same standard as the Do 24K-2, retaining the R-1820-G102 engines. The first example was delivered to the Luftwaffe in August 1941 and these aircraft served in the air-sea rescue role.

HOISTED AIRCRAFT
A loading crane at a flying-boat base on the French side of the English Channel lifts a Dornier Do 24 flying boat out of the water. Further production in the Netherlands yielded the Do 24T series, which were powered by three 746kW (1,000hp) BMW-Bramo 323R-2 Fafnir engines.

Henschel Hs 126 (1937)

TYPE • *Reconnaissance* **COUNTRY** • *Germany*

SPECIFICATIONS

DIMENSIONS:	Length: 10.9m (35ft 7in); Wingspan: 14.5m (47ft 7in); Height: 3.8m (12ft 4in)
WEIGHT:	3,090kg (6,820lb) maximum take-off
POWERPLANT:	1 × 656kW (880hp) BMW 132Dc radial engine
MAX SPEED:	356km/h (221mph)
RANGE:	998km (620 miles)
SERVICE CEILING:	8,530m (28,000ft)
CREW:	2
ARMAMENT:	2 × 7.92mm (0.31in) MG 17 machine guns (one forward firing, one in rear of cockpit); 5 × 10kg (22lb) bombs or 1 × 50kg (110lb) bomb

The Henschel Hs 126 two-seat short-range reconnaissance aircraft traces its lineage to the same company's parasol-winged Hs 122 that was developed in 1935 as a successor to the Heinkel He 45 and He 46, powered by a 492kW (660hp) Siemens SAM 22B engine.

Above: This Hs 126B-1 flew with 2.(Heeres-)/Aufklärungsgruppe 14 as part of the Fliegerführer Afrika unit – the scout and liaison unit detached to General Rommel's HQ – during July 1941.

POWERPLANT
The initial production Hs 126A-1 was generally similar to the A-0 pre-production model, but was powered by a 656kW (880hp) BMW 132Dc radial engine.

HENSCHEL HS 126A-1
An Hs 126A-1 flown by 9.(Heeres-)/Lehrgeschwader 2, active from Chalons, Belgium, in June 1940.

RECONNAISSANCE
For reconnaissance work, a single Zeiss camera in a rear-fuselage bay was supplemented by a handheld camera in the rear cockpit.

FOREIGN SERVICE
Six Hs 126A-1s were employed for combat trials in Spain in 1938 and, following use by the Condor Legion, were passed on to the Spanish Nationalist air arm, while 16 more examples were delivered to Greece. The Hellenic Air Force examples saw combat against Italian aircraft during the early stages of the Balkans campaign in April 1941.

HENSCHEL HS 126B-1
The improved Hs 126B-1 arrived in service in summer 1939 with additional radio equipment and either the 634kW (850hp) Bramo 323A-1 or 671kW (900hp) Bramo 323A-2 engine.

Blohm und Voss BV 138 (1938)

TYPE • *Seaplane* **COUNTRY** • *Germany*

SPECIFICATIONS (BV 138C-1)

Dimensions:	Length: 19.85m (65ft 1in); Wingspan: 26.94m (88ft 5in); Height: 5.9m (19ft 4in)
Weight:	17,650kg (38,967lb) maximum take-off
Powerplant:	3 × 656kW (880hp) Junkers Jumo 205D 6-cylinder diesel engines
Max speed:	285km/h (177mph)
Range:	1,220km (760 miles)
Service ceiling:	5,000m (16,000ft)
Crew:	6
Armament:	2 × 20mm (0.79in) MG 151 cannons (nose turret and rear fuselage); 1 × 13mm (0.51in) MG 131 machine gun (behind centre engine nacelle); 1–3 × 7.92mm (0.31in) MG 15 machine guns (optional); up to 6 × 50kg (110lb) bombs or 4 × 150kg (330lb) depth charges (optional)

The origins of the Blohm und Voss BV 138 can be traced back to the Ha 138 – the first flying-boat design from the Hamburger Flugzeugbau GmbH company, designed under the capable leadership of Richard Vogt.

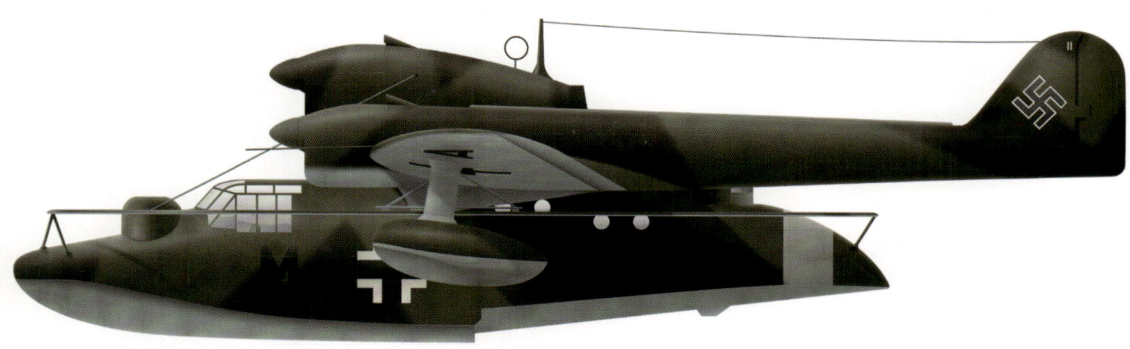

Above: Equipped for mine warfare, this BV 138 MS was on strength with 1. Minensuchstaffel, part of Minensuchgruppe 1, operating along the Baltic Coast in 1944.

Powerplant
The C-series that appeared in March 1941 introduced a new powerplant in the form of three Jumo 205D engines as well as further structural strengthening.

BV 138C-1 Armament
As well as the armament of the BV 138B-1, the C-1 added a 13mm (0.51in) MG 131 cannon in a position behind the centre engine nacelle.

Hull improvements
Compared to its predecessor, the BV 138 featured a much-enlarged hull, with improved planning surfaces.

MINESWEEPER
One unusual development of the flying boat was the BV 138MS for the minesweeping mission. Based on the airframe of BV 138B-0 pre-production aircraft, the BV 138MS had its armament removed and a degaussing loop of duralumin running around the airframe; this was provided with field-generating equipment to detonate mines below the aircraft. A handful of these conversions were completed during 1942–43.

BLACK SEA PATROL
A BV 138C operated by 3.(F)/SAGr 125 from Constanza patrols coastal waters around the Black Sea. The previous five-man crew was increased to six in the C-series and some of these aircraft were additionally equipped with FuG 200 Hohentwiel radar for maritime surveillance.

Curtiss SBC Helldiver (1938)

TYPE • *Naval bomber* **COUNTRY** • *United States*

The final front-line combat biplane in US service, the Curtiss SBC Helldiver was the last of a distinguished line of Curtiss carrier biplanes. Surprisingly, the design originally flew as a monoplane aircraft.

SPECIFICATIONS

Dimensions:	Length: 8.58m (28ft 2in); Wingspan: 10.36m (34ft 0in); Height: 3.18m (10ft 5in)
Weight:	3,462kg (7,632lb) maximum take-off
Powerplant:	1 × 630kW (850hp) Wright R-1820-34 Cyclone 9-cylinder air-cooled radial piston engine
Max speed:	377km/h (234mph)
Range:	652km (405 miles)
Service ceiling:	7,300m (24,000ft)
Crew:	2
Armament:	1 × 7.6mm (0.3in) M1919 Browning machine gun fixed forward-firing in nose; 1 × 7.6mm (0.3in) M1919 Browning machine gun flexibly mounted in rear cockpit; up to 454kg (1,000lb) bombload

Left: An SBC-3 Helldiver VS-3 in flight c.1939. The pace of aviation development was such that all the SBCs had been replaced by the SBD Dauntless on carriers before the US entered the war in December 1941.

Colouring
The blue engine cowling and fuselage band indicate this was the leader of the squadron's 3rd section, while the unit badge below the windscreen depicts a frigatebird in flight.

Armament
The Helldiver had one 7.62mm (0.3in) M1919 Browning machine gun fixed forward-firing in the nose, one 7.62mm (0.3in) M1919 Browning machine gun flexibly mounted in the rear cockpit, and up to 454kg (1,000lb) bombload.

SBC-3 Helldiver
Pictured as it appeared in 1937, the red tail surfaces of this Helldiver of VS-5 signify that the aircraft was serving aboard USS *Yorktown*.

REDESIGN
The Helldiver started life as the Curtiss Model 73, a two-seat parasol monoplane carrier fighter with a folding wing. Rejected for the fighter role, the aircraft was proposed as a scout bomber but the parasol wing failed during dive-bombing tests, although the pilot was able to land the damaged machine. In response Curtiss proposed reworking the aircraft as a biplane, the second lower wing adding strength to the design at the expense of the wing-folding ability. The Navy accepted the change.

SBC-4 HELLDIVER
The US Navy ordered 83 production examples of the Helldiver, which began entering service in 1937. A further 124 of the improved SBC-4 were ordered in January 1938.

Vought OS2U Kingfisher (1938)

TYPE • *Floatplane* **COUNTRY** • *United States*

SPECIFICATIONS

DIMENSIONS:	Length: 10.24m (33ft 7in); Wingspan: 10.94m (35ft 11in); Height: 4.47m 14ft 8in)
WEIGHT:	2,722kg (6,000lb) maximum take-off
POWERPLANT:	1 x 340kW (450hp) Pratt & Whitney R-985-AN2 Wasp Junior 9-cylinder air-cooled radial piston engine
MAX SPEED	275km/h (171mph)
RANGE:	1,461km (908 miles)
SERVICE CEILING:	5,500m (18,200ft)
CREW:	2
ARMAMENT:	1 x 7.62mm (0.3in) Browning M1919 machine gun fixed forward-firing in forward fuselage; 1 x 7.62mm (0.3in) Browning M1919 machine gun flexibly mounted in rear cockpit; up to 295kg (650lb) bombload

The US Navy's standard shipboard floatplane for the majority of the war, the unassuming Vought OS2U Kingfisher proved reliable and versatile and served for considerably longer than had been planned originally.

Left: When it entered service in August 1940, the Vought OS2U was the first catapult-launched monoplane to be operated by the US Navy.

POWERPLANT
The aircraft was powered by a single 340kW (450hp) Pratt & Whitney R-985-AN2 Wasp Junior nine-cylinder air-cooled radial piston engine.

CONSTRUCTION
The OS2U was the first production aircraft to be constructed using spot welding, a process Vought had developed in conjunction with the Naval Aircraft Factory.

FLOAT
The Kingfisher featured interchangeable float or wheeled undercarriage and operated from both catapult-equipped ships and shore bases throughout its career.

US NAVY SERVICE

The OS2U Kingfisher became the standard aircraft operating in the gunnery-spotting observation and air–sea rescue role from the US Navy's capital ships. Battleships normally carried three aircraft, although the powerful new Iowa-class battleships featured four OS2Us apiece when they were commissioned.

ROLLING OUT
Ground crew roll a Vought OS2U Kingfisher out of its hangar at a Naval Air Station, c.January–May 1942. Note that the plane has a depth charge under each wing. In service the OS2U was popular, proving robust and dependable.

Curtiss P-36 & Hawk Model 75 (1938)

TYPE • *Fighter* **COUNTRY** • *United States*

SPECIFICATIONS (P-36A)

Dimensions:	Length: 8.69m (28ft 6in); Wingspan: 11.38m (37ft 4in); Height: 2.57m (8ft 5in)
Weight:	2,726kg (6,010lb) maximum take-off
Powerplant:	1 × Pratt & Whitney R-1830-17 Twin Wasp 14-cylinder air-cooled radial piston engine
Max speed:	504km/h (313mph)
Range:	1,006km (625 miles)
Service ceiling:	10,000m (32,800ft)
Crew:	1
Armament:	1 × 7.62mm (0.3in) M1919 machine gun and 1 × 12.7mm (0.5in) M2 Browning machine gun fixed firing forward in upper front fuselage decking

Although it scored the first USAAF air-to-air victories of World War II, the P-36 would see very little front-line use in US service, but the aircraft proved hugely successful in French and Finnish hands, fighting both for and against the Allies.

Above: A P-36C in olive drab and neutral grey, early 1942. The tail designator is restricted to the aircraft number (22) and last four digits of the serial number (38-191).

Powerplant
The aircraft was powered by a Pratt & Whitney R-1830-17 Twin Wasp 14-cylinder air-cooled radial piston engine.

P-36A Hawk
This P-36A was part of the 79th Pursuit Squadron, 20th Pursuit Group, based at Moffett Field, California, November 1939. The tail designator indicates it is the 21st aircraft.

HAWK 75
While the P-36 was entering service with the USAAC, Curtiss was engaged in an active marketing campaign for a simplified export version with fixed landing gear and a Wright Cyclone engine. It was dubbed the Hawk 75 to capitalize on the excellent reputation of Curtiss's earlier Hawk biplane fighters. Thirty fixed-gear Hawk 75-Ms were acquired by China as well as a production licence for the Hawk 75A-5, broadly equivalent to the P-36A with retractable undercarriage, though only a few examples were actually completed.

Hardpoints
Some later P-36 aircraft were fitted with an optional hardpoint under each wing, each capable of carrying up to 69kg (152lb) of ordnance.

CURTISS P-36A
An American Curtiss P-36A fighter plane in flight. Of all the nations that flew the various derivatives of the Model 75 in combat, its country of origin made the least use of the Curtiss fighter.

Blackburn Skua (1938)

TYPE • *Naval bomber* **COUNTRY** • *United Kingdom*

Through it was principally designed as a carrier-borne dive-bomber, the Blackburn Skua doubled as a naval fighter, but it proved to be ineffective in each of those roles and was withdrawn from front-line service in 1941.

SPECIFICATIONS (Skua Mk II)

DIMENSIONS:	Length: 10.85m (35ft 7in); Wingspan: 14.07m (46ft 2in); Height: 3.81m (12ft 6in)
WEIGHT:	3,732kg (8,228lb) loaded
POWERPLANT:	1 × 664kW (890hp) Bristol Perseus XII radial engine
MAX SPEED:	362km/h (225mph)
RANGE:	1,223km (760 miles)
SERVICE CEILING:	6,160m (20,200ft)
CREW:	2
ARMAMENT:	4 × 7.7mm (0.303in) MGs in wings; 1 × Lewis rear gun; 1 × 227kg (500lb) bomb beneath fuselage

Left: On 1 September 1939, the FAA had 232 aircraft, and of these most were inferior to their RAF counterparts. The most modern type in the fighter, dive-bomber and fighter-reconnaissance role was the Blackburn Skua, operational with Nos 800, 801, 803 and 806 Squadrons, which had just 36 aircraft.

STABILITY
Stability problems with the prototype resulted in the aircraft's nose being lengthened 73cm (2ft 5in) and the horizontal tail surfaces extended.

WATERTIGHT COMPARTMENTS
The Skua was fitted with watertight compartments beneath the two-man cockpit to give the aircraft sufficient buoyancy to allow the crew to escape in the event of a ditching.

SKUA MK II
The Skua Mk II was the production variant of the Skua Mk I prototype. This example belonged to No. 5 Maintenance Unit, Kemble, 1939.

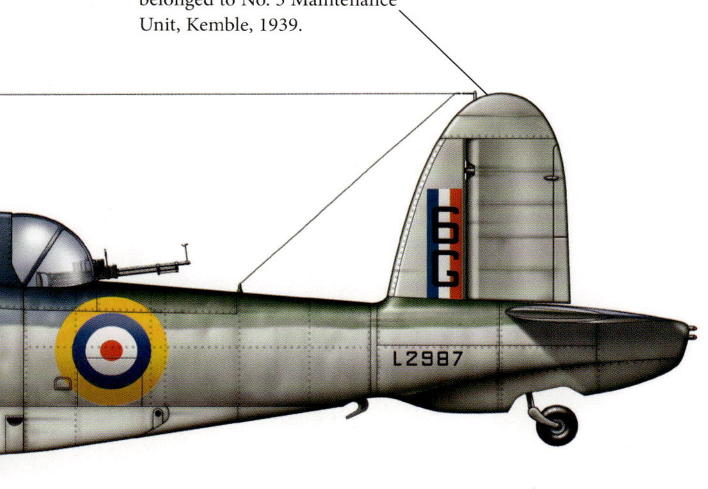

FAA AIRCRAFT
Having a fleet of mostly obsolete types in 1940, the Fleet Air Arm (FAA) adapted land-based RAF fighters for aircraft carrier use, with varying degrees of success. They had more luck with American-built naval fighters and torpedo bombers. Although withdrawn from front-line use during 1941, the Skua was the first aircraft in history to sink an enemy capital ship during wartime.

FLAWED AIRCRAFT
Typifying the flawed concepts prevalent in pre-war naval aircraft, the Skua was a fighter and dive-bomber derived from the Roc fighter. Although it had forward-firing wing guns, unlike the Roc, the engine was the same and so the power-weight ratio was even worse.

Short Sunderland Mk III (1938)

TYPE • *Seaplane* **COUNTRY** • *United Kingdom*

Just as the Short S.23 C-class 'Empire' flying boat marked a startling advance on all previous civil transport aircraft in Imperial Airways service, so its military derivative, the Sunderland, marked an equally great advance on marine aircraft in the RAF.

SPECIFICATIONS (Sunderland Mk III)

DIMENSIONS:	Length: 26.01m (84ft 4in); Wingspan: 34.38m (112ft 9.5in); Height: 10.02m (32ft 10.5in)
WEIGHT:	Empty 15,649kg (34,500lb)
POWERPLANT:	4 × Bristol Pegasus XVIII 9-cylinder air-cooled radial piston engines, 794kW (1,065hp) each
MAX SPEED:	340km/h (210mph) at 2,000m (6,500ft)
RANGE:	2,860km (1,777 miles)
CEILING:	5,200m (17,200ft)
CREW:	9–11
ARMAMENT:	Up to 12 × 7.7mm (0.303in) Browning machine guns; up to 2,000lb (910kg) of bombs, mines and depth charges internally

Left: A Mk III Sunderland from No. 230 Sqn. Sometimes nicknamed 'The Pig' by its crews, on account of its ungainly appearance, the Sunderland was also dubbed 'The Flying Porcupine' by Luftwaffe pilots who tried to attack it.

BOW TURRET
In the bows was an FN.11 turret with a single VGO (Vickers gas-operated) machine gun with a winching system for retracting the turret aft so that the big anchor could be passed out through a bow hatch.

SUNDERLAND MK III
This Sunderland served with No. 201 Squadron, RAF Coastal Command, based in Castle Archdale, County Fermanagh, Northern Ireland.

ANTENNAE
Remaining in service to 1944, this flying boat carries the early type of overfuselage antennae associated with air-to-surface search radar.

SPACIOUS CABIN
In the original Sunderland Mk I the normal crew was seven, accommodated basically on two decks with comprehensive provision for prolonged habitation, with six bunks, galley, workshops and stowage for a considerable quantity of equipment. At the upper level it was possible to walk aft from the two-pilot flight deck past the cubicles of the radio operator and navigator and through the deep front spar into the domain of the flight engineer.

SUNDERLAND MK IIIA
Despite its great bulk, the Sunderland's hull was well shaped. Hydrodynamically, a new feature was the bringing of the planing bottom to a vertical knife-edge at the rear (second) step, thereafter sweeping the bottom line smoothly up and back to the tail.

Handley-Page Hampden (1938)

TYPE • *Bomber* COUNTRY • *United Kingdom*

SPECIFICATIONS

DIMENSIONS:	Length: 16.33m (53ft 7in); Wingspan: 21.08m (69ft 2in); Height: 4.55m (14ft 11in)
WEIGHT:	Maximum take-off 10,206kg (22,500lb)
POWERPLANT:	2 × 750kW (1,000hp) Bristol Pegasus XVIII 9-cylinder air-cooled radial piston engines
MAX SPEED:	398km/h (247mph)
RANGE:	2,770km (1,720 miles)
CEILING:	5,800m (19,000ft)
CREW:	4
ARMAMENT:	1 × fixed forward-firing 7.7mm (0.303in) Browning machine gun in nose; up to five 7.7mm (0.303in) Vickers K machine guns in flexible mounts; up to 1,800kg (4,000lb) bombload or mines or one 457mm (18in) torpedo

Designed along with the Vickers Wellington to Air Ministry specification B.9/32, Handley Page Hampden was the result of a unique but flawed approach to pre-war bomber design, its decent performance compromised by terrible ergonomics for the crew.

Left: The H.P. 52 prototype, K4240, was finished in a glossy grey-green colour scheme for its first public appearances at the RAF Display at Hendon and the SBAC show at Hatfield, both in July 1936.

CREW COMPARTMENT
The Hampden Mk I was operated by a four-man crew all located in the 'pod' section of the fuselage. This was so narrow that it was impossible for anyone to exchange seats and so a badly wounded pilot could not be replaced.

LAYOUT
The Hampden was highly original in its approach to the Ministry specification for a twin-engined bomber, with tapered wings and, most distinctively, the rear half of the fuselage tapering into a slim boom carrying the twin-tail empennage.

SOVIET HAMPDEN TB MK. I
Formerly operated by 455 Squadron RAAF (Royal Australian Air Force) and wearing standard RAF night-bomber camouflage with painted-out roundels and squadron codes, Hampden TB.1 'White 30' was based at Vaenga near Murmansk in 1942.

MARITIME PATROLS

After the mauling of convoy PQ-17 in July 1942, urgent means were sought to protect future convoys venturing through the Arctic Sea. To this end Operation *Orator* saw RAF Coastal Command fly their Hampden TB.1 torpedo bombers to Vaenga, near Murmansk, to supply anti-shipping cover to the next convoy, PQ-18, on its approach to the USSR, deterring German surface raiders.

HANDLING
Two Handley Page Hampdens of No. 61 Squadron in flight on 12 October 1941. Although the Hampden offered excellent handling qualities and almost fighter-like manoeuvrability, its shortcomings were exposed early on, when five out of 11 Hampdens from No. 144 Sqn were lost to German fighters over the Heligoland Bight area on 29 September 1939.

Brewster F2A Buffalo (1938)

TYPE • *Fighter* **COUNTRY** • *United States*

The US Navy's first monoplane fighter delivered a significant upgrade in performance over the biplanes that preceded it. Unfortunately, in operational contexts the Brewster F2A Buffalo failed to live up to its initial promise.

SPECIFICATIONS (F2A-1)

DIMENSIONS:	Length: 7.92m (26ft 0in); Wingspan: 10.67m (35ft); Height: 3.56m (11ft 8in)
WEIGHT:	Maximum take-off 3247kg (7159lb)
POWERPLANT:	1 × 700kW (940hp) Wright R-1820-34 Cyclone 9-cylinder air-cooled radial engine
MAX SPEED:	501km/h (311mph)
RANGE:	2486km (1545 miles)
CEILING:	10,100m (33,200ft)
CREW:	1
ARMAMENT:	2 × 12.7mm (0.5in) M2 Browning MGs fixed forward-firing in wings; 1 × 12.7mm (0.5in) M2 Browning machine gun and 1 × 7.7mm (0.3in) .30 AN/M2 Browning fixed forward-firing in cowling

Above: Although the F2A-2 seen here was faster than the previous F2A-1, accompanying weight growth resulted in a shortfall in other areas, particularly manoeuvrability.

BREWSTER BUFFALO MK I
Serving with 453 squadron of the Royal Australian Air Force, AN210 was based at Sembawang, Singapore, in November 1941. Buffaloes of this unit were stripped of equipment to save around 450kg (1000lb) of weight and improve performance.

POWERPLANT
In the F2A-1 power was delivered from a 700kW (940hp) Wright R-1820-34 Cyclone nine-cylinder air-cooled radial engine.

DESIGN
The Buffalo possessed a fully flush riveted stressed skin construction, split flaps and a hydraulically powered retractable undercarriage.

EXCESS WEIGHT

The Buffalo suffered from excessive weight, which often proved too much for the Buffalo's landing gear. Undercarriage failures were commonplace, resulting in the withdrawal of the F2A from US carriers. F2As were still aboard USS *Saratoga* at the time of Pearl Harbor. However, all had been transferred to shore-based roles within a month. The Buffalo also saw Finnish, British and Belgian service (it was the British who bestowed the 'Buffalo' nickname).

F2A-3 BUFFALO
The F2A-3 saw yet more weight added to the airframe, mostly to lengthen the fuselage to fit in a larger fuel tank, but it utilized the same engine as the F2A-2. As a result the performance, which was by now hardly sparkling by contemporary standards, was lowered further.

Vickers Wellington (1938)

TYPE • *Bomber* **COUNTRY** • *United Kingdom*

SPECIFICATIONS (Wellington Mk III)

Dimensions:	Length: 18.54m (60ft 10in); Wingspan 26.26m (86ft 2in); Height 5.33m (17ft 6in)
Weight:	12,927kg (28,500lb) loaded
Powerplant:	2 x 783kW (1050hp) Bristol Pegasus XVIII 9-cylinder radial engines
Max Speed:	378km/h (235mph)
Range:	2905km (1805 miles)
Ceiling:	5486m (18,000ft)
Crew:	6
Armament:	2 x 7.7mm (0.303in) Browning MGs in both nose and tail; 2 x 7.7mm (0.303in) beam guns; 2041kg (4500lb) bombload

An immensely strong warplane capable of surviving crippling battle damage, the Vickers Wellington was the Royal Air Force's most advanced bomber at the outbreak of World War II and was at the forefront of the British bomber effort for the first half of the war.

Above: (Top) A Wellington Mk III and (bottom) a Wellington Mk IA.

Radar
To aid its submarine-hunting activities, this Wellington is fitted with an ASV Mk III radar (with its antenna in the chin radome).

Wellington GR Mk XIV
This aircraft is of No. 304 (Polish) Squadron, operating within RAF Coastal Command out of Chivenor, late 1944.

Leigh Light
To illuminate U-boats at night, a Leigh Light installation is in a retractable installation just to the rear of the weapons bay; it could be lowered from its location in the fuselage.

MARITIME VARIANT
Although as early as late 1941 Coastal Command had employed modified Wellington Mk ICs for torpedo and mine-laying work, it was during the spring of 1942 that the first true general reconnaissance Wellingtons entered service with RAF Coastal Command. The first land-based maritime patrol and anti-submarine aircraft were GR Mk VIIIs, powered by Pegasus VIII radial engines and equipped with ASV Mk II radar.

COOKIE BOMB
A Wellington is loaded with the largest bomb in its arsenal: the 1818kg (4000lb) high-capacity (HC) bomb, used to deliver massive ground blast effects.

Blackburn Roc (1938)

TYPE • *Naval fighter* **COUNTRY** • *United Kingdom*

SPECIFICATIONS

DIMENSIONS:	Length: 10.85m (35ft 7in); Wingspan: 14.02m (46ft 0in); Height: 3.68m (12ft 0in)
WEIGHT:	3606kg (7950lb) loaded
POWERPLANT:	1 × 675kW (905hp) Bristol Perseus XII radial engine
MAX SPEED:	359km/h (223mph)
RANGE:	1304km (810 miles)
CEILING:	5485m (18,000ft)
CREW:	2
ARMAMENT:	4 × 7.7mm (0.303in) MGs in dorsal turret

Essentially the naval counterpart of the land-based Boulton Paul Defiant, the Roc was based on the turret fighter concept and suffered the same basic failings as the Defiant, including a poor power/weight ratio and a lack of agility.

Left: The Roc was a deeply flawed concept that featured a rear machine-gun turret for defence.

POWERPLANT
The single 675kW (905hp) Bristol Perseus XII nine-cylinder air-cooled radial engine struggled to cope with the aircraft's total weight.

TURRET GUNS
The primary defensive armament of the Roc consisted of four 7.7mm (0.303in) Browning machine guns in a Boulton Paul Type A power-operated dorsal turret.

BLACKBURN ROC
L3075 served with 806 Squadron, one of relatively few units to use the Roc operationally. The 806 Squadron flew fighter patrols and dive-bombing attacks over the Dunkirk evacuation beaches with both Skuas and Rocs.

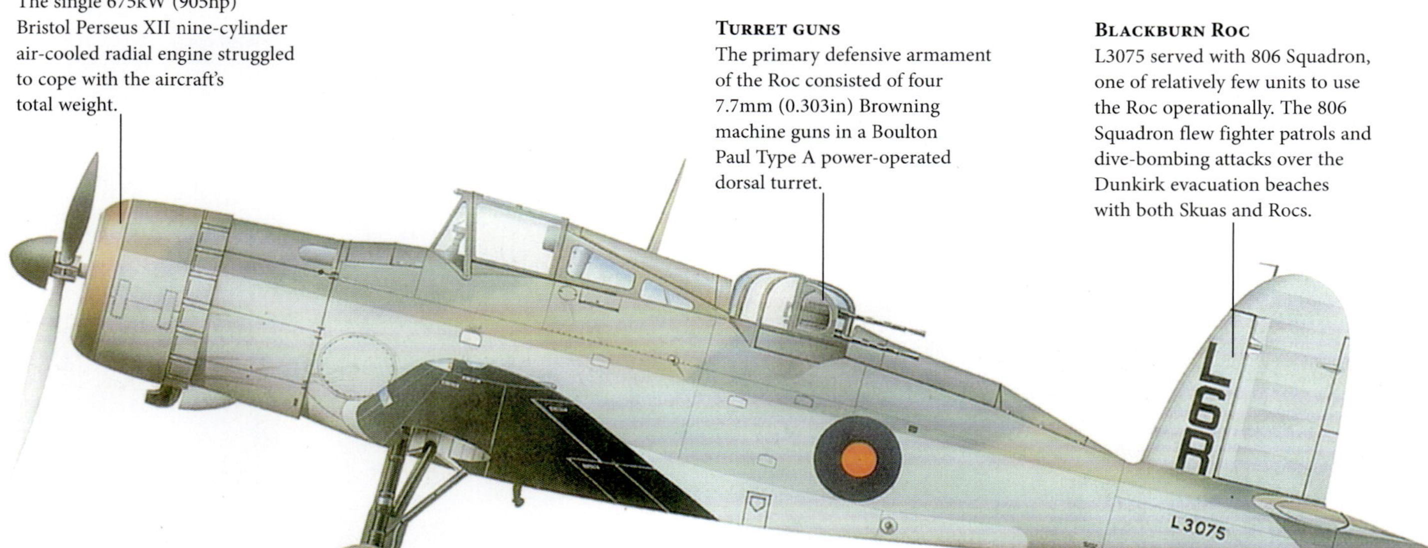

POOR REPUTATION
The Blackburn B-25 Roc was a British Fleet Air Arm fighter aircraft designed by Blackburn Aircraft Ltd. It took its name from the mythical bird of the tales of the Arabian Nights, the Roc. Derived from the Blackburn Skua and developed in parallel, the Roc had its armament in a turret. The Roc came to be viewed as inferior to existing aircraft such as the Skua and the type had only brief front-line service.

PERFORMANCE
While the Roc was certainly pleasant to fly, it could barely exceed 322km/h (200mph) and endurance was reduced in comparison to the Skua due to the turret replacing the fuselage fuel tanks of the Skua.

Fiat G.50 Freccia (1938)

TYPE • *Fighter* **COUNTRY** • *Italy*

The G.50 entered Italian service in early 1938 and was rushed to Spain to take part in operational trials. It proved one of the best fighters of the war, but was not much faster than the CR.42 biplane and by 1944 was becoming obsolescent.

SPECIFICATIONS

Dimensions:	Length 7.79m (25ft 7in); Wingspan: 10.96m (35ft 11in); Height: 2.96m (9ft 9in); Wing area: 18.2 sq m (196 sq ft)
Weight:	Empty: 1,975kg (4,354lb); Maximum: 2,706kg (5,965lb)
Powerplant:	1 x 625kW (838hp) Fiat A.74 RC38 radial piston engine
Max speed:	484km/h (301mph)
Range:	670km (418 miles)
Service ceiling:	9,835m (32,258ft)
Crew:	1
Armament:	2 x 12.7mm (0.5in) Breda-SAFAT machine guns

Above: A G.50 Freccia flying with 20° Gruppo in Belgium in 1940, part of the Corpo Aereo Italiano (Italian Air Corps, CAI).

Performance
The 25kW (838hp) Fiat A.74 RC38 radial piston engine delivered a maximum speed of 484km/h (301mph), which by 1944 had been outclassed by new generations of fighters.

Armament
The armament of the G.50 consisted of just two 12.7mm (0.50in) Breda-SAFAT machine guns. The aircraft did not have hardpoints for further ordnance.

Finnish Freccia
About 35 G.50s were exported to Finland just prior to the war, and for many years they proved themselves capable of handling the best of Soviet fighters, with a very high kill-to-loss rate.

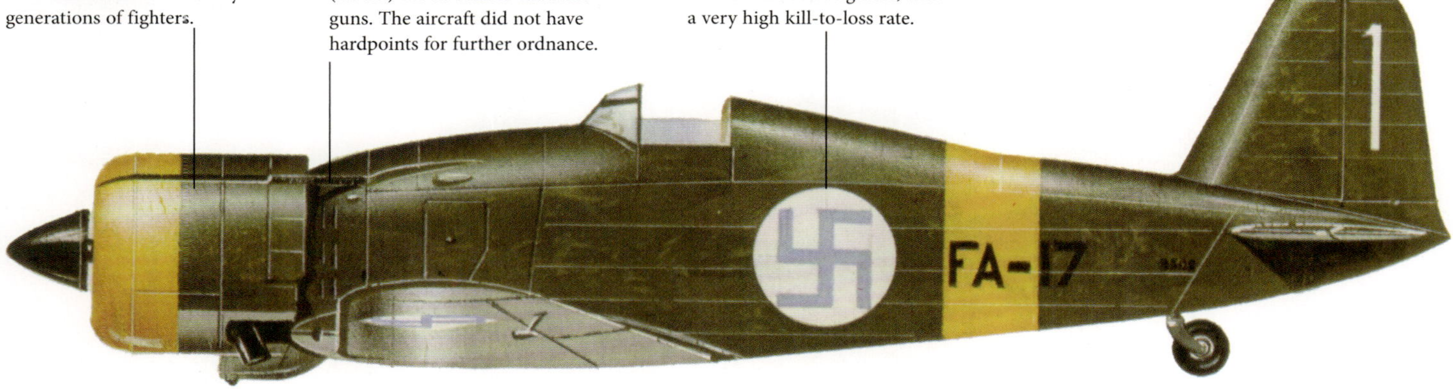

OPEN COCKPIT
One seemingly anachronistic feature of the G.50 was its open cockpit. Initially, the aircraft was fitted with an enclosed greenhouse-type canopy. This, however, was not popular with its pilots, as it tended to gather dust scratches that obscured vision and also trapped engine fumes. Seeing that many pilots were therefore flying with the cockpit open, Fiat subsequently installed an open cockpit on 200 of the aircraft.

WIDESPREAD SERVICE
First tested in combat during the Spanish Civil War, the radial-engined Fiat G.50 subsequently saw service in North Africa, the Balkans and southern Russia, as well as in Finland in the hands of the Finnish Air Force.

Mitsubishi Ki-21 'Sally' (1938)

TYPE • *Bomber* **COUNTRY** • *Japan*

SPECIFICATIONS (Ki-21-Ia)	
Dimensions:	Length: 16.00m (52ft 6in); Wingspan: 22.50m (73ft 9.75in); Height: 4.35m (14ft 3.5in)
Weight:	7916kg (17,452lb) maximum take-off
Powerplant:	2 × 634kW (850hp) Nakajima Ha-5 Kai radial piston engines
Max speed:	432km/h (268mph) at 4000m (13,125ft)
Range:	2700km (1680 miles)
Ceiling:	8600m (28,215ft)
Crew:	5–7
Armament:	3 × 7.7mm (0.303in) machine guns; bombload of up to 1000kg (2205lb)

At the time of its appearance, the Ki-21 helped bring the Imperial Japanese Army Air Service into the modern era, and although it was obsolescent by 1943 the aircraft remained popular with its crews and continued to serve until the end of the war.

Above: An anonymous Mitsubishi Ki-21-IIb as it appeared in Imperial Japanese Army service in 1944.

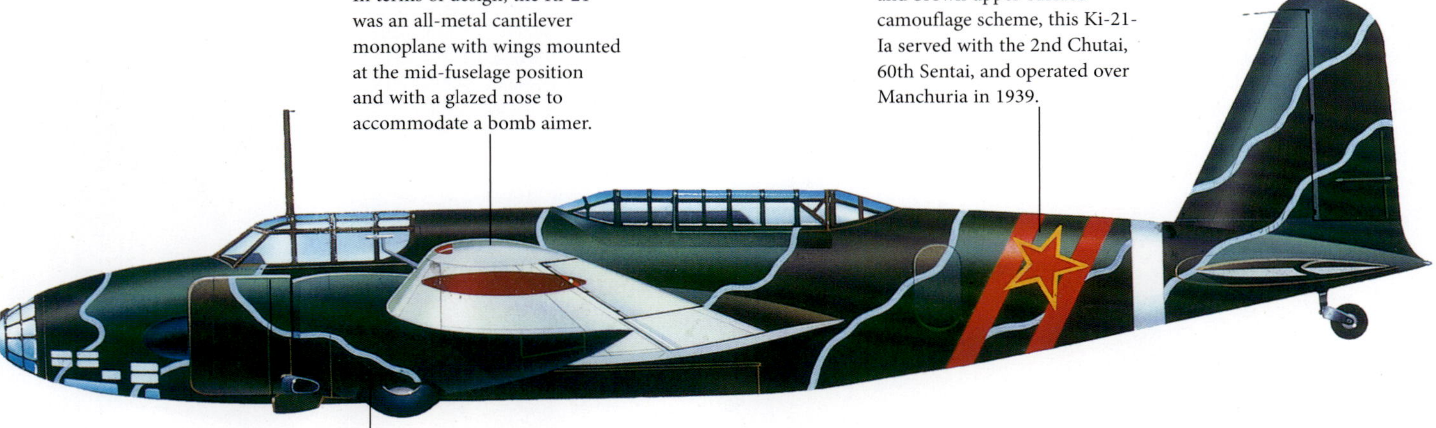

Layout
In terms of design, the Ki-21 was an all-metal cantilever monoplane with wings mounted at the mid-fuselage position and with a glazed nose to accommodate a bomb aimer.

Ki-21-Ia
Wearing an overall olive green and brown upper-surface camouflage scheme, this Ki-21-Ia served with the 2nd Chutai, 60th Sentai, and operated over Manchuria in 1939.

Powerplant
By the third prototype, the powerplant had settled on the 634kW (850hp) Nakaijima Ha-5 radial piston engine; this prototype also had a re-profiled hemispherical nose and a redesigned rear fuselage.

COMBAT EXPERIENCE

Once tested under combat conditions in China, it became apparent that the basic aircraft was lacking defensive armament. The result of these lessons was the Ki-21-Ib (Army Type 97 Heavy Bomber 1b), which upped the number of defensive machine guns from three to five through the addition of a single machine gun firing from lateral positions on either side of the rear fuselage, plus a remotely controlled weapon in a tail barbette.

KI-21 IN FLIGHT
The final production figures for the Ki-21 amounted to 2063 aircraft built, of which 1713 were constructed by Mitsubishi and the remainder by Nakajima.

Blohm und Voss BV 138 (1938)

TYPE • *Seaplane* **COUNTRY** • *Germany*

SPECIFICATIONS (BV 138C-1)

Dimensions:	Length: 19.85m (65ft 1in); Wingspan: 26.94m (88ft 5in); Height: 5.9m (19ft 4in)
Weight:	17,650kg (38,967lb) maximum take-off
Powerplant:	3 x 656kW (880hp) Junkers Jumo 205D 6-cylinder diesel engines
Max speed:	285km/h (177mph)
Range:	1220km (760 miles)
Ceiling:	5000m (16,000ft)
Crew:	6
Armament:	2 x 20mm (0.79in) MG 151 cannons (nose turret and rear fuselage); 1 x 13mm (0.51in) MG 131 machine gun (behind centre engine nacelle); 1–3 x 7.92mm (0.31in) MG 15 machine guns (optional); up to 6 x 50kg (110lb) bombs or 4 x 150kg (330lb) depth charges (optional)

The origins of the Blohm und Voss BV 138 can be traced back to the Ha 138 – the first flying-boat design from the Hamburger Flugzeugbau GmbH company, designed under the capable leadership of Richard Vogt.

Above: Equipped for mine warfare, this BV 138 MS was on strength with 1. Minensuchstaffel, *part of* Minensuchgruppe *1, operating along the Baltic Coast in 1944.*

Powerplant
The C-series that appeared in March 1941 introduced a new powerplant in the form of three Jumo 205D engines as well as further structural strengthening.

BV 138C-1 Armament
As well as the armament of the BV 138B-1, the C-1 added a 13mm (0.51in) MG 131 cannon in a position behind the centre engine nacelle.

Hull improvements
Compared to its predecessor, the BV 138 featured a much-enlarged hull, with improved planning surfaces.

MINESWEEPER

One unusual development of the flying boat was the BV 138MS for the minesweeping mission. Based on the airframe of BV 138B-0 pre-production aircraft, the BV 138MS had its armament removed and a degaussing loop of Duralumin running around the airframe; this was provided with field-generating equipment to detonate mines below the aircraft. A handful of these conversions were completed during 1942–43.

BLACK SEA PATROL
A BV 138C operated by 3.(F)/ SAGr 125 from Constanza patrols coastal waters around the Black Sea. The previous five-man crew was increased to six in the C-series and some of these aircraft were additionally equipped with FuG 200 Hohentwiel radar for maritime surveillance.

CANT Z.1007 Alcione (1939)

TYPE • *Bomber* **COUNTRY** • *Italy*

Italy's pre-war aircraft designers had a particular penchant for the trimotor design. One of the most important bombers of this type in Italian service was the three-engined CANT Z.1007 *Alcione* (Kingfisher).

SPECIFICATIONS (CANT Z.1007bis)

Dimensions:	Length: 18.35m (60ft 2.5in); Wingspan: 24.8m (81ft 4.33in); Height: 5.22m (17ft 5in)
Weight:	Empty: 9396kg (20,715lb); Maximum take-off: 13,621kg (30,029lb)
Powerplant:	3 x 746kW (1000hp) Piaggio P.XI 14-cylinder two-row radial engines
Max speed:	466km/h (290mph)
Range:	1750km (1087 miles)
Ceiling:	8200m (26,900ft)
Crew:	5
Armament:	1 x 12.7mm (0.5in) trainable MG in dorsal turret; 1 x 12.7mm rearward-firing MG in ventral step position; 1 x 7.7mm (0.3in) lateral-firing MG in each two beam position; internal bombload 1200kg (2646lb)

Above: A CANT Z.1007 bis bomber of the Italian Regia Aeronautica turns its engines over in preparation for a bombing mission over Malta. The photograph was taken in Sicily in 1941.

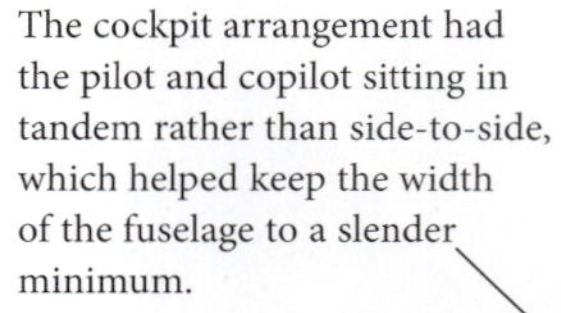

Cockpit layout
The cockpit arrangement had the pilot and copilot sitting in tandem rather than side-to-side, which helped keep the width of the fuselage to a slender minimum.

Turret
The aircraft was fitted with a Caproni-Lanciani Delta manually powered Isotta Fraschini dorsal turret, armed with a single 12.7mm (0.5in) Scotti or Breda-SAFAT machine gun.

Night camouflage
This Z.1007 bis wears night camouflage for attacks against Allied ports and targets on the North African coast in early 1943.

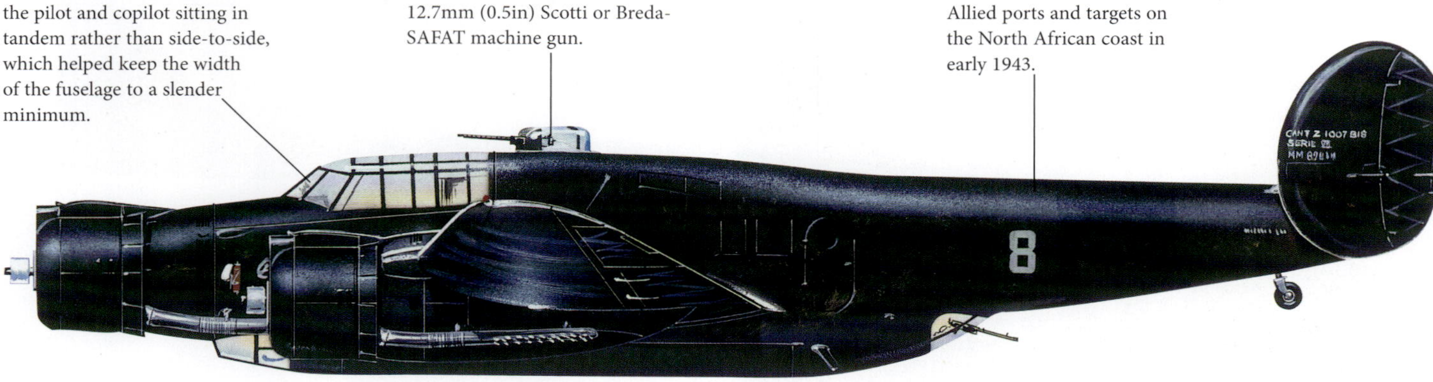

WAR SERVICE
The Z.1007 was first used operationally from August 1940, flying out from bases in Sicily to strike against Allied convoys heading to Malta and against the island itself. By 1942, when these operations ceased, the Italians had taken heavy losses of aircraft, including of Z.1007s. Apart from minor service in the Battle of Britain, the Alciones served principally over the Balkan theatre, specifically over Greece and Yugoslavia.

ALLIED AIRCRAFT
A CANT Z.1007 bis bomber of the Italian Co-belligerent Air Force, photographed over southern Italy in late 1944. After the Italian Armistice of September 1943, many of the surviving Z.1007s were used in operations against German forces.

Mitsubishi A6M Reisen 'Zero' (1939)

TYPE • *Naval fighter* **COUNTRY** • *Japan*

Popularly known as the 'Zero', the Mitsubishi A6M was the world's most capable carrier-based fighter at the time of its appearance, out-performing all land-based contemporaries. Latterly outclassed, it remained in service until the end of the war.

SPECIFICATIONS (A6M2)

DIMENSIONS:	Length: 9.06m (29ft 9in); Wingspan: 12m (39ft 4.5in); Height: 3.05m (10ft)
WEIGHT:	2796kg (6164lb) maximum take-off
POWERPLANT:	1 × 708kW (950hp) Nakajima NK1C Sakae 12 radial piston engine
MAX SPEED:	534km/h (332mph) at 4550m (14,930ft)
RANGE:	1867km (1160 miles)
CEILING:	10,000m (32,810ft)
CREW:	1
ARMAMENT:	2 × 7.7mm (0.303in) machine guns; 2 × 20mm (0.79in) cannon

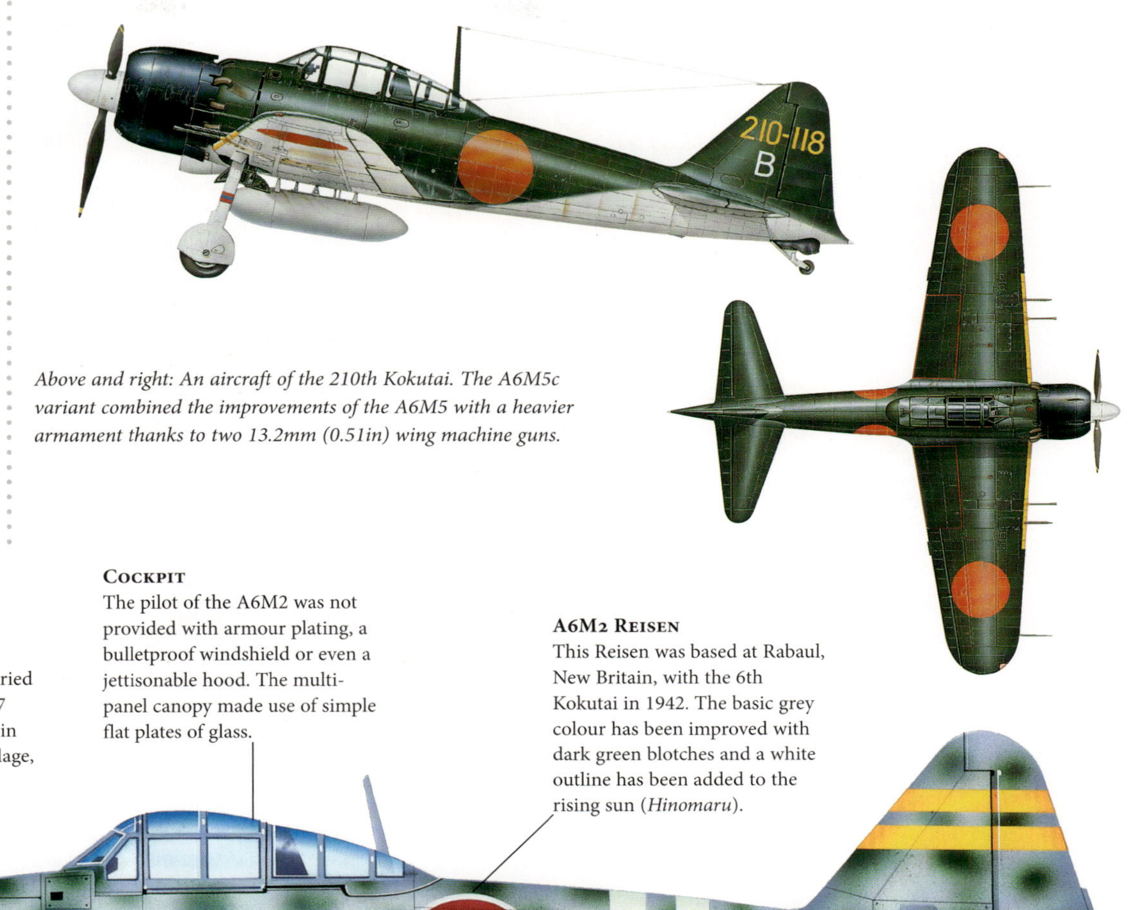

Above and right: An aircraft of the 210th Kokutai. The A6M5c variant combined the improvements of the A6M5 with a heavier armament thanks to two 13.2mm (0.51in) wing machine guns.

ARMAMENT
In addition to the two 20mm (0.79in) cannon that were carried in the wings, a pair of Type 97 machine guns were mounted in the decking of the upper fuselage, forward of the cockpit.

COCKPIT
The pilot of the A6M2 was not provided with armour plating, a bulletproof windshield or even a jettisonable hood. The multi-panel canopy made use of simple flat plates of glass.

A6M2 REISEN
This Reisen was based at Rabaul, New Britain, with the 6th Kokutai in 1942. The basic grey colour has been improved with dark green blotches and a white outline has been added to the rising sun (*Hinomaru*).

CHINA TESTING

The Mitsubishi A6M Reisen (Zero fighter) first flew on 1 April 1939; after 15 aircraft had been evaluated in combat in China, the type was accepted for service with the Japanese Naval Air Force in July 1940, entering full production in November as the A6M2 Model 11. Sixty-four Model 11s were completed, and were followed by the Model 21 with folding wing tips.

WANING SUPERIORITY

The A6M2 soon showed itself to be clearly superior to any fighter the Allies could put into the air in the early stages of the Pacific War. In later years, however, the aircraft and their pilots were totally outclassed. In 1942, the Americans had allocated the code name 'Zeke' to the A6M, but as time went by the name 'Zero' came into general use.

Ilyushin Il-2 Shturmovik (1939)

TYPE • *Fighter-bomber* **COUNTRY** • *Soviet Union*

SPECIFICATIONS (Il-2M3)

Dimensions:	Length: 11.6m (38ft 1in); Wingspan: 14.6m (47ft 11in); Height: 4.2m (13ft 9in)
Weight:	6380kg (14,065lb) maximum take-off
Powerplant:	Mikulin AM-38F V-12 liquid-cooled piston engine, 1285kW (1720hp)
Max Speed:	414km/h (257mph)
Range:	720km (450 miles)
Ceiling:	5000m (18,045ft)
Crew:	2
Armament:	2 × 23mm (0.9in) forward-firing cannon; 2 × 7.62mm (0.3in) forward-firing machine guns; 1 × 7.62mm machine gun in rear cockpit; plus up to 600kg (1320lb) of disposable stores underwing

Built in greater numbers than any other military aircraft in history, the Il-2 was a war-winner for the Soviets, with more than 36,000 built between 1941 and 1955. The ground-attacker was capable of defeating the best-protected German tanks.

Right: The original version of the Il-2, first flown in TsKB-55P prototype form in December 1940, was rushed into service during 1941 as a single-seater with the gun armament of two 23mm (0.9in) ShVAK cannon with 420 rounds and two 7.62mm (0.3in) ShKAS machine guns with 1500 rounds.

Starter mechanism
The circular metal tube projecting from the Shturmovik's spinner is not a cannon or machine gun but a Hucks starter dog used for turning over and firing the engine, in much the same way as a vehicle starting handle.

Cockpit armour
The pilot was seated in an armoured tub with a thickness of 5–12mm (0.2–0.5in); this extended to protect the engine. The armour was capable of defeating all small-arms fire.

Artwork
Il-2s featured more unofficial artwork and slogans than most VVS aircraft, usually on the fuselage. This eagle-adorned two-seater was operating with an unknown unit in Latvia during 1944.

FOREIGN SERVICE
The Il-2 was quite possibly the most important aircraft to serve the VVS (Russian Air Force) – over 36,000 were built and more than 10,000 were lost in combat. In addition to the USSR, Il-2s served with Czech, Polish and Yugoslavian forces during the war, with Mongolia, Hungary and Bulgaria flying them after 1945. Post-war, the aircraft received the NATO reporting name 'Bark'.

TAXIING OUT
The large undercarriage fairings of the Il-2 left the undercarriage partially uncovered, which meant that a pilot could make a belly landing without causing too much damage to the aircraft. Passengers are known to have been carried in the fairings in extreme circumstances (the rescue of a downed pilot, for example), the undercarriage remaining in the down position.

North American B-25 Mitchell (1939)

TYPE • *Bomber* **COUNTRY** • *United States*

The US Army Air Force's (USAAF) definitive light/medium bomber of World War II, the B-25 may have served in more campaigns than any other type in that conflict. It also gave good service in US Navy and Allied hands, and flew the 'Doolittle Raid' against Japan in April 1942.

SPECIFICATIONS (B-25J)

Dimensions:	Length: 16.13m (52ft 11in); Wingspan: 16.13m (67ft 7in); Height: 4.8m (17ft 7in)
Weight:	Empty: 9580kg (21,120lb); Maximum: 19,000kg (28,460lb)
Powerplant:	2 × 1380kW (1850hp) Wright R-2600-29 radial piston engines
Max speed:	442km/h (275mph)
Range:	2172km (1350 miles)
Ceiling:	7600m (25,000ft)
Crew:	5
Armament:	9 × 12.7mm (0.5in) machine guns; 1 × 7.62mm (0.303in) machine gun; up to 2700kg (6000lb) of bombs

Above: The Mitchell medium bomber was of US origins, but used by the RAF in tactical support of the ground forces of the 21st Army Group in 1944.

Cockpit
The B-25 was flown by two crew, comprising the aircraft commander in the left-hand seat and co-pilot/navigator in the right-hand seat. The B-25C/D was equipped with an autopilot.

B-25A Mitchell, 17th BG
The 17th Bomb Group was the first USAAF unit to receive the new B-25 medium bomber (24 built). Production of the following B-25A, with self-sealing fuel tanks, totalled only 40 aircraft.

Wings
The basic B-25 Mitchell had a cantilever wing comprising a two-spar centre section, which was permanently attached to the fuselage and contained integral fuel tanks and the engine mounts/nacelles, single-spar outer wing sections and detachable wing tips.

STRAFER VARIANT

The B-25J was the major production Mitchell variant and was built with either a so-called 'glass nose' or an eight-gun, solid 'strafer nose'. Its other main distinctive feature was the relocation of the top turret to a position behind the cockpit. For strafing attacks, the solid gun nose was supplemented by 'package' guns on the fuselage sides. Exported examples reached 16 countries during and after the war.

DOOLITTLE RAID
USAAF B-25B bombers are parked tightly on the flight deck of USS *Hornet* (CV-8), while en route to the launch point for the feted 'Doolittle Raid' on Tokyo, 18 April 1942, planned and led by Lieutenant Colonel James Doolittle.

Dewoitine D.520 (1939)

TYPE • *Fighter* COUNTRY • *France*

SPECIFICATIONS (D.520C.1)	
DIMENSIONS:	Length: 8.76m (28ft 8.75in); Wingspan: 10.20m (33ft 5.5in); Height: 2.57m (8ft 5.25in)
WEIGHT:	2783kg (6134lb) loaded
POWERPLANT:	1 x 634kW (850hp) Hispano-Suiza 12Y-45 liquid-cooled V-12
MAX SPEED:	535km/h (332mph)
RANGE:	900km (553 miles)
CEILING:	11,000m (36,090ft)
CREW:	1
ARMAMENT:	1 x 20mm (0.79in) Hispano-Suiza HS.404 cannon; 4 x 7.5mm (0.295in) MAC1934 MGs

Its early development marred by official indifference, the D.520 was scarcely a match for the Bf 109, yet its pilots fought with great bravery and skill to bring the type respectability during the Battle of France in 1940.

Left: This D.520 is camouflaged in the standard French Air Force scheme of May 1940. Aircraft serving with the Vichy French Air Force at a later date carried horizontal red and yellow identification stripes on the tail fin, rear fuselage and nose, forward of the wing leading edge.

POWERPLANT
Power for the D.520 came from either a Hispano-Suiza 12Y-45 or a 12Y-49 engine, rated at 634kW (850hp) and 612kW (820hp) respectively, and driving different propellers.

COCKPIT
The cockpit was set well aft, giving excellent downward vision in flight. However, taxiing could be tricky, requiring much weaving to retain a semblance of forward visibility.

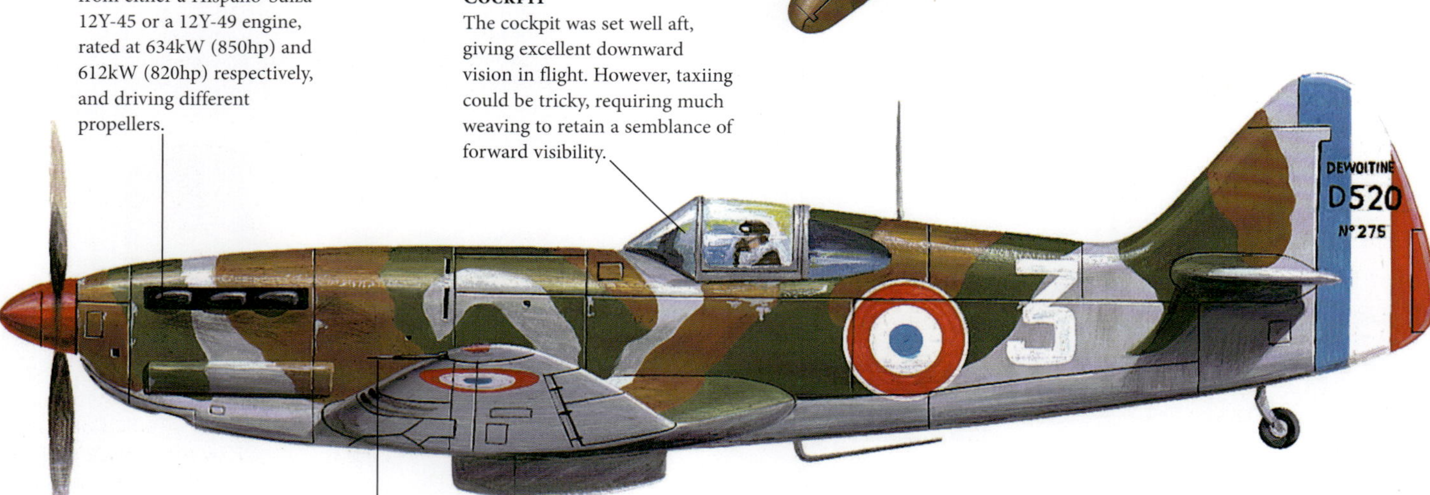

ARMAMENT
By comparison with other French fighters, the D.520 was well armed with one Hispano-Suiza HS.404 20mm (0.79in) cannon, with 60 rounds, and four wing-mounted 7.5mm (0.295in) MAC 1934 M39 machine guns, each with 675 rounds.

AXIS ALLEGIANCE

After the fall of France, and the establishment of the collaborationist Vichy regime, large numbers of D.520s were sent to North Africa, some being dispatched to participate in the 1941 Syrian campaign against British and Free French forces. Flying alongside Luftwaffe fighters, the D.520s were involved in the fight against the Allies during the Operation *Torch* landings of November 1942.

VICHY FLYER
German and French aircrew stand next to Dewoitine D.520s after the French defeat in 1941. The D.520 fought a heroic, yet ultimately futile, effort against the superior Messerschmitt Bf 109 during the Battle of France.

Arado Ar 196 (1939)

TYPE • *Floatplane* **COUNTRY** • *Germany*

SPECIFICATIONS (Ar 196A-5)

Dimensions:	Length: 11m (36ft 1in); Wingspan: 12.4m (40ft 8in); Height: 4.45m (14ft 7in)
Weight:	3720kg (8201lb) maximum take-off
Powerplant:	1 × 716kW (960hp) BMW 132K 9-cylinder radial piston engine
Max speed:	311km/h (193mph)
Range:	1080km (570 miles)
Ceiling:	7010m (23,000ft)
Crew:	2
Armament:	1 × 7.92mm (0.31in) MG 17 machine gun (nose); 2 × 8mm (0.32in) MG 81Z machine guns (rear cockpit); 2 × 20mm (0.8in) MG FF cannon (wings); 2 × 50kg (110lb) bombs

Although it exerted only a minor influence on World War II, the Arado Ar 196 was nevertheless an important type. Evolving through a number of float configurations, the aircraft soon entered service, replacing the venerable He 60.

Below: The Arado Ar 196 had a broad-chord wing with an unswept leading edge and a slight taper on the trailing edge.

Control surfaces
The aircraft had wide-span ailerons outboard, with relatively small flaps inboard. All control surfaces were fabric-covered, the rest of the wing being a metal-skinned two-spar structure.

Powerplant
The pre-production Ar 196A-0 adopted a 716kW (960hp) BMW 132K, which remained the standard powerplant for all subsequent variants.

Arado Ar 196A-5
An Ar 196A-5 from 4./*Seeaufklärungsgruppe* 126 that operated from Vukovar, Croatia, in January 1944.

AR 196A-3
The Ar 196A-3 incorporated further improvements to the series including structural strengthening, additional radio equipment and a new three-blade variable-pitch propeller.

FLOAT ARRANGEMENT
Four Ar 196 prototypes were carefully evaluated in 1937–38, but there was indecision over the preferred float arrangement. The central float was considered preferable in operations from choppy water, but the stabilizing floats could easily dip into the sea during take-off, resulting in pronounced asymmetric drag. It was decided to standardize on the twin-float arrangement.

Ilyushin Il-4 (1939)

TYPE • *Bomber* **COUNTRY** • *Soviet Union*

SPECIFICATIONS	
Dimensions:	Length: 14.76m (48ft 5in); Wingspan: 21.44m (70ft 4in); Height: 4.10m (13ft 6in)
Weight:	Maximum take-off 12,120kg (26,720lb)
Powerplant:	Two Tumanksy M-88B 14-cylinder air-coooled radial engines
Max Speed:	410km/h (250mph)
Range:	3800km (2400 miles)
Ceiling:	8700m (28,500ft)
Crew:	4
Armament:	1 x 7.62mm (0.3in) ShKAS machine gun in nose; 1 x 12.7mm (0.5in) Berezin UBT machine gun in dorsal turret; 1 x 7.62mm (0.3in) ShKAS machine gun in ventral hatch; up to 2700kg (6000lb) of bombs or mines or 1 x 940kg (2100lb) Type 45-36 torpedo

Starting life as the DB-3F, the Il-4 represented a complete redesign and after initial engine problems it served effectively for the duration of the Great Patriotic War, Berlin becoming a regular destination for the bombers in the later war years.

Left: An Il-4 dorsal turret gunner peers out through the open turret; the conditions for these gunners when operating during the Soviet winters can only be imagined.

Defensive armament
The aircraft's primary defence against a rear attack was one 12.7mm (0.5in) Berezin UBT machine gun set in a dorsal turret.

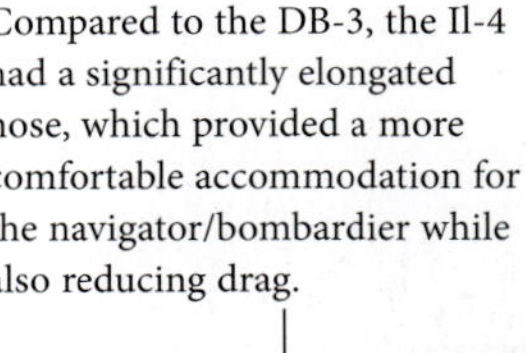

Nose
Compared to the DB-3, the Il-4 had a significantly elongated nose, which provided a more comfortable accommodation for the navigator/bombardier while also reducing drag.

Performance
Performance was improved by the adoption of a thinner wing of greater area and the fitment of two Tumansky M-88 engines in place of the M-87s of the DB-3B.

REDESIGN

The DB-3 had given the VVS (Russian Air Force) its first all-metal long-range bomber, but it was difficult to build and had proved unreliable in service. Ilyushin sought to eradicate these problems while improving performance with the DB-3F. It was a totally new design featuring a rebuilt structure, greatly influenced by the latest US construction methods. The DB-3 was redesignated Il-4 in spring 1942.

IL-4 AIRCREW
Differentiated from predecessor variants by its more streamlined and glazed nose, the Il-4 provided the backbone of the Soviet Union's longer-range bomber capability throughout World War II.

Aichi D3A 'Val' (1939)

TYPE • *Naval bomber* **COUNTRY** • *Japan*

SPECIFICATIONS

DIMENSIONS:	Length 10.2m (33ft 5in); Wingspan: 14.37m (47ft 2in); Height: 3.8m (12ft 8in)
WEIGHT:	Empty 2570kg (5666lb); Maximum 4122kg (9100lb)
POWERPLANT:	1 x 969kW (1300hp) Mitsubishi Kinsei 54 radial piston engine
MAX SPEED:	430km/h (267mph)
RANGE:	1352km (840 miles)
CEILING:	10,500m (34,450ft)
CREW:	2
ARMAMENT:	2 x 7.7mm (.303in) Type 97 machine guns and 1 x 7.7mm (.303in) Type 92 machine gun; up to 250kg (550lb) bombload

One of the outstanding Japanese warplanes of World War II, the D3A 'Val' played a crucial role in the attack on Pearl Harbor and actually sank more tonnage of Allied shipping than any other Axis type of aircraft.

Left: The second of two prototype D3As is pictured here fitted with the Mitsubishi Kinsei 3 14-cylinder radial engine. Other improvements included an increase in wingspan of 40cm (16in).

DORSAL FIN
Directional instability problems were eradicated by the addition of a large dorsal fin. This made the aircraft highly manoeuvrable.

POWERPLANT
The original Nakajima Hikari 1 radial engine was replaced in production aircraft by the 745kW (1000hp) Kinsei 43 or 798kW (1070hp) Kinsei 44.

FIXED UNDERCARRIAGE
Despite the inherent drag of a fixed undercarriage, this was retained as retractable landing gear would have added to the weight.

INDIAN OCEAN

The D3A was, in its heyday, a highly effective aircraft capable of carrying a single 250kg (551lb) bomb under the fuselage and two 60kg (132lb) bombs beneath the wings. Between 4 and 9 April 1942, D3A1s in the Indian Ocean sank not only the British cruisers HMS *Cornwall* and *Dorsetshire* and the aircraft carrier *Hermes*, but also two destroyers, a corvette, an auxiliary vessel, two oilers and 11 merchant vessels.

SALVAGED D3A
US sailors salvage an Aichi D3A from the waters of Pearl Harbor c.1942. Of the 135 D3A1s (known as 'Vals' to the Allies) used during the 7 December 1941 attack, 15 were shot down, but they caused great destruction at Wheeler Field air base as well as to the US battleships.

Nakajima Ki-43 Hayabusa 'Oscar' (1939)

TYPE • *Fighter* **COUNTRY** • *Japan*

SPECIFICATIONS (Ki-43-IIb)

DIMENSIONS:	Length: 8.92m (29ft 3.25in); Wingspan: 10.84m (35ft 6.75in); Height: 3.27m (10ft 8.75in)
WEIGHT:	2590kg (5710lb) maximum take-off
POWERPLANT:	1 x 858kW (1150hp) Nakajima Ha-115 radial piston engine
MAX SPEED:	530km/h (329mph) at 4000m (13,125ft)
RANGE:	3200km (1988 miles)
SERVICE CEILING:	11,200m (36,745ft)
CREW:	1
ARMAMENT:	2 x 12.7mm (0.5in) machine guns; up to 2 x 250kg (551lb) bombs underwing

Like its naval counterpart, the Mitsubishi Zero, the Nakajima Ki-43 *Hayabusa* ('Peregrine Falcon', Allied code name 'Oscar') was in action from the first day of Japan's war until the last, by which time it was woefully outclassed by the latest Allied fighters.

Above and right: The Ki-43 was a cantilever low-wing monoplane with retractable tailwheel landing gear. Here we see two views of a colourful Ki-43-IIb flown by the leader of the Headquarters Chutai of the 77th Sentai during operations in Burma in the winter of 1943–44.

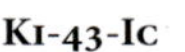

PROPELLER
The initial production variant, designated Army Type 1 Fighter Model 1A, was fitted with a fixed-pitch two-blade wooden propeller, but this was soon replaced by a two-pitch, two-blade metal unit.

BODY
A versatile fighter, the Hayabusa's main drawback was its lack of adequate armament and any form of armour protection, which made it extremely vulnerable to enemy fire.

KI-43-IC
Colourful Chutai markings adorn this 'Oscar' belonging to the 1st Chutai, 50th Sentai, based at Tokorozawa in June 1942.

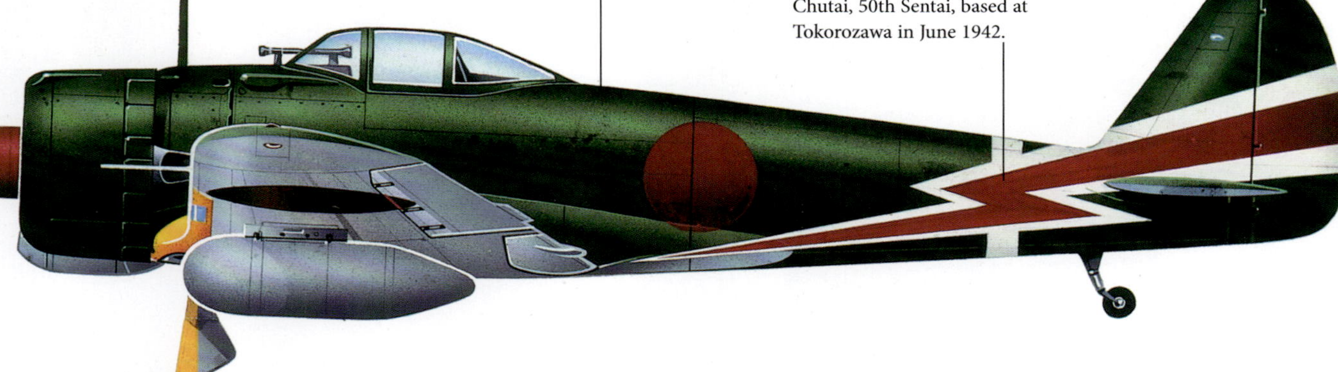

VARIANTS

The prototype Ki-43 flew in January 1939 and 716 early production models were produced: the Ki-43-I, Ki-43-Ia, Ki-43-Ib and Ki-43-Ic, the last two having a better armament. In 1942 the much-improved model Ki-43-II appeared in three subvariants, the Ki-43-IIa and -IIb, and the Ki-43-Kai. The final model was the Ki-43-III, the only variant to include cannon in its armament.

OSCAR IN CHINA
Shining under the Chinese sun, this Ki-43-II is of the 2nd Chutai (indicated by the red diagonal tail stripe), 25th Sentai. The 'Oscar' was one of the most mass-produced aircraft of the war; 5900 were manufactured up until the end of World War II.

Polikarpov I-153 (1939)

TYPE • *Fighter* **COUNTRY** • *Soviet Union*

In the 1930s, the Soviet designer Nikolai N. Polikarpov was at the forefront of Soviet fighter design, and at the outbreak of the war in the east it was aircraft of his design that were the mainstay of the Soviet Air Force's fighter squadrons.

SPECIFICATIONS

Dimensions:	Length: 6.17m (20ft 3in); Wingspan: 10.00m (32ft 9.5in); Height: 2.80m (9ft 2.25in)
Weight:	Empty 1348kg (2972lb); Maximum take-off 2110kg (4652lb)
Powerplant:	746kW (1000hp) Shvetsov M-62 9-cylinder radial
Max Speed:	444km/h (276mph) at 3000m (9845ft)
Range:	880km (547 miles)
Ceiling:	10,700m (35,105ft)
Crew:	1
Armament:	4 x 7.62mm (0.30in) machine guns, plus a light bombload of 6 x air-to-ground rockets

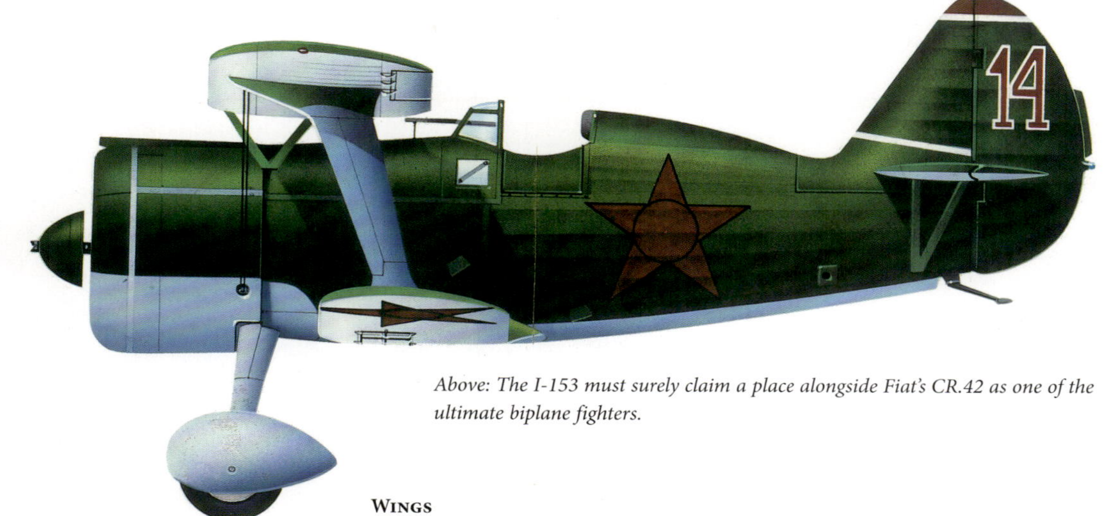

Above: The I-153 must surely claim a place alongside Fiat's CR.42 as one of the ultimate biplane fighters.

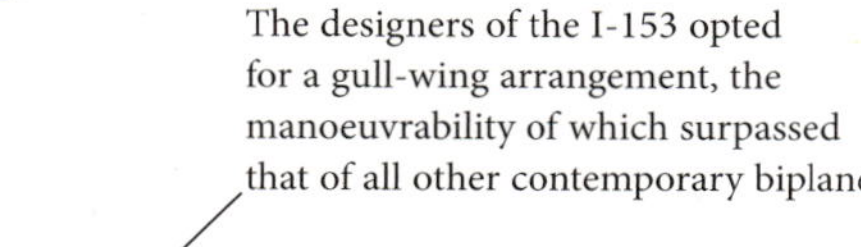

Wings
The designers of the I-153 opted for a gull-wing arrangement, the manoeuvrability of which surpassed that of all other contemporary biplanes.

Armament
The I-153 was armed with four synchronized machine guns, firing along canals lying between the engine cylinders. Small numbers were later fitted with two 20mm (0.79in) cannon.

Undercarriage
The I-153's retractable undercarriage was a novel feature in a biplane. Both legs retracted rearward into the underside of the fuselage, the wheels being turned 90 degrees during the process until they lay flat. As with many other Soviet aircraft, there was provision to fit skis instead of wheels.

THE SEAGULL

The I-153, dubbed *Chaika* (Seagull) because of its distinctive wing shape, was a first-rate combat aircraft and was subsequently to prove its worth in air fighting, being able to out-turn almost every aircraft that opposed it in action. The I-153 saw its first action in the 1939 Sino-Soviet incident, and was heavily involved in the 'Winter War' between Russia and Finland in 1939–40.

FINLAND, 1941

This I-153 was damaged after a forced landing in Finland on 25 June 1941. The I-153 was quickly withdrawn from first-line Soviet AF units after the German invasion of the USSR, but the Finns were still using captured I-153s as first-line fighters up to 1944. It was the last single-seat fighter biplane to be series produced in the USSR.

Curtiss P-40 Kittyhawk (1939)

TYPE • *Fighter* **COUNTRY** • *United States*

SPECIFICATIONS (P-40D)	
Dimensions:	Length: 10.16m (33ft 4in); Wingspan 11.38m (37ft 4in); Height 3.76m (12ft 4in)
Weight:	Empty 2722kg (6000lb); Maximum take-off 5171kg (11,400lb)
Powerplant:	1014kW (1360hp) Allison V-1710-81 V-12 engine
Max Speed:	609km/h (378mph) at 3200m (10,500ft)
Range:	386km (240 miles)
Ceiling:	11,580m (38,000ft)
Crew:	1
Armament:	6 × 12.7mm (0.50in) machine guns, plus a bombload of up to 3 × 227kg (500lb) bombs

The most important American fighter of the early-war years, the Curtiss P-40 did not possess outstanding performance but was agile, tough and dependable. Built in large numbers, it served with distinction in the air forces of many nations.

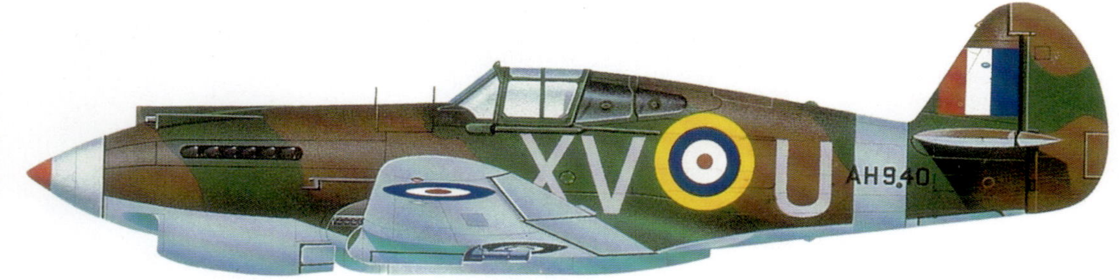

Above: A Curtiss Tomahawk Mk IIB of No. 414 Squadron, RAF, in early 1941.

Air intake
The inlet duct above the Allison engine allowed air into the carburettor, which was situated at the rear of the engine.

Armament
The P-40's armament of six 12.7mm (0.50in) machine guns was standard on most American-built fighters of World War II. Each gun was provided with 235 rounds.

NZ Kittyhawk
Curtiss Kittyhawk IV (P-40N) NZ3237 'E' from 19 squadron RNZAF at Guadalcanal and Torokina in late 1944. It was flown by Allan 'Skip' Watson, who named it 'Esma Lee' after a girl he knew in Auckland.

NAMINGS
The Curtiss P-40 was operated under several different names, depending on the user and on the variant. The initial aircraft, a development of the Curtiss P-36 Hawk, was labelled Warhawk in the United States, a term subsequently applied from 1941 to all US variants. The P-40 was adopted by British and Soviet forces, and they gave the aircraft the names Tomahawk for P-40, P-40B and P-40C variants and Kittyhawk for P-40D and later variants.

US P-40E
Displaying the short-lived red-bordered 'star and bar' insignia of July–September 1943, this Warhawk was photographed flying from Randolph Field. The serial number identifies it as a P-40E-1, a repossessed Kittyhawk Mk IA built for Lend-Lease to Britain; a P-40K-type fin has been fitted.

Lockheed Hudson (1939)

TYPE • *Reconnaissance* **COUNTRY** • *United States*

SPECIFICATIONS (GR Mk IIIA)

Dimensions:	Length: 13.50m (44ft 4in); Wingspan: 19.96m (65ft 6in); Height: 3.62m (11ft 10in)
Weight:	7930kg (17,500lb) loaded
Powerplant:	2 x 895kW (1200hp) Wright Cyclone 9-cylinder radial engines
Max speed:	397km/h (246mph)
Range:	3150km (1960 miles)
Ceiling:	7470m (24,500ft)
Crew:	6
Armament:	7 x 7.7mm (0.303in) Browning MGs (two in nose, two in dorsal turret, two in beam, one ventral); 340kg (750lb) of bombs or depth charges

Developed in response to a British requirement for a maritime patrol aircraft, the Lockheed Hudson reached the squadrons of RAF Coastal Command in time to combat the developing U-boat threat against the UK's merchant fleet.

Left: This Lockheed A-29 is seen in US Army Air Force (USAAF) colours of early 1942. Initially, all 800 A-29/A-29A aircraft were allocated to the RAF under Lend-Lease, but with the crisis in the Pacific and the Far East, a large number were repossessed and pressed into service with the USAAF.

Dorsal turret
The main defence against enemy fighters was provided by the dorsal turret, a Boulton Paul 'C' type mounting a pair of Browning 7.62mm (0.30in) machine guns.

Glazed nose
The glazed nose was occupied by the navigator, who had a seat and a table for his charts. Under his seat was a flat pane window for bomb-aiming.

Engines
Hudsons were powered by either Wright Cyclone or Pratt & Whitney Twin Wasp radial engines. The scoop above the engine is for the carburettor, while the intake under the engine is to cool the oil.

CLANDESTINE OPS

The Lockheed Hudson was primarily a maritime patrol aircraft, developed from the Lockheed Model 14 commercial airliner. Hudsons were also used, however, for clandestine operations, ferrying agents to and from France. The RAF's No. 161 (Special Duties) Squadron used several Hudsons in this capacity until the end of the war, latterly dropping supplies to agents in Germany itself.

AT-18 GUNNERY TRAINER
The AT-18 gunnery trainer was equipped with a Martin turret, with a pair of 12.7mm (0.5in) machine guns and provision for target-towing. The later AT-18A was a navigation trainer.

Boulton Paul Defiant (1939)

TYPE • *Fighter* **COUNTRY** • *United States*

SPECIFICATIONS (Defiant Mk II)

DIMENSIONS:	Length: 10.77m (35ft 4in); Wingspan: 11.99m (39ft 4in); Height: 4.39m (14ft 5in)
WEIGHT:	Empty: 2849kg (6282lb); Maximum: 3900kg (8600lb)
POWERPLANT:	1 × 954kW (1280hp) Rolls-Royce Merlin XX V-12 piston engine
MAX SPEED:	504km/h (313mph)
RANGE:	748km (465 miles)
CEILING:	10,242m (33,600ft)
CREW:	2
ARMAMENT:	4 × 7.7mm (0.303in) Browning machine guns

The Defiant was designed as a bomber destroyer with a four-gun powered turret, but no forward-facing armament. It was heavier than a Spitfire or Hurricane, but had much the same engine. Defiants were withdrawn as day fighters after suffering heavy losses in August 1940.

Above: The Defiant had considerably more success as a night-fighter. The Defiant II had a larger fin, a more powerful Merlin engine and, most importantly, an AI Mk IV air intercept radar. This example served with No. 151 Squadron at Wittering, Cambridgeshire.

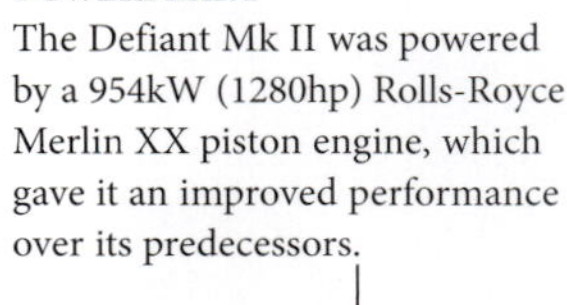

POWERPLANT
The Defiant Mk II was powered by a 954kW (1280hp) Rolls-Royce Merlin XX piston engine, which gave it an improved performance over its predecessors.

GUNNERY CONTROL
The gunner could rotate the turret directly forward and transfer firing control of the guns to the pilot, with the guns firing along each side of the cockpit canopy, although this was rarely done.

TURRET WEAPONS
The Defiant was armed with four 7.7mm (0.303in) Browning machine guns set in a hydraulically powered dorsal turret, with 600 rounds per gun.

TURRET FIGHTER
The Defiant was a British interceptor aircraft designed as a 'turret fighter', intended to intercept enemy bombers operating without, or separated from, fighter escort. In combat, it was indeed found to be effective at destroying bombers, but its lack of forward-firing armament meant that it was horribly vulnerable to the Luftwaffe's single-seat Messerschmitt Bf 109 fighters. It found more success, however, when converted to a night-fighter.

MK I DEFIANTS, 264 SQN
Boulton Paul Defiant Mk Is of No. 264 Squadron RAF. Although the turret armament looked fearsome, the aircraft could not defend itself adequately against German fighters. In one early action in May 1940, five out of six Defiants were shot down in a single mission when attacked frontally by Bf 109s.

Douglas DB-7/A-20 Havoc/Boston (1939)

TYPE • *Bomber* **COUNTRY** • *United States*

Blooded in battle in every theatre of war and sighted on every continent, the Douglas Havoc/ Boston was a fast and agile aircraft that proved to be an exceptional attack bomber. It saw widespread service in the air arms of many nations.

SPECIFICATIONS (A-20G Havoc)

Dimensions:	Length 14.63m (48ft); Wingspan 18.69m (61ft 4in); Height 5.51m (18ft 1in)
Weight:	Maximum take-off 13,608kg (30,000lb)
Powerplant:	2 × 1194kW (1600hp) Wright R-2600-23 Twin Cyclone 14-cylinder air-cooled radial piston engines
Max Speed:	523km/h (325mph)
Range:	1521km (945 miles)
Ceiling:	7200m (23,700ft)
Crew:	3
Armament:	6 × 12.7mm (0.5in) Browning M2 fixed forward-firing MGs, and three similar weapons in power-operated dorsal turret, one rearward-firing through ventral tunnel; up to 1814kg (4000lb) of bombs

Above: A Douglas A-20G of the 646th Bomb Squadron, 410th Bomb Group, US Ninth Army Air Force, Gosfield, 1944.

Design
The essential design was conventional, with a slender, aluminium alloy, semi-monocoque fuselage and a single-spar, aluminium alloy wing with fabric-covered control surfaces.

Soviet A-20G
The Soviet Union received 3125 aircraft of the DB-7 series as part of US Lend-Lease deliveries, many of them receiving a number of local modifications such as the Soviet dorsal turret evident here.

Forward armament
The A-20G was armed with six forward-firing 12.7mm (0.50in) Browning machine guns, which were ideal for heavy strafing runs against ground targets.

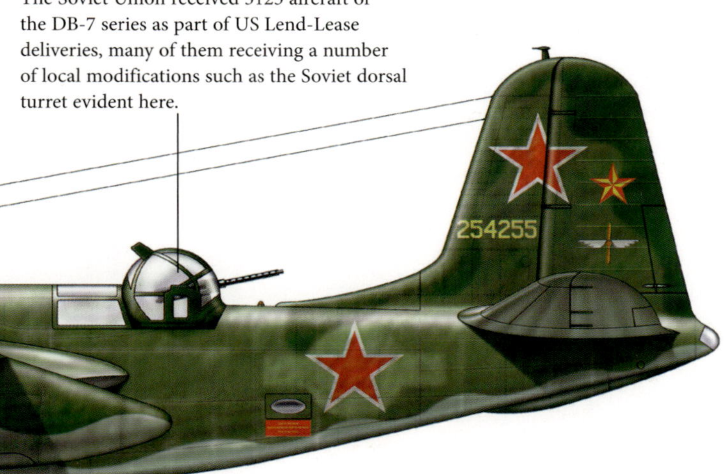

NAMING

The Boston/Havoc was in US Army Air Corps (USAAC), RAF, French and Soviet service. During its career, there was confusion and overlap between the company team DB-7 and the USAAF designation A-20, and between the names Boston and Havoc. Many RAF machines officially had both names, the UK's involvement starting with a 20 February 1940 contract for 150 aircraft.

D-DAY MISSION
This A-20G-20 served with a unit of the Ninth Air Force, which took its place alongside the Eighth Air Force in operations in the ETO and flew more than 100,000 combat missions in the run-up to D-Day.

Reggiane Re.2000 and Re.2001 (1940)

TYPE • *Fighter* **COUNTRY** • *Italy*

The Reggiane Re.2000 Falco I was introduced into service in 1940 as an all-metal, low-wing monoplane fighter. Although it gave good service to the Italian Air Force, it had problems that were largely remedied in a more advanced design, the Re.2001 Falco II.

SPECIFICATIONS (Re.2001 Serie III)

DIMENSIONS:	Length: 8.36m (27ft 5in); Wingspan: 11m (36ft 1in); Height: 3.15m (10ft 4in)
WEIGHT:	Empty: 2495kg (5501lb)
POWERPLANT:	1 × 864kW (1159hp) Alfa Romeo R.A.1000 R.C.41-I Monsone V-12 inverted liquid-cooled piston engine (licence-built Daimler-Benz DB 601Aa)
MAX SPEED:	542km/h (337mph)
RANGE:	1100km (680 miles)
CEILING:	11,000m (36,000ft)
CREW:	1
ARMAMENT:	2 × 12.7mm (0.50in) Breda-SAFAT machine guns in upper cowling; 2 × 7.7mm (0.303in) Breda-SAFAT machine guns in wings

Above: The Re.2001 Falco II pictured here flew in the 362 Squadriglia, *22* Gruppo Autonomo.

POWERPLANT
The Re.2000 powerplant was a Piaggio P.XI RC 40 radial engine, generating 735kW (986hp) and allied to a Piaggio-built three-blade, constant-speed, variable-pitch propeller.

PERFORMANCE
The Re.2000 had a stressed-skin construction and some advanced aerodynamic features, including an elliptical wing profile that gave it good manoeuvrability.

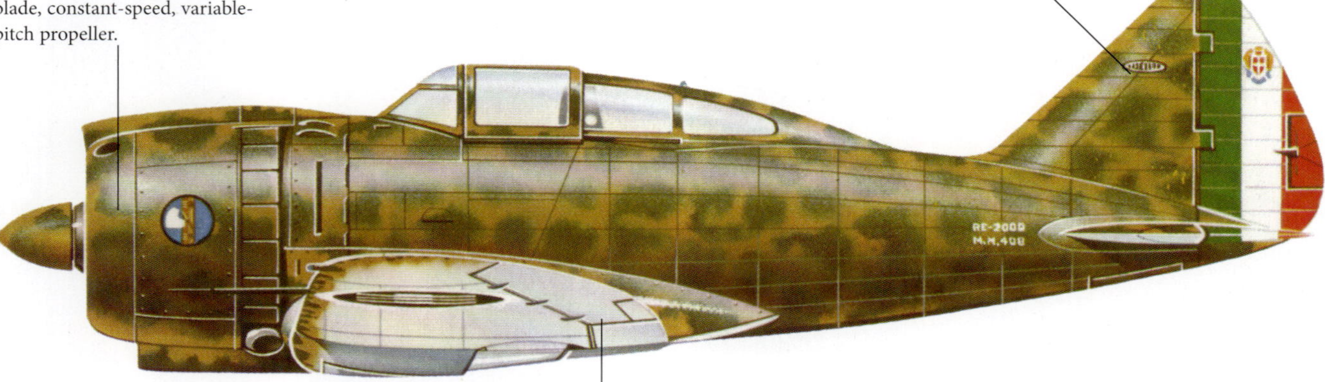

FUEL STORAGE
The Re.2000's fuel was stored entirely in its wings. This was one of the vulnerabilities that were addressed in the development of the Re.2001.

ENGINE SOLUTIONS

The Re.2000's potential could not initially be realized for lack of adequate power, Italy having ignored the advisability of developing potent Vee engines for aviation use. The Piaggio engine used in the aircraft also had a poor reputation for reliability. Solutions were found in the licensed production of German engines, and an early development was the Re.2001 Falco II, first flown in June 1940.

HUNGARIAN FALCO
Hungary not only purchased Re.2000s during the early war period, but also became a licensed producer. In total, Hungary manufactured 204 of their own aircraft, named the MÁVAG Héja II.

Fairey Albacore (1940)

TYPE • *Torpedo bomber* **COUNTRY** • *United Kingdom*

SPECIFICATIONS (Albacore Mk I)

DIMENSIONS:	Length 12.13m (39ft 10in); Wingspan: 15.24m (50ft 0in); Height: 4.65m (15ft 3in)
WEIGHT:	5820kg (12,830lb) maximum take-off
POWERPLANT:	1 × 794kW (1065hp) Bristol Taurus II or 1 × 840kW (1130hp) Bristol Taurus XII 14-cylinder air-cooled radial piston engine
MAX SPEED:	272km/h (169mph)
RANGE:	1497km (930 miles)
CEILING:	6309m (20,700ft)
CREW:	2 or 3
ARMAMENT:	1 × 7.7mm (0.303in) Browning machine gun fixed forward-firing in starboard wing; 1 or 2 × 7.7mm (0.303in) Vickers K MGs flexibly mounted in rear cockpit; up to 907kg (2000lb) bombload or 1 × 730kg (1610lb) torpedo

Although planned as a replacement for the Fairey Swordfish, the Albacore never achieved the same fame as its illustrious predecessor and in many respects was a less useful aircraft in its intended torpedo-bomber role.

Left: An Albacore on a carrier deck. From late 1941 until the summer of 1943, Albacores played a significant role in the defence of Malta, seeing relentless action attacking Axis shipping.

POWERPLANT
Power came from a 794kW (1065hp) Bristol Taurus II or an 840kW (1130hp) Bristol Taurus XII 14-cylinder air-cooled radial piston engine.

CENTRE OF GRAVITY
Poor stalling characteristics were cured before the aircraft entered service by moving the centre of gravity further aft.

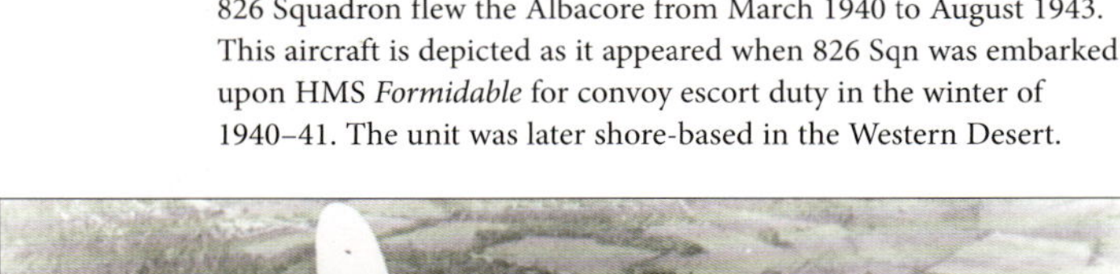

ALBACORE MK I
826 Squadron flew the Albacore from March 1940 to August 1943. This aircraft is depicted as it appeared when 826 Sqn was embarked upon HMS *Formidable* for convoy escort duty in the winter of 1940–41. The unit was later shore-based in the Western Desert.

RELIABILITY
Initial deliveries to units began in December 1939 and the Albacore's operational use commenced during March 1940, although early service use was plagued by reliability issues affecting the Taurus engine, which were bad enough to result in all Albacores being grounded for a month during the summer of 1940. The problems were largely ironed out but an unfortunate reputation for poor reliability would nonetheless dog the Taurus for the remainder of its service life.

HANDLING
The Fairey Albacore proved generally pleasant to fly with a superb view of the surroundings for the pilot and generally good deck-landing characteristics.

Martin PBM Mariner (1940)

TYPE • *Seaplane* **COUNTRY** • *United States*

The PBM Mariner was built as a patrol and bomber flying boat, but variants were created for the Coast Guard and surplus aircraft sold to several nations. The Uruguayan Navy even obtained three PBM-5Es in the mid-1950s and used them for search-and-rescue duties.

SPECIFICATIONS (PBM-1)

DIMENSIONS:	Length: 23.50m (77ft 2in); Wingspan: 36m (118ft 0in); Height: 5.33m (17ft 6in)
WEIGHT:	25,425kg (56,000lb) loaded
POWERPLANT:	2 × 1300kW (1700hp) Wright R-2600-12 14-cylinder radial engines
MAX SPEED:	330km/h (205mph)
RANGE:	4800km (3000 miles)
CEILING:	6040m (19,800ft)
CREW:	7
ARMAMENT:	4 × 12.7mm (0.5in) MGs; 1800kg (4000lb) of bombs or depth charges or 2 × Mark 13 torpedoes

LANDING FLOATS
The PBM-1 Mariner was equipped with retractable wing landing floats that were hinged inboard.

Above: A US Navy PBM-5 in 1945. With two rather than four engines, and a bombload of 3629kg (8000lb) rather than 5443kg (12,000lb), the Mariner was smaller and lighter than the heavyweight Coronado, and was designed for operations over shorter ranges.

PBM-1 MARINER
The PBM-1 was the first production model of the Mariner family, and only 20 of this variant were built.

ARMAMENT
The Mariner was especially heavily armed, with four 12.7mm (0.5in) machine guns (one each in nose and dorsal turrets and blisters amidships) and 1800kg (4000lb) of bombs or depth charges or two Mark 13 torpedoes.

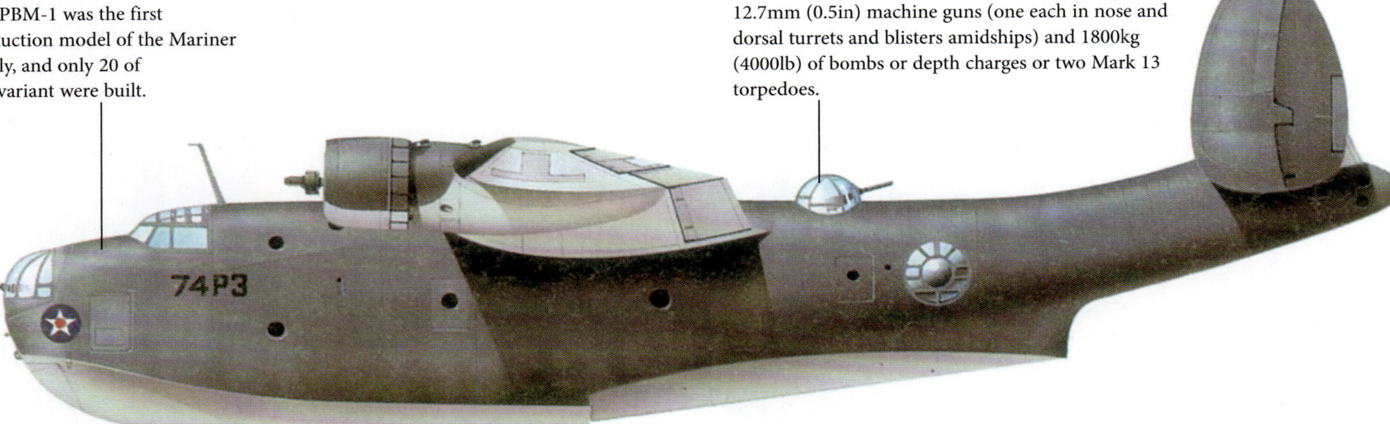

HISTORY
Designed in 1936, the Martin PBM Mariner was of huge importance to the Allied war effort. It was of a very advanced design, with high wing loading and retractable stabilizing floats built into the wing tips. The most prolific variant was the PBM-3, which had its own subvariants. The PBM-3B (32 built) was supplied to the RAF under the Lend-Lease Act as the Mariner GR Mk I.

PBM-3
A Martin PBM-3 Mariner flies past Sugarloaf Mountain, Brazil, in 1943. Compared to the PBM-1, the PBM-3 had longer nacelles, each possessing a bay for four 227kg (500lb) bombs or depth charges, and fixed rather than retractable underwing stabilizing floats.

North American P-51 Mustang (1940)

TYPE • *Fighter* **COUNTRY** • *United States*

SPECIFICATIONS (P-51D)

DIMENSIONS:	Length: 9.83m (32ft 3in); Wingspan: 11.28m (37ft 0in); Height: 4.16m (13ft 8in)
WEIGHT:	5493kg (12,100lb) maximum take-off
POWERPLANT:	1 x 1110kW (1490hp) Packard (Rolls-Royce) V-1650-7 Merlin 12-cylinder liquid-cooled piston engine
MAX SPEED	703km/h (437mph)
RANGE:	2655km (1650 miles) with external fuel tanks
CEILING:	12,800m (42,000ft)
CREW:	1
ARMAMENT:	6 x 12.7mm (0.5in) Browning M2 MGs fixed forward-firing in wings; up to 908kg (2000lb) bombload; later production aircraft fitted with provision for 3 rocket launch tubes under each wing

With a strong claim to be the finest piston-engined fighter of World War II, the superlative P-51 emerged from potential obscurity when re-engined with the British-designed Merlin powerplant. It became a war-winning long-range escort after its service entry in late 1943.

Above: The pilot of the P-51D sat under an aft-sliding, blown 'bubble' canopy, which provided improved visibility compared to the standard canopy on the high-backed P-51B/C.

PRINCESS ELIZABETH
The P-51B 'Princess Elizabeth' was flown by the US fighter ace 1st Lt. William Whisner of the 487th Fighter Squadron, 352nd Fighter Group.

FUEL
Both the P-51B and P-51C could carry a 454kg (1000lb) bomb under each wing or external fuel tank, their fuel capacity being improved by the addition of a 322 litre (85 US gal) fuselage tank on later production aircraft.

AIR SUPERIORITY
P-51Bs of the 354th Fighter Group flew their first operational escort mission from England in December 1943. The first P-51Ds arrived there in the late spring of 1944 and quickly became standard equipment for the US Army Air Force Eighth Fighter Command. In the Pacific, Mustangs operating from the captured Japanese islands of Iwo Jima and Okinawa had the task of escorting B-29s to their targets and neutralizing the Japanese air force on the ground.

MUSTANG ACE
The Mustang was flown by many of the United States Army Air Force's top-scoring aces in the European Theater of Operations. Exemplifying the breed was Captain Don Gentile, 336th Fighter Squadron, 4th Fighter Group, US Army Eighth Air Force, a remarkable fighter leader who scored 15.5 kills on Mustangs.

Yakovlev Yak-1 (1940)

TYPE • *Fighter* **COUNTRY** • *Soviet Union*

SPECIFICATIONS (Yak-1 early production)	
DIMENSIONS:	Length: 8.48m (27ft 10in); Wingspan: 10m (32ft 10in); Height: 2.64m (8ft 8in)
WEIGHT:	Maximum take-off 2844kg (6269lb)
POWERPLANT:	1 × 783kW (1050hp) Klimov M-105PA V-12 liquid-cooled piston engine
MAX SPEED:	560km/h (348mph)
RANGE:	700km (430 miles)
CEILING:	9900m (32,500ft)
CREW:	1
ARMAMENT:	1 × 20mm (0.8in) ShVAK cannon; 2 × 7.62mm (0.3in) ShKAS machine guns

Early Yak-1s were outclassed by their German opponents, but the type soon developed a reputation for reliability and became popular with Russian pilots. It turned out to be ideally suited to the operational conditions it would encounter during the Great Patriotic War.

Above: With 8720 built, the Yak-1 was the most numerous of the Yakolev fighter family. From October 1942 a cutdown rear fuselage and bubble canopy were fitted.

ARMAMENT
The standard armament of the Yak-1 was a pair of 12.7mm (0.50in) machine guns in the upper front fuselage and a 20mm (0.8in) ShVAK cannon in the nose, firing through the propeller boss.

AIRFRAME
The airframe of the Yak-1 was lightweight, giving rise to a generation of fast and manoeuvrable interceptors; on the other hand, the more robust Yak-7A was developed into a succession of heavier tactical fighters like the Yak-9.

ENEMY KILLS
Mikhail Baranov was the leading Soviet ace of 1942, flying this Yak-1 over Stalingrad marked with 27 victory stars and the slogan '*Smert Fascistam*' ('Death to Fascists') rather crudely applied to the rear fuselage.

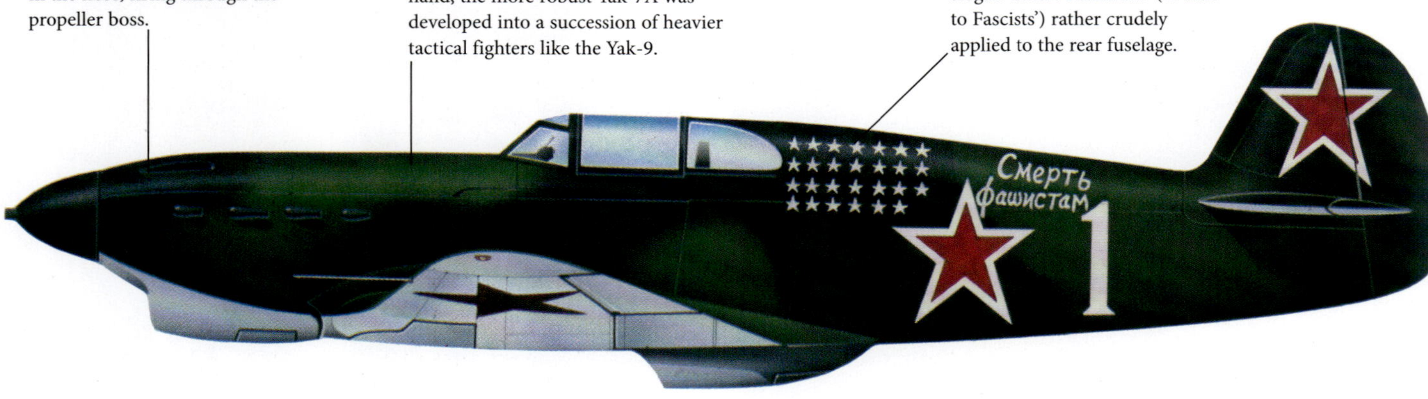

AIR SUPERIORITY

The Russians were late in developing really effective monoplane fighters that were in the same class as Britain's Hurricane and Spitfire and Germany's Bf 109, but Aleksandr Yakovlev's attractive designs soon redressed the situation. The Yak-1, which made its first public appearance on 7 November 1940, evolved into the improved Yak-7 and Yak-9; the latter could take on the best of late-war Luftwaffe fighter aircraft.

DESIGN SIMPLICITY

Ordered into production as the Yak-1 a mere month or so after the prototype's first flight, the aircraft was small, simple and of mixed wood and metal construction to minimize demand on strategic light alloy and steel supplies.

Douglas SBD Dauntless (1940)

TYPE • *Naval bomber* **COUNTRY** • *United States*

SPECIFICATIONS (SBD-3)

DIMENSIONS:	Length: 9.96m (38ft 8in); Wingspan: 12.66m (41ft 6in); Height: 4.14m (13ft 7in)
WEIGHT:	Empty: 2878kg (6345lb); Maximum: 4717kg (10,400lb)
POWERPLANT:	1 x 746kW (1000hp) Wright R-1820-52 Cyclone piston engine
MAX SPEED:	402km/h (250mph)
RANGE:	2165km (1345 miles)
CEILING:	8260m (27,100ft)
CREW:	2
ARMAMENT:	2 x 12.7mm (0.5in) and 2 x 7.62mm (0.3in) Browning machine guns

By the end of the war in the Pacific, the venerable Dauntless dive-bomber was showing its age; nonetheless, its contribution to victory in a succession of key naval battles cannot be overstated and its tally of Japanese shipping is unmatched.

Above and right: Both fin and tailplane employed stressed-skin construction. Elevators and rudders were fabric-covered, and tabs were provided on the control surfaces of the tail.

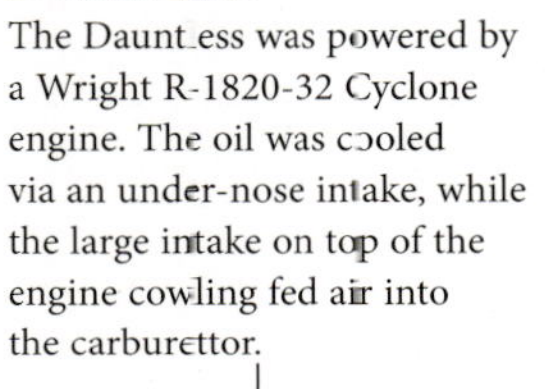

POWERPLANT
The Dauntless was powered by a Wright R-1820-32 Cyclone engine. The oil was cooled via an under-nose intake, while the large intake on top of the engine cowling fed air into the carburettor.

PILOT POSITION
The pilot sat high in the cockpit with an armoured backplate but no bulletproof windscreen. A telescopic sight was used for aiming both bombs and guns.

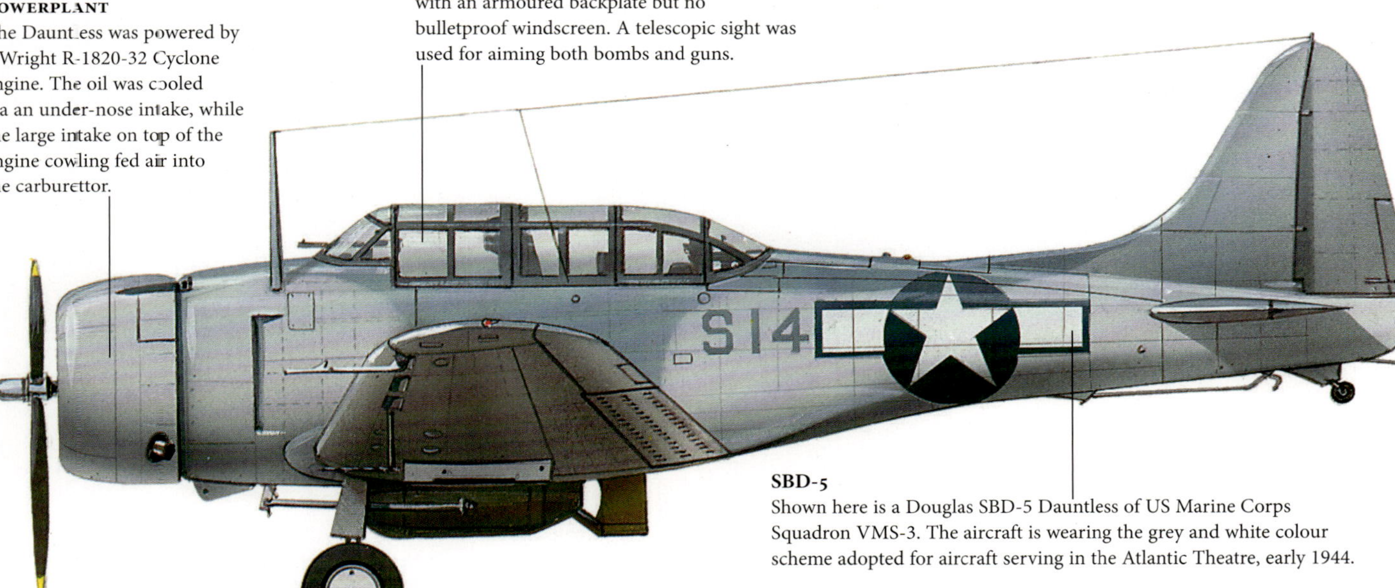

SBD-5
Shown here is a Douglas SBD-5 Dauntless of US Marine Corps Squadron VMS-3. The aircraft is wearing the grey and white colour scheme adopted for aircraft serving in the Atlantic Theatre, early 1944.

MARINE DAUNTLESS
Delivery of the SBD-1 to the US Marine Corps began in mid-1940 and this version was followed by the SBD-2 and SBD-3, with extra fuel tankage, protective armour and autopilot. The attrition rate of the Dauntless squadrons was the lowest of any US carrier aircraft in the Pacific, thanks to the SBD's ability to absorb an amazing amount of battle damage.

DOUGLAS SBD-4 DAUNTLESS, 1943
The SBD-4 was delivered between October 1942 and April 1943. It had improved radio navigation aids, an electric fuel pump and an improved Hamilton Standard Hydromatic constant-speed, fully feathering propeller.

Focke-Wulf Fw 200 Condor (1940)

TYPE • *Maritime bomber* **COUNTRY** • *Germany*

SPECIFICATIONS (Focke-Wulf Fw 200C-1)

DIMENSIONS:	Length: 23.46m (76ft 11in); Wingspan: 32.82m (107ft 8in); Height: 6.3m (20ft 8in)
WEIGHT:	22,700kg (50,045lb) maximum take-off
POWERPLANT:	4 × 620kW (830hp) BMW 132H radial piston engines
MAX SPEED:	360km/h (224mph)
RANGE:	4440km (2795 miles)
CEILING:	6000m (19,685ft)
CREW:	5
ARMAMENT:	3 × 7.92mm (0.31in) MG 15 machine guns; 1 × 20mm (0.8in) MG FF cannon; 4 × 250kg (551lb) bombs or 2 × 1000kg (2205lb) mines

Designed as a four-engined long-range airliner, the Fw 200 was adapted to fill a Luftwaffe requirement for a maritime patrol aircraft. Only built in small numbers, the Fw 200's effect on Allied shipping earned it the sobriquet 'Scourge of the Atlantic'.

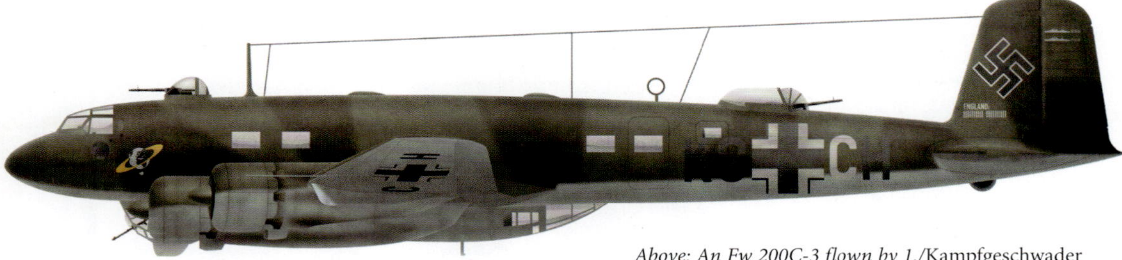

*Above: An Fw 200C-3 flown by 1./*Kampfgeschwader *40 based at Bordeaux-Mérignac, France, in 1940. This Condor was posted missing during a mission over the Atlantic on 24 July 1941.*

FORWARD CUPOLA
The forward-firing 7.92mm (0.31in) MG 15 machine gun in the fully enclosed forward cupola was manned by the co-pilot when the aircraft was threatened by frontal attack.

GONDOLA
The Condor's weapons bay was situated in the ventral gondola; the rear gun position immediately behind it was manned by the flight engineer. On armed reconnaissance missions, four 250kg (551lb) bombs were normally carried, two on the outboard engine nacelles and two on wing racks.

STORAGE
The Condor's rear fuselage was used as a storage area for small stores like flares, light buoys or direction-finding buoys. These were dropped through a hatch in the fuselage underside.

MISSILE CARRIER
The final operational variant of the Condor was the Fw 200C-6, developed from the C-3 to carry a Henschel Hs 293B air-to-surface missile under each outer engine nacelle, the underwing bomb racks being removed. The combination of Hs 293 and Fw 200 was first used operationally on 28 December 1943. The total number of Condors produced during the war years was 252.

PATROL PREPARATIONS
Posed in front of their Condor, which already has its propellers turning, these KG 40 crewmen review their map details before leaving their base in Bordeaux-Mérignac, France, on another long maritime patrol.

Mitsubishi Ki-46 'Dinah' (1940)

TYPE • *Reconnaissance* **COUNTRY** • *Japan*

SPECIFICATIONS (Ki-46 III)

Dimensions:	Length: 11.00m (36ft 1in); Wingspan: 14.70m (48ft 233in); Height: 3.88m (12ft 8.75in)
Weight:	Empty 3263kg (7194lb); Maximum take-off 5800kg (12,789lb)
Powerplant:	2 x 787kW (1055hp) Mitsubishi Ha.102 14-cylinder radials
Max Speed:	604km/h (375mph) at 8000m (26,245ft);
Range:	2474km (1537 miles)
Ceiling:	10,720m (35,170ft)
Crew:	2
Armament:	1 x 7.7mm (0.303in) machine gun

Known to the Allies by the code name 'Dinah', the Mitsubishi Ki-46 was one of the best reconnaissance aircraft of World War II, and aerodynamically one of the most perfect aircraft produced by any of the belligerents.

Above and right: Early versions of the Ki-46 had a pronounced step between the nose and the pilot's windscreen. This was eliminated in the Ki-46-III. An extra fuel tank was also fitted in front of the cockpit.

Crew positions
The Ki-46's pilot and gunner were seated in two cockpits separated by a large fuel tank. To meet performance requirements, the aircraft's designers adopted a fuselage of small diameter.

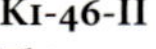

Ki-46-II
This example of the major production version of the 'Dinah' served with the 76th Dokuritsu Hiko Chutai based in the East Indies in 1943.

Engine layout
Special close-fitting cowlings were developed for the Ki-46's engines. This resulted in a substantial improvement in the pilot's sideways vision and also brought about a reduction in drag, as well as contributing to the design of the fully retractable landing gear.

HEAVY FIGHTER

The Ki-46 was designed specifically as a high-altitude reconnaissance aeroplane to meet a 1937 requirement, and the prototype made its maiden flight in November 1939. Versions of the Ki-46 developed as heavy fighters for the air defence of Japan featured a 37mm (1.46in) Ho-203 cannon mounted obliquely in the upper fuselage, designed to fire forward and upward into the underside of a B-29 bomber.

CAPTURED KI-46
A captured Ki-46 lies forlorn on a battlefield in the Pacific. The Ki-46-III-Kai was thrown into battle against the B-29 bombers that were attacking Japan on an almost daily basis in 1945.

Petlyakov Pe-8 (1940)

TYPE • *Bomber* **COUNTRY** • *Soviet Union*

The only modern four-engined bomber developed by the USSR, the Pe-8 was an impressive performer. But like the Luftwaffe and the Italian Air Force, the Soviet Air Force in World War II was geared to tactical support, and paid little attention to strategic bombers.

SPECIFICATIONS

DIMENSIONS:	Length: 23.2m (76ft 1in); Wingspan: 39.13m (128ft 5in); Height: 6.2m (20ft 4in)
WEIGHT:	35,000kg (77,162lb) maximum take-off
POWERPLANT:	4 x 999kW (1340hp) Mikulin AM-35A V-12 liquid-cooled piston engines
MAX SPEED:	443km/h (275mph)
RANGE:	3700km (2300 miles)
CEILING:	9300m (30,500ft)
CREW:	11
ARMAMENT:	2 x 7.62mm (0.3in) ShKAS MGs in nose turret; 1 x 12.7mm (0.5in) Berezin UBT in port and starboard inner engine nacelle turret; 1 x 20mm (0.78in) ShVAK in dorsal turret; 1 x 20mm (0.78in) ShVAK in rear turret; up to 5000kg (11,000lb) bombload

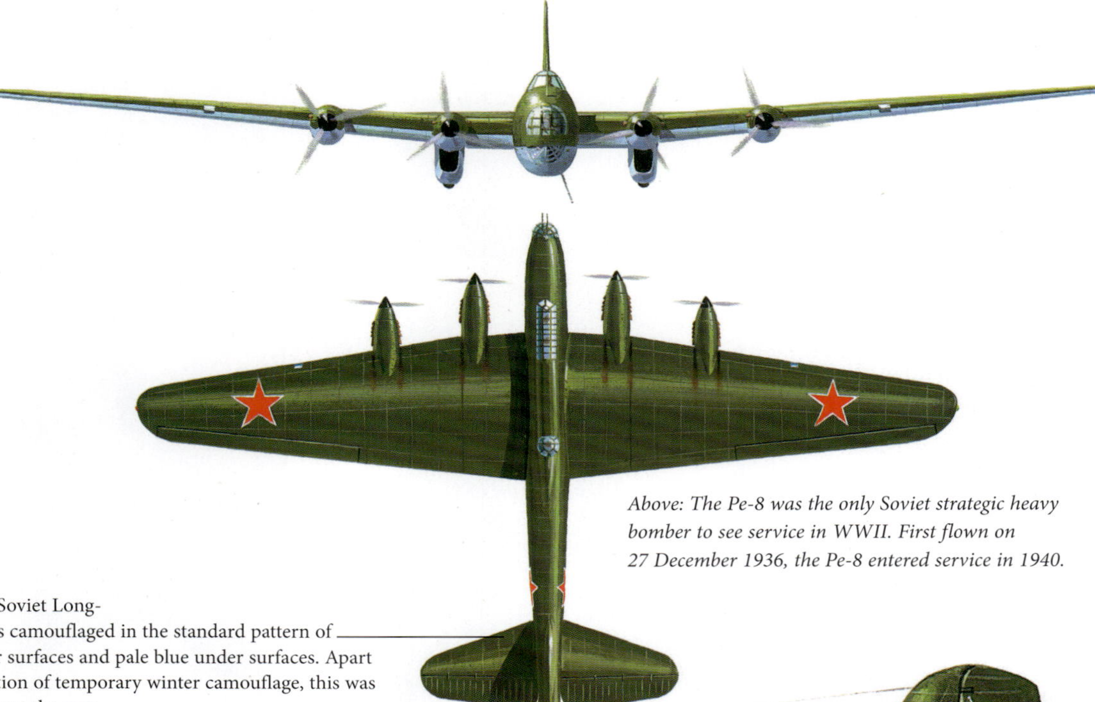

Above: The Pe-8 was the only Soviet strategic heavy bomber to see service in WWII. First flown on 27 December 1936, the Pe-8 entered service in 1940.

COLOURING
This Pe-8 of the Soviet Long-Range Aviation is camouflaged in the standard pattern of dark green upper surfaces and pale blue under surfaces. Apart from the application of temporary winter camouflage, this was retained throughout the war.

BOMB BAY
The Pe-8's bomb bay could accommodate a 5000kg (11,023lb) FAB-5000NG blast bomb. On the eve of the Battle of Kursk in July 1943, Pe-8s were used to drop these weapons on concentrations of German tanks and other armoured vehicles.

GUN POSITIONS
An unusual feature of the Pe-8 was that it had machine gun positions built into the rear of the two inboard engine nacelles. Gunners found these positions cramped and smelly, but they had the advantage of being warm.

LONG DISTANCE

The Pe-8 was dogged by engine difficulties throughout its career and various powerplants were tried, including M-30B diesel engines. From 1943, production Pe-8s were fitted with Mikulin M-82FN fuel injection engines, but the problems persisted and production ended in 1944 after 79 examples had been built. Despite its troubles, the Pe-8 made some notable long-distance flights, including a round trip of more than 17,700km (11,000 miles) between Moscow and Washington.

PE-8, EASTERN FRONT, 1944
Early in its service life, the Pe-8 performed well and was difficult to intercept, the loss rate in 1942 being only one in 106 missions, but as the war progressed, German defences improved and losses more than doubled by 1944.

Martin Maryland (1940)

TYPE • *Bomber* **COUNTRY** • *United States*

SPECIFICATIONS (Maryland Mk II)

Dimensions:	Length: 14.22m (46ft 8in); Wingspan: 18.69m (61ft 4in); Height: 4.57m (15ft 0in)
Weight:	7624kg (16,809lb) loaded
Powerplant:	2 x 895kW (1200hp) Pratt & Whitney Twin Wasp radial piston engines
Max speed:	447km/h (278mph)
Range:	2897km (1800 miles)
Ceiling:	9449m (31,000ft)
Crew:	3
Armament:	4 x 7.7mm (0.303in) Browning MGs; 2 x single Vickers K MGs; up to 907kg (2000lb) of bombs

Aircraft like the Martin Maryland light bomber showed what was possible using massive two-row radial engines and by accepting longer take-off and landing distances and the need for concrete runways.

Below: Delivered to US standard, but fitted with an Armstong Whitworth dorsal turret, the Maryland Mk I was operated from Malta primarily in the long-range reconnaissance role, deep into the Mediterranean and around Italy's coast.

SAAF Maryland Mk II
South Africa was a primary operator of the Maryland, and No. 24 Squadron was one of three detailed for operations over Crete from 23 May 1941. In November, the squadron transitioned to the more capable Douglas Boston.

Anglicized version
The Mk II version of the Maryland introduced Vickers K machine guns into the defensive armament and changed US instrumentation for British imperial measurements.

Crew
The Maryland had a three-man crew, with a navigator/bombardier at the very front of the aircraft, a pilot in the cockpit and a radio operator/gunner in the turret.

FRENCH MARYLAND
Known to the British as the Maryland, the Model 167 was first manufactured for the French in two forms, as the Model 167F reconnaissance bomber (115 ordered) and Model 167A.3 attack-bomber (100 ordered, of which 76 were delivered to the UK after the fall of France).

PHOTO-RECCE
Designed as an attack bomber in 1938, the US-made Martin XA-22 failed to win any production contracts with the US Army Air Force. In 1939 Martin looked for buyers overseas, and under the designation Model 167 (the Maryland) sales were made to Britain, France and South Africa. A key role of the Maryland in British service was as a photo-reconnaissance aircraft, it being faster than the Blenheim.

Bristol Beaufighter (1940)

TYPE • *Heavy fighter* **COUNTRY** • *United Kingdom*

SPECIFICATIONS (TF Mk X)

DIMENSIONS:	Length: 12.70m (41ft 8in); Wingspan: 17.63m (57ft 10in); Height: 4.83m (15ft 10in)
WEIGHT:	11431kg (25,200lb) loaded
POWERPLANT:	2 × 1320kW (1770hp) Bristol Hercules XVII radial piston engines
MAX SPEED:	488km/h (303mph)
RANGE:	2366km (1470 miles)
CEILING:	4570m (15,000ft)
CREW:	2
ARMAMENT:	4 × 20mm (0.8in) cannon; 6 × 7.7mm (0.303in) MGs in wings; 1 × 7.7mm (0.303in) Vickers MG in dorsal turret; 2 × 113kg (250lb) bombs

The Blenheim was barely fast enough to catch most German bombers, so the next platform developed was the more powerful Bristol Beaufighter, which entered service in November 1940 and became one of the most successful multi-role aircraft of World War II.

Above: One of the favourite weapons of Beaufighter strike squadrons was the 76mm (3in) rocket fitted with either an 11kg (25lb) solid armour-piercing or 27kg (60lb) explosive-filled semi-armour-piercing warhead.

ASV RADAR
Coastal Command Beaufighters often carried ASV (air to surface vessel) radar to locate shipping targets. This aircraft is fitted with ASV Mk III, which was of limited use due to the blanking effect of the engine nacelles.

BEAUFIGHTER TF MK X
The Beaufighter TF Mk X pictured here served with No. 489 Squadron, RNZAF, which was part of the Coastal Command Strike Wing based at Dallachy, Scotland.

TORPEDO CONFIGURATION
The Torpedo Beaufighter, known as the Torbeau, was fitted with Fairey-Youngman wing dive brakes installed between the ailerons and the wing root fairings.

ANTI-SHIP BEAUFIGHTERS
The TF Mk X torpedo bomber and the Mk XIC, which was not equipped to carry torpedoes, were fitted with 1320kW (1770hp) Hercules XVII engines and had a dorsal cupola containing a rearward-firing 7.7mm (0.303in) machine gun. Production of the TF Mk X, which was the most important British anti-shipping aircraft from 1944 to the end of the war, totalled 2205 aircraft, while 163 aircraft were completed to Mk XIC standard.

CANADIAN FORMATION
No. 404 Sqn, Royal Canadian Air Force, flew Beaufighters from September 1942. They received the TF Mk Xs, as seen here, in September 1943, although from September 1944 it was one of the Banff Strike Wing squadrons and was re-equipped with Mosquitoes just prior to VE Day.

Handley Page Halifax (1940)

TYPE • *Bomber* **COUNTRY** • *United Kingdom*

SPECIFICATIONS (Halifax Mk III)

DIMENSIONS:	Length: 21.82m (71ft 7in); Wingspan: 30.07m (98ft 8in); Height: 6.32m (20ft 9in)
WEIGHT:	Empty 17,690kg (39,000lb); Maximum take-off 30,845kg (68,000lb)
POWERPLANT:	4 x 1204kW (1615hp) Bristol Hercules VI or XVI 14-cylinder two-row radial engines
MAX SPEED:	454km/h (282mph) at 4115m (13,500ft)
RANGE:	3194km (1985 miles)
CEILING:	7315m (24,000ft)
CREW:	7
ARMAMENT:	5 x 7.62mm (0.30in) machine guns, plus an internal bombload of 6577kg (14,500lb)

Second of the four-engined heavy bombers to enter service with the RAF in November 1940, the Handley Page Halifax was one of the famous triad, comprising the Halifax, Avro Lancaster and Short Stirling, which mounted Bomber Command's night-bombing offensive against Germany.

Above: A Halifax B.Mk III of No. 466 Squadron, Royal Australian Air Force, No. 4 Group, RAF Bomber Command, Driffield, Yorkshire, 1944. The yellow-striped fin-and-rudder units were identifying marks of No. 4 Group's aircraft in 1944.

ENGINES
The Halifax Mk III was fitted with Bristol Hercules engines, but the earlier marks, with Rolls-Royce Merlins, had a longer range, and these were retained by the special duties squadrons for infiltrating agents into enemy territory.

DORSAL TURRET
The dorsal turret was a Boulton Paul A Mk III mid-upper turret, armed with four 7.62mm (0.30in) guns with 1160 rounds each. The teardrop fairing on top of the fuselage between cockpit and dorsal turret housed the direction finder aerial.

RADOME
The later marks of Halifax carried a large radome under the fuselage housing H2S ground mapping radar. Both Halifax and Lancaster were originally intended to have a ventral gun turret in this position.

ENGINE UPGRADE
In 1943 the Halifax's Merlin engines were replaced by four 1204kW (1615hp) Bristol Hercules XVI radial engines in the Halifax Mk III, which remained in the front line up to the end of the war. The next operational variants were the Mks VI and VII, the former powered by the 1249kW (1675hp) Hercules 100 and the latter using the Mk III's Hercules XVI.

STANDARD BOMBER
From the time of their introduction into operational service, Halifax bombers were in continuous use by Bomber Command, equipping at their peak usage no fewer than 34 squadrons in the European theatre, and four more in the Middle East.

Short Stirling (1940)

TYPE • *Bomber* **COUNTRY** • *United Kingdom*

SPECIFICATIONS (Stirling III)

DIMENSIONS:	Length: 26.6m (87ft 3in); Wingspan: 30.2m (99ft 1in); Height: 8.8m (28ft 10in)
WEIGHT:	31750kg (70,000lb) loaded
POWERPLANT:	4 × 1030kW (1375hp) Bristol Hercules radial engines
MAX SPEED:	410km/h (255mph)
RANGE:	3750km (2330 miles)
CEILING:	5030m (16,500ft)
CREW:	7
ARMAMENT:	8 × 7.7mm (0.303in) Browning MGs (two in the nose, four in the tail, two dorsal); up to 8164kg (18,000lb) of bombs

Throughout its operational life, the Short Stirling suffered from an Air Ministry instruction dictating that its wingspan should be reduced so that the aircraft would fit inside existing hangars. Its altitude performance suffered accordingly.

Below: The Stirling suffered from troublesome undercarriage retraction motors, which proved inadequate for the task. The main wheels were the largest fitted to an operational aircraft during World War II.

WINGS
Though stable in flight and surprisingly manoeuvrable, thanks to its high wing loading, the Stirling had a poor operational ceiling when loaded, often being hard pushed to climb above 3660m (12,000ft).

CODE LETTERS
This Stirling carries the code letters of No. 7 Squadron, the first to equip with the type in August 1940. The squadron was then at RAF Leeming, in Yorkshire, but in October 1940 it moved to Oakington, near Cambridge, and remained there for the rest of the war.

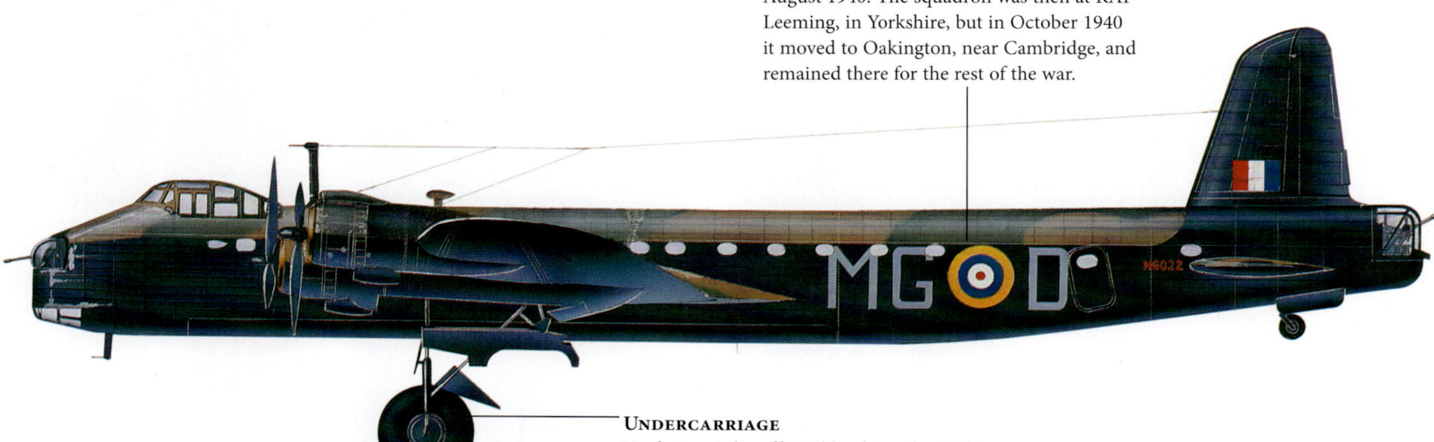

UNDERCARRIAGE
To shorten take-offs and landings the Stirling was fitted with a very tall undercarriage. This improved lift during the take-off run, but made ground handling tricky.

FIRST STIRLINGS
The Stirling eventually equipped seven squadrons in No. 3 Group, RAF Bomber Command. No. 7 Sqn was the first of these, receiving Stirlings in August 1940, the unit taking the new bomber on its first operation, to attack an oil storage depot at Rotterdam, on the night of 10/11 February 1941. The main aircraft on this page, N3641, coded 'MG-D', was one of the No. 7 Sqn Stirlings.

MISSION BRIEFING
A No. 149 Sqn crew confers with a meteorological officer prior to another sortie. Dorsal turret-equipped Stirling bombers generally carried a crew of six. The rear turret seen here carried four 7.7mm (0.303in) Browning machine guns for rear defence.

Douglas Boston III (1940)

TYPE • *Bomber* **COUNTRY** • *United States*

SPECIFICATIONS	
Dimensions:	Length: 14.63m (48ft 0in); Wingspan: 18.69m (61ft 4in); Height: 5.36m (17ft 7in)
Weight:	12,338kg (27,200lb) loaded
Powerplant:	2 x 1194kW (1600hp) Wright Cyclone R-2600-23 air-cooled radial piston engines
Max speed:	546km/h (339mph)
Range:	1755km (1090 miles)
Ceiling:	7650m (25,100ft)
Crew:	3
Armament:	Up to 8 x 12.7mm (0.5in) MGs; 1814kg (4000lb) of bombs

Initially used as the Havoc, as a night-fighter and nocturnal intruder, the Douglas DB-7 saw greater RAF service as the Boston in the light bomber role, scoring notable successes in cross-Channel raids and in the Mediterranean theatre.

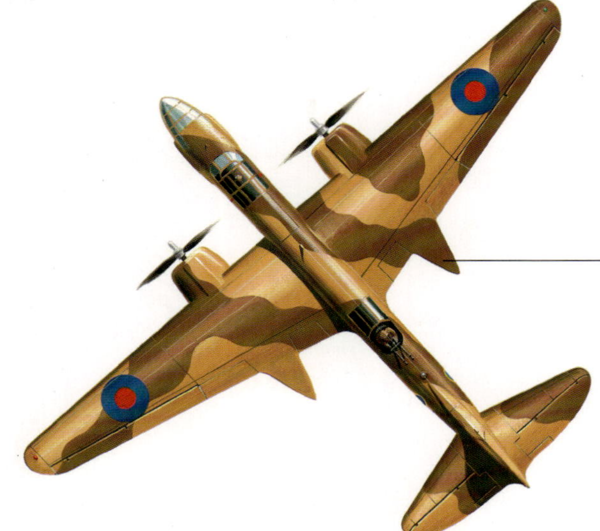

Left: The Douglas Boston attack bomber was used by 18 RAF squadrons in 1942–43, in most cases replacing the Bristol Blenheim.

Streamlining
The Boston's designers paid great attention to producing an aircraft with maximum streamlining. This was particularly noticeable in the engine nacelles, which were equipped with aerodynamic fairings.

Dorsal gunner
The Boston's dorsal gunner sat in a relatively exposed position. Because of the extreme conditions, aircraft supplied to Russia were fitted with a fully enclosed ball-type dorsal turret.

Insignia
The insignia carried by this Boston show it to be an aircraft of No. 18 Squadron, camouflaged for operations in the Mediterranean theatre. The squadron operated in Italy from October 1943 until the end of the war.

CONVERSION
US DB-7s with R-1830-S3C4-G engines were designated Boston Mk IIs in RAF service. Considered unsuitable for use as bombers, the RAF Mk IIs became Havoc Mk I night-fighters, while 100 ex-French DB-7As became Havoc Mk IIs, distinguished by longer nacelle tails. Conversion work was undertaken at the Burtonwood Aircraft Repair Depot near Liverpool, the main facility for erecting aircraft brought in from the United States.

COMBAT SORTIE
RAF Boston IIIs make their way to targets over Europe. Britain's 'own' Boston deliveries began in the early summer of 1941, introducing the Boston Mk III light bomber, in which role it entered service later that year as a Blenheim replacement in No. 88 (Hong Kong) Sqn, followed by No. 226 Sqn.

Grumman F4F Wildcat (1940)

TYPE • *Naval fighter* COUNTRY • *United States*

SPECIFICATIONS (F4F-4)

DIMENSIONS:	Length: 8.85m (29ft 0in); Wingspan: 11.59m (38ft 0in); Height: 3.44m (11ft 4in)
WEIGHT:	3978kg (8762lb) maximum take-off
POWERPLANT:	1 × 895kW (1200hp) Pratt & Whitney R-1830-86 Twin Wasp 14-cylinder air-cooled radial piston engine
MAX SPEED:	515km/h (320mph)
RANGE:	2051km (1275 miles) with external tanks
CEILING:	10,370m (34,000ft)
CREW:	1
ARMAMENT:	6 × 12.7mm (0.5in) AN/M2 Browning machine guns fixed forward-firing in wings; up to 90kg (200lb) bombload

The F4F Wildcat was the US Navy's most important fighter at the time of the United States's entry into World War II in December 1941 after the Japanese attack on Pearl Harbor, and it remained in production right through the war.

Above: The F4F-4 utilized Grumman's patented 'sto-wing' system, which allowed the wings to swing through 90 degrees to be stored pointing backwards alongside the fuselage.

F4F-4 WILDCAT
This F4F-4 was flown by Captain Marian E. Carl, the first Marine ace of World War II. Carl served with VMF-223 on Guadalcanal, where a handful of pilots proved to have the measure of the Japanese. He amassed a tally of 16.5 victories in Wildcats, to which he later added two kills while flying F4U Corsairs.

COLOUR SCHEME
This Wildcat carries the standard early war shipboard colour scheme of non-specular blue/grey with a light grey underside. From March 1944 US Navy aircraft were painted all over in a much darker sea-blue gloss finish.

FIREPOWER
Whereas the F4F-3 had a rather inadequate armament of four Browning 12.7mm (0.50in) machine guns, the F4F-4 carried six. It could also carry two 113kg (250lb) bombs on underwing racks.

US NAVY WILDCATS

The first US Navy Wildcats entered service in December 1940. In the USA, delivery of the Wildcat was slow, and at the time of the Japanese attack on Pearl Harbor only 183 F4F-3s and 65 F4F-3As were in service with the US Navy and Marine Corps. The principal production Wildcat, the F4F-4, which featured folding wings, entered service at the end of 1941.

FLIGHT OF WILDCATS
The portly Wildcat should have been no match for the better performing and more manoeuvrable Zero, yet its ruggedness, better guns and the innovative tactics of its pilots carried the day.

Lavochkin-Gorbunov-Gudkov LaGG-3 (1940)

TYPE • *Fighter* **COUNTRY** • *Soviet Union*

SPECIFICATIONS

Dimensions:	Length: 8.81m (28ft 11in); Wingspan: 9.8m (32ft 2in); Height: 2.54m (8ft 4in)
Weight:	Maximum take-off 3190kg (7033lb)
Powerplant:	1 × 924kW (1239hp) Klimov M-105PF liquid-cooled V-12 engine
Max Speed:	589km/h (366mph)
Range:	1000km (620 miles)
Ceiling:	9700m (31,800ft)
Crew:	1
Armament:	1 × 12.7mm (0.50in) Berezin BS machine gun, 1 × 20mm (0.78in) ShVAK cannon; 2 × 50kg (110lb) bombs or 6 × RS-82 or RS-132 rockets

The LaGG-3 in the form it began to roll off the production line in 1940 was, at best, an immature combat aircraft. The overweight and underpowered aircraft was unloved by those who flew it and derided by its enemies.

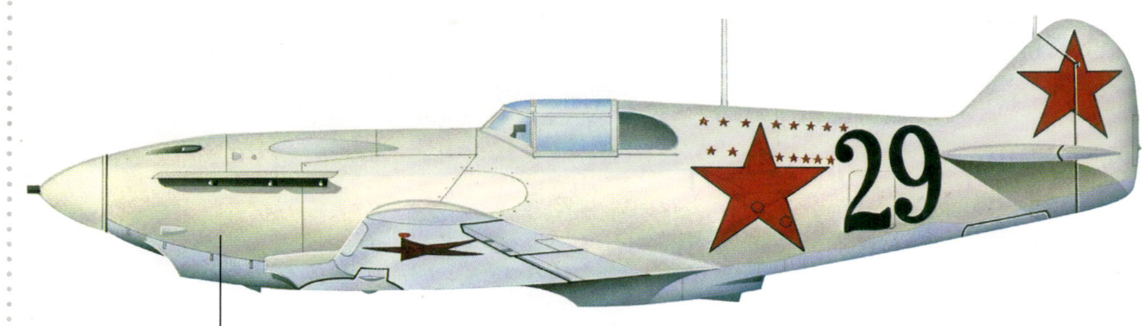

Above: Shown in temporary winter finish during late 1942, this LaGG-3 was flown by 15-victory ace Gerasim Grigoryev of 178 IAP over Moscow.

Airframe
The LaGG-3's only real advantage remained the immensely strong, fire-resistant airframe that could absorb remarkable amounts of punishment and remain airworthy.

Performance
Compared to its great rival, the Yak-1, the LaGG-3 was marginally inferior in speed and climb rate but enjoyed a slightly better range.

LaGG-3
'White 57' was built in August 1942 and forced down by Finnish pilot Altto Tervo the following month. It was repaired and entered operational service with the Finns as LG-3.

FLAWED FIGHTER
Design flaws meant that the LaGG-3 had a collection of serious flight challenges. It was liable to develop a violent spin without warning in a steep banking turn, also it had a tendency to nose-up on approach to land and would stall at the slightest provocation. The undercarriage was prone to collapse, the view from the cockpit was poor (a situation exacerbated by the opacity of Russian acrylic at the time), the hydraulics were unreliable, brakes seized, engines leaked oil, the gun firing mechanism often failed and initial build quality was deficient.

DOWNED IN FINLAND
This LaGG-3 of 524 IAP was shot down by Finnish anti-aircraft fire on 6 March 1942. Repaired by the Finns, this aircraft, coded LG-1, scored the only confirmed kill by a LaGG-3 in Finnish service when it shot down a Soviet LaGG-3 on 16 February 1944.

Yakovlev Yak-3 (1940)

TYPE • *Fighter* **COUNTRY** • *Soviet Union*

SPECIFICATIONS

DIMENSIONS:	Length: 8.5m (27ft 11in); Wingspan: 9.2m (30ft 2in); Height: 2.64m (8ft 8in)
WEIGHT:	2697kg (5946lb) maximum take-off
POWERPLANT:	1 × 960kW (1290hp) Klimov VK-105PF2 V-12 liquid-cooled piston engine
MAX SPEED:	646km/h (401mph)
RANGE:	550km (340 miles)
CEILING:	10,400m (34,100ft)
CREW:	1
ARMAMENT:	1 × 20mm (0.789n) ShVAK cannon; 2 × 12.7mm (0.5in) Berezin UBS machine guns

The last Yak fighter to be developed during the war was the Yak-3, which had started life as the Yak-1M, with the M standing for *Moskit* (Mosquito). This was a lightened version, intended to maximize air-to-air combat performance.

AERODYNAMICS
Compared to previous Yaks, the Yak-3 had wings of reduced span and aerodynamic improvements, most obviously the relocation of the oil cooler from under the nose to the wing roots.

Above: Featuring a stylized winged sword on the nose, Yak-3 'White 100' was flying with 492 IAP as the unit entered Germany in early 1945.

FIREPOWER
By 1945 much effort was being expended on improving the armament, culminating in the Yak-3P that featured three Berezin B-20 20mm (0.78in) cannon – two in the nose decking and one firing through the airscrew hub.

YAK-3
The Yakolev Yak-3 'Blue 24' was based in East Prussia by April 1945, and was operated by the 7 Guards Fighter Aviation Regiment (GvIAP) of the 303 Fighter Aviation Division (IAD).

GAME-CHANGER
By the start of 1945, considerable numbers of the new fighter were available – in January the VVS (Russian Air Force) reported 735 Yak-3s on strength. The Yak-3 delighted its pilots, and for the first time the German fighter pilots admitted a Soviet fighter was superior to their own. A 1944 Luftwaffe general directive famously advised pilots to 'avoid combat below 5000m (16,400ft) with Yakovlev fighters lacking an oil cooler under the nose.'

EARLY PRODUCTION
First flown in February 1943, the Yak-1M (the basis for the Yak-3) was tested against captured examples of the Fw 190 A-4 and Bf 109 G-2 and was found to possess better performance than either at low and medium altitude.

Fairey Fulmar (1940)

TYPE • *Reconnaissance* **COUNTRY** • *United Kingdom*

SPECIFICATIONS (Fulmar Mk II)

DIMENSIONS:	Length: 12.24m (40ft 2in); Wingspan: 14.14m (46ft 4.5in); Height: 3.25m (10ft 8in)
WEIGHT:	4627kg (10,200lb) maximum take-off
POWERPLANT:	1 x 970kW (1300hp) Rolls-Royce Merlin 30 V-12 liquid-cooled piston engine
MAX SPEED:	440km/h (272mph)
RANGE:	1255km (780 miles)
CEILING:	8300m (27,200ft)
CREW:	2
ARMAMENT:	8 x 7.7mm (0.303in) or 4 x 12.7mm (0.5in) Browning machine guns fixed forward-firing in wings; up to 226kg (500lb) bombload

Despite the inevitable performance limitations imposed by its two-seat design, the Fairey Fulmar proved remarkably successful in combat and shot down more enemy aircraft than any other Fleet Air Arm (FAA) fighter.

Above: Fulmar Mk I. The Fulmar entered FAA service in June 1940, with the same powerplant and armament as the Hurricane, but a larger airframe and second crewman.

POWERPLANT
From January 1941 production switched to the Mk II variant that featured a more powerful Merlin 30 engine delivering an additional 198kW (265hp) of power.

TWO-SEATER
The two-seat layout allowed for the aircraft to readily take on reconnaissance and spotting duties and the Navy was always keen to utilize a multi-purpose aircraft given the restricted space on carriers.

FAIREY FULMAR MK I
Fulmar N1860 is shown as it appeared when it was serving with 808 squadron at Dhekalia, Egypt, in March or April 1941. Shore-based Fulmar operations were relatively limited due to the aircraft's poor performance against German Messerschmitt Bf 109s and Vichy French Dewoitine D.520s.

COMBAT DEBUT
The first front-line unit had received three Fulmars only by June 1940, replacing three Blackburn Rocs of 886 Sqn aboard HMS *Illustrious*. The Fulmar made its combat debut on 2 September 1940 when four Italian Savoia Marchetti SM.79 trimotor torpedo bombers and a Cant Z.501 flying boat were all shot down by Fulmars operating off *Illustrious* on its way to join the Mediterranean Fleet.

WINNING DESIGN
To create the Fulmar, Marcel Lobel, chief designer at Fairey, proposed a fighter version of his pre-existing P.4/34 light bomber prototype that had demonstrated excellent performance and handling.

Dornier Do 217 (1940)

TYPE • *Bomber* **COUNTRY** • *Germany*

Drawing heavily on the Do 17 design, Dornier produced a bigger, heavier bomber in the shape of the Do 217. Although it was overshadowed in its primary role by the He 111 and Ju 88, it nevertheless proved adept at anti-shipping strikes.

SPECIFICATIONS (Do 217N-1)

DIMENSIONS:	Length: 17.67m (57ft 11in); Wingspan: 19m (62ft 4in); Height: 4.8m (15ft 8in)
WEIGHT:	Maximum take-off 15,000kg (33,000lb)
POWERPLANT:	2 × 1,380kW (1,850hp) DB603A piston V12 aero engines
MAX SPEED:	525km/h (326mph)
RANGE:	1,755km (1,090 miles)
CEILING:	8,400m (27,600ft)
CREW:	4
ARMAMENT:	4 × 20mm (0.79in) MG 151 cannon and 4 × 7.92mm (0.31in) MG 17 machine guns (nose); 1 × 13mm (0.51in) MG 131 machine gun (dorsal turret); 1 × 7.92mm (0.31in) MG 13 (ventral position)

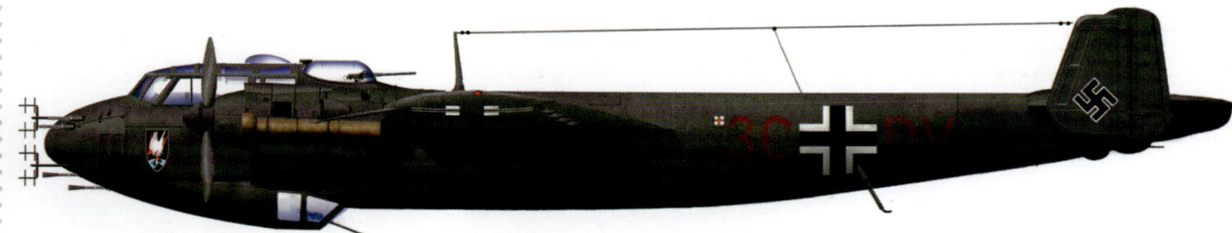

Above: Do 217N-1 3C+DV was operated by II./Nachtjagdgeschwader 4 from a base in Germany in late 1943.

COCKPIT
In autumn 1942 the next major version appeared in the form of the Do 217K. The initial-production Do 217K-1 introduced a new glazed nose and an unstepped cockpit.

ARMAMENT
This variant had a twin-barrelled 7.92mm (0.31in) MG 81Z machine gun in the nose, two 7.92mm (0.31in) MG 81s (beam positions), two 7.92mm (0.31in) MG 131s (dorsal turret and ventral position) and a 2,500kg (5,511lb) internal bombload.

DORNIER DO 217K-1
Do 217K-1 4452 'Yellow G' wears the unit markings of 3./Kampfgeschwader 2, based in France during 1943–44.

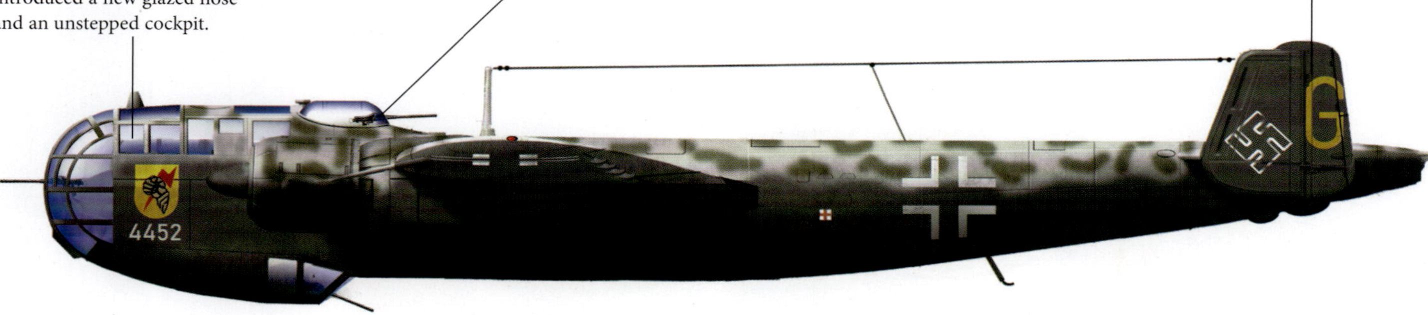

DIVERSIFICATION

The Do 217 was Dornier's response to a 1937 requirement for a long-range warplane optimized for the heavy level and dive-bombing roles. Some 800 Do 217 Es were built, before being succeeded by 950 Do 217Ks. Variants included bombers, anti-shipping bombers, high-altitude reconnaissance aircraft and a missile-launching aircraft. The aircraft also proved able to carry some of the more exotic weapons fielded by the Luftwaffe.

NIGHT-FIGHTER
Following some success with night-fighting Do 17s and 215s, Dornier fitted a new nose to its Do 217 bomber to produce an interim night-fighter variant. Few wartime aircraft packed a harder punch – this N-2 shows the four-cannon, four-gun nose armament, as well as the antennas for the FuG 212 Lichtenstein C-1 radar.

Macchi MC.202 Folgore / Macchi MC.205V Veltro (1941)

TYPE • *Fighter* COUNTRY • *Italy*

SPECIFICATIONS (MC.202)

Dimensions:	Length: 8.85m (29ft 1in); Wingspan: 10.58m (34ft 8.5in); Height: 3.49m (11ft 5in)
Weight:	Empty: 2,491kg (5,492lb); Maximum: 2,930kg (6,460lb)
Powerplant:	1 × 864kW (1175hp) Alfa Romeo R.A.1000 R.C.41I inverted V-12 piston engine
Max speed:	600km/h (372mph)
Range:	765km (475 miles)
Service ceiling:	11,500m (37,730ft)
Crew:	2
Armament:	2 × 12.7mm Breda-SAFAT machine guns; 2 × 7.7mm Breda-SAFAT machine guns; up to 160kg (350lb) of bombs

The *Folgore* (Thunderbolt) was a fairly straightforward conversion of the MC.200 (the second Italian monoplane fighter) with a DB 601 engine, although availability of these engines was always a problem.

Above: The MC.205 prototype was an MC.202 conversion that first flew in April 1942 with the new engine as well as larger outer wing panels. The new fighter entered production and was built to the extent of 262 MC.205V Veltro (Greyhound) aircraft that were committed to combat from July 1943.

MC.202 Folgore
The type entered service in the summer of 1941 and this MC.205 of 151° Squadriglia was flown by eight-victory ace Ennio Tarantola.

Armament
The MC.202 was armed with two 12.7mm (0.5in) Breda-SAFAT machine guns, two 7.7mm (0.31in) Breda-SAFAT machine guns and up to 160kg (350lb) of bombs.

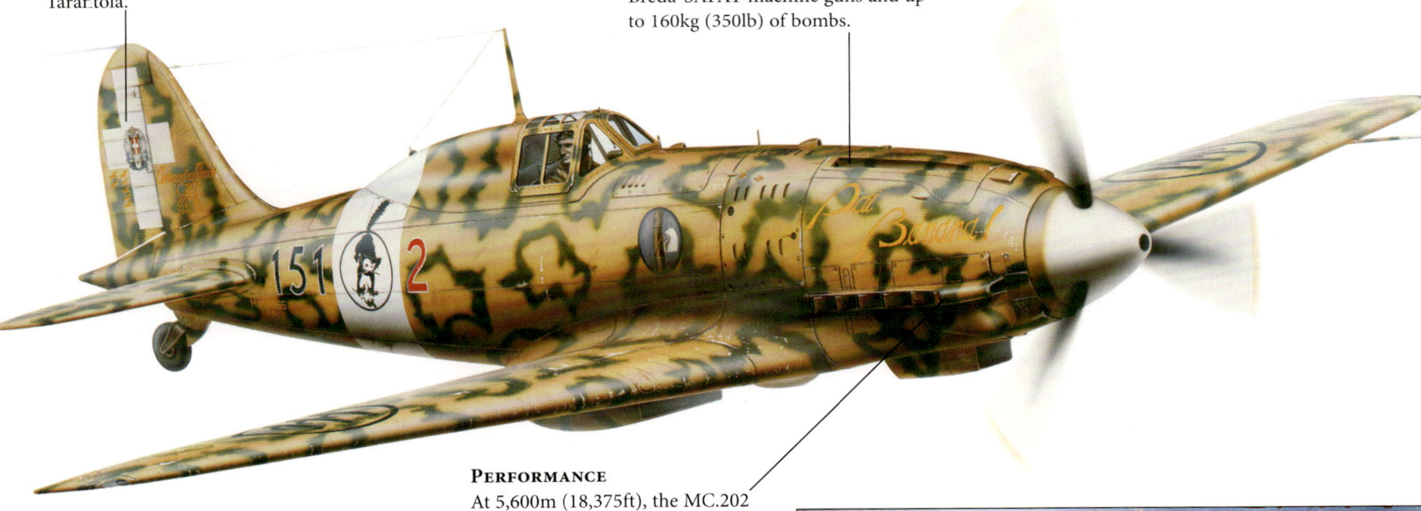

Performance
At 5,600m (18,375ft), the MC.202 could achieve an admirable maximum speed of 600km/h (373mph). The aircraft climbed to 5,000m (16,405ft) in 4 minutes 40 seconds.

AIR DEFENCE

Throughout early 1943, the Allies concentrated heavy attacks on Sicily. Folgores, with their light armament, had little or no effect on the heavily armed US bombers and only achieved moderate success with head-on attacks. The massive Allied attacks destroyed over 1,000 Italian aircraft and the few remaining MC.202s could do little to oppose the Allies when they landed on 10 July.

FOLGORES IN NORTH AFRICA

After having retreated across Libya in November 1941, the Italian Folgores gained air superiority over Tobruk, contributing to the taking of the town by Axis forces in June 1942.

Mitsubishi G4M 'Betty' (1941)

TYPE • *Bomber* **COUNTRY** • *Japan*

So lightly protected that it was known to US fighter pilots as 'the Honorable One-shot Lighter', the G4M (codenamed 'Betty' by the Allies) tried to get too much range from too small an aircraft. Despite this it was by far the most important Imperial Japanese Navy bomber.

SPECIFICATIONS (G4M1 Model 11)

DIMENSIONS:	Length: 20.00m (65ft 7.5in); Wingspan: 25.00m (82ft 0.25in); Height: 6.00m (19ft 8.25in)
WEIGHT:	9,500kg (20,944lb) loaded
POWERPLANT:	2 × 1,141kW (1,530hp) Mitsubishi MK4A Kasei 11 radial piston engines
MAX SPEED:	428km/h (266mph) at 4,200m (13,780ft)
RANGE:	6,033km (3,749 miles)
SERVICE CEILING:	Unavailable
ARMAMENT:	4 × 7.7mm (0.303in) machine guns; 1 × 20mm cannon; maximum bombload of 1,000kg (2,205lb)

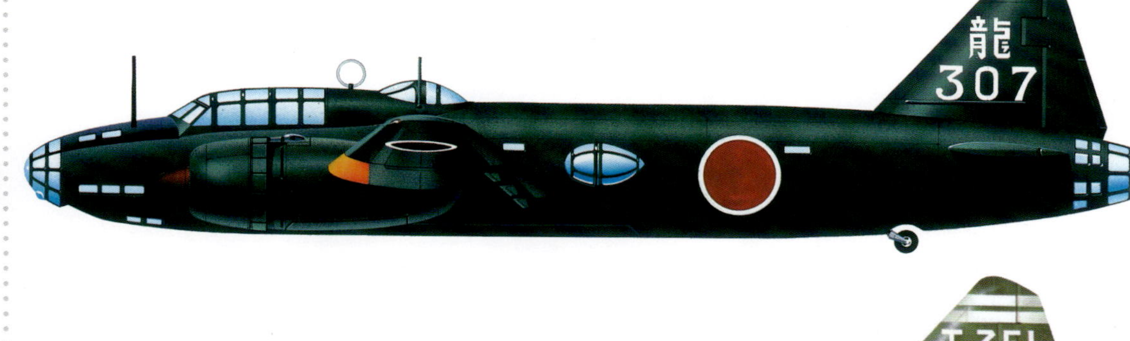

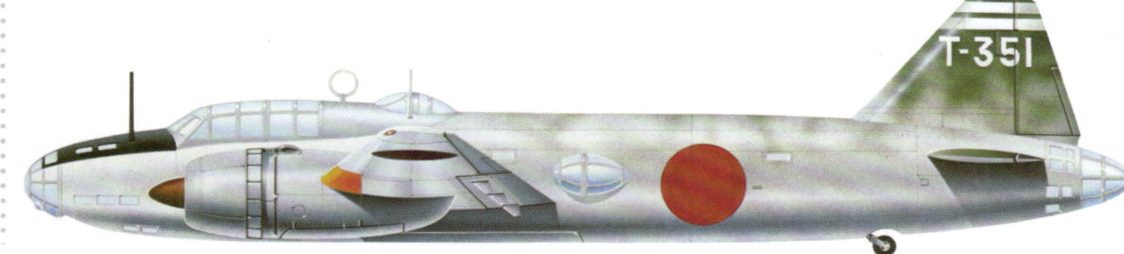

Above: Both of these aircraft are G4M1s. The G4M1 Model 11 at the bottom was based on Rabaul at the time of the US landings in 1942.

G4M2 MODEL 24A
Compared to the first variants, this variant included a laminar-flow wing, increased tailplane area, rounded wing and tail tips, increased nose glazing and additional defensive armament.

POWERPLANT
Another new powerplant was introduced in the G4M2 Model 24a, powered by a pair of 1,362kW (1,825hp) Mk4T Kasei 25 engines.

OHKA MISSILE
Assigned to the 702nd Hikotai, 763rd Kokutai, and shown carrying an Ohka missile, this aircraft was camouflaged overall dark green and was captured at Clark Field, Philippines, in 1944.

POWER PROJECTION

The G4M was the ultimate expression of the Imperial Japanese Navy Air Force's desire to project land-based air power from its island garrisons deep into the Pacific Ocean. However, this range came at the expense of crew protection. Entering service in 1941, production totalled 1,200 G4M1 variants, such as Convoy Fighter escort, Model 11 attack bomber, trainers and transport aircraft.

VULNERABLE BETTY
The G4M 'Betty' was the most important Japanese bomber of the war, with extremely long range and good defensive armament. Its Achilles heel was poor damage tolerance and a tendency to catch fire when hit.

Nakajima Ki-49 *Donryu* 'Helen' (1941)

TYPE • *Bomber* COUNTRY • *Japan*

SPECIFICATIONS (Ki-49-IIa)

DIMENSIONS:	Length: 16.50m (54ft 1.5in); Wingspan: 20.42m (67ft 0in); Height: 4.25m (13ft 11.25in)
WEIGHT:	11,400kg (25,133lb) maximum take-off
POWERPLANT:	2 x 1,119kW (1,500hp) Nakajima Ha-109 radial piston engines
MAX SPEED:	492km/h (306mph) at 5,000m (16,405ft)
RANGE:	2,950km (1,833 miles)
SERVICE CEILING:	9,300m (30,150ft)
CREW:	8
ARMAMENT:	5 x 7.7mm (0.303in) machine guns; 1 x 20mm cannon; maximum bombload of 1,000kg (2,205lb)

Nakajima's *Donryu* (Storm Dragon) was the result of an ambitious programme to develop a heavy bomber that could operate without fighter escort, using speed and defensive armament for survival. In the event, the production Ki-49 was found somewhat wanting.

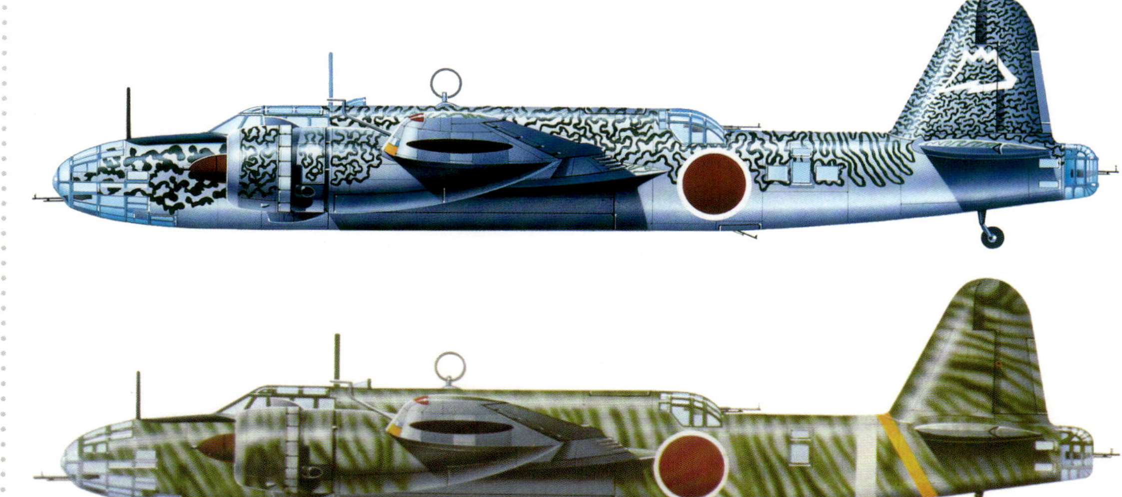

Above: Two Ki-49-IIa aircraft. (Top) A disruptive 'snake-weave' camouflage pattern on an aircraft of the 1st Chutai, 7th Sentai, in 1943. (Bottom) Stationed in north-east China in September 1944, this Donryu was flown by the 3rd Chutai, 95th Sentai, wearing 'palm-frond' camouflage.

UNDER-POWERED
Combat service revealed that the Ki-49-I was under-powered, and as a result longer-range missions could only be flown with a significantly reduced bombload.

SURVIVABILITY
The Ki-49-I's defensive armament was found to be generally effective, and its self-sealing fuel tanks added to its survivability.

KI-49-I
In late 1943, this Ki-49-I aircraft was serving in a training role with the Hamamatsu Army Flying School.

FALLING SHORT

The Donryu was planned from 1938 as a replacement for the Mitsubishi Ki-21, but it proved so indifferent that it supplemented rather than replaced the older type. The aircraft was always hampered by its poor performance. In particular, speed at low and medium altitudes was deemed unsatisfactory. The inability of the Ki-49 to fulfil its intended role as a heavy bomber meant that it was relegated to secondary roles in the later stages of the war.

'HELENS' IN FORMATION
Total production of the Donryu amounted to 819 aircraft, comprising 769 built by the parent company and 50 more manufactured by Tachikawa. The Allied reporting name 'Helen' was applied to all variants.

Lockheed P-38 Lightning (1941)

TYPE • *Heavy fighter* **COUNTRY** • *United States*

The mighty P-38 was something of an anomaly among the US Army Air Force in World War II: a genuinely successful heavy fighter that was equally capable in the long-range escort role or as a hard-hitting ground-attack aircraft in both European and Pacific theatres.

SPECIFICATIONS (P-38J)

DIMENSIONS:	Length: 11.53m (37ft 10in); Wingspan: 15.85m (52ft); Height: 2.99m (9ft 10in)
WEIGHT:	5,806kg (12,800lb) (empty)
POWERPLANT:	2 × 1063kW (1,425hp) Allison V-1710-91 12-cylinder V-type
MAX SPEED:	667km/h (414mph) at 7,620m (25,000ft)
RANGE:	3,600km (2,260 miles)
CEILING:	13,400m (44,000ft)
CREW:	1
ARMAMENT:	1 × 20mm (0.79in) cannon and 4 × 12.7mm (0.5in) machine guns in the nose; bombload of 2 × 726kg (1,600lb) bombs or 10 × 70mm (2.75in) rockets

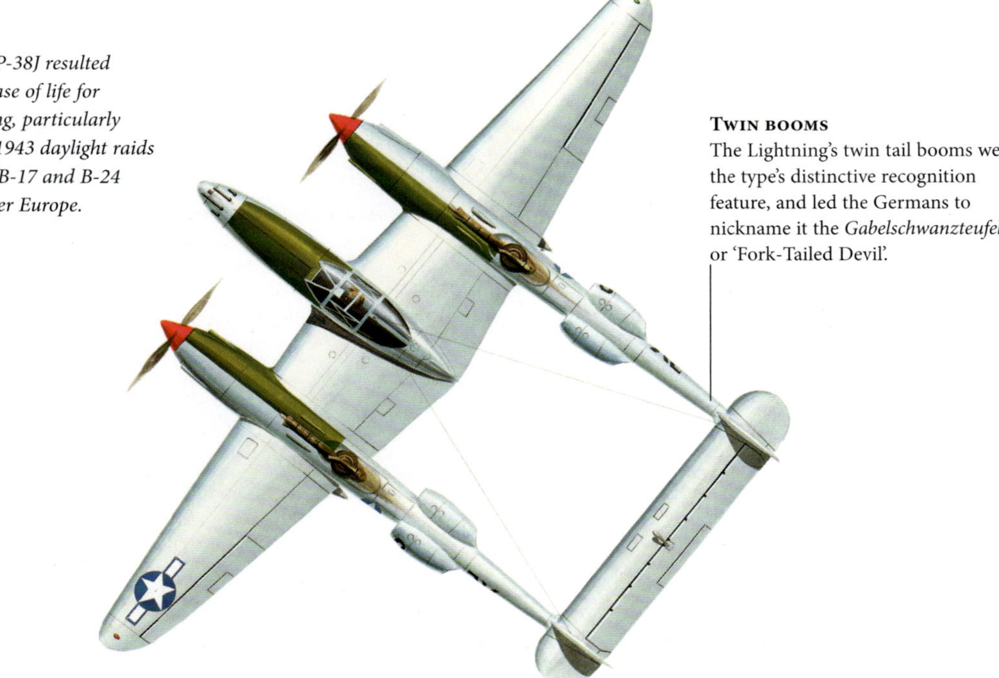

Right: The P-38J resulted in a new lease of life for the Lightning, particularly during the 1943 daylight raids by USAAF B-17 and B-24 bombers over Europe.

TWIN BOOMS
The Lightning's twin tail booms were the type's distinctive recognition feature, and led the Germans to nickname it the *Gabelschwanzteufel* or 'Fork-Tailed Devil'.

SUPERCHARGERS
The P-38 Lightning had supercharged engines. In the early part of the war the RAF wanted to buy substantial numbers of P-38s, but orders were cancelled when the Americans refused to fit the superchargers, which were deemed to be secret.

RAISED COCKPIT
From the raised cockpit of the P-38 the pilot had an excellent view forward, unobstructed by a propeller. The canopy hinged backwards and had downward-winding side windows.

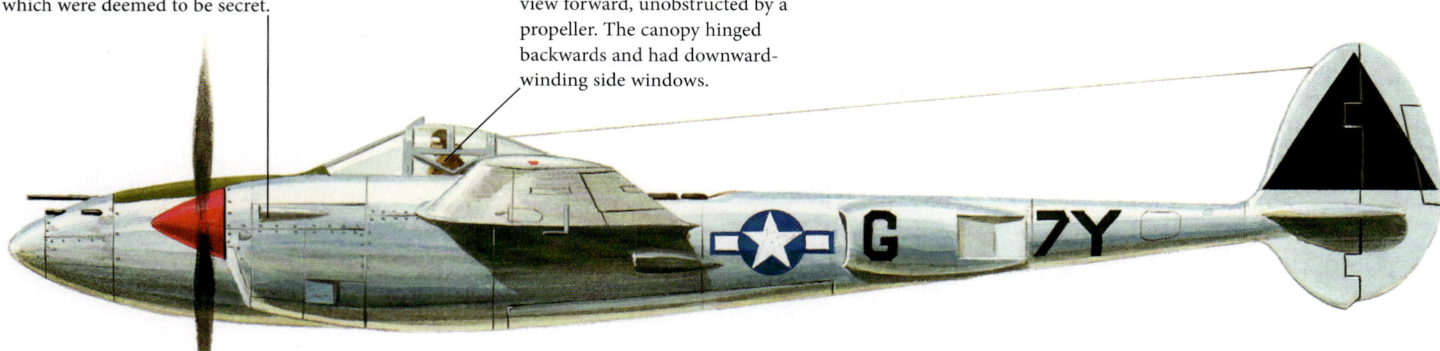

INTERCEPTOR
The P-38 was designed to meet a 1937 USAAC specification calling for a high-altitude interceptor capable of 580km/h (360mph) at 6,100m (20,000ft) and 467km/h (290mph) at sea level. While the P-38J here is equipped with the standard 'fighter' nose, a number of J-models were adapted for use in the light bomber role, for which they were fitted with an alternative glazed nose to the centre nacelle for use by a bomb aimer.

P-38H IN FLIGHT
P-38Hs were the first to have the bar added to the national insignia. Uprated 1,063kW (1,425hp) V-1710-89/-91 engines powered the 375 P-38Hs, which also introduced automatic oil radiator flaps to solve a major engine overheating problem. This factory-fresh example is seen on a test flight from Lockheed's Burbank facility in California, prior to delivery to the USAAF.

Focke-Wulf Fw 190 (1941)

TYPE • *Fighter* **COUNTRY** • *Germany*

SPECIFICATIONS (Fw 190A)

DIMENSIONS:	Length 8.84m (29ft); Wingspan 10.50m (34ft 5.5in); Height 3.96m (13ft)
WEIGHT:	Empty 3,170kg (7,000lb); Maximum take-off 4,900kg (10,805lb)
POWERPLANT:	1,566kW (2,100hp) BMW 801D-2 radial engine
MAX SPEED:	654km/h (406mph) at 6,000m (19,685ft)
RANGE:	1,470km (915 miles)
CEILING:	11,400m (37,401ft)
CREW:	1
ARMAMENT:	2 x 7.92mm (0.31in) machine guns and up to 4 x 20mm (0.79in) cannon in wings, plus provision for under-fuselage and underwing bombs and rockets

At the time of its combat appearance, the Fw 190 was the most capable fighter in service, offering a winning combination of performance and manoeuvrability. Further development ensured it retained its prowess until the end of the war.

Above: This Fw 190A-6 was flown by Leutnant Emil Lang, who served with 5./Jagdgeschwader 54 'Grünherz' ('Green Hearts'). The aircraft was operated on the Eastern Front in October 1943.

FOCKE-WULF FW 190A-4
Major Hubertus von Bonin flew the Fw 190A-4 while serving as commander of Jagdgeschwader 54. The aircraft was operating from Krasnogvardeysky in August 1943.

TAILFIN
The robust fin comprised two spars: one vertical along the rear and one angled along the leading edge. The rudder ran the full length of the fin.

ARMAMENT
As built, early production Fw 190s were armed with four Rheinmetall Borsig MG.17 machine guns mounted in the upper fuselage and wing roots.

NIGHT FIGHTER

Night-fighting was a specialist role for which the Fw 190A-5/U2 was developed. This was used for *Wilde Sau* (Wild Boar) tactics in which day fighters were used at night, especially in order to counter the 'window' jamming employed by RAF bombers. The prime exponent of Wilde Sau was JG 300, which operated both Fw 190s and Bf 109Gs.

FW 190 VARIANTS

The Fw 190 spawned many variants between its entry into service in August 1941 and the end of the war, such as the A-4s seen here. The A-1 was followed into production by the A-2, with a longer span and heavier armament, and the A-3 fighter bomber. The Fw 190A-4 had a methanol-waterpower boost system. The final variant was the Fw 190A-8.

Republic P-47 Thunderbolt (1941)

TYPE • *Fighter* **COUNTRY** • *United States*

SPECIFICATIONS (P-47D)	
DIMENSIONS:	Length: 10.99m (36ft 1in); Wingspan: 12.43m (40ft 9in); Height: 4.44m (14ft 7in)
WEIGHT:	7,938kg (17,500lb) maximum take-off
POWERPLANT:	1 × 1,500kW (2,000hp) Pratt & Whitney R-2800-59 18-cylinder air-cooled radial piston engine
MAX SPEED:	686km/h (426mph)
RANGE:	1,660km (1,030 miles) with external tanks
CEILING:	13,000m (42,000ft)
CREW:	1
ARMAMENT:	8 × 12.7mm (0.5in) M2 Browning machine guns; up to 1,100kg (2,500lb) of bombs or 6 zero-length rockets under wings with drop tanks or 10 rockets without drop tanks

The pugnacious P-47 was one of the stand-out Allied fighters of World War II, equally adept as a long-range bomber escort over occupied Europe or as a potent ground-attack aircraft in theatres that ranged from the Mediterranean to Burma.

Above: Operating in a basic plain metal finish with only small areas of olive drab on the upper fuselage, the P-47D was used late in World War II primarily for the heavy fighter-bomber role.

P-47D THUNDERBOLT
This is the original pattern of P-47D with a framed canopy sliding to the rear over the 'razorback' upper decking of the rear fuselage.

PROPELLER
The aircraft had a large 3.9m (13ft) diameter Curtiss Electric propeller.

225416

DROP TANKS
Even with underwing drop tanks, as seen here, the P-47D Thunderbolt possessed an operational range that was adequate rather than exceptional.

GROUND ATTACK
In all, P-47 production amounted to 15,675 aircraft. A significant number were adapted for ground-attack duties, the P-47D featuring provision for underwing racks that could carry a pair of 454kg (1,000lb) bombs, in addition to the 568 litre (125 US gallon) drop tank under the fuselage. P-47Ds from later production batches had increased external stores capacity, including up to 10 127mm (5in) rockets.

P-47N THUNDERBOLT
This P-47N was fitted with eight 12.7mm (0.5in) machine guns and was capable of carrying bombs and underwing rocket projectiles, both visible here.

De Havilland Mosquito (1941)

TYPE • *Heavy fighter* **COUNTRY** • *United Kingdom*

Immortalized as the 'Wooden Wonder' on account of its construction, the Mosquito was the RAF's most flexible warplane of World War II, excelling in a wide variety of tactical roles and seeing service well into the 1950s.

SPECIFICATIONS (PR.Mk XVI (F-8))

Dimensions:	Length: 12.65m (41ft 6in); Wingspan: 16.50m (54ft 2in); Height: 4.65m (15ft 3in)
Weight:	11,756kg (25,917lb) maximum take-off
Powerplant:	2 × 1276kW (1710hp) Rolls-Royce Merlin 12-cylinder piston engines
Max speed:	657km/h (408mph)
Range:	1,963km (1,220 miles)
Service ceiling:	9,449m (31,000ft)
Crew:	2
Armament:	4 × 20mm (0.8in) Hispano cannon; 4 × 7.7mm (0.303in) Browning MGs

Above: The Mosquito B.Mk IV Series II of No. 105 Squadron, RAF Bomber Command, based at Marham in 1943. The first of these aircraft had been delivered to the unit in late 1942.

Crew
The crew of two were seated side by side in the cockpit, with the pilot on the left. Bulged canopy sides improved rearward vision and an astrodome was provided for navigation by sextant.

Wing planform
One of the Mosquito's major recognition features was its distinctive wing planform, with engine nacelles extending forward of the fuselage nose.

Mosquito PR.Mk XVI (F-8)
Here is a USAAF-operated reconnaissance Mosquito of the 653rd Bombardment Squadron, 25th Bombardment Group, Watton, mid-1944.

MULTI-ROLE AIRCRAFT
Built as a private venture, and allowed to go ahead only because it used mainly 'non-strategic' materials (spruce and balsawood), the Mosquito was one of the most versatile aircraft of the war. The bomber and reconnaissance variants used their speed rather than armament for self-protection, while the night-fighter, fighter-bomber and anti-shipping models packed a heavy punch with machine guns, cannon and rockets. The Mosquito was licence-built in Canada and Australia

PREPARING FOR A MISSION
Ground crew and flight crew gather in preparation for a raid. The Mosquito bomber could carry the same bombload to Berlin as a Lancaster, but with two crew rather than seven.

Avro Lancaster (1941)

TYPE • *Bomber* COUNTRY • *United Kingdom*

SPECIFICATIONS (Lancaster B.Mk I)

DIMENSIONS:	Length: 21.18m (69ft 6in); Wingspan: 31.09m (102ft 0in); Height: 6.10m (20ft 0in)
WEIGHT:	31,751kg (70,000lb) maximum take-off
POWERPLANT:	4 x 1,223kW (1,640hp) Rolly-Royce Merlin XXIV V-12 piston engines
MAX SPEED:	462km/h (287mph)
RANGE:	4,070km (2,530 miles) with bombload
CEILING:	5,790m (19,000ft)
CREW:	7
ARMAMENT:	8 x 7.7mm (0.303in) machine guns, plus bombload comprising one bomb of up to 9,979kg (22,000lb) or smaller bombs up to a total weight of 6,350kg (14,000lb)

The most celebrated British heavy bomber of World War II, the Lancaster found fame for daring missions such as the 'Dambusters' raid and the attack on the *Tirpitz*, but achieved greatest impact through its harrowing night-time strategic bombing campaign against Germany.

Above: (Top) Avro Lancaster B.Mk III. (Bottom) Another of the specially adapted 'dams raid' aircraft, this machine was otherwise a standard Lancaster Mk III.

LANCASTER B.MK III
The Lancaster Mks I and III were fitted defensively with power operated nose and dorsal turrets, each carrying two 7.7mm (0.303in) machine guns, and a power-operated tail turret carrying four 7.7mm (0.303in) machine guns.

TWIN FINS
Compared to the Manchester with its triple fins, the production Lancaster employed a twin-fin tail unit, with tailfins of considerably increased height.

PAYLOAD
The Lancaster possessed good payload/range performance, and was the only British bomber of World War II large enough to carry the 5,443kg (12,000lb) 'Tallboy' and 9,979kg (22,000lb) 'Grand Slam' earthquake bombs.

DAMBUSTERS

In early 1943, Wing Commander Guy Gibson, No. 5 Group RAF, was selected to recruit the best Bomber Command pilots to form a new, elite squadron for a special mission The result was No. 617 Squadron, tasked with a low-altitude Lancaster attack on three dams in the heart of Germany's Ruhr region, using specialized 'bouncing bombs'. The dams raid of May 1943 was a propaganda success, but its strategic impact was limited.

STANDING READY

The Lancaster was the best of the RAF's four-engined 'heavies', and the best remembered. Derived from the Manchester, which had twin engines (neither of them reliable), the Lancaster entered service early in 1942. Able to fly higher and further than the Halifax or Stirling, it became the mainstay of Bomber Command.

Consolidated B-24 Liberator (1941)

TYPE • *Bomber* **COUNTRY** • *United States*

SPECIFICATIONS (B-24D)

Dimensions:	Length: 20.22m (66ft 4in); Wingspan: 33.52m (109ft 11in); Height: 5.46m (17ft 11in)
Weight:	Maximum take-off: 29,029kg (64,000lb)
Powerplant:	4 × 895kW (1,200hp) Pratt & Whitney R-1830-43 Twin Wasp 14-cylinder air-cooled radial piston engines
Max Speed:	488km/h (303mph)
Range:	3,700km (2,300 miles)
Ceiling:	9876m (32,400ft)
Crew:	10
Armament:	1 × 12.7mm (0.5in) Browning M2 MG in nose, ventral tunnel, and one in each of the left and right waist positions; 2 × 12.7mm (0.5in) Browning M2 MGs in both top turret and tail turret; up to 5,806kg (12,800lb) of bombs

Although never as famous as the Flying Fortress, the B-24 was an altogether more versatile machine, and in some respects more capable. More B-24s were built than any other US combat aircraft in history.

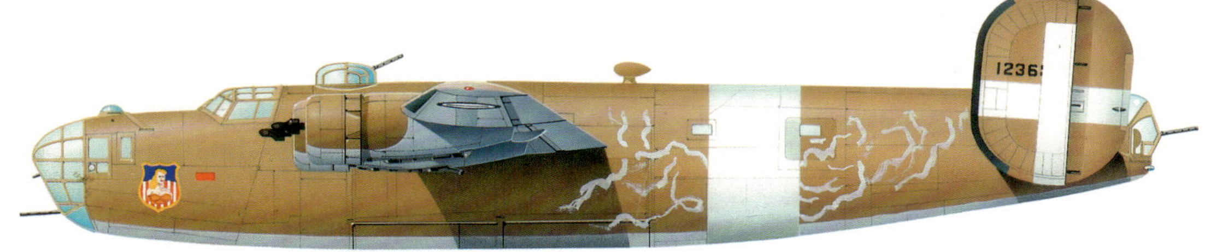

Above: (Top) B-24D of the 93rd Bomb Group, US Eighth Army Air Force. (Bottom) B-24D of the 98th Bomb Group, IX Bomber Command / USAAF, Benghazi, Libya, 1943.

Aspect ratio
With its wing characterized by a high aspect ratio, the B-24 was aerodynamically efficient, and its primary advantage over the B-17 was therefore greater range.

Fuselage
The deep fuselage of the B-24 was less streamlined than that of the B-17 Flying Fortress, and the Liberator tended to burn more easily when seriously hit.

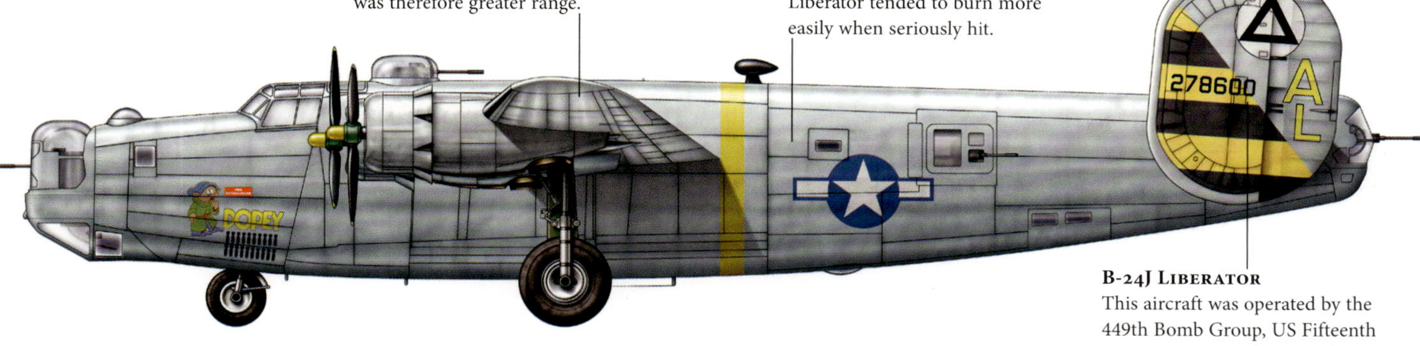

B-24J Liberator
This aircraft was operated by the 449th Bomb Group, US Fifteenth Army Air Force, Mediterranean theatre, late 1944.

PLOESTI
The first major production version, the B-24D with R-1830-43 engines, appeared late in 1941. A policy decision to concentrate B-24s in the Pacific resulted in most of the 2,738 B-24Ds being deployed against Japan. However, the Eighth and Ninth Air Forces in Europe and North Africa also received the aircraft, one of their outstanding raids being the attack on the Ploesti oil refineries in Romania on 1 August 1943.

LONG-RANGE CAPABILITY
The B-24 Liberator was notable for its long range, which made it ideal for operations in the Pacific and for attacks on targets in the Balkans from bases in North Africa.

Mikoyan-Gurevich MiG-1 (1941)

TYPE • *Fighter* **COUNTRY** • *Soviet Union*

SPECIFICATIONS

Dimensions:	Length: 8.16m (26ft 9in); Wingspan: 10.2m (33ft 6in); Height: 2.62m (8ft 7in)
Weight:	3,319kg (7,317lb) maximum take-off
Powerplant:	1 × 1,007kW (1,350hp) Mikulin AM-35A V-12 liquid-cooled piston engine
Max speed:	657km/h (408mph)
Range:	580km (360 miles)
Service ceiling:	12,000m (39,000ft)
Crew:	1
Armament:	1 × 12.7mm (0.5in) Berezin UB machine gun; 2 × 7.62mm (0.3in) ShKAS machine guns

The MiG-1's origins lay in a January 1939 requirement for a fighter intended to achieve its maximum performance at altitudes above 6,000m (19,685ft). Designed for the high-altitude role, this first MiG fighter was produced in very small numbers before being supplanted by the MiG-3.

Right: The glaring red outer wing panels. These were an identification aid to fellow Soviet pilots and a visible feature for would-be rescuers if the aircraft came down in snow. They were soon deleted.

Control
The aircraft was difficult to control in various parts of the flight envelope, largely due to its centre of gravity being well aft.

Top speed
Originally known as I-200s, the first 100 aircraft were redesignated MiG-1 after their designers. Entering service in 1940, the production I-200 had a 630km/h (391mph) top speed.

Cockpit
Following the tradition of earlier Russian fighters, the MiG-1's pilot sat in an open cockpit, which did not make for comfort at high speeds and high altitudes. The MiG-3 had a fully enclosed cockpit.

MIG-3
MiG-1 test flights showed that the aircraft had a high performance. The MiG-1 was redesignated MiG-3 after the 100th machine had been produced, the main improvements being a fully enclosed cockpit and the addition of an auxiliary fuel tank. Because of the increased combat radius that resulted, MiG-3s were used extensively for fighter reconnaissance.

PERFORMANCE
Although the MiG-1 had a good performance, it was handicapped by the overall length of the engine, which resulted in poor pitch and directional stability. Although constant attempts were made to improve the MiG series of fighters, they never matched the designs of Yakovlev and Lavochkin.

Armament
The MiG-1's armament was sacrificed to compensate for the weight of the engine, a great disadvantage when confronted with the heavily armed fighters of the Luftwaffe in 1941. The armament was later increased in the MiG-3. The single 12.7mm (0.50in) machine gun was mounted under the nose.

Petlyakov Pe-2 (1941)

TYPE • *Dive-bomber* **COUNTRY** • *Soviet Union*

Soviet combat aircraft design made massive strides in the early 1940s, and nowhere was this better revealed than in the elegant Petlyakov Pe-2, which performed a multitude of tasks on the Eastern Front.

SPECIFICATIONS (Pe-2FT)

DIMENSIONS:	Length: 12.78m (41ft 11in); Wingspan 17.11m (56ft 1.33in); Height 3.42m (11ft 2.5in)
WEIGHT:	Empty 5,950kg (13,119lb); Maximum take-off 8,520kg (18,783lb) loaded
POWERPLANT:	2 × 940kW (1,260hp) Klimov VK-105PF 12-cylinder V-type
MAX SPEED:	580km/h (360mph) at 4,000m (13,125ft)
RANGE:	1,315km (817 miles)
CEILING:	8,800m (28,870ft)
CREW:	3
ARMAMENT:	6 × 7.62mm (0.30in) or 12.7mm (0.50in) machine guns; 1,600kg (3,527lb) of bombs

Above: The ventral 12.7mm (0.50in) machine gun seen here was aimed by the radio operator with the aid of a periscope, which had a visual arc of 120 degrees.

AERODYNAMIC BALANCE
The vane above the forward edge of the turret immediately to the rear of the cockpit was an aerodynamic balance area to offset the drag of the 12.7mm (0.5in) machine gun as the turret was traversed, obviating the need for the turret to be power-operated.

PETLYAKOV PE-2FT
The Pe-2FT, described in the specifications above, had a 7.62mm (0.30in) machine gun mounted in the rear of the cockpit; this was operated by the navigator/bombardier.

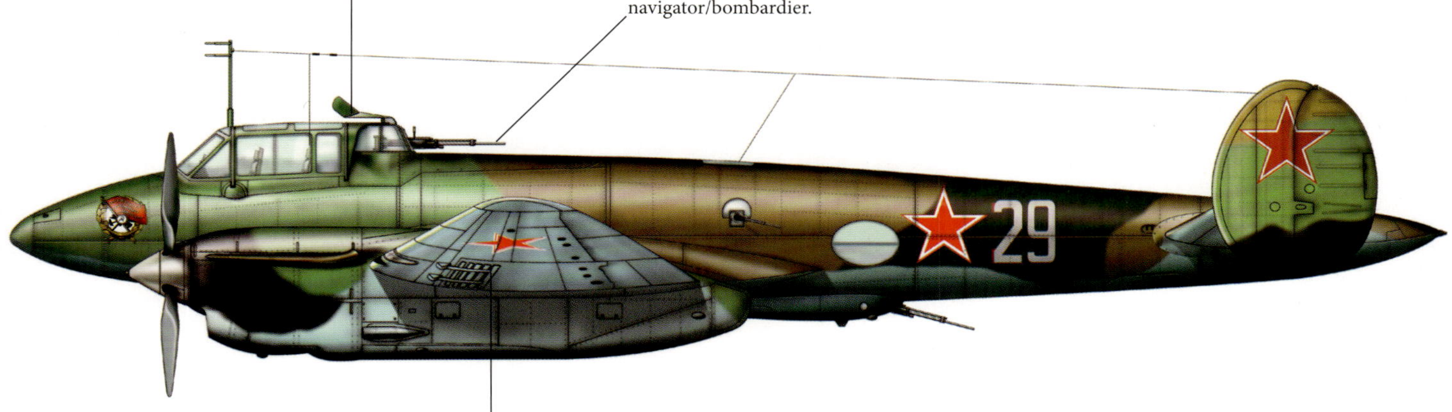

AIR BRAKES
The Pe-2 was equipped with slatted dive-brakes in its wings to slow it to an acceptable speed during a dive-bombing attack.

HIGH PERFORMANCE

In its initial production variant, the Pe-2 was an impressive performer. Its level speed was identical to the Bf 109E, its excellent manoeuvrability belied its fighter origins. In a dive-bombing attack the nose glazing allowed the pilot to visually acquire the target before initiating the dive, recovery being automatic.

EASTERN FRONT, 1944
A Pe-2 aircrew prepare for a bombing sortie during the first months of 1944. The Pe-2 was capable of carrying an internal bombload of 600kg (1,323lb) and a further 400kg (882lb) externally.

Supermarine Seafire (1941)

TYPE • *Naval fighter* **COUNTRY** • *United Kingdom*

SPECIFICATIONS (Seafire F Mk III)

Dimensions:	Length: 9.2m (30ft 3in); Wingspan: 11.23m (36ft 10in); Height: 3.49m (11ft 6in)
Weight:	3,280kg (7,232lb) maximum take-off
Powerplant:	1 × 1,182kW (1,585hp) Rolls-Royce Merlin 55 V-12 liquid-cooled piston engine
Max speed:	578km/h (359mph)
Range:	748km (465 miles)
Service ceiling:	11,000m (36,000ft)
Crew:	1
Armament:	2 × 20mm (0.79in) Hispano cannons; 4 × 12.7mm (0.5in) Browning machine guns fixed forward-firing in wings; up to 226kg (500lb) bombload or 8 × 27kg (60lb) rockets under wing

The most-produced British carrier fighter of World War II, the Supermarine Seafire was a superlative aircraft in the air but ill-suited to deck landing. Despite this impediment it enjoyed widespread use and a long career.

Above: Seafire Mk III PR256 S146 of No. 894 Naval Air Sqn, Royal Navy, based on HMS Indefatigable.

Elliptical wings
The Seafire had the same elegant lines of the Spitfire. In folding-wing variants, the wing folded just inboard of the cannon mounting, the hinges being formed at the top boom of the front spar and at the rear spar.

SEAFIRE ROLES
Seafire deployments were diverse, encompassing land-based as well as carrier operations. Seafire units provided part of the escort for anti-shipping strikes off the Norwegian coast, in particular the well-known attacks on the German battleship *Tirpitz* in mid-1944. Prior to the Normandy landings (Operation *Overlord*), Seafires provided a fighter escort for RAF Typhoons on cross-Channel fighter-bomber sorties and carried out gunnery spotting for naval guns offshore. Seafires also made tactical reconnaissance and bombing sorties over invasion beachheads.

Underwing bombs
Seafires could carry two 113kg (250lb) bombs under the wings or a single 227kg (500lb) bomb under the fuselage. Provision was also made for the fitting of a 30-gallon drop tank in place of the single bomb.

Seafire MB270
MB270 was serving aboard HMS *Attacker* during operations off Crete in September 1944. A month later, MB270's career ended when it missed the arrester wires on landing and was written off following the barrier strike.

SEAFIRE MK IIC
The Seafire Mk IIc was the first folding-wing variant of the aircraft, built in December 1942. Remarkably, the new design was only 8.6kg (19lb) heavier than the standard-wing aircraft it replaced.

Martin B-26 Marauder (1941)

TYPE • *Bomber* **COUNTRY** • *United States*

SPECIFICATIONS (B-26C)

DIMENSIONS:	Length: 17.75m (58ft 3in); Wingspan: 21.64m (71ft); Height: 6.05m (19ft 10in)
WEIGHT:	Maximum take-off: 16,783kg (37,000lb)
POWERPLANT:	2 × 1,491kW (2,000hp) Pratt & Whitney R-2800-43 Double Wasp air-cooled radial piston engines
MAX SPEED:	454km/h (282mph)
RANGE:	1,850km (1,150 miles)
SERVICE CEILING:	6,614m (21,700ft)
CREW:	7
ARMAMENT:	11 × 12.7mm (0.50in) machine guns plus bombload of up to 1,814kg (4,000lb)

Dubbed the 'Widow Maker' after a series of early crashes, the B-26 went on to become one of the USAAF's most important medium bombers. By 1944, Ninth Air Force examples had the lowest loss rate in the European Theater of Operations.

Above: Here is a B-26G Marauder of the 585th Bomb Squadron, 394th Bomb Group, US Ninth Army Air Force, in Cambrai, France, 1944.

WING REDESIGN
Later-production B-26Bs and the B-26C incorporated a redesign of the wing, increasing the span and reducing wing loading. Despite decreasing the maximum speed slightly, the new wing led to a considerably shortened take-off distance.

DEFENSIVE ARMAMENT
The Marauder was heavily armed defensively, with up to 11 12.7mm (0.5in) Browning M2 machine guns in either flexible or turreted mounts.

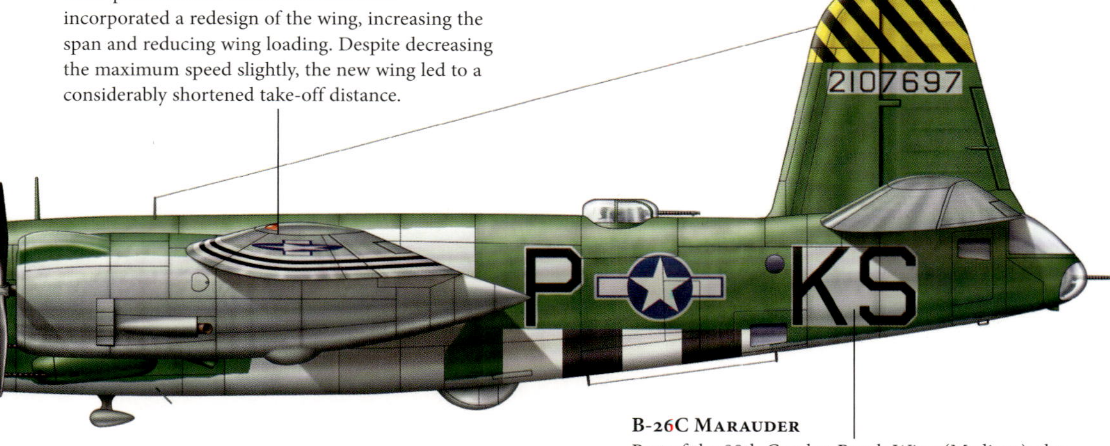

B-26C MARAUDER
Part of the 98th Combat Bomb Wing (Medium), the four squadrons of the 397th Bomb Group flew the B-26C version of the Marauder medium bomber, itself identical to the B-26B except for being built in Omaha rather than Baltimore.

DESIGN CHALLENGE

The Marauder was ordered in response to the March 1939 USAAC Circular Proposal 39-640, calling for a twin-engined medium bomber with a max speed of 560km/h (350mph), a range of 4,800km (3,000 miles) and a bombload of 910kg (2,000lb). This was a tough specification, and the Martin design team responded with an aerodynamically advanced design that featured a tricycle undercarriage and a notably small wing.

558TH BOMB SQUADRON
This B-26B-50-MA served with the 558th Bomb Sqn, 387th Bomb Group, operating out of the UK. The early-model Marauders gained a terrible reputation for accidents, in part due to the type's relatively short wings and tail surfaces, which caused long take-off runs. Later variants like the 'big wing' B-26G reversed this trend and the Marauder eventually had the lowest overall loss rate of any US bomber.

Messerschmitt Me 210/410 (1941)

TYPE • *Heavy fighter* **COUNTRY** • *Germany*

SPECIFICATIONS (Me 210A-0)

Dimensions:	Length: 12.2m (40ft); Wingspan: 16.3m (53ft 6in); Height: 4.2m (13ft 9in)
Weight:	Maximum take-off 9,705kg (21,396lb)
Powerplant:	2 × 783kW (1050hp) Daimler-Benz DB 601A engines
Max Speed:	463km/h (288mph)
Range:	1,818km (1,130 miles)
Ceiling:	8,900m (29,200ft)
Crew:	2
Armament:	2 × 13mm (0.51in) MG 131 machine guns and 2 × 20mm (0.79in) MG 151 cannon firing forward; 2 × 13mm (0.51in) MG 131 firing to the rear

As early as 1938, the Reichsluftfahrtministerium (German Ministry of Aviation, RLM) were planning for a replacement for the Bf 110 heavy fighter. In the summer, Messerschmitt was awarded a contract for its Me 210 design.

Above and left: With its neatly cowled engines and purposeful nose contours, the Me 210 looked the part, but it was plagued with vicious and unpredictable handling qualities.

Messerschmitt Me 410
Developed from the unsuccessful Me 210, the Me 410 *Hornisse* (Hornet) was a fast and powerful twin-engined fighter and reconnaissance platform, although it was not built in great numbers.

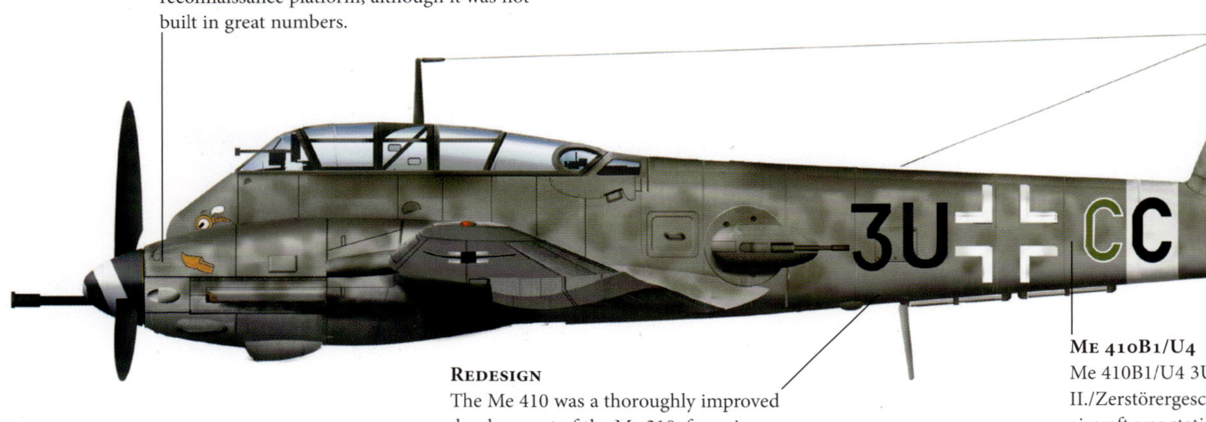

Redesign
The Me 410 was a thoroughly improved development of the Me 210, featuring a lengthened rear fuselage of new design and a wing fitted with automatic leading-edge slats.

Me 410B1/U4
Me 410B1/U4 3U+CC was operated by Stab II./Zerstörergeschwader 26 in 1944. The aircraft was stationed at Königsberg-Neumark.

ADVANCED DESIGN

The Me 210 was an advanced design, with the cockpit right at the front of the fuselage sitting above the gun armament and a small bomb bay. The Daimler-Benz DB 601F engines were mounted on the front of the low-set mainplane, the propellers sitting forwards of the fuselage. On either side of the rear fuselage was an MG 131 13mm (0.51in) machine gun, controlled remotely by the gunner.

ME 410, EASTERN FRONT
Red Army soldiers study the prominent 50mm (2in) cannon on a captured Me 410. This weapon had a formidable effect when applied to strafing armoured and soft-skinned vehicles.

Bell P-39 Airacobra (1941)

TYPE • *Fighter* **COUNTRY** • *United States*

SPECIFICATIONS (P-39Q Airacobra)

DIMENSIONS:	Length: 9.19m (30ft 2in); Wingspan: 10.36m (34ft); Height: 3.78m (12ft 5in)
WEIGHT:	Maximum take-off 3,810kg (8,400lb)
POWERPLANT:	1 × 890kW (1,200hp) Allison V-1710-85 V-12 liquid-cooled piston engine
MAX SPEED:	626km/h (389mph)
RANGE:	845km (525 miles)
SERVICE CEILING:	11,000m (35,000ft)
CREW:	1
ARMAMENT:	1 37mm (1.45in) M4 cannon; 4 × 12.7mm (0.5in) Browning M2 machine guns; up to 230kg (500lb) bombload

The Airacobra was an unusual design that proved disappointing in US and British service. By chance, it turned out to be particularly well suited to conditions on the Eastern Front and was by far the most successful Lend-Lease fighter to serve the USSR.

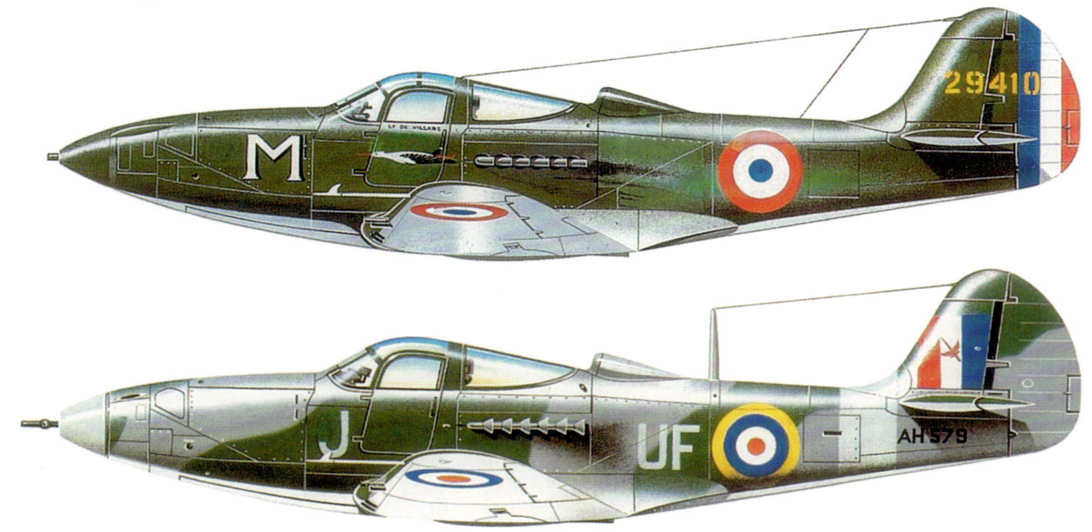

Above: Airacobras served with French and British air forces (as seen here), but their most outstanding export service was in the hands of the Soviet Union.

COCKPIT DOOR
One of the more unusual features of the Bell Cobras was their car-type entry doors. The jettisonable door unit was much the same as that fitted to an automobile, with the normal opening handle and a winding handle for opening the window.

BELL P-39L AIRACOBRA
The wheel turned full circle as the US forces flew Airacobra aircraft initially delivered to the UK as Airacobra Mk I warplanes. The Airacobra's strength and heavy armament made it a good attack fighter.

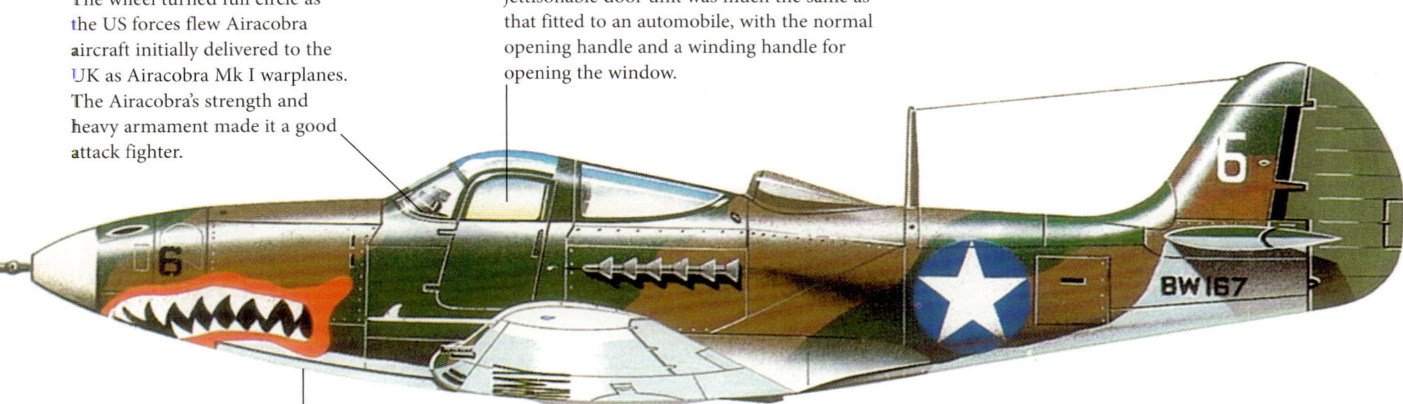

UNDERCARRIAGE
In the light of combat experience with the P-39, the nose undercarriage leg fork was strengthened, beginning with the P-39L model. This was a nonsteerable, self-castoring unit.

LAYOUT
The unconventional Bell P-39 Airacobra was designed around its main gun, a powerful 37mm (1.45in) Colt M4 cannon that was an ideal heavy strafing weapon. The P-39 also reversed normal practice by placing the engine behind the pilot and driving the propeller via a 3m (9ft 11in) long shaft that ran between the pilot's legs. This freed up the entire nose of the aircraft for weapon carriage.

P-39Q
The P-39Q represented the final attempt to mould the Airacobra into a world-class fighter. This is a P-39Q-20, most of which were built for the USSR and delivered without guns, although this example was destined for the USAAF and retained its armament.

Yermolaev Yer-2 (1941)

TYPE • *Bomber* **COUNTRY** • *Soviet Union*

The Yermolaev Yer-2 was derived from a highly advanced prototype trainer. Despite being built in relatively small numbers, the Yermolaev Yer-2 was an important design that saw intensive combat on the Eastern Front.

SPECIFICATIONS

Dimensions:	Length: 16.42m (53ft 10in); Wingspan: 23m (75ft 6in); Height: 4.82m (15ft 10in)
Weight:	Maximum take-off 18,580kg (40,962lb)
Powerplant:	2 × 1,100kW (1,500hp) Charomskiy ACh-30B V-12 liquid-cooled diesel piston engines
Max Speed:	507km/h (315mph)
Range:	5,500km (3,417 miles)
Ceiling:	7,200m (23,600ft)
Crew:	4
Armament:	1 × 12.7mm (0.5in) Berezin UBT flexibly mounted in nose; 1 × 12.7mm (0.5in) Berezin UBT on flexible ventral mount; 1 × 20mm (0.78in) ShVAK cannon in dorsal turret; up to 5,000kg (11,023lb) bombload

Above: The original airliner was redesigned as the DB-240, standing for Dalny Bombardirovshcik *(long-range bomber), but became the Ye-2 on production.*

Armament
The DB-240 offered an excellent range with a 1,000kg (2,205lb) bombload and the defensive armament was considered good, with multiple heavy machine guns and a 20mm (0.79in) cannon in the dorsal turret.

Design
The Yer-2 was developed from the Stal-7 – designed by Italian-born engineer Roberto Ludvigovich Bartini, development of which had passed to his deputy, Vladimir Yermolaev.

Engines
Performance was not quite as good as expected due to the aircraft being forced to use Klimov M-105s rather than the higher-powered M-106s it was designed for, as the M-106 was suffering from insuperable cooling problems. The aircraft was later fitted with efficient Charomskiy ACh-30 diesel engines.

FIRST MISSION

The Yer-2's initial production life was short, with only 128 constructed when in August 1941 Zavod 18 switched to building the more urgently required Il-2. In the same month the Yer-2 entered combat for the first time: on 10 August three of the aircraft bombed Berlin and one was subsequently shot down in error by I-16s on its return to Soviet airspace.

LATE PRODUCTION

After a pause in production in August 1941, Yer-2 production was reinitiated towards the end of 1943. Production difficulties delayed service entry and the first bombing mission of the new Yer-2 occurred on 7 April 1945.

Grumman F6F Hellcat (1942)

TYPE • *Naval fighter* **COUNTRY** • *United States*

SPECIFICATIONS F6F-5 Hellcat)

DIMENSIONS:	Length: 10.24m (33ft 7in); Wingspan 13.05m (42ft 9.66in); Height 3.99m (13ft 1in)
WEIGHT:	Empty 4,191kg (9,239lb); Maximum take-off 7,025kg (15,487lb) loaded
POWERPLANT:	1,491kW (2,000hp) Pratt & Whitney R-2800-10W radial engine
MAX SPEED:	612km/h (380mph) at 7,132m (23,400ft)
RANGE:	1,521km (945 miles)
CEILING:	11,369m (37,300ft)
CREW:	1
ARMAMENT	6 × 12.7mm (0.50in) machine guns or 2 × 20mm (0.79in) cannon and 4 × 12.7mm (0.50in) machine guns, plus provision for 2 × 453kg (1,000lb) bombs or 6 × 127mm (5in) rocket

Credited with more combat victories than any other carrier fighter in history, the large and rugged F6F Hellcat fighter effectively established the US Navy's aerial ascendency over their Japanese foes.

Above: Most of the Hellcat's service took place over the Pacific, but this 800 Sqn RAF example in full invasion stripes was operating off HMS Emperor, *covering Operation* Dragoon, *the landings in southern France during August 1944.*

F6F-3 HELLCAT
Alexander Vraciu was a notable pilot with VF-16, the fourth most successful USN pilot of the war with 19 victories, all claimed while flying Hellcats, including this F6F-3 during the spring of 1944.

CANOPY
The pilot sat under a sliding canopy and was well protected by armour, particularly to the rear. However, no rear-view mirror was provided, and rearward visibility was lacking.

ARRESTER HOOK
The Hellcat's arrester hook was a 'Sting' unit projecting from the extreme rear of the fuselage.

PACIFIC FIGHTER

The Hellcat made its first flight in June 1942. In the Pacific, the Hellcat played a key role in all US naval operations. A more powerful variant, the F6F-5, was fitted with a Pratt & Whitney R-2800-10W engine, capable of developing an emergency power of 1,640kW (2,200hp) by using water injection. The F6F-5 began to reach the Pacific task forces in the summer of 1944.

CRASH-LANDING
November 1943, and an F6F explodes into flames on the flight deck of USS *Enterprise* after crash-landing. The catapult officer, Lt. Walter Chewning, climbed up the side of the aircraft to help the pilot, Ensign Byron Johnson, escape from the flaming cockpit.

Vought F4U Corsair (1942)

TYPE • *Fighter* **COUNTRY** • *United States*

SPECIFICATIONS (F4U-5N)	
DIMENSIONS:	Length: 110.5m (34ft 7in); Wingspan: 12.49m (41ft); Height: 4.49m (14ft 9in)
WEIGHT:	Maximum takeoff 6,398kg (14,106lb)
POWERPLANT:	1 × 1,790kW (2,400hp) Pratt & Whitney R-2800-32W Double Wasp 18-cylinder air cooled radial piston engine
MAX SPEED:	756km/h (470mph)
RANGE:	1,790km (1,120 miles)
CEILING:	11,247m (36,900ft)
CREW:	1
ARMAMENT:	4 × 20mm (0.79in) AN/M3 fixed forward firing in wings; up to 1,452kg (3,200lb) bombload or 8 × 127mm (5in) rockets

The F4U had a troubled introduction to service in World War II, but by the end of the conflict it was challenging for a place among the best single-seat fighters of the war. It remained a viable ground-attack aircraft and night-fighter during the subsequent fighting in Korea.

Above: The first Corsairs built by Goodyear were designated FG-1, and in British Fleet Air Arm service became the Corsair Mk IV, of which 977 were delivered.

ARMAMENT
The Corsair was fitted with four 20mm (0.79in) M3 cannon starting with the F4U-1C in mid 1943, but this armament was not initially popular and suffered from teething issues. The F4U-5N could also carry two 454kg (1,000lb) bombs or napalm tanks, eight 127mm (5in) HVAR rockets or eight 300mm (11.75in) Tiny Tim rockets.

VOUGHT F4U-1A
This Corsair was operating over Bougainville in November 1943 with VF-17, the 'Jolly Rogers'. It was flown by Frederick 'Big Jim' Streig who was to shoot down six Japanese aircraft by the end of the conflict, all with the F4U.

CORSAIR CONSTRUCTION
Apart from the highly cranked wing, which could be folded for storage below the carrier deck, the fighter utilized a broadly conventional airframe of all-metal construction. The FG-1 version differed in having fixed rather than folding wings.

DEPLOYMENT
The first F4U-1 was delivered to the USN on 31 July 1944. Carrier trials began in September 1942 and the first Corsair unit, Marine Fighting Squadron VMF-214, was declared combat-ready in December, deploying to Guadalcanal in February 1943. The Corsair became operational with Navy Fighting Squadron VF-17 in April 1943.

WING DESIGN
Designed with an inverted gull wing to keep span and main landing gear lengths as short as possible, the F4U Corsair was planned as a carrier-borne fighter, but matured as a superlative ground-attack and close-support fighter that saw service mainly in the Pacific theatre.

Northrop P-61 Black Widow (1942)

TYPE • *Heavy fighter* **COUNTRY** • *United States*

Without doubt one of the finest night-fighters of the war, the P-61 was one of the few Allied aircraft specifically designed for the task. The Black Widow served with distinction in the Pacific, often as a night intruder on offensive missions against land and sea targets.

SPECIFICATIONS (P-61B Black Widow)

DIMENSIONS:	Length: 15.11m (49ft 7in); Wingspan: 20.12m (66ft 0in); Height: 4.46m (14ft 8in)
WEIGHT:	13,472kg (29,700lb) maximum take-off
POWERPLANT:	2 x 1,491kW (2,000hp) Pratt & Whitney R-2800-65 radial piston engines
MAX SPEED:	589km/h (366mph)
RANGE:	4,506km (2,800 miles)
CEILING:	10,090m (33,100ft)
CREW:	3
ARMAMENT:	4 x 20mm (0.79in) cannon, plus 4 x 12.7mm (0.5in) machine guns in later aircraft, and provision to carry up to 4 x 726kg (1,600lb) bombs

Right: The P-61 had a massive spread of wing, even bigger than that of today's F-15, and a crew area considerably more spacious than most medium bombers.

RADAR
The SCR-720 radar was an advanced piece of equipment, having anti-jamming features which would seek out an enemy aircraft even if the latter were using countermeasures.

RADIO OPERATOR
The radar operator had the best position in the P-61, installed above and behind the pilot with an excellent forward view.

DORSAL TURRET
The streamlined four-gun dorsal turret caused aerodynamic buffeting when fitted to the P-61A, but a slight lengthening of the nose in the P-61B cured the problem.

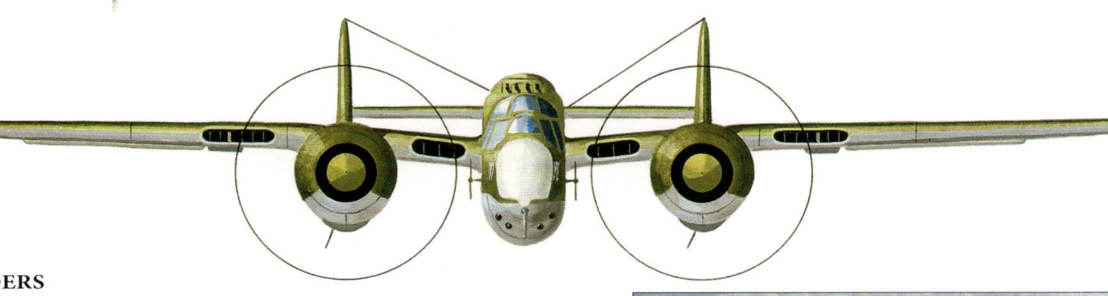

WIDOW INTRUDERS

The first production P-61A Black Widow aircraft appeared in early 1941. Although always classed as a night-fighter, the P-61B version that followed saw increasing use as a night intruder, and was capable of carrying weapons loads including four 726kg (1,600lb) bombs, or four 1136 litre (300 US gallon) drop tanks under the wings.

P-61A BLACK WIDOW
This aircraft is from the first batch of production P-61As. Early P-61A operations were plagued by the unserviceability of the aircraft's Pratt & Whitney R-2800-65 engines.

Hawker Typhoon (1942)

TYPE • *Fighter-bomber* **COUNTRY** • *United Kingdom*

SPECIFICATIONS (Mk IB)

Dimensions:	Length: 9.73m (31ft 11in); Wingspan: 12.67m (41ft 7in); Height: 4.66m (15ft 4in)
Weight:	4,010kg (8,840lb)
Powerplant:	Napier Sabre IIC liquid-cooled H-24 piston engine, 1,685kW (2,260hp)
Max Speed:	663km/h (412mph)
Range:	821km (510 miles)
Ceiling:	10,729m (35,200ft)
Crew:	1
Armament:	4 × 20mm (0.79in) Hispano Mk II cannon; 8 × RP-3 air-to-ground rockets; 2 × 227kg (500lb) or 2 × 454kg (1,000lb) bombs

An interceptor that initially failed, the Hawker Typhoon was nearly cancelled before it blossomed into the finest close-support aircraft of World War II. With its pugnacious snub nose, four long-barrelled cannon and whining Sabre engine, the big fighter-bomber wreaked havoc on its foes.

Above & right: The Typhoon's underwing hardpoints could accommodate eight 27kg (60lb) rockets, as illustrated, or two bombs of up to 453kg (1,000lb) in weight. The four 20mm (0.79in) Hispano cannon were armed with 120 rounds per gun.

Armament
The Typhoon was very heavily armed with four 20mm (0.79in) Hispano Mk II cannon, eight RP-3 air-to-ground rockets, and two 227kg (500lb) or two 454kg (1,000lb) bombs.

Typhoon Mk IB
Poor rearward visibility was improved by replacing the solid fairing behind the cockpit with a transparent version. This preceded the design of an entirely new 'teardrop' canopy.

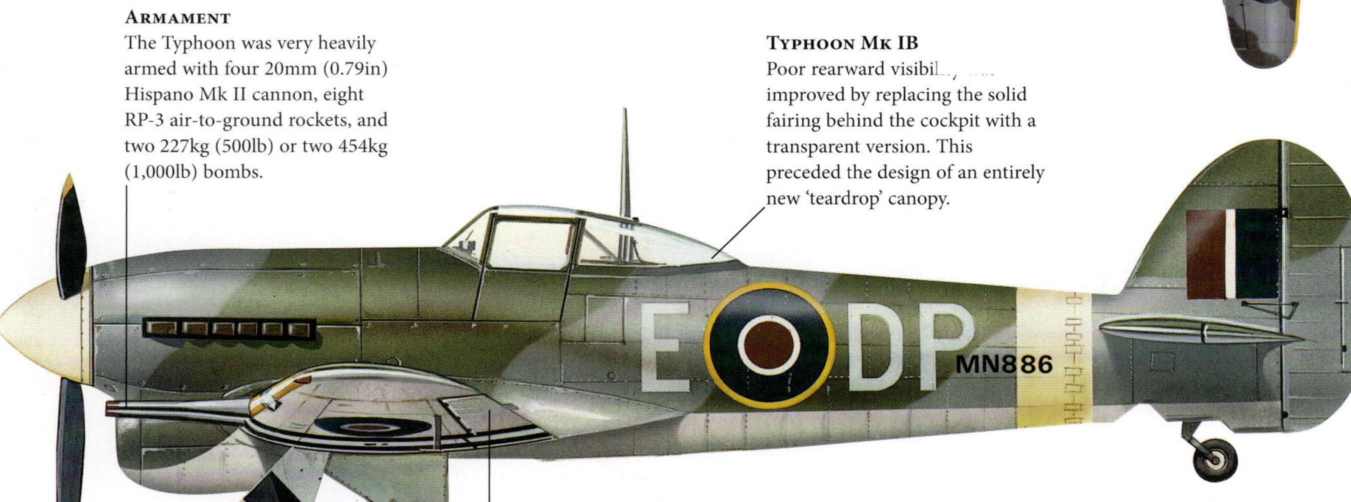

Wing
The Typhoon's wing was built around an immensely strong two-spar structure. Mounted in the port wing just outboard of the landing light was a gun camera to record rocket and cannon strikes.

PROBLEMS
The Hawker Typhoon was designed to combat heavily armed and armoured escort fighters like the Messerschmitt Bf 110. The first of two prototypes flew for the first time on 24 February 1940. However, the aircraft suffered from constant teething troubles, and the first Typhoon squadron did not become operational until May 1942.

WARLOAD
Armed with eight rocket projectiles, this early Mk IB demonstrates a typical Typhoon warload. The worn paintwork is clearly evident even at this early stage and is a testimony to the Typhoon's demanding low-level mission.

Junkers Ju 290 (1942)

TYPE • *Maritime patrol* **COUNTRY** • *Germany*

SPECIFICATIONS (Ju 290A-5)

DIMENSIONS:	Length: 28.64m (94ft 0in); Wingspan: 42m (137ft 10in); Height: 6.83m (22ft 5in)
WEIGHT:	44,969kg (99,140lb) maximum take-off
POWERPLANT:	4 × 1,300kW (1,700hp) BMW 801D 14-cylinder air-cooled radial piston engines
MAX SPEED:	439km/h (273mph)
RANGE:	6,148km (3,820 miles)
SERVICE CEILING:	6,000m (19,685ft)
CREW:	9
ARMAMENT:	2 × 20mm (0.79in) MG 151/20 cannons (dorsal turrets); 1 × 20mm MG 151/20 (tail); 2 × 20mm MG 151/20s (waist); 1 × 20mm MG 151/20 (gondola); 2 × 13mm (0.51in) MG 131 machine guns (gondola); 3,000kg (6,600lb) of disposable stores

The Ju 290 emerged from the Ju 89 four-engine bomber, three prototypes of which were under construction as of 1936. The bomber was cancelled the following year and Junkers instead developed a civil version as the Ju 90.

Left: This Junkers Ju 290A-2 is seen here in October 1945, having been captured by the British and tested by the RAF.

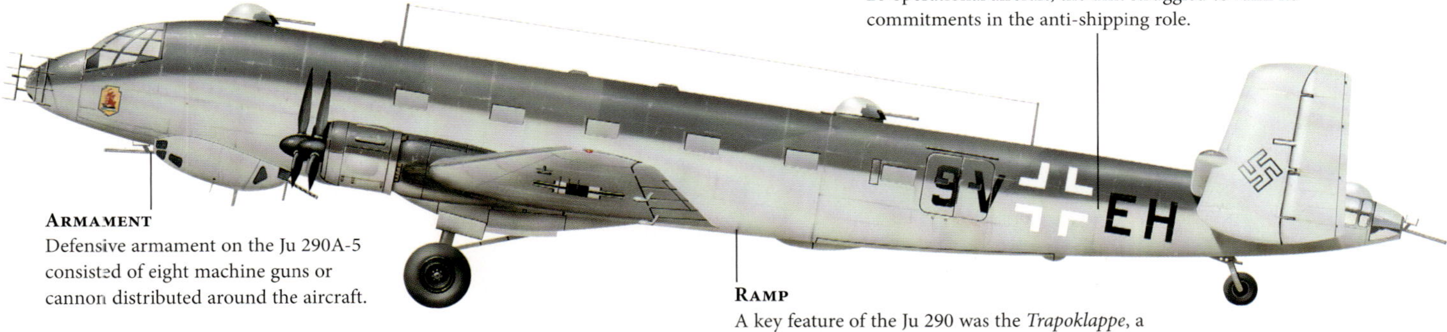

JU 290A-5
This aircraft flew with Fernaufklärungsgruppe 5 from Mont-de-Marsan in France. With never more than 20 operational aircraft, the unit struggled to fulfil its commitments in the anti-shipping role.

ARMAMENT
Defensive armament on the Ju 290A-5 consisted of eight machine guns or cannon distributed around the aircraft.

RAMP
A key feature of the Ju 290 was the *Trapoklappe*, a hydraulically operated ramp that raised the cabin to the level position for ground loading, while also providing a ramp for vehicles to drive straight up into the cabin.

VARIANTS

The first two Ju 290A-0 pre-production aircraft were followed by five examples of the Ju 290A-1, an armed transport, while the Ju 290A-2 was the first of the long-range maritime reconnaissance subvariants, adding an aft dorsal turret, revised navigation equipment and FuG 200 Hohentwiel search radar; three were built. After five Ju 290A-3s had been completed with low-drag Focke-Wulf gun turrets, there followed a similar number of Ju 290A-4 aircraft, with another Focke-Wulf gun turret in the forward dorsal position.

IMPROVEMENTS

Shortcomings encountered in initial subvariants were addressed in the subsequent Ju 290A-5, which added protection for the fuel tanks, armour around the flight crew and improved waist gun positions. The crew complement was increased from seven to nine, adding dedicated gunners.

Kawasaki Ki-45 Toryu (1942)

TYPE • *Bomber* **COUNTRY** • *Japan*

SPECIFICATIONS (Ki-45 Kai-c)

Dimensions:	Length: 11.00m (36ft 1in); Wingspan 15.02m (49ft 3in); Height 3.70m (12ft 1.33in)
Weight:	Empty 4,000kg (8,820lb); Maximum take-off 5,500kg (12,125lb) loaded
Powerplant:	2 × 805kW (1,080hp) Mitsubishi Ha-102 14-cylinder radials
Max Speed:	540km/h (336mph) at 5,000m (16,405ft)
Range:	2,000km (1,243 miles)
Ceiling:	10,000m (32,810ft)
Crew:	2
Armament:	1 × 37mm (1.46in) cannon; 2 × 20mm (0.79in) cannon; 1 × 7.92mm (0.31in) machine gun

The Kawasaki Ki-45 *Toryu* (Dragon Slayer), after a protracted development programme, became one of the most effective Japanese combat aircraft of World War II, but despite its performance its full potential was never realized.

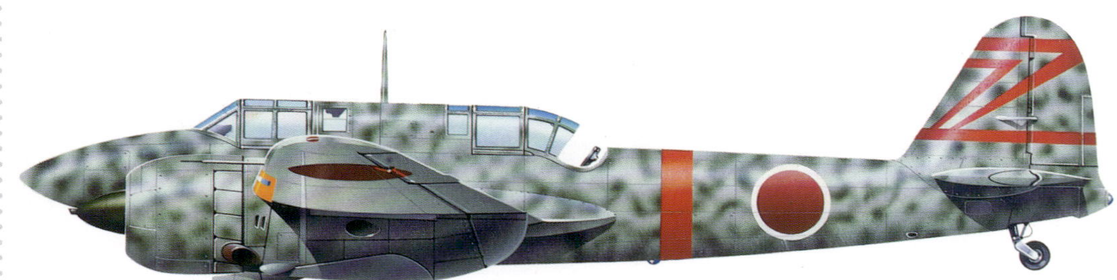

Above: This Kai-c aircraft flew with the 2nd Chutai, 27th Sentai, based in the Philippines in November 1944.

Engines
The Ki-45 Kai-c was powered by two reliable Mitsubishi Ha102 radial engines. The nacelles housing these were longer than those of earlier variants.

Top cannon
The night fighter version (not shown) of the Toryu was equipped with a pair of 20mm (0.79in) cannon, obliquely mounted in the upper fuselage between the two cockpits, enabling the pilot to attack an enemy bomber from below.

Ki-45 Kai-c
An aircraft of the 1st Chutai, 5th Sentai, based at Kashiwa, Chiba Prefecture, in spring 1943.

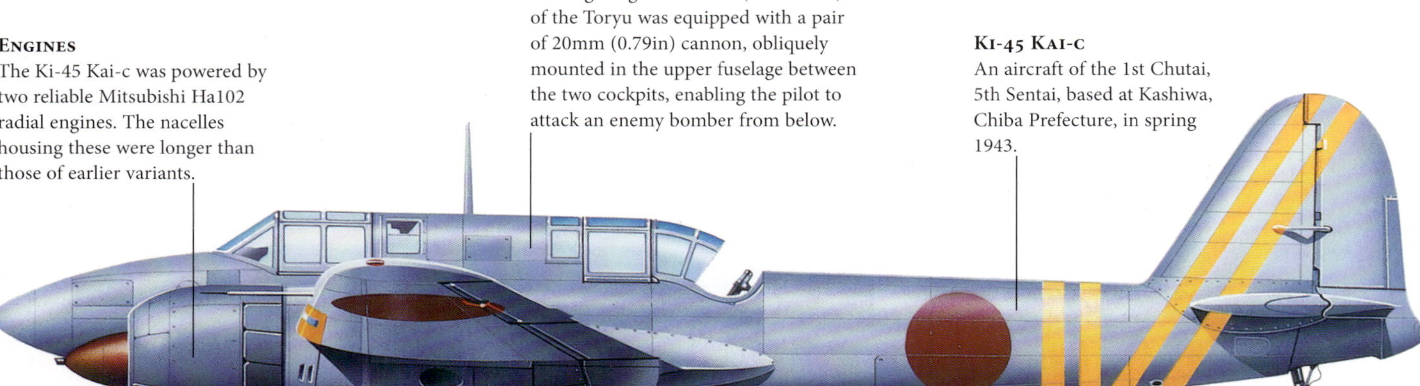

HISTORY

The Kawasaki Ki-45 Toryu prototype first flew in January 1939. The development programme continued slowly and the aircraft did not enter service until the autumn of 1942 as the Ki-45 Kai-a fighter and the Ki-45 Kai-b ground-attack and anti-shipping strike aircraft, the 'Kai' suffix denoting 'improved'. The Ki-45 Kai-c was a night-fighter version, while the Kai-d was an improved ground-attack/anti-shipping variant.

TOP-MOUNTED CANNON
The Ki-45 in the immediate foreground displays the upward-firing 20mm (0.79in) cannon. Although the Ki-45 was a capable aircraft, many of this type were expended in kamikaze attacks during the final months of the war. Total production of the Toryu was 1,675 aircraft, of which 477 were night-fighters. The Toryu received the Allied codename 'Nick'.

Kawasaki Ki-61 Hien (1942)

TYPE • *Fighter* **COUNTRY** • *Japan*

SPECIFICATIONS (Ki-61-I-KAIc)

DIMENSIONS:	Length: 8.75m (28ft 8.5in); Wingspan 12m (39ft 4.25in); Height 3.7m (12ft 1.75in)
WEIGHT:	Empty 2,210kg (4,872lb); Maximum take-off 3,250kg (7,165lb)
POWERPLANT:	1 x 876kW (1,175hp) Kawasaki Ha-40 (Army Type 2) 12-cylinder inverted-Vee engine
MAX SPEED:	592km/h (368mph)
RANGE:	1,100km (684 miles)
CEILING:	11,600m (37,730ft)
CREW:	1
ARMAMENT:	2 x 20mm cannon and 2 x 12.7mm (0.5in) machine guns; up to 500kg (1,102lb) of bombs

The only front-line Japanese combat aircraft to deviate from the radial engine, the Kawasaki Ki-61 *Hien* (Swallow) was dubbed the 'Tony' by the Allies. It was frequently mistaken for the Messerschmitt Me 109, although all it had in common was the (Kawasaki-built) DB 601 engine.

Above: A Ki-61c (top) and Ki-61b show some of the flamboyant markings applied from front-line 'Tony' fighters.

WING RATIO
Another feature that made the Ki-61 stand out from other Japanese fighters was its high aspect ratio wing; this showed the influence of Dr Vogt, a German designer who had been closely involved with Kawasaki and who became chief designer of Blohm & Voss.

ENGINE
The Ki-61 Daimler-Benz DB.601A was chosen because reports from the air fighting in Europe seemed to indicate that the liquid-cooled engine was superior to the air-cooled variety.

KI-61-IB
An aircraft of the 1st Chutai, 244th Sentai, led by Major Kobayashi and stationed at Chofu and Narumatsu in 1945. Captain Takada was the 1st Chutai leader.

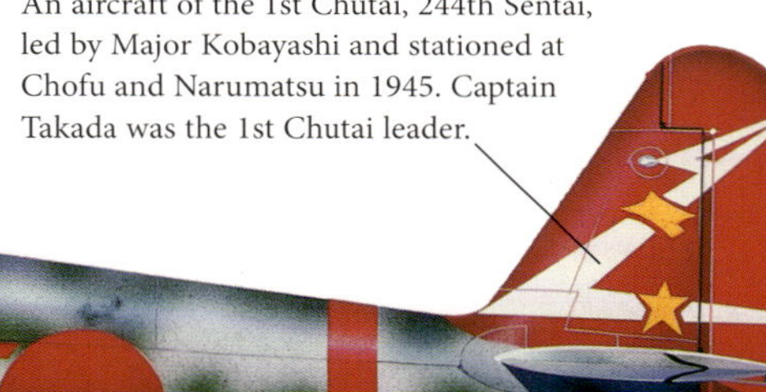

VARIANTS
Designed to replace the Nakajima Ki-43 *Hayabusa* (Oscar) in Japanese Army service, the Kawasaki Ki-61 began to reach front-line air units in August 1942. The principal versions were the Ki-61-I (1,380 aircraft built in two subvariants, differentiated by their armament; the Ki-61 Kai, with a lengthened fuselage and different armament fits (1,274 built); and the Ki-61-II, optimized for high-altitude operation with a Kawasaki Ha-140 engine (374 built).

LAST STAND
This Ki-61-I of the 37th Sentai was among those that fought in the last stages of the defence of the Philippines, before being forced to redeploy to Formosa and Okinawa in the last year of the war.

Curtiss SB2C Helldiver (1942)

TYPE • *Dive-bomber* **COUNTRY** • *United States*

SPECIFICATIONS (Curtiss SB2C-1C)

Dimensions:	Length: 11.18m (36ft 8in); Wingspan: 15.16m (49ft 9in); Height: 4.01m (13ft 2in)
Weight:	Maximum takeoff 7,388kg (16,287lb)
Powerplant:	1 × 1,400kW (1,900hp) Wright R-2600-20 Twin Cyclone 14-cylinder air-cooled radial piston engine
Max Speed:	462km/h (287mph)
Range:	1,786km (1,110 miles)
Ceiling:	7,370m (24,179ft)
Crew:	2
Armament:	2 × 20mm (0.79in) AN/M2 cannon in wings; 2 × 7.62mm (0.3in) M1919 Browning machine guns flexibly mounted in rear cockpit; up to 910kg (2,000lb) bombload or one 910kg (2,000lb) Mark XIII torpedo in internal bomb bay

The Curtiss SB2C Helldiver weathered a protracted development, problematic service introduction and an appalling reputation to become one of the most successful naval aircraft of the entire war, making a signal contribution in the Pacific theatre.

Right: Although the Helldiver was effective in its role, it was not liked by its pilots, who had a number of derogatory nicknames for it. Neither was it liked by ground crews, who found it difficult to service.

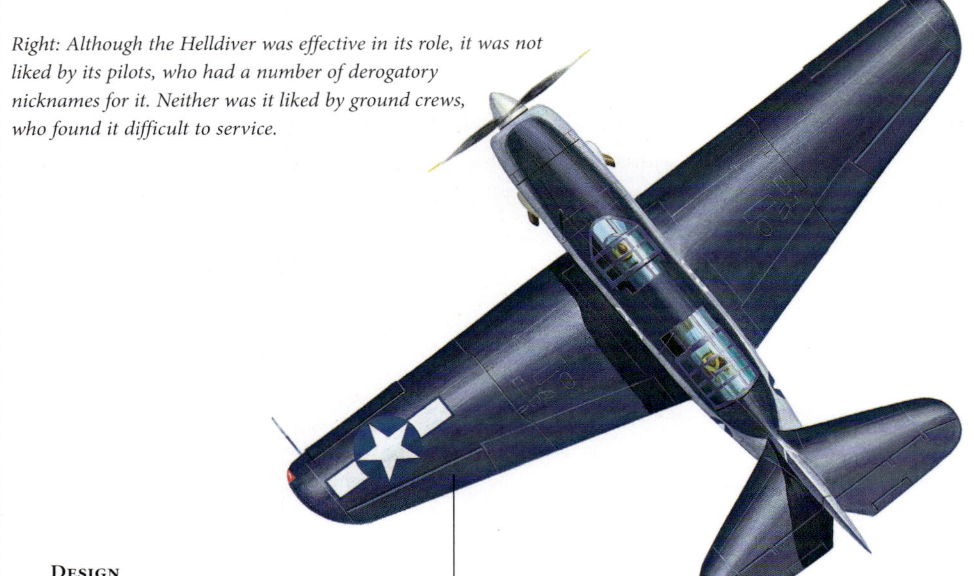

Design
The SB2C was a low-wing cantilever monoplane largely of metal construction, the outer wing panels folding upward for carrier stowage.

Powerplant
The Helldiver was powered by the Wright Twin Cyclone radial engine, a very reliable powerplant on which crews could depend during their long overwater missions.

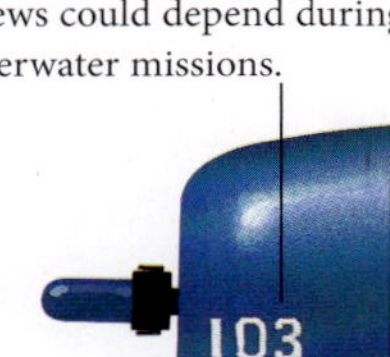

Bomb bay
The Helldiver could accommodate one torpedo or a bombload of 454kg (1,000lb) in its fuselage weapons bay; 454kg (1,000lb) of bombs could also be carried on underwing racks.

RABAUL ATTACK

The SB2C Helldiver was designed as a replacement for the SBD Dauntless, which had achieved fame in the Battle of Midway in June 1942. Because of delays caused by the crash of the prototype, the first production Helldiver did not fly until June 1942 and although the aircraft entered service with the US Navy in December 1942, it did not make its operational debut until 11 November 1943, in an attack on the Japanese-held island of Rabaul.

SB2C-5
A Curtiss SB2C-5 Helldiver scout-bomber, of Bombing Squadron Ten (VB-10), USS *Intrepid* (CV-11), flies over Tientsin, China, as the city is reoccupied by the Allies, 5 September 1945.

Grumman TBF Avenger (1942)

TYPE • *Torpedo bomber* **COUNTRY** • *United States*

SPECIFICATIONS (TBF-1C)

DIMENSIONS:	Length: 12.19m (40ft); Wingspan 16.51m (54ft 2in); Height 5.00m (16ft 5in)
WEIGHT:	Empty 4,788kg (10,555lb); Maximum take-off 7,876kg (17,364lb)
POWERPLANT:	1,268kW (1,700hp) Wright R-2600-8 Cyclone 14-cylinder radial engine
MAX SPEED:	414km/h (257mph) at 3,660m (12,000ft)
RANGE:	1,780km (1,105 miles)
CEILING:	6,525m (21,400ft)
CREW:	3
ARMAMENT:	3 x 12.7mm (0.50in) machine guns; 1 x 7.62mm (0.30in) machine gun; torpedo, bomb and rocket load up to 1,134kg (2,500lb)

Although it had a disastrous start to its operational career at the Battle of Midway in June 1942, when five out of six aircraft were shot down in an attack on the Japanese task force, the Avenger went on to become one of the best ship-borne torpedo bombers of World War II.

Above: This TBF-1 was the sole survivor of the Avenger's disastrous combat debut when six VT-8 TBF-1s from USS Hornet*, on detachment to Midway Island, attacked the Japanese fleet without fighter escort on 4 June 1942.*

FUSELAGE
The Avenger's fuselage was of oval section and semi-monocoque construction, built up from a series of angle frames and stamped bulkheads all covered by a smooth metal skin.

CREW
The TBF was operated by a crew of three: the pilot, a turret gunner and a busy third crew member who served as the bombardier, radioman and ventral gunner.

GRUMMAN AVENGER MK II
Although strongly associated with the war in the Pacific, the Avenger also served in Europe. This example in full invasion stripes was based at RNAS Donibristle during June 1944.

SUBVARIANTS
Subvariants of the Avenger included the TBF-1C, some of which were fitted with two wing-mounted 20mm (0.79in) cannon, the TBF-1B, which was supplied to the Royal Navy under Lend-Lease and was initially known as the Tarpon, the TBF-1D and TBF-1E with ASV radar, and the TBF-1L with a searchlight in the bomb bay. Final wartime versions were the camera-equipped TBM-3P and the TBM-3H, with search radar.

SINGLE-ENGINE DESIGN
As the largest single-engined aircraft to serve in World War II, the Avenger represented a massive step-up in capability and complexity compared to the TBD Devastator. Production of the TBF-1 and TBM-1, including subvariants, amounted to 2,290 and 2,882 aircraft, respectively.

Heinkel He 177 (1942)

TYPE • *Bomber* **COUNTRY** • *Germany*

SPECIFICATIONS (He 177A-5)

DIMENSIONS:	Length: 22m (72ft 2in); Wingspan: 31.44m (103ft 2in); Height: 6.4m (21ft)
WEIGHT:	Maximum take-off 31,000kg (68,300lb)
POWERPLANT:	2 × 2,133kW (2,860hp) Daimler-Benz DB 610 24-cylinder liquid-cooled piston engines
MAX SPEED:	565km/h (351mph)
RANGE:	1,540km (960 miles)
CEILING:	8,000m (26,000ft)
CREW:	6
ARMAMENT:	1 × 7.92mm (0.31in) MG 81; 2 × 20mm (0.79in) MG 151 cannon; 4 × 13mm (0.51in) MG 131; 2,000kg (4,410lb) bombload, LT 50 torpedos or Hs 293 missiles

The Heinkel He 177 heavy bomber, with one of the most distinctive silhouettes in the Luftwaffe fleet, traces its origins back to the P.1041 project for a long-range bomber that emerged amid mid-1930s plans to field a strategic bombing force for the Luftwaffe.

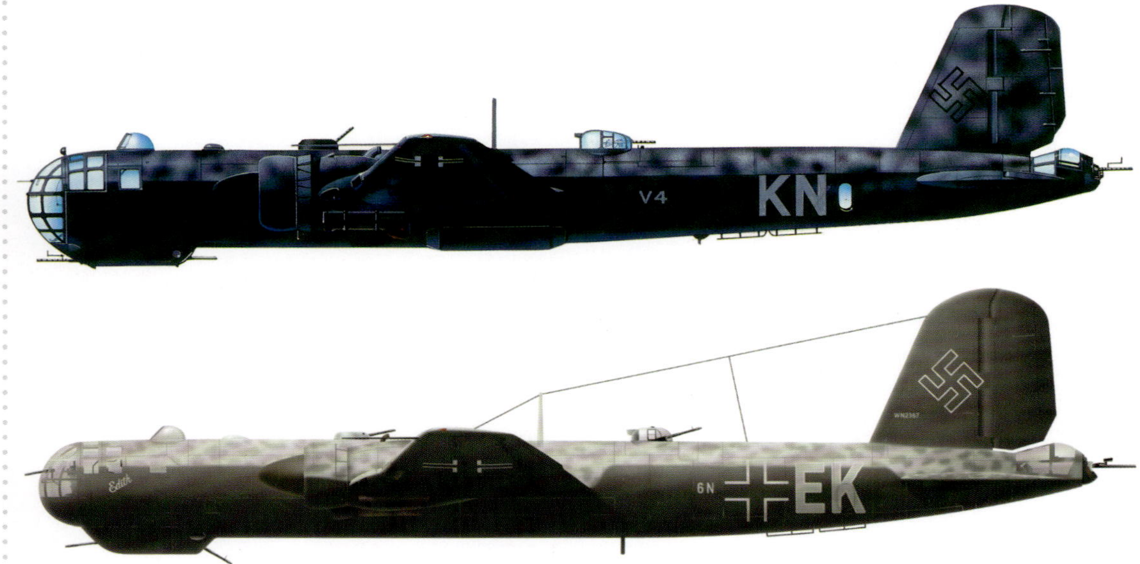

Above: (Top) An He 177A-5/R-6 and (bottom) an He 177A-3/R-2. The He 177s wore a variety of overwater camouflage.

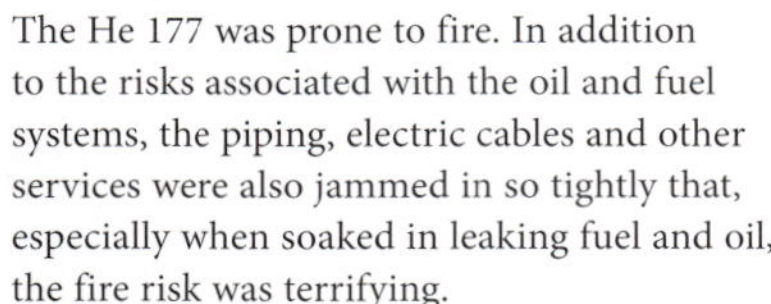

FIRE RISK
The He 177 was prone to fire. In addition to the risks associated with the oil and fuel systems, the piping, electric cables and other services were also jammed in so tightly that, especially when soaked in leaking fuel and oil, the fire risk was terrifying.

POWERPLANT
The He 177A-5 standardized on the DB 610 engine (coupled DB 603s) as opposed to the DB 606 (coupled DB 601s) of the earlier variants.

HE 177A-5/R2 GREIF
This machine hailed from the 4. Staffel, II Gruppe of Kampfgeschwader 100, during the time the unit was based at Bordeaux-Mérignac, France, in 1944.

ADVANCED WEAPONRY

The heavy-lifting power of the Heinkel He 177 meant that it was able to lift all manner of experimental and advanced Luftwaffe weaponry. The weapons carried by the He 177A-3 specifically included the Henschel Hs 293 radio-controlled missile and, in the A-3/R7 and all A-5 versions, a range of anti-ship torpedoes, including the LT 50 glider torpedo.

HE 177A-5
This He 177A-5 is seen in Allied marking, having been captured in France in September 1944. The challenging requirement that ultimately led to the He 177 demanded a maximum speed of 540km/h (335mph) and the ability to carry a 2,000kg (4,410lb) bombload over a radius of 1,600km (995 miles) at a cruising speed of 500km/h (310mph).

Lavochkin La-5 (1942)

TYPE • *Fighter* **COUNTRY** • *Soviet Union*

SPECIFICATIONS (La-5FN)

Dimensions:	Length: 8.67m (28ft 5in); Wingspan: 9.8m (32ft 2in); Height: 2.54m (8ft 4in)
Weight:	Maximum take-off 3,402kg (7,500lb)
Powerplant:	1 x 1,380kW (1,850hp) Shvetsov M-82FN 14-cylinder air-cooled radial engine
Max Speed:	648km/h (403mph)
Range:	765km (475 miles)
Service ceiling:	11,000m (36,000ft)
Crew:	1
Armament:	2 x 20mm (0.79in) ShVAK cannon; 2 bombs up to 100kg (220lb) each

When the La-5 appeared in service it was the first Soviet fighter with superior performance to the Bf 109G. The most widely used series of radial-engined fighters in the Soviet air force inventory, 9,920 were built during the Great Patriotic War.

Above: This is an early example without the later variants' cut-down rear fuselage and revised canopy, which offered much improved all-round fields of vision.

Cooling
The radial engine of the fighter was extremely closely cowled, sufficient engine cooling being achieved through the use of fans mounted in front of and behind the engine.

Canopy
The canopy of the La-5 offered excellent all-round vision, but was difficult to open at high speeds. Consequently, some pilots flew with their canopies open.

Lavochkin La-5FN
'White 69' of 1 Czechoslovak IAP was flown by former 310 Squadron RAF Spitfire pilot Ladislav Valousek over Ukraine during September 1944. The diamond marking on the engine cowl is a stylized representation of the Cyrillic letters 'FN', denoting the engine variant.

IMPROVEMENTS
An extensive conversion of the LaGG-3, the early La-5 aircraft suffered serious performance shortfalls due to shoddy workmanship. However, once these difficulties had been overcome, the aircraft began to take on Fw 190s and Bf 109Gs on equal terms. Many improvements were gradually introduced, the most important being to cut down the rear fuselage and later to introduce the more powerful ASh-82F engine in the La-5F.

FUSELAGE NUMBERS
Outsize fuselage numbers such as the white '77' featured on this aircraft were common on Soviet fighters. Several camouflage and colour schemes were also applied to the La-5 during World War II.

Nakajima Ki-44 Shoki (1942)

TYPE • *Fighter* **COUNTRY** • *Japan*

SPECIFICATIONS (Ki-44-IIb)

DIMENSIONS:	Length: 8.80m (28ft 10.5in); Wingspan: 9.45m (31ft 0in); Height: 3.25m (10ft 8in)
WEIGHT:	2,995kg (6,603lb) maximum take-off
POWERPLANT:	1 × 1,133kW (1,520hp) Nakajima Ha-109 radial piston engine
MAX SPEED:	605km/h (376mph) at 5,200m (17,060ft)
RANGE:	1,700km (1,056 miles)
SERVICE CEILING:	11,200m (36,745ft)
CREW:	1
ARMAMENT:	4 × 12.7mm (0.5in) machine guns

As the fastest-climbing Japanese fighter of World War II to see quantity production, the Ki-44 interceptor held the line in the defence of the homeland when the US Army Air Force began its bombing offensive with the B-29 Superfortress.

Above: (Top) A Ki-44-I assigned to an Air Training Division at Akeno airfield, Mie prefecture in 1944. (Bottom) A Ki-44-IIb flown within the Eastern Defence Sector, Japan, in early 1945.

POWERPLANT
In its initial form, the Ki-44 was powered by a 932kW (1,250hp) Nakajima Ha-41 radial engine, this being chosen as the most powerful option then available.

PERFORMANCE
Compared to its predecessors, the Ki-44 lacked manoeuvrability and its high landing speed could be hazardous.

KI-44-IIB
An example of the 'Tojo' used for homeland defence in late 1944. The operating unit was the 23rd Sentai, and the aircraft served in the Eastern Defence Sector.

BOMBER INTERCEPTOR
Known as the *Shoki* (Demon), the Nakajima Ki-44 interceptor had the appearance of a beefed-up Ki-43, and was strongly influenced by the company's previous fighter design. Compared to the Ki-43, however, the design of the Ki-44 stressed speed and rate of climb rather than agility, which made it ideal for the bomber-interceptor mission in which it would see most of its service.

CAMOUFLAGED KI-44S
Design and development of the Ki-44 was more or less contemporaneous with that of the Ki-43, but the project differed in its requirements, the specification calling for the ability to climb to 4,000m (13,125ft) in less than five minutes, and a top speed of 600km/h (373mph).

Henschel Hs 129 (1942)

TYPE • *Ground attack* **COUNTRY** • *Germany*

SPECIFICATIONS (Hs 129B-3)	
DIMENSIONS:	Length: 9.75m (32ft 0in); Wingspan: 14.2m (46ft 7in); Height: 3.25m (10ft 8in)
WEIGHT:	5,250kg (11,574lb) maximum take-off
POWERPLANT:	2 × 522kW (700hp) Gnome-Rhône 14M 4/5 radial engines
MAX SPEED:	407km/h (253mph)
RANGE:	690km (430 miles)
SERVICE CEILING:	9,000m (30,000ft)
CREW:	1
ARMAMENT:	1 × 75mm (2.96in) BK 7.5 (Bordkanone 7.5)

The Henschel Hs 129 was intended to meet a German Air Ministry requirement for a twin-engine aircraft armed with at least one 20mm (0.79in) cannon for the ground-attack mission and protected by extensive armour.

Above: This Hs 129B-3 was flown by 14.(Panzerjäger)/Schlachtgeschwader 9, one of only two operational units to fly the B-3 with the BK 7.5 cannon carried in a jettisonable fairing.

SUBVARIANTS
Subvariants of the B-1 included the Hs 129B-1/R1 with provision for two 50kg (110lb) bombs or 96 anti-personnel bomblets and the Hs 129B-1/R2 armed with a 30mm (1.18in) MK 101 cannon under the fuselage.

HENSCHEL HS 129B-1
8./Schlachtgeschwader 1's fleet included this Hs 129B-1, based at El Aluin, Tunisia, in February 1943.

POWERPLANT
The powerplant on the Hs 129B-1 consisted of two 522kW (700hp) Gnome-Rhône 14M 4/5 radial engines delivering a maximum speed of 407km/h (253mph).

EARLY DESIGN
The prototype Hs 129 first flew in spring 1939 and was characterized by a triangular-section fuselage that offered limited space for the cockpit – accommodation was notably cramped, but the single pilot was provided with a windscreen of 75mm (2.95in) armoured glass, while the nose itself was constructed of armour plating. A total of three prototypes underwent Luftwaffe evaluation, each being powered by a pair of 347kW (465hp) Argus As 410 engines.

EXAMINATION
British ground crew technicians examine the engine and propeller on a captured Hs 129B at RAF Collyweston in Northamptonshire, UK. The proposed Hs 129A-1 initial-production variant was abandoned in favour of the Hs 129B-1. This featured a number of improvements, including more powerful 522kW (700hp) Gnome-Rhône 14M 4/5 radial engines.

Mitsubishi J2M *Raiden* (1943)

TYPE • *Fighter* **COUNTRY** • *Japan*

SPECIFICATIONS (J2M3)

Dimensions:	Length: 9.95m (32ft 7.75in); Wingspan: 10.82m (35ft 5.25in); Height: 3.95m (12ft 11.5in)
Weight:	3,945kg (8,695lb) maximum take-off
Powerplant:	1 × 1,357kW (1,820hp) Mitsubishi MK4R-A Kasei 23a radial piston engine
Max speed:	595km/h (370mph) at 5,900m (19,360ft)
Range:	1,055km (655 miles)
Service ceiling:	11,700m (38,385ft)
Armament:	4 × 20mm cannon; 2 × 60kg (132lb) bombs on underwing racks

First flown in March 1942, the *Raiden* (Thunderbolt) was designed as the land-based successor to the A6M Reisen. It failed to live up to its initial promise, was very slow in development, and finally entered service with performance little better than that of its legendary predecessor.

Left: Over the Philippines in World War II, a Mitsubishi J2M Raiden 'Jack' is evaluated by a pilot from the US Technical Air Intelligence Center (TAIC).

Armament
The J2M3 version became the major production model, which featured revised armament: four 20mm (0.79in) cannon plus two 60kg (132lb) bombs on underwing racks.

J2M3
This *Raiden* J2M3 was flown by the Imperial Japanese Navy's 302nd Kokutai, which was based in the Japanese home islands by the last year of the war.

3D-153

Design
The *Raiden* was a cantilver low-wing monoplane with a retractable tailwheel landing gear. It was a forward-looking design, but one that would be bogged down in developmental delays.

RAIDEN AT WAR

Development problems meant that the *Raiden* was slow to arrive in service; only 14 aircraft had been delivered by March 1943, six months after production had been approved. By that time, the J2M3 had emerged as the major production variant, and this was deployed to the Philippines. Thereafter, the bulk of the type's combat service would be recorded over the Japanese home islands, where it excelled as a bomber-destroyer.

J2M3 *RAIDEN*
A Mitsubishi J2M3 *Raiden,* codenamed 'Jack' by the Allies, sits abandoned in the Pacific in 1945. The aircraft saw its most important service in the defence of the Japanese homeland.

Nakajima B6N *Tenzan* 'Jill' (1943)

TYPE • *Torpedo bomber* **COUNTRY** • *Japan*

SPECIFICATIONS (B6N2)

DIMENSIONS:	Length: 10.87m (35ft 8in); Wingspan: 14.90m (48ft 10.5in); Height: 3.80m (12ft 5.5in)
WEIGHT:	5,650kg (12,456lb) maximum take-off
POWERPLANT:	1 x 1,380kW (1,850hp) Mitsubishi MK4T Kasei 25 radial piston engine
MAX SPEED:	480km/h (298mph)
RANGE:	3,045km (1,892 miles)
SERVICE CEILING:	9,040m (29,660ft)
CREW:	3
ARMAMENT:	2 x 7.7mm (0.303in) machine guns plus bombload or torpedo of up to 800kg (1,764lb)

The B6N *Tenzan* (Heavenly Mountain) was Japan's standard carrier-based torpedo bomber during the latter stages of the war. It was an evolution of the Nakajima B5N and was considerably heavier and more powerful than its illustrious forebear.

Above: A Nakajima B6N 'Jill' takes off from a Japanese fleet carrier armed with a heavy torpedo.

POWERPLANT
The troubled B6N programme suffered a further setback when the Mamoru engine was removed from production, forcing a switch to the Mitsubishi Mk4T Kasei 25.

FOLDING WING
Designed like its predecessor, the B5N, for operations from carrier decks, the B6N2 *Tenzan* featured a wing which folded at mid-span for easy storage on and beneath the crowded decks of Japanese fleet carriers.

CARRIER LANDINGS
The aircraft's high landing speed and wing loading meant it was only able to operate from the Navy's larger carriers.

NEW ENGINE
The B6N was designed to meet a 1939 Navy requirement and was externally very similar to the B5N that preceded it. The primary advance was the use of a new engine, the Nakajima Mamoru 11 radial, providing some 80 per cent more power than the Sakae 11 unit used in the B5N. The first two prototypes of the B6N were ready to commence flight-testing in spring 1941.

B6NS AT WAR'S END
These Nakajima B6N *Tenzans* were photographed on a Japanese airfield in September 1945, as the war drew to a close. When production ended, Nakajima had built a total of 1,268 B6Ns of all versions.

Junkers Ju 188 (1943)

TYPE • *Bomber* **COUNTRY** • *Germany*

SPECIFICATIONS (Ju 188A-3)

DIMENSIONS:	Length: 14.9m (49ft 0.5in); Wingspan: 22m (72ft 2in); Height: 4.45m (14ft 7in)
WEIGHT:	14,510kg (31,989lb) maximum take-off
POWERPLANT:	2 × 1,290kW (1,730hp) Jumo 213A-1 radial engines
MAX SPEED:	499km/h (310mph)
RANGE:	2,400km (1,490 miles)
SERVICE CEILING:	9,347m (30,665ft)
CREW:	4
ARMAMENT:	1 × 20mm (0.8in) MG 151/20 cannon (dorsal turret); 2 × 13mm (0.5in) MG 131 machine guns; FuG 200 Hohentwiel sea-search radar; provision for 3,000kg (6,600lb) bombload

Intended as the successor to the prolific Ju 88, the design of the Ju 188 was already well advanced by the outbreak of World War II when the company had examined a potentially stretched Ju 85B and Ju 88B.

Above: The Ju 188D-2 version was differentiated by its FuG 200 radar fitted for maritime operations.

RADAR
This Ju 188 is equipped with a FuG 200 Hohentwiel radar, which was capable of detecting ships up to a distance of 10km (6.2 miles).

ARMAMENT
The D-series encompassed the Ju 188D-1 and D-2, both of which were equipped for reconnaissance duties and which had no forward-firing MG 151 cannon, in a bid to improve high-altitude performance.

JUNKERS JU 188D-2
This aircraft served with 1.(Fern) Staffel/Aufklärungsgruppe 124 at Kirkenes, Norway. It was deployed as a maritime patroller.

ENGINE CHOICE

From the outset, the Ju 188 was intended to be suitable for either BMW 801 or Junkers Jumo 213 engines, to ensure that production wouldn't be interrupted by a shortage of either one of these powerplants. While it was originally anticipated that production would begin with the Jumo-engined Ju 188A-1 bomber, in the event the aircraft was launched into series production in Ju 188E-1 form, a bomber version powered by a pair of 1,193kW (1,600hp) BMW 801ML engines.

D-SERIES CHANGES
Other changes in the D-series of the Ju 188 included a three-man crew (the bomber aimer and forward gun were removed) and additional fuel capacity.

BOMBING UP
A Ju 188 is loaded with underwing bombs. In all, more than 1,000 Ju 188s of all variants were completed and more than half of these were destined to serve in the reconnaissance role. While the aircraft had only a limited impact on the war, it was judged to be superior to the Ju 88 in most respects, with improved handling – especially at high operating weights.

Messerschmitt Me 323 Gigant (1943)

TYPE • *Transport* **COUNTRY** • *Germany*

SPECIFICATIONS (323D-1 Gigant)

Dimensions:	Length: 28.2m (92ft 6in); Wingspan: 55.2m (181ft 1in); Height: 10.15m (33ft 4in)
Weight:	Maximum take-off 43,000kg (94,799lb)
Powerplant:	6 x 868kW (1,164hp) Gnome-Rhône 14N-48 14-cylinder radial piston engines
Max Speed:	285km/h (177mph)
Range:	1,000km (620 miles)
Ceiling:	4,000m (13,000ft)
Crew:	5, plus 120 troops or 9,750kg (21,495lb) load
Armament:	2 x 7.92mm (0.31in) MG 15, MG 81 or 13mm (0.51in) MG 131 machine guns in cockpit; 2 x 7.92mm (0.31in) MG 15s in waist (optional)

With the sudden realization that existing assets would be insufficient to the task of invading Great Britain, the Luftwaffe ordered a giant aircraft to transport men, supplies and vehicles. The immense *Gigant* (Giant) family dwarfed all other contemporary aircraft.

Left: The Gigant was versatile and could carry a range of cargo. Different combat zones called for different types of supplies. For example, on the Eastern Front, the aircraft airlifted horses needed to pull gun carriages and other heavy equipment on muddy, unpaved roads.

Engines
A number of Me 323E-2s were given six 1,007kW (1,350hp) Junkers Jumo 211R engines, with the resulting conversion redesignated Me 323F-1.

Structure
The aircraft's fabric-covered metal tube structure allowed it to survive a fair deal of battle damage, but did not offer much protection for the 120 troops or 80 stretcher patients it could carry.

Cargo doors
The front of the aircraft was hinged in the middle, allowing it to open for loading and unloading of cargo, vehicles or troops.

GLIDER CONVERSION

The Me 323 Gigant actually began life as the audacious Me 321, an enormous invasion transport glider with a wingspan of 55m (180ft) and a capacity for loads of up to 20,000kg (44,092lb). Continued problems on take-off (it was made airborne by a bomber aircraft tug and rocket assistance) led to the decision to develop a powered version, the Me 323. The Me 323D began to be produced in series from August 1942.

ME 323D-6
This view of a Messerschmitt Me 323D-6 Gigant shows its impressive cargo-carrying capabilities. The aircraft, however, suffered innumerable problems, leading to its eventual demise.

Fiat G.55 Centauro (1943)

TYPE • *Fighter* **COUNTRY** • *Italy*

The Fiat G.55 *Centauro* (Centaur) fighter aircraft was developed by Fiat for the Italian Air Force in World War II. It was generally able to fight well, but all of its variants had defects that made them vulnerable to Allied fighters.

SPECIFICATIONS

DIMENSIONS:	Length: 9.37m (30ft 9in); Wingspan 11.85m (38ft 10.5in); Height 3.77m (12ft 4in)
WEIGHT:	Empty 2,630kg (5,799lb); Maximum take-off 3,718kg (8,197lb)
POWERPLANT:	1,100kW (1,475hp) Daimler Benz DB 605A 12-cylinder V-type
MAX SPEED:	620km/h (385mph) at 7,400m (24,300ft)
RANGE:	1,650km (1,025 miles)
CEILING:	12,700m (41,700ft)
CREW:	1
ARMAMENT:	2 × 12.7mm (0.50in) machine guns and 3 × 20mm (0.79in) cannon

This page: The G.55 Centauro was Fiat's successor to its G.50 fighter, but with a higher performance and equipped with an inline engine.

ARMAMENT
The G.55 carried three 20mm (0.79in) cannon and two 12.7mm (0.50in) machine guns, the latter mounted in the upper-forward fuselage. One of the three cannon was centrally mounted to fire through the propeller boss.

COCKPIT
Unlike its predecessor, the G.50, the Fiat G.55 had a fully enclosed cockpit. Downward visibility was poor, and the long nose seriously restricted the pilot's view ahead while on the ground.

AIR INTAKE
The G.55 was fitted with an air intake mounted below the fuselage, in much the same configuration as that of the P-51 Mustang (for which it was sometimes mistaken).

LATECOMER

Fitted with a DB.605A engine and featuring an enclosed cockpit, the G.55 was undoubtedly the best wartime fighter produced in Italy, but it did not enter production until 1943, with the result that only a few had been delivered before the Armistice. Production continued after this, however, and most of the 130 or so aircraft that were completed served with the pro-German Italian Socialist Republic forces.

GERMAN CENTAUR
A G.55 Centauro painted in German markings. The G.55s gave a good account of themselves against Allied fighters like the Spitfire and Mustang, but problems ranging from armament layout to balance impacted otherwise excellent performance characteristics.

Bell P-63 Kingcobra (1943)

TYPE • *Fighter* **COUNTRY** • *United States*

SPECIFICATIONS (P-63A)

DIMENSIONS:	Length: 9.96m (32ft 8in); Wingspan 11.68m (38ft 4in); Height: 3.84m (12ft 7in)
WEIGHT:	Empty 2,892kg (6,375lb); Maximum take-off 4,763kg (10,500lb)
POWERPLANT:	988kW (1,325hp) Allison V-1710-95 V-type
MAX SPEED:	657km/h (408mph) at 7,452m (24,450ft)
RANGE:	724km (450 miles)
CEILING:	13,105m (43,000ft)
CREW:	1
ARMAMENT:	1 x 37mm (1.46in) gun and 4 x 12.7mm (0.50in) guns; provision for 3 x 227kg (500lb) bombs

Although bearing a close resemblance to the P-39 and sharing the same unconventional layout, the Kingcobra was in fact a completely new design. Over two-thirds of all P-63s produced were supplied to the Soviet Union.

Above: Seen here is one of the many P-63s supplied to the Soviet Union under Lend-Lease arrangements. Auxiliary fuel tanks could be attached to the underwing hardpoints, providing extra range for the long ferry flight to the USSR via Alaska.

ENGINE
The Allison engine was situated in the middle fuselage bay, driving a long crankshaft that passed between the pilot's legs.

LAMINAR FLOW WING
Though there were obvious similarities, the P-39 and P-63 were entirely different aircraft. The latter's enlarged vertical fin and four-bladed propeller were obvious visual differences, but perhaps more significant was the more efficient laminar flow wing.

ARMAMENT
The P-63 carried five guns: a single 37mm (1.5in) M10 cannon in the propeller hub, a pair of 12.7mm (0.5in) machine guns above the nose and a second pair of podded '50 calibres' under the wings.

LEND-LEASE FIGHTERS

The aircraft was intended to succeed the P-39 Airacobra in the fighter and fighter-bomber roles, but only 332 were in fact delivered to the USAAF and were used as ground-based gunnery targets. No Kingcobra ever saw combat with the USAAF. Of the 1,725 P-63A and 1,227 P-63C Kingcobras built, 2,421 were supplied to the USSR under Lend-Lease, proving to be excellent ground-attack aircraft, and 300 were allocated to the Free French Air Force.

BELL P-63E KINGCOBRA
The Bell P-63 Kingcobra was a wholly new fighter design using the essential layout of the P-39 Airacobra and introducing the laminar-flow wing and taller tail tested on the XP-39E. The Kingcobra was about 12 per cent larger than the P-39.

Messerschmitt Me 262 (1944)

TYPE • *Jet fighter* **COUNTRY** • *Germany*

SPECIFICATIONS (Me 262A-1a)

DIMENSIONS:	Length: 10.61m (34ft 9in); Wingspan: 12.50m (41ft); Height: 3.83m (12ft 7in)
WEIGHT:	6,775kg (14,936lb) maximum take-off
POWERPLANT:	2 × Junkers Jumo 004B-1 turbojets, 8.8kN (1,890lb)
MAX SPEED:	870km/h (541mph)
RANGE:	845km (525 miles)
SERVICE CEILING:	11,000m (36,090ft)
CREW:	1
ARMAMENT:	4 × 30mm (1.18in) cannon

Assured its place in history as the first jet fighter to enter service, the Luftwaffe's Me 262 was the most advanced fighter to reach operational status during World War II, and ushered military aviation into the jet age.

Above: This Me 262A-1a carries the insignia of Jagdgeschwader (JG) 7, the Luftwaffe's first and only fully operational jet fighter Geschwader. Its pilots included some of the world's first jet fighter aces.

ME 262A-2A
This aircraft flew with 1./Kampfgeschwader 51 'Edelweiss' (KG 51) in March 1945.

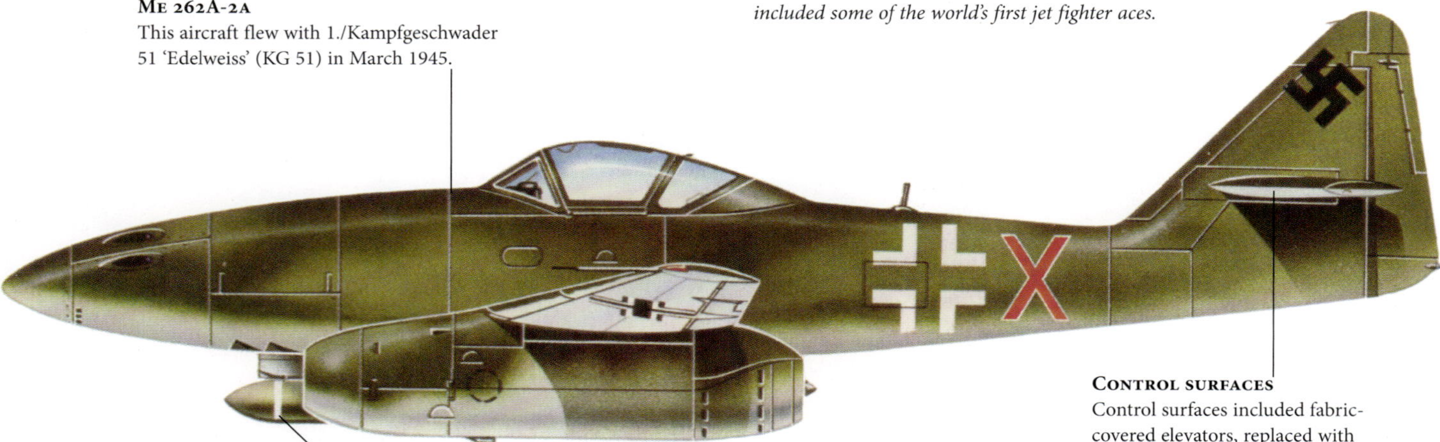

CONTROL SURFACES
Control surfaces included fabric-covered elevators, replaced with stronger metal skins on later production aircraft. The powerful rudder was required to maintain directional stability.

ARMAMENT
The Me 262A-2a fighter-bomber was similar to the Me 262A-1a, but with two racks for 250kg (551lb) bombs and two-gun armament.

NIGHT-FIGHTER ROLE

The Me 262 saw some limited success in the night-fighter role. A dedicated night-fighter model appeared before the end of the war, in the form of the radar-equipped Me 262B-1a/U1. As a daytime bomber-destroyer, the Me 262 could also be armed with 24 underwing R4M unguided rockets. Ultimately, however, the Me 262 was a case of 'too little, too late'.

ME 262B-1A
It is believed that only 15 or so Me 262B-1a tandem two-seat trainers were converted into Me 262B-1a/U1 night-fighters. This example (Werk/nr 110306) was briefly operated in the defence of Berlin by the Kommando Welter.

Boeing B-29 Superfortress (1944)

TYPE • *Bomber* **COUNTRY** • *United States*

SPECIFICATIONS (B-29B)

DIMENSIONS:	Length: 30.18m (99ft); Wingspan: 43.36m (142ft 3in); Height: 9.01m (29ft 7in)
WEIGHT:	64,003kg (141,100lb) maximum take-off
POWERPLANT:	4 × Wright R-3350- 57 radial piston engines, 1641kW (2200hp)
MAX SPEED:	576km/h (358mph)
RANGE:	6,598km (4,100 miles)
CEILING:	9,695m (31,800ft)
CREW:	10–11
ARMAMENT:	12 × 12.7mm (0.5in) machine guns in remote-controlled turrets; 1 × 20mm (0.79in) cannon and 2 × 12.7mm (0.5in) machine guns in tail; plus bombload of up to 9,072kg (20,000lb)

Even without the atomic missions that the type flew against Japan in August 1945, the B-29 – the most advanced heavy bomber of the war – can be considered a war-winner on account of the devastating raids it conducted against the Japanese mainland in the preceding months.

Left: A B-29 Superfortress named for Fleet Admiral Chester W. Nimitz, Commander-in-Chief, Pacific Fleet and Pacific Ocean Areas (CINCPAC-POA), lands at the island of Guam for his use in 1945.

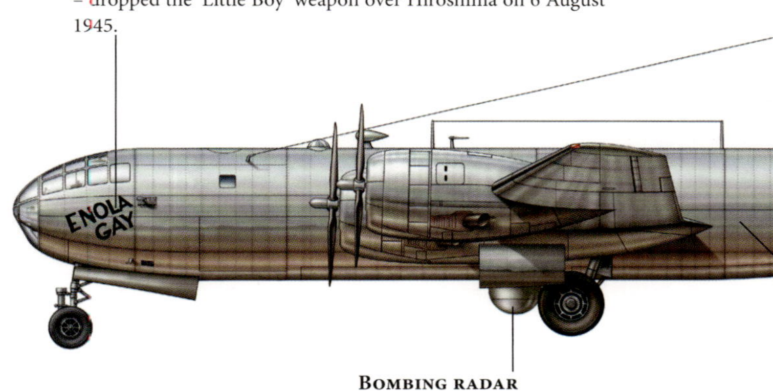

ENOLA GAY
A new era in warfare began when a Silverplate B-29 ('Silverplate' was the code name for B-29s adapted to drop atomic bombs) – named 'Enola Gay' after the mother of the pilot, Paul Tibbetts – dropped the 'Little Boy' weapon over Hiroshima on 6 August 1945.

PRESSURIZED
The B-29 Superfortress was the first aircraft in quantity production with a pressurized fuselage, enhancing crew comfort during long flights.

BOMBING RADAR
The B-29 was equipped with the very accurate AN/APQ-13 bombing radar located between the two bomb bays. This was often deleted from wartime photos for security reasons.

DEVASTATING RAIDS

During their initial nine months of service, the B-29s were employed mainly for high-level daylight raids. However, tactics switched in March 1945, when they began low-level night attacks from the Mariana Islands. These were the most destructive raids of the war in terms of casualties, with the first night-time incendiary raid on Tokyo killing around 80,000 people.

IN FLIGHT

The product of the most expensive single arms programme of the war, the B-29 was, by a considerable margin, the most advanced bomber to see service during the conflict. It remains the only aircraft to have used a nuclear weapon in anger.

Arado Ar 234 (1944)

TYPE • *Jet bomber* COUNTRY • *Germany*

SPECIFICATIONS (Ar 234B-2)

DIMENSIONS:	Length: 12.64m (41ft 5in); Wingspan 14.41m (46ft 3in); Height 4.29m (14ft 1in)
WEIGHT:	Empty 5,200kg (11,466lb); Loaded 9,850kg (21,715lb)
POWERPLANT:	2 x 800kg (1,764lb) thrust BMW 003A-1 turbojets
MAX SPEED:	742km/h (461mph) at 6,000m (19,685ft);
RANGE:	1,630km (1,013 miles)
SERVICE CEILING:	10,000m (32,810ft)
CREW:	1
ARMAMENT:	2 x 20mm (0.79in) MG 151 in belly pod; 2 x rearward-firing 20mm (0.79in) cannon

The Arado Ar 234 was the world's first jet bomber. Entering service in the reconnaissance role in July 1944, the Blitz made flights over Britain and France almost undetected. As a bomber it was also quite successful, but operations were hampered by attacks on airfields and fuel supplies.

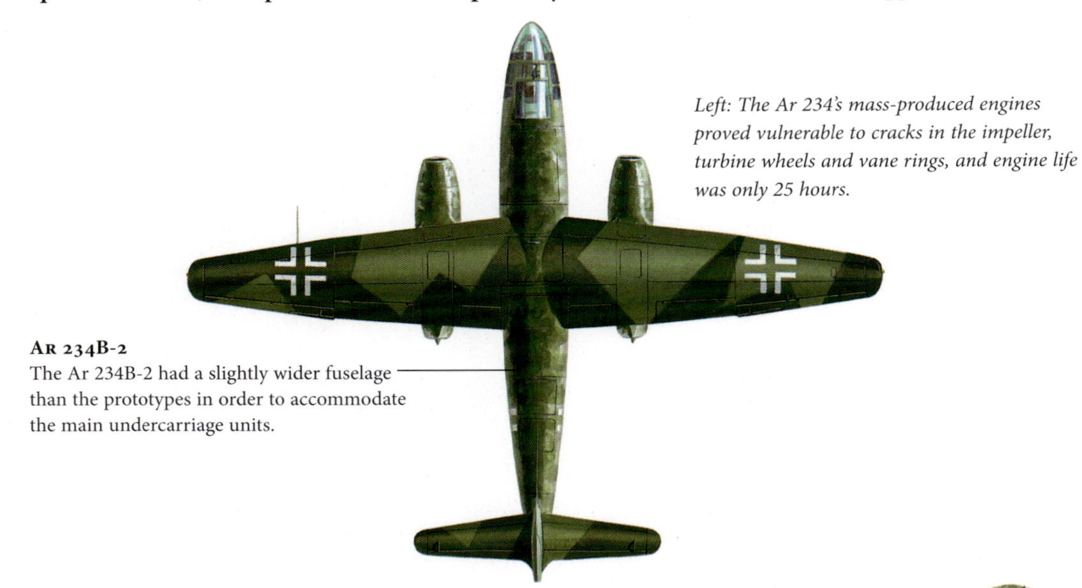

Left: The Ar 234's mass-produced engines proved vulnerable to cracks in the impeller, turbine wheels and vane rings, and engine life was only 25 hours.

AR 234B-2
The Ar 234B-2 had a slightly wider fuselage than the prototypes in order to accommodate the main undercarriage units.

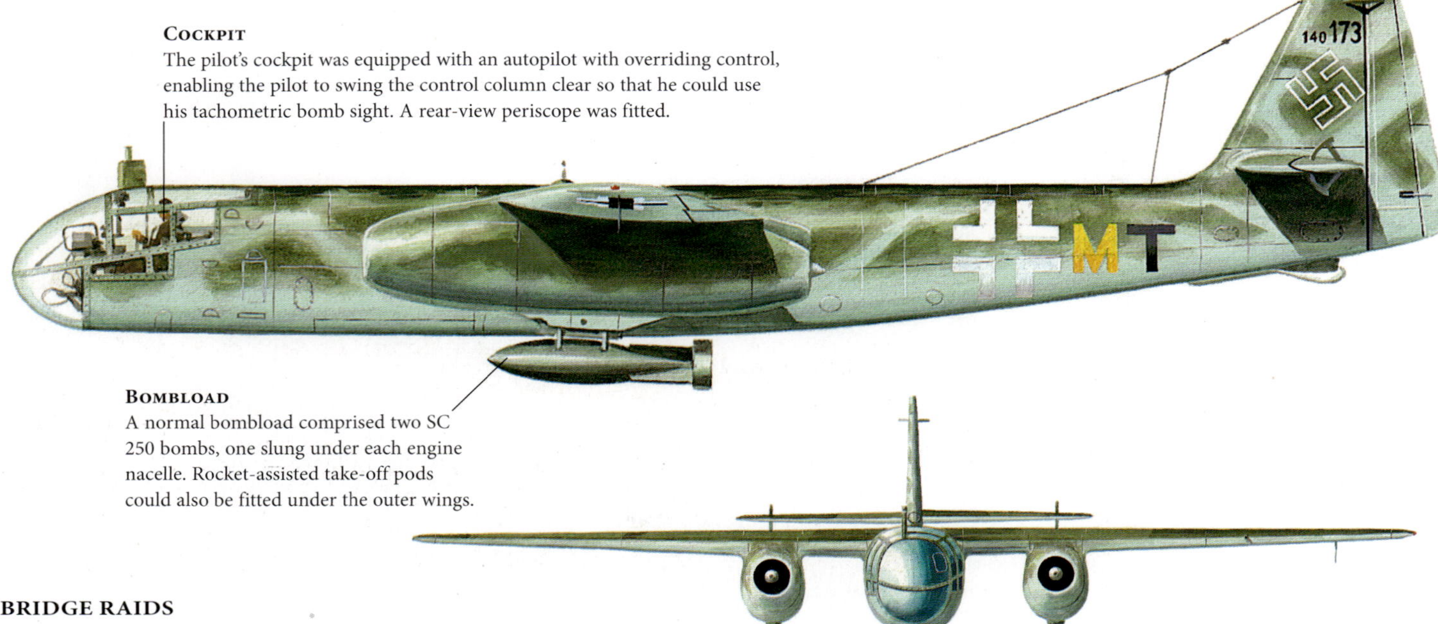

COCKPIT
The pilot's cockpit was equipped with an autopilot with overriding control, enabling the pilot to swing the control column clear so that he could use his tachometric bomb sight. A rear-view periscope was fitted.

BOMBLOAD
A normal bombload comprised two SC 250 bombs, one slung under each engine nacelle. Rocket-assisted take-off pods could also be fitted under the outer wings.

BRIDGE RAIDS
The Arado 234B-2 was the world's first jet bomber, and followed the unarmed Ar 234B-1 reconnaissance version into service. The Ar 234B-2 flew its first combat missions with KG 76 during the German offensive in the Ardennes in December 1944. The jet bombers were extremely active in the early weeks of 1945, one of their most notable missions being a 10-day series of attacks on the Ludendorff Bridge at Remagen.

AR 234C
The more powerful Ar 234C variant was fitted with four BMW 004B turbojets, but only 19 of these had been completed when the war ended.

Messerschmitt Me 163 Komet (1944)

TYPE • *Rocket fighter* COUNTRY • *Germany*

SPECIFICATIONS (Me 163B-1a)

Dimensions:	Length: 5.85m (19ft 2in); Wingspan: 9.4m (30ft 7in); Height: 2.76m (9ft)
Weight:	Empty 1,900kg (4,190lb); Maximum take-off 4,310kg (9,502lb)
Powerplant:	1,700kg (3,749lb) thrust Walter 109-509A-2 rocket motor
Max Speed:	955km/h (593mph)
Range:	35.5km (22 miles)
Service ceiling:	12,100m (39,690ft)
Crew:	1
Armament:	2 x 30mm (1.18in) cannon

The remarkable and revolutionary Me 163 rocket-powered interceptor was yet another example of German ingenuity, but despite its impressive (albeit short-range) performance, it came too late to alter the course of the air war.

Right: Taking off on its jettisonable trolley, the Komet would climb to 9,760m (32,020ft). Time to the Komet's operational ceiling of 12,100m (39,690ft) was a mere 3.35 minutes. Maximum powered endurance was eight minutes.

Cockpit
The pilot sat in a primitive cockpit with a reflector gunsight for aiming the cannon. Rear visibility was limited, but this was of little importance when the rocket motor was running.

Armament
The Komet was armed with a pair of MK 108 30mm (1.18in) cannon in the wingroots, which gave it a mighty punch. But the high closing speed of the aircraft gave the pilot approximately three seconds of firing time.

Me 163B-1a
'White 54' was an Me 163B-1a assigned to 14./Jagdgeschwader 400 based at Brandis in Germany in late 1944 and early 1945.

ROCKET INTERCEPTOR

The Me 163 was perhaps the most radical and futuristic of World War II aircraft. The concept of the short-endurance, high-speed interceptor powered by a rocket engine was certainly valid. Bereft of a horizontal tail and with an extremely short fuselage, the Me 163 was propelled by two extremely volatile liquids. By May 1944, these tiny aircraft were devastating US bomber formations.

ME 163B
Messerschmitt Me 163B VD+E was the eighth prototype aircraft of the Me 163B. A unique rocket-powered fighter, the Me 163 Komet was derived from a long period of studies into tailless sailplane design undertaken by Alexander Lippisch, beginning around 15 years before the outbreak of the war.

Mitsubishi Ki-67 *Hiryu* (1944)

TYPE • *Bomber* **COUNTRY** • *Japan*

Although classed as a heavy bomber, the Mitsubishi Ki-67 was roughly in the same class as the Martin B-26 Marauder. An excellent design, it appeared too late to have a decisive effect on the Pacific air war.

SPECIFICATIONS (Ki-67-I)

Dimensions:	Length: 18.70m (61ft 4.25in); Height 7.70m (25ft 3in)
Weight:	Empty 8,650kg (19,073lb); Maximum take-off 13,765kg (30,347lb)
Powerplant:	2 × 1,417kW (1,900hp) Mitsubishi Ha.104 18-cylinder radials
Max Speed:	537km/h (334mph) at 6,000m (19,685ft)
Range:	3,800km (2,361 miles)
Service ceiling:	9,470m (31,069ft)
Crew:	6–8
Armament:	1 × 20mm (0.79in) cannon and 5 × 12.7mm (0.50in) machine guns; bomb or torpedo load of 1,070kg (2,359lb)

This page: The Ki-67 Hiryu *(Flying Dragon) was unquestionably the best bomber to see service with the Imperial Japanese Army, combining excellent performance with good defensive firepower.*

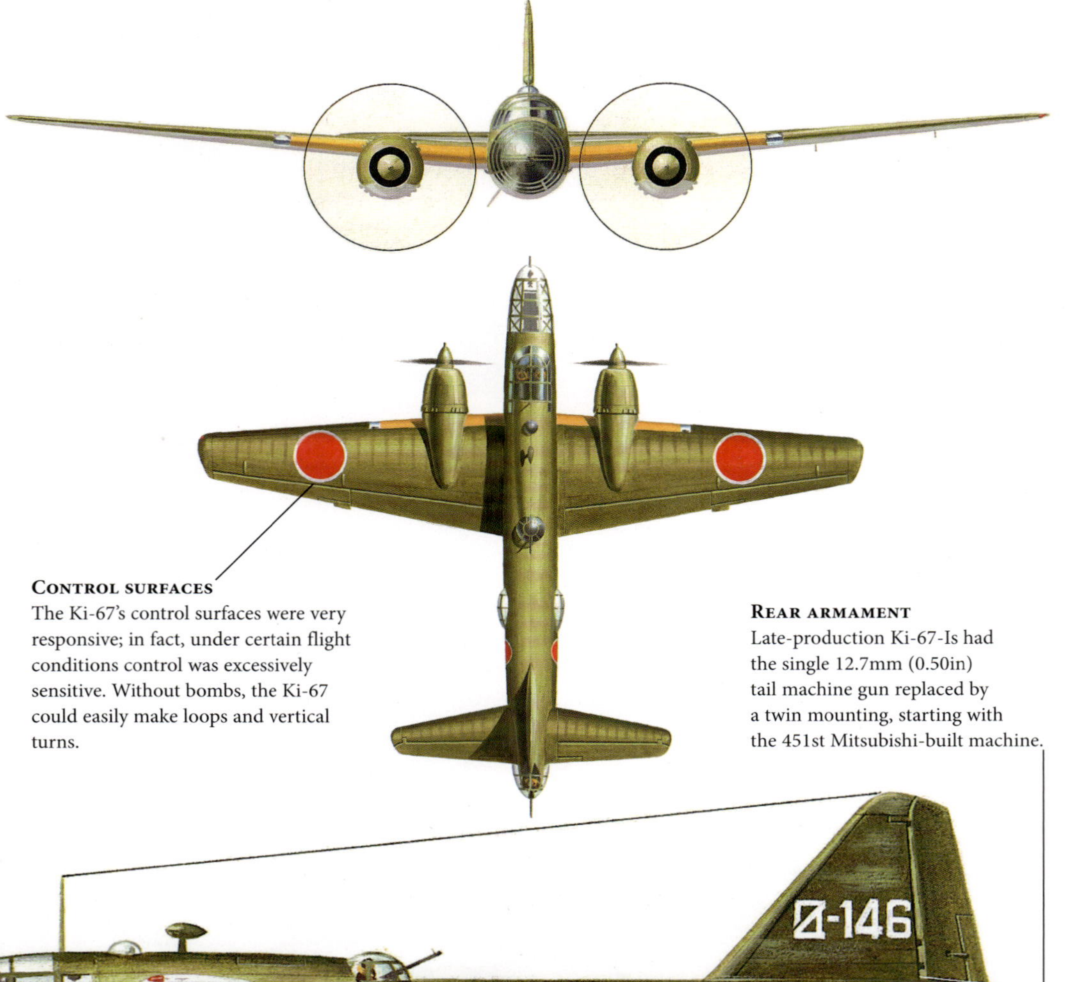

Control surfaces
The Ki-67's control surfaces were very responsive; in fact, under certain flight conditions control was excessively sensitive. Without bombs, the Ki-67 could easily make loops and vertical turns.

Rear armament
Late-production Ki-67-Is had the single 12.7mm (0.50in) tail machine gun replaced by a twin mounting, starting with the 451st Mitsubishi-built machine.

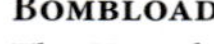

Bombload
The *Hiryu* had a respectable bombload and a capacious weapons bay. Ki-67s operated in China, and in 1945, using Iwo Jima as a refuelling point, they made repeated attacks on B-29 bases in the Marianas.

MANY VARIANTS

Production of the Ki-67 totalled 698 aircraft, serving as bombers, torpedo bombers, reconnaissance aircraft, interceptors, ground-attack aircraft and suicide bombers. The interceptor was designated Ki-109 and was not a success, only 22 being completed.

KI-67
As a torpedo bomber, the Ki-67 was particularly active during the air-sea battle off Formosa in October 1944 and during the American landings on Okinawa in 1945.

Yokosuka MXY-7 Ohka (1944)

TYPE • *Anti-ship aircraft* **COUNTRY** • *Japan*

SPECIFICATIONS

DIMENSIONS:	Length: 6.07m (19ft 10.33in); Wingspan: 5.12m (16ft 9.5in); Height 1.16m (3ft 9.5in)
WEIGHT:	Empty 440kg (970lb); Loaded 2,140kg (4,718lb)
POWERPLANT:	3 x solid-fuel Type 4 Mk 1 Model 20 rockets with total thrust of 800kg (1,764lb)
MAX SPEED:	927km/h (576mph) in terminal dive
RANGE:	37km (23 miles)
SERVICE CEILING:	Not applicable
CREW:	1
ARMAMENT:	1 x 1,200kg (2,646lb) warhead

The notion of a pilot deliberately sacrificing his life as an act of war was foreign to western minds in World War II, but the Japanese brought the concept to grim reality in their Special Attack Corps, whose ultimate development was the *Ohka* (Cherry Blossom) suicide bomb.

Above: The wingspan of the Ohka Model 22, an improved version, was less than that of the Model 11, and its warhead limited to 600kg (1,323lb). This version was to have been powered by a turbojet engine.

WARHEAD
The initial version of the Ohka was fitted with a 1,200kg (2,646lb) warhead and was designed to be transported to within a few miles of its target in the bomb bay of a specially modified Navy Type 1 Attack Bomber Model 24J (G4M2e).

CONSTRUCTION
The tiny aircraft was built of wood and non-critical metal alloys, and great care was taken in planning to enable it to be mass-produced by unskilled labour.

ROCKET MOTORS
After release from its parent aircraft, the Ohka accelerated towards its target under the power of three solid-propellant rockets mounted in the tail, which could be fired either singly or together.

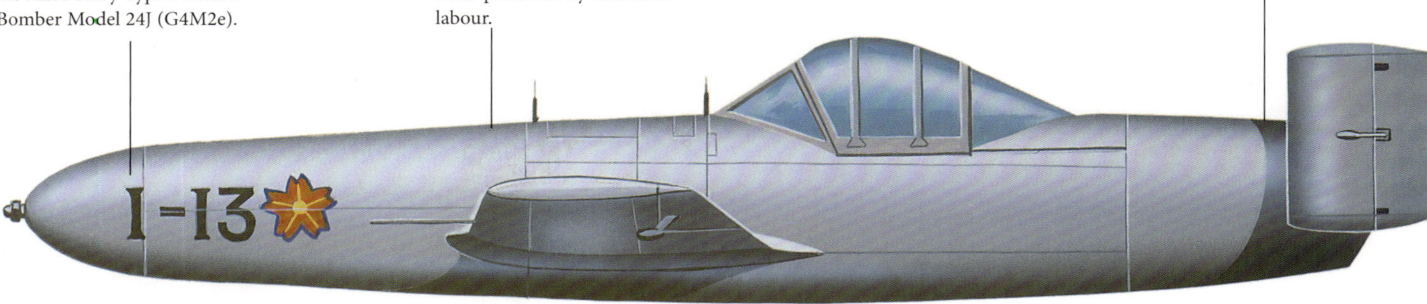

COMBAT SUCCESS

First success for the Ohka came on 1 April 1945, when Ohkas damaged the US battleship *West Virginia* and three transport vessels. The first ship to be destroyed by an Ohka was the destroyer *Mannert L. Abele*, lost off Okinawa on 12 April. Several further versions of the Ohka were proposed, including the turbojet-powered Model 33, but none materialized in operational form before the end of the war.

DEFEATED JETS
US personnel inspect captured Ohka jets at the end of the war. In objective military terms the concept of the Ohka was sound enough, but the lack of suitable carrier aircraft meant the weapon consistently failed to break through the dense Allied fighter screen.

Lavochkin La-7 (1944)

TYPE • *Fighter* **COUNTRY** • *Soviet Union*

SPECIFICATIONS	
Dimensions:	Length: 8.6m (28ft 3in); Wingspan: 9.8m (32ft 2in); Height: 2.54m (8ft 4in)
Weight:	Maximum take-off 3,400kg (7,496lb)
Powerplant:	1,380kW (1,850hp) Shvetsov M-82FN 14-cylinder air-cooled radial
Max Speed:	661km/h (411mph)
Range:	635km (395 miles)
Service ceiling:	10,450m (34,280ft)
Crew:	1
Armament:	2 × cowl-mounted 20mm (0.79in) ShVAK cannons or 3 × 20mm Berezin B-20 cannons; up to 200kg (440lbs) bombload

The ultimate in Soviet WWII piston-engined fighters, the Lavochkin La-7 was produced in large numbers during the last year of the war, and was popular with its pilots. The La-7 maintained the hard-won Soviet air superiority over the Eastern Front.

This page: Both the La-5FN and La-7 were powered by the Shvetsov M-82FN radial engine. It had two banks of 14 cylinders each, with two-stage supercharging and direct fuel injection.

Cockpit
The pilot's relatively high position in the cockpit gave good all-round visibility apart from when taxiing, when the forward view was obscured by the long fuselage nose.

Synchronized guns
The La-7 carried two cannon in its upper fuselage decking, synchronized to fire through the propeller disc.

Design
The Lavochkin La-7 was not a new design, but represented a relatively modest aerodynamic refinement of the proven La-5 airframe.

AIR SUPERIORITY
Although able to carry a 100kg (220lb) bomb under each wing, the La-7s exemplary air-to-air abilities meant that virtually all of the 5,753 built saw service exclusively in the air superiority role. A further 582 two-seaters were built for training as the La-7UTI. As well as Soviet service, the La-7 saw brief service with Czech forces shortly before the end of the war.

AERIAL VIEW
The La-7 was a tough, capable fighter that soon proved its worth as Soviet forces gained offensive momentum on the Eastern Front.

Tupolev Tu-2 (1944)

TYPE • *Bomber* **COUNTRY** • *Soviet Union*

SPECIFICATIONS (Tu-2S)

DIMENSIONS:	Length: 13.8m (45ft 3in); Wingspan: 18.86m (61ft 11in); Height: 4.13m (13ft 7in)
WEIGHT:	Maximum take-off 11,768kg (25,944lb)
POWERPLANT:	2 × 1,380kW (1,850hp) Shvetsov ASh-82 14-cylinder air-cooled radial piston engines
MAX SPEED:	528km/h (328mph)
RANGE:	2,020km (1,260 miles)
CEILING:	9,000m (30,000ft)
CREW:	4
ARMAMENT:	2 × fixed forward-firing 20mm (0.79in) ShVAK cannon in the wings, 3 × 12.7mm (0.5in) flexibly mounted rear-firing Berezin UBT machine guns in rear cockpit canopy, dorsal and ventral hatches; up to 3,000kg (6,600lbs) bombload

The Tu-2 was tailored to meet a requirement for a high-speed bomber or dive-bomber, with a large internal bombload and speed similar to that of a single-seat fighter. It was produced in torpedo, interceptor and reconnaissance versions.

Below: The Tu-2 series (here a Tu-2S) was optimized for mass production by a demand for the minimum number of parts, the use of very accurate drawings and tooling to ensure accuracy of fit, and pre-prepared wiring looms and pipe runs.

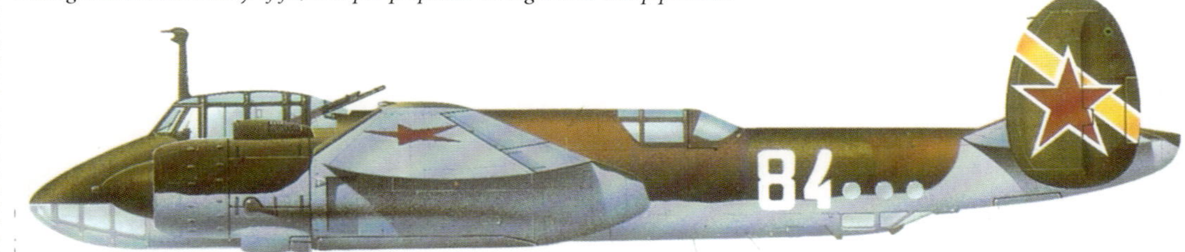

ENGINES
The Tu-2S was powered by two 1,380kW (1,850hp) Shvetsov ASh-82FN radial piston engines.

FLIGHT DECK
The pilot and navigator sat back-to-back on the flight deck. The prominent mast attached to the canopy contained the pitot tube, as well as acting as an attachment for the radio aerial.

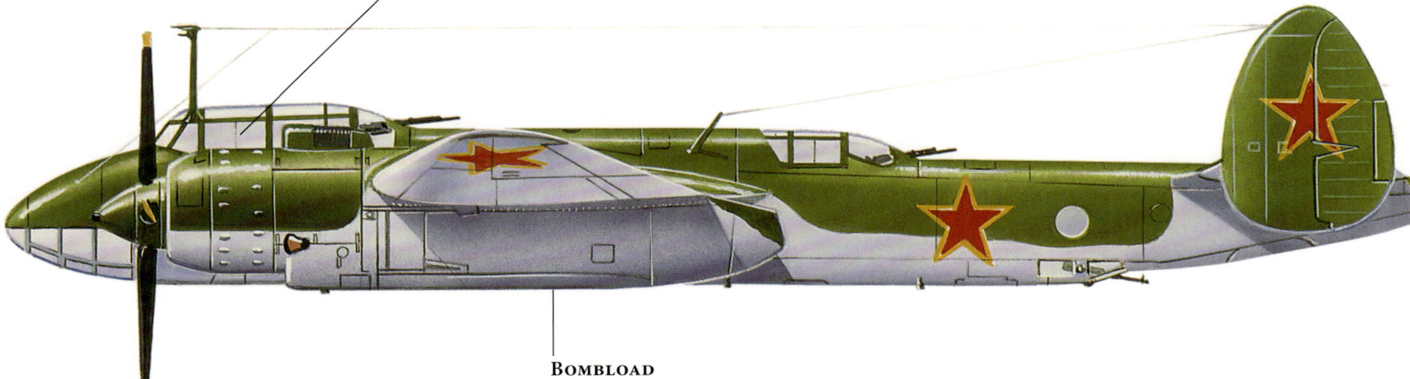

BOMBLOAD
The long bomb bay could accommodate a single 1,000kg (2,205lb) bomb or several smaller weapons. Additional large bombs were carried under the wing roots on racks, while smaller bombs could be carried on five racks on each side, outboard of the engine.

POST-WAR SERVICE

After World War II, the Tu-2 proved to be an ideal test vehicle for various powerplants, including the first generation of Soviet jet engines. Production continued after 1945, some 3,000 aircraft eventually being delivered to various Soviet Bloc air forces. The last Tu-2 model was the ANT-68, a high-altitude version that saw limited service as the Tu-10.

PROTOTYPE
Samolyet 103U was the second Tu-2 prototype, with a raised canopy and lengthened fuselage with accommodation for a fourth crew member, firing a ShKAS from a lower rear fuselage hatch. The 103U had provision for 10 RS rockets underwing.

Hawker Tempest (1944)

TYPE • *Fighter* **COUNTRY** • *United States*

SPECIFICATIONS

Dimensions:	Length: 10.26m (33ft 8in); Wingspan: 12.5m (41ft 0in); Height: 4.9m (16ft 1in)
Weight:	6,142kg (13,540lb) loaded
Powerplant:	1 × 1,626kW (2,180hp) Napier Sabre IIA H-type piston engine
Max speed:	686km/h (426mph)
Range:	2,092km (1,300 miles)
Service ceiling:	10,975m (36,000ft)
Crew:	1
Armament:	4 × 20mm (0.8in) Hispano cannon in wings; up to 907kg (2,000lb) disposable stores (either 2 bombs or 8 rockets for ground attack role)

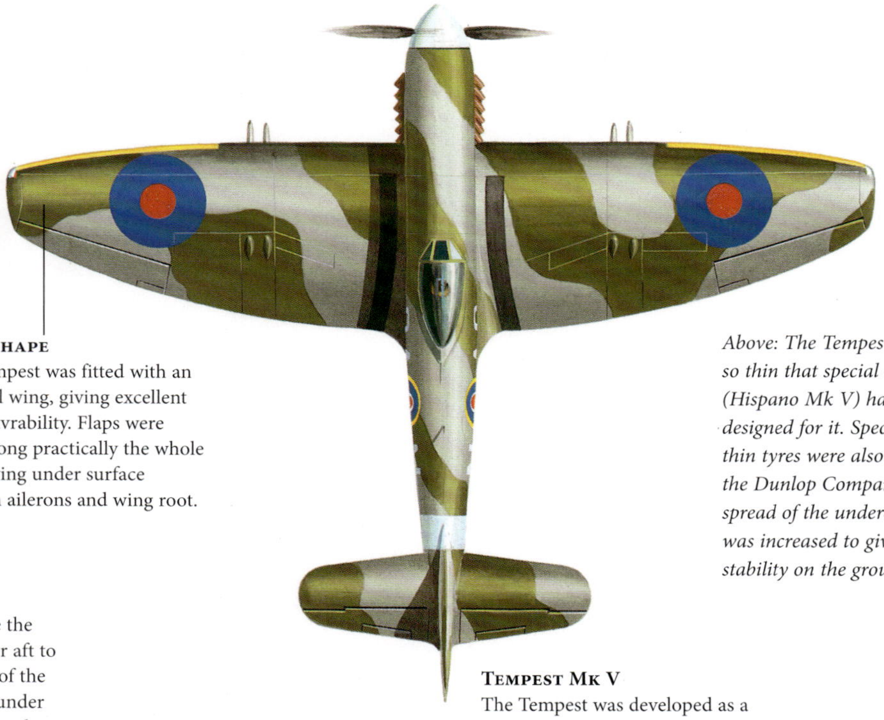

A product from the drawing board of Hawker's prestigious designer, Sir Sydney Camm, the Tempest was built to remedy the problems of the earlier Typhoon. The resulting design proved to be the RAF's best low-/medium-altitude fighter.

Wing shape
The Tempest was fitted with an elliptical wing, giving excellent manoeuvrability. Flaps were fitted along practically the whole of the wing under surface between ailerons and wing root.

Above: The Tempest's wing was so thin that special cannon (Hispano Mk V) had to be designed for it. Special ultra-thin tyres were also devised by the Dunlop Company, and the spread of the undercarriage was increased to give extra stability on the ground.

Cockpit
In redesigning the Typhoon to produce the Tempest, the cockpit was moved further aft to improve pilot visibility, which was one of the Typhoon's shortcomings. The pilot sat under a one-piece sliding canopy, its size reduced to the absolute minimum in order to reduce drag.

Tempest Mk V
The Tempest was developed as a refined version of the Typhoon, with a thinner wing and longer fuselage. It was one of the fastest fighters of the war, and entered service with No. 486 (NZ) Sqn (illustrated) in January 1944.

V-1 KILLER
In April 1944 the Tempest was the fastest and most powerful fighter in the world, and in the summer of 1944 it was thrown into battle against the V-1 flying bombs that were now being launched against London. Between them, the Tempest squadrons claimed the destruction of nearly 600 V-1s. The Tempest squadrons subsequently moved to the Continent with 2nd TAF and became a potent addition to the Allies' striking power.

TEMPEST MK V
No. 501 Squadron received the Tempest Mk V in August 1944. During this month it absorbed the FIU and became the only Tempest unit specializing in night operations against the V-1 flying-bombs.

Dornier Do 335 Pfeil (1944)

TYPE • *Heavy fighter* **COUNTRY** • *Germany*

SPECIFICATIONS (Do 335A-0)

Dimensions:	Length: 13.85m (45ft 5in); Wingspan: 13.8m (45ft 3in); Height: 5m (16ft 5in)
Weight:	Maximum take-off 9,600kg (21,164lb)
Powerplant:	2 × 1,417kW (1,900hp) Daimler-Benz DB 603E-1 V-12 liquid-cooled piston engines
Max Speed:	763km/h (474mph)
Range:	1,395km (867 miles)
Service Ceiling:	11,400m (37,400ft)
Crew:	1
Armament:	1 × engine-mounted 30mm (1.18in) MK 103 cannon plus 2 × 20mm (0.79in) MG 151/20 cannon; up to 1,000kg (2,200lb) bombload in internal weapons bay

A tandem-engine layout had been patented by Claudius Dornier in 1937 and led to feasibility trials with the Göppingen Gö 9 research aircraft designed by Ulrich Hütter and built by Schempp-Hirth in 1939.

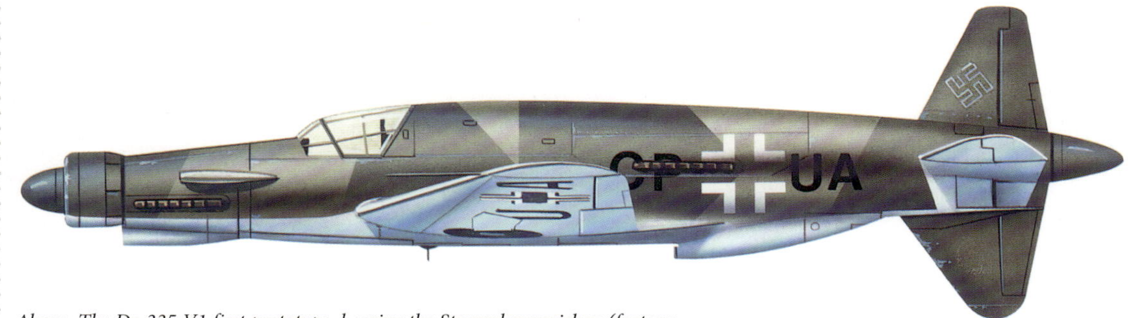

Above: The Do 335 V1 first prototype, bearing the Stammkennzeichen (factory radio code) of CP+UA, was flown on 26 October 1943 by test pilot Flugkapitän Hans Dieterle.

Layout
By placing the engines at the front and rear rather than on the wings, the power was delivered inline with the fuselage, increasing the aircraft's manoeuvrability.

Do 335A-0
Here is the seventh of 10 pre-production aircraft, most of which went to Eprobungskommando (EK) 335 for evaluation.

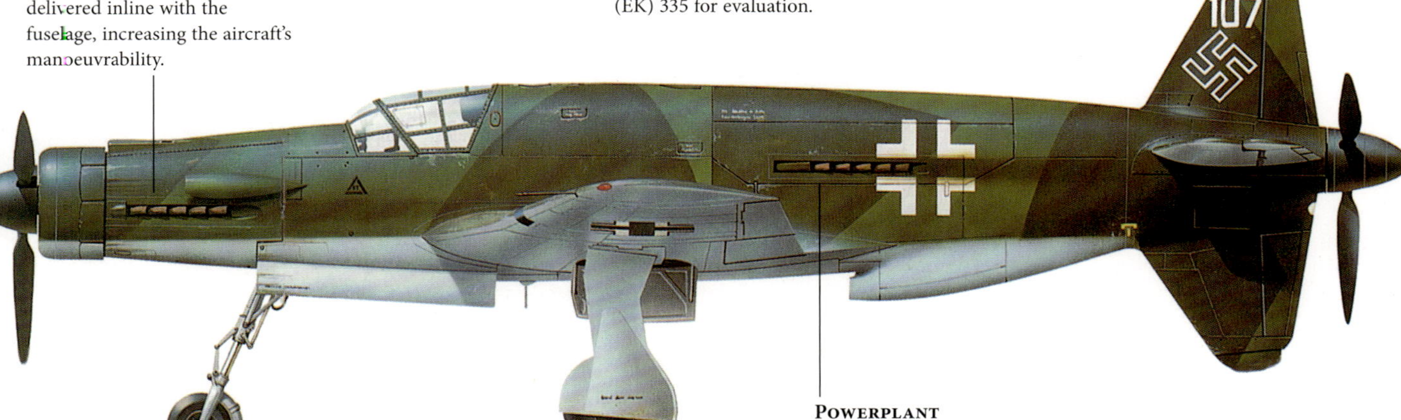

Powerplant
Power was provided by two 1,342kW (1,800hp) Daimler-Benz DB 603 engines, one in the rear fuselage driving a three-bladed pusher propeller and the other in the nose with a three-bladed tractor propeller.

VARIANTS
The full-production Do 335A-1 first appeared in late autumn 1944, with the definitive DB 603E-1 engine. A single example of the unarmed Do 335A-4 reconnaissance version was also completed. The Do 335A-6 was next to appear, as the first of a night-fighter version. The last of the Do 335 variants were the Do 335A-10 and A-12 trainers, both of which featured the second cockpit that was introduced on the Do 335A-6 night-fighter.

DO 335A-0
After nine prototypes, work began on a pre-production batch of 10 Do 335A-0 aircraft, the first of which was ready for evaluation in mid-1944.

Nakajima Ki-84 Hayate (1944)

TYPE • *Fighter* **COUNTRY** • *Japan*

The finest Japanese fighter to see large-scale service during World War II, the Ki-84 offered a superb balance of agility, speed and firepower and it was afforded highest-priority production status as Japan's military was forced on to the defensive from 1944.

SPECIFICATIONS (Ki-84-Ia)

Dimensions:	Length: 9.92m (32ft 6.5in); Wingspan: 11.24m (36ft 10.5in); Height: 3.39m (11ft 1.5in)
Weight:	3,890kg (8,576lb) maximum take-off
Powerplant:	1 × 1,416kW (1,900hp) Nakajima Ha-45 radial piston engine
Max speed:	631km/h (392mph) at 6,120m (20,080ft)
Range:	2,168km (1,347 miles)
Service ceiling:	10,500m (35,350ft)
Crew:	1
Armament:	2 × 12.7mm (0.5in) machine guns; 2 × 20mm cannon; 2 × 250kg (551lb) bombs on underwing racks

Above: Here we see a Ki-84-Ia (bottom) and Ki-84-Ib (top) with the typically colourful late-war fin markings.

Armament
This initial production model featured an armament of two 12.7mm (0.5in) machine guns in the fuselage and two wing-mounted 20mm (0.79in) cannon.

Ki-84-Ia
A Ki-84 operated by the 183rd *Shimbu-Tai* (Special Attack Group) based at Tatebayashi, Japan, in August 1945.

Layout
The aircraft was a conventional low-wing monoplane with its tailplane set characteristically ahead of its vertical tail surfaces.

HIGH PERFORMANCE

Even when not involved in accidents, the reliability of production Ki-84s seldom matched those of the hand-built service trials machines. For the Allies, however, this was a fortunate turn of events as, immediately upon entering service, the Hayate had proved to be a potent foe with performance closely matching that of the most advanced Allied aircraft (F4U, P-38J/L, P-47D, P-51D) and superior to types such as the F6F Hellcat.

PRE-PRODUCTION
This is one of the initial pre-production batch of 83 Ki-84s, seen at Tachikawa in August 1943 from where it was flown by the Army Air Arsenal as a service trials aircraft. All IJA aircraft wore large *Hinomaru* ('meatball') insignia.

Kawasaki Ki-100 (1945)

TYPE • *Fighter* **COUNTRY** • *Japan*

SPECIFICATIONS (Ki-100-1a)

DIMENSIONS:	Length: 8.82m (28ft 11.25in); Wingspan: 12m (39ft 4.5in); Height: 3.75m (12ft 3.63in)
WEIGHT:	Empty: 2,525kg (5,567lb); Maximum take-off: 3,495kg (7,705lb)
POWERPLANT:	1 × 1,118kW (1,500hp) Mitsubishi Ha-112-II two-row radial engine
MAX SPEED:	580km/h (360mph)
RANGE:	2,000km (1,367 miles)
SERVICE CEILING:	11,000m (36,090ft)
CREW:	1
ARMAMENT:	2 × 20mm (0.79in) forward-firing cannon in forward fuselage; 2 × 12.7mm forward-firing MGs in wing; external bombload of 500kg (1,102lb)

Problems with the Ki-61-II forced Kawasaki to store a number of airframes for lack of the appropriate engines and, in an inspired piece of improvisation, combined the Ki-61-II Kai airframe with the Mitsubishi Ha-112-II radial engine.

Below: The Ki-100-1b was a new-build aircraft that utilized the airframe that had been developed for the Ki-61-III. This featured a cut-down rear fuselage and an all-round 'bubble' canopy.

KI-100-1A
An aircraft of the 3rd Chutai, 59th Sentai. Chutai colours were blue for the 1st, red for the 2nd and yellow for the 3rd.

POWERPLANT
For all its bulk, the new radial installation, as a result of lower weight and therefore reduced wing and power loadings, produced much improved handling characteristics and only slightly reduced performance compared to the Ki-61-II.

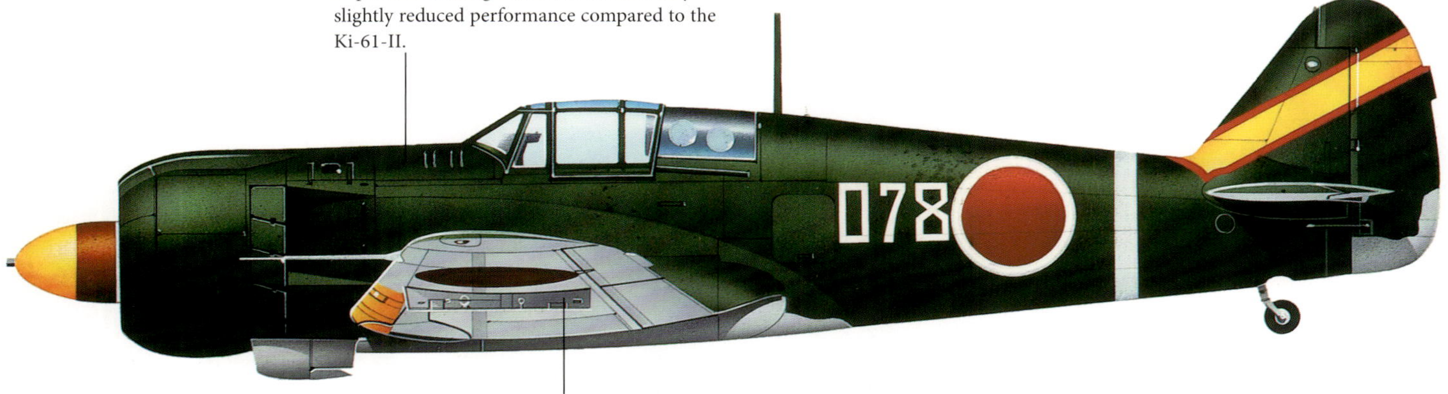

ARMAMENT
The Ki-100 was armed with two 12.7mm (0.5in) machine guns, two 20mm (0.79in) cannon plus two 250kg (551lb) bombs on underwing racks.

RAPID DEVELOPMENT

In November 1944, Kawasaki was instructed to adapt the Ki-61-II Kai aircraft to mount the 1,119kW (1,500hp) Mitsubishi Ha-112-II 14-cylinder radial. This was accomplished in less than 12 weeks. The new aircraft, redesignated the Ki-100, first flew in prototype form on 1 February 1945. Accelerated flight tests were followed by an order to adapt all the engineless Ki-61-II Kais, and 272 Ki-100-Ias were delivered to home-based fighter units between March and June 1945.

KI-100-1 OTSU
From March 1945, there were two subvariants of the Ki-100, including the Ki-100-1b (Ki-100-1 Otsu) with an all-round vision canopy, as seen here. In service the Ki-100 was hailed by pilots and ground crew as the best and most reliable Imperial Japanese Army fighter of the war.

Heinkel He 162 (1945)

TYPE • *Jet fighter* **COUNTRY** • *Germany*

SPECIFICATIONS (He 162A-2)	
DIMENSIONS:	Length: 9.05m (29ft 8in); Wingspan: 7.2m (23ft 7in); Height: 2.6m (8ft 6in)
WEIGHT:	Maximum take-off 2,803kg (6,180lb)
POWERPLANT:	1 × BMW-109-003E-1 Sturm axial flow jet engine, 800kg (1,764lb) static thrust
MAX SPEED:	889km/h (553mph) at sea level (with emergency boosted thrust)
RANGE:	975km (606 miles)
SERVICE CEILING:	12,000m (39,000ft)
CREW:	1
ARMAMENT:	2 × 20mm (0.78in) MG 151/20 cannon

The Heinkel He 162 'Salamander' was developed and flown in an extraordinarily short period of time, the factory requiring only 38 days between receiving detailed drawings and the maiden flight of a prototype on 6 December 1944.

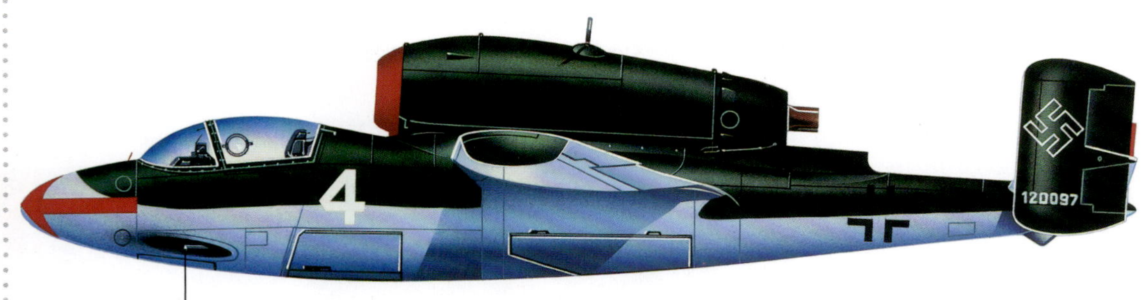

Above: He 162A-1 'White 4' was operated by a front-line unit, 1./Jagdgeschwader 1, based at Leck. This particular aircraft, Werknummer 120097, was captured by the Allies and tested by the RAF after the war.

ARMAMENT
While the He 162 V6 prototype had been armed with a pair of 30mm (1.18in) MK 108s, intended for the He 162A-1, in the He 162A-2 the armament was switched back to two MG 151/20s, with a consequent reduction in airframe vibration.

HE 162 V-10
The tenth prototype Salamander was flown by the Erprobungskommando 162, the test unit for the type, based at Rechlin in Germany.

POWERPLANT
The power plant was a single BMW 003 turbojet, mounted directly above the high-mounted wing, giving the aircraft a top-heavy profile.

FIRST FLIGHT
On its first flight, this turbojet-engined interceptor demonstrated a top speed of 840km/h (520mph). The aircraft had been devised by Nazi officials as a *Volksjäger* ('people's fighter'). From the outset, it was intended to be small, agile enough to outmanoeuvre numerically superior Allied fighter opposition, and requiring only limited skilled labour and minimal scarce strategic materials for its manufacture.

HE 162A-2
This He 162A-2 was allocated to 3. Staffel/JG 1 at its Leck base in May 1945. By this time, the 50 aircraft had been reorganized into one single Gruppe: Einsatz-Gruppe I./JG 1; many pilots from other fragmented units at Leck were absorbed by this new Gruppe.

Focke-Wulf Ta 152 (1945)

TYPE • *Fighter* COUNTRY • *Germany*

SPECIFICATIONS (Ta 152H-1)

DIMENSIONS:	Length: 10.82m (35ft 6in); Wingspan: 14.44m (47ft 5in); Height: 3.36m (11ft)
WEIGHT:	Maximum take-off 4,727kg (10,421lb)
POWERPLANT:	1 x 1,530kW (2,050hp) Junkers Jumo 213E-1 liquid-cooled piston engine
MAX SPEED:	760km/h (472mph)
RANGE:	2,000km (1,200 miles)
SERVICE CEILING:	15,100m (49,500ft) with GM-1 boost
CREW:	1
ARMAMENT:	1 x 30mm (1.18in) MK 108 cannon; 2 x 20mm (0.8in) MG 151/20 cannon

Reflecting Kurt Tank's overall design responsibility for the Fw 190 family, and a change in fighter aircraft designations ordered by the Reichsluftfahrtministerium (German Air Ministry), the Ta 152 name was introduced for the ultimate 'long nose' development of the series.

Below: The Ta 152C-1's DB 603 engine had its air inlet on the left, diverging from the H-1's Jumo engine, with its inlet situated on the right.

DERIVATIVES
Other derivatives of the basic Ta 152 included the Ta 152S-1, a two-seat conversion trainer, and the Ta 152E that was planned as a reconnaissance fighter version of the Ta 152C, again with the standard wing.

TA 152H-1
The H variant of the Focke-Wulf Ta 152 was a high-altitude fighter. Small numbers were operated by Jagdgeschwader 301, primarily to provide cover over Messerschmitt Me 262 bases while the jets were taking off and landing.

ARMAMENT
C-series Ta 152s boasted four MG 151/20 guns, enhancing firepower but compromising speed and agility. Meanwhile, H-series variants prioritized speed, featuring only two cannons and the hub-firing weapon for bomber interception.

AIRFRAME INNOVATION
The Ta 152 was developed from the Fw 190D, with the aim of further improving performance at high altitude through a series of airframe refinements. The basic structure was inherited from the 'Dora', except for the flap and undercarriage systems which featured hydraulic, rather than electrical, actuation. Production versions comprised the Ta 153C-1 with standard wing, the C-2 with improved radio equipment and the C-3 with revised armament.

CAPTURED TA 152H-1
This captured Ta 152H-1 has now been given a new RAF livery. Long-span wings gave the Ta 152H, the final variant of the Fw 190/Ta 152 family, a superb high-altitude performance. Fortunately for the Allies, only a few made it into action.

Junkers Ju 88 Mistel (1945)

TYPE • *Composite bomber* **COUNTRY** • *Germany*

SPECIFICATIONS (Mistel 1)

Dimensions:	Length: 14.36m (47ft 1in); Wingspan: 20.08m (65ft 9in); Height: 13.97m (45ft 9in)
Weight:	33,780kg (74,472lb) loaded
Powerplant:	1 x 993kW (1,332hp) DB 601E radial piston engine; 2 x 1,051kW (1,410hp) Jumo 211 J-1 radial piston engines
Max Speed:	380km/h (236mph)
Range:	650km (1,025 miles)
Service ceiling:	10,655m (34,950ft)
Crew:	1
Armament:	3,800kg (8,380lb) hollow-charge device

The *Mistel* (Mistletoe) was a composite aircraft consisting of an explosives-packed surplus bomber flown to a launch point by a fighter mounted on top. Mistels were inaccurate and caused negligible damage on the few occasions they were used.

Above: This Mistel 1 combination comprised a Ju 88A-4 with a Bf 109F-2. The warhead was typically a 3,800kg (8,380lb) hollow-charge device with a long standoff fuse, fitted in the nose of the bomber. The ideal release point was judged to be around 1,000 metres (0.6 miles) from the target.

Mistel 2
Operated by an unknown unit, this Mistel 2 combination consisted of a Ju 88G-1 and an Fw 190F-8/U3.

Torpedo
The Fw 190F-8/U3 aircraft also carried a 1,400kg (3,100lb) BT-1400 heavy torpedo, which relied on forward momentum rather than propulsion to travel through water.

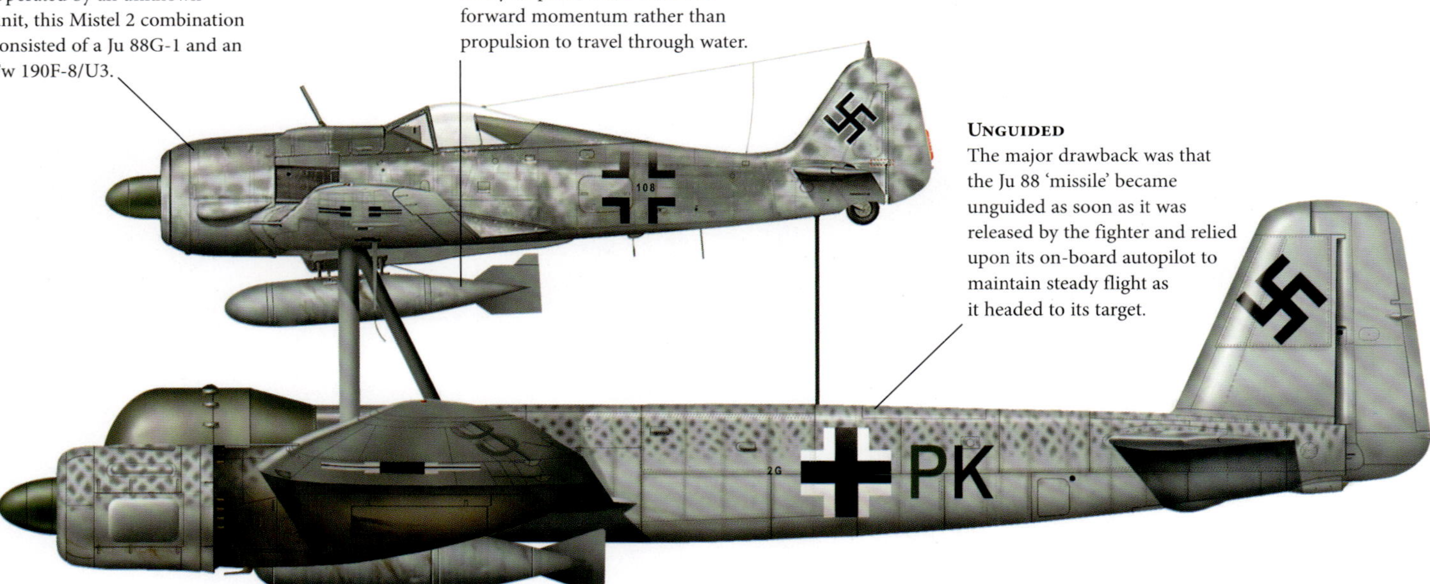

Unguided
The major drawback was that the Ju 88 'missile' became unguided as soon as it was released by the fighter and relied upon its on-board autopilot to maintain steady flight as it headed to its target.

COMPOSITE AIRCRAFT
Several different composites were completed, including the Mistel 1 that was used operationally and which combined the Ju 88A-4 with a Bf 109F; it was also available in a training version as the Mistel S-1. The Mistel 2 (and S-2) combined the Ju 88G-1 with an Fw 190A-8 or Fw 190F-8/U3, while the Mistel 3a (and S-3a) combined the Ju 88A-6 with an Fw 190A-6.

OPERATIONS
The Mistel was first put to operational use on 24/25 June 1944, when the composite aircraft were launched in an attack against Allied blockships that formed part of the Mulberry temporary harbour in the Baie de la Seine, France. In total, around 250 of these composite aircraft were completed, but the lack of terminal guidance ensured that their effectiveness was limited.

Douglas A-26 Invader (1945)

TYPE • *Bomber* **COUNTRY** • *United States*

SPECIFICATIONS (A-26B)

DIMENSIONS:	Length: 15.62m (51ft 3in); Wingspan: 21.34m (70ft 0in); Height: 5.56m (18ft 3in)
WEIGHT:	15,876kg (35,000lb) loaded
POWERPLANT:	2 × 1,491kW (2,000hp) Pratt & Whitney radial piston engines
MAX SPEED:	571km/h (355mph)
RANGE:	2,253km (1,400 miles)
SERVICE CEILING:	6,735m (22,100ft)
CREW:	3
ARMAMENT:	6 × 12.7mm (0.5in) MGs (two each in nose, dorsal and ventral positions); up to 1,814kg (4,000lb) of bombs

The Invader fought in more wars than any other aircraft type. Americans flew it in World War II, Korea and Vietnam, while other air arms took the A-26 to war in Indo-China, Algeria, Biafra, Cuba, the Congo and a dozen other conflicts.

Above: An A-26 Invader makes a bombing run over Germany, dropping a stick of bombs on the Siegfried Line in the winter of 1945.

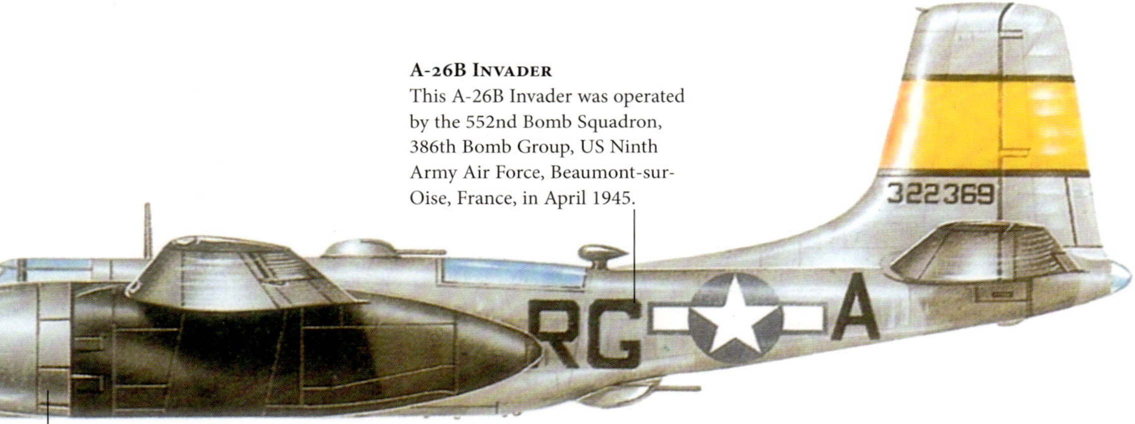

FIREPOWER
The A-26B had six 12.7mm (0.5in) machine guns in the nose (later increased to eight), remotely controlled dorsal and ventral turrets, each with two 12.7mm (0.5in) guns and up to 10 more 12.7mm (0.5in) guns in underwing and underfuselage packs.

A-26B INVADER
This A-26B Invader was operated by the 552nd Bomb Squadron, 386th Bomb Group, US Ninth Army Air Force, Beaumont-sur-Oise, France, in April 1945.

FAST BIRD
Heavily armoured and able to carry up to 1,814kg (4,000lb) of bombs, the A-26B, with its maximum speed of 571km/h (355mph) at 4,570m (15,000ft) was the fastest Allied bomber of World War II.

INITIAL PROBLEMS
Pilots were delighted with the aircraft's manoeuvrability and ease of handling, but the A-26 began life with a needlessly complex and fatiguing instrument array, a weak nose gear that collapsed easily, and an early cockpit canopy that was difficult to hold in the 'open' position for bail-out. Time and attention resolved these problems, and A-26 pilots took pride in mastering a demanding but effective bombing machine.

553RD BOMBARDMENT SQUADRON, USAAF
The A-26 Invader was conceived by Douglas as a replacement for the DB-7 (A-20) series. Similar in configuration to its predecessor, but more streamlined, powerful and better armed, the Invader reached the European theatre in late 1944.

Tanks & Armoured Fighting Vehicles

During World War II, armour became the true vanguard of land warfare. Experiments in armoured doctrine and AFV technology during the inter-war years mainly produced new generations of fast but light tanks, often little more than tracked machine-gun carriers. While light tanks remained useful for reconnaissance and infantry support, the experience of wartime combat shifted the focus more onto armour (for survivability) and firepower (for long-range killing), producing landmark medium and heavy tanks such as the American M4 Sherman, Soviet T-34 and German Tiger I. In the European and Mediterranean theatres and on the Eastern Front, the mass and the firepower of available armour often decided the outcome of battles.

T-34 ATTACK
Soviet T-34 tanks prepare to launch an attack, moving in a close formation. The T-34 represented a very Soviet way of thinking about armour; it was a rugged, capable tank, often less sophisticated than German tanks, but produced in vast numbers.

TK/TKS Tankette (1931)

TYPE • *Tankette* COUNTRY • *Poland*

SPECIFICATIONS (TK)

DIMENSIONS:	Length: 2.58m (8ft 5in); Width: 1.78m (5ft 10in); Height: 1.32m (4ft 4in)
WEIGHT:	2.43 tonnes (2.39 tons)
ENGINE:	29.8kW (40hp) Ford A 4-cylinder petrol
SPEED:	46km/h (28.58mph)
RANGE:	200km (124 miles)
ARMOUR:	4–8mm (0.16–0.31in)
ARMAMENT:	1 x 7.92mm (0.31in) Hotchkiss wz.25 MG
CREW:	2

The TK tankette was developed from the Carden-Loyd carrier series. The TKS closely resembled the TK tankette but incorporated a number of improvements, including thicker armour, a more powerful engine and wider tracks.

Right: Around 300 TK tankettes were built between 1931 and 1933.

RECONNAISSANCE TANK
This TKS tankette belonged to the Reconnaissance Tank Squadron, 62nd Armoured Battalion, Podolska Cavalry Brigade, of the Poznan Army.

MACHINE GUN
The 7.92mm (0.31in)Hotchkiss wz.25 machine gun was supplied with 2000 rounds of internally stored ammunition. The weapon had a cyclical rate of 450–600rpm.

ARMOUR
On the TKS, the maximum depth of armour was raised to 10mm (0.39in), sufficient to stop many small-arms rounds but providing little protection against heavier cannon shells.

POLISH ARMOUR

The first Polish-crewed tanks were 150 Renault FT-17s that were delivered in 1919–20. In 1929, modified versions of Vickers-Carden-Loyd tankettes (TK and TKS) and Vickers six-ton tanks (generally known as the Vickers E) were adopted after extensive trials. These formed the mainstay of the *Bron Pancerna*, or Armoured Forces, an organization set up in 1930 to administer all tanks, armoured cars and armoured trains.

TK TANKETTE PROTOTYPE
This trials photograph taken during the 1930s shows the diminutive size of the TK tankette. By 1935, a total of nine armoured battalions had been formed in Poland, although these were actually deployed in company units (usually of 13 vehicles each), tasked with supporting infantry divisions and cavalry brigades.

BT-5 (1932)

TYPE • *Fast tank* **COUNTRY** • *Soviet Union*

SPECIFICATIONS

DIMENSIONS:	Length: 5.58m (18ft 4in); Width: 2.3m (7ft 7in); Height: 2.25m (7ft 5in)
WEIGHT:	10.2 tonnes (11.24 tons)
ENGINE:	298kW (400hp) M5 petrol
SPEED:	100km/h (62mph)
RANGE:	200km (124 miles)
ARMOUR:	6–14mm (0.24–0.55in)
ARMAMENT:	1 x 37mm (1.46in) Model 1930 gun; 1 x 7.62mm (0.3in) DT MG
CREW:	3

A prevalent feature of 1930s Soviet tank doctrine was the significance placed on the fast tank concept. Such vehicles relied on their impressive speed and mobility to survive, while conducting rapid exploitation-style operations.

Left: BT-5TU Command Tank. Finished in a two-tone olive and off-white camouflage scheme, this vehicle is the command variant of the BT-5 with its distinctive rail antenna.

MAIN ARMAMENT
The main weapon on the BT-5 light tank was improved to a 45mm (1.8in) gun from the 37mm (1.46in) gun of the earlier BT-2. The weapon was heavier than those of most opposing light tanks.

SLOPED ARMOUR
During the 1930s, the Soviets began developing tanks with sloped armour, maximizing the protection afforded with such designs. The BT-5 had a design influence over the later T-34 medium tank.

SUSPENSION
The BT tanks' impressive speed stemmed from their use of the radical American-designed Christie suspension system. This featured vertical-coil springs that supported the large non-bogie road wheels around which the track ran tightly, making upper track return rollers unnecessary.

SOVIET DOCTRINE
Soviet armoured warfare doctrine emphasized mobility to rapidly exploit success. The Soviet light tanks of the 1930s partially fulfilled this role, but they lacked sufficient firepower, protection and mobility. Therefore, the Soviets designed the BT fast tank series. These were marginally heavier and better armed than the light tanks, but were also much faster, which boosted survivability.

BT-7 TANKS IN MANOEUVRES
BT-7 tanks on manoeuvre in the late 1930s. The BT-7 variant was introduced in 1935, with thicker armour and a new Mikulin M-17T engine, which was a licensed copy of a BMW engine.

T-26 (1933)

TYPE • *Light tank* **COUNTRY** • *Soviet Union*

SPECIFICATIONS

Dimensions:	Length: 4.9m (16ft 1in); Width: 3.4m (11ft 2in); Height: 2.31m (7ft 6in)
Weight:	9.4 tonnes (10.36 US tons)
Engine:	67kW (90hp) GAZ-T26 4-cylinder petrol
Speed:	35km/h (22mph)
Range:	130km (81 miles)
Armour:	6–15mm (0.24–0.59in)
Armament:	1 x 45mm (1.77in) 20K Model 1932 (later Model 1934) L/46 gun; 1 x coaxial 7.62mm (0.3in) DT Model 1929 machine gun
Crew:	3

After the T-26 Model 1931, the next version of the T-26 was the Model 1933, which introduced several key modifications. The most obvious difference was that in this design the twin turrets of the Model 1931 were replaced by a large, centrally positioned single turret.

Left: As Model 1933 production unfolded, the Soviets introduced minor improvements, thus creating the new Model 1936. This variant featured the improved 20K Model 1934 gun.

Armament
This variant featured an improved version of the 45mm (1.77in) gun, the Model 1938, along with enhanced optical equipment.

T-26 Model 1938
The Model 1938 featured a redesigned conical turret. The variant retained the Model 1936's hull, however.

Armour
While this variant of the T-26 had the same 15mm (0.59in) plates as before, the turret's side plates were sloped, thus enhancing the tank's survivability.

BRITISH ADAPTATION

In the late 1920s Red Army planners launched a programme to re-equip the USSR's tank arm. In common with many other nations, the USSR decided upon an infantry support tank for its non-cavalry units and, after attempting without success to develop a new design, decided on the mass production of a British commercial model, the Vickers six-ton Type E light tank. This was named the T-26, and the first examples of the British model arrived during 1930, receiving the designation T-26A-1.

KNOCKED-OUT T-26
The Model 1933 was the most widely produced of all Soviet tanks before 1941, with about 5500 built. They were, inevitably, lost in great numbers during the German Operation *Barbarossa*; here we see a T-26 knocked-out and abandoned.

T-37 (1933)

TYPE • *Amphibious light tank* **COUNTRY** • *Soviet Union*

During the 1930s, the Soviets produced more amphibious light tanks than any other nation; most of these modestly armed and lightly armoured tanks succumbed during the 1941 Axis invasion of the Soviet Union.

SPECIFICATIONS (T-37A)

Dimensions:	Length: 3.75m (12ft 4in); Width: 2.1m (6ft 11in); Height: 1.82m (6ft)
Weight:	3.2 tonnes (3.53 US tons)
Engine:	30kW (40hp) GAZ-AA petrol
Speed:	35km/h (22mph)
Range:	185km (115 miles)
Armour:	3–10mm (0.12–0.39in)
Armament:	1 x 7.62mm (0.3in) DT Model 1929 machine gun
Crew:	2

Left: This T-37A tank has been finished in a mottled winter disruptor camouflage scheme, with dappled whitewash applied over its standard olive green finish.

Turret armament
The tank featured a tall cylindrical turret atop the hull and centre-right that mounted a 7.62mm (0.3in) DT machine gun.

Engine
The T-37A was powered by a 30kW (40hp) GAZ-AA engine that delivered a power-to-weight ratio of 9.4kW/tonne (11.4hp/ton).

T-37A profile
This side view ably illustrates both the tank's distinctive track arrangement and its large cylindrical turret.

CONFIGURATION

The tall T-37A had a distinctive flat and shallow hull superstructure that sloped slightly upwards from the front of the vehicle towards the back. The T-37A featured a track suspension system based on a large frontal drive-wheel, two pairs of medium-sized horizontally sprung six-spoke bogie road wheels, a large six-spoke rear idler wheel and two track-top return rollers per side; the rear idler was positioned lower than the front driving-wheel.

CROSSING RIVER
To enable it to cross water, the tank incorporated several specialized features, such as hollow track float-covers, rear mudguard 'water wings' and a retractable three-bladed propeller.

L-3/35 Lf Flamethrower (1933)

TYPE • *Tankette* COUNTRY • *Italy*

SPECIFICATIONS

Dimensions:	Length: 3.2m (10ft 6in); Width: 1.42m (4ft 8in); Height: 1.3m (4ft 3in)
Weight:	3.3 tonnes (3.64 US tons)
Engine:	1 x Fiat 4-cylinder petrol, developing 30kW (40hp)
Speed:	42km/h (26mph)
Range:	120km (75 miles)
Armour:	6–14mm (0.24–0.55in)
Armament:	1 x flamethrower
Crew:	2

The Carro Veloce 29 (CV 29) began a series of Italian tankettes, later redesignated the L3. Basic L3s featured a Breda 13.2mm (0.52in) machine gun, but the L3/35 Lf flamethrower version was the most prevalent of the series.

Right: A front view of the L3/35 Lf shows the offset flame gun to the right and the driver's hatch to the left.

Armour
The vehicle had a maximum armour depth of 14mm (0.55in) on the hull, sufficient to stop small-arms rounds and shell splinters.

Powerplant
The L3/35F was powered by a Fiat 4-cylinder petrol, developing 30kW (40hp) and giving a top speed of 42km/h (26mph).

Flamethrower
The flamethrower barrel extended from the left of the barbette, and the L3/35 Lf had its own internal flame-liquid tank.

DESIGNATION

In 1929, the Italian Army purchased 25 British Carden-Loyd Mk VI tankettes for use in mountainous terrain. Subsequently, Fiat-Ansaldo produced their own version, the Carro Veloce 29 (CV 29), which began an entire series of Italian tankettes. In 1938, the variants numbered CV 3/33 and 3/35 were redesignated as L3.

FLAMETHROWER TANK
The most basic L3s were armed with a Breda 13.2mm (0.52in) machine gun, but the L3/35Lf flamethrower version became the most prevalent of the L3 series.

15cm sIG 33 (1933)

TYPE • *Self-propelled gun* **COUNTRY** • *Germany*

The 15cm sIG 33 (*schweres Infanterie Geschütz* 33) was the standard German heavy infantry gun from the late 1920s until the end of the war, but was always plagued by problems caused by its excessive weight.

SPECIFICATIONS (sIG 33 Ausf B)

Dimensions:	Length: 4.67m (15ft 4in); Width: 2.06m (6ft 9in); Height: 2.8m (9ft 2in)
Weight:	8.5 tonnes (9.37 US tons)
Engine:	Maybach NL38TR petrol, 75kW (100hp)
Speed:	40km/h (25mph)
Range:	140km (87 miles)
Armour:	5–13mm (0.2–0.51in)
Armament:	1 x 15cm (5.9in) *schweres Infanterie Geschütz* 33
Crew:	4

Left: A 15cm sIG 33 (Sf) auf Panzerkampfwagen I Ausf B of the 5th Panzer Division, Russia, 1943.

sIG 33 Bison II
The Bison II was a more practical design using an enlarged Panzer II hull. It was designed in 1940, but only 12 were completed in November/December 1941 for combat trials in North Africa.

Reliability
The sIG Bison II type was ill suited to the desert conditions of North Africa and suffered frequent breakdowns due to over-heating.

Armament
Both variants of the sIG 33 were armed with the powerful but relatively short-ranged 15cm (5.9in) *schweres Infanterie Geschütz* 33 with 10 rounds.

INFANTRY GUN

The sIG 33 was the largest-calibre weapon ever designed as an infantry gun. Development began in 1927, but the design was not approved for service until 1933, and it was 1936 before the first units received their guns. Although it was officially described as a gun, the sIG 33 was in fact a howitzer with a short (L/11) barrel, which restricted maximum range to 4700m (5140yd).

SIG 33 IN FRANCE
The vehicle's overall height, apparent here, was 2.8m (9ft 2in), and its high centre of gravity made it unstable, limiting its off-road mobility. The chassis was also badly overloaded, resulting in frequent breakdowns.

Char de Cavalerie 38H / Hotchkiss H-39 (1934)

TYPE • *Light tank* **COUNTRY** • *France*

SPECIFICATIONS

Dimensions:	Length: 4.23m (13ft 10in); Width: 1.96m (6ft 5in); Height: 2.16m (7ft 1in)
Weight:	12.1 tonnes (11.9 tons)
Engine:	90W (120hp) Hotchkiss 1938 6-cylinder petrol
Speed:	36.5km/h (22.7mph)
Range:	150km (93 miles)
Armour:	Up to 45mm (1.77in) thick
Armament:	1 x 37mm (1.5in) SA-38 gun, plus 1 x coaxial 7.5mm (0.295in) MG
Crew:	2

Fitted with the 37mm (1.46in) SA 38 L/33 gun, the H-39 was a respectable performer by the standards of the 1930s. Its only major disadvantage was that the commander had to work the gun as well as lead the vehicle.

Right: Germans parade captured H-39s in Paris following the fall of France in June 1940.

Armament
From April 1940, the L/35 37mm (1.5in) SA-38 gun was fitted to all new vehicles, with older H-39s being refitted with the weapon as supplies became available.

Performance
The H-39 could achieve a maximum speed of 36.5km/h (22.7mph), its reasonable pace fitting with French armoured cavalry doctrine of the 1930s.

Armour
The H-39 was a further development of the H-38 with armour up to 45mm (1.77in) thick. By 1940, however, even this increased thickness was largely obsolete against German armour.

ORIGINS

The origins of this tank can be found in 1933 with a requirement for a light infantry tank to partner the SOMUA S-35. The Hotchkiss prototype of 1934 was then rejected by the infantry in favour of the Renault R-35, but was then accepted by the cavalry as the Char de Cavalerie 35H before finally being accepted by the infantry as the Char H-35. The type thereby became one of the most important French tanks of the day. After 400 had been produced from 1936 onward, the basic model was supplemented by the H-38 and then the H-39.

GERMAN SERVICE
This American soldier is examining an H-39 that had been pressed into German service, as indicated by the *Panzerfaust* anti-tank weapon strapped to the side of the vehicle's hull.

Type 95 Kyugo (1934)

TYPE • *Light tank* **COUNTRY** • *Japan*

SPECIFICATIONS

DIMENSIONS:	Length: 4.38m (14ft 4in); Width: 2.06m (6ft 9in); Height: 2.18m (7ft 2in)
WEIGHT:	7.4 tonnes (8.16 US tons)
ENGINE:	1 x 6-cylinder air-cooled Mitsubishi NVD 6120 diesel powerplant generating 89kW (120hp)
SPEED:	45km/h (28mph)
RANGE:	250km (156 miles)
ARMOUR:	6–14mm (0.24–0.55in)
ARMAMENT:	Main: 1 x 37mm (1.45in) Type 98 gun; Secondary: 2 x 7.7mm (0.303in) Type 97 machine guns
CREW:	3

When the Japanese Army called for a light or cavalry tank to support its infantry operations, the resulting Type 95 performed capably until confronted with the superior firepower and armour protection of Soviet, American and British tanks.

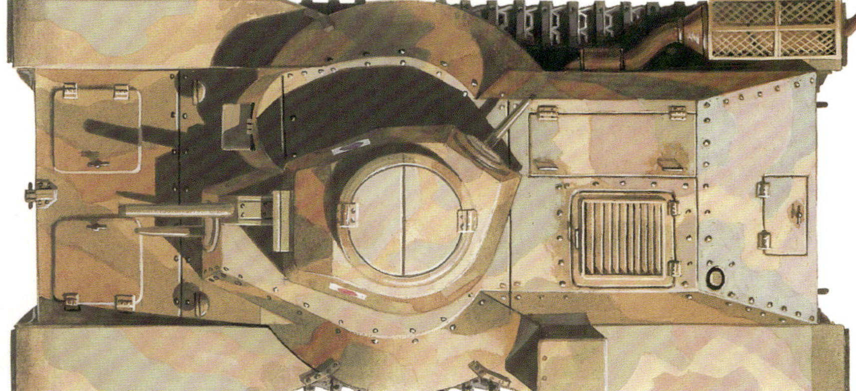

Left: The high silhouette of the Type 95 tank was especially pronounced from the rear, adding to the tank's vulnerability in combat. Both the heavier weapons of enemy tanks and high-velocity anti-tank guns deployed by opposing armies took their toll on the Type 95.

TURRET
Characteristic of Japanese tank designs of the 1930s, the Type 95 turret was irregularly shaped and quite cramped, requiring the commander to direct the crew in combat and operate the main 37mm (1.45in) gun.

MAIN ARMAMENT
The Type 95 light tank initially mounted the Type 94 37mm (1.45 in) gun; however, its disappointing penetrating power resulted in a transition to the Type 98 37mm (1.45in) gun, which supplied greater muzzle velocity.

ENGINE
A six-cylinder air-cooled Mitsubishi NVD 6120 diesel engine powered the Type 95 light tank, producing 89kW (120hp). It was mounted at the rear of the hull.

PRODUCTION RUN
Identified popularly as the Ha-Go, Ke-Go or Kyugo, the Type 95 was initially produced by Mitsubishi Heavy Industries. Subsequently, Hitachi Industries, the Kokura Arsenal, Kobe Seikosho, and the Sagami Arsenal each produced the tank in quantity. Although there is some dispute as to the length of the Type 95 production run, either until 1943 or the actual end of World War II, up to 2300 are believed to have been completed.

CAMOUFLAGE
Camouflage was important to the survival of a Kyugo crew; the thin armour of the Type 95, only 6–14mm (0.24–0.55in) thick, offered little protection against the standard main weapons of opposing tanks.

Universal Carrier (1934)

TYPE • *Armoured personnel carrier* **COUNTRY** • *United Kingdom*

SPECIFICATIONS

Dimensions:	Length: 3.76m (12ft 4in); Width: 2.11m (6ft 11in); Height: 1.63m (5ft 4in)
Weight:	4.06 tonnes (4 tons)
Engine:	63.4kW (85hp) Ford V8 8-cylinder petrol
Speed:	52km/h (32mph)
Range:	258km (160 miles)
Armour:	7–10mm (0.28–0.39in)
Armament:	1 x 14mm (0.55in) Boys anti-tank rifle, plus 1 or 2 x 7.7mm (0.303in) Bren MGs
Crew:	3

Almost invariably referred to as the 'Bren Carrier', the Universal Carrier was an indispensable addition to the British Army's light armour, used extensively for resupply, casualty evacuation and a thousand and one other tasks.

Right: A Universal Carrier of the 16th Australian Infantry Brigade, 6th Australian Division, Western Desert Force.

AA MOUNT
The Universal Carrier was subjected to a vast range of modifications by its users. This example has a Bren gun carried on the AA mount, supplementing the hull-mounted gun.

ENGINE
The Universal Carrier's engine – a 63.4kW (85hp) Ford V8 eight-cylinder petrol – was placed in the centre of the vehicle, making life deafening for the driver and gunner.

ITALIAN THEATRE
This Universal Carrier served with the 2nd Battalion Rifle Brigade, 61st Infantry Brigade 6th Armoured Division in the Italian theatre.

RECONFIGURATION
The Bren Carrier was more correctly known as the Universal Carrier. Produced between 1934 and 1960, it was used to transport a two-man Bren-gun team, although initially it was designed as a gun tractor for a Vickers machine gun and a four-man crew. It was the advent of the Bren gun in 1936 that put paid to its gun-tractor days. Configured with the Bren, the vehicle could provide lightly armoured mobile fire support.

VICKERS ARMED CARRIERS
The Universal Carrier was found to be useful in every theatre of war in which the British fought. The 13-vehicle Carrier Platoons in each infantry battalion were always in demand for a bewildering variety of tasks. These carriers are armed with Vickers heavy machine guns.

SdKfz 222 (1934)

TYPE • *Armoured car* **COUNTRY** • *Germany*

SPECIFICATIONS

DIMENSIONS:	Length: 4.8m (14ft 9in); Width: 1.95m (6ft 5in); Height: 2m (6ft 7in)
WEIGHT:	4.877 tonnes (5.38 US tons)
ENGINE:	Horch/Auto Union 108 8-cylinder petrol, 66kW (89hp)
SPEED:	80km/h (50mph)
RANGE:	300km (187 miles)
ARMOUR:	14.5–30mm (0.6–1.2in)
ARMAMENT:	1 × 20mm (0.79in) KwK 30 or KwK 38L/55 plus 1 × coaxial 7.92mm (0.31in) MG34 machine gun with 1050 rounds
CREW:	3

The SdKfz 222 was a more powerfully armed development of the SdKfz 221 wheeled vehicle fitted with an enlarged open-topped turret mounting a 2cm (0.79in) KwK 30 automatic cannon and a coaxial 7.92mm (0.31in) MG34 machine gun.

Left: An SdKfz 222 of the 21st Panzer Division, Deutsches Afrikakorps, deployed to Libya in autumn 1941.

ARMAMENT
This Leichter *Panzerspähwagen* SdKfz 222 is seen here in the type's usual form, armed with a 2cm (0.79in)cannon and a 7.92mm (0.31in) MG 34 machine gun.

ADAPTATIONS
Later in the war the thickness of the front hull plates was increased from 14.5mm (0.57in) to 30mm (1.2in) and the 20mm cannon mounting was adapted to provide more elevation for use against aircraft targets.

PERFORMANCE
As well as having a maximum road speed of 85km/h (50mph), the SdKfz 222 had a fording capability of 0.6m (24in).

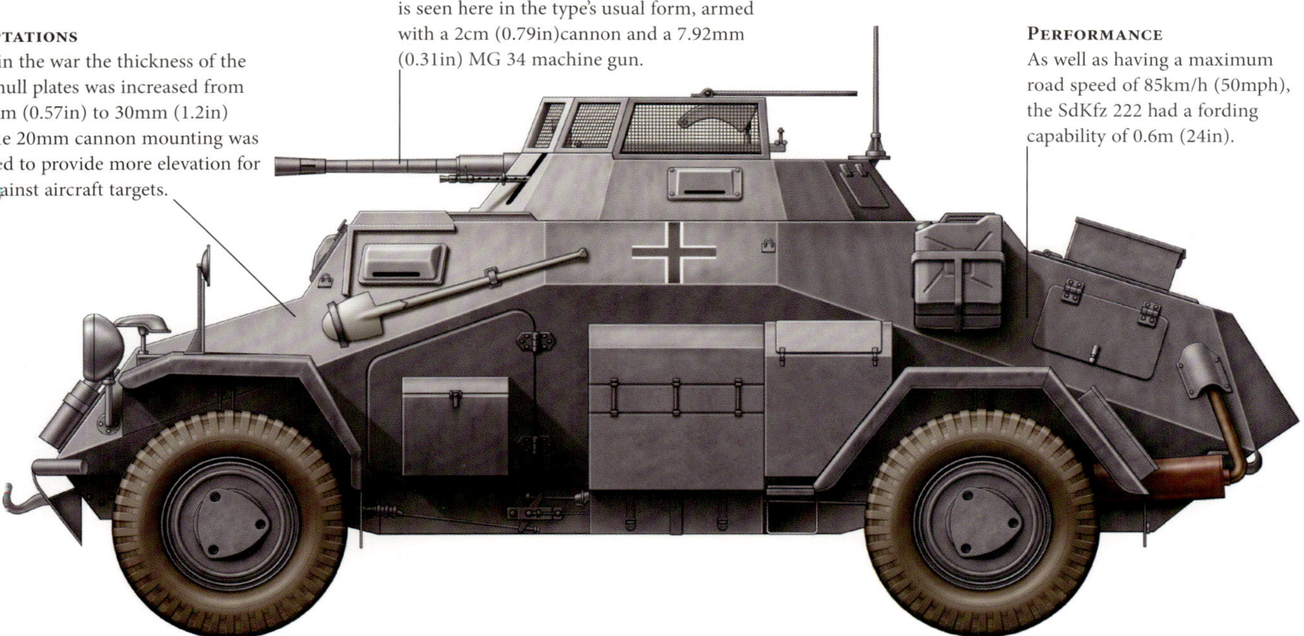

WAFFENWAGEN
From the SdKfz 221 evolved the SdKffz 222 armoured car, having a slightly larger armoured turret with an open top and the potential to mount a slightly heavier armament. The first SdKfz 222 appeared in 1938 and thereafter was adopted as the standard German armoured car for use by the new divisional reconnaissance units. The SdKfz 222 was initially referred to as a *Waffenwagen*, or weapons vehicle.

RECONNAISSANCE UNIT
Here we see a family of vehicles within a German reconnaissance unit in France in 1939/40 – SdKfz 222, 223 and 231 (8-Rad) armoured cars together with a motorcycle and sidecar.

SdKfz 231 (1934)

TYPE • *Armoured car* **COUNTRY** • *Germany*

SPECIFICATIONS

Dimensions:	Length: 5.85m (19ft 2in); Width: 2.2m (7ft 3in); Height: 2.35m (7ft 8.5in)
Weight:	8.3 tonnes (9.15 US tons)
Engine:	Magirus M206 6-cylinder petrol, 52.2kW (70hp)
Speed:	70km/h (44mph)
Range:	300km (187 miles)
Armour:	5–8mm (0.2–0.31in)
Armament:	1 x 20mm (0.79in) KwK 38 L/55 with 20 × 10-round magazines plus 1 x coaxial 7.92mm (0.31in) MG 34 machine gun with 1500 rounds
Crew:	4

These armoured cars were initially based on a Daimler-Benz 6 × 4 truck chassis modified to allow steering from either end and fitted with an armoured hull and turret.

Below: The poor cross-country performance of the 6×4 armoured cars was recognized as soon as they entered service, and an official requirement for an improved design was issued in 1934, resulting in the '8-rad' design seen here.

Cannon
The turret of the SdKfz 231 originally mounted a KwK 30 20mm (0.79in) cannon, but later the KwK 38 was fitted, with a higher rate of fire.

Front shield
Later in the war, some SdKfz 231s were fitted with a nose-mounted '*Pakschutz*', an 8mm (0.31in) armoured shield that also served as a storage bin.

Powerplant
The SdKfz 231 was powered by a Daimler-Benz, Bussing-NAG or Magirus water-cooled petrol engine developing between 45 and 60kW (60 and 80hp).

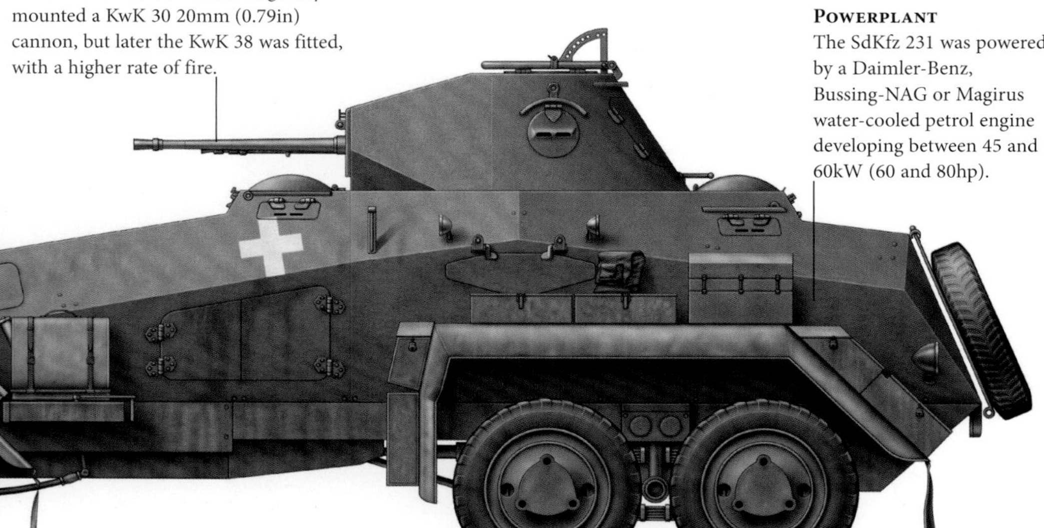

RUSSIAN ORIGINS

The SdKfz 231 6×4 heavy armoured car had its origins at the Kazan test centre established in the Soviet Union during the 1920s. At the centre the German automobile industry developed an 8×8 armoured car chassis that proved to be too expensive for further development, so a 6×4 chassis was tried instead. This model used a truck chassis as its basis, originally a Daimler-Benz product, but later Büssing-NAG and Magirus chassis engines were employed.

SDKFZ 231, SS WIKING DIVISION
The six-wheeled armoured cars were under-powered and had only limited cross-country capabilities. But when used on roads they were as good as anything else available.

Panzer I (1935)

TYPE • *Light tank* **COUNTRY** • *Germany*

SPECIFICATIONS (Ausf B)

Dimensions:	Length: 4.42m (14ft 6in); Width: 2.06m (6ft 9in); Height: 1.72m (5ft 8in)
Weight:	5.8 tonnes (6.39 US tons)
Engine:	Maybach NL38TR 6-cylinder inline petrol, 74.5kW (100hp)
Speed:	40km/h (25mph)
Range:	170km (106 miles)
Armour:	6–13mm (0.24–0.51in)
Armament:	2 x 7.92mm (0.31in) MG13 machine guns with 90 × 25-round magazines
Crew:	2

Development of the Panzer I began in 1932. The first turretless tanks were delivered to the *Kraftfahrlehrkommandos* (Motorization Training Commands) at Zossen and Ohrdurf two years later for driver training.

Left: German troops crouch behind a Panzer I during operations in Poland in 1939.

Panzer I Ausf B
Panzer I Ausf A and Ausf B models were clearly obsolescent by the time of the French campaign of 1940; by mid-1941, only 74 remained with Panzer units.

Engine
Mechanical reliability was improved compared to the Ausf A by a new transmission and the replacement of the air-cooled Krupp engine by the more powerful water-cooled six-cylinder Maybach NL38TR.

Hull
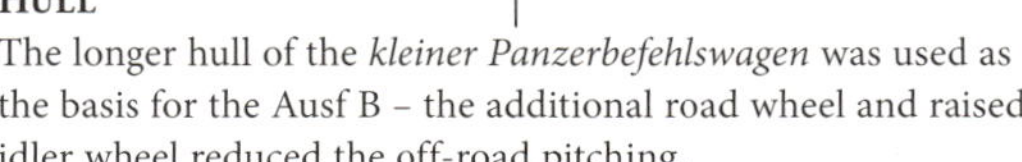
The longer hull of the *kleiner Panzerbefehlswagen* was used as the basis for the Ausf B – the additional road wheel and raised idler wheel reduced the off-road pitching.

PRODUCTION

In 1933 the German Army issued a requirement for a light armoured vehicle that could be used for training purposes. After trials, the Army Weapons Department accepted a Krupp design for further development. The Army Weapons Department gave the tank the cover name of *Landwirtschäftlicher Schlepper* (industrial tractor). The first batch of 150 vehicles was ordered, and production commenced in July 1934 under the designation PzKpfw I(MG) (SdKfz 101) Ausf A.

PANZER PRODUCTION LINE
The PzKpfw I entered service in 1935 and 675 were completed by mid-1937 when production ended to free up factory space for the PzKpfw II. Both the Ausf A and the Ausf B saw extensive service in 1939/40.

T-35 (1935)

TYPE • *Heavy tank* COUNTRY • *Soviet Union*

The first Soviet attempt to produce an effective indigenous heavy tank design – the five-turreted T-35 behemoth – produced a visually impressive vehicle ideal for propaganda purposes, yet one that was tactically disappointing.

SPECIFICATIONS (Model 1936)

DIMENSIONS:	Length: 9.72m (31ft 11in); Width: 3.2m (10ft 6in); Height: 3.43m (11ft 3in)
WEIGHT:	43 tonnes (47.4 US tons)
ENGINE:	373kW (500hp) M-17M petrol
SPEED:	30km/h (19mph)
RANGE:	150km (93 miles)
ARMOUR:	11–30mm (0.43–1.18in)
ARMAMENT:	1 x 76.2mm (3in) Model 1927/32 gun; 2 x 45mm (1.77in) 20K Model 1932 gun; 2 x 7.62mm (0.3in) DT machine gun
CREW:	11

Left: T-25 Model 1939: this modified variant incorporated sloped turret side armoured plates as well as a roof-mounted anti-aircraft machine gun.

ARMAMENT
The main weapon of the T-35 was housed in the largest of five turrets (right). Two small turrets contained 45mm (1.8in) cannon and 7.62mm (0.3in) machine guns, while two still smaller ones mounted single 7.62mm (0.3in) machine guns.

T-35 MODEL 1936
The main turret of the T-35 heavy tank was identical to that of the T-28 medium tank, as was the 76.2mm (3in) main gun.

ENGINE
The mammoth T-35 heavy tank was powered by a 12-cylinder petrol Mikulin M-17M engine generating 373kW (500hp). Critics assert that the tank was underpowered for its prodigious 45-tonne (49.6-ton) weight.

IN SERVICE

In service the T-35 was disappointing. The tank was hard to manoeuvre and it proved difficult to employ the five weapons accurately when in motion. The T-35s that were completed were mainly used for propaganda: these behemoths made a fine show during the annual May Day parades. The few T-35s that entered combat during *Barbarossa* were soon either knocked out or abandoned.

CAPTURED T-35
A German examines a captured T-35 with curiosity. Despite the formidable size of the T-35, its interior was quite cramped. The crew of either 11 or 12 were crammed into tight quarters, restricting efficiency during combat conditions.

Hotchkiss H-35 (1935)

TYPE • *Light tank* **COUNTRY** • *France*

SPECIFICATIONS

Dimensions:	Length: 4.22m (13ft 10in); Width: 1.96m (6ft 5in); Height: 2.62m (8ft 7in)
Weight:	10.6 tonnes (10.43 tons)
Engine:	55.91kW (75hp) Hotchkiss 1935, 6-cylinder petrol
Speed:	27.4km/h (17mph)
Range:	150km (93 miles)
Armour:	13–34mm (0.51–1.34n)
Armament:	1 x 37mm (1.5in) SA-18 gun, plus 1 x coaxial 7.5mm (0.295in) MG
Crew:	2

Roughly 400 H-35s were in service in September 1939. It was intended to update them with improved vision devices and the L/35 37mm (1.5in) SA-38 gun. The programme was never completed and many tanks went into action in their original configuration.

Left: The H-35 (seen here), H-38 and H-39 were all used in action in France after the German invasion of May 1940, and in general gave a moderately good account of themselves despite their indifferent armament.

Radio
This H-35 was one of the relatively small number of radio-equipped French tanks in 1940. Widespread reliance on verbal briefings and flag signals played an important part in slowing the tempo of French armoured operations.

Char de Cavalerie 35H (H-35)
This tank served with the 1re DLM/4e Cuirassiers during the battle for France, May–June 1940.

Insignia
Some French tank battalions and regiments used colourful symbols. The 4e Régiment de Cuirassiers, for example, adopted a red and white Joan of Arc badge.

ORIGINS

The original H-35 was a small vehicle with a crew of two, and it was lightly armed with only a 37mm (1.46in) short-barrel gun and a 7.5mm (0.295in) machine gun. The armour was also light, ranging in thickness from 12 to 34mm (0.47 to 1.34in). The tank was also under-powered by a Hotchkiss petrol engine delivering a maximum speed of just 28km/h (17.4mph).

ON PARADE
H-35 light tanks on parade during the 'Phoney War' period, late 1939. The small size of the vehicle is apparent from the size of the drivers' faces, framed in the open hull hatches.

Mark VIB Light Tank (1936)

TYPE • *Light tank* **COUNTRY** • *United Kingdom*

SPECIFICATIONS	
Dimensions:	Length: 4.01m (13ft 2in); Width: 2.08m (6ft 10in); Height: 2.26m (7ft 5in)
Weight:	5.08 tonnes (5 tons)
Engine:	65.6kW (88hp) Meadows 6-cylinder petrol
Speed:	56km/h (34.78mph)
Range:	200km (124 miles)
Armour:	4–15mm (0.16–0.59in)
Armament:	1 x 12.7mm (0.5in) Vickers HMG, plus 1 x coaxial 7.62mm (0.3in) Vickers MG
Crew:	3

Although the Mk VIB's nimbleness and speed made it effective as a reconnaissance vehicle, its thin armour and feeble armament caused heavy losses in France in 1940 when it was forced to act in the role of 'substitute cruiser or infantry tank'.

Right: A Mk VIB. Over 200 of these tanks were in service with the British Expeditionary Force (BEF) in France in May 1940.

Mk VIB
Mounting a 12.7mm (0.5in) and later a 15mm (0.59in) machine gun with a 7.92mm (0.31in) machine gun, the Vickers light tank was adequate only for armoured scouting.

Mobility
The chief strength of the Vickers light tanks was their mobility. The Mk VIB could move at a brisk pace, achieving a maximum speed of 56km/h (34.78mph).

Armour
All the Vickers Mk VI light tanks used a simple hull with riveted armour, which was up to 15mm (0.59in) thick.

VICKERS LIGHT TANKS

The Vickers light tanks had their origins in a series of tankettes produced by Carden-Loyd during the 1920s. One of these, the Carden-Loyd Mk VIII, acted as the prototype for the Vickers Light Tank Mk I. Only a few of these innovative vehicles were made, but they provided a great deal of insight into what would be required for later models. The Light Tank Mk I had a two-man crew and a small turret for a single 7.7mm (0.303in) machine gun.

MK VI TANKS, WESTERN DESERT
The Mk I led via the Light Tank Mk IA (better armour) to the Light Tank Mk II (improved turret and modified suspension) which appeared in 1930, and this formed the basis for later versions up to the Light Tank Mk VI. All manner of changes to items such as upgraded firepower, engine cooling and vision devices were introduced on this late mark.

Panzer II (1936)

TYPE • *Light tank* COUNTRY • *Germany*

Originally intended to bridge a gap in German tank design as heavier, more powerful machines were developed, the *Panzerkampfwagen* II became a mainstay of the German armoured force during campaigns in Poland and France.

SPECIFICATIONS (Ausf F)	
DIMENSIONS:	Length: 4.64m (15ft 3in); Width: 2.30m (7ft 6.5in); Height: 2.02m (6ft 7.5in)
WEIGHT:	9.5 tonnes (10.47 US tons)
ENGINE:	1 x Maybach 6-cylinder petrol powerplant delivering 104kW (140hp)
SPEED:	55km/h (34mph)
RANGE:	200km (125 miles)
ARMOUR	35mm (1.37in) front; 20mm (0.79in) side; 14.5mm (0.57in) rear; 5mm (0.19in) underside
ARMAMENT:	1 x 20mm (0.79in) KwK 30 cannon; 1 x 7.92mm (0.31in) MG 34 machine gun
CREW:	3

ARMOUR PROTECTION
The armour protection of the PzKpfw II was initially 11–30mm (0.43–1.2in) thick. Combat experience in the Spanish Civil War, however, and the heavy guns of Allied tanks prompted progressive increases in armour as later variants were developed.

PANZER IIC
This Panzer II Ausf C was deployed to North Africa as part of the 21st Panzer Division, Afrika Korps, in 1941.

ENGINE
The original powerplant of the PzKpfw II was a 97kW (130hp) petrol engine. When this was deemed inadequate, it was replaced by a six-cylinder Maybach petrol engine generating 104kW (140hp).

COMBAT CHARACTER
During the opening months of World War II, the PzKpfw II delivered the ideal combination of speed and firepower to execute the rapid ground advance of the German Blitzkrieg. Although its main gun was lighter than those of opposing armoured forces, particularly the French Char B1-bis, Somua S-35 and Renault R35, which mounted 75mm (2.95in), 47mm (1.85in) and 37mm (1.45in) weapons respectively, the PzKpfw II was fast and quite manoeuvrable in a cross-country advance.

PRODUCTION LINE
The Panzer II formed the backbone of the German armoured divisions during the invasion of France, with about 1000 being in front-line service. The tank was also used in the invasion of the USSR in the following year, although by that time it was obsolete.

Panzer 35(t) (1936)

TYPE • *Light tank* **COUNTRY** • *Germany/Czechoslovakia*

SPECIFICATIONS

Dimensions:	Length: 4.9m (16ft); Width: 2.1m (6ft 10in); Height: 2.35m (7ft 8in)
Weight:	11.6 tonnes (12.79 US tons)
Engine:	1 x Skoda T11 engine
Speed:	35km/h (21.7mph)
Range:	190km (118 miles)
Armour:	8–25mm (0.31–0.98in)
Armament:	1 x 3.7cm (1.46in) KwK 34(t) gun; 2 x 7.92mm (0.31in) MGs
Crew:	4

The PzKpfw 35(t) light tanks had a powerful 37mm (1.46in) gun renowned for its accuracy, and carried a mix of 72 high explosive and anti-tank rounds. After occupying Czechoslovakia, the Germans pressed it into service, adding a radio set.

Right: A Panzer 35(t) of the 6th Panzer Division, on the Eastern Front in the summer of 1941.

Turret
The one-man turret was universally condemned by the Germans. Some ammunition stowage racks were removed from the turret to make space for a loader.

Layout
As originally designed, the type had a three-man crew, with the commander in the turret and the driver and radio-operator in the hull.

Panzer 35(t)
This Panzer 35(t) is of the 1st Light Division, and is seen as it was operating in Poland in September 1939.

CZECH TANK
In October 1934 the Czech army placed an order for two prototypes of a medium tank called the S-11-a (or T-11), which were completed in the following year. This evolved into the LT vz 35. Gradually, most of the vehicle's many faults were overcome and the vehicle gained a good reputation. The Germans took over the remaining vehicles when they occupied Bohemia and Moravia in 1939, giving them the designation *Panzerkampfwagen* 35(t). A further 219 were built by Skoda for the Wehrmacht.

PANZER 35(T) IN RUSSIA
A Panzer 35(t) of the 6th Panzer Division is seen here on the advance through a burning village on the Eastern Front during the invasion of the Soviet Union in 1941.

Somua S-35 (1936)

TYPE • *Cavalry tank* **COUNTRY** • *France*

SPECIFICATIONS

Dimensions:	Length: 5.38m (17ft 7.8in); Width: 2.12m (6ft 11.5in); Height: 2.62m (8ft 7in)
Weight:	17.4 tonnes (19.2 US tons)
Engine:	V8 petrol engine
Speed:	40.7km/h (25.3mph)
Range:	Road: 230km (143 miles); Off-road: 130km (80 miles)
Armour:	20–47mm (0.79–1.85in)
Armament:	Main gun: 47mm (1.8in) gun; Coaxial: 7.5mm (0.29in) machine gun
Crew:	3

The Somua S-35 was superior in many ways to the German Panzers, mounting a powerful gun by the standards of the time. It was not any deficiency in its design that prevented the Somua S-35 from achieving its potential – it was simply overtaken by events.

Left: French Forces of the Interior (FFI) fighters pose on a Somua S-35 tank captured and marked with the emblem of the FFI in August 1944 in Paris.

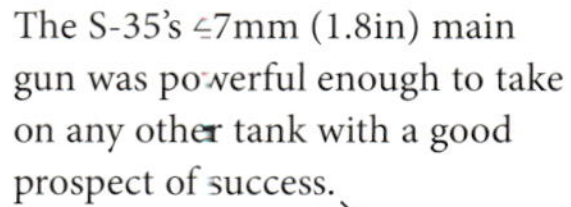

Main gun
The S-35's 47mm (1.8in) main gun was powerful enough to take on any other tank with a good prospect of success.

Side hatch
Lack of turret hatches forced the commander to exit the tank and position himself on the upper surface when not 'buttoned up'.

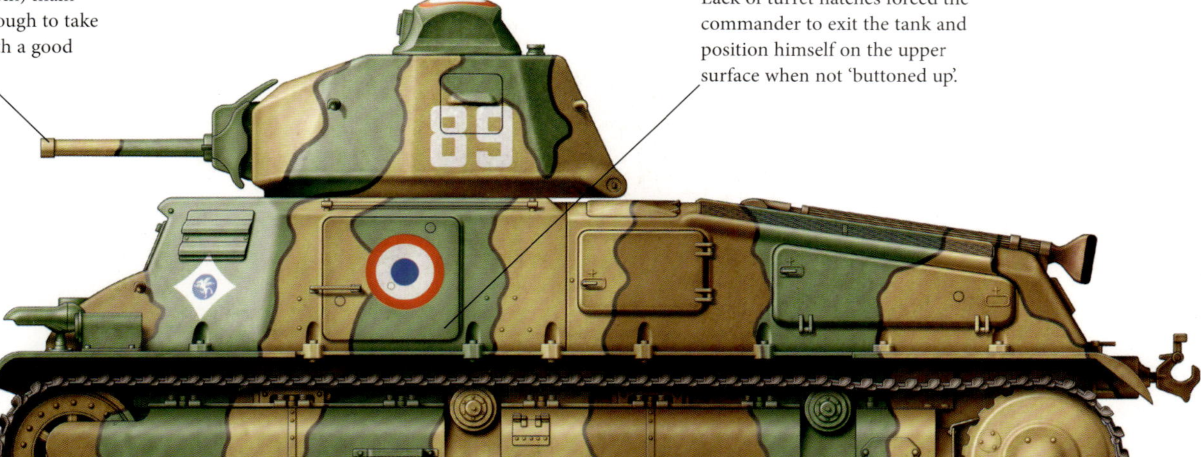

Armour
Cast armour sections were fitted over much of the tank, giving good protection but making the vehicle expensive to produce.

FAST CAVALRY TANK
The Somua S-35, entering service in 1935, was a new departure for the French Army. Up until its introduction, the cavalry were required to refer to their armoured vehicles as *automitrailleuse*, or armoured cars, whether they had tracks or not. The S-35 was explicitly a cavalry tank, intended to do what cavalry did best. It was fast and had a good operating radius, enabling it to undertake mobile operations.

GERMAN S-35S
Captured S-35s in German service are paraded on the Champs-Élysées in Paris in 1940. Production of the S-35 had been slow and there were only around 250 in front-line service by the time the Germans invaded.

M2 Light Tank (1936)

TYPE • *Light tank* **COUNTRY** • *United States*

SPECIFICATIONS

Dimensions:	Length: 4.43m (14ft 6in); Width: 2.47m (8ft 1in); Height: 2.64m (8ft 8in)
Weight:	11.8 tonnes (13.0 US tons)
Engine:	186kW (250hp) up-rated Wright/ Continental R670-9A petrol (gasoline)
Speed:	58km/h (36mph)
Range:	322km (200 miles)
Armour:	6.4–25.4mm (0.25–1in)
Armament:	1 x 37mm (1.46in) M5; 5 x 7.62mm (0.3in) M1919A4 MG
Crew:	4

The Light Tank M2 grew out of the T1 project of the late 1920s. During 1933, the Rock Island Arsenal (RIA) manufactured the first prototype T2 vehicle. This featured a Vickers-Horstman suspension with two sets of paired bogie wheels connected by leaf springs.

Right: Seen here in 1938, the M2A2 variant – dubbed by its crews the 'Mae West' – featured two side-by-side turrets, one of which mounted a heavy machine gun and the other, a medium machine gun.

M2A4
A USMC M2A4 light tank in the drab olive camouflage scheme used during the 1942–43 Guadalcanal campaign. The vehicle's compact size is attested to by the size of the externally mounted heavy machine gun.

Powerplant
The vehicle was powered by a 186kW (250hp) up-rated Wright/ Continental R670-9A seven-cylinder air-cooled radial petrol engine.

Crew
Weighing 11.8 tonnes (13 tons), the M2A4 light tank had a crew of four: the vehicle commander/loader, the gunner, the driver and the co-driver.

VARIANTS
During 1935, RIA produced 19 modified M2 tanks. These were essentially T2A1s with a smaller one-man turret with a single 7.62mm (0.3in) Browning M1919A4 machine gun; a similar weapon was fitted to the hull front. During 1936–37, American firms then manufactured 237 M2A2 variants. These vehicles were distinctive in that they sported twin rectangular-shaped side-by-side turrets, each mounting a single Browning M1919A4 machine gun.

TANK ON TRIAL
An M2 light tank on test, c.1940. On the side of the turret is a pair of white crossed swords, which designates that this tank belongs to the US Cavalry branch of the US Army. The tank's hull floor was conspicuously high above the ground; this distance equated to four-fifths of its road wheels' height.

Renault R-35 (1936)

TYPE • *Light infantry tank* **COUNTRY** • *France*

SPECIFICATIONS

Dimensions:	Length: 4.55m (14ft 11in); Width: 2.2m (7ft 2.5in); Height: 2.3m (7ft 6.5in)
Weight:	14.5 tonnes (15.98 US tons)
Engine:	134.2kW (180hp) Renault 4-cylinder
Speed:	42km/h (26mph)
Range:	160km (99 miles)
Armour:	30–43mm (1.18–1.69in)
Armament:	1 x 37mm (1.45in) SA-18 gun; 1 x coaxial 7.5mm (0.295in) MG
Crew:	2

The R-35 was a 1934 design intended to replace the venerable Renault FT-17 as the French Army's standard infantry support tank. Production began in 1936, but technical difficulties with the turrets delayed deliveries and the FT-17 had to remain in service for far longer than expected.

Left: An R-35 of the 21e Bataillon de Chars de Combat. For its day, the R-35 was a sound enough vehicle, and was typical of contemporary French design.

Crew positions
The driver's position was forward, while the commander in the cast turret had to act as his own loader and gunner firing the 37mm (1.45in) L/21 gun.

Char Léger 35R (R-35)
This vehicle belonged to the 24e Bataillon de Chars de Combat, 4e Division Cuirassée de Réserve (DCR) in 1940.

Armour
By the standards of 1940, the R-35 was an exceptionally well-protected light tank, with much of the vehicle covered with 40mm (1.57in) of armour, giving a high degree of immunity to contemporary German tank and anti-tank guns.

BACKGROUND

The Renault R-35 light tank had its origins in a design known originally as the ZM, produced late in 1934 in answer to a French army request for a new infantry support tank to supplement and eventually replace the ageing Renault FT-17 which dated back to World War I. Trials of the new tank started in early 1935, and in that same year the design was ordered into production before its evaluation had been completed as Germany appeared to be in a mood for conflict.

SPOILS OF WAR
German soldiers examine an abandoned French Renault R-35. Large numbers of R-35s fell into German hands virtually intact. These were put to use by garrison units in France with the designation PzKpfw 35-R(f), many later passing to driver and other tank training schools.

Matilda II (1937)

TYPE • *Infantry Tank* **COUNTRY** • *United Kingdom*

The Matilda II was slow as it was intended for the direct support of infantry units, a role in which speed was not essential. Overall it was a sound tank and proved to be far more reliable than many of its contemporaries.

SPECIFICATIONS

Dimensions:	Length: 5.61m (18ft 5in); Width: 2.59m (8ft 6in); Height: 2.52m (8ft 3in)
Weight:	26.92 tonnes (29.67 US tons)
Engine:	2 x 64.8kW (87hp) AEC 6-cylinder diesel
Speed:	13km/h (8mph)
Range:	258km (160 miles)
Armour:	20–78mm (0.79–3.1in)
Armament:	1 x 40mm (1.57in) 2pdr Ordnance Quick-Firing (OQF) gun; 1 x coaxial 7.92mm (0.31in) Besa MG
Crew:	4

Right: A Matilda II of the 7th Royal Tank Regiment (RTR) in France, 1940.

Matilda II
This Matilda carries the prominent white-red-white recognition stripes applied to many British AFVs in North Africa.

Variant fittings
Matildas were fitted with a variety of devices to create new variants, including mine flails, mine rollers, dozer blades, flamethrowers and searchlights.

Performance
The Matilda was never fast and was notably undergunned by the standards even of 1940, but had the priceless benefit of offering its crew excellent protection and great mechanical reliability.

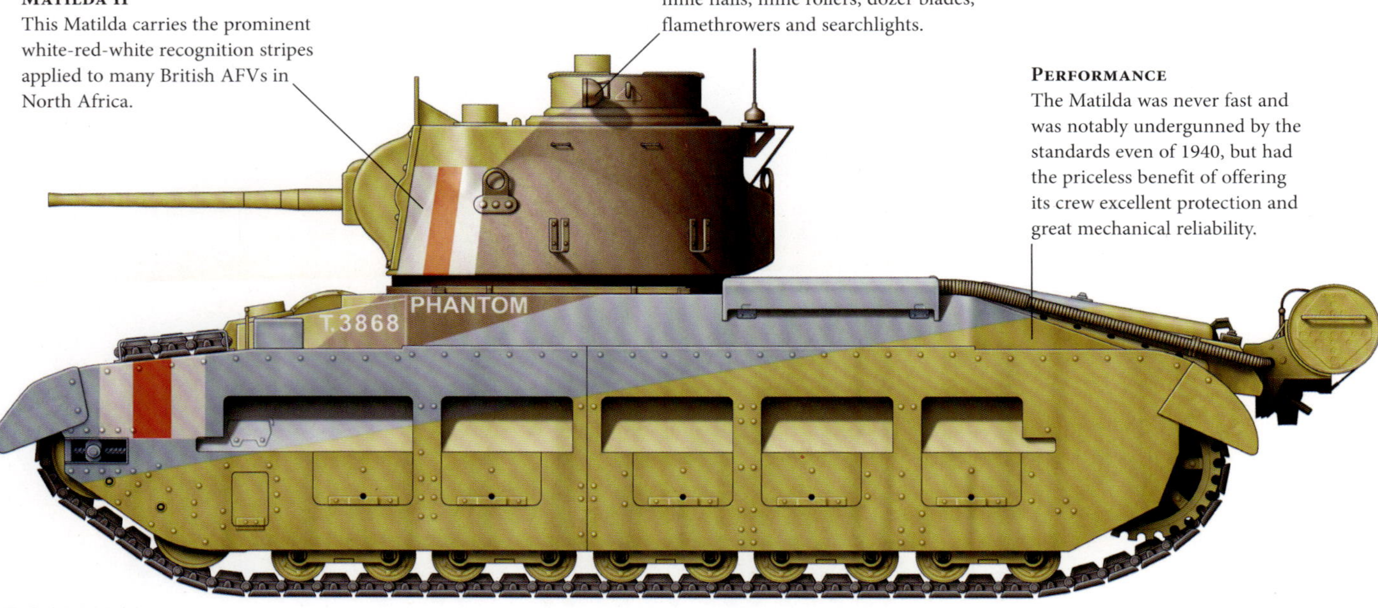

HEAVY VARIANT
The Matilda I was intended only as an interim type before the A12 Infantry Tank Mk II became available. This project began in 1936 and the first examples were completed in 1938. The Mk II, known later as Matilda II, was a much larger vehicle than the Matilda I with a four-man crew, a turret mounting a 2pdr (40mm/1.57in) gun and cast armour (varying in thickness from 20 to 78mm/0.8 to 3.1in) capable of defeating all known anti-tank projectiles.

WESTERN DESERT
In their first major actions, Matildas were found to be virtually immune to all Italian weapons, except for heavy artillery. Even direct hits by the 13.6kg (30lb) high explosive shells of 100mm (3.9in) howitzers rarely inflicted serious damage.

Char B1 bis (1937)

TYPE • *Heavy Tank* COUNTRY • *France*

SPECIFICATIONS

Dimensions:	Length: 6.63m (21ft 9in); Width: 2.52m (8ft 3in); Height: 2.84m (9ft 4in)
Weight	31.5 tonnes (34.72 US tons)
Engine:	1 x Renault 6-cylinder inline petrol delivering 229kW (307hp)
Speed:	Road: 28km/h (17.5mph); Cross-country: 21km/h (13mph)
Range:	Road: 135km (85 miles); Cross-country: 100km (60 miles)
Armour:	14–60mm (0.55–2.36in)
Armament:	1 x 75mm (2.95in) ABS SA35 L/17; 1 x 47mm (1.85in) SA35 L/32; 1 x 7.5mm (0.3in) Chatellerault Mle. 31 MG
Crew:	4

The Char B1 bis was a much-improved development of the earlier Char B. Orders were placed in 1937 for a total of 1,144 vehicles, but only 369 examples of the B1 bis had been delivered for service by June 1940.

Left: A Char B1 bis of the 47e Bataillon de Chars de Combat, 4e DCR / 47e Bataillon de Chars de Combat. The B1 bis rapidly acquired a fearsome reputation among German troops from its ability to shrug off repeated hits from tank and anti-tank guns.

Crew positions
The four crewmen were dispersed throughout the interior of the tank, making effective communications problematic.

Innovations
The Char B1 bis offered several innovative technological advances. Among these were an electric starter and self-sealing fuel tanks.

Armour
Armour protection 14–60mm (0.55–2.36in) thick was provided by riveted and welded nickel-steel plating.

ARMAMENT
The heavy armament of the Char B1 bis included a 47mm (1.85in) SA35 L/32 gun in a fully traversing turret, a formidable 75mm (2.95in) ABS SA35 L/17 howitzer fixed in azimuth in the front of the hull, a coaxially mounted 7.5mm (0.3in) Chatellerault Mle. 31 machine gun and a second 7.5mm machine gun in a flexible mount. The tank carried 72 rounds of 47mm ammunition and 74 rounds for the 75mm howitzer.

COMMANDER'S CHALLENGE
The Char B1 presented some significant operational challenges for the crew. The tank commander occupied the confined and cramped turret and was responsible for both laying and firing the 47mm (1.85in) gun, an overburden in combat.

Type 97 Chi-Ha (1937)

TYPE • *Medium Tank* **COUNTRY** • *Japan*

SPECIFICATIONS

DIMENSIONS:	Length: 5.5m (18ft); Width: 2.33m (7ft 8in); Height: 2.23m (7ft 4in)
WEIGHT:	14.3 tonnes (15.76 US tons)
ENGINE:	127kW (170hp) Mitsubishi Type 97 V-12 diesel engine
SPEED:	Road: 39km/h (24mph)
RANGE:	Road: 240km (149 miles); Cross-country: 210km (130 miles)
ARMOUR:	8–33mm (0.31–1.2in)
ARMAMENT:	1 x 57mm (2.24in) gun; Secondary: 2 x 7.7mm (0.3in) Type 97 machine guns
CREW:	4

The Japanese Type 97 Medium Chi-Ha was as good as any contemporary Allied light tank, but unfortunately for its crews it remained in production long after it had been surpassed by superior Allied designs.

MAIN GUN
The Chi-Ha's main armament was a 57mm (2.24in) Type 97 cannon, backed up by two 7.7mm (0.3in) Type 97 machine guns, one in the bow and one in the rear of the turret.

Left: The thickest armour was on the vertical parts of the turret and was 33mm (1.2in) steel. Elsewhere, the armour was mainly 25mm (0.9in) thickness.

HE SHELLS
The Chi-Ha was mainly used in the infantry support role and was supplied with high explosive (HE) shells. These were largely useless against heavier Allied tanks.

SUSPENSION
The Chi-Ha's suspension was refined compared to previous Japanese tanks, but still gave the crew an uncomfortable ride over uneven terrain.

SHINHOTO
A successful development of the Chi-Ha was the Shinhoto ('modified turret') Chi-Ha, which had the turret of the Type 1 medium tank and a 47mm (1.45in) high-velocity gun. This more effective version was produced until the war's end, along with specialist variants, such as bridgelayers, mine flail tanks and command tanks.

INVASION OF CHINA
Type 97 Chi-Ha tanks roll through a Chinese city in the 1930s. A medium tank by Japanese standards, the Chi-Ha was chosen after being evaluated with the three-man Type 97 Chi-Ni.

BT-7 (1937)

TYPE • *Fast Tank* **COUNTRY** • *Soviet Union*

SPECIFICATIONS (BT-7 Model 1937)

Dimensions:	Length: 5.66m (18ft 6in); Width: 2.29m (7ft 6in); Height: 2.42m (7ft 11in)
Weight:	14 tonnes (15.4 US tons)
Engine:	373kW (500hp) Milukin M17-T V-12 petrol
Speed:	86km/h (53mph)
Range:	250km (155 miles)
Armour:	6–15mm (0.24–0.59in)
Armament:	1 x 45mm (1.77in) 20K Model 1932 gun; 1 x 7.62mm (0.3in) coaxial DT machine gun
Crew:	3

The Soviet BT-7 light tank of 1935 was a logical development of the BT-5, incorporating various refinements as a result of the lessons learned during border conflicts in the Far East in the early 1930s. The tank was both fast and agile.

Below: A BT-7 Model 1937. This, the mass-production version of the BT-7, featured a redesigned sloping-sided conical turret. This tank has been painted with three-tone camouflage and served in eastern Poland in 1939.

Turret
The BT-7A featured a redesigned and enlarged drum-shaped turret in comparison with the standard BT-7 tank, which was based on that mounted on the T-28.

BT-7A
The BT-7A 'artillery tank' was armed with a 76mm (3in) howitzer for the close support role. The 76mm (3in) HE shell was far more effective against AT guns or field defences than the rounds fired by the standard BT tanks.

Hull
This new turret of the BT-7A was mounted upon a hull identical to that of the BT-7. Additional internal turret space was required to fit a larger weapon.

RADIO TANK
The Soviet KhPZ factory produced about one-tenth of the BT-7A production run as platoon commanders' vehicles. These carried a wireless radio set, with the distinctive horseshoe-shaped rail antenna along the tank's turret top edge. Because of the large space required to house the radio set, these vehicles only carried 40 rounds for its 76.2mm (3in) gun.

COMBINED ARMS
By the start of Operation *Barbarossa* in June 1941, there were around 2,500 BT-7s in service, mainly Model 1937s and BT-7Ms (a diesel-powered rather than petrol-powered variant); over 80 per cent of these tanks were destroyed, captured or abandoned during the bitter battles that raged in 1941.

T-28 (1938)

TYPE • *Heavy Tank* **COUNTRY** • *Soviet Union*

The T-28 became the standard Soviet medium tank design of the latter part of the 1930s; as soon as the T-34 medium tank entered service in 1940, however, the T-28 was totally eclipsed and production ended in 1940.

SPECIFICATIONS (Model 1934)

DIMENSIONS:	Length: 7.44m (24ft 5in); Width: 2.81m (9ft 3in); Height: 2.82m (9ft 3in)
WEIGHT:	28 tonnes (30.86 US tons)
ENGINE:	373kW (500hp) V-12 Milukin-M17 petrol
SPEED:	37km/h (23mph)
RANGE:	220km (137 miles)
ARMOUR:	10–30mm (0.39–1.18in)
ARMAMENT:	1 x 45mm (1.77in) 20K Model 1932 gun; later short-barrelled 76.2mm (3in) KT-28 howitzer; 3 x 7.62mm (0.3in) DT Model 1927 machine guns
CREW:	6

Right: This view of the T-28 illustrates the positioning of the two auxiliary turrets below and in front of the main turret.

MAIN GUN
The main gun was a short 76.2mm (3in) weapon that was replaced in some cases by a longer gun of the same calibre.

MACHINE GUN
The ball-mounted machine gun faced to the rear on early T-28s, but later models had an ammunition bustle at the turret rear and the machine gun was relocated to the front quarter.

TRENCH CROSSING
The T-28's many wheels and long ground footprint gave it good trench-crossing ability. Unfortunately, this was not needed, as it was used mainly in the defensive role.

EXPERIMENTS

There were several experimental versions of the T-28, including some self-propelled guns and 'specials' such as bridging and assault engineering tanks. None of these experimental variants proceeded past the prototype stage, but experience with them was of great importance when later variations on production tanks were contemplated. In fact, the T-28 was of more value as an educational tank than as a combat tank. Its service life was short, spanning only the years from 1939 to 1941.

CAPTURED T-28

In 1941 the T-28 tanks demonstrated themselves to be of only limited combat value. Their large slab sides and stately performance made them notably easy prey for the German anti-tank artillery arm.

SdKfz 251 (1938)

TYPE • *Armoured Personnel Carrier* **COUNTRY** • *Germany*

SPECIFICATIONS

DIMENSIONS:	Length: 5.8m (19ft); Width: 2m (6ft 7in); Height: 1.75m (5ft 9in)
WEIGHT:	7.81 tonnes (8.61 US tons)
ENGINE:	Maybach HL42 TUKRM 6-cylinder petrol engine, 100hp (75kW)
SPEED:	Maximum road speed of 53km/h (33mph)
RANGE:	Road range of 180km (112 miles)
ARMOUR:	6–14.5mm (0.24–0.57in)
ARMAMENT:	Differed according to variant
CREW:	2

The SdKfz 251 entered service in 1939 as an armoured personnel carrier. There were 22 special-purpose variants: rocket-launcher, flamethrower, anti-tank, communications vehicle, observation post, ambulance and infrared searchlight carrier.

Left: A front view of the SdKfz 251. The standard personnel carrier version could carry 10 fully equipped troops and had a crew of two; note the two vision slits at the front.

ARMOUR
Armour was only 14.5mm (0.57in) at its thickest, which was adequate against heavy machine gun bullets and anti-tank shells.

ARMAMENT
The base SdKfz 251 had its own armament of a fixed MG 34 machine gun, but there was also a mount for the infantry squad's machine gun.

HULL
Later models had simplified hull construction to speed production, notably all-welded armour as opposed to mainly riveted plates.

MANY VARIANTS

The 251 came in many variants. The 251/1 was fitted with wooden racks for 320mm (12.6in) infantry support rockets, a weapon sometimes known as the 'Stuka on foot'. The 251/16 had dual flamethrower guns. The 251/20 had a large infrared searchlight and was used in conjunction with the IR night sights on some Panther tanks. The 251/22 was a tank-destroyer version with a 75mm Pak 40 anti-tank gun.

RUSSIAN OFFENSIVE
Panzer high tide: Panzergrenadiers in SdKfz 251 half-tracks and Panzer IIIs advance across the Russian steppe in the summer of 1942. The half-tracks gave the ability for mechanized infantry support to the heavy armour.

Tank, Cruiser, Mk II (A10) (1938)

TYPE • *Cruiser Tank* **COUNTRY** • *United Kingdom*

SPECIFICATIONS (Mk 1A)

Dimensions:	Length: 5.51m (18ft 1in); Width: 2.54m (8ft 4in); Height: 2.59m (8ft 6in)
Weight:	13.97 tonnes (15.4 US tons)
Engine:	1 x 111.9kW (150hp) AEC Type 179 6-cylinder petrol engine
Speed:	26km/h (16mph)
Range:	161km (100 miles)
Armour:	6–30mm (0.24–1.19in)
Armament:	1 x 40mm (1.57in) 2pdr gun; 2 x 7.92mm (0.31in) Besa MGs (1 coaxial and 1 ball-mounted in hull front)
Crew:	5

In 1934, Vickers designed the Cruiser Tank Mk I (A9), and this entered production in 1937, albeit on a fairly limited scale. It was followed by the Heavy Cruiser Tank Mk II, which had begun life as the A10 Infantry Tank.

Left: The multi-colour diagonal pattern of camouflage was applied to many British tanks in the North African and Balkans theatre.

Secondary armament
The first models of the A10 were armed with Vickers machine guns in the hull, but later these were changed in preference for Besa machine guns.

Performance
The Mk II (A10) had significantly upgraded armour compared to its predecessor, the Mk I (A9), but this resulted in a slow maximum speed of 26km/h (16mph).

Suspension
The A10 might have been slow, but its suspension proved to be durable in the unforgiving conditions of the North African desert. Track breakages were common, however.

CRUISER TANKS

In the early 1930s, the British Army, which had previously focused on developing dual-role medium tanks, decided to develop two separate types of armoured fighting vehicle, one an infantry tank to operate in support of ground forces and the other a 'cruiser' tank, whose role was to seek and destroy other tanks and vehicles. The cruiser tank was designed to exploit gaps in the enemy's defences created by heavier armour or artillery, and penetrate behind enemy lines, relying on speed for survival. To achieve this, it had to sacrifice armour.

A10 IN NORTH AFRICA

The campaigns in the Western Desert, 1940–2, were synonymous with armoured warfare. The flat wastes of desert may seem to be ideal tank country, but this was far from the case. Sand caused many problems, clogging engine parts and turret mechanisms, while victory usually went to the tanks with the longer-range guns.

T-40 (1938)

TYPE • *Amphibious Light Tank* **COUNTRY** • *Soviet Union*

SPECIFICATIONS

DIMENSIONS:	Length: 4.43m (13ft 6in); Width: 2.51m (8ft 3in); Height: 2.12m (6ft 11in)
WEIGHT:	5.5 tonnes (6.1 US tons)
ENGINE:	63kW (85hp) GAZ-202 petrol
SPEED:	45km/h (28mph)
RANGE:	450km (280 miles)
ARMOUR:	3–13mm (0.12–0.51in)
ARMAMENT	1 x 12.7mm (0.5in) DShK Model 1938 heavy machine gun; 1 x 7.62mm (0.3in) DT coaxial machine gun
CREW:	2

During the late 1930s, the latest Soviet amphibious light tank design, the T-40, incorporated enhanced lethality and slightly greater survivability; these modest improvements, however, could not prevent the design from still being out-classed by 1941.

Left: The T-40 was designed to replace the T-37. Flotation tanks were fitted at the rear, but its thin armour meant it fared poorly during the fighting in Finland in 1939.

DSHK
Firing the B-30 armour-piercing round, the DShK could penetrate up to 16mm (0.6in) of vertical armour plate at 300m (985ft).

AMPHIBIOUS
A rear screw-propeller, two rudders and the tracks enabled the waterproofed T-40 to cross large rivers and lakes.

HULL
This side view of a T-40 in whitewashed winter camouflage highlights its high slope-sided hull superstructure.

DESIGN

From 1938 to 1940, the Soviets designed an improved amphibious scout tank, the T-40, to replace the outclassed T-37A and T-38, which lacked adequate firepower and lethality. The T-40 was a squat rectangular vehicle with a tall, slope-sided rectangular hull superstructure. The track suspension consisted of a large front track driving sprocket wheel, four large non-bogie road wheels, a large rear idler wheel and three top-track return rollers.

T-40 WINTER ASSAULT
T-40s advance alongside Red Army infantry in winter conditions in Finland. To speed production of the tank, from 1940 the Soviets also produced a simplified up-armoured land-only version, the T-40S, which lacked amphibious features and a radio, but also had turret armour increased to 20mm (0.79in).

T-38 (1938)

TYPE • *Light Tank* **COUNTRY** • *Soviet Union*

SPECIFICATIONS

Dimensions:	Length: 3.78m (12ft 4in); Width: 2.33m (7ft 8in); Height: 1.63m (5ft 4in)
Weight:	3.3 tonnes (3.63 US tons)
Engine:	30kW (40hp) GAZ-AA petrol (gasoline)
Speed:	40km/h (25mph)
Range:	170km (109 miles)
Armour:	4–9mm (0.16–0.35in)
Armament:	1 x 7.62mm (0.3in) DT Model 1929 machine gun
Crew:	2

A total of 1,340 T-38s were produced between 1936 and 1939 and were widely used by reconnaissance units. Some of these vehicles were fitted with a 20mm (0.79in) ShVAK cannon in place of the usual DT MG, but few survived the first months of the war.

Right: The T-38's large cylindrical turret was positioned atop the centre-left of the rectangular flat hull roof.

Armament
During 1938–39, some 150 up-gunned tanks, designated the T-38RT, were produced with the long-barrelled 20mm (0.79in) automatic-fire ShVAK cannon.

Engine
The T-38 had the same 30kW (40hp) GAZ-AA engine as the T-37A, giving it an operational range of 170km (109 miles) and a top road speed of 40km/h (25mph).

Light armour
The T-38's light 3–9mm (0.12–0.35in) armour kept its weight to just 3.3 tonnes (3.6 tons), making it air-transportable.

SOVIET TANKETTES

During the 1920s and 1930s, the tankette was of continuing attraction for Soviet tank designers. By the late 1930s, the Red Army had tested and dropped the one-man tankette, and was at the usual stage where the tankette had been developed into the two-man light tank. By the time the Germans attacked in 1941, the Red Army had invested fairly heavily in the light tank, and the models in service came from years of development.

T-38 ON DISPLAY
Designed during 1934–36, the T-38 amphibious light scout tank was a development of the T-37A. It was a marginally squatter vehicle than its predecessor, but visually both tanks looked quite similar.

Panzer 38(t) (1938)

TYPE • *Light Tank* **COUNTRY** • *Germany/Czechoslovakia*

SPECIFICATIONS

DIMENSIONS:	Length: 4.61m (15ft 1in); Width: 2.135m (7ft); Height: 2.252m (7ft 5in)
WEIGHT:	9.85 tonnes (10.86 US tons)
ENGINE:	1 x Praga EPA 6-cylinder water-cooled inline petrol powerplant delivering 112kW (150hp)
SPEED:	Road: 42km/h (26.1mph); Off-road: 15km/h (9.32mph)
RANGE:	Road: 250km (160 miles); Cross-country: 100km (62.14 miles)
ARMOUR:	8–50mm (0.31–1.97in)
ARMAMENT:	1 x Czech 37mm (1.45in) Skoda A7 gun; 2 x 7.92mm (0.31in) ZB-53 machine guns
CREW:	4

After occupying Czechoslovakia, the German Army ordered production of the LT vz 38, the standard Czechoslovakian light tank, to continue. Redesignated the Panzer 38(t), the design proved one of the world's best in German service early in the war.

Left: The turret and hull of the Panzer 38(t) were of riveted construction rather than welded and some ancillary components of the tank were bolted to the superstructure.

MAIN ARMAMENT
The Czech 37mm (1.45in) Skoda A7 gun turret mounted atop the Panzer 38(t) was heavier than the primary weaponry of other light tanks early in World War II, providing a definite edge in combat situations.

ARMOUR
On early versions of the Panzer 38(t), armour protection varied from 8mm (0.31in) in less vulnerable areas to 30mm (1.18in) of frontal thickness. Later production models provided increased crew protection with armour up to 50mm (1.97in).

ENGINE
The Praga EPA six-cylinder water-cooled inline petrol engine delivered 112kW (150hp) and the Panzer 38(t) reached a top road speed of 42km/h (26.1mph).

STOLEN PROPERTY
One of the most notable weapons to emerge from the Czech arsenal emblazoned with the German cross was the LT vz 38 light tank, the standard armoured fighting vehicle of the Czech Army. The Germans redesignated the tank as the Panzer 38(t), with the 't' designating *tschechisch*, the German word for Czechoslovakian. An efficient design, the Panzer 38(t) was originally conceived following specifications issued by the Czech military in 1935 for a new light tank.

PANZER 38(T), VITEBESK
This photograph illustrates the small dimensions of the Panzer 38(t) relative to its crew. While the tank was quickly outclassed as a combat vehicle, it continued to be widely used as a reconnaissance vehicle. In that role the Germans fitted some chassis with the turret of the SdKfz 222 light armoured car, complete with its 20mm (0.79in) cannon.

M3 Scout Car (1938)

TYPE • *Armoured Car* **COUNTRY** • *United States*

SPECIFICATIONS (M3A1)

Dimensions:	Length: 5.62m (18ft 5in); Width: 2m (6ft 8in); Height: 1.99m (6ft 6in)
Weight:	5.62 tonnes (6.2 US tons)
Engine:	82kW (110hp) Hercules JXD petrol (gasoline)
Speed:	72km/h (45mph)
Range:	402km (250 miles)
Armour:	6.4–12.7mm (0.25–0.5in)
Armament:	1 x 12.7mm (0.5in) M2HB HMG; 1 x 7.62mm (0.3in) M1919A4 MG
Crew:	2 (+6 troops)

The M3 Scout Car (or the White Scout Car in British Army parlance) was initially designated as the M2A1, a modified variant of the M2 Scout Car; some 22 of the latter were built during 1935–38. The M3's main tactical roles were reconnaissance and screening.

Above: This M3A1, vehicle 'T17', serving with the Free French forces, has a lowered skate rail for its 12.7mm (0.5in) Browning M2HB heavy machine gun.

Engine
The M3 was powered by the standard 71kW (95hp) Hercules JXD six-cylinder petrol (gasoline) engine, which permitted it to reach a maximum road speed of 89km/h (55mph).

Armoured plates
This US Army M3 Scout Car, sporting a three-tone camouflage scheme, has been fitted with armoured plates to the driving compartment's side window areas.

Armament
In terms of armament, the arrangement of the machine guns varied. Many M3s were armed with a mix of 12.7mm (0.5in) Browning M2HB heavy machine gun and one or two 7.62mm (0.3in) Browning M1919A4 machine guns, all fitted to a skate mount.

M3A1
During early 1939, WMC developed an improved and widened variant of the M3 designated the M3A1, which at 5.62 tonnes (5.5 tons) weighed significantly more than its predecessor. American firms subsequently mass-manufactured the M3A1 through to summer 1944, by which time 20,918 examples had been completed. Thousands of these vehicles were dispatched to America's Allies.

M3 SCOUT CAR
During 1938–39, WMC manufactured 100 M3s. This design was a compact protected scout car with a front and rear pair of driving road wheels shielded by large curving fenders. The centre of the vehicle sported a shallow raised driving position, while the rear half comprised the open-topped troop-carrying compartment, the sides of which sloped down to the vehicle's vertical hull rear face that housed the exit/entry door.

Pantserwagen M39 (1939)

TYPE • *Armoured Car* **COUNTRY** • *Netherlands*

The M39 was a DAF-designed armoured car that was just entering Dutch service at the time of the German invasion. It seems likely that no more than a dozen or so M39s were completed, of which one or two may have seen action alongside the earlier M36 and M38 armoured cars in 1940.

SPECIFICATIONS

Dimensions:	Length: 4.75m (15ft 7in); Width: 2.08m (6ft 10in); Height: 2.16m (7ft 1in)
Weight:	5.8 tonnes (6.4 US tons)
Engine:	Ford Mercury V8, 95hp
Speed:	75km/h (47mph) forwards; 50km/h (31mph) backwards
Range:	200–225km
Armour:	5–10mm
Armament:	1 x 37mm (1.45in) Bofors cannon; Secondary: 2 x 7.92mm (0.31in) Paw m-20 No.1 Lewis machine gun, 1 x 7.92mm (0.31in) Paw m-20 No.2 modified Lewis machine gun
Crew:	5

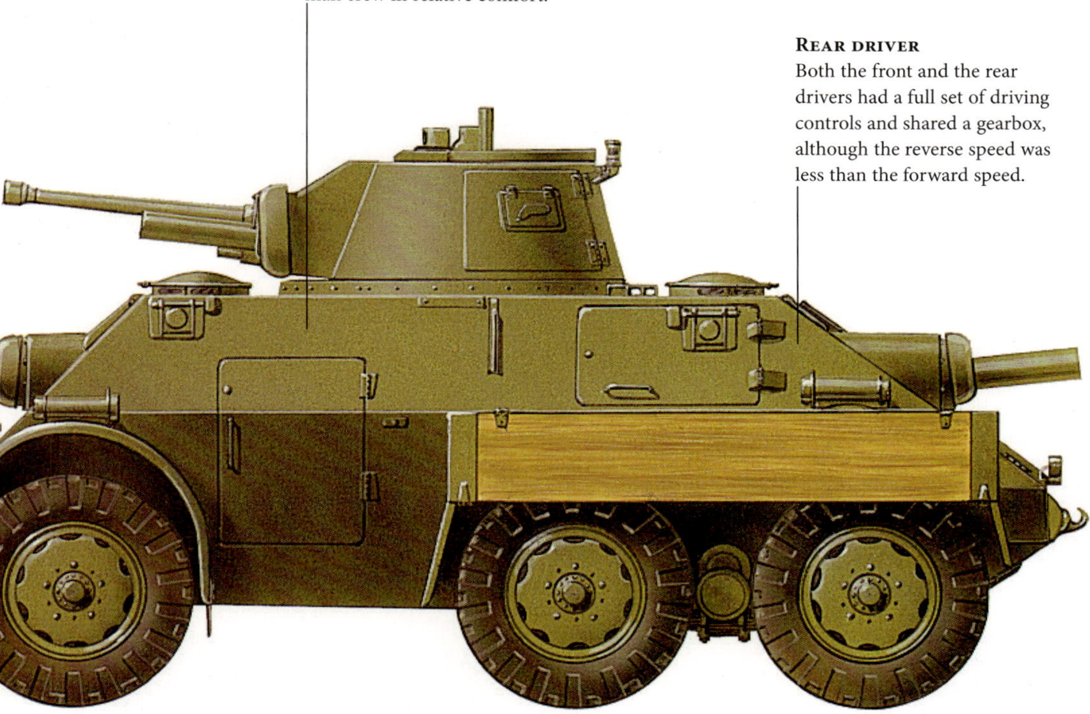

Internal space
The M39 was designed with a large internal space that could hold the five-man crew in relative comfort.

Rear driver
Both the front and the rear drivers had a full set of driving controls and shared a gearbox, although the reverse speed was less than the forward speed.

Machine guns
The two machine guns were placed in ball mounts but fired out through an extended tube that allowed for 30 degrees of traverse.

M39 OFF-ROAD TRIALS
The rapid takeover of the Netherlands by Germany in 1940 meant that the M39's combat career was short-lived. M39s were subsequently pressed into German service as Pz. SpWg L202h.

DESCRIPTION

The M39 was produced by the DAF company in the build-up to World War II, resisting Dutch Army requests to license-build British armoured cars. It was a well-made 6x4 armoured car with an all-welded hull, a rear-mounted Ford Mercury V8 engine and a well-sloped glacis plate. A useful set of driving controls at the rear of the vehicle allowed the rear machine-gunner to control the vehicle in reverse in an emergency.

M2 Half-track (1939)

TYPE • *Armoured Personnel Carrier* **COUNTRY** • *United States*

SPECIFICATIONS

Dimensions:	Length: 5.96m (19ft 7in); Width: 1.96m (6ft 5in); Height: 2.3m (7ft 7in)
Weight:	8.7 tonnes (9.6 US tons)
Engine:	110kW (147hp) White 160AX petrol (gasoline)
Speed:	72km/h (45mph)
Range:	322km (200 miles)
Armour:	6.4–12.7mm (0.25–0.5in)
Armament:	1 x 7.62mm (0.3in) M1919A4 MG
Crew:	3 (+7 troops)

During the late 1930s, the US Ordnance Department evaluated the concept of half-tracked artillery tractors using French Citroën-Kégresse vehicles. In 1939, WMC married the rear-located tracked running gear of the T9 half-tracked truck to the M3 Scout Car's front wheel arrangement.

Below: The M4A1 mortar half-track was based upon the M2; it was designed to provide infantry support via a mobile 81mm (3.1in) mortar mounted in the rear.

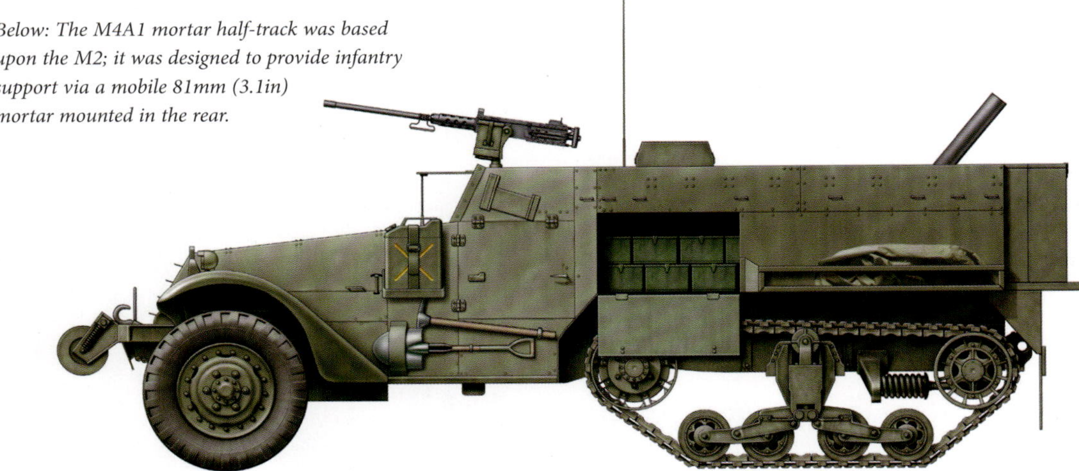

Camouflage
This M2, seen in Tunisia in January 1943, has a relatively unusual camouflage scheme of khaki 'clouds' daubed over the base olive drab finish.

Drive layout
The front nose section of the M2 featured a single large rubber-tyred road wheel pairing. The remaining two-thirds of the hull featured tracked running gear.

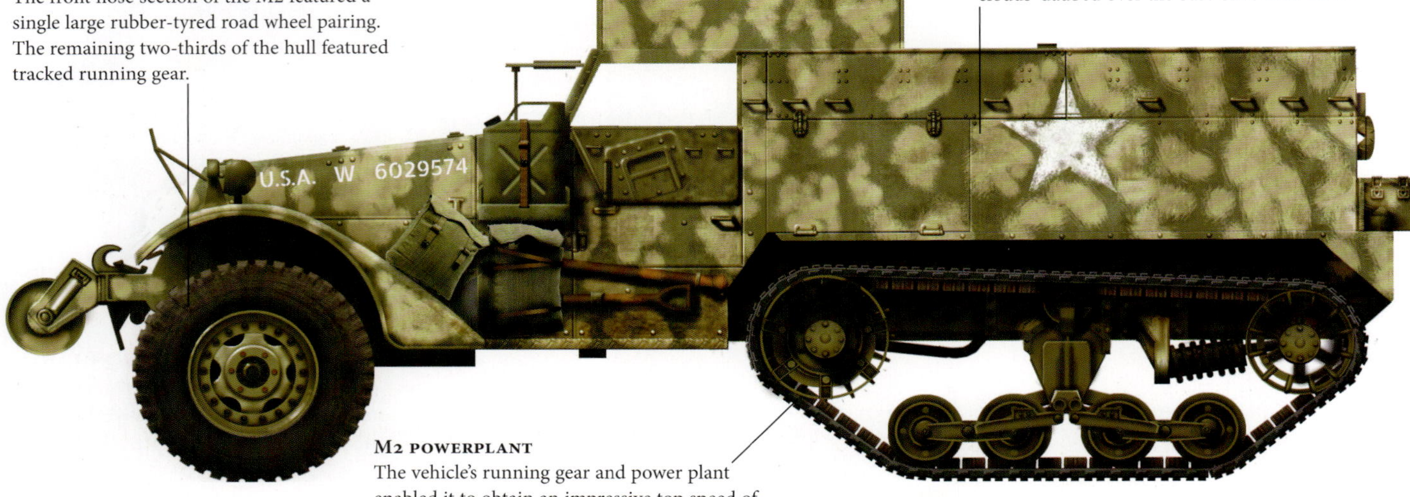

M2 powerplant
The vehicle's running gear and power plant enabled it to obtain an impressive top speed of 72km/h (45mph) on tarmacked roads.

M2A1 DIFFERENCES
At 8.9 tonnes (8.8 tons), the M2A1 weighed slightly more than its M2 predecessor. The main difference between the two was that the M2A1 did away with the skate rail. Instead, the 12.7mm (0.5in) Browning M2HB heavy machine gun was fixed to its own substantial M49 ring mount, with a low shield-rail, situated above the co-driver's right-side seat.

FACTORY FRESH
From October 1943 onwards, Autocar and White Motor Company (WMC) transferred their manufacturing efforts from the M2 to the improved M2A1 half-track car. In total, these firms produced 1,643 M2A1s and converted a further 1266 M2s in the process of manufacture to the M2A1 configuration.

KV-2 (1939)

TYPE • *Heavy Tank* COUNTRY • *Soviet Union*

The KV-2 was built to assault fixed emplacements. It was effective, but its great weight and size proved its downfall, and only 330 were built. It appeared in two forms – a battle tank with a 76.2mm (3in) gun and an 'artillery tank' with a massive 152mm (5.9in) howitzer.

SPECIFICATIONS

Dimensions:	Length: 6.79m (22ft 3in); Width: 3.32m (10ft 11in); Height: 3.65m (12ft)
Weight:	53.1 tonnes (58.54 US tons)
Engine:	1 x 410kW (550hp) V-2K V-12 diesel engine
Speed:	26km/h (16mph)
Range:	140km (87 miles)
Armour:	Up to 110mm (4.33in)
Armament:	1 x 152mm (5.98in) gun; 3 x MGs
Crew:	6

Right: The 152mm weapon of the KV-2 fired at a muzzle velocity of 508m (1,667ft) per second for the AP projectile and 432m (952ft) per second for the HE projectile.

Main gun
The 152mm (5.98in)weapon was provided with 36 rounds of ammunition.

Turret
The turret was high and slab-sided, constructed of thick armour up to a maximum thickness of 76.2mm (3in) on the front and sides.

Mobility
Another deficiency of the KV-2 was its very poor cross-country mobility: the KV-2 was more than 6 tonnes heavier than the KV-1 but had no more power.

HEAVY GUN

The Soviets appreciated that the KV-1 had the makings of an effective heavy tank, but one with indifferent firepower. To make the KV-2A the designers added a large and totally unwieldy turret carrying a 122mm (4.8in) M1938 L/22.7 howitzer. The 122mm weapon had been installed in only a few vehicles before it was superseded by the 152mm (6in) M1938 L/24.3 howitzer, the largest-calibre weapon ever installed in a mass-production tank.

MONSTER TAMED
German troops examine a captured KV-2 in 1941. The tall, slab-sided turret of the KV-2 was vulnerable to attack as it presented a large and tempting target. In addition, the turret was virtually unmovable except when the tank was on level ground.

Mk III Valentine (1939)

TYPE • *Infantry Tank* **COUNTRY** • *United Kingdom*

SPECIFICATIONS

Dimensions:	Length: 5.41m (17ft 9in); Width: 2.63m (8ft 7.5in); Height: 2.273m (7ft 5.5in)
Weight:	16.96 tonnes (18.7 US tons)
Engine:	1 x AEC A190 6-cylinder diesel generating 98kW (131hp)
Speed:	Road: 24km/h (15mph); Off-road: 12.9km/h (8mph)
Range:	145km (90 miles)
Armour:	8–65mm (0.31–2.55in)
Armament:	1 x 2pdr (40mm/1.57in) QF gun; 1 x 7.92mm (0.31in) Besa machine gun
Crew:	3

Derived from a previous Vickers design, the A10, the Mk III Valentine Infantry Tank was available in large numbers at a critical time for Great Britain and the Commonwealth nations as a potential Nazi invasion of Britain loomed.

Left: The Valentine was regarded by the Red Army as the best British tank supplied under Lend-Lease. A total of 3,782 Valentines of all marks were shipped to Soviet Russia between 1941 and 1945, of which 320 were lost en route.

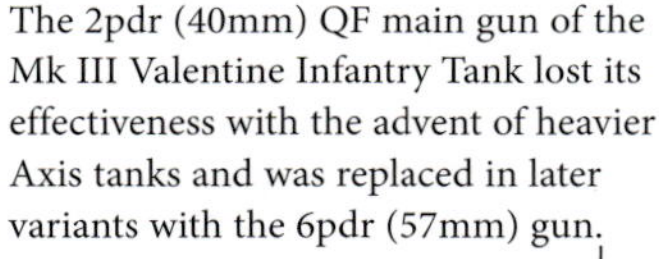

Armament
The 2pdr (40mm) QF main gun of the Mk III Valentine Infantry Tank lost its effectiveness with the advent of heavier Axis tanks and was replaced in later variants with the 6pdr (57mm) gun.

Armour
The armour protection of the Mk III Valentine Infantry Tank varied from 8–65mm (0.31–2.55in), heavier than the A10 Cruiser Tank from which the Valentine was derived.

Engine
The AEC A190 six-cylinder diesel engine of the Mk III Valentine Infantry Tank generated 103kW (131hp). It was replaced in later variants with an American GMC diesel engine.

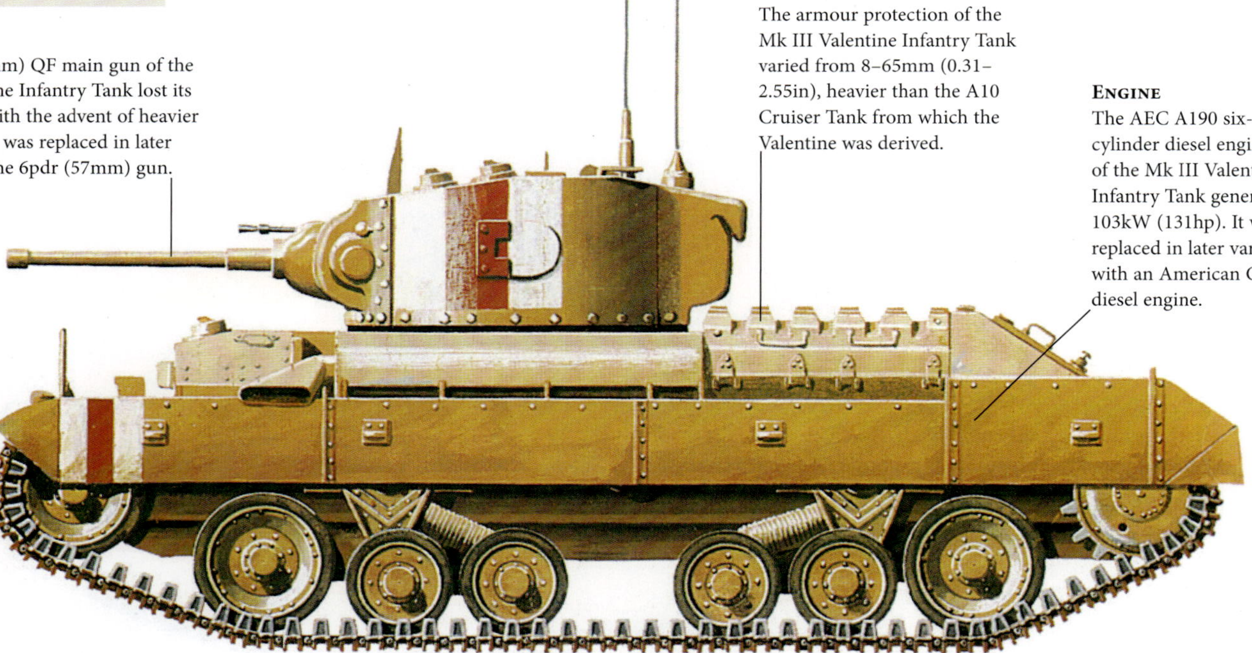

VALENTINE VARIANTS

In total, 11 different marks of the original Valentine were produced during World War II. One of the tank's greatest virtues was its ability to accept substantially heavier weaponry. While Marks I–VII mounted the 2pdr gun, the 57mm (2.24in) 6pdr QF was introduced with the Mark VIII and continued up to the Mark X. With the Mark XI, a 75mm (2.95in) QF gun was mounted.

KNOCKED-OUT VALENTINE

A Valentine burns in the Western Desert. Valentine tanks saw extensive service with Commonwealth forces in the Mediterranean, the North African desert and in Burma, where it was superior to most Japanese tanks. It was, however, relatively slow and inferior to newer tank designs entering service by 1943.

Fiat-Ansaldo M11/39 (1939)

TYPE • *Light Tank* **COUNTRY** • *Italy*

SPECIFICATIONS

Dimensions:	Length: 4.73m (15ft 6in); Width: 2.18m (7ft 2in); Height: 2.3m (7ft 7in)
Weight:	11.1 tonnes (12.3 US tons)
Engine:	1 x SPA 8 T diesel engine producing 78.3kW (105bhp)
Speed:	33.3km/h (20.7mph)
Range:	200km (124 miles)
Armour:	6–30mm (0.24–1.18in)
Armament:	1 x 37mm (1.46in) gun; 2 x 8mm (0.315in) Breda MGs
Crew:	3

This light tank had a poor 37mm (1.46in) gun, hull-mounted with a small two-man turret above, which housed a pair of machine guns. Developed as a light infantry support AFV, it was used as a medium tank in the Western Desert, far beyond its capabilities.

Right: Here we see captured Fiat-Ansaldo tanks in Eritrea in May 1941; a spare set of track treads are coiled up between the guards.

Australian M11/39
This tank is a captured Italian vehicle put into use by the 6th Australian Division Cavalry Regiment.

Armament
The tank's armament consisted of one 37mm (1.45in) Vickers-Terni L/40 in a limited-traverse mount in the hull front, plus two 8mm (0.31in) machine guns in the turret.

Insignia
The large white kangaroo recognition markings were applied to the front, sides and rear of all captured AFVs used by the regiment to minimize the risk of 'friendly fire'.

COMBAT LOSSES

The M11/39 was a poorly designed vehicle developed in the late 1930s as a 'breakthrough tank' for the Italian Army. By the time it went into action in 1940, it was already obsolescent and took heavy losses from British 2pdr tank and anti-tank guns. A small number of M11/39s and the later M13/40s were captured in running order and issued to the 6th Australian Division Cavalry Regiment to support their Universal Carriers in the assault on Tobruk in January 1941.

TANK TRANSPORT
This M11/39 is on a towed trailer for transportation; weighing just 11.1 tonnes (12.3 US tons), it was a truly 'light' tank, although its weight reflected a problematic deficit in armour protection.

Cruiser Tank Mk IV (A13 Mk II) (1940)

TYPE • *Cruiser Tank* **COUNTRY** • *United Kingdom*

SPECIFICATIONS Mk IVA (A13 Mk II)

Dimensions:	Length: 6.02m (19ft 9in); Width: 2.59m (8ft 6in); Height: 2.59m (8ft 6in)
Weight:	15.04 tonnes (16.56 US tons)
Engine:	1 x 253.64kW (340hp) Nuffield Liberty V12 petrol engine
Speed:	48km/h (30mph)
Range:	145km (90 miles)
Armour:	6–30mm (0.24–1.19in)
Armament:	1 x 40mm (1.57in) 2pdr gun; 1 x coaxial 7.92mm (0.31in) Besa MG
Crew:	4

A turning point in British tank design came with the 1936 decision to develop new cruiser tanks based on the suspension system devised in the US by J. Walter Christie. This led to the A13 designed by Nuffield.

Left: An A13 Cruiser Tank of the 2nd Dragoon Guards (Queen's Bays), 2nd Armoured Brigade, 1st Armoured Division.

Coaxial machine gun
The Mk IVA introduced a 0.312in Besa coaxial machine gun in place of the original Vickers weapon.

Mk IVA (A13 Mk II)
This particular tank belonged to the 2nd Royal Tank Regiment (RTR), 4th Armoured Brigade, 7th Armoured Division, Western Desert Force.

Shortcomings
As with the Mk III, range was too limited for effective independent operations, and the angular design of the box-like hull and V-sided turret provided many shot traps.

EMPEROR

T15228

3

A13 DEVELOPMENT

The 14,429kg (31,810lb) prototype of the A13 was completed in 1937 and immediately displayed excellent performance as a result of the Christie suspension combined with a high power-to-weight ratio. Only moderate armour was provided, however, as the tank was intended to rely on performance and agility as the main platforms of its protection, and the armament was also modest. Deliveries of this Cruiser Tank Mk III began in December 1938 and the production programme was completed in 1939.

CRUISER TANK MK IVA
Tank officers consult a map in front of a Mk IVA, named 'Churchill', of 1st Armoured Division, February 1941. The Cruiser Tank Mk III was used in France during 1940 and in North Africa during 1941, and proved a failure because of its noticeably inadequate armour. It was this failing that the Cruiser Tank Mk IV (A13 Mk II) was designed to overcome through the thickening of the armour, increasing the protective basis to 20 or 30mm (0.79 or 1.18in) in important areas.

Panzer III (early model) (1940)

TYPE • *Medium Tank* **COUNTRY** • *Germany*

SPECIFICATIONS (Ausf C)	
DIMENSIONS:	Length: 5.85m (19ft 2in); Width: 2.82m (9ft 3in); Height: 2.42m (7ft 11in)
WEIGHT:	16 tonnes (17.64 US tons)
ENGINE:	Maybach HL108TR 12-cylinder inline petrol, 171.5kW (230hp)
SPEED:	40km/h (25mph)
RANGE:	165km (102 miles)
ARMOUR:	5–15mm (0.2–0.59in)
ARMAMENT	1 x 37mm (1.45in) KwK 36 L/46.5 with 121 rounds plus 3 x 7.92mm (0.31in) MG34 machine guns
CREW:	5

During the era of German rearmament in the 1930s, the Panzerkampfwagen III was developed as a lighter medium tank to operate in company with the heavier PzKpfw IV. Soon, however, the PzKpfw III developed a much broader role in the field.

Below: A Panzer III Ausf A, Poland, September 1939.

PANZER III AUSF E
A Panzer III Ausf E of the 2nd Panzer Division. The Ausf E was the first model to enter production after the outbreak of war, and soon gave way on the production line to the Ausf F.

ENGINE
Later versions of the Panzer III were powered by a 186kW (250hp), 12-cylinder Maybach HL 120 TRM engine, which generated a top speed of about 40km/h (24.85 mph).

IMPROVEMENTS
Variants A to D were prototype models constructed in 1937 and 1938. With A to C the torsion-bar suspension was refined and with D and F heavier armour, a higher-performance engine and an improved commander's cupola were installed.

CREW POSITIONS
The interior of the PzKpfw III was spacious compared to other contemporary tanks, although space was diminished as larger main weapons were installed in succeeding variants. The driver was positioned forward and to the left in the hull, while a radio operator/machine-gunner was seated to the right. Three crewmen – the commander, gunner and loader – occupied the turret, which was centred on the hull.

KNOCKED-OUT PANZER III
A PzKpfw III lies knocked out on an Eastern Front battlefield. The Panzer III was developed from the German Army requirement for each armoured battalion to be equipped with three companies of relatively light medium tanks and one company of heavier, more powerful support tanks. It was numerically the most important German tank during the invasion of the Soviet Union.

SdKfz 250 (1940)

TYPE • *Armoured Personnel Carrier* **COUNTRY** • *Germany*

SPECIFICATIONS (SdKfz 250/1)

Dimensions:	Length: 4.56m (15ft 1in); Width: 1.95m (6ft 5in); Height: 1.98m (6ft 6in)
Weight:	5.89 tonnes (6.49 US tons)
Engine:	Maybach HL 42 TRKM 6-cylinder inline petrol, 74.5kW (100hp)
Speed:	60km/h (37mph)
Range:	320km (199 miles)
Armour:	6–14.5mm (0.24–0.57in)
Armament:	2 x 7.92mm (0.31in) MG34 or MG42 machine guns with 2,010 rounds
Crew:	2, plus 4 infantrymen

The SdKfz 250 provided mobility for infantry and other units operating with Panzer divisions. Variants included a communications vehicle, mobile observation post and specialized weapons carriers, mounting anti-aircraft or anti-tank guns.

Right: An SdKfz 250/3 radio command vehicle. The versatility of the SdKfz 250 led to the development of at least a dozen variants.

SdKfz 250/9

The SdKfz 250/9 was a variant of the basic SdKfz 250 with a turret-mounted 20mm (0.79in) cannon. It was widely used by the Wehrmacht in the armoured reconnaissance role, particularly on the Eastern Front, with the first examples appearing in May 1943.

Steering

The sophisticated steering system used front wheel steering for gentle turns, supplemented by progressively harsher track braking the further the steering wheel was turned.

Tracks

Each track ran on four overlapping and interleaved double road wheels with torsion bar suspension – the so-called Schachtellaufwerk design used by nearly all German half-tracks.

SERIES REQUIREMENT

This series was developed to meet a 1939 requirement for a 'light armoured troop carrier'. The type was intended to transport an infantry *Halbgruppe* (half squad), primarily within reconnaissance units. The first 39 vehicles only entered service in June 1941. These resembled small versions of the SdKfz 251 series half-tracks but had superior speed and agility thanks to their significantly higher power/weight ratio.

SDKFZ 250/3 LEICHTE FUNKPANZERWAGEN

This radio communications variant of the 250 series was used by both the *Heer* and the *Luftwaffe*. Vehicles were used by Luftwaffe liaison teams to direct close-air support operations and were fitted with two radios: an FuG7 with a 2m (6ft 6in) rod aerial was used for ground-to-air communications, and an FuG8 formed part of the divisional radio net. Early models of the FuG8 used the distinctive frame antenna seen here, while later versions had an 8m (26ft 2in) star aerial.

Panzer IV (early model) (1940)

TYPE • *Medium Tank* **COUNTRY** • *Germany*

SPECIFICATIONS (Ausf F1)

Dimensions:	Length: 5.91m (19ft 5in); Width: 2.88m (9ft 5in); Height: 2.68m (8ft 10in)
Weight:	22 tonnes (24.25 US tons)
Engine:	1 x 12-cylinder inline Maybach HL 120 TRM water-cooled petrol engine generating 220kW (296hp)
Speed:	42km/h (26mph)
Range:	Road: 240km (150 miles); Cross-country: 120km (75 miles)
Armour:	15–50mm (0.59–1.97in)
Armament:	1 x short-barrelled 75mm (2.95in) L/24 gun; 2 x 7.92mm (0.31in) MG 34 machine guns
Crew:	5

The workhorse of the German armoured forces during the war, the Panzer IV was originally intended as an infantry support tank; however, it later assumed a tank-fighting combat role as Allied armoured vehicles became more powerful.

Left: The Ausf D variant, introduced in October 1939, was protected by thicker armour, and an external mantlet or gun shield protected the 75mm (2.95in) KwK.

Panzer IV Ausf E
The asymmetrical construction of the PzKpfw IV included a turret that was offset 66.5mm (2.6in) from the tank's centre to allow the torque shaft to clear the rotary base junction.

Engine
The 12-cylinder inline Maybach HL 120 TRM water-cooled petrol engine of the PzKpfw IV generated 296hp (220kW) and a top road speed of 42km/h (26mph).

Mobility
Wider tracks and modified front sprockets and rear idler wheels assisted with handling the PzKpfw IV in difficult terrain. Ice springs were added for manoeuvrability in winter weather.

ARMOURED BACKBONE
The PzKpfw IV became the backbone of the Wehrmacht's Panzer arm and was produced throughout the war. In total, nearly 9,000 vehicles were built, the basic chassis remaining the same in all models – heavier armour and armament being added as requirements changed. Despite the extra weight, it retained a good power-to-weight ratio throughout its production life and thus had good mobility.

STIFF COMPETITION
The Panzer IV was the only German tank in production throughout the war. It emerged in many enhanced variants, with upgraded armour, armament and mobility, which kept it able to compete with the best of Allied armour.

Sturmgeschütz III (1940)

TYPE • *Assault gun* **COUNTRY** • *Germany*

SPECIFICATIONS (Ausf G)	
Dimensions:	Length: 6.77m (22ft 2in); Width: 2.95m (9ft 8in); Height: 2.16m (7ft 1in)
Weight:	23.9 tonnes (26.35 US tons)
Engine:	Maybach HL120TRM 12-cylinder inline petrol, 223.7kW (300hp)
Speed:	40km/h (25mph)
Range:	155km (96 miles)
Armour:	11–80mm (0.31–3.15in)
Armament:	1 x 75mm (2.95in) StuK 40 L/48 (late production models only); 2 x 7.92mm (0.31in) MG34 machine guns (1 x coaxial and 1 on loader's hatch)
Crew:	4

The *Sturmgeschütz* III (StuG III) was one of the most successful German AFVs of the entire war. Approximately 9500 vehicles were produced from January 1940 to March 1945, and as early as the spring of 1944, StuG III units claimed the destruction of 20,000 Allied tanks.

Below: A StuG III Ausf G. As the role of the StuG III evolved to one of tank destroyer, its armament was up-gunned to a higher-velocity, long-barrelled 75mm (2.95in) L/43 and L/48 cannon.

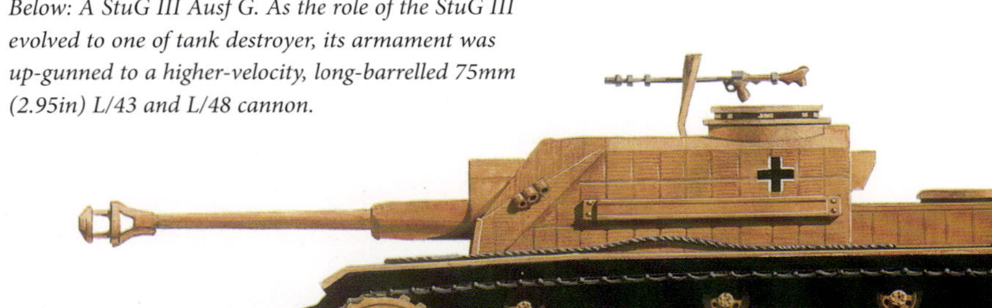

Driver's position
The StuG was based on the chassis of the Panzer III. The driver's station was unaltered from that of the tank, but behind him was now a very cramped compartment, which made fighting with hatches down an extremely arduous experience.

Silhouette
The low profile of the StuG III made the vehicle easy to conceal, while the addition of armour plating was effective against hollow charge shells.

StuG III Sdkfz 142/1
This variant was up-gunned with the powerful 75mm (2.95in) StuK 40, which was capable of destroying any Allied tank.

ORIGIN STUDY

In 1935 an initial study was drafted by then-Colonel Erich von Manstein and submitted to General Ludwig Beck, suggesting that *Sturmartillerie* ('assault artillery') units should be used in a direct-fire support role for infantry divisions. The idea was favourably received and, on 15 June 1936, Daimler-Benz AG received an order to develop an armoured infantry support vehicle equipped with a 75mm (2.95in) gun in a limited traverse mounting protected by a fully enclosed fighting compartment. This led to the StuG III, which entered service in 1940.

STUG COLUMN
Sturmgeschütz units were considered to be the elite artillery units of the German Army. Overall, the Sturmgeschütz series proved highly successful and served on all fronts as assault guns and tank destroyers.

KV-1 (1940)

TYPE • *Heavy tank* **COUNTRY** • *Soviet Union*

SPECIFICATIONS

Dimensions:	Length: 6.68m (21ft 11in); Width: 3.32m (10ft 11in); Height: 2.71m (8ft 11in)
Weight:	43.6 tonnes (48.1 US tons)
Engine:	473kW (600hp) V-2 12-cylinder diesel
Speed:	35km/h (22mph)
Range:	160km (99 miles)
Armour:	25–90mm (0.98–3.54in)
Armament:	1 x 76.2mm (3in) L-11 L/32 gun; 3 x 7.62mm (0.3in) DT machine guns (1 coaxial, 1 turret rear, 1 hull front)
Crew:	5

During Operation *Barbarossa*, the occasional counter-attacks made in strength by the potent new Soviet heavy tank design, the KV-1 – supported by T-34s – inflicted considerable shock on the Axis invaders.

Below: A KV-1 Model 1941. Sporting new radial road wheels, the Model 1941 typically mounted either the longer-barrelled F-34 or ZiS-5 gun in a redesigned and up-armoured welded turret with modified mantlet.

Gun mantlet
The most obvious external difference between this model and its predecessor, the Model 1939, was that they had differently shaped gun mantlets.

Armour
The KV-1 Model 1940 – with armour up to 75mm (2.9in) thick – proved almost impervious to German tank and AT guns in the first few months of *Barbarossa*.

Kv-1 Model 1940
The other external feature that differentiated the Model 1940 from its predecessor was that it lacked the two canisters per side of lubricant that had been fitted on the Model 1939's rear fenders.

SOLID FOUNDATION
Although the KV tanks were prone to mechanical failure and some critics maintained that their main armament lacked the firepower of opposing heavy tanks, they were the product of sound design concepts and rendered vital service with the Red Army during the bleakest period following the German invasion. They also established a basis for the improved Stalin tanks that were to come.

KV-1 IN MOSCOW
A KV-1 rolls through Moscow streets to the front in December 1941. The tank had a 76.2mm (3in) main gun and was used by the Red Army for the breakthrough role in which its lack of speed was not a handicap.

Marmon Herrington (1940)

TYPE • *Armoured car* **COUNTRY** • *South Africa*

SPECIFICATIONS (Mk II)

Dimensions:	Length: 4.88m (16ft); Width: 1.93m (6ft 4in); Height: 2.286m (7ft 6in)
Weight:	6 tonnes (6.61 US tons)
Engine:	1 x Ford V-8 petrol engine
Speed:	80.5km/h (50mph)
Range:	322km (200 miles)
Armour:	12mm (0.47in)
Armament:	1 x 7.7mm (0.303in) Vickers machine gun; 1 x 14mm (0.55in) Boys anti-tank rifle; 1 x 7.7mm (0.303in) Bren machine gun
Crew:	4

The Marmon Herrington saw extensive service in the Western Desert against Rommel's Afrika Korps. Well-liked and sturdy, it was effective despite light armour and armament, being relatively easy to maintain. It was fitted with many different weapons in the field.

Left: This Marmon Herrington Mk II in desert guise is armed in typical fashion with a Vickers water-cooled machine gun, a Bren air-cooled machine gun and a Boys 13.97mm (0.55in) turret-mounted anti-tank rifle.

Marmon Herrington Mk II
Marmon Herrington armoured cars were built in South Africa using a variety of imported components. Almost 900 Mark IIs were produced, the majority of which were sent to North Africa.

Crew
The vehicle had a crew of four housed in what was a fairly roomy hull. This vehicle belonged to the South African Armoured Car Regiment.

Layout
The Mk II, known to the British as the armoured car, Marmon Herrington, Mk II, was a fairly simple but effective conversion of the original truck chassis to take the new 4x4 transmission and a well-shaped armoured hull.

FIELD MODIFICATIONS

When they were first issued to South African and British units in North Africa, the Marmon Herringtons were the only armoured cars available in any numbers. They proved to be surprisingly effective vehicles, but their 12mm (0.47in) armour was too thin and the armament was too light. The troops in the field made their own changes to the armament and all manner of weapons sprouted from the turrets or from the open hulls once the turrets had been removed.

SOUTH AFRICAN FORCES, 1942
One of the more common weapon fits to the Marmon Herrington was a captured Italian 20mm (0.79in) Breda cannon, but Italian and German 37mm (1.45in) and 45mm (1.77in) tank or anti-tank guns were also used. One vehicle mounted a British 2pdr (40mm/1.57in) tank gun, and this became the preferred armament for later marks.

Chevrolet WA (1940)

TYPE • *Truck* **COUNTRY** • *Canada*

SPECIFICATIONS

DIMENSIONS:	Length: 6.579m (21ft 7in); Width: 2.49m (8ft 2in); Height: 3m (9ft 9in)
WEIGHT:	3.048 tonnes (3.36 US tons)
ENGINE:	1 x Ford V-8 petrol engine developing 71kW (95hp)
SPEED:	80km/h (50mph)
RANGE:	274km (170 miles)
ARMOUR:	None
ARMAMENT:	2 x machine guns, various calibres
CREW:	1

The Chevrolet WA was produced with either wood or steel bodies and used in an enormous number of roles, from ambulances to mobile gun carriages. Many were adapted for use by special forces, such as the Long Range Desert Group (LRDG) in North Africa.

Right: An LRDG patrol in the Western Desert utilizes the Chevrolet WA to cross the scorching landscape. The lead vehicle has a Boys anti-tank rifle mounted.

WEAPONRY
A vast assortment of weaponry was carried by the LRDG, ranging from machine guns to anti-tank and light AA guns.

LRDG CHEVROLET WA
This Chevrolet is typical of the wide range of 'soft-skinned' vehicles used by the LRDG for raiding and reconnaissance missions far behind enemy lines.

ENGINE
The chief strengths of the Chevrolet WA were durability and mobility, the latter provided by a Ford V-8 petrol engine delivering a top speed of 80km/h (50mph).

WORKHORSES
The LRDG used a variety of light vehicles during their operations in North Africa. The Chevrolet truck proved particularly useful, however, because it not only offered speed and mobility but also could carry the weight of food, water, fuel, ammunition, equipment, personal effects and weapons necessary for long-range missions to distant enemy objectives. The total payload of the vehicle was about 1364kg (3000lb).

MACHINE-GUN ARMAMENT
Allied soldiers of the LRDG in their 30cwt Chevrolet truck man a Lewis gun (left) and a modified Browning Mk II aircraft machine gun (right), in the Western Desert, North Africa, in 1942.

Daimler Scout / Armoured Car (1941)

TYPE • *Armoured car* **COUNTRY** • *United Kingdom*

SPECIFICATIONS (Scout Mk II)

DIMENSIONS:	Length: 3.23m (10ft 5in); Width: 1.72m (5ft 8in); Height: 1.5m (4ft 11in)
WEIGHT:	3.22 tonnes (3.55 US tons)
ENGINE:	41kW (55hp) Daimler 6-cylinder petrol
SPEED:	89km/h (55mph)
RANGE:	322km (200 miles)
ARMOUR:	5–30mm (0.2–1.18in)
ARMAMENT:	1 x 7.62mm (0.3in) machine gun
CREW:	2

The Daimler Scout/Armoured Car became the standard equipment for many reconnaissance regiments. Armed with a 2-pounder (40mm) gun, it had limited combat capability but proved to be an excellent and reliable reconnaissance vehicle in all theatres.

Right: This Daimler Scout Car Mk II has been fitted with a 7.62mm (0.3in) Browning machine gun in place of the more usual Bren.

TURRET MODIFICATIONS
A number of Daimlers were modified in 1944–45 by having their turrets removed and pintle-mounted machine guns fitted to produce 'heavy scout cars', which were widely known as 'SODs' – 'Sawn-Off Daimlers'.

FOUR-WHEEL DRIVE
The four-wheel drive used double-coil springs on each wheel, although the early idea of using four-wheel steering was discarded as being too complex.

ARMAMENT
Alongside the 2pdr (40mm) gun, the turret of the Daimler Scout also mounted a coaxial 7.92mm (0.3in) Besa machine gun.

DEVELOPMENT
When the BSA Scout Car was undergoing its initial trials, it was decided to use the basic design as the foundation for a new vehicle to be called the Tank, Light, Wheeled. Daimler took over the development of the project, and the result was a vehicle that resembled the diminutive Scout Car but was nearly twice as heavy and had a two-man turret. Development started in August 1939 and the first prototypes were running by the end of the year. The first production vehicles emerged in April 1941, known as the Armoured Car, Daimler Mk I.

DAIMLER ARMOURED CAR
The Daimler Armoured Car was basically a Scout Car (the two were developed in parallel) enlarged to accommodate a turret mounting a 2pdr (40mm) gun. It underwent surprisingly few changes once in service. An Armoured Car, Daimler Mk II version was later introduced with a new gun mounting, a slightly revised radiator arrangement and an escape hatch through the engine compartment for the driver.

M3 Half-track (1941)

TYPE • *Half-track* **COUNTRY** • *United States*

SPECIFICATIONS (M3)

Dimensions:	Length: 6.16m (20ft 3in); Width: 1.96m (6ft 5in); Height: 2.3m (7ft 7in)
Weight:	9.1 tonnes (10.03 US tons)
Engine:	110kW (147hp) White 160AX petrol (gasoline)
Speed:	72km/h (45mph)
Range:	322km (200 miles)
Armour:	6.4–12.7mm (0.25–0.5in)
Armament:	1 x 7.62mm (0.3in) M1919A4 MG
Crew:	3 (+10 troops)

The American M3 half-track was officially designated as the Carrier, Personnel, Half-track, M3. In essence, the design was an elongated M2 half-track with 25cm (10in) added to the length of the troop compartment.

Right: This M3 half-track has its canvas canopy erected to protect the troops from inclement weather; note also the anti-ditching roller sticking out from the vehicle's hull nose.

Range
The half-track carried 230 litres (51 US gal) in its fuel tanks, enabling it to obtain a maximum operational range on one fuel load of 322km (200 miles).

Armoured ambulance
The versatile M3 was frequently employed as an armoured ambulance. This vehicle was operated by the Medical Battalion of the US 4th Infantry Division.

Troop carrying
The standard M3 featured a lengthened and redesigned troop-carrying compartment compared to the M2. Its capacity was up to 10 troops, seated in two inward-facing rows of five seats.

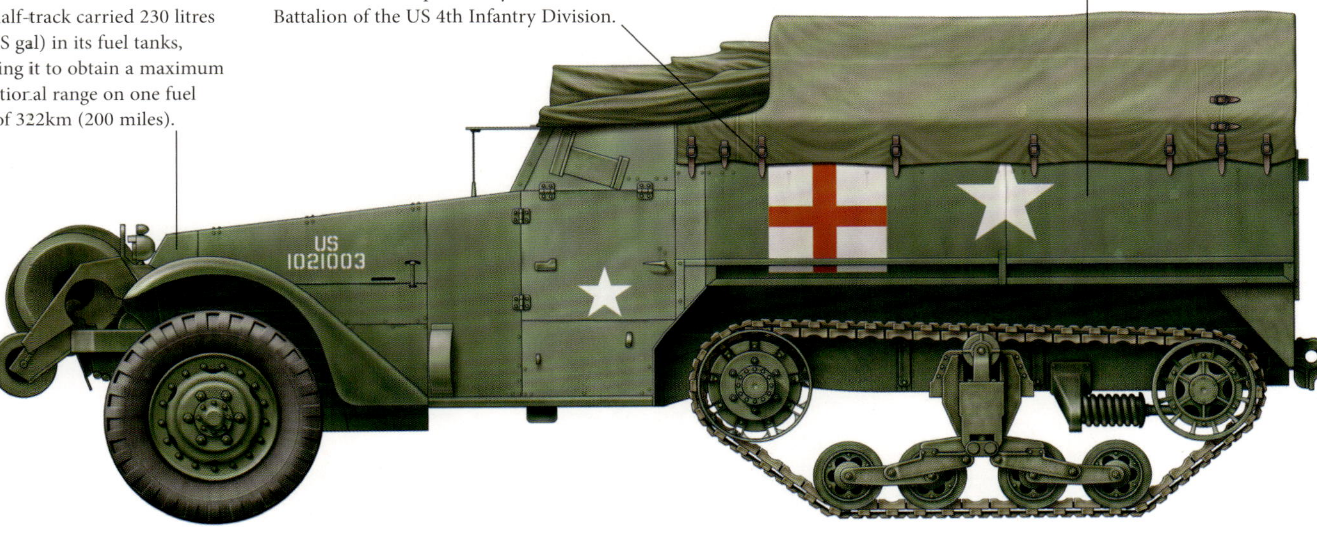

M2/M3 DIFFERENCES
Commencing May 1941, Autocar, Diamond T and WMC manufactured a total of 12,391 M3s. Similar to the M2 half-track, the front of the M3 variant featured a single large front rubber-tyred road wheel pairing, while the remaining two-thirds of the hull sported tracks. The M3's VVS suspension and running gear were largely similar to that of the M2 and also featured a large open-spoked rear idler wheel that had a double horizontal spring coil.

M3A1 TROOP CARRIER
During October 1943, the first M3A1 half-tracks entered American Army service; this design was slightly heavier at 9.3 tonnes (9.2 tons). The main difference between the two designs was that the M3A1 dispensed with the M25 pedestal mount and instead featured an M49 or M49A1 ring mount.

M3 Stuart (1941)

TYPE • *Light tank* **COUNTRY** • *United States*

SPECIFICATIONS (M3A3)	
DIMENSIONS:	Length: 4.53m (14ft 10in); Width: 2.24m (7ft 4in); Height: 2.39m (7ft 10in)
WEIGHT:	14.7 tonnes (16.2 US tons)
ENGINE:	186kW (250hp) up-rated Wright/Continental W670-9A petrol (gasoline) or 191kW (250hp) Guiberson T-1020 diesel
SPEED:	58km/h (36mph)
RANGE:	217km (135 miles)
ARMOUR:	9.5–51mm (0.375–2in)
ARMAMENT:	1 x 37mm (1.46in) M5; 2 or 3 x 7.62mm (0.3in) M1919A4 MG
CREW:	4

The M3 American light tank was developed as an infantry support vehicle with excellent speed and effective armament, and served with the US, British and Soviet armies in both the European and Pacific theatres during World War II.

Left: Speed was the primary advantage the tank possessed in the face of superior enemy forces. Thicker sloped armour increased the survivability of the M3A3, seen here.

M3A3
This M3A3 with redesigned hull is seen here during August 1944 sporting the red, white and blue tactical insignia of the First Free French Army.

ARMAMENT
Throughout the service life of the M3 light tank, the 37mm (1.45in) M6 gun was its main armament, unsuitable for tank versus tank combat, but adequate against other targets in infantry support.

SUSPENSION
The vertical volute spring suspension was characteristic of American armoured vehicles of the World War II era. It featured rear idlers that were on the ground, reducing pressure and providing better support for the rear of the M3A3.

MULTIPLE THEATRES

British crews in North Africa grew fond of the M3; it helped the British and later American forces to win the North African campaign. In the Pacific, the M3 light tank was effective as an infantry support vehicle, penetrating thick jungle and negotiating terrain that heavier tanks could not. The M3 was powerful enough to neutralize Japanese tanks, machine-gun nests, bunkers and troop concentrations as American troops fought their way, island by island, across the theatre.

M3A1 STUART

The four-crew M3A1 sported enhanced lethality modifications. These included an altered turret design that featured an internal basket in which the two turret crew sat and rotated with the turret. The M3A1 also featured the 37mm (1.46in) M6 L/56.6 as standard but married to an improved gun vertical stabilizer.

T-60 (1941)

TYPE • *Light tank* **COUNTRY** • *Soviet Union*

SPECIFICATIONS

Dimensions:	Length: 4.29m (14ft 1in); Width: 2.46m (8ft 1in); Height: 1.89m (6ft 2in)
Weight:	5.2 tonnes (5.73 US tons)
Engine:	52kW (70hp) GAZ-202 6-cylinder petrol
Speed:	45km/h (27mph)
Range:	435km (270 miles)
Armour:	7–35mm (0.28–1.38in)
Armament:	1 x 20mm (0.79in) TNSh L/82.4 automatic-fire cannon; 1 x 7.62mm (0.3in) coaxial DT machine gun
Crew:	2

The next generation of Soviet light tanks sported somewhat enhanced survivability thanks to their modest yet well-sloped armour; they also had increased firepower and were more economical to produce. Despite this, they were still semi-obsolescent by summer 1941.

Right: The Model 1942 variant featured solid, rather than spoked, road wheels, as well as thicker frontal armour.

Turret
The hexagonal angular turret, offset to the left, mounted a long-barrelled TNSh 20mm (0.79in) L/82.4 automatic-fire cannon and a coaxial DT machine gun.

Track suspension
Weighing 5.2 tonnes (5.73 US tons), this two-man vehicle featured a track suspension arrangement of one drive, four road and one rear idler wheel plus three return rollers on each side.

Angled armour
The tank also sported angular well-sloped – albeit light – armour on the shallow hull superstructure; the latter gave the tank a low silhouette.

NEW DESIGN

During the late 1930s, the Soviets concluded that their T-26 light tanks were inadequate. In 1938, therefore, design work commenced on prototype replacement vehicles that would mount a more potent 20mm (0.79in) gun as well as light yet well-sloped armour. By 1941, this design work culminated in the emergence of the T-50 and T-60. While the diesel-powered T-50 had its production run curtailed after just 69 vehicles, that year the T-60 successfully entered into mass production.

T-60 TANK RIDERS
Soviet infantry sit precariously on the hulls of T-60s. Crucially, the Soviets found that the T-60 could be easily and cheaply manufactured, which was essential given the catastrophic tank casualties suffered during the *Barbarossa* campaign in 1941. In a 14-month production run, the Soviets delivered 6292 T-60s, including 1500 Model 1942 variants, before manufacturing capacity was switched to the improved T-70.

T-34 Model 1941 (1941)

TYPE • *Medium tank* **COUNTRY** • *Soviet Union*

SPECIFICATIONS

Dimensions:	Length: 5.92m (19ft 5in); Width: 3m (9ft 10in); Height: 2.45m (8ft)
Weight:	26.5 tonnes (29.2 US tons)
Engine:	373kW (500hp) Model V-2-34 diesel
Speed:	55km/h (34mph)
Range:	300km (186 miles)
Armour:	15–60mm (0.59–2.4in)
Armament:	76.2mm (3in) F-34 L/40.5 gun; 2 x 7.62mm (0.3in) DT machine guns (1 coaxial, 1 hull front)
Crew:	4

With its excellent trade-off between lethality, survivability, mobility, usability and ease of production, the T-34 became the mainstay of the Soviet tank force, with 57,300 vehicles manufactured between 1940 and 1945.

Left: In 1941, Soviet development teams improved the already promising T-34 Model 1940 design with the introduction of the up-gunned and up-armoured Model 1941, shown here in summer camouflage.

Penetration
At a range of 1000m (3280ft), the F-34 gun, when firing armour-piercing high explosive (APHE) rounds, could penetrate 60mm (2.36in) of vertical armour – enough to knock out most extant German tanks.

Armour
The Model 1941 had an improved distribution of armour in comparison to its predecessor. The front glacis plates were 45–47mm (1.77–1.85in) thick and sloped at 60 degrees.

Engine
All Model 1941 tanks were powered by the new 373kW (500hp) V-2-34 38.3 litre (8.4 US gal) V-12 diesel engine.

LETHALITY
In early 1941, the next T-34 variant, the Model 1941 (T-34B), entered mass production. Instead of the L-11 gun, this tank mounted the newly developed 76.2mm (3in) F-34 gun in a box mantlet. This weapon's greater barrel length – 40.5 rather than 30.5 calibres – enabled its rounds to develop greater muzzle velocity, thus increasing its lethality.

WINTER OFFENSIVE 1941/42
The incorporation of the new gun and turret front armour thickened to 60mm (2.4in) increased the Model 1941's weight to 26.5 tonnes (29.2 tons), although the Model 1941 still achieved the same performance as its lighter predecessor.

Panzer IV Ausf F1 (1941)

TYPE • *Medium tank* **COUNTRY** • *Germany*

SPECIFICATIONS	
DIMENSIONS:	Length: 5.92m (19ft 4in); Width: 2.84m (9ft 3in); Height: 2.68m (8ft 8in)
WEIGHT:	24.6 tonnes (27.11 US tons)
ENGINE:	1 x Maybach HL120TRM engine
SPEED:	42km/h (26mph)
RANGE:	200km (124.3 miles)
ARMOUR:	10–30mm (0.4–1.2in)
ARMAMENT:	1 x 75mm (2.95in) KwK 37 L/24 gun; 2 x 7.92mm (0.31in) MG34
CREW:	5

The Panzer IV Ausf F1 marked an attempt to rationalize the armour layout of the Panzer IV series. The armour depth was increased to 50mm (1.96in) on the mantlet and turret front for the first time. The F2 variant was also fitted with a more powerful long-barrelled gun.

Left: A front view of the Panzer IV Ausf F1. The frontal hull armour was 50mm (1.97in) in thickness.

ARMAMENT
The main armament of the PzKpfw IV Ausf F included two subvariants, the F1 and F2. The F1 mounted the short-barrelled 75mm (2.95in) L/24 gun and the F2 the long-barrelled 75mm L/43 gun (shown here).

WEIGHT
The weight of the Panzer IV increased as a larger, more powerful engine was installed and additional armour fitted. Wider tracks were also fitted to reduce ground pressure.

ENGINE
The Ausf F models were powered by a Maybach HL120TRM 12-cylinder inline petrol engine generating 223.7kW (300hp) and a top speed of 42km/h (26mph).

FIREPOWER
When the PzKpfw III was authorized for production, its 37mm (1.45in) main weapon was deemed sufficient to take on enemy tanks. The heavier weapon of the PzKpfw IV was intended to neutralize gun emplacements, fixed fortifications and troop concentrations that could slow the progress of the German Blitzkrieg, the coordinated offensive action by aircraft, artillery, tanks and ground troops that swept across Poland and then France and the Low Countries in 1939 and 1940.

PANZER IV AUSF F2
Little serious work was carried out on up-gunning the Panzer IV until November 1941, when the flood of reports from the Eastern Front complaining about the Panzer IV's ineffectiveness against the T-34 and KV-1 compelled urgent action. The 75mm (2.95in) KwK 40 L/43 gun was fitted to the Panzer IV Ausf F2, which entered service in March 1942.

Carro Armato L6/40 (1941)

TYPE • *Light tank* COUNTRY • *Italy*

SPECIFICATIONS	
DIMENSIONS:	Length: 3.78m (12ft 5in); Width: 1.92m (6ft 4in); Height: 2.03m (6ft 8in)
WEIGHT:	6.9 tonnes (7.61 US tons)
ENGINE:	1 x SPA 18 D petrol, 52.2kW (70bhp) engine
SPEED:	42km/h (26.1mph)
RANGE:	200km (125 miles)
ARMOUR:	6–30mm (0.24–1.18in)
ARMAMENT:	1 x 20mm (0.79in) Breda cannon; 1 x 8mm (0.315in) Breda MG
CREW:	2

The Fiat L6/40 light tank, roughly equivalent to the Panzer II, was developed from the L3. Several versions were produced, including flamethrower and command tank variants. The most successful was a self-propelled gun version, the Semovente 47/32.

Right: The L6/40 had a prominent boarding step on the track guards.

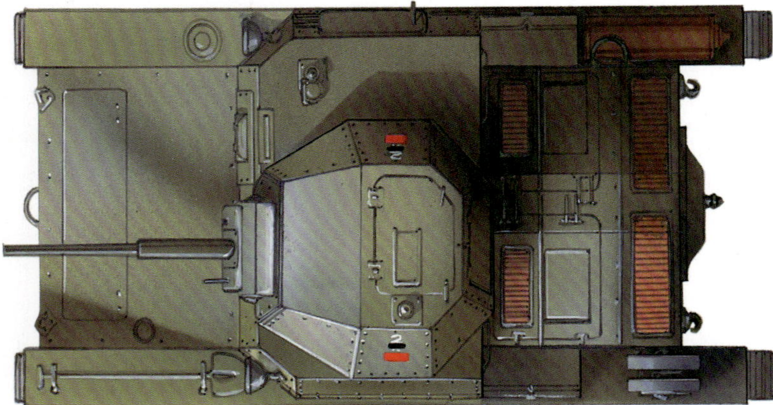

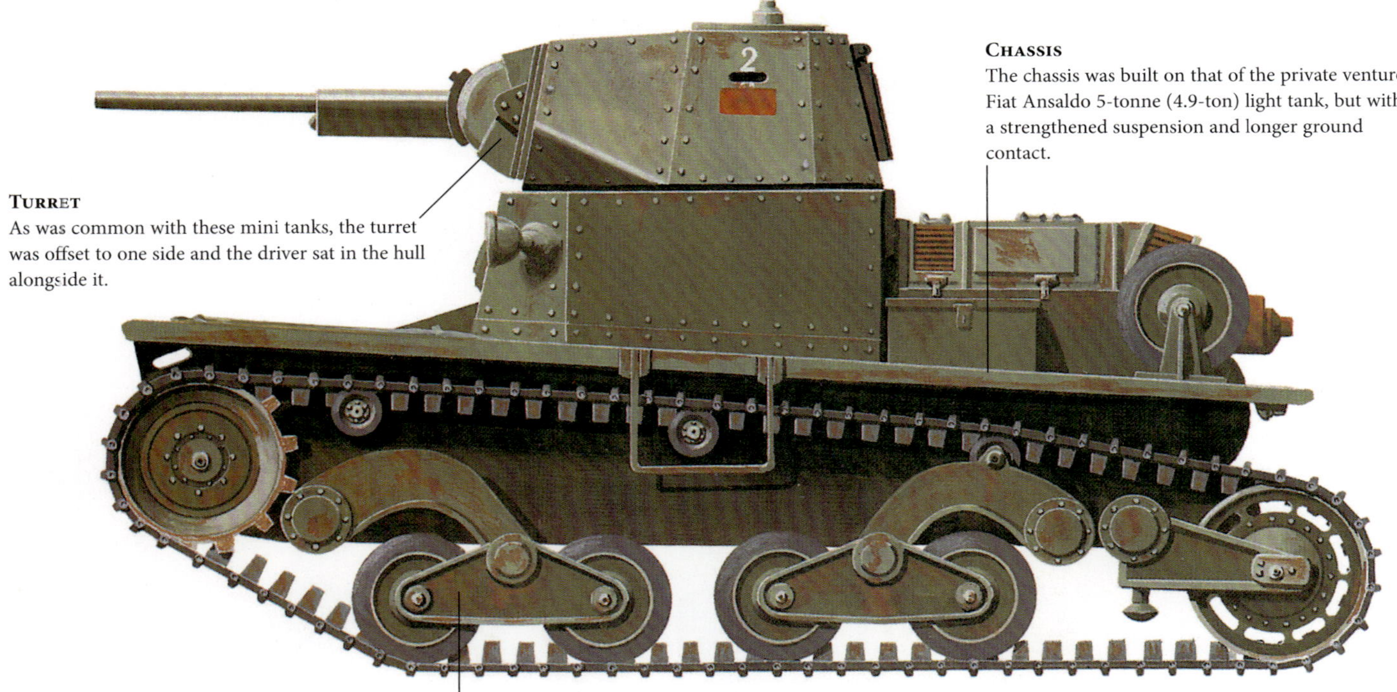

CHASSIS
The chassis was built on that of the private venture Fiat Ansaldo 5-tonne (4.9-ton) light tank, but with a strengthened suspension and longer ground contact.

TURRET
As was common with these mini tanks, the turret was offset to one side and the driver sat in the hull alongside it.

SUSPENSION
The torsion bar suspension had double-wheel bogies and trailing suspension arms.

ARMAMENT OPTIONS

Designed to replace the L3 (CV 33) light tank, the Fiat L6/40 had as its basis a Fiat-Ansaldo tracked chassis intended for export. In 1936, two armed prototypes were delivered for testing. They had either two 8mm (0.31in) machine guns or one 37mm (1.46in) cannon in the turret plus a sponson-mounted machine gun. The production vehicles had a 30mm (0.79in) Breda cannon and one machine gun.

CAPTURED L6/40
This photograph, taken in Kocevje, Yugoslavia, in December 1943, shows German troops operating a captured L6/40. Lacking in medium and heavy tanks, the Italians were forced to use light tanks where they were unsuited.

AEC Mk III (1941)

TYPE • *Armoured car* **COUNTRY** • *United Kingdom*

SPECIFICATIONS	
DIMENSIONS	Length: 5.61m (18ft 5in); Width: 2.70m (8ft 11in); Height: 2.69m (8ft 10in)
WEIGHT:	12.7 tonnes (14.0 US tons)
ENGINE:	AEC A195 6-cylinder diesel engine, 178kW (05hp)
SPEED:	Road: 58km/h (38mph)
RANGE:	Road: 400km (250 miles)
ARMOUR:	16–65mm (0.63–2.56in)
ARMAMENT:	Main: 1 × QF 75mm (2.95in) cannon; Secondary: 1 × 7.92mm (0.31in) Besa machine gun, 1 × 7.62mm (0.303in) Bren light machine gun
CREW:	4

The AEC armoured cars were heavily armed and effective vehicles, packing the weaponry of a heavy tank. They were adaptable to larger guns as these became available. After the war, some AEC IIIs were supplied to Belgium for its reconnaissance regiments.

Right: One of the few faults of this car was its high profile and angular appearance, which made it hard to conceal in the observation role.

CAMOUFLAGE
Camouflage netting was applied to the turret of this AEC Mk III. Local foliage is threaded through the netting to provide some concealment in wooded terrain.

M3 GUN
The AEC Mk III had the 75mm (2.95in) M3 gun used on American medium tanks such as the M3 and many M4 Shermans.

DRIVE SETTING
The AECs had selectable two- or four-wheel drive and steering with front-wheel drive used only for road travel.

BUS BUILDER

Designed (and built) by a bus manufacturer without any official requirement, the AEC armoured cars proved to be the equal of many tanks of their day and served with distinction in North Africa and Europe. In 1941, the AEC (Associated Engineering Company) of Southall, West London, built an armoured car based on information they had gleaned on fighting in North Africa. This Mk I car was virtually a wheeled tank, with heavy armour, a powerful engine and a 40mm (2pdr) gun, equivalent to that used by most tanks in the desert.

MK III ON MANOEUVRES
Following the Mk I, armament was increased on subsequent models in parallel with developments in tank guns. The AEC Mk II was given a three-man electrically traversed turret and a 57mm (6pdr) gun, but the Mk III had a 75mm (2.95in) M3 cannon.

Cruiser Tank Mk VI, Crusader Mk I (A15) (1941)

TYPE • *Cruiser tank* **COUNTRY** • *United Kingdom*

SPECIFICATIONS

Dimensions:	Length: 5.99m (19ft 8in); Width: 2.64m (8ft 8in); Height: 2.23m (7ft 4in)
Weight:	19.73 tonnes (21.75 US tons)
Engine:	Nuffield 12-cylinder Liberty L-12 water-cooled petrol engine generating 254kW (340hp)
Speed:	Road: 43.4km/h (27mph); Off-road: 24km/h (15mph)
Range:	204km (127 miles)
Armour:	Up to 51mm (2in) in Mk III
Armament:	Main: 1 x 6pdr (57mm/2.24in) QF gun; Secondary: 1 x 7.92mm (0.31in) Besa machine gun
Crew:	3

The British Crusader tanks were conceived between the world wars as rapid exploitation armoured vehicles that would exploit breaches in enemy defensive lines created by heavier weapons and then slash into rear areas to create havoc.

Right: Crusaders on the move in the Western Desert; the dust raised by armoured forces created an easy locator for enemy attack aircraft.

Armour protection
The essence of the cruiser tank lay in its speed, which was achieved by the sacrifice of armour. Early Crusaders were thinly protected with up to 40mm (1.57in) of armour, while later variants were slightly improved to 51mm (2in).

Main armament
The Mk VI Crusader I Cruiser tank was armed with a weak 2pdr (40mm/1.57in) QF gun, which was ineffective against a new generation of German tanks. The Crusader III introduced the more powerful 6pdr (57mm/2.24in) QF gun.

Engine
The Nuffield 12-cylinder Liberty L-12 water-cooled petrol engine of the Crusader series was prone to overheating, while its Nuffield constant mesh transmission often broke down.

CRUISER TANK CONCEPT
For British tacticians in the 1930s, the concept of the cruiser tank was logical. The cruisers would utilize speed to demoralize the enemy, striking deep behind the lines. But the benefits of speed and mobility came at a high price. Cruiser tanks would have to sacrifice their armour protection to execute their mission efficiently. In addition, lighter weaponry was essential, as the additional weight of heavy guns would diminish combat effectiveness.

TRIAL CRUSADER MK I
The Crusader series of tanks were sleek, streamlined and looked to all the world like first-class armoured fighting vehicles. However, the harsh climate of the North African desert laid bare their shortcomings.

Cruiser Tank Mk VI, Crusader Mk III (1941)

TYPE • *Cruiser tank* **COUNTRY** • *United Kingdom*

SPECIFICATIONS

DIMENSIONS:	Length: 6.3m (20ft 8in); Width: 2.64m (8ft 8in); Height: 2.24m (7ft 4in)
WEIGHT:	20.07 tonnes (22.12 US tons)
ENGINE:	253.64kW (340hp) Nuffield Liberty Mark IV V12 petrol
SPEED:	44km/h (27mph)
RANGE:	161km (100 miles)
ARMOUR:	7–51mm (0.28–2.01in)
ARMAMENT:	1 x 57mm (2.24in) 6pdr (57mm/2.24in) OQF gun; 1 x coaxial 7.92mm (0.31in) Besa MG
CREW:	3

The Crusader was thinly armoured and lacked firepower, and reliability was a problem. Once replaced by the M4 Sherman, it was adapted for a variety of roles, such as anti-aircraft tank, recovery vehicle, combat engineer tank and artillery tractor.

Right: Here we see a Crusader III in Tunisia in 1943, serving with the 6th Armoured Division near Bou Arada.

PROTECTION
The Crusader III was somewhat slower than its predecessors due to the weight of the larger gun; therefore, armour protection was largely unchanged.

MAIN GUN
The 6pdr's anti-tank performance was better than that of the US 75mm (2.9in) in the Lee/Grant and Sherman.

PERFORMANCE
The maximum cross-country speed of the Crusader III was 24km/h (15mph), while its top road speed was 43.4km/h (27mph).

IN COMBAT
The Crusader III, which became the definitive fighting variant of the series, made its combat debut at the pivotal Battle of El Alamein in October 1942 and during the 1770km (1100-mile) pursuit of the German *Panzerarmee Afrika* into Tunisia. About 100 of the Crusader III participated in the great El Alamein victory, and the introduction of the 6pdr QF gun with 65 rounds of ammunition at long last gave the Crusader the ability to destroy the German PzKpfw III and IV tanks then deployed by the Germans in North Africa.

6-POUNDER GUN
The first towed 6pdr anti-tank guns were issued to front-line units in May 1942, but the Crusader III, which carried the 6pdr as its main armament, was not ready until August of that year.

Churchill tank (1941)

TYPE • *Heavy tank* **COUNTRY** • *United Kingdom*

Conceived as an infantry support tank that would take on obstacles on a battlefield reminiscent of World War I trench warfare, the Churchill Mk IV evolved into a versatile fighting vehicle that fulfilled a variety of combat and support roles.

SPECIFICATIONS

Dimensions:	Length: 7.44m (24ft 5in); Width: 2.44m (8ft); Height: 3.45m (11ft 4in)
Weight:	39 tonnes (42.98 US tons)
Engine:	Bedford Twin-Six Petrol developing 261kW (350bhp)
Speed:	Road: 25km/h (15.5mph); Off-road: 13km/h (8mph)
Range:	259km (161 miles)
Armour:	19–89mm (0.75–3.5in)
Armament:	Main: 1 x OQF 6 pdr (57mm/2.24in) L/43 Mk. V Gun; Secondary: 2 x 7.92mm (0.31in) Besa MGs; 1 x 7.7mm (0.303in) Bren machine gun
Crew:	5

Right: The Churchill Mk III (seen here) was an immediate predecessor to the Mk IV.

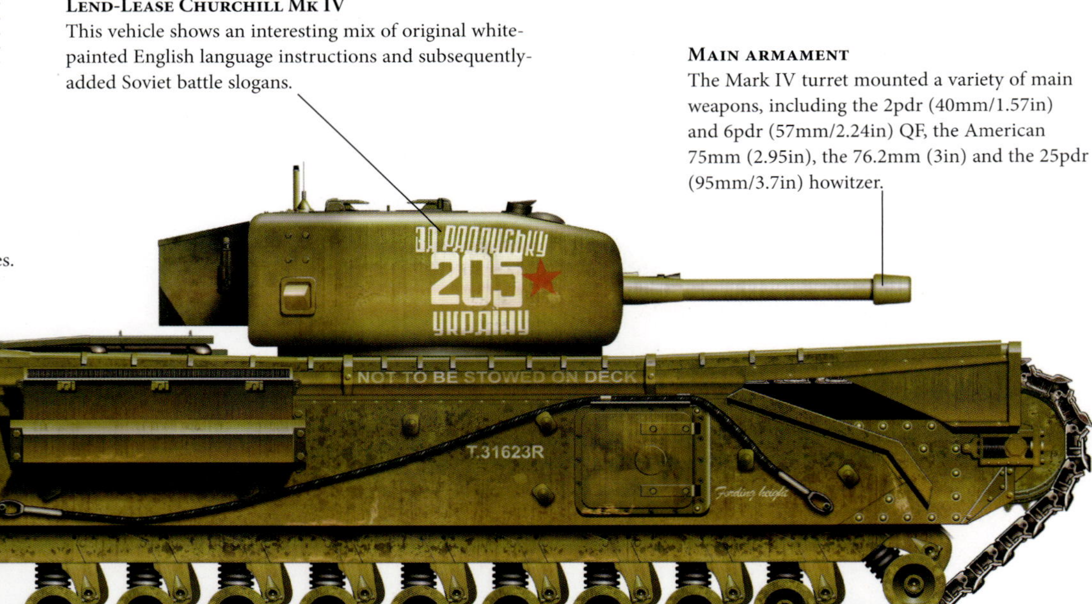

Lend-Lease Churchill Mk IV
This vehicle shows an interesting mix of original white-painted English language instructions and subsequently-added Soviet battle slogans.

Main armament
The Mark IV turret mounted a variety of main weapons, including the 2pdr (40mm/1.57in) and 6pdr (57mm/2.24in) QF, the American 75mm (2.95in), the 76.2mm (3in) and the 25pdr (95mm/3.7in) howitzer.

Suspension
The coiled spring suspension of the Churchill Mk IV included 11 bogies covered by panniers and each mounting a pair of 254mm (10in) wheels. It proved most effective in providing traction on various surfaces.

SOVIET TACTICS

The Soviets organized the Churchill tanks they received from the British into 10 separate Guards Armoured Breakthrough Regiments, numbered in the range 10th–82nd Regiments. Each unit was equipped with 21 Churchills and staffed by 214 personnel. During 1942–44, these regiments fought in operations to lift the siege of Leningrad, the battle to surround Stalingrad, the titanic clash of armour at Kursk and the liberation of Kiev and Orel.

NORMANDY BOCAGE
Churchill tanks (left-hand column) negotiating the lanes of Normandy, 1944. During the course of World War II, nearly 7400 Churchill infantry tanks of all marks were produced. The specialized vehicles derived from the original included several that were instrumental during the Allied landings in Normandy on 6 June 1944 and the ensuing campaign in Western Europe.

M3 Lee / Grant (1941)

TYPE • *Medium tank* **COUNTRY** • *United States*

SPECIFICATIONS	
DIMENSIONS:	Length: 5.64m (18ft 6in); Width: 2.72m (8ft 10in); Height: 3m (10ft)
WEIGHT:	27 tonnes (29.76 US tons)
ENGINE:	1 x General Motors 6046 12-cylinder diesel combining two GM 6-71 engines and generating 313kW (420hp)
SPEED:	40km/h (25mph)
RANGE:	Road: 240km (160 miles); Cross-country: 150km (90 miles)
ARMOUR:	12.5–76mm (0.49–3in)
ARMAMENT:	1 x 75mm (2.95in) M2 L/31 cannon in sponson hull mount; Secondary: 1 x 37mm (1.45in) M6 turret-mounted cannon; up to 3 x 7.62mm (0.3in) Browning M1919A4 machine guns
CREW:	6 or 7

In the rush to provide additional armoured firepower to counter German tanks in North Africa, American designers adapted an existing hull to carry a sponson-mounted 75mm (2.95in) gun, resulting in the M3 Lee/Grant.

Right: The unorthodox appearance of the M3 light tank was largely due to the urgency with which the tank was produced.

TURRET
The small turret of the M3 could not accommodate a gun heavier than 37mm (1.45in). The British made some modifications, eliminating the commander's cupola and lengthening the turret to hold radio equipment.

MAIN ARMAMENT
The M3 medium tank carried a 75mm (2.95in) gun mounted in a sponson in the hull and a 37mm (1.45in) cannon in the turret.

T24203

SUSPENSION
The vertical volute suspension, common among American tanks, was improved in later M3 models with the addition of heavy bogies rather than springs.

COMBAT DEBUT
The combat debut of the M3 medium tank occurred at Gazala in North Africa in 1943. The Germans had no warning that a heavier Allied tank mounting a 75mm (2.95in) gun was in the field and were startled at the appearance of the M3. The Grant tanks at Gazala quickly added substantial firepower and actually engaged German tanks while remaining safely out of range of the towed 50mm (1.97in) Pak 38 anti-tank guns deployed by the Germans.

FACTORY-FRESH M3
The riveted construction of some M3s presented an additional hazard for Allied crewmen. When an enemy round hit the tank, it was not uncommon for the rivets to fracture and fly about the interior of the vehicle with devastating results.

Howitzer Motor Carriage T12 (1941)

TYPE • *Gun carriage* **COUNTRY** • *United States*

SPECIFICATIONS

DIMENSIONS:	Length: 6.16m (20ft 3in); Width: 1.96m (6ft 5in); Height: 2.3m (7ft 7in)
WEIGHT:	9.1 tonnes (10.03 US tons)
ENGINE:	110kW (147hp) White 160AX petrol (gasoline)
SPEED:	68km/h (42mph)
RANGE:	322km (200 miles)
ARMOUR:	6.4–12.7mm (0.25–0.5in)
ARMAMENT:	1 x 75mm (2.95in) M1897A4; 1 x 7.62mm (0.3in) M1919A4 machine gun
CREW:	4

The T12 was an early US Army half-tracked self-propelled gun (SPG)/improvised tank destroyer. Based on the M3 half-track chassis, the T12 featured a 75mm (2.95in) M1897A4 gun fixed above and behind the driver's cab position in a T30 mounting with a small gun shield.

Below: Two features help differentiate the T12 from its sister M3 half-track SPG conversion, the T30: the T12's 75mm (2.95in) howitzer had a much longer barrel and its small gun shield was of a distinctive three-sided wing-like design.

MAIN GUN
The gun had a limited arc, with a traverse to the left or right of only 22 degrees; to engage targets beyond this traverse, the vehicle itself would have to be moved.

ARMOUR
Its protection comprised armoured plates of between 6.4mm (0.25in) and 12.7mm (0.5in) thickness; this provided inadequate crew survivability.

CHARACTERISTICS
The T12 weighed 9.1 tonnes (9 tons) and was powered by a 110kW (147hp) White 160AX petrol (gasoline) engine.

T12 GUN CREW
This T12 is manned by an African American gun crew.

FIRE SUPPORT
WMC produced 2203 T12s, many of which served in the North African and Italian campaigns. By 1944, the vehicle's anti-armour capabilities were inadequate against the newer, better-protected German Panzer IV (Models H–M), V and VI tanks; it was thus increasingly used in an indirect fire-support role. The T12 proved a better tank-killer in the Pacific theatre against the less well-protected Japanese AFVs and delivered effective service during the 1943–45 battles of Tarawa, Saipan and Okinawa.

Ram Kangaroo (1941)

TYPE • *Armoured personnel carrier* **COUNTRY** • *Canada*

SPECIFICATIONS

DIMENSIONS:	Length: 5.79m (19ft); Width: 2.78m (9ft 1in); Height: 2.47m (8ft 1in)
WEIGHT:	29 tonnes (31.97 US tons)
ENGINE:	1 x Continental R-975 9-cylinder diesel, developing 298kW (399hp)
SPEED:	40km/h (25mph)
RANGE:	230km (140 miles)
ARMOUR:	Up to 88mm (3.46in)
ARMAMENT:	1 x 7.62mm (0.3in) machine gun
CREW:	2 (+ 8 troops)

The Ram Kangaroo was essentially a Canadian Ram tank, converted into an armoured personnel carrier. The turret was removed, benches were fixed in the interior alongside ammunition racks and a standard infantry No. 19 wireless set was fitted.

Left: With the original tank turret removed, the silhouette of the Kangaroo was relatively low, helping improve survivability.

ARMOUR
Using the chassis and hull of the Ram tank meant that the crew and infantry inside were protected by armour up to 88mm (3.46in) thick.

INFANTRY COMPARTMENT
With the Ram's turret and main gun apparatus removed, there was space inside the hull for eight fully equipped infantry.

PERFORMANCE
Powered by its Continental engine, a fully loaded Ram Kangaroo had a top speed of 40km/h (25mph).

KANGAROO TANKS

'Kangaroo' was a generic name for a broad range of Allied armoured personnel carriers created by converting the chassis of other vehicles. There were Kangaroos built from Churchills, M7 Priest self-propelled guns and Shermans. This vehicle was essentially a turretless Canadian Ram tank, which was developed in 1942 and 1943 but was quickly rendered obsolete by the introduction of the US Sherman tank.

TROOP DEPLOYMENT
Ram Kangaroos were light and mobile vehicles, and joined the ranks of several similar Allied tank conversions. They served in the European Theatre of Operations (ETO) until the end of the European war in May 1945.

LVT-1 (1941)

TYPE • *Amphibious vehicle* **COUNTRY** • *United States*

The design of the first American military amphibious landing vehicle, designated the Landing Vehicle Tracked, Mk. 1 (LVT-1) Alligator, originated in the civilian world as an amphibious rescue vehicle.

SPECIFICATIONS

Dimensions:	Length: 6.55m (21ft 6in); Width: 3m (9ft 10in); Height: 2.48m (8ft 2in)
Weight:	14 tonnes (15.43 US tons)
Engine:	89kW (120hp) Lincoln-Zephyr V-12
Speed:	32km/h (20mph)
Range:	241km (150 miles) on land
Armour:	None
Armament:	None or 1–2 x 12.7mm (0.5in) M2HB HMG; 1–2 x 7.62mm (0.3in) M1919A4 machine gun
Crew:	3 (+ 18 troops)

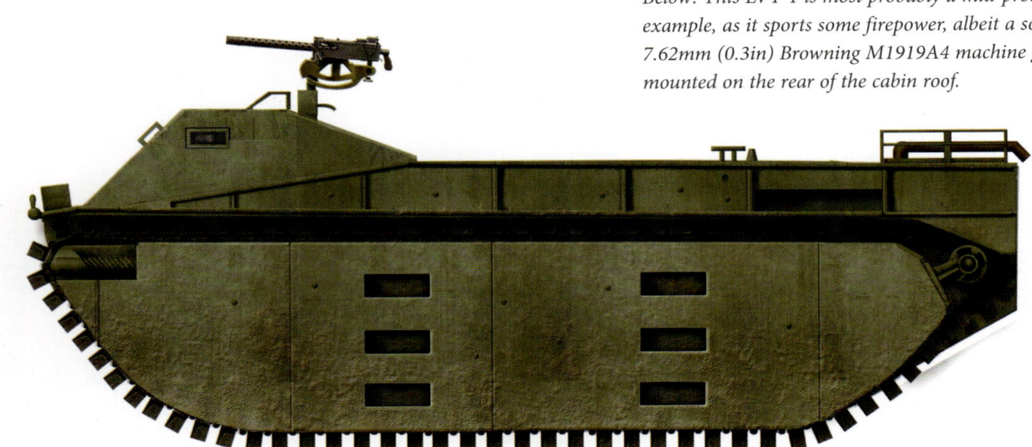

Below: This LVT-1 is most probably a mid-production example, as it sports some firepower, albeit a solitary 7.62mm (0.3in) Browning M1919A4 machine gun mounted on the rear of the cabin roof.

LVT-1 Alligator
This late-production USMC LVT-1, vehicle '49', sports a cabin-top Browning M2HB heavy machine gun; here it features a mottled three-tone brown-olive-indigo camouflage scheme during the November 1943 Battle for Tarawa.

Vehicle nose
The vehicle front had a sharp chevron-shaped nose to aid seaworthiness; this nose also featured two high-power lamps.

Capacity
The early LVT-1s weighed 14 tonnes (15.43 US tons) and could carry 18 fully laden troops or 2.1 tonnes (2.07 tons) of cargo.

SWAMP VEHICLE

Back in 1933, engineer Donald Roebling developed an amphibious emergency rescue vehicle to be used in Florida's Everglades swamps. Subsequently, during 1940, the US Navy and US Marine Corps developed and tested the first three LVT-1 military prototypes. These test vehicles were powered by an 89kW (120hp) Lincoln-Zephyr V12 engine. Next, during the second half of 1941, the Food Machinery Corporation (FMC) manufactured the first batch of 200 LVT-1 production vehicles.

AMPHIBIOUS TRAINING

The vehicle had a maximum height of 2.33m (7ft 8in) and a width of up to 3m (9ft 10in); typically, it moved through water submerged to the height of the top track, meaning that four-fifths of its mass was typically underwater when in amphibious mode.

LVT-2 (1942)

TYPE • *Amphibious vehicle* **COUNTRY** • *United States*

SPECIFICATIONS	
DIMENSIONS:	Length: 7.95m (26ft 1in); Width: 3.25m (10ft 8in); Height: 2.5m (8ft 2in)
WEIGHT:	15.1 tonnes (16.65 US tons)
ENGINE:	186kW (250 hp) up-rated Wright/ Continental W670-9A petrol (gasoline)
SPEED:	30km/h (19mph)
RANGE:	241km (150 miles) on land
ARMOUR:	None
ARMAMENT:	2–3 x 12.7mm (0.5in) M2HB HMG; 1–2 x 7.62mm (0.3in) M1919A4 MG
CREW:	3 (+ 16 troops)

Combat experience with the LVT-1 proved its concept but also pointed out potential improvements in terms of armour, firepower and seaworthiness. This led to the development of the redesigned LVT-2 Water Buffalo.

Below: The Buffalo's 'main armament' of a 12.7mm (0.5in) heavy machine gun was frequently replaced with a 20mm (0.79in) cannon.

PROFILE
In comparison with its LVT-1 predecessor, this view of an LVT-2 reveals its shallower, more streamlined hull superstructure and more compact cabin.

TROOP COMPARTMENT
The centrally located troop-carrying compartment remained open and could house up to 16 fully laden troops or 2.7 tonnes (2.65 tons) of cargo.

SUSPENSION
There were similarities with the LVT-1's track and suspension, but the lozenge-shaped sponson had been modified and there were differences in the rigid suspension format; the grousers were now bolted on.

WORKHORSE

Weighing 15.1 tonnes (16.65 US tons), the LVT-2 had a more powerful rear-located 186kW (250hp) Wright/Continental W670-9A engine. This increased the vehicle's maximum speed through water slightly to 10km/h (6mph). American firms produced 2963 LVT-2s between 1942 and 1944, and they saw wide service in both the European and Pacific theatres.

US MARINE CORPS
US Marines jump over the sides of an LVT-2 as it nears a beach on Kwajalein Atoll, January 1944; later designs incorporated a rear exit ramp that enabled the troops being transported to disembark without exposing themselves unduly to enemy fire.

LVT(A)-1 (1942)

TYPE • *Amphibious vehicle* **COUNTRY** • *United States*

SPECIFICATIONS

Dimensions:	Length: 7.95m (26ft 1in); Width: 3.25m (10ft 8in); Height: 3.07m (10ft 1in)
Weight:	14.9 tonnes (16.42 US tons)
Engine:	95kW (124hp) Hercules WXLC-3 petrol (gasoline)
Speed:	32km/h (20mph)
Range:	201km (125 miles) on land
Armour:	6.4–51mm (0.25–2in)
Armament:	37mm (1.46in) M6; 3 x 7.62mm (0.3in) M1919A4 MG
Crew:	6

When the Americans developed an up-armoured LVT variant they added the suffix (A) to indicate the modifications. The first such vehicle, the LVT(A)-1, was an up-armoured fire support variant of the LVT-2.

Right: US Marines assaulting the Pacific island of Tarawa in November 1943 hunker down behind an LVT(A)-1 as it provides fire support.

Survivability
The LVT(A)-1 also incorporated enhanced survivability upgrades. The hull decking comprised 6.4mm (0.25in) thick plates while the hull front and turret front had armour that was 51mm (2in) thick.

Machine guns
On the flat rear hull were mountings for a further two 7.62mm (0.3in) M1919A4 machine guns, each protected by a small shield.

Camouflage
This vehicle sports an unusual disruptive two-tone camouflage scheme of randomly shaped olive and khaki patches.

FIRE SUPPORT

Early amphibious assault experiences indicated that landing vehicles with more potent firepower were required. This led to the development of the LVT(A)-1, which was similar to a light submersible tank in that it had no troop-carrying capacity. The LVT(A)-1's shallow flat-topped superstructure mounted the same turret as seen on the M3A1 Stuart light tank. This turret contained in an M44 mounting the standard 37mm (1.46in) M6 L/53 cannon and to the right a coaxial 7.62mm (0.3in) M1919A4 machine gun.

NIGHT-TIME GUNNERY

An LVT(A)-1 unleashes a ferocious stream of fire from its primary and secondary armament. The plethora of firepower led to an increased crew of six, comprising the commander, driver and four gunners.

DUKW (1942)

TYPE • *Amphibious vehicle* **COUNTRY** • *United States*

SPECIFICATIONS	
Dimensions:	Length: 9.45m (31ft); Width: 2.44m (8ft); Height: 2.69m (8ft 10in)
Weight:	6.2 tonnes (6.83 US tons)
Engine:	70kW (94hp) General Motors 270
Speed:	80km/h (50mph)
Range:	644km (400 miles) on land
Armour:	None
Armament:	None or 1 x 12.7mm (0.5in) M2HB HMG
Crew:	5 (+ 25 troops)

During 1942, the General Motors Corporation (GMC) developed a wheeled (rather than tracked) amphibious utility vehicle designated by the codename DUKW; in common parlance, it became known as 'the Duck'.

Right: DUKW amphibious trucks transport cargo across the beach at Anzio in Italy, on 15 April 1944. Vehicles such as the DUKW made repeated mass amphibious landings possible.

Powerplant
The front third of the vehicle housed the power plant, a 70kW (94hp) GM 270 six-cylinder engine. The engine powered both the road wheels and – via a long transmission shaft – the propeller housed at the hull rear.

Hold
A full two-thirds of the boat was given over to its open hold, which could carry up to 25 troops or a 2.4-tonne (2.3-ton) cargo load.

Hull
GMC welded a watertight and streamlined all-steel thinly armoured hull onto this chassis. This rectangular hull had flat sides, a horizontal floor, a curved front nose and an upwardly curving rear.

AMPHIBIOUS
The vehicle was based on GMC's ACKWX two-tonne (1.8-ton) cab-over-engine military truck, employing existing design to enable economic mass production. The vehicle could travel an incredible 93km (58 miles) across water, making it capable, for example, of crossing the English Channel during the June 1944 Allied invasion of German-occupied Normandy. Behind the engine came the open plywood driver's station.

INVASION OF GUAM, 1944
Between December 1942 and September 1945, GMC manufactured 21,137 DUKWs, some 4000 of which were sent to America's Allies. The DUKW saw extensive combat service in both the European and Pacific theatres.

Carro Armato M15/42 (1942)

TYPE • *Medium tank* **COUNTRY** • *Italy*

SPECIFICATIONS

Dimensions:	Length: 4.92m (16ft 2in); Width: 2.2m (7ft 3in); Height: 2.4m (7ft 10in)
Weight:	14.6 tonnes (16.1 US tons)
Engine:	1 x SPA 8TM41 V8 diesel engine developing 108kW (145bhp) at 1900rpm
Speed:	35km/h (22mph)
Range:	200km (124.3 miles)
Armour:	6–42mm (0.24–1.65in)
Armament:	1 x 47mm (1.85in) gun; 2 x MGs
Crew:	4

The Fiat Carro Armato M15/42 medium tank was an upgrade of the M13/40, fitted with a more powerful diesel engine and air filters to cope with desert sand conditions. The engine gave the tank a higher top speed than its predecessor.

Left: The earlier M13/40 and M14/41 had a large entrance hatch on the left side of the upper hull. The M15/42 relocated this to the other side.

Turret
The turret had a powered traverse for the first time on an Italian medium tank. The gun was the high-velocity long-barrelled Model 47/40 47mm (1.85in) gun.

Petrol engine
Unlike its predecessors, the M15/42 had a petrol engine. This was more prone to fire, but it simplified battlefield logistics.

Machine guns
The M15/42 usually had four machine guns, two of which were in a dual mount in the hull. Another was coaxial with the main gun and the fourth could be fitted on an anti-aircraft mount.

LIMITED NUMBERS

The M13/40 was developed into the M14/41 and the definitive M15/42, with its long-barrelled 47mm (1.85in) gun, heavily armoured mantlet, more powerful petrol engine, better sand filters and more external stowage. Only 82 M15/42s were built, however, compared to 2000 of the M13/40 and M14/41 combined. From March 1943, the chassis were used for self-propelled guns.

M15/42 IN PROFILE
The M15/42 was the final development of the medium tank series begun with the M11/39. By the time it appeared in 1942, its armour and armament were obsolescent. Despite its faults, however, it was the best Italian tank of the war to be produced in any quantity.

15cm sIG 33 (Sf) auf PzKpfw 38(t) Grille (1942)

TYPE • *Self-propelled gun* **COUNTRY** • *Germany*

SPECIFICATIONS (Ausf H, 138/1)

Dimensions:	Length: 4.61m (15ft 1in); Width: 2.16m (7ft 1in); Height: 2.4m (7ft 10in)
Weight:	11.5 tonnes (12.68 US tons)
Engine:	Praga EPA 6-cylinder petrol, 91.9kW (123.3hp)
Speed:	35km/h (22mph)
Range:	185km (115 miles)
Armour:	8–25mm (0.31–1in)
Armament:	1 x 15cm schweres Infanterie Geschütz 33 with 15 rounds; 1 x 7.92mm (0.31in) MG34 machine gun
Crew:	5

The limitations of the early self-propelled heavy infantry guns turned attention to a version based on the versatile Panzer 38(t). Development of this variant began in 1942 and proved to be relatively straightforward.

Left: Mounting the main weapon so far forward placed a considerable load on the front suspension units and caused a significant degree of nose-heaviness in handling.

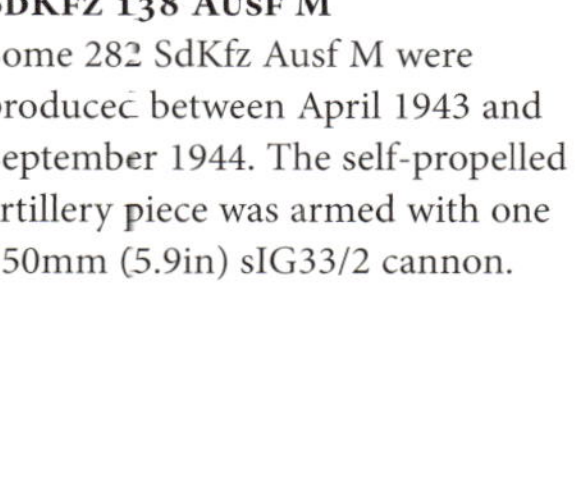

SdKfz 138 Ausf M
Some 282 SdKfz Ausf M were produced between April 1943 and September 1944. The self-propelled artillery piece was armed with one 150mm (5.9in) sIG33/2 cannon.

Fighting compartment
The tank's turret and superstructure were removed to create space for an enlarged open-topped fighting compartment for the sIG 33 on a limited traverse mounting.

Side armour
The side armour of the fighting compartment was extended to enclose the engine decks in order to give sufficient space for ammunition stowage.

DEVELOPMENT

An initial order was placed for 200 examples of what was officially designated the 15cm *Schweres Infanteriegeschütz 33 (Sf) auf Panzerkampfwagen* 38(t) Ausf H (SdKfz 138/1). Understandably, the type was generally known as the *Grille* ('cricket'). It had been intended to use the new Panzer 38(t) Ausf M hull with a centrally mounted engine. However, delays with this version forced the use of the then-current Ausf H hull with its conventional rear-mounted engine.

WAFFEN-SS 'GRILLE', 1944
A Waffen-SS Panzer 38(t) lays down fire on a distant target. A total of 91 vehicles (including a single prototype) were built between February and April 1943 using both newly completed and repaired hulls.

Marder I and II (1942)

TYPE • *Self-propelled gun* **COUNTRY** • *Germany*

SPECIFICATIONS (Marder II SdFfz 132)

DIMENSIONS:	Length: 5.65m (18ft 6in); Width: 2.3m (7ft 6in); Height: 2.6m (8ft 6in)
WEIGHT:	11.5 tonnes (12.68 US tons)
ENGINE:	Maybach HL62TRM 6-cylinder inline petrol, 104kW (140hp)
SPEED:	55km/h (34mph)
RANGE:	220km (137 miles)
ARMOUR:	5–30mm (0.2–1.18in)
ARMAMENT:	1 x 75mm (2.95in) Pak 36(r) L/51.5; 1 x 7.92mm (0.31in) MG34 machine gun
CREW:	4

The Marder I appeared after the Marder II and III. In May 1942, it was decided to rebuild 60 of the 300 or so serviceable ex-French Lorraine 37L armoured supply vehicles as *Panzerjäger* armed with the 75mm (2.95in) Pak 40.

Right: A Marder II Ausf D (SdFfz 132), camouflaged for operations around Kursk in the summer of 1943.

MARDER II AUSF F
By May 1942, the Panzer II was still being produced at a rate of 50 per month and, as the type was at best obsolescent, its future was seriously questioned. Within a month, it had been decided to switch production to a new *Panzerjäger* based on the hull of the Panzer II Ausf F.

PAK 40/2
The Pak 40/2 retained the upper part of its field carriage and was mounted on girders to help absorb its recoil.

FIGHTING COMPARTMENT
The design retained much of the Panzer II hull with an open fighting compartment protected by 30mm (1.18in) (front) and 10mm (0.39in) (side) plates.

PANZERJÄGER
Even in the pre-war era, German anti-tank units were given considerable importance, with an emphasis on their offensive potential rather than a purely defensive role. This offensive doctrine was formalized in April 1940 when all *Panzerabwehr* (anti-tank) units were redesignated *Panzerjäger* (tank-hunter) units to coincide with the introduction of the first German self-propelled anti-tank gun, the Panzerjäger I. The Marder vehicles were a series of Panzerjäger adaptations in service between 1942 and 1945.

MARDER CONVERSIONS
The project of developing the Marder I was assigned to Major Alfred Becker, a talented engineer who made such a success of the conversion that a total of 170 vehicles were produced in July/ August 1942.

T17E1 Staghound I (1942)

TYPE • *Armoured car* **COUNTRY** • *United States*

SPECIFICATIONS

Dimensions:	Length: 5.49m (18ft); Width: 2.69m (8ft 10in); Height: 2.36m (7ft 9in)
Weight:	13.92 tonnes (15.34 US tons)
Engine:	GMC 270 6-cylinder petrol engine, 97hp (72kW)
Speed:	Road: 89km/h (55mph)
Range:	Road: 724km (450 miles)
Armour:	9–44mm (0.35–1.73in)
Armament:	Main: 1 x 37mm (1.5in) M6 cannon; Secondary: 2–3 x 7.62mm (0.3in) M1919 Browning machine guns
Crew:	5

The Staghound was fast, manoeuvrable and easy to operate and maintain. The Mk II was fitted with a tank howitzer and the Mk III with the turret from a Crusader tank. Other variants included a mine-clearer and command car.

Right: A top view of the T17E1 shows its armament and stowage profile to good effect. The Staghound was powerful, fast and well armed. The 'Staghound' name was actually a British label applied to the T17E1.

STOWAGE
The Staghound had stowage hooks for extra fuel containers and crew equipment such as bedrolls and tools.

SEARCHLIGHT
The roof-mounted searchlight was useful for visibility for the driver and crew but also for target acquisition by the gunner at night.

ESCAPE HATCH
An advantage of armoured cars over tanks is that an entry/escape hatch can be fitted in the lower fuselage side.

QUALITIES
The Staghound, with its high speed, good range, thick armour and hydraulically traversed turret, was a popular and effective weapon. It was adaptable for a number of uses, including anti-aircraft (the Staghound AA with twin 12.7mm (0.5in) guns) and anti-tank (Staghound Mk III with a Crusader turret and 75mm (2.95in) gun). The Staghound was built in the United States but used entirely by British and Commonwealth forces during the war.

CANADIAN STAGHOUND
In France, August 1944, a Canadian T17E1 Staghound of the 18th Armoured Car Regt, 12th Manitoba Dragoons passes a knocked-out King Tiger of the 503 *Panzerabteilung*.

M5 Stuart (1942)

TYPE • *Light tank* **COUNTRY** • *United States*

SPECIFICATIONS

DIMENSIONS:	Length: 4.34m (14ft 3in); Width: 2.24m (7ft 4in); Height: 2.59m (8ft 6in)
WEIGHT:	15.1 tonnes (16.6 US tons)
ENGINE:	Twinned 110kW (148hp) Cadillac 44T24 petrol (gasoline)
SPEED:	58km/h (36mph)
RANGE:	161km (100 miles)
ARMOUR:	9.5–51mm (0.375–2in)
ARMAMENT:	37mm (1.46in) M6; 3 x 7.62mm (0.3in) M1919A4 MG
CREW:	4

Between April and December 1942, a total of 2076 M5 Stuarts were built. It was distinguished from its M3 predecessor by the raised rear decking, modified to accommodate the twin Cadillac engines and relocated fuel tanks.

Right: A 3rd US Armored Division M5 Stuart moves through the Vauterie hamlet of Saint-Fromond, Normandy, June 1944. In a surreal twist, nearby a child's doll has been placed on a stone next to the bullet-pocked wall of a house.

REDESIGN
The 15.1-tonne (16.6-US ton) M5A1 featured a redesigned elongated turret, with the M20 bracket mounting for the external Browning machine gun being moved to the right side of the turret roof rear.

M5A1
This American M5A1, dubbed 'Annie B' by its crew, prominently displays on its hull side the multi-coloured shield that is the tactical symbol of the 66th Armored Regiment.

RUNNING GEAR
The M5A1's running gear was identical to its predecessor. However, the modestly increased weight did somewhat raise the tank's ground pressure rating.

RANGE AND SPEED
The twin Cadillac 44T24 engines provided the M5 Stuart with better mobility than the M3A3. The former could obtain a top road speed of 58km/h (36mph), some 8km/h (5mph) more than the M3A3. However, since the M5 had a reduced fuel capacity, its maximum operational range on a single tank was merely 161km (100 miles), 35 per cent less than the 217km (135 mile) range of the M3A3.

M5A1 STUART ON PATROL, 1944
The M5A1 provided useful service in the tactical roles of reconnaissance and scouting during 1943–45 in the Italian and Northwest Europe campaigns, as well as in the Pacific. As the M24 Chaffee entered service in Europe in late 1944 and early 1945, it replaced many of the surviving M5 and M5A1 Stuarts then in front-line service.

M22 Locust (1942)

TYPE • *Airborne tank* **COUNTRY** • *United States*

SPECIFICATIONS

Dimensions:	Length: 3.94m (13ft); Width: 2.25m (7ft 5in); Height: 1.84m (6ft)
Weight:	7.3 tonnes (8.05 US tons)
Engine:	121kW (162hp) Lycoming O-435T petrol (gasoline)
Speed:	56km/h (35mph)
Range:	180km (110 miles)
Armour:	9.5–25mm (0.375–1in)
Armament:	37mm (1.46in) M6; 1 x 7.62mm (0.3in) M1919A4 MG
Crew:	3

During 1941/42, the Americans developed an air-deployable light tank design in response to a British request for a Tetrarch tank replacement. A key requirement was that the vehicle could be carried by the existing Douglas C-54 Skymaster transport aircraft or the British Hamilcar glider.

Right: The M22 was a compact vehicle with tall tracks, and on top of these a shallow flat-topped superstructure.

Crew
The tank was manned by a crew of three: the commander/loader was in the turret-right position, the gunner in the turret-left and the driver in the hull-left.

Main gun
The forward-positioned cylindrical turret mounted the ubiquitous 37mm (1.46in) M6 cannon as carried in the M3/M5 Stuart light and M3 Lee/Grant medium tanks.

Powerplant
The vehicle was powered by a 121kW (162hp) Lycoming O-435T six-cylinder petrol (gasoline) engine. This power plant enabled it to reach a top speed of 56km/h (35mph).

FAILED DESIGN
Ultimately, the Locust turned out to be an unsatisfactory design. It took 24 minutes to load an M22 onto a Skymaster transport because the turret had to be removed. It also proved to be mechanically unreliable and its armour protection was woefully inadequate for combat in 1944. Just 22 American M22 tanks were deployed to Europe during 1944. In addition, eight glider-borne British Locust tanks participated in Operation *Varsity* in March 1945.

AIR-TRANSPORTABLE
A US Army M22 Locust is loaded into the nose of a British RAF General Aircraft Hamilcar military glider on a runway ahead of a training flight from an air station in England during World War II in March 1945.

SU-76 (1942)

TYPE • *Self-propelled gun* **COUNTRY** • *Soviet Union*

SPECIFICATIONS (SU-76/SU-12)

DIMENSIONS:	Length: 5m (16ft 5in); Width: 2.7m (8ft 10in); Height: 2.1m (6ft 11in)
WEIGHT:	10.3 tonnes (11.4 US tons)
ENGINE:	2 x mated (in parallel) 52kW (72hp) GAZ-202 6-cylinder petrol
SPEED:	45km/h (28mph)
RANGE:	354km (240 miles)
ARMOUR:	16–35mm (0.59–1.4in)
ARMAMENT:	1 x 76.2mm (3in) ZiS-3Sh L/42.6 gun
CREW:	3

Manufactured in two basic designs, the SU-76 light assault gun (at first also known as the SU-12) became, after the famous T-34 medium tank, the most produced Soviet armoured fighting vehicle of World War II.

Left: In the centre-front of the fighting compartment, the SU-76 mounted the large and potent long-barrelled 76.2mm (3in) ZiS-3Sh L/42.6 variant of the ZiS-3 L/41 divisional cannon.

MANTLET
Perhaps the most externally distinctive feature of the SU-76 was the extremely large and very long gun mantlet that projected well forward of the fighting compartment's frontal face.

LAYOUT
The engine, fuel tanks and driver's station were at the front of the vehicle, permitting the construction of a spacious, lightly armoured, closed-topped fighting compartment that covered the rear half of the vehicle.

ENGINE
The SU-76 was powered by the same paired 52kW (72hp) GAZ-202 engines as in the T-70 tank.

EARLY DESIGN

The first model of the SU-76 was an attempt to produce a light self-propelled gun by mounting the 76.2mm (3in) ZiS-3 gun on a lengthened T-70 chassis. The power-train was nearly identical to that of the early T-70 light tank, with two commercial GAZ-202 engines each powering one track through separate, unsynchronized transmissions. This proved to be a mechanical nightmare and was a major factor in cancelling production in March 1943 after only 360 units had been completed.

MUSEUM SU-76
The core SU-76 model was replaced in large numbers by the redesigned SU-76M. A revised power-train dramatically improved the type's mechanical reliability and the replacement of the SU-76's enclosed fighting compartment by an open-topped design cured the problems with engine and gun fumes.

KV-1S (1942)

TYPE • *Heavy tank* **COUNTRY** • *Soviet Union*

SPECIFICATIONS

Dimensions:	Length: 7.41m (24ft 4in); Width: 2.87m (9ft 5in); Height: 3.25m (10ft 8in)
Weight:	43.4 tonnes (47.8 US tons)
Engine:	485kW (650hp) V-2K 12-cylinder diesel
Speed:	43km/h (26mph)
Range:	250km (155 miles)
Armour:	20–82mm (0.79–3.2in)
Armament:	1 x 76.2mm (3in) ZiS-5 gun; 4 x 7.62mm (0.3in) DT machine guns (1 coaxial, 1 hull front, 1 turret rear, 1 turret roof)
Crew:	5

In an attempt to improve the lumbering manoeuvrability of the up-armoured KV-1 Model 1942 tank, the Soviets designed a new variant, termed the KV-1S (with the 'S' standing for *skorostnoy*, meaning 'speedy'), with lighter armour and enhanced speed.

Left: This side view of a KV-1S from spring 1943 sports a fading winter white camouflage scheme.

Radio Antenna
This KV-1S heavy tank is most unusual in having a palm-headed radio antenna on its front hull side decking.

Turret
The KV-1S had a slightly smaller and lighter turret with rounded edges and a rear face that sloped outwards; it also incorporated for the first time a commander's cupola with all-round vision blocks.

Road Wheels
The last batches of the design, the Model 1943, featured redesigned road wheels that returned to the no-holed solid-disc design seen in early KV-1 tanks.

INFANTRY SUPPORT

In the middle and later phases of the war against the Axis invaders (namely 1942–45), Soviet infantry adopted the tactic of moving into contact with the enemy by standing or sitting on a tank's hull decking. To facilitate these tactics and reduce the risk of soldiers falling off as the vehicle manoeuvred, tanks such as the KV-1S incorporated horizontal handrails on the turret and hull sides onto which soldiers could hold.

KV-1S COLUMN
In this propaganda photo, a column of KV-1S tanks of the 6th Guards Armoured Breakthrough Regiment advance to the front line in the spring of 1943.

T-70 (1942)

TYPE • *Light tank* **COUNTRY** • *Soviet Union*

SPECIFICATIONS (T-70M)

DIMENSIONS:	Length: 4.29m (14ft 1in); Width: 2.32m (7ft 7in); Height: 2.04m (6ft 8in)
WEIGHT:	12.67 tonnes (14 US tons)
ENGINE:	GAZ-203 = 2 x 52kW (70hp) GAZ-202 6-cylinder petrol
SPEED:	45km/h (28mph)
RANGE:	354km (220 miles)
ARMOUR:	10–45mm (0.39–1.77in)
ARMAMENT:	1 x 45mm (1.77in) L/46 20K Model 1938 gun; 1 x 7.62mm (0.3in) coaxial DT machine gun
CREW:	2

After the shock of the *Barbarossa* Axis invasion in the summer of 1941, the Soviets rushed the T-70 tank into mass production. It was essentially an up-armoured, up-gunned and up-powered modification of the existing T-60.

Right: Although the T-70's turret was offset to the left, the gun's positioning meant that it remained close to the vehicle's centreline.

ARMOUR
The T-70 sported superior levels of protection compared to the T-60, with sloped armoured plates up to 45mm (1.77in) thick on the turret.

UPGRADE
Subsequently, the improved T-70M incorporated much-enhanced running gear, a modified turret and reduced main armament round stowage.

MAIN GUN
The T-70 mounted the potent rapid-fire long-barreled 45mm (1.77in) 20K Model 1938 gun (as fitted to the T-26 Model 1938 and 1939).

INVASION RESPONSE

In October 1941, the Soviets began developing an improved version of the T-60, designated the T-70. Given the catastrophic tank losses inflicted by the Axis invaders, the Soviets were desperate to rush this improved design into mass production. To expedite development, the Soviets retained many of the T-60's design features. The GAZ factory completed the first prototype in December 1941, and after hurried pre-production trials, full-scale T-70 production commenced in March 1942.

T-70 ON THE EASTERN FRONT
The T-70 was the final Soviet light tank to enter service in quantity during the war. While the 45mm (1.77in) gun and thicker armour were welcome advances on earlier designs, the retention of a one-man turret severely limited the type's battlefield performance.

T-34 Model 1942 (1942)

TYPE • *Medium tank* **COUNTRY** • *Soviet Union*

SPECIFICATIONS	
Dimensions:	Length: 5.92m (19ft 5in); Width: 3m (9ft 10in); Height: 2.45m (8ft)
Weight:	28.5 tonnes (31.4 US tons)
Engine:	373kW (500hp) Model V-2-34 diesel
Speed:	55km/h (34mph)
Range:	465km (289 miles)
Armour:	20–70mm (0.79–2.76in)
Armament:	1 x 76.2mm (3in) F-34 L/40.5 gun; 2 x 7.62mm (0.3in) DT machine guns (1 coaxial, 1 hull front)
Crew:	4

Produced in slightly different versions by different factories, the T-34 Model 1942 incorporated a number of design modifications primarily intended to speed up and rationalize the manufacturing process.

Right: This Model 1942 tank was built at the Stalingrad Tractor Zavod (STZ) factory. By the autumn of 1942, STZ had produced about 3600 T-34s.

Mantlet
Turrets manufactured by STZ featured a box-shaped configuration distinguished by its outwards-sloping flat-faced design.

Glacis plate
The Model 1942 was differentiated from its predecessors due to its redesigned sloping hull front glacis plate.

Tracks and road wheels
Many Model 1942s were fitted with all-metal road wheels, yet some had rubber-rimmed ones. Some tanks had 500mm (19.7in) wide tracks, while others were fitted with 550mm (21.7in) tracks.

'SHLEMAN' PRESS

The T-34 Model 1942 tanks manufactured at UZTM's 'Uralmash' factory in Sverdlovsk had distinctive turrets with rounded edges, a slightly waved bottom edge and a non-flat-faced gun mantlet. This was thanks to the presence of 'Shleman', the huge 9071 tonne (10,000 ton) steel press employed on the UZTM plant's production line. This press could transform a single large piece of 45mm (1.77in) thick hardened steel into a 'stamped' pressed turret.

T-34S ON OFFENSIVE
The T-34 Model 1942 was essentially the same as the Model 1941 but incorporated numerous small changes to simplify production. Here a T-34 unit manoeuvres through sparse woodland during an attack on German positions.

T-34 Model 1943 (1942)

TYPE • *Medium tank* **COUNTRY** • *Soviet Union*

SPECIFICATIONS

Dimensions:	Length: 6.68m (21ft 11in); Width: 3.0m (9ft 10in); Height: 2.45m (8ft)
Weight:	26.5 tonnes (29.2 US tons)
Engine:	V-2-34 V-12 38.8-litre (8.5-gallon) diesel engine delivering 375kW (500hp)
Speed:	53km/h (33mph)
Range:	400km (250 miles)
Armour:	15–60mm (0.59–2.24in)
Armament:	1 x 76.2mm (3in) ZIS5 F-34 gun; 2 x 7.62mm (0.3in) DT machine guns
Crew:	4

In early 1943, further sequential modifications to the existing T-34 design were incorporated into the production process, resulting in vehicles retrospectively designated the Model 1943. These variants were known to the Germans as the T-34D, T-34E and T-34F tanks.

Above: The high ground clearance and proven Christie suspension of the T-34 medium tank made it ideal for mobile warfare across the vast Russian steppes.

Radio
Increasingly larger proportions of the Model 1943 production were outfitted with a 9R wireless radio set, supported by a whip antenna mounted on the front-right hull edge.

Main armament
The main weapon of the T-34 Model 1943 was the 76.2mm (3in)M1940 F-34 gun.

Road wheels
Whereas many Model 1942 tanks had all-steel road wheels, most Model 1943 tanks featured a particular mix of road-wheel designs: the first and last (fifth) road wheels had rubberized rims, whereas the remaining three were made entirely from steel.

TURRET CUPOLA
The first Model 1943 tanks (T-34D) had the same 'Mickey Mouse' turret-roof twin hatches as seen in the final Model 1942 production batch. However, subsequent Model 1943s (also known as T-34Es) featured a raised drum-shaped commander's cupola on the left of the turret roof to replace the previous flush-level commander's hatch. This innovation afforded the vehicle commander better all-round observation and situational awareness.

T-34 ON THE MOVE
During 1944, production of the 76.2mm (3in)-gunned T-34 was gradually phased out in favour of the up-gunned T-34/85. According to some sources, the final batches of T-34/76 tanks (as they were then often called to differentiate them from the T-34/85) were designated the T-34 Model 1944 (or T-34G according to the Germans).

Panzer VI Tiger I Ausf E (1942)

TYPE • *Heavy tank* **COUNTRY** • *Germany*

SPECIFICATIONS

DIMENSIONS:	Length: 8.45m (27ft 8in); Width: 3.7m (12ft 1in); Height: 2.93m (9ft 7in)
WEIGHT:	56.9 tonnes (62.74 US tons)
ENGINE:	Maybach V-12 HL 230 P45 engine, generating 522kW (700hp)
SPEED:	45.4km/h (28.2mph)
RANGE:	Road: 195km (121 miles); Off-road: 110km (68 miles)
ARMOUR:	25–120mm (0.98–4.7in)
ARMAMENT:	1 x 88mm (3.5in) KwK 36 L/56 high-velocity gun; 2 x 7.92mm (0.31in) MG 34 machine guns
CREW:	5

Introduced as the Panzerkampfwagen VI Ausf H (later redesignated Ausf E), but commonly known as the Tiger I, this tank gave excellent service in Tunisia, on the Eastern Front and in Northern Europe despite several technical problems.

Above: The Tiger (such as the one pictured here) was first encountered in Tunisia by the British Army, and from then on appeared on all of the German fronts.

MAIN ARMAMENT
The high-velocity 88mm (3.5in) KwK 36 L/56 mounted in the Tiger turret was adapted from a successful anti-aircraft gun that had already been used in an improvised anti-tank role.

ARMOUR PROTECTION
At 100mm (3.9in) and 120mm (4.7in) respectively, the heavy armour of the Tiger I frontal hull and turret were substantially thicker than that of any other German tank.

ENGINE
After 250 Tigers were produced, the early 12-cylinder Maybach HL 210 P45 engine was replaced by the Maybach V-12 HL 230 P45 engine, generating 522kW (700hp).

MASS PRODUCTION
When it began mass production of the Tiger I in August 1942, the Henschel factory at Kassel already had eight years' experience of manufacturing AFVs (armoured fighting vehicles), although the massive Tiger was very different from the little Panzer Is that it had started building in 1934. During the war years, the factory employed 8000 workers in AFV production and operated around the clock, working two 12-hour shifts. Each six-hour stage in the manufacturing process was referred to as a *takt*, and there were nine such *takte* in producing the Tiger I.

ARDENNES OFFENSIVE
Grinding up the earth beneath their mass, SS-manned Tiger I Ausf E tanks advance through the snow-covered Ardennes forest during the great and late German offensive there in December 1944.

M3 Lee Canal Defence Light (CDL) (1942)

TYPE • *Special purpose tank* **COUNTRY** • *United Kingdom*

SPECIFICATIONS

DIMENSIONS:	Length: 6.15m (20ft 2in); Width: 2.64m (8ft 8in); Height: 3.24m (10ft 8in)
WEIGHT:	27.8 tonnes (27.4 tons)
ENGINE:	254kW (340hp) Wright/Continental R975-EC2 petrol (gasoline)
SPEED:	34km/h (21mph)
RANGE:	193km (120 miles)
ARMOUR:	20–78mm (0.79–3.1in)
ARMAMENT:	1 x 75mm (2.95in) M2; 13 million candle-power (163.36 million lumen) searchlight; 1 x 7.62mm (0.3in) M1919A4 MG
CREW:	4

During 1940–42 the British developed a novel armoured warfare dimension: tanks that shone powerful lights intended to temporarily blind the enemy. This top-secret project was disguised under the innocuous-sounding cover name of Canal Defence Light (CDL).

Right: This rare top-secret M3 Lee variant is easily identified by the tall cylindrical turret that mounted its 'secret weapon': a very powerful searchlight.

SEARCHLIGHT
In the centre of the CDL turret front was a vertical searchlight aperture. To compensate for this visual difference, British-manufactured CDL turrets sported a dummy 37mm (1.46in) cannon to the aperture's right.

TURRET
On top of the front-left hull roof was a tall cylindrical CDL turret with a rounded right-hand side and a flat left-hand side.

CHASSIS
In terms of external appearance, the chassis of the four-crew M3 Lee CDL tank was identical to standard M3/M3A1 tanks.

DAZZLE EFFECT

Back in 1937 the concept of an armoured fighting vehicle that 'fired' dazzling light had been demonstrated. However, it was not until 1940 that Britain developed a CDL variant of the Matilda Mk II tank, whose rotating turret mounted a powerful searchlight. As 304 Matilda CDL vehicles were constructed, simultaneously design work unfolded during 1942 on a CDL variant of the M3 Lee/Grant tank.

CANDLE POWER

The M3's CDL turret housed a 13 million candle-power (163.36 million lumen) carbon-arc searchlight and the solitary turret crewman. An entire brigade of Matilda, Churchill, M3 Lee and M4 Sherman CDL tanks deployed to Normandy during 1944, but these strange vehicles were never employed in combat in this bespoke specialized role.

M4 Sherman (1942)

TYPE • *Medium tank* **COUNTRY** • *United States*

The M4 was designed as the successor to the M3 Lee/Grant medium tank and development on it started in March 1941. The prototype T6 used the existing M3 chassis but with a new superstructure, and on top of this a turret that sported a low-velocity 75mm (2.95in) M3 gun.

SPECIFICATIONS (M4A3)	
DIMENSIONS:	Length: 5.92m (19ft 5in); Width: 2.62m (8ft 7in); Height: 2.74m (9ft)
WEIGHT:	30.8 tonnes (33.94 US tons)
ENGINE:	336kW (450hp) Ford GAA V-8 petrol (gasoline) engine
SPEED:	46km/h (29mph)
RANGE:	210km (130 miles)
ARMOUR:	12.7–89mm (0.5–3.5in)
ARMAMENT:	75mm (2.95in) M3; 1 x 12.7mm (0.5in) M2HB HMG; 2 x 7.62mm (0.3in) M1919A4 MG
CREW:	5

Left: M4A3 of the Free French Division. This variant possessed a welded hull and was powered by a 336kW (450hp) Ford GAA V-8 petrol engine.

ARMOUR
The armour protection of the Sherman generally could not stand up to the 75mm (2.95in) and 88mm (3.5in) high-velocity shells of the German Panther and Tiger. Armour ranged from 9mm (0.35in) on the turret top to 50mm (1.97in) on the frontal hull and 89mm (3.5in) on the turret front.

AMMUNITION STORAGE
Up to 90 rounds of 75mm (2.95in) ammunition were carried aboard the M4A3 Sherman – in later models in 'wet' storage, reducing the potential of a catastrophic explosion if the tank took a serious hit.

M4A3E8
The M4A3E8 (or 'Easy Eight') was fitted with the stronger horizontal volute spring suspension (HVSS).

SHERMAN VARIANTS
The first production model was the M4A1 (Sherman II) with a fully cast rather than a cast/welded hull; variants were the M4A2 (Sherman III) with a welded hull, the M4A3 (Sherman IV) and the M4A4 (Sherman V). All versions had different engines, all progressively more powerful. The British modified some Shermans for special tasks. The M4A3 was the type most favoured by the US Army. It differed from the M4A2 in the design of its turret and suspension (using a more effective horizontal volute spring system) and in its armament, employing the more powerful 75mm (2.95in) gun.

OCCUPATION FORCE
German civilians look on as a column of M4A3 Sherman tanks of the 70th Infantry division of the United States Seventh Army drive down Dachauer Strasse in Munich, Germany, following the city's occupation on 30 April 1945.

Panzer III Ausf J (1942)

TYPE • *Medium tank* **COUNTRY** • *Germany*

SPECIFICATIONS	
DIMENSIONS:	Length: 6.28m (20ft 7in); Width: 2.95m (9ft 8in); Height: 2.5m (8ft 2in)
WEIGHT:	21.5 tonnes (23.7 US tons)
ENGINE:	223.7kW (300hp) Maybach HL120TRM 12-cylinder inline petrol
SPEED:	40km/h (25mph)
RANGE:	155km (96 miles)
ARMOUR:	10–50mm (0.39–1.96in)
ARMAMENT:	1 x 50mm (1.97in) KwK 39 L/60
CREW:	5

The Ausf J was the first Panzer III variant to be retrofitted with the more effective L/60 gun. Many earlier vehicles were fitted with the 50mm (1.97in) gun in place of their 37mm (1.46in) weapon, which soon disappeared from service.

Right: A front view of the Ausf J. Note how the Ausf J had triple smoke dischargers on the forward corners of the turret.

MAIN GUN
The 50mm (1.97in) cannon was a small calibre by 1942 but was still able to defeat most Allied light tanks.

ARMOUR
The Ausf J was the first of the Panzer III series to be built with 50mm (1.97in) frontal armour, a significant increase in the forward protection for the crew.

AMMUNITION STOWAGE
Compared to the Ausf F model, the Ausf J had a prominent turret bustle for stowage of ammunition for the main gun.

HITLER'S ORDER

As early as August 1940, Hitler had ordered that future Panzer IIIs should receive the high-velocity 50mm (1.96in) KwK 39, but the Ordnance Department chose to fit the better KwK 38. Hitler was unaware of the decision until he attended a tank demonstration in April 1941 and saw that none of the latest Panzer IIIs had been rearmed as he had instructed. He furiously demanded the immediate installation of the KwK 39, but relatively few tanks were thus modified.

PANZER III AUSF J, EASTERN FRONT
In early 1942, Ausf Js with the new gun were issued to motorized infantry detachments and to the Panzer battalions that had been hard hit in late 1941 after the Soviet army regrouped.

Hummel (1942)

TYPE • *Self-propelled gun* **COUNTRY** • *Germany*

SPECIFICATIONS	
Dimensions:	Length: 7.17m (23ft 6in); Width: 2.97m (9ft 9in); Height: 2.81m (9ft 3in)
Weight:	24 tonnes (26.46 US tons)
Engine:	Maybach HL120 TRM V-12 petrol, 221kW (296hp)
Speed:	42km/h (26mph)
Range:	215km (133 miles)
Armour:	10–30mm (0.39–1.18in)
Armament:	1 x 15cm (5.9in) sFH 18/1 L/30; 1 x 7.92mm (0.31in) MG34 machine gun
Crew:	6

The *Hummel* (Bumble Bee) was a hybrid of the PzKpfw III and IV hulls, with a lightly armoured open superstructure. A popular weapon, it was used on all fronts, having plenty of room for the crew of five and the mobility to keep up with the Panzer divisions.

Above: Late-production models had a redesigned front superstructure, with fully enclosed positions for the radio operator and driver.

Stowage
The Munitionsträger was a standard production vehicle without the howitzer. A 10-mm (0.39-in) plate was fitted to cover the gun mount) but fitted with racks in order to carry 40 rounds of 150mm (5.9in) ammunition.

Munitionsträger
As the Hummel could carry only 18 rounds of main armament ammunition, the Munitionsträger Hummel (ammunition carrier Hummel) was developed.

Production
The Hummel proved to be highly successful and remained in service throughout the war. Total production amounted to 714 vehicles, plus a further 150 ammunition carriers.

DEVELOPMENT
Development of the Hummel began in July 1942. Initial studies concentrated on mounting a 105mm (4.13in) howitzer on the hull of the Panzer III or Panzer IV. The improved solution, however, was to mount the 15cm (5.9in) sFH 18 L/30 howitzer on the specially designed Geschützwagen III/IV, which used elements of both the Panzer III (driving and steering system) and Panzer IV chassis (suspension and engine).

KURSK OFFENSIVE, 1943
A battery of heavily camouflaged Hummel vehicles sit deployed in open scrub terrain; the crews' apparently relaxed countenance seems to suggest that no tactical engagement is imminent.

Semovente DA 75/18 (1942)

TYPE • *Self-propelled gun* **COUNTRY** • *Italy*

SPECIFICATIONS	
DIMENSIONS:	Length: 5.04m (16ft 6in); Width: 2.23m (7ft 4in); Height: 1.85m (6ft 1in)
WEIGHT:	13.1 tonnes (14.44 US tons)
ENGINE:	SPA 15-TM-41 V-8 petrol engine, developing 145hp (108kW)
SPEED:	38km/h (24mph)
RANGE:	Road: 230km (143 miles)
ARMOUR:	6–50mm (0.24–2in)
ARMAMENT:	1 × 75mm (2.95in) Obice da 75/18 Mod. 34; 1 × 8mm (0.31in) Breda Mod. 38 or 6.5mm (0.25in) Breda Mod. 30 machine gun
CREW:	3

The DA 75, also known as the M41 self-propelled gun, was intended as a counter to the Soviet T-34, but was never in fact sent to serve on the Eastern Front. Most of the vehicles were used in Sicily against US and British forces.

Left: The low profile of the DA 75 is apparent here in this front-view image. The basic purpose of these vehicles was to provide mobile assault artillery and anti-tank fire. One of their biggest issues was the limited number of shells they carried – 44 in total.

PROFILE
The DA 75 was a low-profile vehicle with a very flat roof. There were few fittings for attaching ancillary equipment, such as tools or crew bedding.

OFFSET GUN
The gun was offset slightly to make room for the driver/gunner, who had only an armoured slit for vision.

STRUCTURE
The Semoventes dispensed with the high turret and the superstructure of the M15/42 and replaced them with a box-like fixed riveted structure with no commander's cupola. Turret access was through a large hinged hatch cover that opened to the rear.

GERMAN SERVICE

About 262 of the DA 75/18 were built during the war years. The improved M43 105/25 was completed in smaller numbers – only about 90 – but sported a much more effective 105mm (4.1in) gun. In German service, the Semovente was renamed Sturmgeschütz M42 mit 75/18 850(i), or StuG M42. Including vehicles built by the Germans, 294 were issued to Wehrmacht divisions in Italy and the Balkans in 1943 and 1944.

DESERT OPERATIONS
The DA 75/18 proved itself in the desert battles in North Africa in 1942/43. It was reliable and its low profile was ideal for improving survivability in the very flat desert hinterlands. The vehicle did not have a coaxial weapon, however, so could be weak against infantry assaults.

M7 Priest (1942)

TYPE • *Self-propelled gun* **COUNTRY** • *United States*

SPECIFICATIONS

DIMENSIONS:	Length: 6.02m (19ft 9in); Width: 2.87m (9ft 5in); Height: 2.95m (9ft 8in)
WEIGHT:	23 tonnes (25.35 US tons)
ENGINE:	260kW (350hp) up-rated Wright/ Continental R975-C1 petrol (gasoline)
SPEED:	39km/h (24mph)
RANGE:	193km (120 miles)
ARMOUR:	12.7–108mm (0.5–4.25in)
ARMAMENT:	105mm (4.1in) M2A1; 1 x 12.7mm (0.5in) M2HB HMG
CREW:	7

The Howitzer Motor Carriage M7 was a heavily modified M3 medium tank hull, fitted with the standard US 105mm (4.1in) howitzer in a thinly armoured, open-topped fighting compartment. In British service, it was referred to as 'the Priest' due to the pulpit-like machine-gun position.

Left: The US Army used Priests from November 1942 until the war's end and in the Korean War, where the M7B2, with a raised gun mount to allow 65 degrees elevation, was the main version.

ARMOUR
The Priest's armour was thin, with a maximum of 25mm (0.98in), and was effective only against small arms fire and shrapnel.

SIDE PLATE
On the M7B1, hinged side plates were added to protect the tips of the vertically stowed ammunition from small arms fire.

POWERPLANT
The up-rated 260kW (350hp) Wright/Continental R975-C1 petrol (gasoline) engine enabled it to obtain a top speed of 39km/h (24mph) on roads.

GUN PULPIT
During 1941–42, the Americans developed the T32, a turretless SPG mounting a 105mm (4.1in) howitzer in an open-topped fighting compartment. After trials, the vehicle incorporated a tall ring mount at the superstructure's front side housing a dual-purpose 12.7mm (0.5in) Browning M2HB heavy machine gun; it was from this mounting's pulpit-like shape that the SPG, now named the M7, in British service was dubbed 'the Priest'.

FIRE SUPPORT
A dug-in and camouflaged Priest delivers long-range fire support. Each US armoured division had three armoured field artillery battalions, each with 18 105mm (4.1in) M7s.

Howitzer Motor Carriage M8 (1942)

TYPE • *Self-propelled gun* **COUNTRY** • *United States*

SPECIFICATIONS

DIMENSIONS:	Length: 4.98m (16ft 4in); Width: 2.32m (7ft 7in); Height: 2.75m (9ft)
WEIGHT:	15.7 tonnes (17.32 US tons)
ENGINE:	Twinned 110kW (148hp) Cadillac 44T24 petrol (gasoline)
SPEED:	42km/h (26mph)
RANGE:	241km (150 miles)
ARMOUR:	9.5–44.5mm (0.375–1.75in)
ARMAMENT:	75mm (2.95in) M2 or M3; 1 x 12.7mm (0.5in) M2HB HMG
CREW:	4

The US Army also developed a range of fully tracked self-propelled guns (SPGs) during the 1939–45 conflict. Some of these designs, like the M8, mounted a howitzer, a short-barrelled indirect-fire artillery piece to deliver fire support of ground troops.

TURRET
On top of the hull roof was mounted a larger rounded-edged cast open-topped turret.

MAIN GUN
This view of an HMC M8 shows the very short barrel length of its 75mm (2.95in) L/18.4 howitzer. Based on the M5 Stuart light tank, its compact size is attested to by the relative size of its turret roof-mounted M2HB heavy machine gun.

WEAPON RANGE
Firing indirectly the M82 High Explosive round with a terminal muzzle velocity of 381m/s (1250ft/s), the howitzer could obtain a maximum range of 8,790m (9,610yd).

CHASSIS
Based on the standard M5 Stuart chassis, the four-crew lightly armoured M8 SPG weighed 15.7 tonnes (17.31 US tons).

FIRE SUPPORT
The 75mm (2.95in) Howitzer Motor Carriage (HMC) M8 was a modified M5 Stuart light tank that mounted a short-barrelled howitzer in a fully rotating turret, thus making it the M5's close support variant. Between late 1942 and early 1944, M8s provided indirect fire support for motorized infantry troops in Europe and the Pacific, but they increasingly became vulnerable to enemy anti-tank fire. During 1944, they were replaced in theatre by the M4(105) and M4A3(105) Sherman close-support tanks.

M8 IN TRANSIT
In total, American firms manufactured 1,778 HMC M8 SPGs: 373 during late 1942, 1,330 during 1943 and 75 vehicles during the final production run in January 1944.

155mm Gun Motor Carriage M12 (1942)

TYPE • *Self-propelled gun* **COUNTRY** • *United States*

SPECIFICATIONS	
Dimensions:	Length: 6.73m (22ft 1in); Width: 2.68m (8ft 10in); Height: 2.88m (9ft 5in)
Weight:	27 tonnes (29.76 US tons)
Engine:	260kW (350hp) up-rated Wright/ Continental R975-C1 petrol (gasoline)
Speed:	34km/h (21mph)
Range:	225km (140 miles)
Armour:	12.7–51mm (0.5–2in)
Armament:	155mm (6.1in) M1917, M1917A1 or M1918 M1
Crew:	6

During 1941–42, the Ordnance Department developed the 155mm (6.1in) Gun Motor Carriage (GMC) M12, a self-propelled gun (SPG) that mounted a 155mm heavy field gun in an open-topped fighting compartment built upon the chassis of the M3 Lee/Grant medium tank.

Right: The M12 featured a vertical volute spring suspension (VVSS) arrangement with three pairs of bogie wheels. The SPG could achieve a top road speed of 34km/h (21mph).

Main gun
The M12 featured a 155mm (6.1in) M1917, M1917A1 or M1918 M1 L/38.2 field gun, all of which had a maximum range of 19,500m (21,325yd).

Earth spade
The prominent large rear-located earth spade was a distinctive feature of the GMC M12; it helped absorb the potent recoil of the vehicle's 155mm (6.1in) gun.

Armour
The SPG was lightly protected, with most plates being just 12.7mm (0.5in) thick, although key frontal areas had 51-mm (2-in) thick armour.

PRODUCTION

The M12 was a World War I-vintage 155mm (6.1in) gun mounted on a heavily modified M3 Lee medium tank. Only 100 vehicles were completed before production ended in 1943, and most were used for training or put into storage. A total of 74 were refurbished and issued to heavy artillery battalions taking part in the Normandy landings. The type proved to be highly successful.

M12 BATTERY
A battery of M12s from the 991st Field Artillery Battalion, 3rd Armoured Division, open fire on German positions at the crossroad town of Bildchen, south-west of Aachen in Germany, during the Allied Siegfried Line campaign on 10 September 1944.

T19 Howitzer Motor Carriage (HMC) (1942)

TYPE • *Self-propelled gun* **COUNTRY** • *United States*

SPECIFICATIONS

Dimensions:	Length: 6.18m (20ft 3in); Width: 2.22m (7ft 3in); Height: 2.55m (8ft 4in)
Weight:	10.5 tonnes (11.57 US tons)
Engine:	1 x White 160AX 6-cylinder diesel, developing 95kW (128hp)
Speed:	65km/h (40mph)
Range:	282km (175 miles)
Armour:	13mm (0.51in) maximum
Armament:	1 x 105mm (4.13in) M2A1 howitzer
Crew:	5 or 6

The T19 HMC was an M3 half-track mounting the M2A1 105mm (4.1in) howitzer. The M3 could only stow eight rounds of 105mm ammunition, while the chassis was only just able to withstand the howitzer's weight and recoil.

Above: In comparison with its sister improvised half-track SPG, the T12, the expedient T30 design (shown here) had a different, shorter-barrelled 75mm (2.95in) gun and a larger three-sided triangular-profiled gun shield.

Main gun

Its main weapon was a 105mm (4.13in) M2A1 howitzer, which had a maximum range of 10,698m (35,097ft) and could fire high explosive (HE), high-explosive anti-tank (HEAT), smoke and illumination rounds.

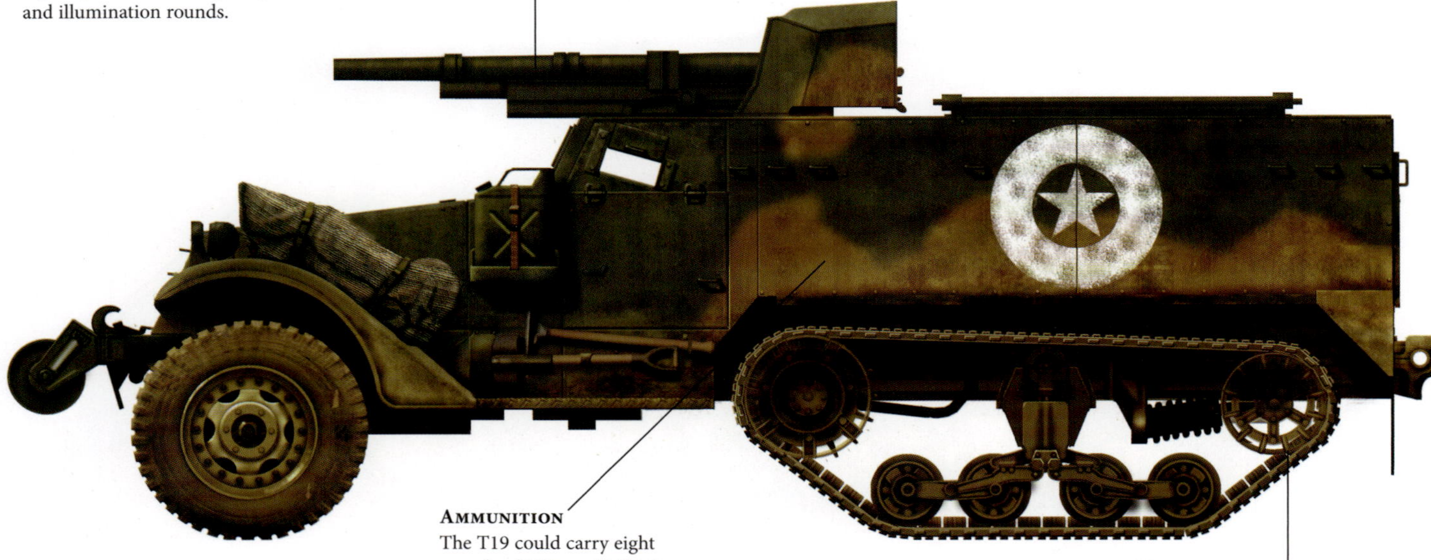

Ammunition

The T19 could carry eight rounds of 105mm (4.13in) ammunition on board, with additional rounds being transported in a towed trailer.

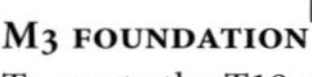

M3 foundation

To create the T19, the howitzer was mounted on an M3 half-track, and the vehicle chassis required considerable strengthening to cope

TRACKED VEHICLES

In addition to tanks, during World War II the US Army developed a range of other fully tracked self-propelled gun (SPG) vehicles. These included tank destroyers, lightly armoured and manoeuvrable armoured fighting vehicles with potent anti-tank cannons; SPGs that mounted artillery such as howitzers and field guns; and self-propelled anti-aircraft gun vehicles (SPAAGs) for mobile air defence purposes.

IN SERVICE

The T19 saw service in North Africa, Italy and northern Europe, but it was replaced by the M7 GMC during 1944. Existing T19s were often stripped of their howitzers to supply the M7 and converted back to standard M3s.

SdKfz 135/1 Lorraine Schlepper (1942)

TYPE • *Self-propelled gun* **COUNTRY** • *Germany*

SPECIFICATIONS

Dimensions:	Length: 5.31m (17ft 5in); Width: 1.83m (6ft); Height: 2.23m (7ft 4in)
Weight:	8.49 tonnes (9.36 US tons)
Engine:	Delahaye 103TT petrol, 51.5kW (69hp)
Speed:	35km/h (22mph)
Range:	120km (75 miles)
Armour:	7–12mm (0.28–0.47in)
Armament:	15cm (5.9in) sFH 13/1 howitzer with 36 rounds; 1 x 7.92mm (0.31in) MG 34 machine gun with 600 rounds
Crew:	4

The Lorraine Schlepper was a French weapons carrier adapted by the Germans as a self-propelled heavy howitzer. Twelve of these vehicles carried the 105mm (4.1in) leFH 18/40 howitzer, 94 were equipped with the 150mm (5.9in) gun and one carried the Soviet 122mm (4.8in) howitzer.

Above: This overhead view shows the open crew fighting compartment, which rendered the crew very vulnerable to overhead shell burst.

Main gun
The 15cm (5.9in) schwere Feldhaubitze (sFH) 13 was a heavy field howitzer, formerly operated as a horse-drawn gun.

Designation
The full German designation for the vehicle was 15cm sFH 13/1 (Sf) auf GW Lorraine Schlepper(f).

Production
It seems likely that an initial batch of 30 of the 15cm (5.9in) 135/1 was completed in June 1942, with further production runs bringing the total to 166.

CONVERSION
The origins of the SdKfz 135/1 lay with a French vehicle, the Tracteur Blindé 37L (Lorraine). This served as a French armoured personnel carrier and artillery tractor, and a total of 315 were captured by the Germans when France was occupied in 1940. Initially, the vehicles were converted into self-propelled anti-tank guns – the original crew compartment was removed and replaced by a gun shield and a Pak 40/1 L-46 75mm (2.95in) cannon.

MUSEUM PIECE
The original German anti-tank version of the Lorraine Schlepper was designated the SdKfz 135. The 135/1 variant was of similar construction but mounted a 150mm (5.9in) howitzer.

Wespe (1943)

TYPE • *Self-propelled gun* **COUNTRY** • *Germany*

The *Wespe* (Wasp) self-propelled howitzer was an effective mobile field gun. The main armament could be used in a direct fire role but was normally elevated to provide indirect support fire. Some Wespes were also produced as specialist ammunition carriers.

SPECIFICATIONS

Dimensions:	Length: 4.81m (15ft 7in); Width: 2.28m (7ft 5in); Height: 2.3m (7ft 6in)
Weight:	11 tonnes (12.13 US tons)
Engine:	1 x 104kW (140hp) Maybach HL62TR inline 6-cylinder petrol engine
Speed:	40km/h (25mph)
Range:	Road: 220km (138 miles)
Armour:	5–30mm (0.19–1.18in)
Armament:	1 x 105mm (4.1in) LeFH 18m L28 gun
Crew:	5

Right: The Wespe was a quick and easy way of using an obsolete tank hull to produce an effective self-propelled howitzer.

Layout
The initial production models were based on the Panzer II Ausf F with the engine moved to the centre of the hull and a reinforced suspension to absorb the howitzer's recoil.

Howitzer
The howitzer had a total traverse of 34 degrees and elevation of –5 to +42 degrees.

Modifications
Later examples were based on a modified chassis with a slightly lengthened hull, and the suspension was strengthened again.

DEVELOPMENT

The opening stages of Operation *Barbarossa* showed that the Panzer II was obsolete as a light tank; in early 1942, it was formally relegated to second-line duties. This decision allowed a number of hulls to be made available for conversion to self-propelled guns, and a prototype Wespe was built mounting the 105mm (4.1in) leFH 18/2 howitzer. Following trials, the Wespe was approved for service.

EASTERN FRONT
All versions carried their main armament on a limited traverse mount in an open-topped fighting compartment that provided very cramped accommodation for the commander and three-man gun crew operating within.

Sherman DD (1943)

TYPE • *Amphibious tank* **COUNTRY** • *United States/United Kingdom*

From 'Duplex Drive', this vehicle was an amphibious Sherman able to swim ashore after launching from a landing craft well offshore to give support to the first waves of infantry immediately on landing. It was most famously used at the Normandy landings on 6 June 1944.

SPECIFICATIONS (M4A1 DD)

Dimensions:	Length: 6.35m (20ft 10in); Width: 2.81m (9ft 3in); Height: 3.96m (13ft)
Weight:	32.3 tonnes (35.59 US tons)
Engine:	373kW (500hp) Ford GAA V8 petrol
Speed:	7.4km/h (4 knots) in water
Range:	240km (149 miles)
Armour:	13–76mm (0.51–3in)
Armament:	1 x 75mm (2.95in) M3 gun; 1 x coaxial 7.62mm (0.3in) MG
Crew:	5

Left: Although the waterproofed canvas flotation screen of the Sherman DD looked fragile, operational experience showed that it could withstand surprisingly rough sea conditions.

British DD
This Sherman DD is a British vehicle of the 13th/18th Royal Hussars. Although best known for their role in the Normandy landings, Sherman DD tanks were also used in the assault crossings of the Rhine and Elbe.

Propellers
The propellers mounted at the rear of the hull provided steady propulsion until the tracks touched the sea bottom and could take over.

Flotation screen
The flotation screen, seen collapsed against the upper hull, was erected before launch into the water to provide buoyancy.

AMPHIBIOUS SOLUTION
The Duplex Drive (DD) tanks provided an answer to the problem of making early delivery of tanks onto the assault beaches before it was safe for tank landing craft to arrive but offered very little margin for error, and many of the tanks foundered. In practice, the DD system was much more suitable for river crossings, and DD Shermans were used during the Rhine crossings of 1945. Although other tanks used the DD system, the Sherman was the standard British army tank for the purpose.

BRITISH DD TANK
Sherman DD tanks of 'B' Squadron, 13th/18th Royal Hussars, 27th Armoured Brigade, support men of No. 4 Army Commando on the Rue de Riva-Bella in Ouistreham, Normandy, on 6 June 1944.

SdKfz 234 (1943)

TYPE • *Armoured car* **COUNTRY** • *Germany*

The SdKfz 234 was designed as an 8x8 armoured car suitable for operations in hot climates. It gave excellent performance and was probably the best vehicle of its type in the war. The 234/2 Puma used the turret intended for the Leopard light tank.

SPECIFICATIONS (SdKfz 234/1)

DIMENSIONS:	Length: 6.02m (19ft 9in); Width: 2.36m (7ft 9in); Height: 2.1m (6ft 11in)
WEIGHT:	11.68 tonnes (12.88 US tons)
ENGINE:	Tatra 103 V-12 diesel, 115.58kW (155hp)
SPEED:	80km/h (50mph)
RANGE:	900km (559 miles)
ARMOUR:	9–30mm (0.35–1.18in)
ARMAMENT:	1 x 20mm (0.79in) KwK 38 L/55 with 48 x 10-round magazines; 1 x coaxial 7.92mm (0.31in) MG34 machine gun with 2400 rounds
CREW:	4

Left: It seems likely that about 100 Pumas were completed by September 1944, when production ended in favour of the simpler SdKfz 234/1.

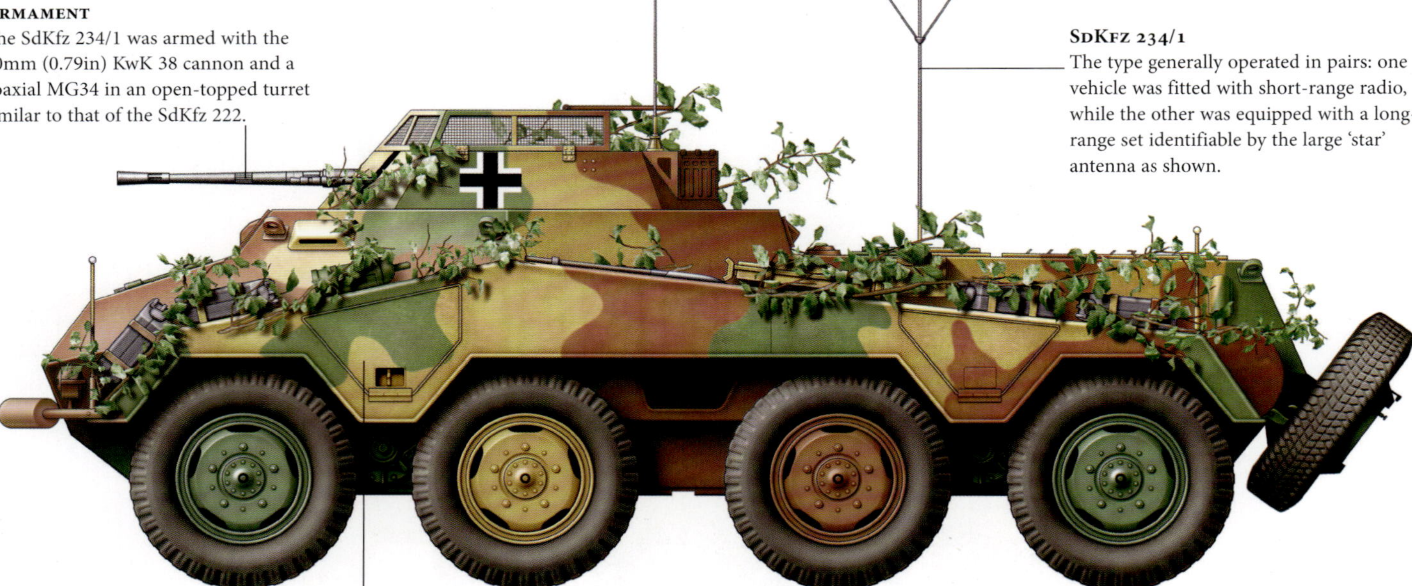

ARMAMENT
The SdKfz 234/1 was armed with the 20mm (0.79in) KwK 38 cannon and a coaxial MG34 in an open-topped turret similar to that of the SdKfz 222.

SDKFZ 234/1
The type generally operated in pairs: one vehicle was fitted with short-range radio, while the other was equipped with a long-range set identifiable by the large 'star' antenna as shown.

RELIABILITY
Once the vehicle was in service, crews appreciated the diesel engine's reliability and improved range, which were particularly important factors in the harsh conditions of the Eastern Front.

PUMA

Studies of reconnaissance operations led Büssing-NAG to redesign their 8-rad armoured cars to incorporate a monocoque hull and an air-cooled engine. The first prototype began trials in mid-1942, but the SdKfz 234/2 Puma entered production in September 1943, well before the SdKfz 234/1. The Puma was fitted with the turret originally intended for the cancelled VK 16.02 Leopard light tank, making it one of the best-armed armoured cars of the mid-war period.

BERLIN, 1945
An SdKfz 234/2 Puma lies abandoned amid the bomb-damaged buildings of the Nollendorf Platz in July 1945, following the Allied occupation of Berlin.

Marder III (1943)

TYPE • *Self-propelled gun* **COUNTRY** • *Germany*

SPECIFICATIONS (SdKfz 139)

DIMENSIONS:	Length: 5.85m (19ft 2in); Width: 2.16m (7ft 1in); Height: 2.5m (8ft 2in)
WEIGHT:	10.67 tonnes (11.76 US tons)
ENGINE:	Praga EPA-2 6-cylinder petrol, 111.85kW (150hp)
SPEED:	42km/h (26mph)
RANGE:	185km (115 miles)
ARMOUR:	10–50mm (0.4–1.97in)
ARMAMENT:	1 x 75mm (2.95in) Pak 36(r) L/51.5 with 30 rounds; 1 x 7.92mm (0.31in) MG37(t) machine gun in hull front with 1200 rounds
CREW:	4

By 1942, the Wehrmacht's requirement for a powerful tank destroyer had become urgent. The result was the Marder III, the best of the series, armed with the 75mm (2.95in) Pak (Panzer Abwehr Kanone) 40 or the captured Soviet 75mm F22 field gun.

Left: A Marder III Ausf H. Protection for the gun crew in the early-production Marder IIIs was limited to an enlarged gun shield.

MARDER III AUSF M
A late-production Marder III. The repositioned fighting compartment gave better weight distribution and eliminated the gun overhang of earlier versions, which markedly improved cross-country mobility.

MAIN GUN
The Marder III mounted its 75mm (2.95in) Pak 40/3 in a central position in the turret, rather than an offset position.

CHASSIS
This Marder III used a chassis derived from that of the Skoda TNHP-S tank, known in German service as the Panzer 38(t).

CONVERSION
In 1941 the reliable Panzer 38(t) was a prime candidate to help meet the insatiable German demand for *Panzerjägers*. The urgency of the requirement prompted the designers to adopt the simplest possible layout for the new vehicle. Almost the entire tank hull was retained with a 76.2mm (3in) Pak 36(r) bolted on top, protected by a three-sided gun shield. A total of 344 were produced between April and October 1942, with a further 19 converted from Panzer 38(t)s during 1943.

KNOCKED-OUT MARDER IIIS
Two knocked-out Marder IIIs lie embedded in the ruins of a collapsed building. Tank destroyers would often use the corners of buildings as positions offering cover, from which to ambush approaching Allied armour.

Panzer III Ausf M/Ausf N (1943)

TYPE • *Medium tank* **COUNTRY** • *Germany*

SPECIFICATIONS (Ausf N)

DIMENSIONS:	Length: 5.65m (18ft 6in); Width: 2.95m (9ft 8in); Height: 2.5m (8ft 2in)
WEIGHT:	23 tonnes (25.35 US tons)
ENGINE:	Maybach HL120TRM 12-cylinder inline petrol, 223.7kW (300hp)
SPEED:	40km/h (25mph)
RANGE:	155km (96 miles)
ARMOUR:	10–70mm (0.39–2.75in)
ARMAMENT:	1 x 75mm (2.95in) KwK 37 L/24; 2 x 7.92mm (0.31in) MG34 machine guns (1 x coaxial and 1 in front hull)
CREW:	5

The PzKpfw III Ausf M and PzKpfw III Ausf N fielded the 75mm (2.95in) L/24 gun, which had been installed in the PzKpfw IV. Production of the PzKpfw III ceased in August 1943, though its chassis formed the basis for several assault guns and self-propelled howitzers.

Left: A late-production Ausf M. A total of 432 Ausf L and Ausf M tanks took part in the Kursk offensive.

PANZER III AUSF N
An Ausf N in winter camouflage, Eastern Front, 1942/43. Late-production Ausf Ms and all Ausf Ns were fitted with smoke dischargers on each side of the turret.

AMMUNITION
A total of 64 rounds of ammunition was carried for the 75mm (2.95in) L/24 gun.

POWERPLANT
The PzKpfw III Ausf N was Maybach powered by an HL120TRM 12-cylinder inline petrol engine, which generated 223.7kW (300hp).

AUSF N FIREPOWER
By 1942/43, the KwK 39 gun was rapidly becoming obsolete, and several proposals were made to maintain the Panzer III's combat effectiveness. These proposals included drastic measures such as retrofitting the turret of the Panzer IV. Eventually, it was decided to fit the 75mm (2.95in) KwK 37 L/24. This armed the 700 tanks produced between June 1942 and August 1943 under the designation Panzer III Ausf N.

SICILY, 1943
A German Panzer III Ausf M roars towards the Allied invasion front in Sicily in July/August 1943, members of the crew taking a ride on the turret, a risky business over uneven terrain.

M5 Half-track (1943)

TYPE • *Half-track* **COUNTRY** • *United States*

SPECIFICATIONS

Dimensions:	Length: 6.33m (20ft 9in); Width: 2.21m (7ft 3in); Height: 2.74m (9ft)
Weight:	9.3 tonnes (10.25 US tons)
Engine:	107kW (143hp) International Harvester RED-450-B petrol (gasoline)
Speed:	68km/h (42mph)
Range:	322km (200 miles)
Armour:	6.4–16mm (0.25–0.625in)
Armament:	1 x 7.62mm (0.3in) M1919A4 MG
Crew:	3 (+ 10 troops)

In December 1942, the Ordnance Department contracted the International Harvester Company (IHC) to manufacture a modified variant of the M3, designated the M5 half-track, to meet surging demand for half-track vehicles among the Allies.

Below: The two most significant differences between the M3 and M5 were that the latter was powered by an IHC-designed petrol (gasoline) engine and that its hull was made from welded rolled homogeneous armour (RHA), often with rounded edges rather than the bolted face-hardened steel of the M2 and M3 with its right-angled edges.

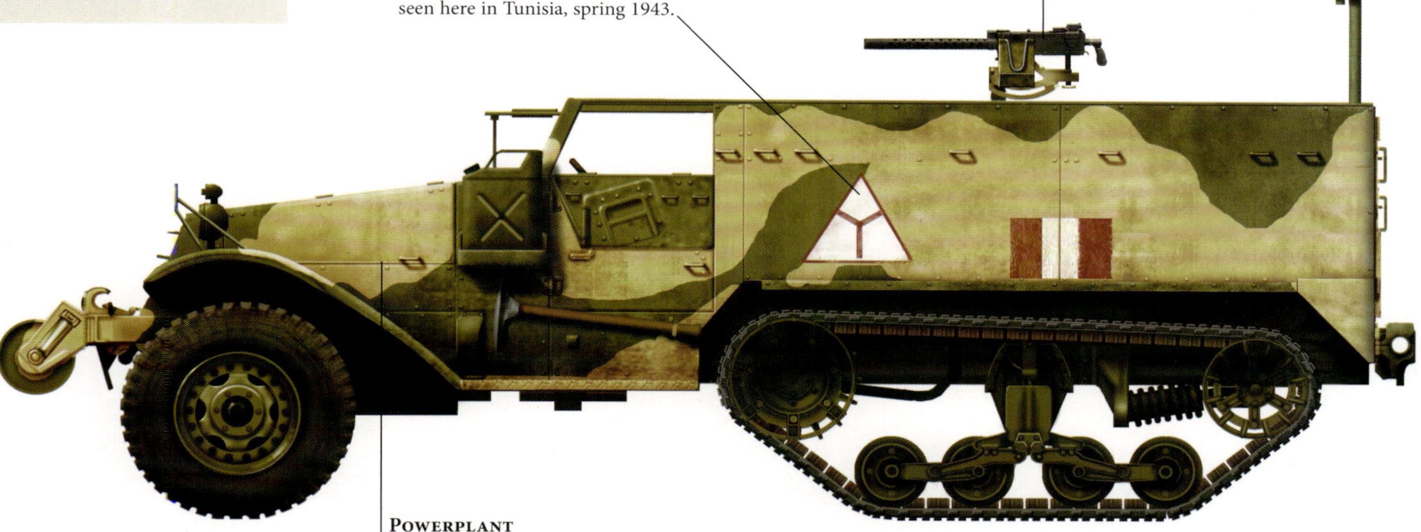

Machine gun
The M5's firepower consisted of a solitary 7.62mm (0.3in) Browning M1919A4 machine gun. This weapon, with all-round traverse, was fitted on an M25 pedestal mount.

Tactical symbol
This M5, like most of its sister vehicles, was exported to an American ally. It appears to bear the red-on-white triangular tactical symbol of the British 1st Infantry Division, seen here in Tunisia, spring 1943.

Powerplant
For its power plant, the three-crewed M5 featured a 107kW (143hp) International Harvester RED-450-B six-cylinder, four-cycle, inline petrol (gasoline) engine.

M5A1
From October 1943, the improved IHC-manufactured M5A1 half-track entered American service. The main difference with the M5A1 subvariant was that it featured lethality upgrades. Similar to the M2A1 and M3A1 vehicles, the M5A1 half-track sported a 12.7mm (0.5in) Browning M2HB heavy machine gun fixed to its own substantial M49/M49A1 pulpit ring mount situated above the co-driver's right-side seat.

BRITISH M5
British soldiers attempt to dig an M5 half-track out of deep mud. In total, IHC constructed 4625 examples of the M5. America sent the majority of these vehicles to its Allies via Lend-Lease, especially to the United Kingdom.

M8 Greyhound (1943)

TYPE • *Armoured car* **COUNTRY** • *United States*

SPECIFICATIONS	
Dimensions:	Length: 5m (16ft 5in); Width: 2.5m (8ft 2in); Height: 2m (6ft 8in)
Weight:	7.9 tonnes (8.71 US tons)
Engine:	82kW (110hp) Hercules JXD petrol (gasoline)
Speed:	90km/h (56mph)
Range:	563km (350 miles)
Armour:	9.5–25mm (0.375–1in)
Armament:	1 x 37mm (1.46in) M6; 1 x 12.7mm (0.5in) M2HB HMG; 1 x 7.62mm (0.3in) M1919A4 MG
Crew:	4

The M8 came from a 1941 Ordnance Department request for a new armoured car design. The project's specifications included a highly mobile 6x6 vehicle with sloped armour, a turret-mounted 37mm (1.46in) M6 cannon as the main armament, and several secondary weapons.

Left: The M8 was manned by a crew of four: the commander (right turret), the gunner (left turret), the driver (hull front left) and the radio operator/co-driver in the hull front right.

Main gun
The front of the turret sported a 37mm (1.46in) M6 cannon aimed via an M70D telescopic sight; the vehicle carried up to 80 rounds of main gun ammunition.

French Foreign Legion
The M8 was also exported to American Allies. The vehicle here was operated by the French Foreign Legion in North Africa.

Armour
To save weight and maintain mobility, the vehicle was only very lightly protected with thin welded-steel RHA plates.

PERFORMANCE
The M8 Greyhound was powered by the up-rated 82kW (110hp) Hercules JXD six-cylinder petrol (gasoline) engine. This enabled the vehicle to reach a top speed of 90km/h (56mph) on tarmacked roads, although its cross-country performance never reached the levels expected of the design. On a single load of fuel, the M8 could obtain a maximum cruising operational range of 563km (350 miles).

NORTHWEST EUROPE, 1944
An M8 moves through a shattered village in north-west Europe. The M8 was a compact vehicle with a shallow mostly welded hull, at the centre of which sat a tall, open-roofed two-man turret.

M20 Armored Utility Car (1943)

TYPE • *Armoured car* **COUNTRY** • *United States*

SPECIFICATIONS	
Dimensions:	Length: 5m (16ft 5in); Width: 2.54m (8ft 4in); Height: 2m (6ft 7in) (estimated)
Weight:	7 tonnes (7.72 US tons) (estimated)
Engine:	1 x 82kW (110hp) Hercules JXD 6-cylinder petrol engine
Speed:	89km/h (55mph)
Range:	563km (350 miles)
Armour:	Up to 19mm (0.75in)
Armament:	1 x 12.7mm (0.5in) AA HMG
Crew:	4

A close cousin of the M8 was the M20 Armored Utility Car, in which the turret was removed and the fighting compartment cut away to allow the interior to be used as a personnel or support vehicle for many purposes, from an observation post to an ammunition carrier for tank units.

Left: This M8 was operated by the HQ 1st Armoured Division (1re Division Blindée), French First Army.

Command vehicle
This modified M20 served as General Patton's personal command vehicle in the Third Army HQ.

Heavy machine gun
The M20 was a variant of the M8 Staghound with its turret removed and replaced by a pintle-mounted 12.7mm (0.5in) Browning M2HB heavy machine gun.

Bazooka
Because the M20 lacked a primary anti-tank weapon, the crew often stored a man-portable Bazooka in the fighting compartment, ready to engage enemy armour.

M20 PRODUCTION

The US Army employed the M8 and M20 widely from the time the first production examples left the production lines in March 1943. By November of that year, more than 1000 had been delivered, and during 1943 the type was issued to British and Commonwealth formations. By the end of the war in Europe, a total of 3791 M20s specifically had been produced.

M20 PERFORMANCE
An M20 stands as part of a monument on Utah Beach, Normandy. The M20, like the M8, had a powerful 6×6 configuration, which gave it exceptional performance on roads. Its off-road handling, however, could be challenging and needed an experienced driver to avoid becoming immobilized.

Panzer V Panther Ausf D (1943)

TYPE • *Medium tank* **COUNTRY** • *Germany*

SPECIFICATIONS

Dimensions:	Length: 8.86m (29ft); Width: 3.4m (11ft 2in); Height: 2.95m (9ft 8in)
Weight:	47.4 tonnes (52.3 US tons)
Engine:	1 x V-12 Maybach HL 230 P30 petrol engine generating 514.5kW (690hp)
Speed:	46km/h (28.6mph)
Range:	200km (124 miles)
Armour:	15–80mm (0.59–3.14in)
Armament:	1 x long-barrelled high-velocity 75mm (2.95in) KwK 42 L/70 gun; 2 x 7.92mm (0.31in) MG 34 machine guns
Crew:	5

After overcoming its early mechanical problems, the Panzerkampfwagen V Panther, with its high-velocity 75mm (2.95in) gun, became, in the opinion of some, the best all-round main battle tank of World War II.

Above: The wide tracks and double torsion bar suspension with interwoven road wheels allowed the PzKpfw V Panther to handle varied types of terrain with relative ease.

Turret
A three-man turret had already been developed when the Panther was being evaluated, and several modifications were introduced. Among these were the addition of a cast commander's cupola and a bracket for an MG 34 anti-aircraft machine gun in later models.

Ammunition storage
Up to 48 rounds of 75mm (2.95in) ammunition were stored in sponsons on either side of the Panther medium tank's hull. No ammunition was routinely stored in the turret.

Armour
Armour in the Panther Ausf D was up to 80mm (3.14in) thick and sloped at 55 degrees to improve its effectiveness in protecting the five-man crew. Side armour generally varied in thickness from 40mm to 50mm (1.57in to 1.97in).

PROWLING PANTHER
The leading Panther tank ace of World War II was SS Oberscharführer Ernst Barkmann. Barkmann halted his Panther in a thick stand of oak trees near the French village of Le Lorey one day in late July 1944. A column of 15 American M4 Sherman tanks and auxiliary vehicles approached; Barkmann waited for the appropriate moment and opened fire. In quick succession, Barkmann destroyed nine Shermans, a fuel truck and several support vehicles. Barkmann was able to withdraw to safety at Le Neufbourg.

NORMANDY DEPLOYMENT
This view of a Panther in Normandy in 1944 shows its frontal armoured slope to good effect. Note also the Zimmerit anti-magnetic mine paste on the tank's exterior, designed to repel the attachment of magnetic mines.

Panzerjäger IV Hornisse / Nashorn (1943)

TYPE • *Self-propelled gun* **COUNTRY** • *Germany*

SPECIFICATIONS	
Dimensions:	Length: 8.44m (27ft 8in); Width: 2.86m (9ft 5in); Height: 2.65m (8ft 8in)
Weight:	24 tonnes (26.46 US tons)
Engine:	Maybach HL120TRM petrol, 221kW (296hp)
Speed:	42km/h (26mph)
Range:	215km (134 miles)
Armour:	10–30mm (0.39–1.18in)
Armament:	1 x 88mm (3.46in) Pak 43/1 L/71 with 24 rounds; 1 x 7.92mm (0.31in) MG34 machine gun
Crew:	5

The Hornisse/Nashorn was a special weapon-carrier vehicle based on the PzKpfw IV chassis and adapted to take the 88mm (3.46in) Pak 43 gun. The high vehicle was difficult to conceal, a problem increased by poor armour. Used at long range, though, it was a potent weapon.

Left: The SdKfz 164 Hornisse was the first Panzerjäger to mount the famous 8.8cm (3.5in) Pak 43/1 and used the same chassis as the Hummel self-propelled artillery vehicle.

MAIN GUN
The main armament was the 88mm (3.46in) Pak 43/1 L/71, which amply fulfilled the requirement to destroy any Soviet AFV at long range.

CREW
The Nashorn carried a crew of five, but only the driver was under complete armour. The rest of the crew were carried in the open fighting compartment with only a canvas cover to protect them from the elements.

DESIGN
The Nashorn was very much one of the interim Panzerjäger designs, for although the gun was mounted behind armour at the front and sides, this armour was relatively thin, and the top and rear were open

NAME AND REPUTATION
Series production of the type began in February 1943. The type was initially known as the *Hornisse* (Hornet) and proved to be highly effective, especially on the Eastern Front where it was able to exploit the Pak 43's long range, destroying T-34s at up to 4000m (4375yd). From 1944, the type officially became the *Nashorn* (Rhinoceros), although both names seem to have been used interchangeably for the rest of the war.

EASTERN FRONT NASHORN
The Hornisse/Nashorn was highly regarded by its crews, who considered it to be far superior to the Porsche Ferdinand/Elefant. After the war, a driver, Gefreiter Hoffmann, recalled that: 'Everybody on the front was talking of it, calling it a wonder-weapon'.

Panzerjäger Tiger (P) Ferdinand/Elefant (1943)

TYPE • *Self-propelled gun* **COUNTRY** • *Germany*

SPECIFICATIONS	
Dimensions:	Length: 8.14m (26ft 8in); Width: 3.38m (11ft 1in); Height: 2.97m (9ft 9in)
Weight:	65 tonnes (71.65 US tons)
Engine:	2 x 221kW (296hp) Maybach HL120TRM petrol
Speed:	30km/h (19mph)
Range:	150km (93 miles)
Armour:	20–200mm (0.79–7.9in)
Armament:	1 x 88mm (3.46in) Pak 43/2 L/71 with 50 rounds; 1 x 7.92mm (0.31in) MG34 machine gun
Crew:	6

The development of the Ferdinand/Elefant was rushed, and many broke down in their first action. The lack of proper armour made it an easy target; and the lack of machine guns meant there was no defence against being disabled in close-quarter combat.

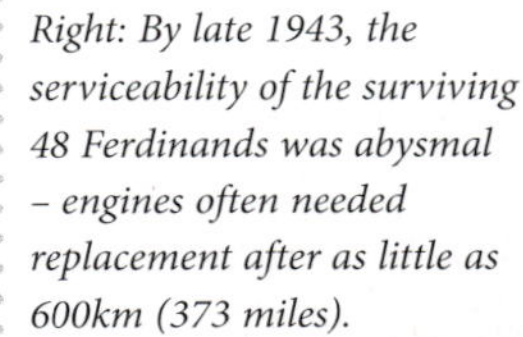

Right: By late 1943, the serviceability of the surviving 48 Ferdinands was abysmal – engines often needed replacement after as little as 600km (373 miles).

Armour
Protection was on a massive scale: 100mm (3.9in) appliqué armour was fitted to the hull front, bringing frontal protection up to a uniform 200mm (7.8in).

Self-defence
The lack of properly designed close-defence weapons was a major fault – except for pistol ports for sub-machine guns, there was no way to stop enemy infantry from getting near to the tank.

Mobility
The Ferdinand's battlefield mobility was limited – although it could cross trenches up to 2.6m (8ft 6in) wide, the driver's limited field of vision made obstacle crossing difficult, especially when under fire.

DEVELOPMENT

When Henschel was awarded the contract to produce the Tiger I in August 1942, its rival Porsche had already started to manufacture its design, the VK 4501 (P). Ferdinand Porsche developed this into a new tank destroyer officially designated Panzerjäger Tiger (P). Despite the name, it was totally unlike the earlier thinly armoured, open-topped Panzerjägers; this was a massive 65-tonne (71.6-ton) AFV, mounting the high-velocity 88mm (3.46in) L/71 gun in a fully enclosed fighting compartment.

CAMOUFLAGED ELEFANT
When the Ferdinands went into action at Kursk in 1943, their armour and armament fully met expectations, with even the heaviest Soviet AFVs being destroyed at ranges of 2,000m (2,187yd) or more. However, losses were significant.

Sturmpanzer IV Brummbär (1943)

TYPE • *Self-propelled gun* **COUNTRY** • *Germany*

SPECIFICATIONS	
DIMENSIONS:	Length: 5.93m (19ft 5in); Width: 2.88m (9ft 5in); Height: 2.52m (8ft 3in)
WEIGHT:	28.2 tonnes (31.09 US tons)
ENGINE:	Maybach HL 120TRM 12-cylinder petrol, 220.7kW (296hp)
SPEED:	40km/h (25mph)
RANGE:	190km (130 miles)
ARMOUR:	10–100mm (0.39–3.94in)
ARMAMENT:	1 x 15cm schweres Infanterie Geschütz 33 with 38 rounds; 1 x 7.92mm (0.31in) MG34 machine gun (late-production vehicles only)
CREW:	5

Based on the Panzer IV, the *Brummbär* (Grizzly Bear) was a heavily armoured mobile howitzer but lacked self-defence. Offering mobile artillery support to infantry, it mounted a 150mm (5.9in) howitzer. Its reliability let it outclass newer designs.

Left: Initial production Sturmpanzers had an MG34 machine gun carried in the fighting compartment, but with no firing mount the commander had to fire from an open hatch.

MAIN GUN
It was decided to develop a more compact 150mm (5.9in) gun to be mounted in Panzer IV hulls. This became the 15cm (5.9in) StuH 43.

SIDE SKIRTS
This example also has side hull skirts (*Schürzen*). The armour panels were mounted on rails and were frequently torn off when moving off-road or manoeuvring through narrow streets.

SUSPENSION
The Sturmpanzer's weight strained the suspension to its limits, causing rapid wear of road wheel tires and frequent failures of the final drives, increasing the already massive workload of unit repair teams.

VALUED WEAPON

Despite its problems, the Brummbär was highly valued. One veteran recalled that it was always considered a 'fire brigade' unit, used when the infantry was in trouble and heavy artillery support was needed. However, while the unit commanders were happy when Brummbärs smashed enemy attacks, the line infantry were glad when they left, as the enemy artillery fire was relentless while the Brummbär was present.

ITALY, 1944
A Brummbär and a Panther Ausf A of Sturmpanzer-Abteilung 216 stand beside an Italian farmhouse in 1944. Production of the Brummbär continued until March 1945, with 306 completed.

SU-122 (1943)

TYPE • *Self-propelled gun* **COUNTRY** • *Soviet Union*

SPECIFICATIONS	
DIMENSIONS:	Length: 6.95m (22ft 10in); Width: 3m (9ft 10in); Height: 2.32m (7ft 7in)
WEIGHT:	30.5 tonnes (33.6 US tons)
ENGINE:	373kW (500hp) V-2 diesel
SPEED:	55km/h (34mph)
RANGE:	300km (186 miles)
ARMOUR:	20–45mm (0.79–1.77in)
ARMAMENT:	1 x 122mm (4.8in) M-30 Model 1938 L/23 field howitzer
CREW:	5

The Soviets employed the proven chassis of the T-34 medium tank as a platform to mount the powerful 122mm (4.8in) field howitzer in an armoured superstructure to create the SU-122 self-propelled gun.

Right: Weighing 30.5 tonnes (33.6 US tons), the SU-122 was protected by well-sloped 20–45mm (0.79–1.77in) thick armour.

GUN MOUNT
The gun was fitted to a large and long box-like gun mantlet, which was mounted low down in the superstructure's well-sloped frontal plate.

FIGHTING COMPARTMENT
The provision of a large fighting compartment, fitted with a 9R radio set, enabled an enlarged crew of five to service the gun's fire with relative ease.

EXTERNAL FUEL
In addition to its internal fuel tanks, the SU-122 was fitted with additional cylindrical external fuel tanks attached to the rear hull.

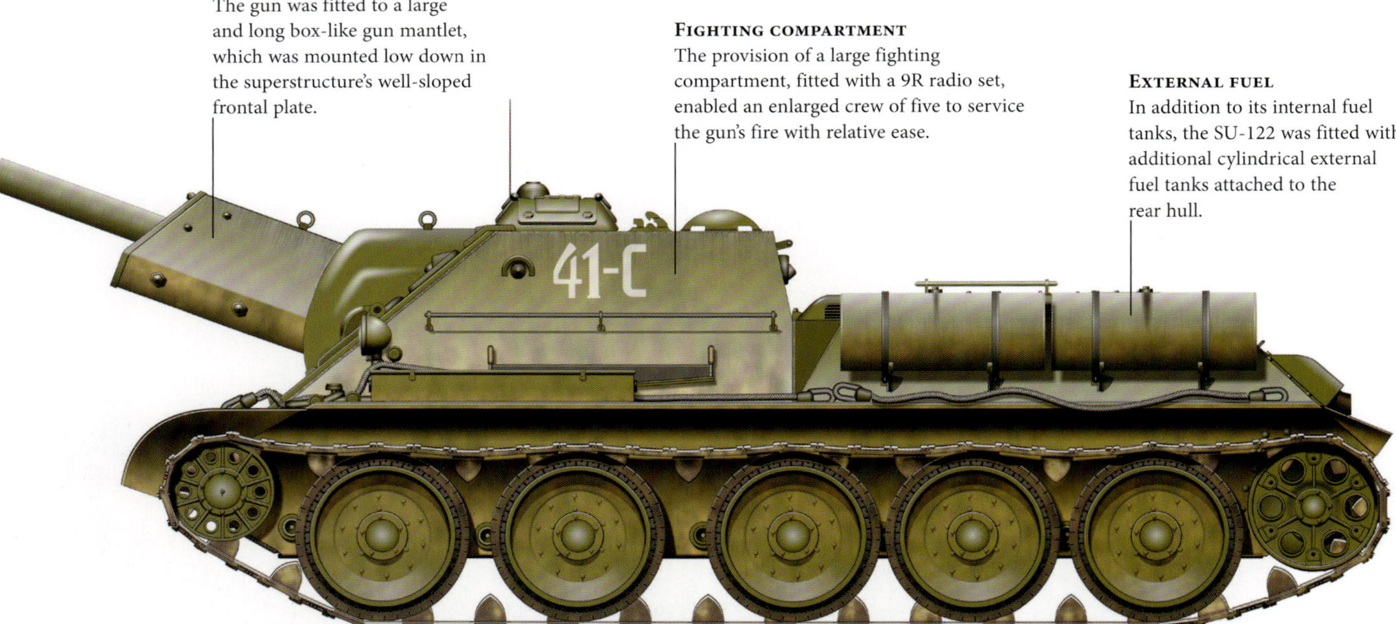

TACTICAL ROLE
The SU-122 first entered production in December 1942 and reached front-line units from early 1943. The vehicle's primary tactical role was to provide direct-fire support for infantry attacking prepared enemy defences. From the summer of 1943, the SU-122's mediocre anti-armour capability was marginally improved by the introduction of a new HEAT (high-explosive anti-tank) round for the M30 gun.

SU-122 ORGANIZATION
During January–November 1943, Soviet factories produced 1150 SU-122 vehicles. These served in Soviet medium SP artillery regiments that consisted of 16 SU-122s plus a T-34 command tank.

SU-85 (1943)

TYPE • *Self-propelled gun* **COUNTRY** • *Soviet Union*

To rush the potent 85mm (3.35in) gun into combat, the Soviets designed an easy-to-manufacture tank destroyer – the SU-85 – that took many of its components from the existing T-34 and SU-122 AFV (armoured fighting vehicle) designs.

SPECIFICATIONS

DIMENSIONS:	Length: 8.15m (26ft 8in); Width: 3m (9ft 10in); Height: 2.45m (8ft)
WEIGHT:	29.6 tonnes (32.6 US tons)
ENGINE:	373kW (500hp) V-2 12-cylinder diesel
SPEED:	55km/h (34mph)
RANGE:	400km (249 miles)
ARMOUR:	20–45mm (0.78–1.77in)
ARMAMENT:	1 x 85mm (3.35in) D-5T L/51.6 gun
CREW:	4

Above: Completed vehicles were typically fitted with rubber-rimmed road wheels, but some featured one or more metal-rimmed wheels due to continuing rubber shortages throughout the war period.

INSIGNIA
The white eagle insignia on this SU-85's superstructure identifies it as belonging to a unit of the Soviet-raised People's Army of Poland (LWP).

PERFORMANCE
Powered by a 373kW (500hp) V-2 diesel engine, and with the T-34's proven Christie vertical coil-spring suspension, the SU-85 could obtain an impressive top road speed of 55km/h (34mph).

GUN MOUNTING
The gun was mounted, offset to the right, in a large mantlet fitted on the front of the shallow slope-sided armoured superstructure.

SU-85M
The last 315 production vehicles in the SU-85 manufacturing run, produced during late 1944, featured several modifications; these vehicles were re-designated as the SU-85M, with the 'M' signifying 'modified' in the Russian language. The main innovation was that these vehicles utilized the up-armoured chassis of the new SU-100 tank destroyer. These SU-85M vehicles also featured a re-designed gun mantlet as well as a modified commander's cupola on the superstructure roof.

LOW PROFILE
At just 2.45m (8ft) high, the vehicle had an impressively low silhouette. This aided its survivability in combat by decreasing the amount of target at which the enemy could fire and making it easier to take advantage of low cover.

KV-85 (1943)

TYPE • *Heavy tank* COUNTRY • *Soviet Union*

As an interim response to encountering the latest German tanks in the battles of summer 1943, the Soviets mounted a more potent 85mm (3.35in) gun in an enlarged turret on top of the KV-1S to produce the KV-85.

SPECIFICATIONS

Dimensions:	Length: 8.6m (28ft 3in); Width: 3.25m (10ft 8in); Height: 2.9m (9ft 6in)
Weight:	46 tonnes (50.7 US tons)
Engine:	473kW (600hp) V-2 12-cylinder diesel
Speed:	35km/h (22mph)
Range:	250km (160 miles)
Armour:	30–110mm (1.18–4.33in)
Armament:	1 x 85mm (3.35in) D-5T L/51.6 gun; 3 x 7.62mm (0.3in) DT machine guns (1 coaxial, 1 turret rear, 1 hull front)
Crew:	4

Above: A production KV-85. During autumn 1943, Soviet factories manufactured just 148 KV-85 heavy tanks.

Armour penetration
Firing the standard anti-armour round, the D-5T gun mounted in the KV-85 could penetrate 100mm (3.94in) of vertical armour at a range of 1000m (3280ft).

Vehicle weight
The additional weight of the larger gun, heavier rounds, enlarged turret and thickened hull frontal armour all combined to push the KV-85 back up to 46 tonnes (50.7 US tons) – more than the KV-1 Model 1941.

Hull
The hull of the KV-85 was essentially a slightly modified KV-1S chassis with its frontal armoured plates increased from 82mm (3.2in) to 110mm (4.33in).

RATIONALE

The Soviet experience of encountering the new German Panther and Tiger tanks in 1943 led them to conclude that Soviet heavy tanks urgently needed to be up-gunned to counter this new threat. While development of the new Iosef Stalin (IS)-1 heavy tank proceeded, the four-man KV-85 was produced as a stop-gap. This design mounted the new 51.6 calibre-long 85mm (3.35in) D-5T gun in an enlarged turret on top of a modified KV-1S hull.

HEAVY TANK
The heavy weight of the KV-85 undermined the very logic of increased mobility that had been behind the introduction of the KV-1S in the first place. Thus, the KV-85's top road speed was consequently reduced to a disappointing 35km/h (22mph).

SU-152 (1943)

TYPE • *Self-propelled gun* **COUNTRY** • *Soviet Union*

SPECIFICATIONS

Dimensions:	Length: 8.95m (29ft 4in); Width: 3.25m (10ft 8in); Height: 2.45m (8ft)
Weight:	45.5 tonnes (50.2 US tons)
Engine:	473kW (600hp) V-2 12-cylinder diesel
Speed:	43km/h (27mph)
Range:	220km (137 miles)
Armour:	20–75mm (0.78–2.95in)
Armament:	1 x 152.4mm (5.98in) ML-20S Model 1938 L/29 gun-howitzer; sometimes 1 x 12.7mm (0.5in) DShK heavy machine gun
Crew:	5

The last of the KV-1 family of vehicles was the mighty SU-152 assault gun. It mounted the colossal 152.4mm (5.98in) gun, a formidable long-range weapon, in a well-protected superstructure fitted to the chassis of the KV-1 tank.

Below: This vehicle featured a monotone drab olive paint scheme while on the Karelian Front in the summer of 1944.

Main gun
At the extreme combat range of 2000m (6560ft), the ML-20S gun could penetrate 110mm (4.3in) of vertical armour. The likelihood of the vehicle achieving a hit at this great range, however, was low due to the provision of mediocre optics and the tactical limitations of the crew.

Fuel tanks
The vehicle was fitted with rear-mounted cylindrical external fuel tanks that boosted its fuel capacity to a considerable 945 litres (208 gal).

Track configuration
The stretching of the upper track over the three high-positioned return rollers is clearly evident in this side view of an SU-152.

SUSPENSION
The SU-152 featured a suspension/track arrangement identical to that of the KV-1. This consisted of six medium-sized solid-disc road wheels per side, each independently connected to a torsion-bar suspension, together with a rear driving wheel and a front idler. The vehicle also had the wide tracks of the KV-1, which helped it maintain reasonable tactical mobility despite its considerable weight.

SU-152 IN COMBAT
The SU-152 gained a reputation within the Red Army for its respectable lethality against German tanks and soon earned the nickname 'Beast Slayer'. Despite this, the SU-152's primary tactical role remained infantry support, where it typically fired HE rounds.

M10 Wolverine (1944)

TYPE • *Tank Destroyer* **COUNTRY** • *United States*

The M10 Wolverine was one of several highly manoeuvrable, lightly protected, fully tracked American direct-fire tank destroyers fitted with a fully rotating turret and armed with a potent anti-tank cannon.

SPECIFICATIONS

DIMENSIONS:	Length: 5.97m (19ft 7in); Width: 3.05m (10ft); Height: 2m (6ft 7in)
WEIGHT:	29.6 tonnes (32.6 US tons)
ENGINE:	General Motors 6046 (twinned 127kW (170hp) GM 6-71) diesel
SPEED:	50km/h (31mph)
RANGE:	300km (186 miles)
ARMOUR:	9.5–57mm (0.375–2.25in)
ARMAMENT:	76mm (3in) M7; 1 x 12.7mm (0.5in) M2HB HMG
CREW:	5

Below: This view of an M10 during late 1944 in a winter camouflage scheme of whitewash randomly applied over olive drab also shows the unusual design of the turret rear.

PENETRATION
Firing the M79 armour-piercing round, at a range of 1,000m (1,094yd), the M7 cannon could penetrate 76mm (3in) of RHA sloped at 30 degrees.

TURRET
Mounted frontally on the hull roof was a large, long open-topped pentagon-shaped angular turret with a distinctive frontal 'beak' and an outwardly sloped rear face.

RUNNING GEAR
The M10 featured the M4 Sherman tank's running gear: three pairs of medium-sized close-spoked road wheels on a bogie arrangement per side, with a front drive sprocket and rear idler wheel.

PRODUCTION

Between September 1942 and December 1943, Fisher and three Ford factories produced 4,993 GMC M10s. This design utilized the chassis of the M4A2 Sherman. Starting in October 1942 and continuing until November 1943, these firms also produced 1,403 M10A1 variants, which were based on the M4A3 Sherman chassis. America eventually sent 514 M10s to Britain and the USSR under the Lend-Lease programme.

BRITISH M10
The British M10 vehicles can be identified by the addition of a muzzle brake at the end of the gun, with a counterweight visible immediately behind this feature.

M18 Hellcat (1944)

TYPE • *Tank Destroyer* **COUNTRY** • *United States*

SPECIFICATIONS

Dimensions:	Length: 5.82m (19ft 1in); Width: 2.87m (9ft 5in); Height: 2.57m (8ft 5in)
Weight:	16.8 tonnes (18.52 US tons)
Engine:	260kW (350 hp) Wright/Continental R975-C1 petrol (gasoline)
Speed:	89km/h (55mph)
Range:	161km (100 miles)
Armour:	12.7–25mm (0.5–1in)
Armament:	76mm (3in) M1A1, M1A1C or M1A2; 1 x 12.7mm (0.5in) M2HB HMG
Crew:	5

Even as the M10 tank destroyer was being developed from 1941 onwards, some senior US military commanders feared that the vehicle was too heavy and too slow to be fully effective as a tank destroyer.

Below: The muzzle brake fitted to its 76mm M1A1 cannon made a late-production M18 – like this one seen at Anzio during May 1944 – even more visually distinctive from the M10 than earlier vehicles.

Machine gun
On the left rear of the turret was a ring mount that sported a dual-purpose 12.7mm (0.5in) Browning M2HB heavy machine gun.

Turret
Using its electromagnetic traverse mechanism, the Hellcat's T23 turret could rotate full circle in just 24 seconds.

Armour
The M18 design kept its combat weight below 17 tonnes (16.7 tons) largely by sporting light armour protection. Most of the hull just had 12.7mm (0.5in)-thick plates, although these were often well sloped.

HELLCAT
The M18 was accepted for mass production in March 1943. It soon became dubbed the Hellcat by US troops. Between August 1943 and October 1944, American firms produced a total of 2,501 M18s (excluding the six T70 pilot vehicles). The five-crew M18 was easily distinguishable from its sister M10 and M36 because it did not use the substantial chassis of the M4 Sherman medium tank. Indeed, its smaller, lighter chassis brought the Hellcat in at the modest combat weight of 16.8 tonnes (18.5 tons).

COMBAT-READY M10
The combat experiences of 1943–44 exposed the inability of the M1A1 cannon to penetrate the frontal armour of the German Panther tank. This was partly mitigated by the introduction of the M93 high-velocity armour-piercing round during late 1944.

Churchill AVRE (1944)

TYPE • *Special Purpose Tank* **COUNTRY** • *United Kingdom*

SPECIFICATIONS

DIMENSIONS:	Length: 7.44m (24ft 5in); Width: 2.44m (8ft); Height: 3.45m (11ft 4in) with log carpet mounted above tank
WEIGHT:	40.72 tonnes (44.88 US tons)
ENGINE:	1 x Bedford Twin-Six petrol engine developing 261kW (350hp)
SPEED:	Road: 20km/h (12.5mph); Cross-country: 12.8km/h (8mph)
RANGE:	144.8km (90 miles)
Armour:	16–102mm (0.62–4in)
ARMAMENT:	1 x Petard 290mm (11.41in) spigot mortar; 1 x 7.92mm (0.31in) Besa machine gun
CREW:	5

The Churchill AVRE (Assault Vehicle Royal Engineers) was developed in 1943 for a variety of uses by combat engineers, who had to overcome natural and man-made obstacles across the beaches of Normandy and into the Third Reich.

Left: An AVRE Churchill Mk III tank from the 49th Division of the 1st Canadian Corps, Canadian Army drives through the battle-damaged streets of Arnhem, the Netherlands, on 13 April 1945.

'BOBBIN'
AVRE Bobbin tanks covered areas of soft sand and clay with canvas matting to allow tanks and troops to pass.

CREW COMPARTMENT
The interior of the Churchill AVRE was modified to allow room for Royal Engineers and their array of gear, including tools, equipment and explosives used to clear obstacles, deploy bridging and perform other tasks.

ENGINE
The Churchill AVRE engine was a single Bedford Twin-Six petrol powerplant that produced 261kW (350hp).

APPLICATIONS

Apart from the log-carpet application, the Churchill AVRE could be put to a broad spectrum of other uses. Its 'Mortar, Recoiling Spigot, Mark II' was ideal for close-range assault operations, blasting reinforced enemy positions. On its front, it could carry a Small Box Girder bridge, which could be laid across ditches or rivers up to 9m (30ft) wide.

PETARD AVRE
This Churchill AVRE tank, moving through Germany towards the city of Düsseldorf, is armed with the 290mm (11.4in) Petard spigot mortar, which used a powerful spring to hurl an 18.1kg (40lb) projectile at enemy fixed emplacements more than 73m (239ft) away.

ISU-122 (1944)

TYPE • *Assault Gun* **COUNTRY** • *Soviet Union*

SPECIFICATIONS

Dimensions:	Length: 9.85m (32ft 4in); Width: 3.07m (10ft 1in); Height: 2.84m (8ft 2in)
Weight:	45.5 tonnes (50.2 US tons)
Engine:	388kW (520hp) V-2-IS diesel
Speed:	37km/h (23mph)
Range:	220km (137 miles)
Armour:	30–120mm (1.18–4.7in)
Armament:	1 x 122mm (4.8in) A-19S Model 1931/37 L/46.5 gun; sometimes 1 x 12.7mm (0.5in) DShK heavy machine gun
Crew:	4 or 5

Marrying powerful guns with 'turretless tanks' based on the IS heavy tank chassis, the Soviets created the ISU family of multi-role assault gun vehicles. The ISU-122 wielded the potent 122mm (4.8in) main gun.

Above: This ISU-122 has been finished in two-tone camouflage and took part in the assault on Berlin in April 1945.

ISU-122S
The modified ISU-122S can be differentiated from its predecessor due to the longer gun with muzzle brake and the 'snoutless' gun mantlet.

Offset cannon
The cannon was offset to the right in the well-sloped front of the casement-style fighting compartment, which was located well forward.

Running gear
The vehicle sported the IS-style torsion-bar suspension and running gear with six independent solid-disc road wheels per side and three high-positioned return rollers.

GUN UPGRADE

The ISU-122 was essentially an ISU-152 with the main armament exchanged for a 122mm (4.8in) A-19S gun. From August 1944, the modified ISU-122S appeared, which mounted the longer-barrelled 122mm (4.8in) D-25S gun fitted in a redesigned mantlet that lacked the low-slung 'snout'. This gun had an improved rate of fire and reduced recoil in comparison with the A-19S gun.

RED ARMY IN BERLIN
ISU-122 heavy assault guns move into the suburbs of Berlin in April 1945. Between March 1944 and November 1945, ChKZ produced 1,735 ISU-122 and 675 ISU-122S vehicles.

ISU-152 (1944)

TYPE • *Assault Gun* **COUNTRY** • *Soviet Union*

SPECIFICATIONS

Dimensions:	Length: 9.18m (30ft 1in); Width: 3.07m (10ft 1in); Height: 2.48m (8ft 2in)
Weight:	47.3 tonnes (52.1 US tons)
Engine:	388kW (520hp) up-rated V-2-IS diesel
Speed:	40km/h (25mph)
Range:	220km (137 miles)
Armour:	30–120mm (1.18–4.72in)
Armament:	1 x 152.4mm (5.98in) ML-20S Model 1938 L/29 gun
Crew:	4 or 5

The Soviets fitted the mighty 152.4mm (5.98in) gun to a heavily protected casement-style armoured superstructure fitted on top of the IS heavy tank chassis to create the renowned ISU-152 multi-role SPG.

Below: This ISU-152, finished off in winter whitewash camouflage, has painted along its barrel the familiar slogan of 'Forward to the destruction of the enemy'.

Machine gun
This late-production ISU-152 incorporates a 12.7mm (0.5in) DShK anti-aircraft machine gun mounted on its fighting compartment roof.

Main gun
In late 1944, the improved ISU-152 Model 1944 was introduced. This modified variant featured the improved ML-20SM gun, significantly increased mantlet armour and the DShK on the hull roof.

Powerplant
The four-man vehicle was powered by a 388kW (520hp) up-rated V-2-IS, and its IS-based chassis featured six road wheels per side, independently connected to torsion bars.

TACTICAL ROLES

The first heavy assault gun variant based on the chassis of the IS heavy tanks that the Soviets developed was the ISU-152. The ISU-152 performed three main tactical roles: firing various armour-piercing (AP) rounds, the vehicle acted as a tank destroyer endeavouring to knock out enemy AFVs; providing direct fire with high-explosive (HE) rounds, the ISU-152 was used for infantry support; finally – again delivering HE via indirect fire – it performed as self-propelled artillery.

UKRAINE OFFENSIVE, 1943
A unit of ISU-152s grind their way across the Ukrainian steppe in 1943. The tank was a heavy one, as it featured 30mm (1.18in) roof armour plates and 75–90mm (2.95–3.54in) side plates. Its frontal protection was 60–90mm (2.36–3.54in) thick, while the armour on the mantlet was 120mm (4.72in) thick.

Sturmgeschütz IV (StuG IV) (1944)

TYPE • *Assault Gun* **COUNTRY** • *Germany*

SPECIFICATIONS	
Dimensions:	Length: 6.7m (21ft 11in); Width: 2.95m (9ft 8in); Height: 2.2m (7ft 3in)
Weight:	23 tonnes (25.35 US tons)
Engine:	Maybach HL120TRM 12-cylinder inline petrol, 223.7kW (300hp)
Speed:	38km/h (23.6mph)
Range:	155km (96 miles)
Armour:	11–80mm (0.31–3.15in)
Armament:	1 x 75mm (2.95in) StuK 40 L/48 with 63 rounds; 1 x 7.92mm (0.31in) MG34 machine gun
Crew:	4

As the war progressed, the StuG III's L/48 gun was inadequate to cope with the latest additions to enemy armoured forces, so the StuG IV – based on the Panzer IV chassis – was developed to accommodate the more powerful L/70 75mm (2.95in) tank gun.

Above: This StuG IV is fitted with extra armour in the form of Schürzen (side skirts) in Russia in the summer of 1944.

Superstructure
Although the superstructure was basically that of the StuG III Ausf G, a new armoured cab was added for the driver with two periscopes and an access hatch in the roof.

Hull space
Surprisingly, the StuG IV weighed a tonne less than the StuG III Ausf G and benefited from a more spacious hull that allowed for the stowage of an additional 19 main armament rounds.

ADDITIONAL ARMOUR

A number of StuG IVs were also fitted with an unusual form of appliqué armour: 150mm (5.9in)-thick concrete slabs attached to the front of the superstructure and driver's cab.

ITALY, 1944
Two StuG IVs move through Italy in 1944. Overall, the type was highly successful – a total of 1,139 were completed by the time production ended in March 1945 – and received many of the same updates as the StuG III, including the roof-mounted remote-controlled machine gun.

Sherman VC Firefly (1944)

TYPE • *Medium Tank* **COUNTRY** • *United Kingdom*

SPECIFICATIONS

Dimensions:	Length: 7.85m (25ft 9in); Width: 2.67m (8ft 9in); Height: 2.74m (8ft 11in)
Weight:	37.8 tonnes (41.68 US tons)
Engine:	350kW (470hp) up-rated Chrysler A57 multibank petrol (gasoline)
Speed:	40km/h (25mph)
Range:	201km (125 miles)
Armour:	15–100mm (0.59–3.9in)
Armament:	1 x 17pdr (76.2mm/3in) QF gun; 1 x 7.62mm (0.3in) Browning M1919A4 machine gun
Crew:	5

Intended as a short-term solution to the need for additional firepower, British designers replaced the main gun of the M4 Sherman with the heavier 17pdr QF and produced a tank, the Firefly, that was effective even against German Tigers and Panthers.

Below: The Sherman VC Firefly entered production in the autumn of 1943 and was available to British forces during the Normandy campaign.

Main armament
The 17pdr (76.2mm/3in) QF anti-tank gun was the most powerful weapon of its kind built by the British during World War II.

Radio bustle
To accommodate the large 17pdr QF gun, the turret of the M4 Sherman tank was modified. Among the changes was the removal of the radio to a bustle at the rear of the turret.

Armour
The armour protection of the Firefly varied from the basic M4 Sherman tank only in the greater thickness of the turret mantlet, which was 13mm (0.5in) thicker.

STINGING FIREFLY
The Firefly's 17pdr QF gun substantially improved the odds of survival in combat with German tanks. When the Sherman VC Firefly entered service with the British 21st Army Group in the spring of 1944, the Germans quickly grew to respect the new Allied tank mounting the QF 17pdr gun. In several documented actions, the Firefly got the best of the heavy German Tiger and medium Panther tanks, particularly when firing from concealed positions.

BRITISH FIREFLY
By D-Day, 6 June 1944, nearly 350 Sherman Firefly tanks were in service with British forces. As the campaign in Normandy came to an end, the number of Fireflies in service topped 400.

Panzer V Panther Ausf G (1944)

TYPE • *Medium Tank* **COUNTRY** • *Germany*

Continuing mechanical and operational problems with the Panzer V Panther Ausf A led to the introduction of a new model, the Ausf G, a total of 3,126 of which were produced from March 1944 to April 1945.

SPECIFICATIONS	
Dimensions	Length: 8.86m (29ft 1in); Width: 3.42m (11ft 3in); Height: 2.98m (9ft 9in)
Weight:	45.5 tonnes (50.17 US tons)
Engine:	Maybach HL230P30 petrol, 515kW (690hp)
Speed:	56km/h (35mph)
Range:	200km (124 miles)
Armour:	16–110mm (0.63–4.33in)
Armament	1 x 75mm (2.95in) KwK 42 L/70; 2 x 7.92mm (0.31in) MG34 machine guns
Crew:	5

Above: The Panther Ausf G featured thickened upper hull side armour and a new front plate, which was strengthened by the removal of the driver's vision port.

232

Armament
The main armament of the Panther was the long-barreled 75mm (2.95in) gun, for which 79 rounds of ammunition were carried.

Skirts
Skirts have been added to this Panther to offer some protection to the wheels, and spare track has been used as auxiliary armour.

Suspension
The Panther's torsion bar suspension was better than the Tiger's, and its sloped armour, a complete departure from earlier German tank design, was reminiscent of the T-34's.

INFRARED PANTHERS

German research into infrared (IR) night-fighting gear had begun in the 1930s, but received little official backing until increasing Allied air superiority forced greater attention to be given to the problems of moving and fighting at night. Prototype IR equipment underwent troop trials in 1943/44 and led to the adoption of the 200mm (7.87in) FG1250 IR searchlight and viewer, fitted to a small number of Panthers on the commander's cupola. It had an effective range of approximately 600m (656yd).

DRIVER'S POSITION
In the Ausf G, although the driver was reliant on a rotating periscope when 'closed down', he now had an adjustable seat and controls that allowed him to drive with his head out of the hatch when not in action.

Jagdpanzer IV (1944)

TYPE • *Tank Destroyer* **COUNTRY** • *Germany*

SPECIFICATIONS	
Dimensions:	Length: 6.85m (22ft 6in); Width: 3.17m (10ft 5in); Height: 1.85m (6ft 1in)
Weight:	25 tonnes (27.56 US tons)
Engine:	Maybach HL120TRM petrol, 221kW (296hp)
Speed:	40km/h (25mph)
Range:	210km (130 miles)
Armour:	10–80mm (0.39–3.15in)
Armament:	1 x 75mm (2.95in) Pak 39 L/48; 1 or 2 x 7.92mm (0.31in) MG42 machine guns
Crew:	4

The Jagdpanzer IV had been under development since late 1942 by Vogtländische Maschinenfabrik AG (VOMAG). It used the Panzer IV chassis 7 (known as BW7), but it was radically different from earlier assault guns and Panzerjägers.

Above: A Jagdpanzer IV operating in Normandy in 1944. The type had a fully enclosed fighting compartment and was protected by up to 80mm (3.14in) of well-sloped frontal and side armour.

Powerplant
The Jagdpanzer IV was fitted with a Maybach HL120TRM petrol engine, delivering 221kW (296hp) of power and a maximum speed of 40km/h (25mph).

Main gun
A few pre-production vehicles received the 75mm (2.95in) L/43, which was replaced by the 75mm (2.95in) Pak 39 L/48 in the initial 769 Jagdpanzer IVs completed between January and November 1944.

Side skirts armour
Side skirts armour could improve the survivability of a vehicle, but as a trade-off the extra weight affected mobility and fuel consumption.

MUZZLE BRAKE
In service the Jagdpanzer IV revealed a particular problem. The gun was very close to the ground, and crews intensely disliked the muzzle brake that kicked up clouds of dust with every shot, betraying the position of even the most carefully camouflaged vehicle. Many units took matters into their own hands and removed the muzzle brakes themselves before a new version of the 75mm (2.95in) L/48 without a muzzle brake became available from May 1944 onwards.

LOW PROFILE
The Jagdpanzer IV had been under development since late 1942 by Vogtländische Maschinenfabrik AG (VOMAG). Using the Panzer IV chassis 7 (known as BW7), the vehicle was an effective and popular tank destroyer, whose low silhouette made it easy to conceal in ambush positions.

Jagdpanzer IV/70 (1944)

TYPE • *Tank Destroyer* **COUNTRY** • *Germany*

SPECIFICATIONS (Jagdpanzer IV/70(V))

Dimensions:	Length: 8.5m (27ft 11in); Width: 3.17m (10ft 5in); Height: 1.85m (6ft 1in)
Weight:	25.8 tonnes (28.44 US tons)
Engine:	Maybach HL120TRM petrol, 221kW (296hp)
Speed:	35km/h (22mph)
Range:	210km (130 miles)
Armour:	10–80mm (0.39–3.15in)
Armament:	1 x 75mm (2.95in) Pak 42 L/70; 1 x 7.92mm (0.31in) MG42 machine gun
Crew:	4

The Jagdpanzer IV was a tank hunter built on the chassis of the Panzer IV with a new low-profile welded superstructure, suitable for ambush tactics. The improved version, the Jagdpanzer IV/70, had a gun with a barrel 70 calibres long.

Left: Despite problems with balance (see below), the IV/70(V) was a formidable tank killer, and VOMAG had completed 930 by the time production ended in March 1945.

Jagdpanzer IV/70(A)
The Jagdpanzer IV/70(A) was taller than the Jagdpanzer IV/70(V), which made it significantly more conspicuous on the battlefield. Its greater height also exposed a large area of relatively thin side armour.

Gun traverse
The 75mm (2.95in) L/70 had a total traverse of 20° and elevation of -5° to +15°. A total of 55 rounds of ammunition for the weapon were carried.

Mess armour
To protect against shaped-charge warheads, wire mesh *Thoma Schürzen* began to replace the earlier solid plate version from September 1944.

IMBALANCE
The weight imbalance imposed by the fitting of such a long gun caused rapid wear of the conventional rubber-tyred front road wheels, and these were replaced by resilient-rim steel road wheels. The sheer length of the L/70 in such a low-slung hull caused its own problems: when moving off-road, the vehicle needed careful handling as crossing even small dips and hollows could result in digging the barrel into the ground.

NETHERLANDS, 1944
A Jagdpanzer IV/70(V) in a suburban street. Judging from the casual attitude of the crew and passers-by, it is well behind the front line. (The ineffectual attempt at camouflage using brushwood would invite rapid destruction in combat.)

Jagdpanther (1944)

TYPE • *Tank Destroyer* **COUNTRY** • *Germany*

SPECIFICATIONS

Dimensions:	Length: 9.9m (32ft 6in); Width: 3.42m (11ft 3in); Height: 2.72m (8ft 11in)
Weight:	46 tonnes (50.7 US tons)
Engine:	Maybach HL120TRM petrol, 221kW (296hp)
Speed:	46km/h (29mph)
Range:	160km (99 miles)
Armour:	16–100mm (0.63–3.94in)
Armament:	1 x 88mm (3.46in) Pak 43/3 L/71 with 50 rounds; 1 x 7.92mm (0.31in) MG34 machine gun
Crew:	5

The Jagdpanther was one of the first purpose-built tank destroyers. Fast, well armoured and mounting a powerful gun, it was able to knock out almost any tank it encountered. Anti-magnetic mine paint and a machine gun helped with close-quarter defence.

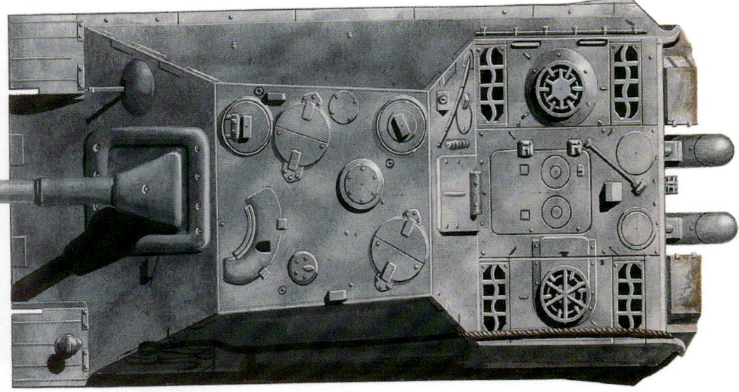

Right: The rear decking of the Jagdpanther was dominated by the central engine hatch and the large circular fan units required to cool the water for the large 23.88-litre Maybach engine.

Armour
Although the Jagdpanther was best protected against frontal fire, the likelihood of attack from the side was not ignored, and good protection was therefore provided on the sides of the vehicle.

Exhausts
The pair of exhausts for the Maybach HL 230 P30 petrol engine were upswept to keep their ends above the water as the Jagdpanther waded across small rivers and streams.

Running gear
The running gear of the Jagdpanther comprised eight interleaved road wheels with torsion-bar suspension, a front-mounted idler and a rear-mounted drive sprocket; there were no track-return rollers.

DEVELOPMENT

Based on the hull and propulsion arrangements of the Panther battle tank, what began life as the 8.8cm Pak 43/3 auf Panzerjäger Panther was renamed as the Jagdpanther at Hitler's suggestion in February 1944. The basic lines of the hull were continued upward and inward to create a large superstructure containing the fighting compartment with its exceptional 8.8cm (3.46in) anti-tank gun, which was a potent tank-killer.

RUSSIA, 1944
A Jagdpanther crosses a Russian plain, possibly on a training exercise. The type proved to be a formidable tank destroyer. The well-sloped frontal armour gave immunity to virtually all Allied anti-tank weapons at normal combat ranges, while the well-proven Pak 43 could penetrate 132mm (5.2in) of armour at ranges up to 2,000m (2,187yd).

Jagdpanzer 38(t) Hetzer (1944)

TYPE • *Tank Destroyer* **COUNTRY** • *Germany*

SPECIFICATIONS

Dimensions:	Length: 6.38m (20ft 11in); Width: 2.63m (8ft 8in); Height: 2.17m (7ft 1in)
Weight:	15.75 tonnes (17.36 US tons)
Engine:	Praga AC-2 6-cylinder petrol, 118kW (158hp)
Speed:	42km/h (26mph)
Range:	177km (115 miles)
Armour:	8–60mm (0.31–2.36in)
Armament:	1 x 75mm (2.95in) Pak 39 L/48 with 41 rounds; 1 x 7.92mm (0.31in) MG34 or MG42 machine gun
Crew:	4

Based on the PzKpfw 38(t) chassis, the Hetzer was a light tank destroyer that appeared in 1943. Small, well protected, with good mobility and able to knock out all but the heaviest tanks, it proved to be a tremendous success.

Left: A top view of the Hetzer. Production continued until the factories were overrun in May 1945, by which time 1577 had been built.

Fighting compartment
The Hetzer was very cramped – the commander was isolated well behind the gun in a confined position.

Mantlet
Early Hetzers had a rather narrow *Saukopf* ('pig's head') mantlet, with flattened sides, which did not adequately protect the inner splash shield when the gun was traversed. This was rapidly replaced by a far better wider mantlet, which remained in production until the end of the war.

Pak 39 gun
The Pak 39 was highly effective, but its very limited traverse (5 degrees left, 11 degrees right) meant that crews had to manoeuvre carefully to track targets while minimizing the exposure of the 20mm (0.79in) side armour.

LOADER'S CHALLENGE
Although the Pak 39 was designed to be loaded from the right, the loader was seated to the left of the gun, so he had to load over the solid deflector screen instead of the low-mounted bar on the right, designed for this purpose. All the loader's controls were mounted on the right side of the breech ring, so he had to lean over the gunner and breech to reach them. Opening the breech to load the first round, unloading the gun and removing jammed cartridge cases required near-acrobatic skills.

KNOCKED-OUT HETZER
An American GI examines a knocked-out Hetzer. The vehicle had some significant vulnerabilities. The original horizontally mounted exhaust system, for example, acted as a trap for grenades and demolition charges lobbed onto the engine decks, although it was later replaced with a vertical exhaust.

M4A3E2 Jumbo assault tank (1944)

TYPE • *Assault Tank* **COUNTRY** • *United States*

SPECIFICATIONS

Dimensions:	Length: 7.54m (24ft 8in); Width: 2.9m (9ft 6in); Height: 2.95m (9ft 8in)
Weight:	38.1 tonnes (41.99 US tons)
Engine:	336kW (450hp) Ford GAA petrol (gasoline)
Speed:	35km/h (22mph)
Range:	161km (100 miles)
Armour:	12.7–152mm (0.4–6in)
Armament:	1 x 75mm (2.95in) M3; 1 x 12.7mm (0.5in) M2HB HMG; 2 x 7.62mm (0.3in) M1919A4 MG
Crew:	5

During the winter of 1943–44, the army identified the need for an up-armoured tank to engage the enemy's Siegfried Line bunkers along Germany's western border. The result was the petrol-engined Sherman M4A3E2, an assault tank later nicknamed 'Jumbo'.

Below: With a standard Ford 336kW (450hp) petrol (gasoline) engine, but working through a modified final drive ratio, the M4A3E2 could obtain a top speed of 35km/h (22mph).

M4A3E2
This M4A3E2 was the first vehicle to break through the German siege of Bastogne on 26 December 1944, a feat enshrined by the crew-painted slogan. Note the extra armour on the hull frontal glacis plate and on the gun mantlet.

Turret
The tank also featured an up-armoured T26 turret with additional armour added to the M26 mounting to create an enlarged gun mantlet, which housed the 75mm (2.95in) M3 gun.

Armour
Fisher welded solid 38mm (1.46in)-thick armour plates to the front hull upper glacis plate and the hull sides, raising the vehicle's protection to 101mm (4in) on the glacis plate and 76mm (3in) on the hull sides.

DESIGN SPEED
With limited time available to create the new tank, the Americans simply modified the existing M4A3 Shermans and skipped the normal design testing process. In March 1944, the Army contracted Fisher to build 250 M4A3E2 assault tanks. During April–July 1944, Fisher produced 254 vehicles, and after testing, they arrived in Allied-liberated northwest Europe during September–October 1944.

TANK CREWS
The crews of M4A3E2 Sherman Jumbos from 747th Tank Battalion (attached to the 29th Infantry Division, US 9th Army) watch as German prisoners of war from the 340th Volksgrenadier Division are marched past near Koslar in the North Rhine-Westphalia region of Germany, December 1944.

LVT-4 (1944)

TYPE • *Amphibious Vehicle* **COUNTRY** • *United States*

SPECIFICATIONS

Dimensions:	Length: 7.95m (26ft 1in); Width: 3.25m (10ft 8in); Height: 2.5m (8ft 2in)
Weight:	16.5 tonnes (18.19 US tons)
Engine:	186kW (250hp) up-rated Wright/Continental W670-9A petrol (gasoline)
Speed:	24km/h (15mph)
Range:	241km (150 miles) on land
Armour:	None or 6.4–12.7mm (0.25–0.5in) appliqué plates
Armament:	1–2 x 12.7mm (0.5in) M2HB HMG; 1–2 x 7.62mm (0.3in) M1919A4 MG
Crew:	3 (+30 troops)

The LVT-4 was a highly capable amphibious assault vehicle, able to carry troops, supplies or artillery as large as a 105mm (4.1in) howitzer. The type was extensively used in river crossings during the final stages of the Italian campaign.

Above: In addition to its three-man crew, the LVT-4 could carry 30 troops, with access to and from the vehicle via a rear door.

Weaponry
The LVT-4 housed a variety of weapons: either one or two centrally positioned 12.7mm (0.5in) Browning M2HB heavy machine guns and one or two 7.62mm (0.3in) M1919A4 machine guns.

Superstructure
The LVT-4 was visually distinguishable from its predecessors by its flat superstructure top, interrupted only by weapon mounts.

Front cabin
The frontal cabin was not raised above the top line of the superstructure and featured three small vision ports instead of large windows.

RIVER ASSAULTS

Some 500 LVT-4 vehicles were transferred to the British Army. To give additional support-fire capability during contested landings, many of these vehicles were fitted with a 20mm (0.79in) Polsten cannon and two 7.62mm (0.3in) Browning machine guns. These vehicles participated in the autumn 1944 amphibious assaults in the Scheldt estuary and the March 1945 attack across the Rhine.

ASSAULT ON OKINAWA
LVT-4s, packed with infantry, make the run-in to the beaches of Okinawa in April 1945. The .50-cal M2HB machine guns are placed behind curved shields to protect the gunners against small-arms fire and shell-splinters.

LVT(A)-4 (1944)

TYPE • *Amphibious Vehicle* **COUNTRY** • *United States*

SPECIFICATIONS

Dimensions:	Length: 7.95m (26ft 1in); Width: 3.25m (10ft 8in); Height: 3.11m (10ft 2in)
Weight:	18.3 tonnes (20.17 US tons)
Engine:	186kW (250hp) Wright/ Continental W670-9A petrol (gasoline)
Speed:	24km/h (15mph)
Range:	241km (150 miles) on land
Armour:	6.4–38mm (0.25–1.5in)
Armament:	1 x 75mm (2.95in) M2; 1 x 12.7mm (0.5in) M2HB HMG; 2–3 x 7.62mm (0.3in) M1919A4 MG
Crew:	6

Experience at Tarawa in November 1943 showed the need for a more heavily armed version of the AMTRAC to support the troop carriers. Various light tank turrets were tried before the definitive LVT(A)-4 and -5, with the turret of the M8 howitzer, appeared.

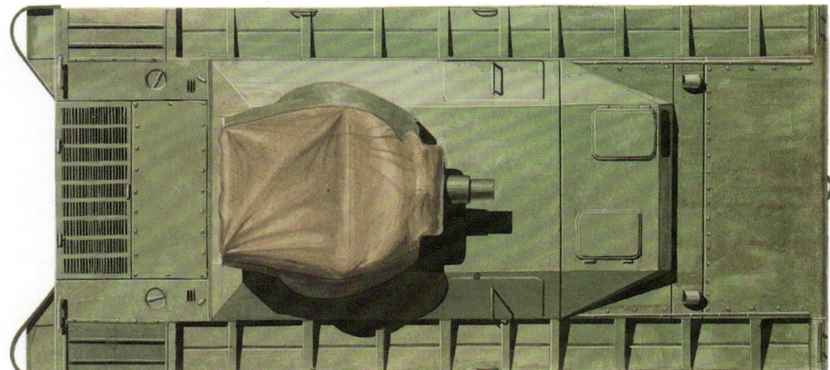

Left: The vehicle carried 100 rounds for its main gun, these being a mix of M48 high explosive and M66 high explosive anti-tank shells.

Turret
The turret of the LVT (A)-4 featured the short-barrelled 75mm L/18.4 M2 howitzer in an M7 mounting.

Powerplant
A 186kW (250hp) Wright/ Continental W670-9A petrol (gasoline) engine was married to a Spicer synchromesh transmission with one reverse and five forward gears.

Armour
The six-crew vehicle had 6mm (0.25in) side and rear armour, 6–12.7mm (0.25–0.5 in) frontal hull armour and a turret front with a thickness of 38mm (1.46in).

FIRE SUPPORT
From late 1944, the LVT(A)-4 provided the USMC's amphibious assault forces with a much-needed enhanced close fire-support capability – in the form of a short-barrelled 75mm M2 L/18.4 howitzer. These vehicles fought in the USMC's 1945 campaigns, such as Iwo Jima and Okinawa. In the war's last weeks, 269 examples of an improved variant, the LVT(A)-5, entered service. This had a gyro-stabilized M3 gun on the new M12 mounting fitted to an electric-powered turret.

IWO JIMA, 1945
An LVT(A)-4 is hoisted from USS *Hansford* (APA-106) off Iwo Jima in the spring of 1945. Although the LVT(A)-1 had provided much-needed fire support for America's 1944 amphibious assaults in the Pacific, the limitations of its 37mm (1.46in) M6 cannon led to the development by March 1944 of the up-gunned LVT(A)-4.

Churchill Crocodile (1944)

TYPE • *Special Purpose Tank* **COUNTRY** • *United Kingdom*

SPECIFICATIONS	
DIMENSIONS:	Length (without trailer): 7.44m (24ft 5in); Width: 2.74m (9ft 0in); Height: 3.45m (11ft 4in)
WEIGHT:	40.6 tonnes (44.73 US tons)
ENGINE:	Bedford 12-cylinder petrol, 261kW (350hp)
SPEED:	Maximum road speed of 20km/h (12.5mph)
RANGE:	Road range of 144km (90 miles)
ARMOUR:	51–152mm (2–6in)
ARMAMENT:	1 x 75mm Ordnance QF main gun; 1 x Flame Projector Unit
CREW:	5

The Churchill Crocodile was a conversion of the Churchill Mk VII adapted for the beach assault role and used in the Normandy invasion as a flamethrower and assault tank. It got its name because it came onto the beach with a motion suggestive of a crocodile crawling out of the water.

Left: This AVRE carries a 'Log Carpet', a more durable version of the 'Bobbin Carpet'.

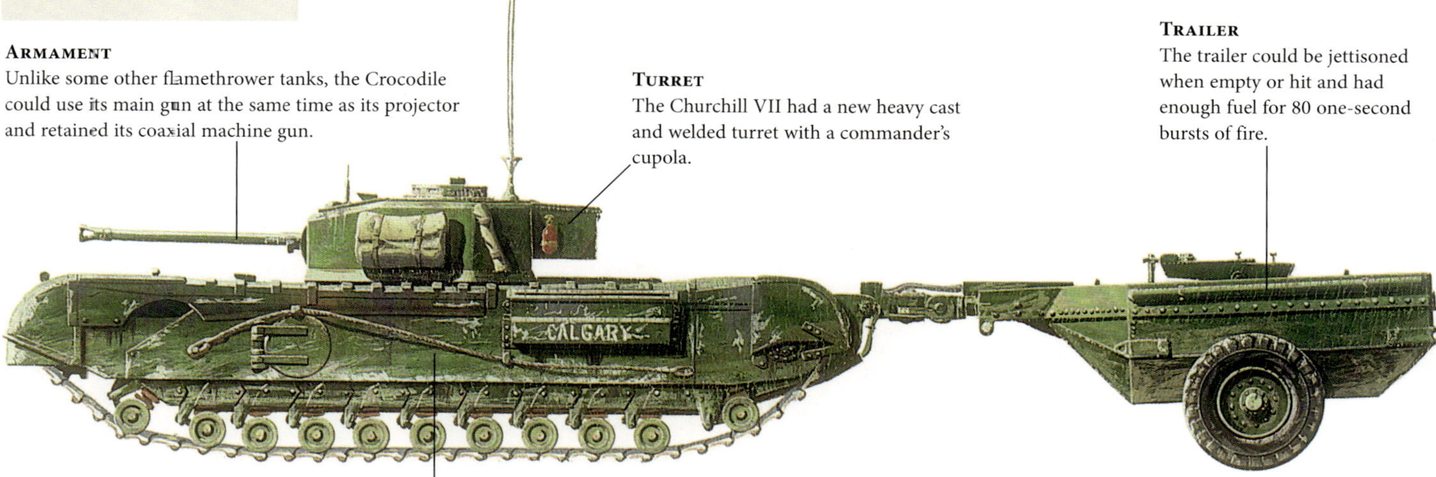

ARMAMENT
Unlike some other flamethrower tanks, the Crocodile could use its main gun at the same time as its projector and retained its coaxial machine gun.

TURRET
The Churchill VII had a new heavy cast and welded turret with a commander's cupola.

TRAILER
The trailer could be jettisoned when empty or hit and had enough fuel for 80 one-second bursts of fire.

HULL
Although superficially similar to earlier models, the Churchill VII was of completely new construction. It had no hull frame, but was constructed from frameless armour plate that was joined to form a rigid structure.

FLAME UNIT
The Churchill Crocodile, of which 800 were made, replaced the hull machine gun with a projector that emitted a jet of flame 73–110m (80–120yd) long. This was fed under pressure by a pipe from the 6.5-tonne (7.3-ton) armoured trailer. On D-Day, the Crocodiles were used against bunkers and machine gun positions on the beach, and later as flamethrowers or conventional tanks, as the situation dictated. Against point positions such as pillboxes or bunkers, the flame weapon was devastating.

FLAMETHROWER 'FUNNIES'
The Churchill Mark VII Crocodile flamethrowing tank was developed under Major-General Percy Hobart, whose vehicles were informally known as 'Hobart's Funnies'. This one is on the move with the British 79th Armoured Division on 12 September 1944 during operations to take Brest in France.

T-34/85 (1944)

TYPE • *Medium Tank* **COUNTRY** • *Soviet Union*

SPECIFICATIONS (T-34/85 Model 1944)

Dimensions:	Length: 6.1m (20ft); Width: 3m (9ft 10in); Height: 2.72m (8ft 11in)
Weight:	32 tonnes (35.3 US tons)
Engine:	373kW (500hp) Model V-2-34 diesel
Speed:	55km/h (34mph)
Range:	350km (217 miles)
Armour:	20–90mm (0.79–3.54in)
Armament:	1 x 85mm (3.35in) ZiS-53 or ZiS-S-53 L/51.5 gun; 2 x 7.62mm (0.3in) DT machine guns, typically coaxial
Crew:	5

The improved firepower of the T-34/85 medium tank came about following analysis of the T-34's performance during the Battle of Kursk in July 1943. Three 85mm (3.35in) weapons were considered before a decision was made to mount the ZIS-S-53.

Left: Stronger springs were installed in the T-34/85's Christie suspension system to deal with the heavier turret weight. The suspension was originally designed by American engineer Walter Christie.

Main armament
When the T-34 medium tank's 76.2mm (3in) L-11 gun and later the long-barrelled F-34 were both deemed insufficient in firepower, the new 85mm (3.35in) ZIS-S-53 cannon was installed and the new variant was dubbed the T-34/85.

Turret
The turret of the T-34/85 was expanded to accommodate three crewmen rather than two, eliminating the need for the tank commander to serve the tank's main weapon.

Engine
The T-34/85 powerplant was essentially the same as that of the early T-34, the reliable 12-cylinder V-2-34 water-cooled diesel engine that generated 500hp (375kW).

SURVIVABILITY
The T-34/85 brought better combat survivability to Soviet armoured forces. The greater range of the new main weapon and its muzzle velocity of 780mps (2,559fps) improved penetration of German armour plating with armour-piercing ammunition. Combat experience revealed the need for additional protection against German anti-tank weapons such as the shoulder-fired Panzerfaust. Additional thin plating or wire mesh was welded into areas around the hull and turret that were susceptible to 'trapping' shells or hollow charges. These were often successful at deflecting otherwise damaging strikes.

FUEL TANKS
The fuel tank capacity of the T-34/85 was reduced from that of the original T-34 due to the redesign of the tank and its added weight. Although the change negatively impacted the T-34/85's range, the firepower gained was worth the price.

SU-100 (1944)

TYPE • *Self-propelled Gun* **COUNTRY** • *Soviet Union*

SPECIFICATIONS	
DIMENSIONS:	Length: 9.45m (31ft); Width: 3m (9ft 10in); Height: 2.25m (7ft 5in)
WEIGHT:	31.6 tonnes (34.8 US tons)
ENGINE:	373kW (500hp) V-2-34M 12-cylinder diesel
SPEED:	35km/h (22mph)
RANGE:	320km (199 miles)
ARMOUR:	20–75mm (0.78–2.95in)
ARMAMENT:	1 x 100mm (3.94in) D-10S L/53.5 gun
CREW:	4

The SU-100 tank destroyer was developed as an up-gunned version of the SU-85. Its powerful 100mm (3.94in) gun meant that the SU-100 was capable of dealing with even the most powerful German tanks, and it remained in service for many years after the war.

Above: The late 1943 introduction of the T-34/85 tank, fitted with the same 85mm (3.35in) weapon as the SU-85, brought the latter's future role into question. Consequently, the Soviets produced the SU-100 tank destroyer.

FRONT PLATE
The plate was located well forward in the vehicle; given the D-10S cannon's length, the vehicle's barrel overhang amounted to 59 percent of the hull's entire length.

EQUIPMENT
Like its predecessor, the SU-100 had no machine gun fitted for close-range defence. It also mounted a 10-RF-26 radio set.

POWERPLANT
Powered by a 373kW (500hp) rated V-2 12-cylinder diesel engine, the SU-100 could reach a top road speed of 35km/h (22mph) and a maximum by-road operating range of 300km (186 miles).

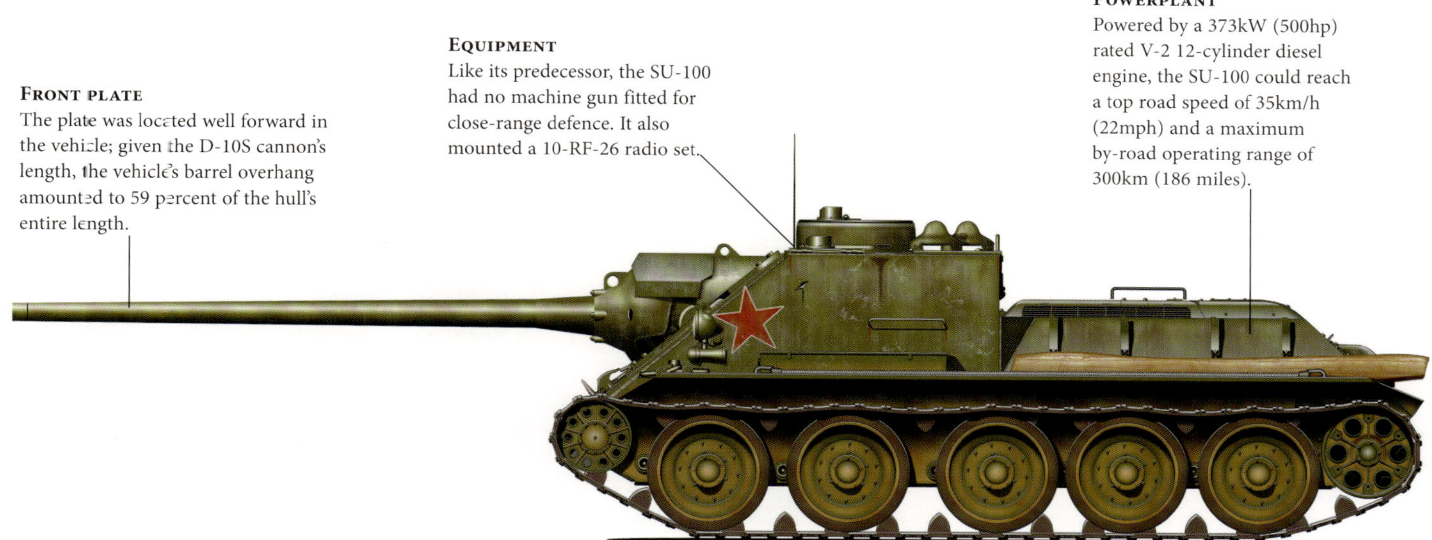

NEW GUN
The four-man SU-100 mounted the new long-barrelled 100mm (3.94in) D-10S Model 1944 cannon. This was fitted, offset to the right, in a large rounded mantlet attached to the superstructure's well-sloped front plate.

SU-100 COLUMN
A unit of SU-100s move in echelon formation on the Eastern Front. During late 1944 and early 1945 the Soviets produced 1,534 SU-100 tank destroyers, many of which participated in the final Soviet advance into central Germany.

IS-2 (1944)

TYPE • *Heavy Tank* **COUNTRY** • *Soviet Union*

The IS-2 tank first saw combat in the spring of 1944. IS-2s were assigned to separate heavy tank regiments, normally of 21 tanks each. These regiments were used to reinforce the most important attack sectors during major offensive operations.

SPECIFICATIONS

Dimensions:	Length: 9.9m (32ft 6in); Width: 3.09m (10ft 2in); Height: 2.73m (8ft 11in)
Weight:	46 tonnes (50.7 US tons)
Engine:	473kW (600hp) V-2-IS 12-cylinder diesel
Speed:	37km/h (23mph)
Range:	240km (149 miles)
Armour:	30–120mm (1.18–4.72in)
Armament:	1 x 122mm (4.8in) A-19 or D-25T L/48 gun; 2 x 7.62mm (0.3in) DT machine guns (1 coaxial, 1 turret rear); sometimes 1 x 12.7mm (0.5in) DShK machine gun on turret roof
Crew:	4

Left: The second heavy tank in the Iosef Stalin heavy tank series, the IS-2, was the first such vehicle to mount the truly formidable new 122mm (4.8in) A-19 gun.

Main gun
The four-man IS-2 design incorporated the long-barrelled 122mm (4.8in) A-19 gun into a forward-positioned turret. This gave the tank a very significant barrel overhang.

Turret
The well-sloped and rounded modified turret narrowed toward the gun mantlet, presenting a smaller area for the enemy to strike.

Suspension
The IS-2 had a standard torsion-bar suspension that supported six independent pairs of road wheels per side; the minor visual difference was that the top track was slightly undulating as it got pulled over the three high-positioned return rollers.

DEVELOPMENT

During October 1943, the Soviets concluded that it was no use having heavy tanks that only fielded the same 85mm (3.35in) weapon as the T-34/85. Although the 100mm (3.94in) BS-3 gun had been shown to be potent, it proved costly to produce. The Soviets instead decided that the corps-level 122mm (4.8in) Field Cannon A-19 Model 1931 should become the main armament to be mounted in its future heavy tanks. This decision, therefore, required the development of a new heavy tank design – and consequently, the IS-122 (later renamed IS-2) tank was born.

BERLIN ADVANCE
A column of IS-2s enters the outskirts of Berlin in April 1945. Soviet factories produced 3,854 IS-2 tanks during a production run that lasted from December 1943 until summer 1945. The design underwent various modifications during its production run.

Sherman Crab Mine-Clearing Tank (1944)

TYPE • *Special Purpose Tank* **COUNTRY** • *United States*

SPECIFICATIONS

Dimensions:	Length: 6.35m (20ft 10in); Width: 2.81m (9ft 3in); Height: 3.96m (13ft)
Weight:	32.28 tonnes (35.57 US tons)
Engine:	1 x Ford GAA V-8 petrol powerplant generating 373kW (500hp)
Speed:	46km/h (28.75mph)
Range:	62km (100 miles)
Armour:	15–76mm (0.59–2.9in)
Armament:	1 x 75mm (2.95in) gun; 1 x 7.62mm (0.3in) Browning machine gun (removed from some tanks)
Crew:	5

The Medium Tank M4, popularly known as the Sherman, has been adapted for specialized service more than any other tank. The Sherman Crab Mine-Clearing Tank utilized a flail to detonate land mines, clearing a path for troops that followed.

Above: Using a rotating bobbin and 43 lengths of chain, the Sherman Crab detonated land mines in its path and marked the passage through a minefield with coloured chalk, smoke or luminous poles periodically fired into the ground automatically.

Hydraulic apparatus
The right arm of the Sherman Crab flail was hydraulically powered, raising and lowering the apparatus as needed. The Mk II variant included a jib that was weighted and balanced to follow the contour of the terrain.

Powerplant
The Sherman Crab's Ford GAA V-8 petrol engine was modified to accept the drive shaft that powered the flail. Operating the flail off the main tank engine was a decided advantage over an external engine that was prone to breakdowns.

CRABS AT WAR
During the Normandy landings on 6 June 1944, the Sherman Crabs of the Westminster Dragoons, 22nd Dragoons, and 1st Lothians and Border Yeomanry were with the first wave of British and Canadian troops to land on Gold, Juno and Sword beaches, clearing mines and engaging German machine-gun nests and bunkers. The Crabs saw service throughout the rest of World War II.

FLAIL TEST
The flail of a Sherman Crab kicks up a cloud of dust and dirt while undergoing extensive testing in April 1944. British designers and engineers used the American M4 medium tank as the basis for the most effective Allied mine clearing tank of the 1939–45 war.

Cruiser Tank Mk VIII, Cromwell (A27M) (1944)

TYPE • *Medium tank* **COUNTRY** • *United Kingdom*

Perpetuating the British line of cruiser tanks, but finally addressing the need for a more powerful gun and increased armour protection, the Cromwell Mk VIII made great strides in combat effectiveness against German tanks.

SPECIFICATIONS

DIMENSIONS:	Length: 6.35m (20ft 10in); Width: 2.9m (9ft 6in); Height: 2.49m (8ft 2in)
WEIGHT:	29 tonnes (31.96 US tons)
ENGINE:	1 x V-12 Rolls-Royce Meteor powerplant generating 447kW (600hp)
SPEED:	61km/h (37.9mph)
RANGE:	Road: 278km (173 miles); Cross-country: 128.75km (80 miles)
ARMOUR:	8–76mm (0.31–2.9in)
ARMAMENT:	1 x 75mm (2.95in) QF gun; 2 x 7.92mm (0.31in) Besa machine guns
CREW:	5

Right: With up to 76mm (2.9in) of armour protection, the Cromwell offered its crew a greater chance of survival on the battlefield.

MAIN ARMAMENT
The 75mm (2.95in) QF gun provided the increased firepower necessary for the Cromwell Mk VIII to somewhat even the odds in tank versus tank combat with a new generation of German armoured vehicles.

SECONDARY ARMAMENT
Most versions of the Cromwell mounted two 7.92mm (0.31in) Besa machine guns, one ball-mounted forward in the hull and the other mounted coaxially in the turret.

ENGINE
The V-12 Rolls-Royce Meteor petrol engine provided power that preserved the Cromwell's speed advantage despite the added weight of a heavier main gun and enhanced armour protection.

IN COMBAT

The Cromwell Mk VIII primarily equipped units of the British 7th Armoured Division. At full strength, the armour complement of a Cromwell regiment included the Mk IV with its 75mm (2.95in) gun, the 95mm (3.74in) howitzer-equipped Mk VIII and the Sherman Firefly, an up-gunned British variant of the American M4 Sherman medium tank. Although its main gun was still inferior to those of the German Tiger and Panther tanks, it was a considerable improvement over previous British cruiser tank models.

CROMWELL ADVANCE
The bocage country of Normandy inhibited the Cromwell's advantage of speed, but once the breakout from the hedgerow was achieved, the tank kept pace with the rapid movement of infantry across France and into Germany. Here a Cromwell displays its speed, raising clouds of dust during a swift advance.

Archer SP gun (1944)

TYPE • *Self-propelled gun* **COUNTRY** • *United Kingdom*

SPECIFICATIONS

DIMENSIONS:	Length: 6.68m (21ft 11in); Width: 2.64m (8ft 8in); Height: 2.24m (7ft 4in)
WEIGHT:	18.79 tonnes (20.71 US tons)
ENGINE:	123kW (165hp) GMC M10 diesel
SPEED:	24km/h (15mph)
RANGE:	145km (90 miles)
ARMOUR:	16–60mm (0.63–2.36in)
ARMAMENT:	1 x 76mm (3in) 17pdr OQF; 1 x 7.7mm (0.303in) Bren MG
CREW:	4

The British Archer was a conversion of the Valentine infantry tank to mount a 17pdr (76mm/3in) anti-tank gun that fired over the rear of the hull. The first examples were used in action late in 1944, and proved to be very useful weapons with a low silhouette.

Below: The 17pdr was carried on a rearward-facing, limited-traverse mount in an open-topped fighting compartment.

LAYOUT
To ensure the gun/chassis combination would not be nose-heavy and unwieldy, it was decided to place the gun in a limited-traverse mounting facing over the rear of the chassis.

SUPERSTRUCTURE
The Valentine could be rapidly adapted for its new gun-carrying role by adding a sloping superstructure, open at the top, on the forward part of the hull.

REAR-FACING GUN
In action the Archer's tank-killing capabilities were soon revealed. The rear-facing gun was seen to be a virtue.

ARCHER CREW

It was March 1943 before the first self-propelled 17pdr Valentine rolled off the production lines. The troops looked at the new vehicle with some trepidation, for the idea of having a gun that faced only to the rear was against established practice. Drivers were also less than enchanted, for they were positioned at the centre-front of the fighting compartment and the gun breech was directly behind their heads: on firing, the breech block came to within a short distance of the back of the driver's head. It was October 1944 before the first of these Valentine/17pdr combinations reached the fighting in Europe. By then the type had become known as the Archer.

ARCHER FIREPOWER

Although the British Army tended to lag behind the Germans in up-gunning its tanks as World War II progressed, an early decision by British planners to make a quantum leap in anti-tank gun calibre, from 57mm (2.24in) in the 6pdr to 76mm (3in), was bold as it was made at a time when the 6pdr was only just getting into production.

Tiger II 'King Tiger' (1944)

TYPE • *Heavy tank* **COUNTRY** • *Germany*

Even as production began on the initial Tiger, the Henschel and Porsche companies were working to develop an even more formidable heavy tank. When Henschel won the contract in October 1943, the result was dubbed the Tiger II or 'King Tiger'.

SPECIFICATIONS

DIMENSIONS:	Length: 7.25m (23ft 10in); Width: 3.72m (12ft 2in); Height: 3.27m (10ft 9in)
WEIGHT:	63.5 tonnes (69.99 US tons)
ENGINE:	1 x V-12 Maybach HL 230 P30 petrol engine producing 514kW (690hp)
SPEED:	38km/h (24mph)
RANGE:	Road: 170km (105 miles); Off-road: 120km (70 miles)
ARMOUR:	40–180mm (1.57–7in)
ARMAMENT:	1 x 88mm (3.5in) KwK 43 L/71 high-velocity gun; 2 x 7.92mm (0.31in) MG 34 machine guns
CREW:	5

Left: The frontal armour of the Tiger II was 150mm (5.9in) thick and sloped 50mm (1.97in), while armour protection for the front of the turret increased to 180mm (7in). Side armour was 80mm (3.15in) thick and sloped at a 25 degree angle.

MAIN GUN
The main weapon of the Tiger II heavy tank was the 88mm (3.5in) KwK 43 L/71 high-velocity gun. The weapon's barrel was over 6m (19ft) long.

AMMUNITION STOWAGE
The Tiger II carried a minimum of 80 rounds of armour-piercing and high-explosive 88mm (3.5in) ammunition.

POWERPLANT
The V-12 Maybach HL 230 P30 petrol engine was also used in Panther medium tanks produced late in the war. In the field, the Maybach powerplant was the source of many mechanical breakdowns.

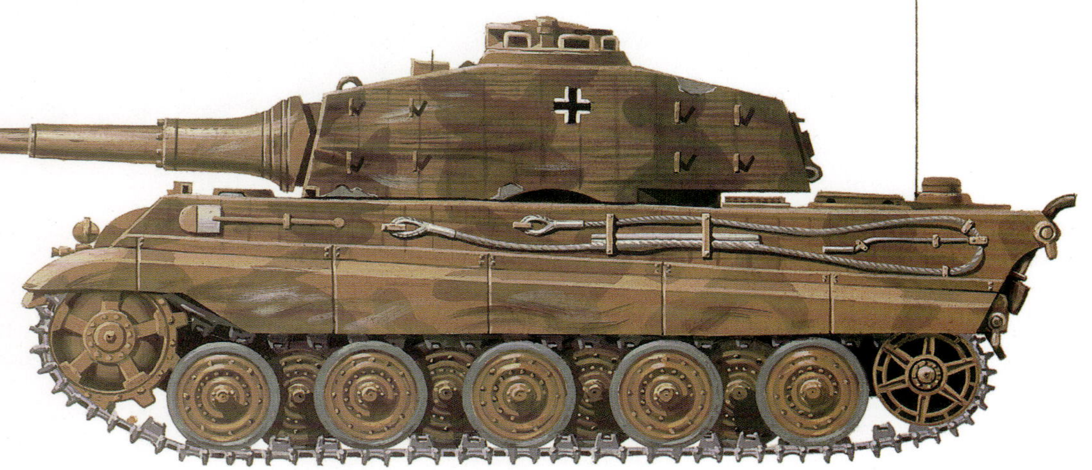

IMPACT
The Tiger II had a significant psychological effect on Allied soldiers who encountered the armoured giant, or those who believed they had. In reality, the Tiger II was never available in great numbers owing to the German penchant for perceived quality over quantity and the damage inflicted on the country's industrial capacity by continuous Allied bombing. Through the course of World War II, fewer than 500 Tiger IIs were actually completed and deployed during a brief production run from late 1943 through the spring of 1945.

MASSED TIGERS
A massed group of Tiger IIs presents a formidable front. Although the Tiger II was a powerful foe in combat, fuel shortages and mechanical failures resulted in a number of the massive tanks being abandoned in the field or destroyed by their crews to prevent capture.

Jagdpanzer VI Jagdtiger (1944)

TYPE • *Tank destroyer* **COUNTRY** • *Germany*

Although the *Jagdtiger* (Hunting Tiger) was the most heavily armed and armoured vehicle deployed during World War II, its ponderous weight, high fuel consumption and inadequate powerplant limited its worth on the battlefield.

SPECIFICATIONS

Dimensions:	Length: 10.65m (34ft 11in); Width: 3.63m (11ft 11in); Height: 2.95m (9ft 8in)
Weight:	70.6 tonnes (77.83 US tons)
Engine:	1 x V-12 Maybach HL 230 P30 petrol engine generating 522kW (700hp)
Speed:	38km/h (24mph)
Range:	Road: 120km (75 miles); Cross-country: 80km (50 miles)
Armour:	25–250mm (0.98–9.8in)
Armament:	1 x 128mm (5in) Pak 44 L/55 gun; 2 x 7.92mm (0.31in) MG 34 machine guns
Crew:	6

Left: The turret of the Tiger II was removed in favour of a high superstructure in the Jagdtiger, while the hull of the heavy tank was lengthened to accommodate another crewman and the heavy main gun.

Main armament
The 128mm (5in) Pak 44 L/55 anti-tank gun was chosen as the primary weapon of the Jagdtiger. It was the heaviest weapon of its kind deployed during World War II.

Powerplant
The V-12 Maybach HL 230 P30 petrol engine was used in Panther medium tanks and the Tiger II heavy tank. The engine was inadequate to power the Jagdtiger efficiently, being the heaviest armoured vehicle deployed during World War II.

Secondary armament
Two 7.92mm (0.31in) MG 34 machine guns protected the Tiger II from infantry attack. One was mounted coaxially in the welded turret, while the other was ball-mounted on the right front hull.

DESTRUCTION

Only about 70 examples of the Jagdpanzer VI Jagdtiger were produced by the Nibelungwerk in St Valentin, Germany. Its combat record was mixed. Mechanical failures accounted for numerous losses among the Jagdtigers, and the inexperience of some crews resulted in disaster. Tiger tank ace Otto Carius remembered a Jagdtiger commander turning broadside rather than towards the enemy and absorbing several hits that resulted in the deaths of all six crewmen.

HIGH SILHOUETTE
The high silhouette of the Jagdtiger made it a conspicuous target on the battlefield. Aside from vulnerability to tank-killer squads, the Hunting Tiger was also especially exposed to being spotted and attacked by Allied fighter-bombers.

M36 Jackson (1944)

TYPE • *Tank destroyer* **COUNTRY** • *United States*

SPECIFICATIONS

DIMENSIONS:	Length: 5.97m (19ft 7in); Width: 3.05m (10ft); Height: 3.28m (10ft 9in)
WEIGHT:	29 tonnes (31.97 US tons)
ENGINE:	336kW (450hp) Ford GAA petrol (gasoline)
SPEED:	42km/h (26mph)
RANGE:	241km (150 miles)
ARMOUR:	12.7–108mm (0.5–4.25in)
ARMAMENT:	90mm (3.54in) M3; 1 x 12.7mm (0.5in) M2HB HMG
CREW:	4

The M36 tank destroyer comprised the hull of an M10A1 with a new turret mounting a 90mm (3.54in) M3 gun, plus a machine gun in an anti-aircraft mounting. The turret was open-topped but fitted with a folding armoured roof kit to protect from shrapnel.

Right: On the rear of the bustle, there was a bracket-mount that sported a dual-purpose 12.7mm (0.5in) Browning M2HB heavy machine gun, for which the vehicle carried 1000 rounds.

TURRET
Externally, the four-crew M36 resembled the M10A1 but with a taller and longer open-topped turret.

MUZZLE BRAKE
From vehicle 601 onwards, M36s featured an M3 cannon fitted with a distinctive double-baffle muzzle brake.

RUNNING GEAR
Powered by a 336kW (450hp) Ford GAA V-8 petrol (gasoline) engine, the M36's running gear sported three pairs of medium-sized close-spoked bogie-suspended VVSS road wheels per side.

PRODUCTION

After extensive field trials held during autumn 1943–44, the design was accepted for mass production under the designation 90mm (3.46in) Gun Motor Carriage (GMC) M36; some authorities allege that troops soon dubbed it the Jackson, after the Confederate US Civil War General. During the period from September 1944 to June 1945, the firms of ALCO, Fisher, Massey Harris, Montreal Locomotive Works and the Grand Blanc Arsenal produced 1413 M36s, many of which were extant M10A1 vehicles converted to the M36 design through the addition of the new turret.

URBAN OPERATIONS
An M36 tank destroyer of the 3rd US Army trains a 90mm gun in the town of Metz (France) during mopping-up operations, 22 November 1944.

M24 Chaffee (1944)

TYPE • *Light tank* **COUNTRY** • *United States*

SPECIFICATIONS	
Dimensions:	Length: 5.49m (18ft); Width: 2.95m (9ft 8in); Height: 2.46m (8ft 1in)
Weight:	18.28 tonnes (20.15 US tons)
Engine:	2 x 82kW (110hp) Cadillac 44T24 V-8 8-cylinder petrol
Speed:	55km/h (34mph)
Range:	282km (175 miles)
Armour:	9–38mm (0.35–1.5in)
Armament:	1 x 75mm (2.95in) gun; 1 x 12.7mm (0.5in) HMG on AA mount; 2 x 7.62mm (0.3in) MGs (1 x coaxial, 1 ball-mounted in hull front)
Crew:	5

The Chaffee was the most advanced light tank of the late-war period, with firepower equivalent to many of the earlier Sherman medium tanks that were still in service. Upgraded versions still serve today with some smaller armies.

Right: A winterized Chaffee. This Chaffee light tank was a vast improvement over its predecessor, the M3 Stuart, mounting a 75mm (2.95in) main gun and a trio of machine guns.

Powerplant
The twin Cadillac Model 44T24 V-8 petrol engines mounted in the rear of the M24 chassis produced plenty of power for the light tank to manoeuvre in reconnaissance and to maintain contact with advancing infantry units.

Armour
The thin armour of the M24, only 38mm (1.5in) at its thickest on the front of the hull, meant it was vulnerable to a variety of German anti-tank weapons.

Main gun
The 75mm (2.95in) M6 gun, adapted from the modified weapon that served aboard the B-25 Mitchell bomber, provided the firepower that had long been lacking in American light tanks.

KOREAN WAR
The greatest combat contribution of the M24 Chaffee came during the Korean War of 1950–53. In the early days of the conflict, the Chaffee was available in quantity and it delivered excellent performance in the reconnaissance and infantry support roles. Again, however, it was sometimes compelled to serve in tank versus tank combat and was overmatched by the superb Soviet-built T-34 medium tanks deployed by North Korean forces.

ARDENNES CAMPAIGN
M24 crews prepare to move out during the German Ardennes Offensive of 1944–45. The M24 reached the battlefields of Europe in November 1944. Its numbers were too few, however, to make a definitive impact on Allied operations before the German surrender.

Sturmmörser Tiger (1944)

TYPE • *Self-propelled gun* **COUNTRY** • *Germany*

The Sturmmörser Tiger, or Sturmtiger, fired a heavy rocket-assisted projectile against fixed targets. It could operate in the direct assault role or provide indirect fire at ranges of up to 6km (3.7 miles). The mortar itself was designed for use by U-boats.

SPECIFICATIONS

DIMENSIONS:	Length: 6.28m (20ft 7in); Width: 3.57m (11ft 9in); Height: 2.85m (9ft 4in)
WEIGHT:	68 tonnes (74.96 US tons)
ENGINE:	Maybach HL230P45 petrol, 514.5kW (690hp)
SPEED:	40km/h (25mph)
RANGE:	120km (74 miles)
ARMOUR:	25–150mm (0.98–5.9in)
ARMAMENT:	1 x 38cm (14.9in) Raketen-Werfer 61 L/5.4; 1 x 7.92mm (0.31in) MG34 machine gun
CREW:	5

HEAVY MORTAR
The original intention was to produce an entirely new vehicle based on the Tiger I hull and armed with a 21cm (8.26in) howitzer, but the howitzer was not available at the time and the 38cm (14.9in) Raketen-Werfer 61 L/5.4 was substituted.

AMMUNITION HOIST
A hoist was fitted to the roof of the fighting compartment to lift the massive rounds from their racks onto the loading tray.

CAMOUFLAGE
This Sturmtiger is in a variation of the 'ambush' camouflage scheme, Reichswald, Germany, February–March 1945. Three new Panzer companies were raised to operate the Sturmtiger: Panzer Sturmmörser Kompanien (PzStuMrKp) (Armoured Assault Howitzer Companies) 1000, 1001 and 1002.

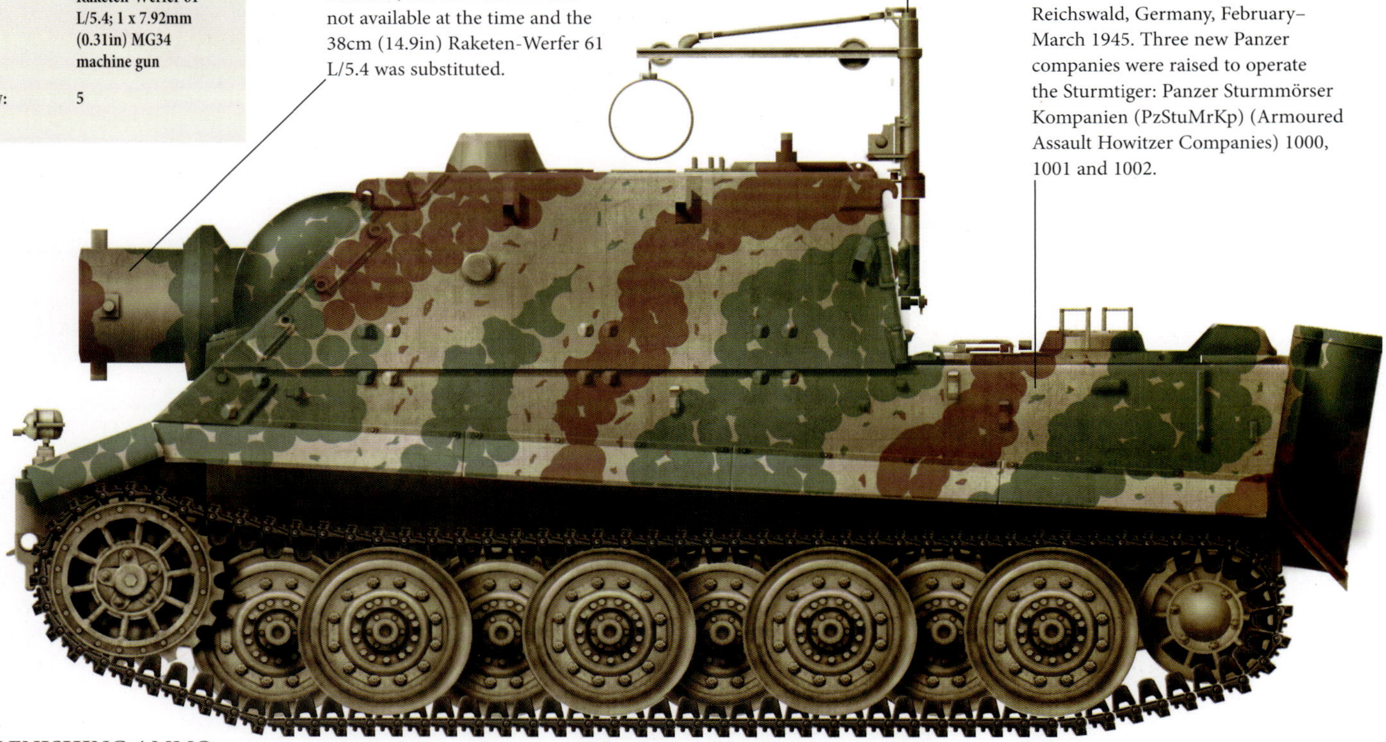

REPLENISHING AMMO
Replenishing ammunition in the Sturmtiger was challenging. It had to be passed through a roof hatch roughly 2.74m (9ft) above ground level. A hand-operated crane was fitted to the rear superstructure to lift the rounds to the loading hatch, but even so 'bombing-up' was a long job demanding back-breaking effort from the entire five-man crew. It was intended that each Sturmtiger would be accompanied by an ammunition carrier based on the Tiger I hull, but only one such carrier was completed.

ABANDONED STURMTIGER
American servicemen examine a disabled Sturmtiger. Although fearsome in appearance, the Sturmtiger proved limited in the defensive role and most were destroyed or captured.

T-44 (1945)

TYPE • *Medium tank* **COUNTRY** • *Soviet Union*

SPECIFICATIONS

Dimensions:	Length: 7.65m (25ft 1in); Width: 3.15m (10ft 4in); Height: 2.45m (8ft)
Weight:	31.9 tonnes (35.2 tons)
Engine:	373kW (500hp) Model V-44 diesel
Speed:	51km/h (32mph)
Range:	300km (186 miles)
Armour:	15–120mm (0.59–4.72in)
Armament:	1 x 85mm (3.35in) D-5T gun; 2 x 7.62mm (0.3in) DTM machine guns, 1 coaxial, 1 hull front
Crew:	4

Entering service in the Red Army in early 1945, the advanced T-44 medium tank further improved and simplified the T-34/85 design and paved the way for the introduction in 1947 of the famous T-54 tank.

Below: The T-44 had a redesigned and shallower chassis, optimized for mass production, with its engine re-orientated onto a novel transverse mounting.

Main gun
The 31.9 tonne (35.2 ton)-vehicle mounted the 85mm (3.35in) D-5T gun (as fitted to the T-34/85 Model 1943) on a redesigned and up-armoured T-34/85 turret.

Armour
In comparison to the T-34/85, the T-44 featured enhanced protection that ranged from 15mm (0.59in) to 120mm (4.72in) thickness.

Suspension
The T-44 abandoned the Christie coil-spring suspension in favour of a more economic torsion bar arrangement that supported five large road wheels per side. The ensuing design had a lower silhouette than its predecessor, as well as sleek well-sloped lines.

MUSEUM T-44
During 1944–45, Soviet designers picked up the T-34M development work (investigating an improved T-34/76) that had been abandoned in 1941. Initially, the 1944 developmental work aimed to produce an improved T-34/85 design, but this morphed into the T-44 medium tank. About 175 T-44 medium tanks were delivered to front-line units before the war's end in May 1945.

T-44-100

During the T-44's development, the designers investigated mounting the more powerful 100mm (3.9in) gun in the new design. When the gun was mounted on the T-44-100, two problems became apparent. First, the long gun fitted to a forward-positioned turret gave the tank a significant barrel overhang. Second, the gun's large breech made the interior of the turret cramped. These experiments, however, did lead to the creation of the T-54 in 1947.

IS-3 (1945)

TYPE • *Heavy tank* **COUNTRY** • *Soviet Union*

The last Soviet heavy tank to enter production before the end of World War II, the IS-3 became operational too late to influence the outcome of the war, but nevertheless became a symbol of the Red Army's military might.

SPECIFICATIONS

Dimensions:	Length: 6.77m (22ft 2in); Width: 3.07m (10ft 1in); Height: 2.44m (8ft)
Weight:	45.8 tonnes (50.5 US tons)
Engine:	1 x V-2-IS V-12 diesel powerplant generating 447kW (600hp)
Speed:	37km/h (22.9mph)
Range:	Road: 160km (100 miles); Cross-country: 120km (75 miles)
Armour:	20–230mm (0.78–9in)
Armament:	1 x 122mm (4.8in) D-25-T gun; 2 x 7.62mm (0.3in) DT or DTM machine guns; 1 x 12.7mm (0.5in) DshK machine gun
Crew:	4

Left: This view shows the extent of the powerful tank-killing 122mm (4.8in) D-25-T gun, which was developed from the M1931/37 field gun.

Turret
The IS-3's rounded cast turret had the resemblance of an overturned soup bowl. The turret was small and restricted crew movement.

Driving compartment
The driver compartment in the front hull of the IS-3 was typical of Soviet AFV designs of this period, offering few concessions to comfort and little storage space.

Gun breech
Unable to pivot fully on its vertical axis, the breech of the main gun limited the ability to depress the weapon completely.

WAR SERVICE

Although the IS-3 bears something of a family resemblance to preceding Soviet tanks, its design was distinctly different. At the end of World War II, fewer than 30 of the new tanks had been completed, but by mid-1946 the number in Red Army service exceeded 2300. Despite its combat participation in World War II being doubtful, a regiment of the 45.8-tonne (50.5-ton) machines participated in a victory parade through Red Square on 7 September 1945.

IS-3 VICTORY PARADE
The crew of an IS-3 take the salute during a victory parade in 1945. The narrow frontal area and low turret of the IS-3 theoretically reduced the probability of detection and the drawing of enemy fire.

M26 Pershing / Super Pershing (1943/1945)

TYPE • *Heavy tank* COUNTRY • *United States*

The M26 was developed as a counter to heavy German tanks in World War II, but arrived only in the closing stages of the conflict. Its 90mm (3.5in) gun could easily penetrate a T-34, which might have been useful if the Cold War had turned hot in the early 1950s.

SPECIFICATIONS (M26 Pershing)

DIMENSIONS:	Length: 6.33m (20ft 9in); Width: 3.51m (11ft 6in); Height: 2.78m (9ft 1in)
WEIGHT:	46.1 tonnes (50.8 US tons)
ENGINE:	336kW (450hp) Ford GAF petrol (gasoline)
SPEED:	34km/h (21mph)
RANGE:	161km (100 miles)
ARMOUR	12.7–110mm (0.5–4.5in)
ARMAMENT:	1 x 90mm (3.5in) M3; 1 x 12.7mm (0.5in) M2HB HMG; 1 x 7.62mm (0.3in) M1919A4 MG
CREW:	5

Right: The M26E4 'Super Pershing' was armed with the 90mm (3.5in) L/70 T15E1 high-velocity gun firing a T44 HVAP round at 1170m/s (3850ft/s) and was capable of penetrating 220mm (8.5in) of rolled homogeneous armour (RHA) at 30 degrees at 914m (1000yd).

MACHINE GUN
A .50-calibre M2H2 machine gun was mounted on top of the turret, for both anti-aircraft and anti-personnel purposes.

COMMUNICATIONS
In terms of communication devices, the Pershing's turret mounted an SCR 5-28 radio set, positioned just behind the tank commander.

M26 PERSHING
The M26 was well protected with armour thickness that ranged from 75mm (2.95in) on parts of the hull sides and up to 102mm (4in) on the hull front.

TIMING

The M26 Pershing has acquired a reputation of always being a little too late to make a difference. Even in the Korean War (1950–53), by the time it was deployed in significant numbers there were few enemy tanks left for it to fight. It stood ready in Europe to repel a Soviet invasion that never came, passing into Belgian service after being phased out by the US military. However, the Pershing marked a maturing of US tank design, which led to the M48 Patton.

CROSSING THE RHINE
The heavy weight of the M26 tank meant that lighter tanks were obliged to spearhead the drive across the Rhine River in 1945. The Pershings followed once the far bank was secure.

Artillery, Anti-Aircraft & Anti-Tank Guns

On the battlefield, artillery was the true killer of World War II. Depending on the theatre (land artillery was less prominent in some Pacific battles), artillery caused between 50 and 70 per cent of all military casualties. While armies might struggle to get results from nimble tactics, massed artillery could still batter the enemy from distance, inflicting attrition or even submission. But artillery was a diverse family. It ranged from direct-fire anti-tank guns to super-long-range railway guns; from small and portable infantry mortars to truck-mounted rocket launchers; from anti-aircraft guns to heavy field howitzers. The design of these weapons sought to perfect the balance between precision, range and effect on target.

15CM SFH 18
Nearly 7000 of the 15cm sFH 18 field howizer were produced by Germany between 1933 and 1945. The type provided the booming heart of German divisional artillery, striking targets out to more than 13km (8 miles) away.

QF 3in 20cwt (1914)

TYPE • *Anti-aircraft* **COUNTRY** • *United Kingdom*

SPECIFICATIONS

Calibre:	76mm (3in)
Weight:	2721kg (6000lb)
Gun length:	3.556m (140.0in)
Elevation:	-10° to +90°
Traverse:	360°
Shell type:	HE: 7.25kg (16lb)
Muzzle velocity:	610m/sec (2000ft/sec)
Effective ceiling:	7163m (23,500ft)
Rate of fire:	16–18rpm

The Ordnance QF 3in 20cwt was the first British purpose-built anti-aircraft gun, designed for naval service and introduced early in 1914. Its peculiar title refers to the weight of the gun itself (20 hundredweight or one ton).

Left: In France in 1940, the Australian Air Minister James Valentine Fairbairn inspects a QF 3in 20cwt anti-aircraft gun in the hands of troops from the British Expeditionary Force (BEF).

Variations
By the beginning of World War II, the 76mm (3in) gun existed in numerous configurations, including a variety of breechblocks and carriages.

AA performance
The 76mm (3in) gun fired a 7.25kg (16lb) shell up to a ceiling of 7163m (23,500ft).

Mounting
The mounting was a rotating pedestal with a base unit which could be bolted down on a ship's deck or a concrete emplacement.

STATIC AND MOBILE

The grandfather of British anti-aircraft weapons was the venerable Ordnance QF 3in 20cwt, which had originally been placed in service with the army as early as 1914. The 76mm (3in) weapon was, by 1939, widely in use as a static and mobile gun, and it was deployed to the continent with the British Expeditionary Force in 1939.

POLISH NAVY
Polish Navy gun crews set to work cleaning a 3in (High Angle) HA 20cwt anti-aircraft gun on board the Polish Navy destroyer ORP *Błyskawica* (Lightning) while in port in Devonport, UK, on 13 September 1940.

15cm sIG 33 (1927)

TYPE • *Infantry* **COUNTRY** • *Germany*

SPECIFICATIONS

CALIBRE:	15cm (5.9in)
WEIGHT:	1688kg (3722lb)
GUN LENGTH:	1.75m (68.8in)
ELEVATION:	0° to +73°
TRAVERSE:	11°
SHELL TYPE:	HE: 28.8kg (63.6lb)
MUZZLE VELOCITY:	240m/sec (790ft/sec)
MAXIMUM RANGE:	4700m (15,420ft)
RATE OF FIRE:	2–3rpm

One of the oldest artillery pieces used by the German Army during World War II, the 15cm (5.9in) sIG 33 had first appeared in 1927, serving as the armament of the Heavy Gun Company of the infantry regiment.

Below: From 1940 onwards, two 15cm (5.9in) sIG 33 guns were allocated to the heavy infantry gun platoon found in Waffen-SS Panzergrenadier and infantry regiments.

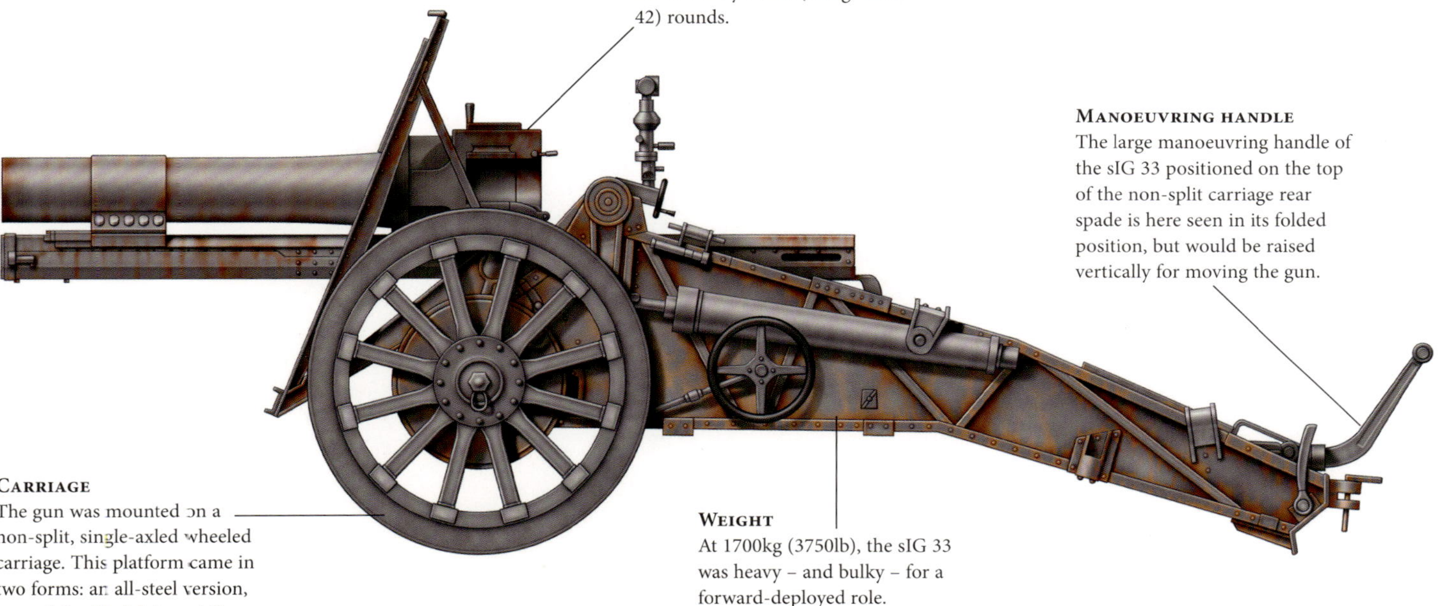

RANGE CAPABILITIES
The short-barrelled (L/11.4) 15cm (5.9in) cannon delivered a high-explosive round out to a maximum range of 4700m (15,420ft); it could also fire smoke, hollow-charge and HEAT sticky bomb (Stielgranate 42) rounds.

MANOEUVRING HANDLE
The large manoeuvring handle of the sIG 33 positioned on the top of the non-split carriage rear spade is here seen in its folded position, but would be raised vertically for moving the gun.

CARRIAGE
The gun was mounted on a non-split, single-axled wheeled carriage. This platform came in two forms: an all-steel version, termed the Model A, and the Model B, which combined steel with lightweight metal alloys.

WEIGHT
At 1700kg (3750lb), the sIG 33 was heavy – and bulky – for a forward-deployed role.

WEIGHT ISSUES
The 15cm Schwere Infanterie Geschütz (sIG) 33 was the heaviest weapon ever to be classified as an 'infantry gun' in any army. Conventional in design, it was simple and robust and gave no trouble even in the worst conditions, but customers complained of the weight. A lightweight version was designed and tested in 1938 but it showed little improvement and, with the outbreak of war, it was abandoned.

EASTERN FRONT
Artillery crew of the SS 'Wiking' Division fuse shells for the 15cm (5.9in) sIG33, in preparation for delivering an offensive bombardment against Red Army troops.

75mm Type 88 (1928)

TYPE • *Anti-aircraft* **COUNTRY** • *Japan*

SPECIFICATIONS	
CALIBRE:	75mm (2.95in)
WEIGHT:	2442kg (5383lb)
GUN LENGTH:	3.315m (10.87ft)
ELEVATION:	0° to 85°
TRAVERSE:	360°
SHELL TYPE:	HE: 6.58kg (14.5lb)
MUZZLE VELOCITY:	720m/sec (2360ft/sec)
CEILING:	7160m (23,500ft)
RATE OF FIRE:	15–20rpm

The 75mm (2.95in) Type 88 dates from 1928 and became the most widely used Japanese air defence gun, both in the defence of Japan itself and with the field armies that were deployed throughout the Pacific.

Below: The Type 88 was an entirely conventional design of gun, mounted on a pedestal fixed to a five-legged platform, and its performance was no more than average for its class.

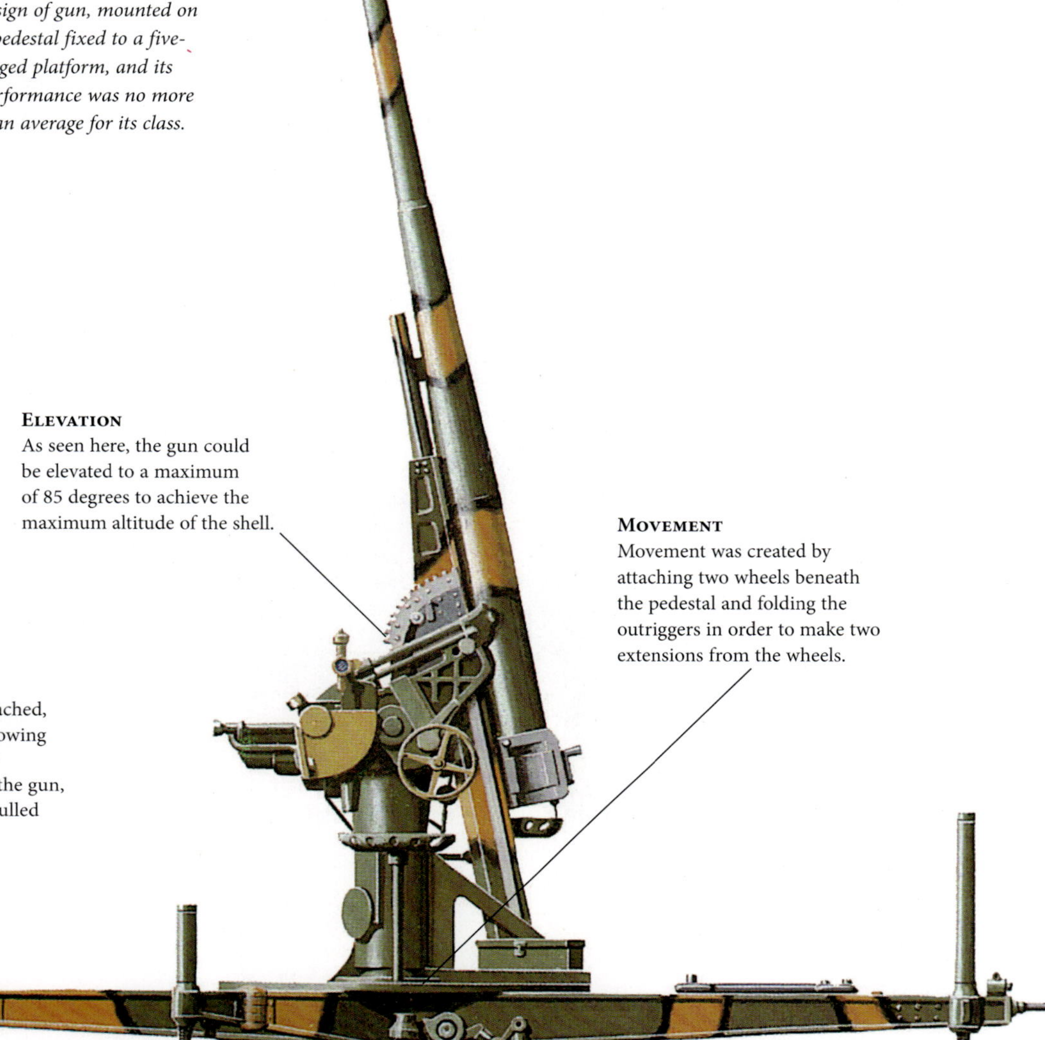

ELEVATION
As seen here, the gun could be elevated to a maximum of 85 degrees to achieve the maximum altitude of the shell.

MOVEMENT
Movement was created by attaching two wheels beneath the pedestal and folding the outriggers in order to make two extensions from the wheels.

TOWING
Once the wheels were attached, one outrigger acted as a towing connection and the other anchored the rear end of the gun, which was elevated and pulled back in its cradle.

MAX CEILING
The Japanese 75mm (2.95in) Type 88 gun dated from the late 1920s and was unsatisfactory by the time large formations of American bombers were flying high above the home islands to deliver their payloads. Its maximum ceiling of 7160m (23,500ft) was too low for effective fire, and its 6.58kg (14.5lb) shell lacked the necessary power.

AIR DEFENCE
From 1943 onwards, the Type 88s were gradually concentrated on the home islands as the Allied aerial threat grew, although they were never enough to cope with the ultimate scale of the onslaught.

QF 2-pounder Mk VII (1930)

TYPE • *Anti-tank* **COUNTRY** • *United Kingdom*

SPECIFICATIONS	
Calibre:	40mm (1.57in)
Weight:	797kg (1757lb)
Barrel length:	2.08m (82in)
Elevation:	-5° to +23°
Traverse:	360°
Shell type:	AP: 907g (2lb)
Muzzle velocity:	808m/sec (2650ft/sec)
Effective range:	1000m (1094yd)
Rate of fire:	20rpm

Developed in the 1930s, this gun was used both as a towed anti-tank gun and as a turret tank gun, because they both had the same targets in mind. What this meant in practice was that the anti-tank gunners were limited because the weapon had to fit into a tank turret.

Right: During World War II, in the Midlands, UK, a three-man Czechoslovakian gun crew practise operating the Ordnance QF 2pdr anti-tank gun.

Penetration
The maximum effective range of the gun was less than 1000m (1094yd), and its penetrating power was just over 5cm (2in) at 457m (500yd).

Elevation and traverse
The elevation of the gun was from a depression of -5° to a maximum elevation +23°, with a traverse of 360°.

Carriage
The 'Ordnance QF 2-pounder Mark IX on Carriage Mark II' required the wheels to be removed when the gun was emplaced for firing.

EARLY AT GUNS

The earliest of the British anti-tank guns, the Ordnance QF 2pdr was developed primarily by Vickers-Armstrong in response to army specifications drafted in 1934. Five years later, the most widely used version of the gun, the Mark III, was delivered. For its firepower, the 2pdr (47mm) was quite heavy and complicated to operate, although it must be said that the intent was for the weapon to be used in static defence rather than mobile warfare.

2PDR IN ACTION, NORTH AFRICA
During the British campaign in France in 1940 and the fighting in the deserts of North Africa, it became painfully obvious that the 2pdr weapon was inadequate to penetrate the armour of front-line German tanks.

203mm Howitzer Model 1931 (B-4) (1931)

TYPE • *Howitzer* **COUNTRY** • *Soviet Union*

SPECIFICATIONS

CALIBRE:	203mm (8in)
WEIGHT:	17,700kg (39,022lb)
GUN LENGTH:	5.087m (16ft 8in) L/25
ELEVATION:	0° to +60°
TRAVERSE:	8°
SHELL TYPE:	HE: 100kg (220lb)
MUZZLE VELOCITY:	607m/sec (1990ft/sec)
RANGE:	18,000m (19,685yd)
RATE OF FIRE:	1 round every 2–3 minutes

The 203mm (8in) Howitzer Model 1931 (B-4) was another member of the 'family' of weapons sharing a common tracked carriage that was developed in the 1930s.

Left: A Soviet-era B-4 on display in a museum. The gun's 2.5m (8ft 2in) height gave it a prominent silhouette.

SHELL CRANE
The heaviest of the M1931's shells could weigh about 150kg (330lb), so the shell-lifting device was necessary for loading.

TOWING
In common with the Russian Br-2 heavy gun, the complete gun could be towed for short distances by a Voroshilovets heavy artillery tractor at speeds of up to 8km/h (5mph).

TRACKED CARRIAGE
The tracked carriage offered the advantage that the gun could be set up and fired straight from towing, and could be manoeuvred relatively easily between shots.

SERVICE

The B-4 was accepted for service in 1934 and probably remained in production until 1944–45, by which time an estimated 870 had been completed. The B-4 also remained in service after the war. It was modernized in the mid-1950s with a new four-wheeled carriage that allowed high-speed towing over long distances without removing the barrel. These updated howitzers remained in service until at least the 1970s.

M1931 203MM HOWITZER
A Red Army gun crew lay their weapon for fire on German positions. Such was the explosive effect of the 203mm (8in) shell that German soldiers nicknamed the gun 'Stalin's sledgehammer'.

7.5cm leichtes Infanteriegeschütz 18 (1932)

TYPE • *Infantry* **COUNTRY** • *Germany*

SPECIFICATIONS

CALIBRE:	75mm (2.95in)
WEIGHT:	400kg (882lb)
GUN LENGTH:	11.2 calibre: 884mm (32.80in)
ELEVATION:	-10° to +75°
TRAVERSE:	12°
SHELL TYPE:	HE: 6.00kg (13.22lb)
MUZZLE VELOCITY:	210m/sec (688ft/sec)
RANGE:	3375m (3690yd)
RATE OF FIRE:	8–12rpm

During the interwar period, the German Army developed a new genre of direct-fire weapon termed the infantry gun (*Infanteriegeschütz*). This was a lightweight, mobile direct-fire-support weapon operated by infantry that could obtain ranges beyond that of mortars.

Left: During the invasion of France in 1940, German infantry demonstrated the portability of the le IG 18 by taking it across a river on a raft.

BREECH
The le IG 18 had an odd 'shotgun' breech mechanism. The barrel lay in a square trough, the rear end of which was the breechblock; opening the breech merely raised the rear end of the barrel clear of the 'block', and as the cartridge was loaded, so the barrel dropped back into place and the breech was closed.

VARIANTS
The le IG 18 came with two types of wheels: the first, with spoked wheels, was designed to be horse-drawn; the second, with filled-in wheels that sported pneumatic tyres, was moved by motor vehicles.

TRANSPORTATION
Two versions of the gun were developed that could be broken down into loads: one for mountain infantry use and the other for paratroops, although only six of the latter were built, as the recoilless gun proved more suitable.

LIGHT GUNS

Between 1927 and 1933, the Germans developed two infantry gun designs: the 75mm (2.95in) le IG 18 light weapon and the 15cm (5.9in) SiG33 heavy device; both were to equip the newly forming cannon companies within an infantry regiment. The Rheinmetall-designed 75mm le IG 18 entered service in 1932. In 1944, a new infantry gun – the 75mm le IG 37 – began to supplement the le IG 18 in front-line German units.

FRANCE, 1940
The crew of an le IG 18 provide cover down a road during the German invasion of France in 1940. The gun had been issued to German infantry battalions after World War I for their own close support, entirely separate from the organic divisional artillery.

15cm sFH 18 (1934)

TYPE • *Howitzer* **COUNTRY** • *Germany*

SPECIFICATIONS

Calibre:	15cm (5.9in)
Weight:	5512kg (12,150lb)
Gun length:	27.5 calibre: 4.125m (13.53ft)
Elevation:	-3° to +45°
Traverse:	64°
Shell type:	HE: 43.5kg (96lb)
Muzzle velocity:	495m/sec (1624ft/sec)
Range:	13,250m (14,490yd)
Rate of fire:	4rpm

Based on a design first conceived during World War I, the 15cm (5.9in) sFH 18 was the primary German heavy howitzer of World War II. Nicknamed 'Evergreen', the weapon remained in service until the 1970s.

Above: On the Eastern Front, troops of the Waffen-SS division 'Totenkopf' lay down fire with a 15cm (5.9in) sFH 18.

Range
The weapon weighed 5512kg (12,150lb) and could fire a 43.5kg (96lb) shell out to a maximum range of 13,250m (14,490yd), which was not particularly impressive for a weapon of this calibre.

Upgrade
In 1942, a modified version of this weapon was developed: the sFH 18M. This gun fired its round with a larger propellant charge to gain additional range. The barrel featured a replaceable chamber liner and a muzzle brake.

Movement
For movement, the split-trail ends were lifted on to a two-wheeled limber and the gun disconnected from the recoil system, pulled back in its cradle and locked to the trails, so as to distribute the weight evenly.

ROCKET SHELL
The backbone of the German medium artillery strength during World War II, the sFH 18 was developed between 1926 and 1930, the howitzer being from Rheinmetall and the carriage from Krupp. It has the distinction of being the first gun ever to be issued with a rocket-assisted shell, in 1941, which gave it a maximum range of 19,000m (20,778yd). However, it was not very accurate and wore out the gun rather rapidly.

SFH 18 GUN BATTERY
Production of the gun commenced in late 1933 and it entered service in 1934. This piece remained the principal German medium field howitzer throughout World War II and was widely used in all campaigns.

8.8cm Flak 18 (1933)

TYPE • *Anti-aircraft* **COUNTRY** • *Germany*

SPECIFICATIONS

CALIBRE:	88mm (3.46in)
WEIGHT:	4983kg (10,987lb)
GUN LENGTH:	4.93m (16.17ft)
ELEVATION:	-3° to +85°
TRAVERSE:	360°
SHELL TYPE:	HE: 9.40kg (20.72lb)
MUZZLE VELOCITY:	820m/sec (2690ft/sec)
CEILING:	8000m (26,245ft)
RATE OF FIRE:	15–18rpm

One of the most celebrated guns of World War II, the German '88' was adopted in 1933, having been designed by Krupp engineers working in the Bofors factory in Sweden. Its reputation stems from its use as an anti-tank gun; as an anti-aircraft gun it was average.

Above: The design of the Flak 18 was highly innovative. The gun was mounted on a novel firing platform of cruciform design, with four outriggers that were extended to provide a stable firing platform.

ANTI-TANK CAPABILITY
Although the weapon was optimized for the anti-aircraft role, it also had a useful ground-combat capability, firing armour-piercing shells. In the ground role, the gun could penetrate 88mm (3.46in) of vertical armour at a range of 2000m (2187yd).

RANGE
The gun fired its high-explosive round with a muzzle velocity of 820m/sec (2690ft/sec) and could obtain a maximum vertical range of 8000m (2690ft).

RATE OF FIRE
With a well-trained crew, the hand-loaded weapon could obtain a rate of fire of 15–18rpm.

EVOLUTION

It appeared originally as the Flak 18 gun, a single-tube barrel on a pedestal, carried on a four-legged platform supported by two two-wheeled limbers for transport. A new three-piece barrel was introduced so that the worn section near the chamber could be easily replaced, and this became the Flak 36. An improved data transmission system from the predictor to the gun was adopted, and this became the Flak 37. The carriage and performance did not change between the three models.

RANGING TARGETS
Near Voronezh, east of Kursk, a member of a German 8.8cm (3.46in) Flak 18 crew uses a stereoscopic rangefinder to spot and range enemy armour. The stripes and aircraft painted on the barrel indicate armour and aircraft kills respectively.

Ordnance ML 3in Mortar (1935)

TYPE • *Mortar* **COUNTRY** • *United Kingdom*

SPECIFICATIONS

Calibre:	76mm (3in)
Weight:	52.4kg (115lb)
Gun length:	1.3m (4ft 3in)
Elevation:	+45° to +80°
Traverse:	11°
Shell type:	4.5kg (10lb)
Muzzle velocity:	198m/sec (650ft/sec)
Range:	Mk 1: 1463m (1600yd); Mk 2: 2560m (2800yd)
Rate of fire:	10rpm

Although the 3-inch Mortar Mk II was initially handicapped by its short range, it was developed into an effective support weapon firing HE, smoke and illuminating rounds, and it remained in British service until the 1960s.

Left: A 3-inch mortar crew from the Queen's Own Royal West Kents in action in Tunisia, 31 January 1943.

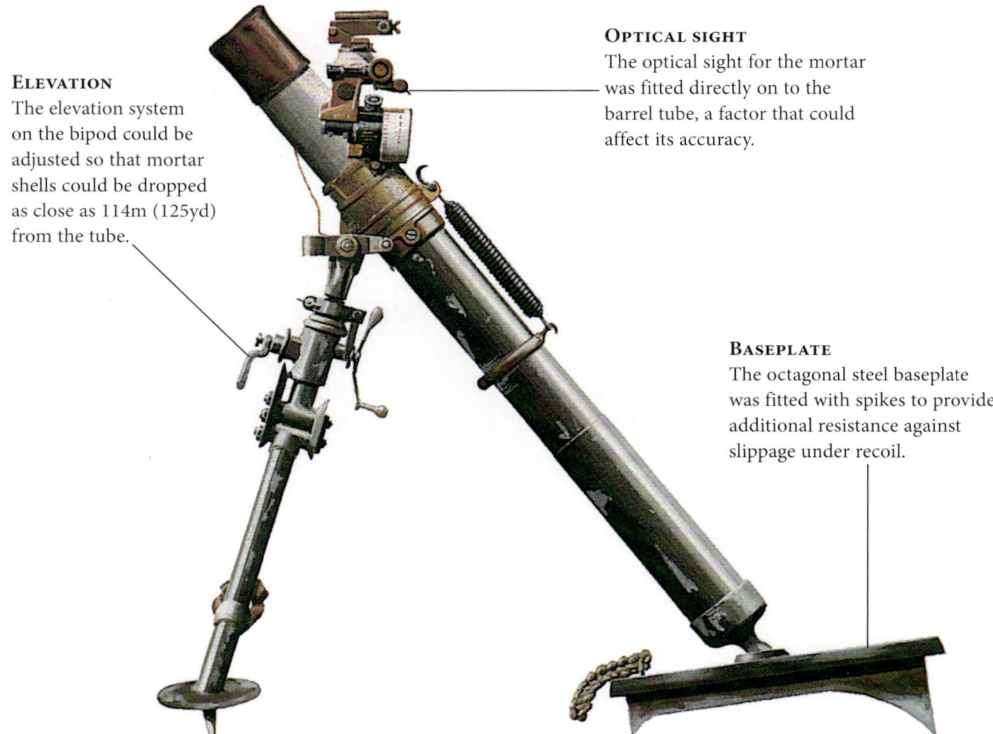

Elevation
The elevation system on the bipod could be adjusted so that mortar shells could be dropped as close as 114m (125yd) from the tube.

Optical sight
The optical sight for the mortar was fitted directly on to the barrel tube, a factor that could affect its accuracy.

Baseplate
The octagonal steel baseplate was fitted with spikes to provide additional resistance against slippage under recoil.

3-IN MORTARS

The first British 3-inch mortar was the original Stokes Mortar, which was first used in 1916. Improved versions of this weapon remained in service for much of the interwar period, but in the early 1930s it was decided that it was in need of complete modernization. Both the mortar and its ammunition were thoroughly updated, incorporating many features of the French Brandt mortars. The new design was formally adopted as the Ordnance, ML Mortar, 3-in Mk II in the late 1930s.

MORTAR CREW, ITALY
This British mortar crew in Italy have dug a shallow ditch to stabilize the weapon. A 'textbook' mortar pit took the crew at least four hours of hard digging, but this was frequently reduced to half an hour's work by blasting a basic pit using six No. 75 grenades.

M1 Mortar (81mm) (1935)

TYPE • *Mortar* **COUNTRY** • *United States*

Developed from the successful French Brandt mortar, the 81mm (3.2in) M1 mortar was one of the defining American infantry support weapons of World War II, its service extending into the early 1950s.

SPECIFICATIONS	
Calibre:	81mm (3.2in)
Weight:	61.7kg (136lb)
Gun length:	1.21m (3ft 11.5in)
Elevation:	+45° to +85°
Traverse:	14°
Shell type:	HE: 3.11kg (6.87lb)
Muzzle velocity:	213m/sec (700ft/sec)
Range:	3000m (3280yd)
Rate of fire:	18–30rpm

Right: Members of a mortar company of the 92nd Division load and fire at German positions, Italian Campaign, 1944.

Mortar carrier
The six-crew M21 was another early-war American self-propelled indirect fire vehicle, but it sported an 81mm (3.2in) M1 mortar.

Traverse
The main tactical constraint of this weapon was that it was manually traversable only through a limited arc when fired from inside the vehicle, which was the preferred option.

Mount
This weapon was mounted facing forwards in the rear of the M2 half-track's rear-located troop compartment.

AMMUNITION TYPES
Like many mortars of World War II, the M1 came with a wide variety of ammunition types to suit different tactical requirements. The most common anti-personnel round was, of course, high-explosive (HE), which came in light and heavy varieties. White phosphorous rounds delivered anti-personnel, incendiary and smoke obscuration effects, while the mortar could also fire chemical smoke and illumination rounds.

BURMA MORTAR TEAM
A US mortar team in Lashio, Burma, in 1945 lay down fire on Japanese lines. Ammunition tubes are stacked all around the perimeter of their properly dug mortar position.

10.5cm leFH 18 (1935)

TYPE • *Howitzer* **COUNTRY** • *Germany*

The 10.5cm (4.13in) leFH 18 was the standard German divisional field piece used throughout World War II; it was designed by the German industrial giant Rheinmetall in 1929–30 and went into service in 1935.

SPECIFICATIONS (leFH 18(M))

Calibre:	10.5cm (4.13in)
Weight:	1985kg (4376lb)
Gun length:	24.8 calibre: 2.61m (102.75in)
Elevation:	-6.5° to +40.5°
Traverse:	56°
Shell type:	HE: 14.25kg (31.41lb)
Muzzle velocity:	540m/sec (1771ft/sec)
Range:	12,325m (13,480yd)
Rate of fire:	4–6rpm

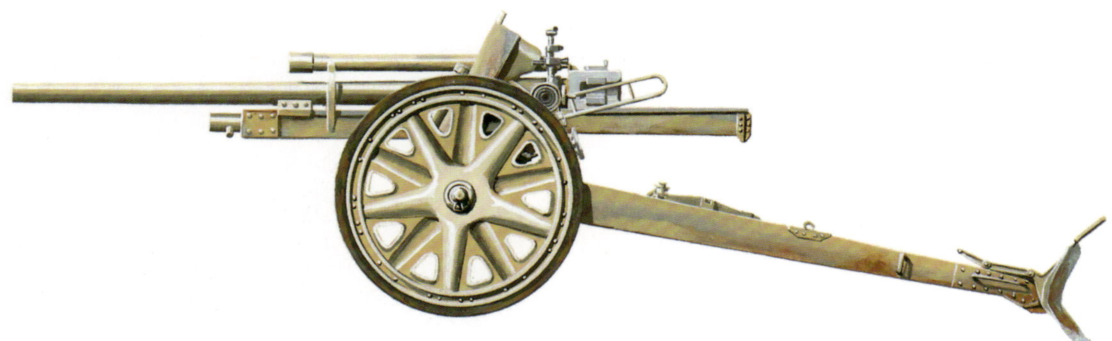

Above: The leFH 18 was a sound orthodox design. It used a split trail with folding spades and a hydro-pneumatic recoil system split above and below the barrel, but retained wooden or pressed-steel wheels and was mostly horse-drawn.

leFH 18(M)
This weapon was derived from the 10.5cm (4.13in) leFH 18, but with the gun barrel fitted with a muzzle brake to enable it to fire more powerful ammunition and thus achieve a greater range without placing excessive stress on the recoil system and carriage.

Recoil buffer
It was found necessary to replace the valves in the recoil buffer and increase the air pressure in the recuperator in order to absorb the extra energy of the leFH 18(M).

Ammunition
A special long-range shell and cartridge were provided, although the original leFH 18 ammunition could still be fired.

REVISED MODEL

In 1935, the German Army asked for a standard 10.5cm (4.13in) field howitzer that could supply a heavier round than the earlier 77mm (3.03in) weapon used during World War I. The requirement was met by Rheinmetall, with its 10.5cm leFH 18. This was a standard export to countries of Eastern Europe, Spain and South America, but when war came, the need for additional range resulted in a revision with a muzzle brake and additional propellant charge. This version, introduced prior to the campaign against Russia, was designated the 10.5cm leFH 18(M).

ATLANTIC WALL
An leFH 18 gun presents its muzzle seaward on the Atlantic Wall. Although augmented by improved models in WWII, the gun remained in use and was kept in service by several European armies for some years after the war ended.

10.5cm Flak 38 (1936)

TYPE • *Anti-aircraft* **COUNTRY** • *Germany*

SPECIFICATIONS

CALIBRE:	10.5cm (4.13in)
WEIGHT:	10,224kg (22,493lb)
GUN LENGTH:	6.648m (21ft 10in)
ELEVATION:	-3° to +85°
TRAVERSE:	360°
SHELL TYPE:	HE 14.8kg (32.6lb)
MUZZLE VELOCITY:	881m/sec (2891ft/sec)
CEILING:	9450m (31,000ft)
RATE OF FIRE:	15–18rpm

During the 1930s consensus among German armaments experts was that an anti-aircraft weapon of heavier calibre than the 88mm was needed, and by the mid-1930s, the Rheinmetall 10.5cm (4.13in) Flak 38 had been selected for production following a competition with Krupp.

Right: A German 10.5cm (4.13in) Flak 38 crew fire at ground targets on the Oder front in 1945.

CEILING
Firing a 15.1kg (33.3lb) projectile to a ceiling of 12,800m (41,995ft), the 10.5cm (4.13in)Flak 38 was nevertheless disappointing in its overall performance and was never used as a field gun on a large scale.

ELECTRIC MOTORS
In 1939, the electric motors were built for alternating current instead of direct, so that they could be driven from the ordinary power supply, and with other changes this became the Flak 39.

DESIGN
The Flak 38 had electro-hydraulic remote power control, power loading and a compact four-legged platform.

EXCESSIVE WEIGHT
The Flak 38 was quickly superseded by the Flak 39, which incorporated an improved fire-control data system. The major shortcoming of both models lay in their considerable weight. The Flak 39 was a hefty 10,240kg (22,575lb) when firing. Coupled with the fact that the weapons' performance was not appreciably better than that of the 88, the weight problem relegated the 10.5cm (4.13in) models to primary use in fixed fortifications.

FLAK 38S IN NORWAY
This 10.5cm (4.13in) Flak 38 battery is set up in a Norwegian valley to intercept Allied air raids passing over the far north of Europe.

8.8cm Flak 41 (1936)

TYPE • *Anti-aircraft* **COUNTRY** • *Germany*

SPECIFICATIONS

Calibre:	88mm (3.46in)
Weight:	7800kg (17,196lb)
Gun length:	6.545m (21ft 5in)
Elevation:	-3° to +90°
Traverse:	360°
Shell type:	HE: 9.40kg (20.73lb)
Muzzle velocity:	1000m/sec (3280ft/sec)
Ceiling:	10,675m (35,025ft)
Rate of fire:	20–25rpm

There were many variants of the 'Flak 88'. In early 1942, the Germans introduced into service a fundamentally new 88mm (3.46in) anti-aircraft gun, the 8.8cm Flak 41. Early teething problems, however, meant the device only got to the front in reasonable numbers in early 1943.

Below: By the time the war ended, the Germans had only placed slightly more than 300 Flak 41s in service. The Flak 41 is not to be confused with the more notable 8.8cm Flak 18, 36 and 37 series.

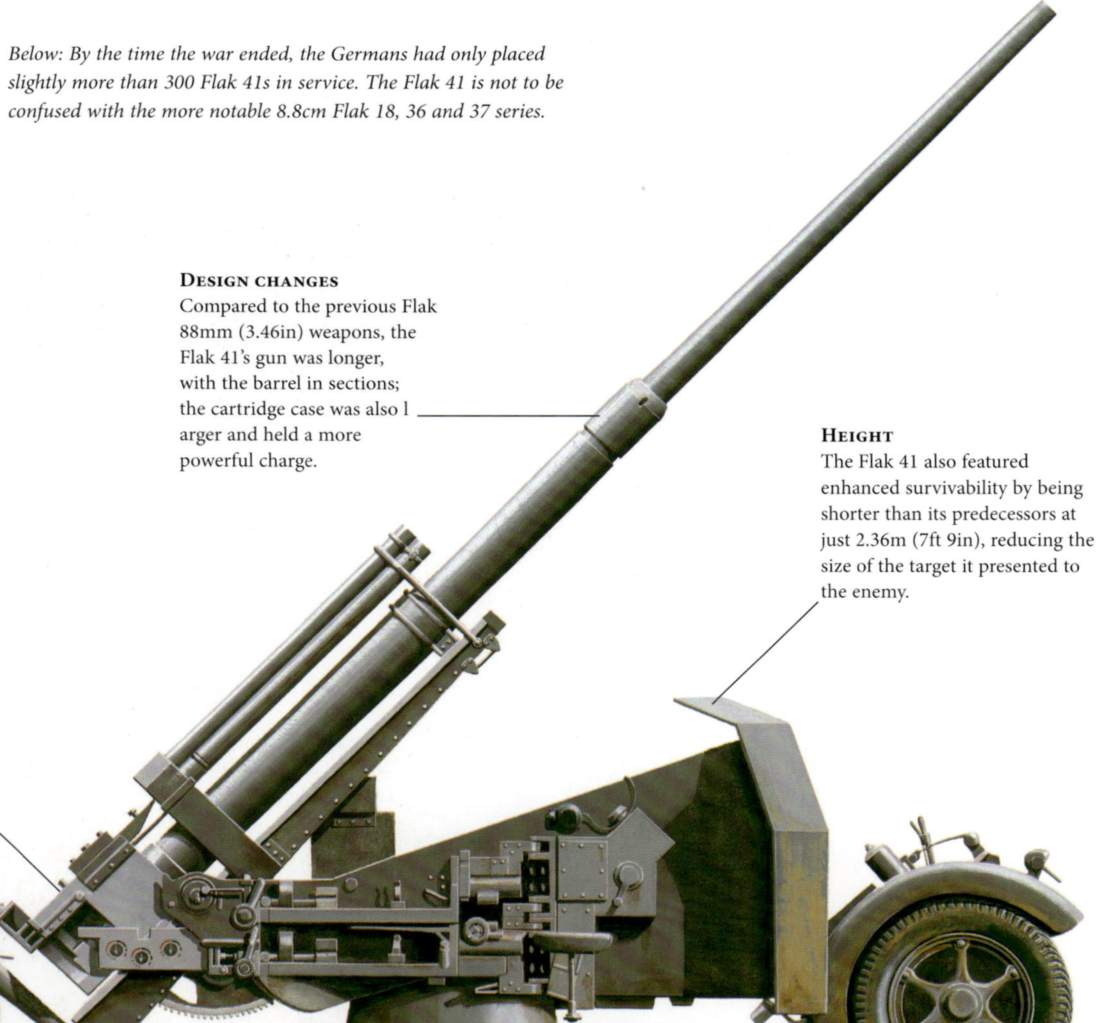

Design changes
Compared to the previous Flak 88mm (3.46in) weapons, the Flak 41's gun was longer, with the barrel in sections; the cartridge case was also l arger and held a more powerful charge.

Height
The Flak 41 also featured enhanced survivability by being shorter than its predecessors at just 2.36m (7ft 9in), reducing the size of the target it presented to the enemy.

Armour penetration
When delivering armour-piercing rounds, the weapon could penetrate 132mm (5.2in) of vertical armour at a range of 2000m (6560ft).

RATIONALE
By the beginning of World War II, the performance of the Flak 37, designed in the early 1930s, was falling behind the improving speed and height of other aircraft, and in 1939 the Luftwaffe (who were responsible for German air defences) issued a specification for a new gun. Accepted by Rheinmetall-Borsig, the Flak 41 was the result. Only the calibre remained; the gun, ammunition and mounting were all new.

ANTI-AIRCRAFT CAPABILITY
Although the Flak 41 did have issues, it was an effective anti-aircraft weapon, firing the 88mm (3.46in) shell to a ceiling of 14,700m (48,230ft) and easily coping with high-flying formations of Allied bombers.

3.7cm Flak 36 and 5cm Flak 41 (1936)

TYPE • *Anti-aircraft* **COUNTRY** • *Germany*

In the late 1930s the Germans developed the 3.7cm Flak 36 anti-aircraft gun, a development of the existing 3.7cm Flak 18. The 37mm (1.46in) flak cannon offered the Germans greater range and hitting power than the existing 20mm (0.79in) weapons.

SPECIFICATIONS (Flak 41)

Calibre:	50mm (1.97in)
Weight:	3100kg (6838lb)
Gun length:	4.686m (184.49in)
Elevation:	-10° to +90°
Traverse:	360°
Shell type:	HE 2.25kg (4.85lb)
Muzzle velocity:	840m/sec (2756ft/sec)
Ceiling:	5600m (18,375ft)
Rate of fire:	180rpm (cyclical)

Above: The sister variant of the SdKfz 7/1 was this vehicle, the SdKfz 7/2; this mounted the 3.7cm Flak 36 on to the 8-tonne (7.6-ton) half-track; the gun could be elevated from -8° through to +85°.

Flak 41
In 1935 the Germans realized that there was a gap in the sky between the lowest engagement range of their 88mm (3.46in) guns and the highest range of the 37mm (1.46in) gun, and they asked Rheinmetall to plug it with this 50mm (1.97in) weapon.

Design faults
Although the design looked good, it proved to have several faults: it was too high and therefore difficult to conceal, it vibrated badly when firing and so was inaccurate, and the sight was complicated and a source of further errors.

Gas operated
The gun was a gas-operated automatic weapon, clip-fed like the Bofors gun, and the mounting was a four-wheeled cruciform.

CORE DESIGN
The first 37mm (1.46in) Flak gun adopted by the German Army used a complicated and expensive four-wheeled carriage, and after some experience with it the Army demanded something simpler. The solution was a two-wheeled trailer unit similar to that used with the Flak 30, and this weapon entered service in 1936 as the 3.7cm Flak 36.

FLAK 36 COASTAL POSITION
The 3.7cm Flak 36 was provided with the Flakvisier 36 sight, a simple device, but then the Flakvisier 40 appeared, a clockwork-driven computing sight that worked out the necessary aim-off and displaced the crosswires in the sight automatically. This was a complex device and the mounting had to be altered in order to fit. Guns with this type of sight became known as the Flak 37.

40mm Bofors (1936)

TYPE • *Anti-aircraft* **COUNTRY** • *United Kingdom*

SPECIFICATIONS (L/60)

CALIBRE:	40mm (1.57in)
WEIGHT:	1981kg (4568lb)
GUN LENGTH:	3m (118in)
ELEVATION:	-5° to +90°
TRAVERSE:	360°
SHELL TYPE:	HE: 907g (2lb)
MUZZLE VELOCITY:	854m (2802ft) per sec
CEILING:	7200m (23,622ft)
RATE OF FIRE:	Up to 140rpm (cyclical)

If there was such a thing as a universally acclaimed anti-aircraft weapon during World War II, it was a gun that had been developed in a neutral country. The Swedish 40mm (1.57in) Bofors became one of the most famous guns in history.

Left: A British 40mm (1.57in) Bofors anti-aircraft gun covers a road as troops pass by in coaches during Exercise Bumper, *a 12-division anti-invasion exercise, on 30 September 1941.*

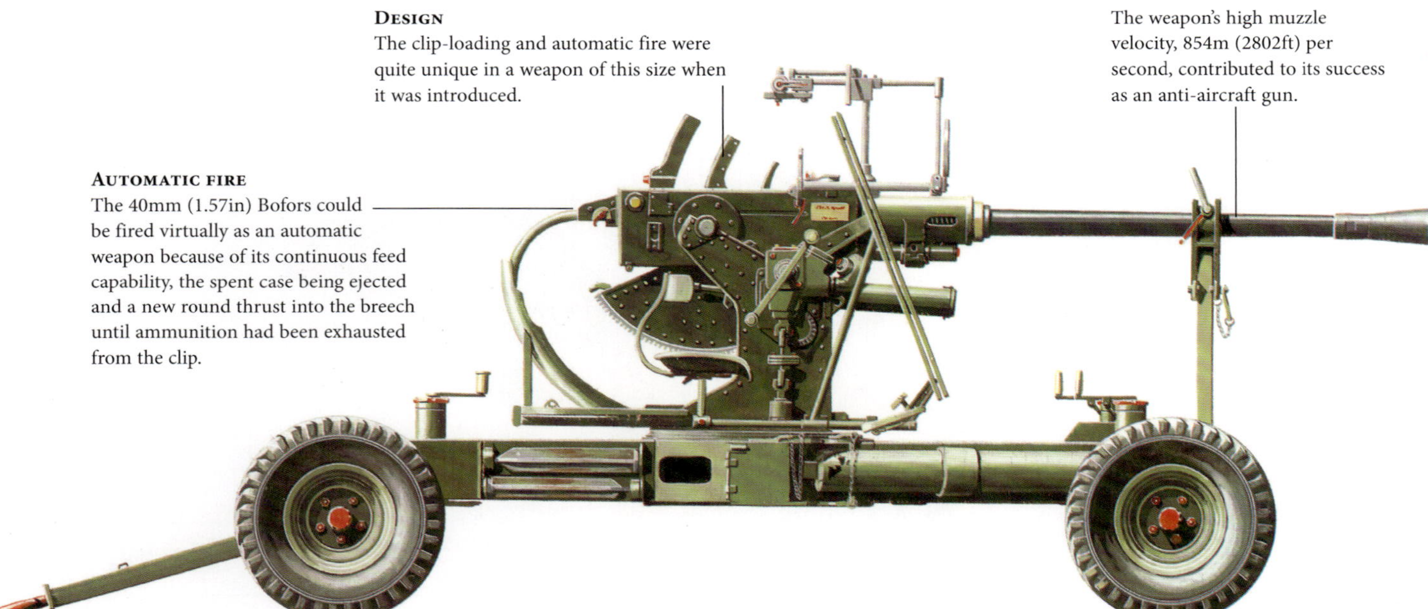

DESIGN
The clip-loading and automatic fire were quite unique in a weapon of this size when it was introduced.

MUZZLE VELOCITY
The weapon's high muzzle velocity, 854m (2802ft) per second, contributed to its success as an anti-aircraft gun.

AUTOMATIC FIRE
The 40mm (1.57in) Bofors could be fired virtually as an automatic weapon because of its continuous feed capability, the spent case being ejected and a new round thrust into the breech until ammunition had been exhausted from the clip.

REPUTATION

The 40mm (1.57in) Bofors L/60 first appeared in 1929. Sales began to pick up in the mid-1930s and by 1939 almost every country in Europe possessed some. The USA adopted the gun in 1941 and it remained in production until the 1950s, when Bofors replaced it with the L/70. It soon built up a reputation for reliability and accuracy, which it has never subsequently lost.

BOFORS CREW, PACIFIC
US Marines in the Pacific ready their Bofors for Japanese air attack. As well as the field mounting pictured, it was used on self-propelled mountings and as a ship-board gun.

Oerlikon 20mm (1937)

TYPE • *Anti-aircraft* **COUNTRY** • *United States*

SPECIFICATIONS	
Calibre:	20mm (0.79in)
Weight:	68.04kg (150lb)
Gun length:	2.2m (7ft 3in)
Elevation:	-15° to +90°
Traverse:	360°
Shell type & weight:	N/A
Muzzle velocity:	820m/sec (2700ft/sec)
Range:	914m (1000yd)
Rate of fire:	450rpm

Another brilliant weapon design from Switzerland, the 20mm (0.79in) Oerlikon cannon was manufactured in the United Kingdom and many other countries, and was one of the most important weapons of its type in use during World War II.

Left: A US Navy Oerlikon crew. The Oerlikon was widely used aboard aircraft and warships of virtually every warring nation. The Germans designated the Oerlikon as the 20mm Flak 28 or 29, while the Italians renamed it the Cannone-Mitraglia da 20 Oerlikon, and the Americans the 20mm Automatic Gun Mk IV.

FEED
The Oerlikon normally used a 60-round drum magazine for the feed system, but a 20-round box magazine was used on some versions.

MOUNTING
Although used mainly as a naval weapon, many were employed by land forces. This is the British HB Mk 1 mounting.

BLOWBACK
The Oerlikon was a blowback-operated gun; the action was assisted by the large recoil springs around the barrel that were a recognition feature of the weapon.

MOUNT VARIATIONS
By 1940, Oerlikons were being pressed into service on land mountings of all kinds. Some of these British mountings were simple in the extreme; others, such as the Haszard semi-mobile mount, were much more 'formal'. Later in the war, a triple-gun mounting with the three guns one over the other was placed into production; some of these types of mounts were later used on trucks.

NAVAL OERLIKONS
Twin 20mm (0.79in) Oerlikons are cleaned aboard the Indian Navy sloop HMIS *Naradba* late in the war. Still in service at sea after more than 70 years, the Oerlikon is now rarely encountered in towed form.

152mm Gun-Howitzer M1937 (ML-20) (1937)

TYPE • *Howitzer* **COUNTRY** • *Soviet Union*

The 152mm Gun-Howitzer M1937 (ML-20) was developed in the mid-1930s to replace a collection of World War I-era 152mm (6in) guns that had been refurbished in 1933, and was among the first weapons to be classed as a 'gun-howitzer'.

SPECIFICATIONS

Calibre:	152mm (6in)
Weight:	7128kg (15,716lb)
Gun length:	4.42m (14.5ft)
Elevation:	-2° to +65°
Traverse:	58°
Shell type:	HE: 43.56kg (96lb)
Muzzle velocity:	655m/sec (2150ft/sec)
Range:	17,265m (18,880yd)
Rate of fire:	3–4rpm

Below: The 'gun-howitzer' could fire at high velocity and flat trajectory like a gun, or at low velocity and on a high, looping trajectory like a howitzer, as the task demanded.

Muzzle brake
As a large-calibre weapon, the M1937 had formidable recoil, an impulse that was somewhat softened by the fitting of a large muzzle brake.

Propellant loads
The M1937 was loaded with separate shell and propellant charges, rather than unitary shells, an arrangement that improved the versatility of its fire.

Carriage
The M1937's carriage was of split-trail type (twin legs forked out when the gun was emplaced), with leaf spring suspension and steel wheels with rubber tyres.

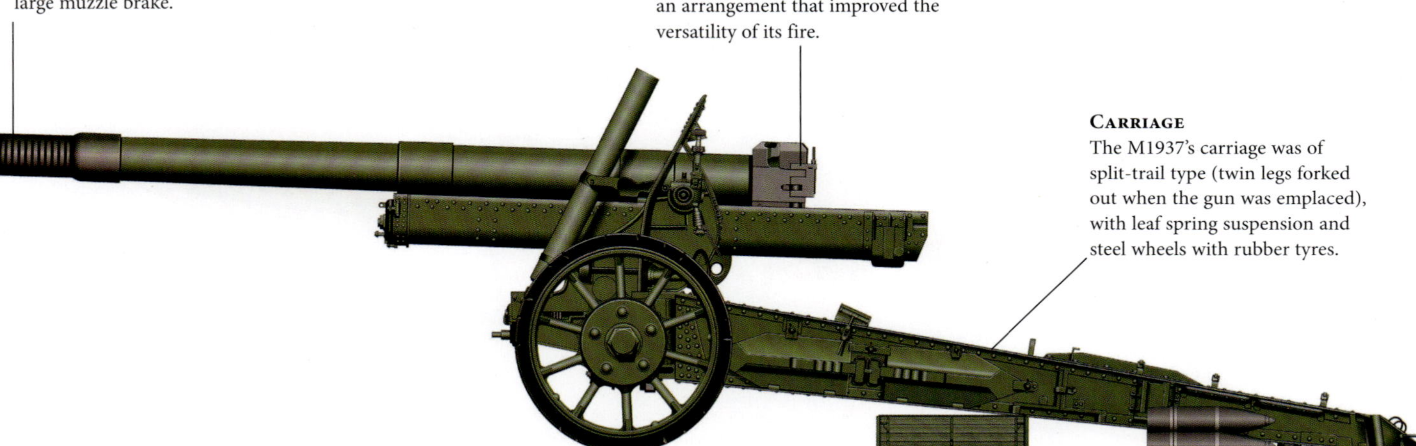

SOVIET SOLUTIONS

As a great deal of Soviet territory was occupied by the Germans, the challenge of maintaining updated artillery was met through the ingenious employment of available manufacturing capacity. The 76mm (3in) field gun M1942, for example, was the marriage of the M1939 gun and a new split carriage. The M1942 holds the distinction of being produced in the largest numbers of any field artillery piece of World War II.

RUSSIAN AND GERMAN USE

A split-trail weapon, with spring balancing 'horns' alongside the barrel, the M1937 was the workhorse of Russian medium artillery throughout World War II and was used by several armies for many years afterwards. The German army was very impressed by them and many captured examples were used against their former owners.

45mm Anti-tank Gun M1937 and M1942 (1937)

TYPE • *Anti-tank* **COUNTRY** • *Soviet Union*

SPECIFICATIONS (Model 1942)

Calibre:	45mm (1.77in)
Weight:	625kg (1378lb)
Gun length:	3.09m (10ft) L/66
Elevation:	-8° to +25°
Traverse:	60°
Shell type:	AP: 1.43kg (3.15lb)
Muzzle velocity:	870m/sec (2854ft/sec)
Range:	4550m (14,927ft)
Rate of fire:	15–20rpm

The M1937 (53-K) originated in the M1932 (19-K), which was a combination of a slightly modified 1-K carriage and a new 45mm (1.77in) barrel. Problems with this design led to an improved gun, redesignated as the 53-K, in 1937.

Above: The 45mm (1.77in) Model 1937 (seen here) replaced the Model 1932's manually operated breech with a semi-automatic breech.

45mm M1942
Despite having a limited anti-tank capability by the end of the war, the M-42 was easy to manhandle and was a useful close-support weapon firing HE and canister rounds.

Shield
The shield was thickened to 7mm (0.27in) to give the gun crew improved protection frommachine-gun fire and shell splinters.

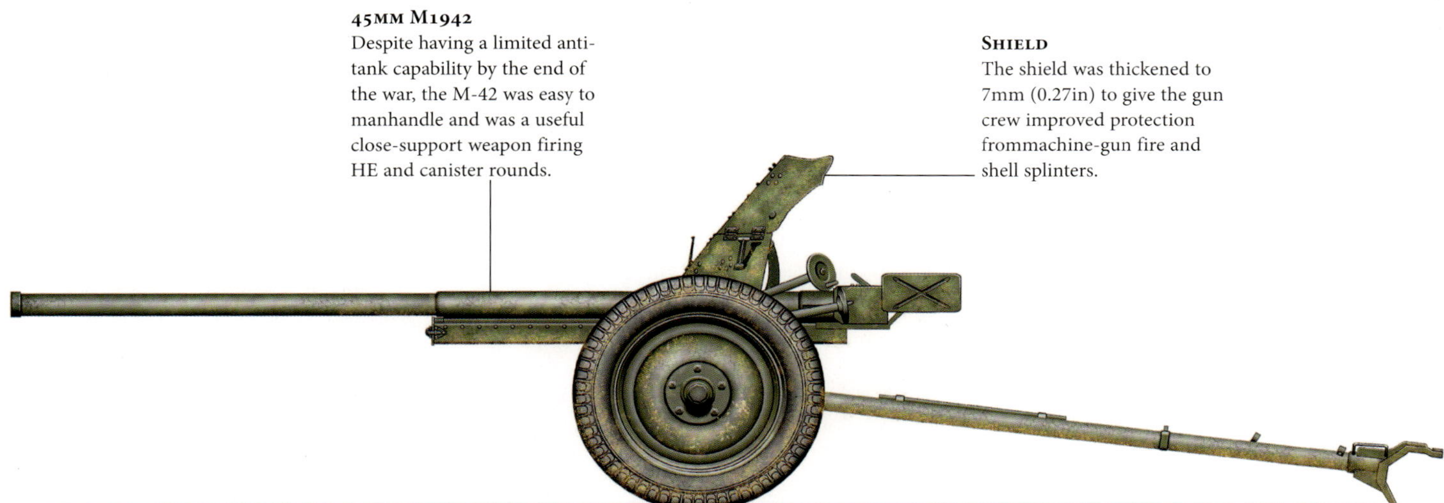

M1942 UPDATE
By 1942, the effectiveness of existing 45mm (1.77in) anti-tank guns was rapidly reducing as the Germans up-armoured their tanks and assault guns. The much-delayed 57mm (2.24in) ZiS-2 anti-tank gun was acknowledged to be the best solution, but as an interim measure, the 45mm (1.77in) gun was updated by fitting a longer (L/66) barrel and being rechambered to take more powerful ammunition. This gun was the Model 1942 (M-42).

ARTILLERY COVER
The three-man crew of a Soviet Model 1937 anti-tank gun give cover to an infantry assault on the Eastern Front. Compared to the Model 1932, the Model 1937 had new sights, firing mechanism and shield mounting fittings.

GrW 34 8cm Mortar (1937)

TYPE • *Mortar* **COUNTRY** • *Germany*

SPECIFICATIONS

Length:	1.14m (3ft 9in)
Weight:	62kg (137lb)
Calibre:	81.4mm (3.2in)
Elevation:	45° to 90°
Traverse:	Up to 23°
Shell weight:	3.5kg (7lb 11oz)
Muzzle velocity:	174m/sec (571ft/sec)
Range:	2400m (2625yd)
Rate of fire:	15–25rpm

The 8cm schwere Granatwerfer 34 (GrW 34) medium mortar was the first such weapon to be developed by the Germans, entering service in 1937, although developmental work had started as far back as 1923.

Above: On the Eastern Front, a German mortar team prepare to fire the 8cm GrW 34.

Traversing gear
Side view of an 8cm GrW 34 medium mortar, with bipod and barrel and base plate; at the top of the bipod is the weapon's traversing gear and elevating mechanism.

Barrel length
The mortar was sizeable, with a barrel length of 1.14m (3ft 9in) and a weight of 62kg (137lb).

Calibre
The mortar was actually an 81.4mm (3.2in)-calibre weapon, despite its designation as an 8cm mortar.

STANDARD MORTAR
The GrW 34 was sturdy enough to survive the rigours of combat and proved a reliable weapon. It soon acquired a good reputation for accuracy, thanks to its RA-35 dial sight, which in contrast to the British mortars had its deflection marked in mils instead of degrees and yards. This medium mortar remained the standard German infantry mortar throughout World War II.

8CM MORTAR CREW, 1940
The GrW 34 was employed in large numbers in every campaign in which the Wehrmacht fought. The weapon was usually operated by a three-man team; here the crew is on the Western Front in 1940.

120mm M1938 Mortar (1939)

TYPE • *Mortar* COUNTRY • *Soviet Union*

SPECIFICATIONS

Calibre:	120mm (4.7in)
Barrel length:	1.862m (73.3in)
Weight as fired:	280kg (617lb)
Elevation:	+45° to +80°
Traverse:	6°
Weight/bomb:	16.0kg (35.2lb)
Muzzle velocity:	272m/sec (892ft/sec)
Range:	6000m (6560yd)
Rate of fire:	10rpm

This is the ancestor of every one of the multitude of 120mm (4.7in) mortars in use today; prior to 1939 the only people in the world to have a mortar of this calibre were the Russians, who treated it as an artillery weapon.

Above: The mortar had an ingenious design of a transporting trailer that could be hooked to the baseplate. It lifted the mortar out of the ground and loaded it on to the trailer bed in one swift move.

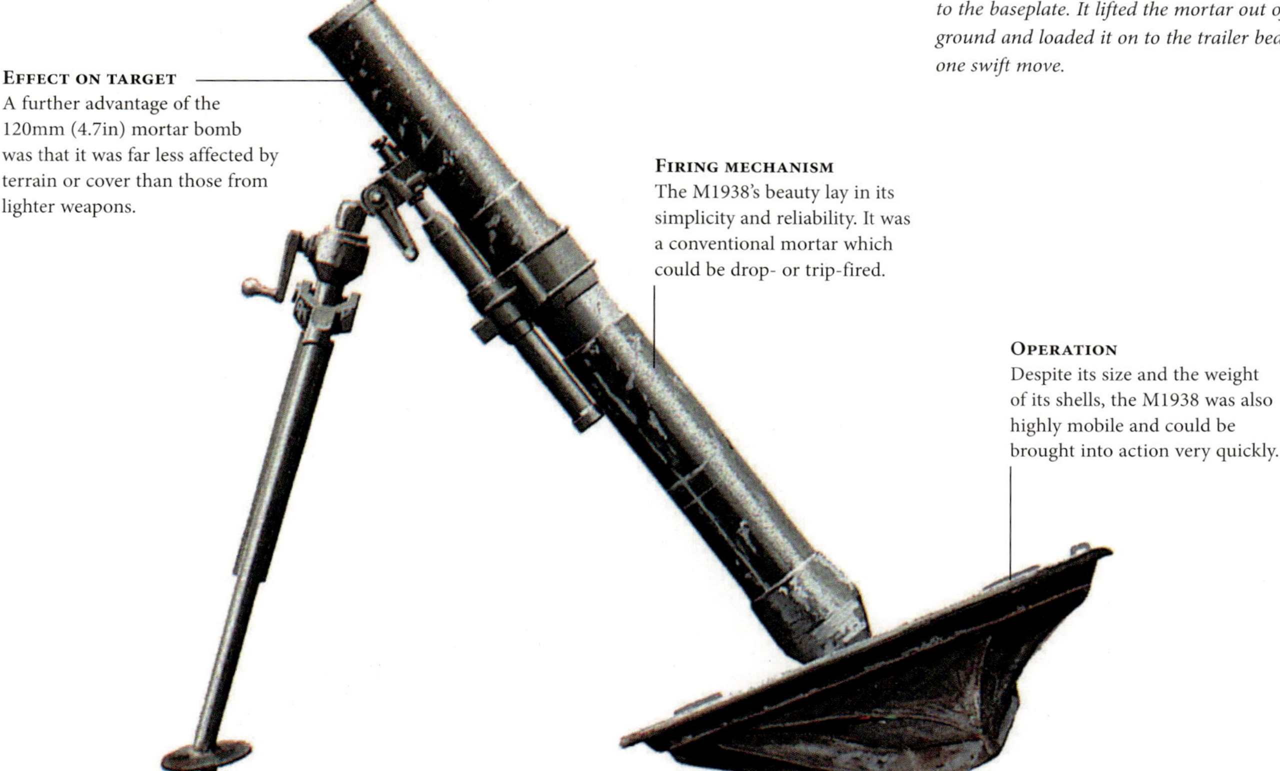

Effect on target
A further advantage of the 120mm (4.7in) mortar bomb was that it was far less affected by terrain or cover than those from lighter weapons.

Firing mechanism
The M1938's beauty lay in its simplicity and reliability. It was a conventional mortar which could be drop- or trip-fired.

Operation
Despite its size and the weight of its shells, the M1938 was also highly mobile and could be brought into action very quickly.

HEAVY MORTAR

The 120mm (4.7in) mortar blurred the distinction between infantry weapons and light artillery pieces. The German Army first encountered this monster the hard way as the Red Army had pioneered the concept with the 120mm Model 1938. The Germans had a taste of its effectiveness in the early stages of Operation *Barbarossa* and were sufficiently impressed to simply copy the type.

SOVIET MORTAR CREW
Soviet 120mm (4.7in) mortars were essentially cheap but effective regimental artillery. In common with virtually all other mortars, they sacrificed range for simplicity, but their firepower was devastating – a 120mm (4.7in) mortar bomb has about the same explosive capacity as a 155mm (6.1in) artillery shell.

37mm 61-K M1939 (1939)

TYPE • *Anti-aircraft* **COUNTRY** • *Soviet Union*

SPECIFICATIONS

Calibre:	37mm (1.46in)
Weight:	2100kg (4600lb)
Gun length:	2.5m (8ft 2in) L/67
Elevation:	-5° to +85°
Traverse:	360°
Shell type:	Frag-T: 730g (1.61lb)
Muzzle velocity:	880m/sec (2900ft/sec)
Ceiling:	5000m (16,000ft)
Rate of fire:	160–170rpm

During the 1930s, the Red Army felt that a 45mm (1.8in) AA gun was rather too large for optimum mobility in the field. In the late 1930s, the Red Army bought a small number of Bofors 40mm (1.57in) AA guns that provided the basis for the development of the very similar 61-K.

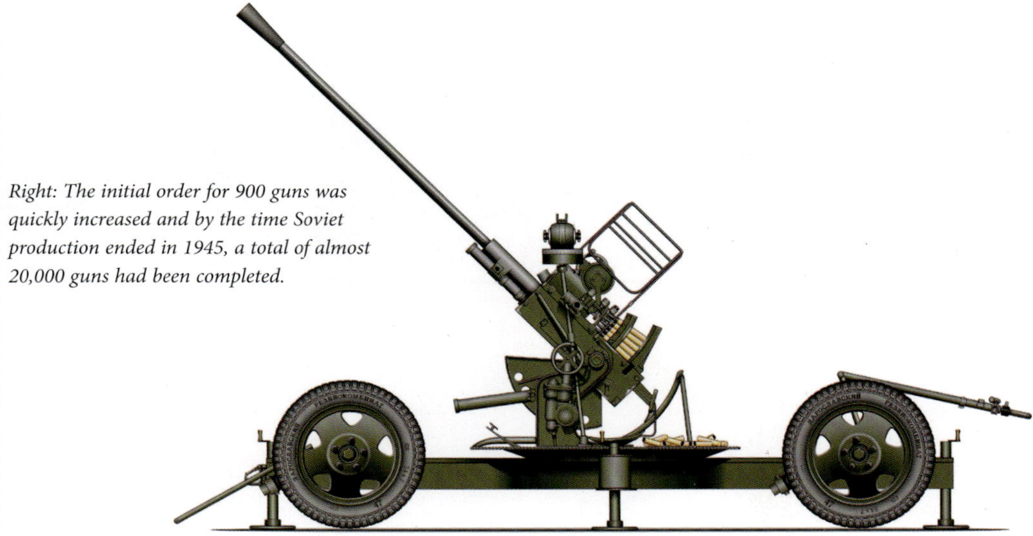

Right: The initial order for 900 guns was quickly increased and by the time Soviet production ended in 1945, a total of almost 20,000 guns had been completed.

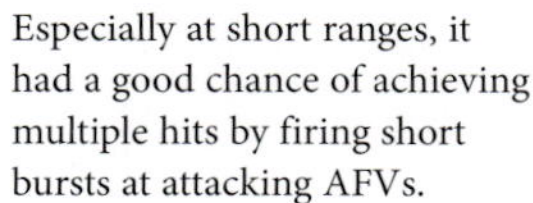

Ground fire
Especially at short ranges, it had a good chance of achieving multiple hits by firing short bursts at attacking AFVs.

Ammunition feed
The ammunition seems to have been derived from that used by the contemporary US 37mm (1.46in) Browning AA gun and was loaded in five-round clips.

Mounting
The gun was mounted on a four-wheeled ZU-7 carriage and closely resembled the 40mm (1.57in) Bofors guns in general appearance.

ANTI-TANK ROLE
Although it was designed as an AA gun, the 61-K's potential in the anti-tank role was also appreciated and priority was given to developing armour-piercing (AP) ammunition – penetration at 500m (1640ft) range was recorded as 37mm (1.46in) of armour sloped at 60°. (The 61-K's high rate of fire in comparison to conventional anti-tank guns would make it a more potent 'tank-killer' than these figures suggest.)

SOVIET GUN CREW
This rather staged photograph shows the ideal composition of a 61-K gun crew. Soviet propaganda claimed that the 61-K batteries shot down a total of 14,657 enemy aircraft, averaging 905 rounds per aircraft destroyed.

122mm Howitzer M1938 (M-30) (1939)

TYPE • *Howitzer* **COUNTRY** • *Soviet Union*

SPECIFICATIONS

CALIBRE:	122mm (4.8in)
WEIGHT:	2450kg (5401lb)
GUN LENGTH:	2.67m (8ft 9in) L/21.9
ELEVATION:	-3° to +63.5°
TRAVERSE:	49°
SHELL TYPE & WEIGHT:	HE-fragmentation: 21.76kg (47.87lb)
MUZZLE VELOCITY:	458m/sec (1503ft/sec)
RANGE:	11,800m (12,904yd)
RATE OF FIRE:	5-6rpm

As the Soviet Union's premier piece of divisional artillery, the 122mm (4.8in) Howitzer M1938 (M-30) had a profound effect on the Red Army's ability to deliver indirect support, especially in the context of the numbers produced.

Left: A Soviet gun crew dig in their M-30. Although it was primarily an indirect fire weapon, the M-30 did have a significant anti-tank capability after the introduction of the BP-460A HEAT shell in mid-1943.

BARREL
The gun did not have a muzzle brake, increasing the recoil but reducing the visual signature of dust raised up from the ground by a muzzle brake's gas redirection.

BREECHBLOCK
The breechblock was of the interrupted-screw type. The rate of fire was approximately 5–6 rounds per minute.

TRAIL
The M-30 had a split trail; in emergencies the gun could be fired with the trail arms together, albeit with a limited traverse.

DEVELOPMENT

By the late 1930s, it was becoming clear to the Soviet military that the Model 1909/37 and the Model 1910/30 howitzers were in need of replacement by an entirely new design. Various 122mm (4.8in) howitzers underwent prolonged service trials in 1938–39, leading to the acceptance of the M-30 in 1940. The design was so successful that production continued until 1960, with more than 19,000 completed.

BATTLE-WINNING GUN
Not only was the M-30 extremely powerful in the anti-personnel role, it was also used to destroy field fortifications, minefields and enemy vehicles, purely with its HE shell.

7.5cm Pak 40 (1940)

TYPE • *Anti-tank* **COUNTRY** • *Germany*

SPECIFICATIONS

Calibre:	7.5cm (2.95in)
Weight:	1.5 tonnes (1.37 tons)
Gun length:	3.7m (12ft 1in)
Elevation:	-5° to +22°
Traverse:	65°
Shell type:	APCBC: 6.80kg (1lb)
Muzzle velocity:	APCBC: 792m/sec (2598ft/sec)
Range:	AP: 2000m (2187yd); HE: 7500m (8202yd)
Rate of fire:	Up to 14rpm

The Pak 40 was a large but low-silhouetted and easy-to-conceal anti-tank gun that resembled its smaller progenitor, the Pak 38. The Pak 40 served on all fronts right through until the war's end in May 1945.

Right: Normandy, France, in 1944. A Pak 40 team position their camouflaged anti-tank gun ready to ambush Allied armour moving across open fields.

Early design
This early-production 7.5cm (2.95in) Pak 40 sports the initial design single-baffle muzzle brake as well as spoked steel wheels; later examples featured one of two slightly modified muzzle-brake designs.

Ballistic performance
Firing the 7.5cm (2.95in) Panzergrenate Patrone 39 armour-piercing, capped, ballistic-capped (APCBC) round at a muzzle velocity of 792m/sec (2598ft/sec), the gun could penetrate 135mm (5.3in) of vertical and 106mm (4.2in) of 30°-sloped armour at 500m (547yd).

Layout
The gun was mounted on a standard-design single-axled, pneumatic-tyred split-trail carriage.

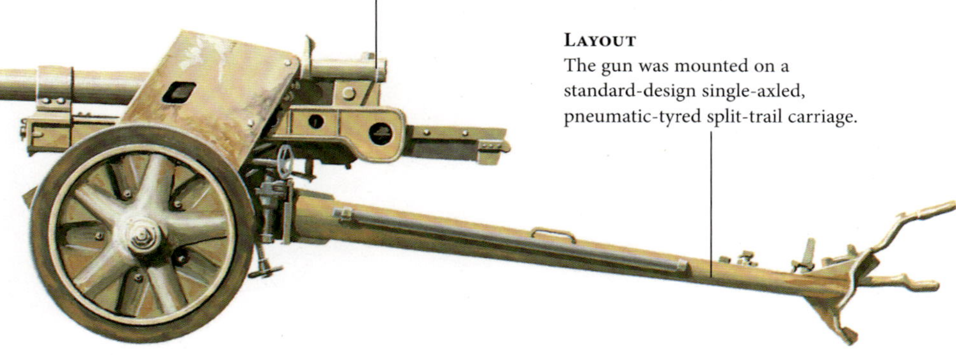

EASTERN FRONT

The first examples of this new weapon, the 7.5cm (2.95in) Pak 40 L/46, were rushed to the Eastern Front just as the Soviet winter 1941–42 counteroffensive erupted. The troops of the hard-pressed and outflanked German defensive 'hedgehogs,' like those at Velikiye Luki, were relieved when they discovered the new weapon's potent tank-killing powers. The only defect was its weight, which led to several being abandoned in retreats during the Russian winter when they became so bogged in mud that the eight-man crew could not move them.

WAFFEN-SS GUN TEAM
A Waffen-SS anti-tank gun team load a Pak 40 on the Eastern Front, 1944. The gun was first issued in 1941 and became the standard anti-tank gun for the remainder of the war; as long as the crew kept their nerve and let the tank get close, they could destroy any Allied tank.

Ordnance QF 25-pounder (1940)

TYPE • *Howitzer* **COUNTRY** • *United Kingdom*

SPECIFICATIONS (Mk II)

Calibre:	87.6mm (3.45in)
Weight:	1800kg (3968lb)
Length:	2.4m (7ft 11in)
Elevation:	-5° to +40°
Traverse:	On carriage 8°; on firing table 360°
Shell type:	HE: 11.3kg (25lb)
Muzzle velocity:	532m/sec (1745ft/sec)
Maximum range:	12,253m (13,400yd)
Rate of fire:	3–8rpm

One of the most famous artillery pieces of World War II, the 25-pounder was designed between the wars to provide the British Army with a versatile weapon that could fulfil the role of both a gun and a howitzer.

Left: A British 25pdr on the Gothic Line in Italy in 1944. The 25pdr fired a shell that weighed 11.3kg (25lb) to a range of 12,253m (13,400yd). It had the propellant charge loaded separately to the shell; 'Normal' and 'Super Charge' propellant loads were available.

Muzzle brake
The use of the muzzle brake made it possible for the gun to fire the heavier propelling charges.

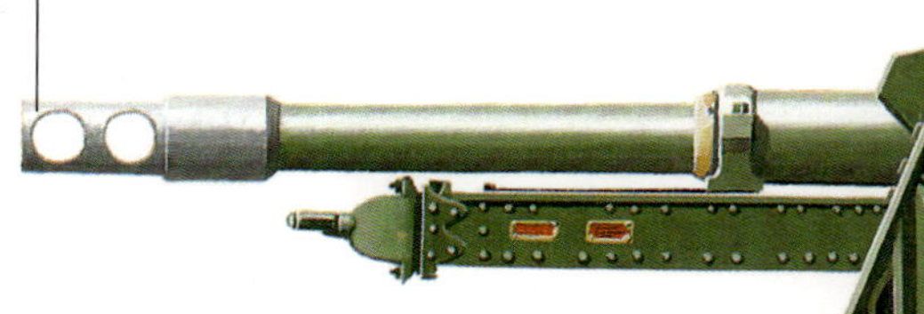

Sighting
As well as an indirect-fire sight, a direct-fire telescope was an integral fitting, used primarily for the anti-tank role.

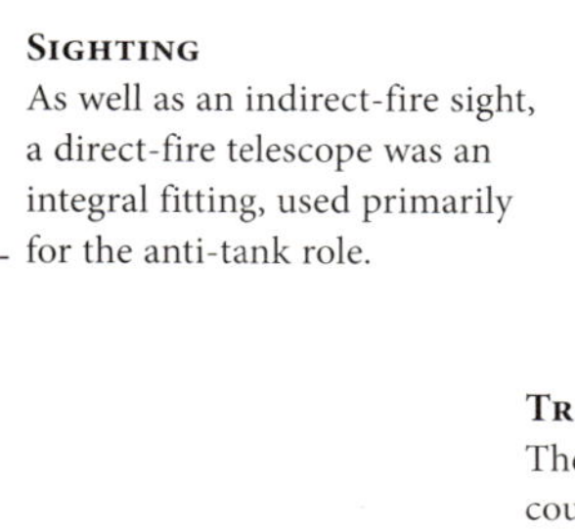

Trail
The trail of the 25pdr gun could be hooked directly to the towing vehicle; it did not need a separate limber.

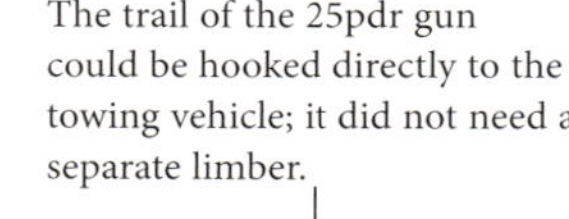

MK I TO MK II
The initial Ordnance QF 25pdrs were essentially heavier guns mounted on the carriages of the old surplus 18pdrs. The carriages had been modernized with pneumatic tyres, and some had been equipped with split trails. A number of these guns, designated Mark I, went to war with the British Expeditionary Force on the continent and were lost during the evacuation at Dunkirk. Simultaneously, however, the Mark II, engineered on a combined basis including gun and carriage, was being deployed with Commonwealth troops and was destined to become one of the best-known artillery pieces of World War II.

LOADERS
A British 25pdr howitzer crew supports an Allied attack between Tilly and Caen during the intensive fighting for Normandy in June 1944.

37mm Gun M3 (1940)

TYPE • *Anti-tank* **COUNTRY** • *United States*

SPECIFICATIONS

Calibre:	37mm (1.46in)
Weight:	413.7kg (912lb)
Barrel length:	2.095m (82.5in)
Elevation:	-10° to +15°
Traverse:	60°
Projectile type:	AP/HE: 870g (1.92lb)
Muzzle velocity:	884m/sec (2900ft/sec)
Range:	457m (500yd)
Rate of fire:	Up to 25rpm

The US 37mm (1.46in) M3 earned the dubious distinction of being obsolete at the time it was issued to combat units headed to North Africa. It was withdrawn from the European theatre in favour of heavier types.

Left: The 37mm (1.46in) M3 had a relatively short range of 457m (500yd) but could to a degree compensate against light armour with a rapid rate of fire.

Penetration
The 37mm (1.46in) cannon penetrated 2.5cm (1in) of armour at a distance of 914m (1000yd) and fired an armour-piercing projectile against hard targets.

Layout
The M3 is distinguished from the Pak 36 by its shorter and more vertical shield, perforated shoulder guard for the gunlayer, and a different towing connection.

Pak 36 influence
Two German Pak 36 guns were bought from Germany to give the US designers guidance in developing the M3, and as a result there is a considerable degree of likeness between the German and American weapons.

PACIFIC USE

The M3 was widely used in the Pacific, uniquely suited for use during amphibious operations and against light Japanese tanks. Firing a variety of shells, it was effective against enemy personnel and in the reduction of bunkers and pillboxes. Nearly 19,000 of the field variant were built during the war, and it was also used as the main armament for US light tanks and armoured cars.

AMPHIBIOUS LANDING
US soldiers roll out an M3 on to a beachhead. Standardized in 1937 and issued in large numbers, the gun was obsolete by the time of Pearl Harbor, but it remained in wide use in the Pacific theatre since it could deal with almost any Japanese tank.

Howitzer M1 and M2 (1940)

TYPE • *Howitzer* **COUNTRY** • *United States*

SPECIFICATIONS (M1)

Calibre:	203mm (8in)
Weight:	14,380kg (14.15 tons)
Gun length:	25 calibre: 5.08m (16.67ft)
Elevation:	-2° to +65°
Traverse:	60°
Shell type:	HE: 90.73kg (200lb)
Muzzle velocity:	595m/sec (1952ft/sec)
Range:	16,925m (18,510yd)
Rate of fire:	1–3 rounds per 2 mins

Originally designed during the interwar years in response to the production of heavy artillery in Germany, the 203mm (8in) Howitzer M1 was used during the Vietnam era and by NATO forces in the 1960s. A prime mover or gun tractor was required to relocate the weapon.

Above: During World War I the US Army had no heavy artillery and so acquired numbers of British 203mm (8in) howitzers. Between the wars they developed this M1 design, which could fit on the same carriage as the 155mm gun M2.

Recoil system
The recoil system adjusted the length of stroke as the gun was elevated; the gun could be uncoupled from the recoil system and pulled back across the trail for travelling, to equalize the weight.

Deployment
To go into action, the limber was removed, the trails opened and the wheels lifted off the ground, giving a solid platform that paid off in accuracy.

155mm M2
The long 155mm (6.1in) barrel was balanced by two hydro-pneumatic cylinders attached to horns above the breech.

155MM GUN M2

The US Army adopted a 155mm (6.1in) gun from the French in 1917; they liked the calibre and in the 1930s developed a modern version, producing one of the finest guns of the war years. The 155mm M2, which inevitably became known as 'Long Tom', was on a split-trail carriage with eight wheels under the gun and a two-wheeled limber for towing.

HEAVY GUNS
A battery of 155mm (6.1in) M1 howitzers from the US Army's 969th Artillery Battalion provide fire support during the Ardennes offensive in December 1944. Primary US heavy artillery pieces with origins during the interwar years were the 203mm (8in) howitzer M1, 240mm (9.4in) howitzer M1 and the 155mm gun M1. They were used for long-range indirect fire capable of smashing fortified positions.

Flakpanzer I / Flak 38 (1941)

TYPE • *Anti-aircraft* **COUNTRY** • *Germany*

SPECIFICATIONS

Dimensions:	Length: 4.02m (13ft 2in); Width: 2.6m (8ft 6in); Height: 1.72m (5ft 8in)
Weight:	5.4 tonnes (5.95 US tons)
Engine:	Krupp M 305 4-cylinder petrol, 44kW (59hp)
Speed:	37km/h (23mph)
Range:	200km (120 miles)
Armour:	6–13mm (0.24–0.51in)
Armament:	1 x 20mm (0.79in) Flak 38
Crew:	4

The Flakpanzer was a mobile anti-aircraft vehicle. Initial design studies for this vehicle type were based on the Panzer I and began in 1940. A total of 24 Ausf A hulls were converted by Stoewer at Stettin in 1941 to produce the Flakpanzer I.

Below: Employed by all branches of the Wehrmacht, the Flak 38 gun appeared mounted on various fixed and mobile platforms.

Gunsight
The gunsight was originally the Flakvisier 38, a reflector sight similar to those used in fighter aircraft. It was electrically linked to the gun's elevation and traverse gears, so that as an aircraft was tracked, the sight automatically calculated 'aim-off' and displaced the graticule of the optical sight accordingly.

Weapon layout
The weapon itself typically consisted of the long-barrelled gun, fitted with a well-sloped dual-angle splinter shield, mounted either on a fixed-firing platform or a Sonderanhänger single-axle wheeled trailer.

Flakpanzer I
This Flakpanzer I was deployed to the Ukraine in the summer of 1941 to participate in the early months of Operation *Barbarossa*.

SDKFZ 10/5
The 2cm (0.7in) Flak 38 appeared in many iterations throughout the German armed forces. Here the flak gun is mounted on the back of a leichter Zugkraftwagen 1t, a vehicle widely used for a variety of roles by both the Werhmacht and Luftwaffe.

2CM FLAK 30/38
The gun's design originated with the Swiss Solothurn ST-5 20mm (0.79in) cannon, which was initially developed into the C/30 for the Kriegsmarine. The main problem with the gun was its rate of fire, which at 120rpm was not particularly fast for a weapon of this calibre. Rheinmetall accordingly developed the 2cm (0.79in) Flak 38, which entered service in 1939. This was a very similar weapon, however, with an increased rate of fire of 220rpm.

82-PM-36 and -37 (1941)

TYPE • *Mortar* **COUNTRY** • *Soviet Union*

SPECIFICATIONS (82-PM-36)

Calibee:	82mm (3.2in)
Weight:	62kg (136.7lb)
Gun length:	1320mm (51.97in)
Elevation:	45° to 85°
Traverse:	6° to 11° (variable with elevation)
Shell type:	HE bomb: 3.4kg (7.5lb)
Muzzle velocity:	N/A
Range:	3000m (9842ft)
Rate of fire:	25–30rpm

Soviet mortars were especially valued weapons as they were simple to produce, relatively lightweight and thus easy to move (an important consideration given the Red Army's perennial shortage of gun tractors).

Above: Harley-Davidson 42WLA with Russian M-72 sidecar and 82mm Model 1937 mortar, Operation Bagration*, summer 1944.*

Shell types
Soviet 82mm (3.2in) mortars primarily fired HE-fragmentation bombs, but phosphorus-filled smoke bombs were also issued.

Model 1936
The 82mm Model 1936 (82-PM-36) was a copy of the French Brandt 81mm (3.1in) mortar, and was virtually identical to it except for the increase in calibre.

German use
Captured examples were fielded by the Germans as the 8.2cm Granatwerfer 274/1(r). German 81mm (3.1in) mortar bombs could be fired from Russian 82mm (3.2in) mortars with some loss of accuracy.

MODEL 1937 DESIGN
Soviet design teams modified the French Brandt design to produce the 82mm Model 1937. A number of changes were made, including the addition of recoil springs between the barrel and bipod to reduce the amount of re-laying required during prolonged firing. The most obvious alteration was the adoption of a new circular base plate, which became one of the main recognition points of Russian mortars. In German hands the type was designated as the 8.2cm Granatwerfer 274/2(r).

MORTAR TEAM
While one of this Soviet mortar team adjusts the aim, the others ready an 82mm (3.2in) shell. A mortar team would also have to be ready to fight as infantry when the moment came.

80cm Schwerer Gustav (1941)

TYPE • *Railway gun* **COUNTRY** • *Germany*

Manufacturer Krupp designed the mammoth 80cm (31.5in) Schwerer Gustav and Dora guns, named for the head of the armaments firm and the wife of the project's senior engineer, as weapons capable of destroying the French Maginot Line fortifications.

SPECIFICATIONS

Calibre:	800mm (31.5in)
Barrel length:	32.480m (106.56ft)
Length over buffers:	42.976m (141ft)
Weight:	1,350,000kg (1328.9 tons)
Elevation:	+10° to + 65°
Traverse:	Nil
Shell:	HE: 4800kg (4.73 tons); CP: 7100kg (6.99 tons)
Muzzle velocity:	HE: 820m/sec (2690ft/sec); CP: 710m/sec (2330ft/sec)
Range:	HE: 47km (29.2 miles); CP: 38km (23.61 miles)
Rate of fire:	c.14 rounds per day

Above & right: It took weeks to assemble or dismantle the gun and demanded the services of over 1200 men, plus an anti-aircraft gun regiment for protectio

Calibre
The largest calibre rifled weapon in history, the Schwerer Gustav was exceeded in calibre by only a few large mortars.

Weight
Weighing nearly 1219 tonnes (1344 US tons), the two guns were capable of firing a shell weighing 6.3 tonnes (7 US tons) a distance of 59.5km (37 miles).

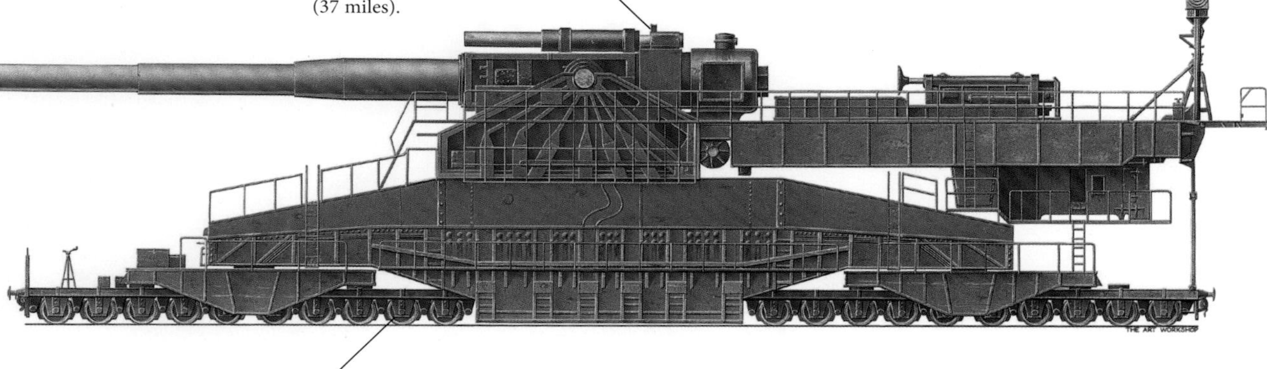

Elevation
Because the gun was on a fixed rail carriage, it was only capable of elevation and not traverse; the latter was provided by a curved section of train track.

DEVELOPMENT

Originally designed to defeat the fortifications of the Maginot Line, the Schwerer Gustav took longer to develop and build than expected and was used solely on the Eastern Front against Sebastopol and other hard targets. Two were built, Gustav and Dora, and a third was still being manufactured when the war ended.

GUN ASSEMBLY
The gun travelled dismantled into its constituent parts and had a special set of four tracks laid at the firing site, two for the gun and two for the assembly cranes.

76mm divisional gun M1942 (ZiS-3) (1941)

TYPE • *Anti-tank* **COUNTRY** • *Soviet Union*

SPECIFICATIONS

CALIBRE:	76mm (3in)
WEIGHT:	1116kg (2460lb)
GUN LENGTH:	42.6 calibre: 3.24m (127.55in)
ELEVATION:	-5° to +37°
TRAVERSE:	54°
SHELL TYPE:	HE: 6.20kg (13.67lb)
MUZZLE VELOCITY:	680m/sec (2230ft/sec)
RANGE:	13,300m (14,545yd)
RATE OF FIRE:	Up to 25rpm

Experience after the German invasion of 1941 convinced the Russians that what they needed was a combination field and anti-tank gun, and they therefore designed this M1942 weapon as their standard field piece.

Left: At Stalingrad, a Soviet gun crew lay direct fire on an urban target using their 76mm (3in) divisional gun M1942 (ZiS-3).

MUZZLE BRAKE
A substantial muzzle brake was fitted to redirect some of the muzzle blast and thereby prevent the recoil from damaging the relatively lightweight carriage.

HEIGHT
All anti-tank guns should have a low profile; the ZiS-3 was no exception, with a height of just 1.37m (4ft 6in).

BREECH
The breech was of the semi-automatic vertical sliding-wedge type, taking fixed ammunition. The ZiS-3 was a fast-firing gun, with a maximum possible rate of 25rpm.

STALIN'S APPROVAL

Design of the ZiS-3 began in late 1940. It was essentially a combination of the F-22 USV's barrel and the carriage of the 57mm (2.2in) ZiS-2 anti-tank gun. Despite a lack of official support, the designer, Vasiliy Grabin, took the enormous risk of authorizing production himself and persuaded the Red Army to accept guns for unofficial combat trials. Enthusiastic reports on these guns prompted an official demonstration attended by Stalin. He was deeply impressed.

DIRECT-FIRE ROLE

The ZiS-3 was frequently used in the direct-fire role. A crewman recalled that: 'Two holes were made to the left and right of the gun's wheels – one for the gunner, the other for the loader. ZIS-3 guns didn't require simultaneous presence of the entire crew near the gun… it was usually enough for only one person to be present.'

105mm Howitzer M2A1 (1941)

TYPE • *Howitzer* **COUNTRY** • *United States*

SPECIFICATIONS

Calibre:	105mm (4.13in)
Weight:	2258kg (4980lb)
Gun length:	22 calibre: 2.31m (90.94in)
Elevation:	-5° to +66°
Traverse:	46°
Shell type:	HE: 14.97kg (33.0lb)
Muzzle velocity:	472m/sec (1548ft/sec)
Range:	11,200m (12,248yd)
Rate of fire:	4rpm

The 105mm (4.13in) Howitzer M2A1 was the standard divisional field piece used throughout World War II by the US Army and it was distributed around the world thereafter. It is still in wide use and the ammunition has become a virtual standard to which other howitzers have been built.

Left: During field exercises, US soldiers wrestle a 105mm (4.13in) M2A1 artillery piece into position. The M2A1 served as the backbone of US artillery in World War II.

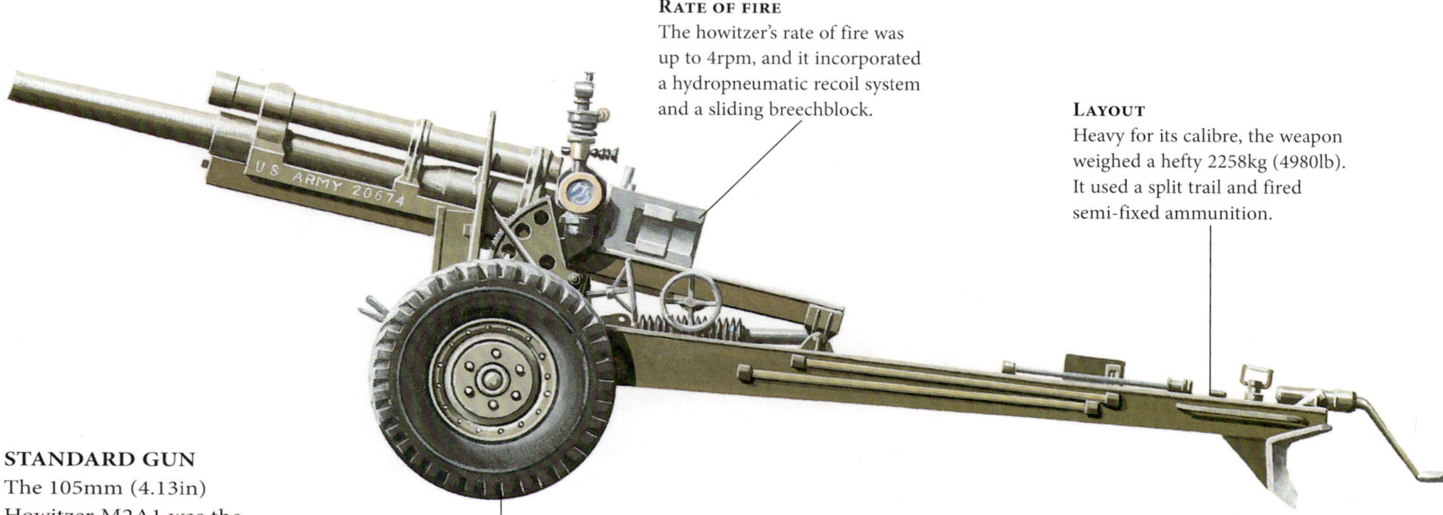

Rate of fire
The howitzer's rate of fire was up to 4rpm, and it incorporated a hydropneumatic recoil system and a sliding breechblock.

Layout
Heavy for its calibre, the weapon weighed a hefty 2258kg (4980lb). It used a split trail and fired semi-fixed ammunition.

Carriage
Mounted on the M2A2 carriage, the wheeled weapon was primarily towed into position by the army's 2.3-tonne (2.2-ton) truck.

STANDARD GUN
The 105mm (4.13in) Howitzer M2A1 was the primary field weapon of US divisional artillery units in World War II. The design for the baseline weapon, the Howitzer M1, was completed in 1928, with the improved M2 variant standardized in 1934 and the M2A1 variant emerging in March 1940. From April 1941 until June 1945, more than 8500 of the M2A1 guns were produced. As well as serving as standard towed field weapons they were mounted on various vehicles to create self-propelled guns.

FIRE MISSION
In the Bruyères area of France in October 1944, a US Army 105mm (4.13in) M2 crew lays down fire on distant German positions. The weight of firepower delivered by US artillery was a decisive factor of the eventual Allied victory in Europe.

Ordnance QF 6-pounder 7cwt (1941)

TYPE • *Anti-tank* COUNTRY • *United States*

SPECIFICATIONS (Mk II)

Calibre:	57mm (2.2in)
Weight:	1144kg (2521lb)
Barrel length:	2.56m (101in)
Elevation:	-5° to +15°
Traverse:	90°
Projectile type:	AP: 2.72kg (6lb); APDS: 1.47kg (3.25lb)
Muzzle velocity:	AP: 821m/sec (2695ft/sec); APDS: 1235m/sec (4050ft/sec)
Range:	1500m (1650yd)
Rate of fire:	15rpm

Although designed in 1938, the Ordnance QF 6pdr 7cwt Gun Mk 2 did not go into production until November 1941, after which it remained in use until the 1950s. It was also adopted by the US Army, as the 57mm M1, and used in several British tanks.

Left: During the infamous Battle of the Bulge in the Ardennes in December 1944, troops of the US Army 26th Infantry Regiment manhandle a 57mm M1 anti-tank gun in the mud (UK QF 6-pounder).

Penetration
The 6pdr improved the survivability of British gun crews with a penetrating power of 6.8cm (2.7in) at a distance of 914m (1000yd).

Ammunition
Originally provided with AP shot, it had a tungsten-cored composite rigid shot for a short time and was then the first gun ever to have a discarding sabot shot as its service round, APDS being issued in June 1944 in time for the Normandy campaign.

Variants
Several variants of the weapon were produced for anti-tank or tank-mounted use. The Mark II and Mark IV were placed in the anti-tank role and distinguished by slightly different barrel lengths.

CALIBRE SELECTION

The selection of a 6pdr weapon was at least partially due to the fact that this had been a standard calibre of the Royal Navy since the late nineteenth century and hence manufacturing equipment was readily available. The design of the gun was complete by 1940 and in April of that year the type was formally accepted as both a tank gun and an anti-tank gun.

CANADIAN 6PDR
Here a Canadian QF 6pdr AT gun crew pull through the barrel with a cleaning rod. British and Commonwealth anti-tank regiments in North Africa began to re-equip with the 6pdr in the spring of 1942 and welcomed the new gun as a vast improvement on the outclassed 2pdr.

Katyusha rocket launcher (1941)

TYPE • *Rocket launcher* **COUNTRY** • *Soviet Union*

SPECIFICATIONS (82mm (3.2in) M-8)

Length:	66cm (26in)
Diameter:	82mm (3.2in)
Total weight:	8kg (17.6lb)
Propellant weight:	1.2kg (2.645lb)
HE weight:	0.5kg (1.1lb)
Maximum range:	5900m (19,356ft)

Soviet artillery rockets, generally known as Katyushas, were developed under the tightest security in the late 1930s. By the end of the war, more than 10,000 Katyusha launchers of all types had been produced together with 12 million rockets in an estimated 200 factories.

Above: BM-13-16 132mm (5.2in) rocket launcher on Studebaker US 6x6 U3. In early 1943, the Red Army adopted the Studebaker 6x6 as the standard vehicle to mount the BM-8 and BM-13 salvo rocket launchers.

BM-8-48 rocket launcher on Studebaker US6 U-3
Each Studebaker US6 truck could fire a salvo of 48 lightweight 82mm (3.2in) M-8 rockets, giving the standard four-vehicle battery devastating short-range firepower.

Studebaker truck
Almost 105,000 Studebaker vehicles were delivered to Russia by the end of the war, many of which were adapted to give the Katyusha a high degree of cross-country mobility.

AREA WEAPON
The Katyusha was not an accurate weapon, at least in terms of the individual rockets, but as an area weapon it had enormous destructive capability. A battery of four BM-13 launchers could fire up to 192 rockets in a few seconds, striking over a 400,000sq m (4,300,000sq ft) impact zone. The downside of the system was that once the rockets were fired, it could take about 50 minutes to reload.

KATYUSHA ROCKETS
The 82mm (3.2in) M-8 rocket was based on the RS-82 air-launched rocket (RS standing for *Reaktivnyy Snaryad*, 'rocket-powered shell'). Converting the RS-82 for ground-to-ground use primarily involved enlarging the warhead and motor, but it remained a simple, fin-stabilized, solid-fuel rocket.

21cm Nebelwerfer 42 (1942)

TYPE • *Rocket launcher* **COUNTRY** • *Germany*

SPECIFICATIONS (Wurfgranate 42)

Calibre:	210mm (8.27in)
Launcher weight:	1100kg (22,425lb)
Length of rocket:	1.249m (49.21in)
Weight of rocket:	109.55kg (241.3lb)
Warhead:	HE: 10.17kg (22.4lb)
Maximum velocity:	320m/sec (1050ft/sec)
Maximum range:	7850m (8585yd)

Under the terms of the Versailles Treaty, Germany could not develop heavy artillery. However, the Treaty said nothing about rockets. Therefore, rockets were developed as a substitute for artillery from 1931 onwards and the Nebelwerfer was one of the products of this programme.

Right: The basic launcher was a six-barrelled device on a split-trail two-wheeled mounting, and the rocket was an ingenious design which had the motor in the front section, exhausting through a ring of vents halfway down the body. The explosive 'warhead' was actually the sail section of the round.

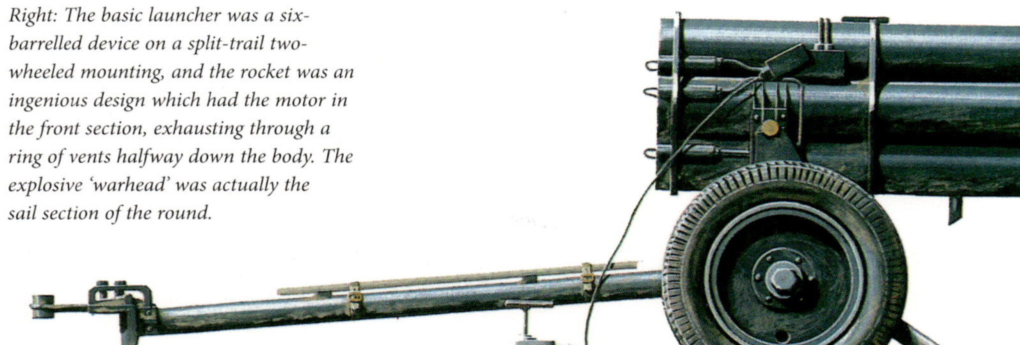

Wurfgranate 41
The 150mm (5.9in) is probably the rightful owner of the Moaning Minnie nickname, and its 2.5kg (5.5lb) warhead could reach targets more than 6858m (7500yd) away.

Ammunition
The 210mm (8.27in) rocket contained a 10kg (22.4lb) high-explosive warhead and ranged to nearly 7850m (8585yd).

Panzerwurfer 42
The Germans mounted a 10-barrel version on the back of an armoured weapons carrier so that the launcher could be moved rapidly after firing. The Opel company built about 300 of these in the latter part of 1942 and they were in use for the rest of the war, particularly on the Eastern Front.

MOANING MINNIES
German rocket systems were originally intended to generate smoke, obscuring troop movements. However, they quickly found purpose in delivering high explosives. To the Allied infantryman, the word *Nebelwerfer* (smoke thrower) came to describe all German rockets. The dull drone made by the rockets in flight also resulted in the nickname 'Moaning Minnies'.

MOUNTED LAUNCHER
The Germans deployed the 150mm (5.9in) Wurfgranate 41 and the 210mm (8.27in) Wurfgranate 42, launched from the multibarrelled Nebelwerfers mounted on the carriage of the Pak 35/36 gun or fixed atop the SdKfz 4/1 half-track.

60mm Mortar M2 (1942)

TYPE • *Mortar* **COUNTRY** • *United States*

SPECIFICATIONS

Calibre:	60mm (2.36in)
Weight in action:	61.7kg (136lb)
Gun length:	726mm (28.6in)
Elevation:	+40° to +85°
Traverse:	7°
Shell type:	HE: 1.33kg (2.94lb)
Muzzle velocity:	158m/sec (518ft/sec)
Range:	3008m (3290yd)
Rate of fire:	18rpm
Crew:	3

The US Army began examining mortars in the late 1920s. They eventually bought a design from Edgar Brandt, the French ordnance engineer, and manufactured it under licence in the United States as the Mortar M2.

Right: At the M2 mortar's optimal angle of elevation, it had a maximum range of 3008m (3290yd).

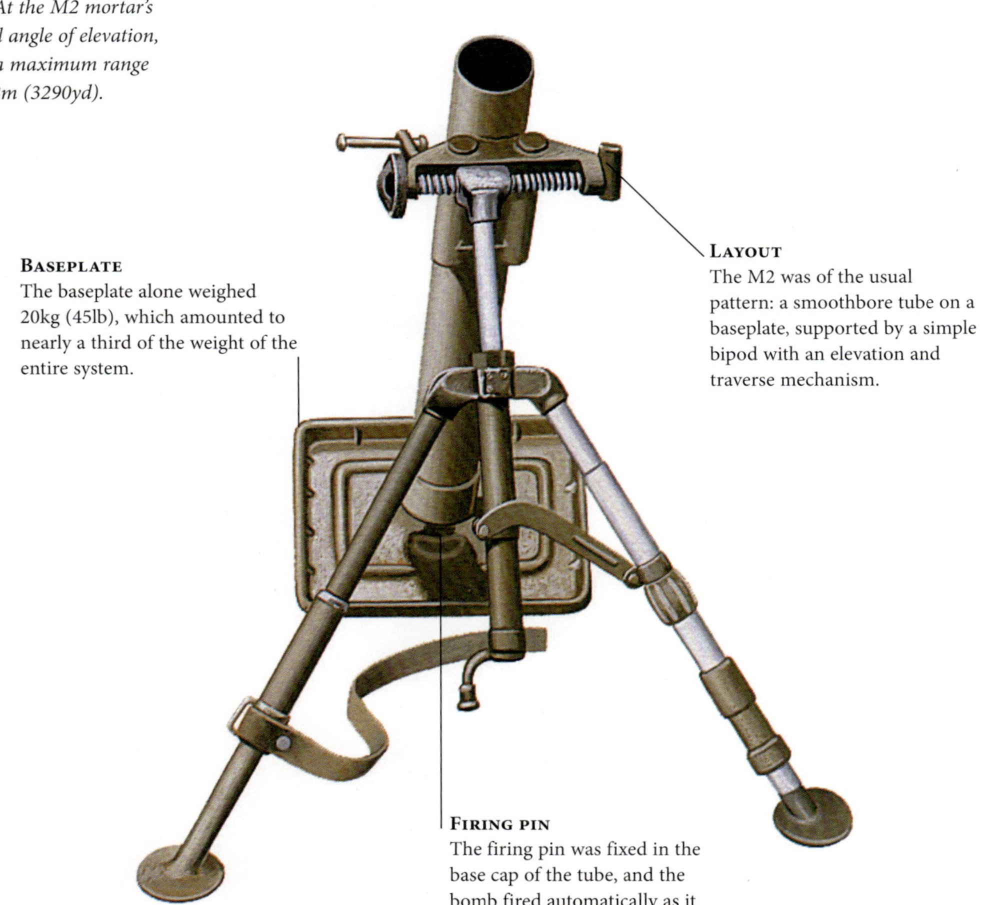

Baseplate
The baseplate alone weighed 20kg (45lb), which amounted to nearly a third of the weight of the entire system.

Layout
The M2 was of the usual pattern: a smoothbore tube on a baseplate, supported by a simple bipod with an elevation and traverse mechanism.

Firing pin
The firing pin was fixed in the base cap of the tube, and the bomb fired automatically as it was dropped down the barrel.

AMMUNITION

The M2 was a basic weapon, fitted with a simple optical sight. It was provided with high explosives (light and heavy varieties), smoke and illuminating bombs. The latter were found to be useful not only for battlefield illumination but also for anti-tank teams, firing the bomb beyond the enemy tank to silhouette it at night. The M57 WP shell could also lay down white phosphorous, which had both obscuration and anti-personnel effects.

SETTING THE RANGE
Two GIs from the US 100th Infantry Battalion prepare to fire a 60mm (2.36in) mortar, 1943. The standard rate of sustained fire was 18rpm, but in extremis, the mortar team could nearly double this rate for short periods.

MGMC AA: M13 / M14 / M16 (1942)

TYPE • *Anti-aircraft* **COUNTRY** • *United States*

SPECIFICATIONS (M16 MGMC)

Dimensions:	Length: 6.5m (21ft 4in); Width: 1.98m (6ft 6in); Height: 2.2m (6ft 8in)
Weight:	9 tonnes (9.9 US tons)
Engine:	110kW (147hp) White 160AX petrol (gasoline)
Speed:	68km/h (42mph)
Range:	282km (175 miles)
Armour:	6–12.7mm (0.25–0.5in)
Armament:	4 x 12.7mm (0.5in) M2-TT-HB HMG
Crew:	5

The Multiple Gun Motor Carriage (MGMC) was a half-tracked, self-propelled, anti-aircraft gun vehicle (SPAAG) based on the M3 half-track chassis. During 1942, the US Army realized it needed to protect its forces from aerial attack, and the M13 was an early response.

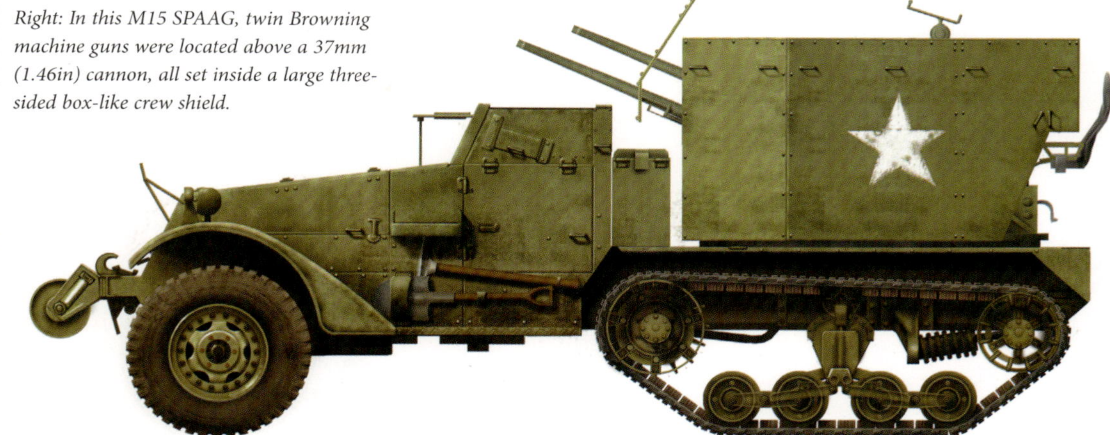

Right: In this M15 SPAAG, twin Browning machine guns were located above a 37mm (1.46in) cannon, all set inside a large three-sided box-like crew shield.

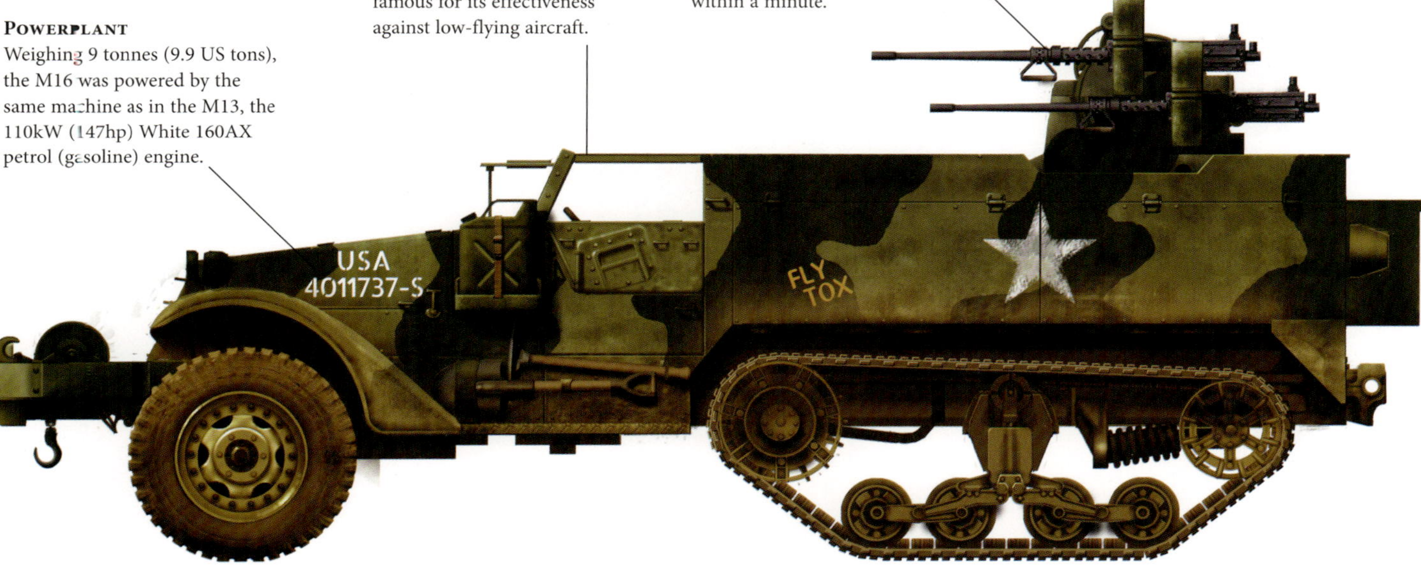

Powerplant
Weighing 9 tonnes (9.9 US tons), the M16 was powered by the same machine as in the M13, the 110kW (147hp) White 160AX petrol (gasoline) engine.

M16 GMC
Nicknamed 'the Meat Chopper', the M16 was famous for its effectiveness against low-flying aircraft.

Firepower
With each gun capable of 575rpm, for short periods the Quadmount could fire an impressive 2300 12.7mm (0.5in) bullets into the air within a minute.

M13
The five-crew M13 was a modified M3 half-track that sported at its rear an M33 Maxson open-topped mounting, which held a pair of remotely controlled 12.7mm (0.5in) Browning M2-TT-HB heavy machine guns, each capable of delivering 570rpm. The 8.2-tonne (8-ton) M13 was powered by a 110kW (147hp) White 160AX petrol (gasoline) engine and could achieve a top speed of 72km/h (45mph).

BROWNING M2-TT-HB
An individual 12.7mm (0.5in) Browning machine gun was a formidable firearm in its own right, but the M16 MGMC brought four of them together in a single modified M33 Maxson Quadmount.

28/32cm Wurfkörper SdKfz 251 / Panzerkampfwagen 35(H) (1942)

TYPE • *Rocket launcher* **COUNTRY** • *Germany*

SPECIFICATIONS (28cm Wurfkörper Spreng)

Length:	1.26m (4ft 2in)
Diameter:	280mm (11in)
Weight:	82kg (181lb)
Weight of explosives:	45.4kg (100lb) (TNT)
Weight of Propellant:	6kg (13lb)
Muzzle Velocity:	149m/sec (489ft/sec)
Range:	1925m (2105yd)

Heavy but short-range 28cm (11in) or 32cm (12.59in) rockets known as Wurfkörper were fitted to tracked vehicles by the Germans. Often the mount was the SdKfz 251, a workhorse of the German armed forces, who nicknamed such vehicles the 'Howling Cow'.

Below: The thin-walled warhead of the 28cm (11in) rocket had a massive blast effect, and the 50 litres (11 gal) of Flammöl of the 32cm (12.59in) rocket created a 'lake of fire' of more than 200sq m (219sq yards).

Rocket load
The standard load was five 28cm (11in) HE and a single 32cm (12.59in) incendiary, but this could be varied according to tactical requirements.

Launch frames
Three rockets were carried on each side of the vehicle – the storage/shipping crates were fitted to swivelling plates that could be clamped at any elevation between 5° and 45°.

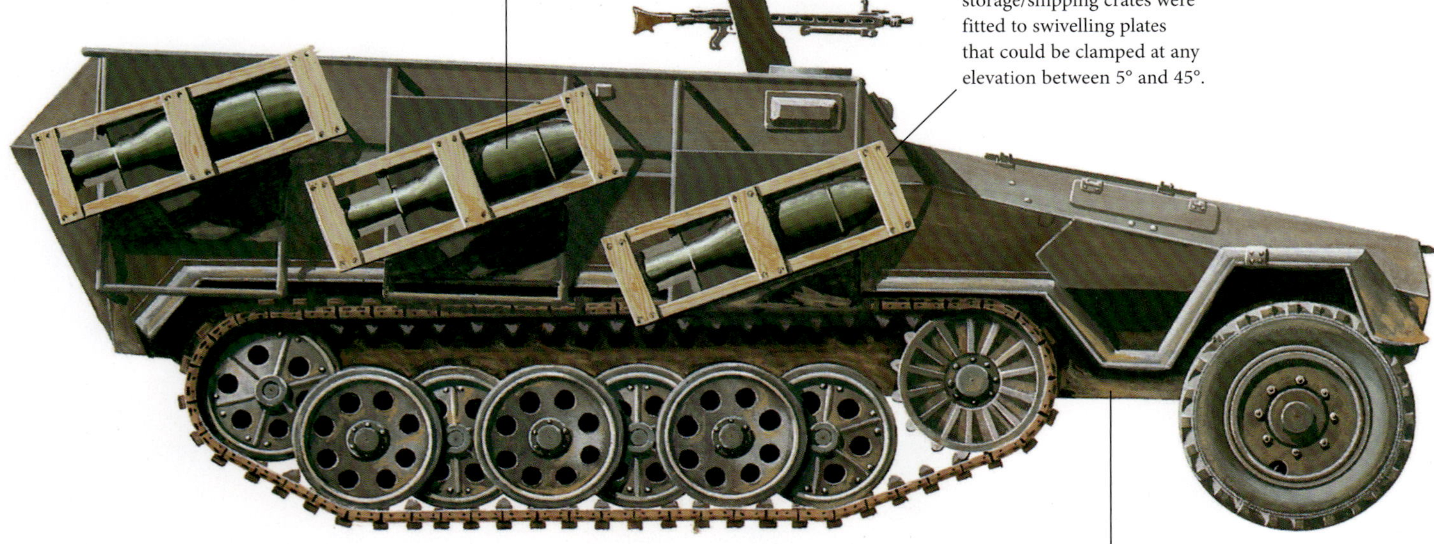

SP launcher
It was quickly recognized that a self-propelled version of the rocket launcher was needed and the six-round Schweres Wurfrahmen launcher was developed for the SdKfz 251 series.

FIRING
The 28/32cm (11/12.59in) rockets were originally intended to be fired directly from their storage/shipping crates, which were mounted on four-round launching frames. Firing drill was as follows: a) The vehicle was pointed at the target and the brakes were applied; b) The rockets were loaded, the plates elevated and clamped in position; c) The crew took cover at least 10m (33ft) away from the vehicle and the rockets were fired electrically.

ROCKET-EQUIPPED PANZER
The heavy rockets could also be mounted onto turreted armour. Here we see a Panzerkampfwagen 35H(f) mit 28/32cm Wurfrahmen in Normandy in the summer of 1944.

Ordnance QF 17-pounder (1942)

TYPE • *Anti-tank* **COUNTRY** • *United Kingdom*

SPECIFICATIONS

Calibre:	76.2mm (3in)
Weight:	2923kg (6444lb)
Gun length:	3.56m (11ft 8in)
Elevation:	-6° to +16.5°
Traverse:	60°
Shell type:	APCBC: 17kg (37.4lb)
Muzzle velocity:	950m/sec (2900ft/sec)
Range:	3000m (3280yd)
Rate of fire:	Up to 10rpm

The Ordnance QF 17pdr was introduced in August 1942 and rushed into service in North Africa on the carriage of the 25pdr to address the threat of the new Tiger tanks. Not until 1943, during the Italian Campaign, did the 17pdr gun reach the battlefield in significant numbers.

Left: A British 17pdr Mk 2 AT gun, here seen in action at Medenine, North Africa, 1943. The weapon became the supreme tank-killer on the Allied side. As the war neared its end, the gun had become standard among the Royal Artillery.

Breech
The breech of the 17pdr was a semi-automatic vertical sliding type, which was proven to be reliable under intense and sustained combat use.

Handling
The weapon appeared to be unwieldy, particularly due to the length of its barrel, vertical breechblock and muzzle brake, but it was actually relatively simple to handle.

Carriage
The standard mount was a very heavy two-wheeled split-trail type, the bulk of the carriage necessary to absorb the gun's hefty recoil.

APPLICATIONS

Primarily a towed anti-tank gun, the 17pdr was also adapted to tanks and self-propelled guns, notably the Valentine Mk I, Archer, M10 Achilles and the Sherman Firefly. When the Firefly arrived at the front lines in 1944, it was one of the most potent armoured vehicles on the battlefield, capable of killing the latest German Panther and Tiger tanks. Large numbers of the 17pdr were also used by the Royal Navy to arm landing craft.

ITALIAN CAMPAIGN
A QF 17pdr is towed within a British column moving through Italy. By 1944, the 17pdr was the British Army's most potent 'tank-killer'. The towed gun was heavy and difficult to bring into action quickly, but self-propelled versions such as the M10 Achilles were in great demand.

152mm Howitzer M1943 (D-1) (1943)

TYPE • *Howitzer* **COUNTRY** • *Soviet Union*

During World War II, in order to speed up production, the Russians frequently 'married' existing guns and carriages to produce new equipment, and the 152mm (6in) Howitzer M1943 (D-1) is a good example. It remained in service until the late 1980s.

SPECIFICATIONS

Calibre:	152mm (6in)
Weight:	3600kg (7937lb)
Gun length:	24.6 calibre: 4.201m (13.76ft)
Elevation:	-3° to +63.5°
Traverse:	35°
Shell type:	HE: 40.0kg (88.2lb)
Muzzle velocity:	508m/sec (1666ft/sec)
Range:	12,400m (13,560yd)
Rate of fire:	3–4rpm

Right: This highly stylized propaganda photograph, 'Fight up to the death' by E. Everihin, shows a battery of M1943 howitzers in action.

Muzzle brake
The DT-3 muzzle brake was essential to lessen the impact of firing on the lighter M-30 carriage.

Recoil system
The D-1's recoil system, straddling the barrel, consisted of a hydraulic buffer and a hydropneumatic recuperator.

Split trail
The split trail was linked directly to the tow vehicle without a limber. On roads, the maximum towing speed was 40km/h (25mph).

DESIGN PROCESS

Design studies for a mobile 152mm (6in) howitzer based on the carriage of the 122mm (4.8in) M-30 and the barrel of the 152mm M-10 began in 1942. The only significant modification was the addition of a muzzle brake to allow the relatively light carriage to absorb the recoil without damage. Trials were carried out in May 1943, and the type was approved for service in August of that year. Production was able to get underway exceptionally quickly using existing stocks of components for the M-30 and M-10.

MASSED ARTILLERY

The D-1 was a very strong design, and more than 2800 were completed between 1943 and 1949. This was, however, not a large number of guns compared with many other similar pieces. For example, 17,526 122mm (4.8in) M1938 (M-30) howitzers were produced between 1940 and 1945 alone.

8.8cm Pak 43 (1943)

TYPE • *Anti-tank* **COUNTRY** • *Germany*

SPECIFICATIONS (Pak 43/41)

CALIBRE:	88mm (3.46in)
WEIGHT:	4380kg (9656lb)
BARREL LENGTH:	6.61m (21.68ft)
ELEVATION:	-5° to +38°
TRAVERSE:	56°
PROJECTILE TYPE:	APCR: 7.30kg (16lb); AP/HE: 10.40kg (22.9lb)
MUZZLE VELOCITY:	APCR: 1130m/sec (3707ft/sec); AP/HE: 1000m/sec (3280ft/sec)
EFFECTIVE RANGE:	4000m (4375yd)
RATE OF FIRE:	6–10rpm

In 1943, the firm Krupp designed a technologically advanced and highly potent successor to the 7.5cm (2.95in) Flak 40, designated the 8.8cm (3.46in) Pak 43 L/71. This weapon is widely regarded as the most effective anti-tank gun of World War II.

Right: An abandoned Pak 43/41 on the Eastern Front. The original Pak 43 gun was slow and difficult to manufacture, so this cheap and cheerful version was built, using the wheels from the 15cm sFH 18 howitzer and the trail legs from the 10.5cm leFH 18 field howitzer.

BARREL
The Pak 43 mounted an extremely long 71-calibre barrel fitted with a muzzle brake. This lethal cannon fired the newly designed 10.4kg (23lb) PzGr 39/43 armour-piercing round at an astonishing muzzle velocity of 1000m/s (3300ft/s).

PLATFORM
The long gun was mounted on a low cruciform platform with a well-sloped splinter-shield to protect the crew. At just 2.05m (6ft 9in) tall, the weapon presented a lower silhouette than did the dual-role 8.8cm (3.46in) Flak, giving it superior survivability.

BREECH
The gun featured an advanced semi-automatic breech-loader and electrical firing circuit that allowed it to obtain a rapid rate of fire of 6–10rpm.

ARMOUR KILLER

With the field army clamouring for this superb tank-killer, production always lagged behind demand, with just 2100 Pak 43s being completed. Although allocated to just a handful of corps- and army-level independent anti-tank battalions, the Pak 43 made its mark on the tactical battlefield despite its small numbers. During the 17 July 1944 Anglo-Canadian Goodwood offensive south-east of Caen, for example, three Pak 43 guns deployed near Cagny knocked out 23 British tanks in under 30 minutes.

CAPTURED PAK 43
US engineers inspect the breechblock of a captured Pak 43. Although the Pak 43/41 was taller than the original Pak 43, and had a more limited traverse, it fired the same ammunition as the Pak 43 and delivered the same outstanding ballistic capability.

3.7cm Flak 43 (1943)

TYPE • *Anti-aircraft* **COUNTRY** • *Germany*

SPECIFICATIONS

Calibre:	37mm (1.46in)
Weight:	1248kg (2752lb)
Gun length:	3.30m (129.9in)
Elevation:	-7.5° to +90°
Traverse:	360°
Shell type:	HE: 635g (22.4oz)
Muzzle velocity:	820m/sec (2690ft/sec)
Ceiling:	4200m (13,780ft)
Rate of fire:	180rpm practical

The German 3.7cm (1.46in) Flak 43 and the Flakzwilling 43 (shown) were developed by Rheinmetall-Borsig as the standard German anti-aircraft weapons for use against low-flying Allied aircraft. The Flakzwilling was an up-gunned version of the Flak 43, adding a second barrel.

Left: A motorized 3.7cm (1.46in) Flak 43 of the Waffen-SS provides aerial overwatch. Production of this weapon continued until the war's last weeks, by which time around 1200 had been completed.

Sighting
A clockwork sight was fitted originally, but in due course it was discovered that this could not cope with the increased speed of aircraft and a new, simpler sight had to be adopted.

Mechanism
The Flak 43 had the body of the Flak 37 gun, but with the addition of the gas-actuated mechanism from an aerial cannon, the MK103, instead of the original recoil-actuated mechanism.

Configuration
The gun was used in a twin configuration, but mounted one above the other, not the usual side-by-side system.

TAKEOVER

Between1942 and 1944, the firms of Dürkropp, DWM and Skoda produced more than 4500 Flak 36 and Flak 37 weapons. Production was terminated in 1944, however, in favour of the more effective Flak 43, which had entered service late the previous year. The Flak 43 combined reduced weight with an increased rate of fire of 230–250rpm delivered by a new gas-operated mechanism.

FLAK 43, EASTERN FRONT, 1944
The 37mm (1.46in) Flak 43 and Flakzwilling 43 arrived in combat areas in early 1944, having been produced in a quarter of the time required for previous models, due to the adoption at Rheinmetall of manufacturing techniques similar to those applied to small arms.

15cm Panzerwerfer 42 (1943)

TYPE • *Rocket launcher* **COUNTRY** • *Germany*

SPECIFICATIONS

Calibre:	150mm (5.9in)
Launcher weight:	800kg (1,764lb)
Length of rocket:	979mm (28.55in)
Weight of rocket:	31.80kg (70lb)
Warhead:	HE: 2.5kg (5.5lb)
Maximum velocity:	342m/sec (1120ft/sec)
Range:	7060m (7725yd)

The Opel company built about 300 15cm (5.9in) Panzerwerfer 42 vehicles in the latter part of 1942. They proved to be of sufficient tactical value that they were in use for the rest of the war, particularly on the Eastern Front.

Left: The Panzerwerfer would often be shadowed by a similar vehicle acting as an ammunition carrier, as seen here.

Half-track
The launcher unit was mounted on the rear of the SdKfz 4/1 half-track – an armoured version of the Maultier half-track.

Launcher
A 10-round launcher was developed as the 15cm (5.9in) Panzerwerfer 42, which entered service in 1943.

SOLUTION
The German Nebelwerfer rocket kicked up a cloud of dirt and debris behind the launcher when the rockets were fired, and left a trail of smoke in the air during their flight, two 'signatures' that could give the location of the launcher. To counter this, the Germans mounted a 10-barrel version on the back of an armoured weapons carrier so that the launcher could be moved rapidly after firing.

RELOAD
The Panzerwerfer 42 featured a 10-tube launcher unit, with a single ripple barrage delivering a devastating area effect on the target. A further 10 missiles would typically be carried within the vehicle for a reload, which took about two minutes.

2cm Flakpanzer 38(t) (1943)

TYPE • *Anti-aircraft* **COUNTRY** • *Germany*

SPECIFICATIONS
(Flakpanzer 38(t) Ausf M)

DIMENSIONS:	Length: 4.61m (15ft 2in); Width: 2.13m (7ft); Height: 2.25m (7ft 5in)
WEIGHT:	9.8 tonnes (10.8 US tons)
ENGINE:	185kW (248hp) Praga AC 6-cylinder petrol
SPEED:	42km/h (26mph)
RANGE:	2200m (7220ft)
ARMAMENT:	1 x 20mm (0.79in) Flak 38 L/65 cannon
RATE OF FIRE:	120–180rpm
CREW:	5

Although the Luftwaffe had established air superiority during the Blitzkrieg campaigns of 1939–40, the Germans recognized the need for light AA weapons that had better mobility than the standard towed guns.

Above: The hull and running gear of the Grille self-propelled heavy infantry gun proved to be extremely reliable and gave the Flakpanzer 38(t) exceptionally good mobility.

FLAKPANZER 38(T)
The Flakpanzer 38(t) anti-aircraft AFV mounted the 2cm (0.79in) Flak 38 L/65 cannon on to the rear of the restructured Panzer 38(t) Model M tank chassis.

PROTECTION
The open-topped fighting compartment was protected by folding upper panels to allow the gun a full 360° traverse at low elevation.

AMMUNITION
Inside the vehicle there was space alongside the five-man crew sufficient to store 1040 rounds of the 20mm (0.79in) ammunition.

MASS PRODUCTION
Under mass production, the Flak 38 became the Army's standard flak weapon and supplanted the 2cm (0.79in) Flak 30. Employed by all branches of the Wehrmacht, it also appeared mounted on various fixed and mobile platforms. The combined total of Flak 30s and 38s in service peaked in March 1944 at 19,692 before declining sharply to 10,531 by February 1945.

INVASION OF DENMARK, 1940
This German gunner is performing the classic role of the battlefield flak weapons – providing air cover for armour and infantry columns. Even at the time of its introduction, it was recognized that the firepower of the Flakpanzer 38(t) was inadequate. The initial solution was to modify the Panzer IV to mount the 20mm (0.79in) Flakvierling 38 and 37mm (1.46in) Flak 43.

160mm Model 1943 (1943)

TYPE • *Mortar* **COUNTRY** • *Soviet Union*

SPECIFICATIONS

Calibre:	160mm (6.3in)
Barrel length:	2896mm (114in)
Weight in action:	1080.5kg (2380lb)
Elevation (max):	50°
Traverse:	17°
Maximum range:	5150m (16,896ft)
Minimum range:	750m (2460ft)
Bomb type and weight:	HE: 41.4kg (90.1lb)
Rate of fire:	3rpm

The Model 1943 mortar started out to be simply a larger edition of the 120mm (4.7in) mortar M38, but it was soon apparent that drop-loading a 40kg (90lb) bomb into a 3m (9ft 11in) barrel was asking a lot of the gunners, and it was re-designed as a breechloading weapon.

Above: A Lend-Lease US6 U3 – a much-appreciated American import – tows a 160mm (6.3in) Model 1943 heavy mortar.

Barrel cradle
The barrel sat in a cradle that was attached to the usual baseplate and tripod, so that it could be hinged forward, rather like a shotgun, to expose the rear end of the barrel for loading.

Loading
The bomb was loaded, retained in place by a catch and the barrel swung back into the cradle, which in effect closed the breech. There was also a substantial recoil system to soak up some of the firing shock and prevent it burying the baseplate too deeply.

Ammunition
The Model 1943 was the largest of all the Red Army's wartime mortars – its 41.4kg (90.1lb) bomb shown here was exceptionally powerful and almost three times the weight of that fired by the 120mm (4.7in) mortar.

SOVIET MORTAR CO.

In offensive operations, the Red Army mortar company's primary role was to lay down supporting fire for the battalion's leading rifle platoons. During the general artillery preparation preceding a Red Army infantry attack, the company concentrated on neutralizing enemy infantry positions and clearing paths for the assault force by blowing gaps through minefields and wire entanglements. As the Soviet infantry deployed, the mortars joined with the artillery in providing general covering fire.

MUSEUM MODEL 1943
The size and range of the Model 1943 made it very much an artillery weapon, which was fitted with wheels for towing by an artillery tractor. Brigades of 32 mortars were fielded as part of the Breakthrough Artillery Divisions raised from 1942 onwards.

Flakpanzer IV (Wirbelwind) (1944)

TYPE • *Anti-aircraft* **COUNTRY** • *Germany*

SPECIFICATIONS

DIMENSIONS:	Length: 5.92m (19.42ft); Width: 2.9m (9.51ft); Height: 2.7m (8.86ft)
WEIGHT:	22 tonnes (24.25 US tons)
ENGINE:	1 x HL 120 Maybach 12-cylinder petrol, developing 200kW (268hp)
SPEED:	38km/h (24mph)
RANGE:	200km (125 miles)
ARMOUR:	60mm (2.36in)
ARMAMENT:	4 x 20mm (0.79in) Flak 38 L/112.5 cannon
CREW:	5

There are two conflicting versions of the Wirbelwind's development – the more prosaic is that it originated with an official requirement issued in early 1944, and the alternative explanation is that it arose from the inventiveness of 12th SS Panzer Division 'Hitlerjugend' (Hitler Youth).

CREW
The vehicle was operated by a five-man crew, consisting of a commander/gunner, two loaders, a driver and a radio operator.

Left: The Wirbelwind was an attempt to enhance the mobile firepower of front-line German units.

GUN MOUNT
Four 20mm (0.79in) Flak 38 L/112.5 cannon were set into a nine-sided armoured turret, which was then mounted on the chassis of battle-damaged Panzer IV tanks.

MOBILITY
Power came from a single HL 120 Maybach 12-cylinder petrol, developing 200kW (268hp), pushing the vehicle to a top speed of 38km/h (24mph).

REQUIREMENT
The official requirement behind the Wirbelwind stated that all future Flakpanzers should have:

- A fully armoured three- or four-man rotating turret.
- At least a twin-barrel weapon installation.
- An overall height of less than 3m (9ft 10in).
- Adequate ammunition stowage.
- Easy access to the turret.
- Good turret ventilation and gun fume extraction.

WESTERN FRONT WIRBELWIND
A Wirbelwind crew in Europe scan the skies vigilantly for Allied airpower. Although the Wirbelwind was developed primarily as an anti-aircraft weapon, it could also provide heavy ground fire, devastating against infantry or light vehicles.

Multiple Gun Motor M19 (1944)

TYPE • *Anti-aircraft* **COUNTRY** • *United States*

SPECIFICATIONS

DIMENSIONS:	Length: 5.81m (19ft 1in); Width: 2.93m (9ft 7in); Height: 2.96m (9ft 8in)
WEIGHT:	17.9 tonnes (19.73 US tons)
ENGINE:	Twinned 148kW (110hp) Cadillac 44T4 petrol (gasoline)
SPEED:	56km/h (35mph)
RANGE:	161km (100 miles)
ARMOUR:	6.4–12.7mm (0.25–0.5in)
ARMAMENT:	2 x 40mm (1.57in) Bofors M2
CREW:	6

The final class of fully tracked self-propelled guns (SPGs) that the US Army developed during the war were self-propelled anti-aircraft guns (SPAAGs). During 1943–44, the Ordnance Department developed the T65E1 prototype SPAAG.

Right: This view of an M19 SPAAG reveals its paired 40mm (1.57in) auto-cannon housed in a fully rotating rear-located turret; note also the torsion-bar suspension.

ELEVATION
The M2 auto-cannon had a wide elevation range of between -3° and +85°.

ARMOUR
The M19 was lightly armoured with RHA plates of 6.4–12.7mm (0.25–0.5in) thickness, some sloped at 45–59°.

AMMUNITION
The six-crew M19 carried 352 rounds for its main armament and it could also tow an M28 ammunition trailer that carried a further 320 rounds.

MASS PRODUCTION
The T65E1 prototype sported two 40mm (1.57in) Bofors M2 auto-cannon in a rear-located fully rotating open-roofed turret mounted on the prototype chassis of the M24 Chaffee light tank. The T65E1 prototype was subsequently accepted for mass production as the Multiple Gun Motor Carriage (MGMC) M19 in May 1944. Cadillac manufactured 285 M19s before the war's end.

M19 PERFORMANCE
The M19 was powered by twinned 148kW (110hp) Cadillac Series 44T4 petrol (gasoline) engines. With running gear of five large road wheels per side on torsion springs, and a twin hydramatic transmission, this SPAAG could obtain a top road speed of 56km/h (35mph).

Warships

Naval power was forever reshaped by World War II. Prior to 1939, the world's navies still regarded the battleship as the premier instrument of global power projection. By the end of the war, however, the great battleships were often regarded as little more than vulnerable liabilities, prey to the new generations of combat aircraft and submarines. Aircraft carriers and submarines became the most important strategic naval assets. In the Atlantic, for example, the chief battle was fought by Allied convoys and their escorts against the predatory German U-boats. In the Pacific, American aircraft carriers steadily – then overwhelmingly – tipped the balance of the maritime conflict, aided by an increasingly capable fleet of US submarines. But beyond battleships, aircraft carriers and submarines, many of the campaigns were dominated by a vast range of amphibious, combat and logistics vessels.

TIRPITZ
Crewmen gather on the deck of the great German battleship *Tirpitz*, while she was moored in a Norwegian fjord, c. 1942–44. One of the ship's 380mm (15in) gun turrets is trained abeam, hinting at the immense firepower the ship commanded.

HMS *Queen Elizabeth* (1915)

TYPE • *Battleship* **COUNTRY** • *United Kingdom*

The Queen Elizabeth's speed and firepower set them apart as a separate battleship squadron, intended to pursue and outflank an enemy fleet and force it into battle with the Grand Fleet. However, they were not used in this way at Jutland.

SPECIFICATIONS

Dimensions:	Length: 195.34m (640ft 11in); Beam: 27.6m (90ft 7in); Draught: 9.1m (29ft 10in)
Displacement:	27,940 tonnes (30,798 US tons)
Propulsion:	Quadruple screws, 4 Parsons geared turbines, 24 Babcock & Wilcox boilers, 55,927kW (75,000shp)
Speed:	46.3km/h (23 knots; 26.5mph)
Range:	9300km (5800 miles; 5000nm) at 12 knots
Armament:	8 × 381mm (15in) guns; 16 × 152mm (6in) guns; 2 × 76mm (3in) AA guns; 4 × 533mm (21in) torpedo tubes
Armour:	Belt: 330–102mm (13–4in); Bulkheads: 152–102mm (6–4in); Barbettes: 254–102mm (10–4in); Turrets: 330–127mm (13–5in)
Complement:	951

Left: His Majesty King George V on board HMS Queen Elizabeth *in 1918, during the final year of World War I.*

Catapult
From 1939 to 1943 an aircraft catapult was installed on the boat deck. Four floatplanes could be carried. But from 1943 the British dispensed with aircraft on battleships, relying on carrier-borne planes for scouting.

Guns
AA guns – 20mm (0.79in) – were fitted on the super-firing turrets; up to 52 of these guns were installed during World War II in addition to 32 40mm (1.6in) eight-barrelled AA guns and 16 four-barrelled heavy machine guns.

Radar
From 1941 Type 273 (sea search) radar was carried on the foremast, the aerial rotating within a protective plastic cylinder.

BIG GUNS
Laid down at Portsmouth Dockyard on 27 October 1912, launched on 16 October 1913 and commissioned on 19 January 1915, *Queen Elizabeth*'s design was influenced by reports and rumours about the battleship designs of other powers, suggesting that the United States and Germany were planning heavier-calibre naval guns. Consequently, 381mm (15in) guns were ordered, and although only eight were to be mounted, it was felt that their weight of impact would more than make up for their number.

AERIAL VIEW
HMS *Queen Elizabeth* is here seen under steam off the US east coast, in June 1943, following her repair and overhaul at the Norfolk Navy Yard. She returned to the UK to again join the Home Fleet for a few months before being sent in January 1944 as flagship of the Eastern Fleet.

Conte di Cavour (1915)

TYPE • *Battleship* **COUNTRY** • *Italy*

SPECIFICATIONS (As built)	
DIMENSIONS:	Length: 237.76m (780ft 3in); Beam: 32.82m (107ft 8in); Draught: 9.6m (31ft 6in)
DISPLACEMENT:	40,724 tonnes (44,891 US tons) standard
PROPULSION:	8 Yarrow boilers, 4 steam turbines, 4 screws developing 95,600kW (128,200shp)
SPEED:	56km/h (30 knots; 35mph)
RANGE:	8480km (4580nm; 5270 miles) at 30km/h (16 knots; 18mph)
ARMAMENT:	9 × 381mm (15in) guns; 12 × 152mm (6in) guns; 4 × 120mm (4.7in)/40 guns; 12 × 90mm (3.5in) anti-aircraft guns; 20 × 37mm (1.5in) guns; 20 × 20mm (0.79in) guns
ARMOUR:	Belt: 280mm (11in) + 70mm (3in); Deck: 90–150mm (3.5–5.9in); Barbettes: 350mm (14in); Turrets: 380mm (15in)
COMPLEMENT:	1830

The *Conte di Cavour* was one of Italy's contributions to the dreadnought era, initially equipped with three triple-gun and two twin-gun turrets mounting 305mm (12in) firepower. The ship was commissioned in 1915 and saw service in both world wars.

Below: Conte di Cavour *saw service over a 30 year period, surviving the British attack on the harbour at Taranto in November 1940.*

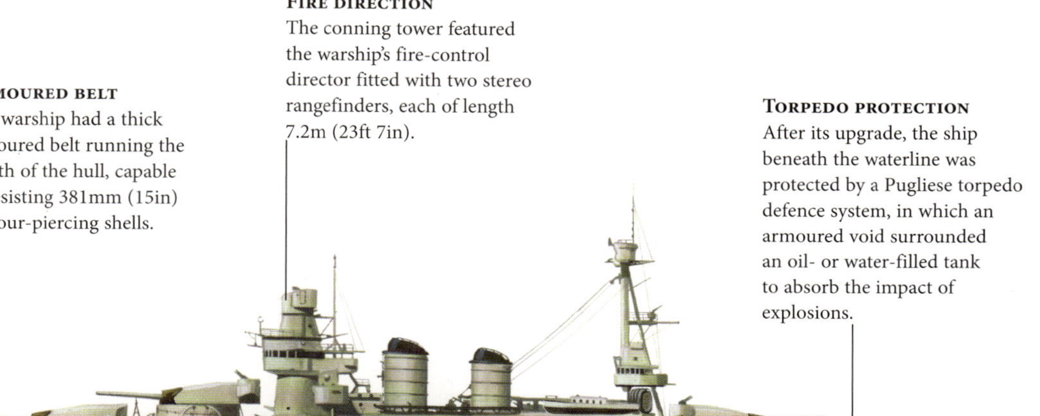

***CONTE DI CAVOUR* OFF NAPLES, 1938**
This photograph of the *Conte di Cavour* was taken as she emerged from her major period of reconstruction. The overall appearance of the ship was now more emphatically modern, and it was faster, bigger, more capably armed and had a large complement.

RECONSTRUCTION
The *Conte di Cavour* underwent a major reconstruction between 1933 and 1937. One of the biggest changes was to remove a triple-gun turret from the amidships position; all main guns were also bored out to 320mm (12.6in) calibre. The ship's bow section was reconfigured, which added another 10m (33ft) to the overal length of the ship. Turbines and boilers were also upgraded.

HMS *Warspite* (1915)

TYPE • *Battleship* **COUNTRY** • *United Kingdom*

SPECIFICATIONS

DIMENSIONS:	Length: 196.2m (643ft 8in); Beam: 27.6m (90ft 7in); Draught: 10.1m (33ft 2in)
DISPLACEMENT:	31,818 tonnes (36,497 US tons)
PROPULSION:	Quadruple screws, 4 Parsons geared turbines, 24 Yarrow boilers, 55,927kW (75,000shp)
SPEED:	46.3km/h (23 knots; 26.5mph)
RANGE:	9300km (5800 miles; 5000nm) at 12 knots
ARMAMENT:	8 × 381mm (15in) guns; 16 × 152mm (6in) guns; 2 × 76mm (3in) AA guns; 4 × 533mm (21in) torpedo tubes
ARMOUR:	Belt: 330–102mm (13–4in); Bulkheads: 152–102mm (6–4in); Barbettes: 254–102mm (10–4in); Turrets: 330–127mm (13–5in)
COMPLEMENT:	1025

Laid down in 1912 as fast battleships to replace battlecruisers as the offensive element of the British battle fleet, the Queen Elizabeth class of dreadnoughts included the *Barham*, *Malaya*, *Valiant* and *Warspite*. A sixth vessel, *Argonaut*, was never built.

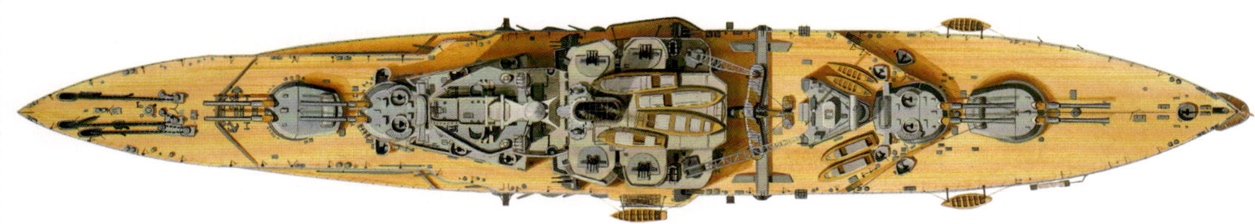

Above: Although they were handsome vessels, their handling was not as good as it might have been. They were seriously overweight because the designers attempted to incorporate too many innovations.

SUPERSTRUCTURE
A distinguishing feature of this class was the heavy tripod foremast and pole-type mainmast. The conning tower was redesigned and enlarged during reconstruction.

FIRE CONTROL
The Queen Elizabeth class had the benefit of a very accurate fire-control system, which had left a profound impression on the Germans at the Battle of Jutland in 1916.

FIREPOWER
The Queen Elizabeth class were the first battleships to mount 381mm (15in) guns. Their firepower was designed to overwhelm any existing enemy battleship.

SURVIVOR
All the Queen Elizabeth class survived World War II except *Barham*, which exploded after being hit by three torpedoes off Sollum on 25 November 1941. Like *Queen Elizabeth*, *Valiant* was badly damaged by Italian frogmen and was further damaged in a series of accidents in 1944, being broken up in 1948. *Malaya* was also broken up in 1948, having survived a torpedo attack in 1941. *Warspite*, having suffered severe damage in the Mediterranean in 1941 and again in 1943, was scrapped in 1947.

WORK ON DECK, 1948
A line of sailors on the foredeck of HMS *Warspite* haul up stores amid piles of chains and cables beneath the warship's famous 381mm (15in) guns in March 1948.

USS *Nevada* (1916)

TYPE • *Battleship* **COUNTRY** • *United States*

The United States' first 'mighty super-dreadnoughts', the two ships of the Nevada class, incorporated a number of new features, including a revised armour arrangement, oil-firing and triple turrets.

SPECIFICATIONS

Dimensions:	Length: 177.8m (583ft 4in); Beam: 29m (95ft 2in); Draught: 8.7m (28ft 6in)
Displacement:	27,941 tonnes (27,500 US tons)
Propulsion:	Twin shafts, 2 Curtis turbines, 19,761kW (26,500shp), 12 Yarrow boilers, 2 geared cruising turbines
Speed:	38km/h (20.5 knots; 23.6mph)
Range:	14,816km (9206 miles; 8000nm) at 19km/h (10 knots)
Armament:	10 × 356mm (14in) guns; 21 × 127mm (5in) guns; 2 × 76mm (3in) AA guns; 2 × 533mm (21in) torpedo tubes
Armour:	Belt: 343–203mm (13.5–8in); Barbettes: 343mm (13.5in); Turrets: 457–127mm (18–5in); Decks: 76–38mm (3–1.5in)
Complement:	864

Left: Nevada *underway off the Atlantic coast of the United States on 17 September 1944. The ship served in both world wars. In 1946 it was used as a target in the Bikini Atoll atomic bomb tests but remained afloat until sunk by an aerial torpedo on 31 July 1948.*

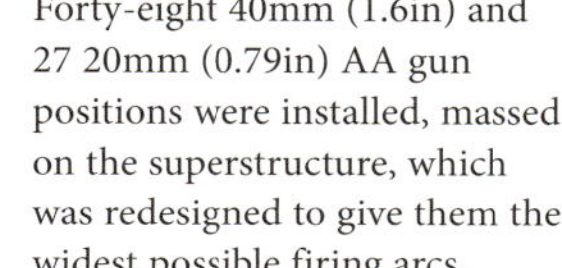

ANTI-AIRCRAFT GUNS
Forty-eight 40mm (1.6in) and 27 20mm (0.79in) AA gun positions were installed, massed on the superstructure, which was redesigned to give them the widest possible firing arcs.

RADAR
This shows *Nevada*'s 1945 appearance after the topmast was heightened in 1943. Both masts carry SRA and SK radar aerials, the latter being added in 1943.

TURRETS
Six of the main guns were in triple turrets, mounted in common cradles, which meant that they could not be individually elevated.

FIRING TESTS
Nevada (BB-36), was laid down at Fore River Shipbuilding Company, at Quincy, Massachusetts, on 4 November 1912, launched on 11 July 1914, and commissioned on 11 March 1916. Firing tests in 1911 showed that light armour was of no value against heavy shells; instead, heavy armour was applied on 122m (400ft) of the waterline, and other vital parts only, on the 'all or nothing' principle that became standard practice in battleship design after 1918.

NEVADA MAIN GUNS
A view across the foredeck towards the turreted main guns. Significant alterations were made to the ship from 1927 to 1929. The secondary battery, originally in casemates below the forecastle deck, was raised to deck level, with the forward and aft guns removed, which made it more usable in rough conditions. The torpedo tubes were taken out and anti-torpedo bulges applied to the hull.

USS *Mississippi* (1916)

TYPE • *Battleship* **COUNTRY** • *United States*

SPECIFICATIONS

Dimensions:	Length: 190.2m (624ft); Beam: 29.7m (97ft 5in); Draught: 9.1m (29ft 10in)
Displacement:	32,513 tonnes (35,839 US tons)
Propulsion:	Quadruple shafts, Curtis turbines, 23,862kW (32,000shp), 9 Babcock & Wilcox boilers
Speed:	38.9km/h (21 knots; 24.2mph)
Range:	15,000km (9200 miles) at 19km/h (10 knots; 11.5mph)
Armament:	12 × 356mm (14in)/50-calibre guns; 14 × 127mm (5in)/51-calibre guns; 4 × 76mm (3in)/50-calibre guns; 2 × 533mm (21in) torpedo tubes
Armour:	Belt: 343–203mm (13.5–8in); Barbettes: 343mm (13.5in); Turrets: 457–127mm (18–5in); Decks: 89–38mm (3.5–1.5in)
Complement:	1084

***Mississippi* was part of the New Mexico class, the first US battleships fitted with clipper bows. The Navy Board had wanted a completely new battleship design, but the government opted for a repetition of the preceding Pennsylvania class, with minor alterations.**

Left: From 1943 through to 1945, Mississippi *was engaged in many actions in the Pacific, bombarding shore positions and supporting troop landings.*

Triple turrets
The 356mm (14in)/50-calibre guns were of a new (at first not entirely satisfactory) design in which each gun in the triple turrets could be trained independently.

Armour
In the manner established with USS *Nevada*, the armour was 'all or nothing', but the bulkheads and the armoured deck were 12.5mm (0.5in) thicker as a result of weight savings elsewhere.

Launcher
The original aircraft test launcher was simply a wooden platform atop 'X' turret. By this time, a catapult and crane have been fitted.

BATTERY POSITION
Mississippi (BB-41) was the first of the class to be laid down, at Newport News, on 5 April 1915, launched on 25 January 1917 and completed on 18 December 1917. Previous battleships had carried their secondary armament in casemates below the conning tower with constant problems of unusability if a high sea was running. In *Mississippi*, the batteries were on the weather deck and suffered far less from wetness; lower-level bow and stern guns in the hull were removed, and the positions plated over.

LATTICE MASTS
On 19 July 1919, *Mississippi* was deployed to the Pacific Fleet at San Pedro, California, remaining there until a refit at Norfolk Navy Yard in 1931–33 when the original lattice masts (seen here) were removed and the foremast replaced by a tower structure.

HMS *Royal Sovereign* (1916)

TYPE • *Battleship* **COUNTRY** • *United Kingdom*

SPECIFICATIONS

Dimensions:	Length: 190.3m (624ft 3in); Beam: 27m (88ft 6in); Draught: 8.7m (28ft 6in)
Displacement:	28,449 tonnes (28,000 US tons)
Propulsion:	Quadruple shafts, Parsons turbines, 29,828kW (40,000shp), 18 Yarrow boilers
Speed:	42.6km/h (23 knots; 26.5mph)
Range:	13,000km (8100 miles) at 19km/h (10 knots; 11.5mph)
Armament:	8 × 381mm (15in)/42-calibre guns; 14 × 152mm (6in)/45-calibre guns; 2 × 76mm (3in) AA guns; 4 × 3-pounder guns; 4 × 533mm (21in) torpedo tubes
Armour:	Belt: 330–25mm (13–1in); Barbettes: 254–102mm (10–4in); Turret faces: 330mm (13in); Conning tower: 280mm (11in)
Complement:	997

Final ship of the Revenge class, *Royal Sovereign* served with the Grand Fleet during World War I and was extensively used on convoy escort in World War II. The five Revenge-class ships were the major part of Britain's 1913 naval programme.

Left: Royal Sovereign *was laid down at Portsmouth on 15 January 1914 (the year after the previous ship of the same name was scrapped), launched on 29 April 1915 and completed in May 1916, just too late to participate in the Battle of Jutland.*

Tower
By 1939, *Royal Sovereign* had a black funnel cowl and clinker screen fitted. The mast was built up as a multi-stage tower.

Platforms
Flying-off platforms were fitted to 'B' and 'X' turrets in 1917. Later, a catapult was fitted on the quarter deck, but this was removed early in World War II.

Profile
The class was designed with a low metacentric height (GM), the aim being a slower roll period, an easier gun-laying capability and therefore more accurate long-range accuracy.

REFIT
The ship was part of the 1st Battle Squadron from 1916 to 1919, first with the Grand Fleet. Following spells in reserve and as a training ship, and a 1937 refit, in which four twin 102mm (4in) guns were mounted and two-pounder pom-pom guns housed in sponsons constructed on each side of the funnel, it steamed huge distances as a convoy escort both in the Atlantic and Far East. By this time, it was obsolescent, certainly no match for the new Japanese battleships.

ROYAL SOVEREIGN SAIL-PAST
Royal Sovereign was a majestic ship in its heyday. In 1944, however, it was secretly handed over to the Soviet Navy and operated as *Archangelsk* in Arctic waters, before being returned to Britain in February 1949. It was sold for breaking in the same year.

Ise (1917)

SPECIFICATIONS

Dimensions:	Length: 205.8m (675ft); Beam: 28.7m (94ft 2in); Draught: 8.8m (29ft 10in)
Displacement:	31,762 tonnes (35,011 US tons)
Propulsion:	Quadruple shafts, Curtis turbines, 33,556kW (45,000shp), 24 Kampon boilers
Speed:	42.6km/h (23 knots; 26.4mph)
Range:	15,000km (9320 miles) at 19km/h (10 knots; 11.5mph)
Armament:	12 × 356mm (14in)/45-calibre guns; 20 × 140mm (5.5in)/50-calibre guns; 4 × 79mm (3.1in) AA guns; 6 × 533mm (21in) torpedo tubes
Armour:	Belt: 305–102mm (12–4in); Barbettes and turrets: 305–203mm (12–8in); Decks: 55–34mm (2.2–1.5in)
Complement:	1360

Beginning its career as a World War I coal-burning battleship, the Japanese battleship *Ise* passed through various changes to end up as a 'battleship carrier' in World War II before being sunk in July 1945.

Left: Laid down at the Kawasaki yard, Kobe, Japan, on 10 May 1915, Ise *was launched on 12 November 1916 and completed on 15 December 1917.*

Crane
More reconstruction took place in 1931–32 at Kure, Japan, with the fitting of a catapult and crane on the fantail. New machinery was installed between August 1935 and March 1937.

AA guns
Final AA armament was eight twin-mount 127mm (5in) guns and 57 Type 96 25mm (1in) guns, 19 of them in triple mountings.

Radar
The battleship was fitted with Type 21 air-search radar and two sets of Type 22 surface-search radar.

BATTLESHIP-CARRIER
After Midway, Japan lacked carrier strength, and *Ise* was converted to a hybrid 'battleship-carrier', with a hangar and 70m (230ft) aircraft deck replacing Nos. 5 and 6 turrets. Twenty-two dive-bombers could be carried. AA armament was increased, and Type 21 air-search and Type 22 surface-search radar fitted. In fact, the ship, completed in this form on 5 September 1943, was never used as a carrier, though participated in the Leyte Gulf battle (23–26 October 1944), when it was damaged by bombs.

WRECK OF THE *ISE*, OCTOBER 1945
From February 1945, the *Ise* remained docked at Kure and was sunk by 16 bombs on 28 July. Remaining partially above water, it was dismantled on site in 1946–47.

HMS *Walker* (W class) (1918)

TYPE • *Destroyer* **COUNTRY** • *United Kingdom*

Launched in November 1917 and commissioned the following February, HMS *Walker* served through and survived all six years of World War II, principally in the role of troopship and convoy escort.

SPECIFICATIONS

Dimensions:	Length: 91m (300ft) overall; Beam: 8.15m (26ft 9in); Draught: 2.7m (8ft 10in)
Displacement:	1117 tonnes (1231 US tons)
Propulsion:	3 Yarrow type water-tube boilers, Brown-Curtis steam turbines, 2 shafts, developing 20,134kW (27,000shp)
Speed:	63km/h (34 knots; 39mph)
Range:	6000km (3500nm; 4039 miles) at 28km/h (15 knots; 17.3mph)
Armament:	4 × QF 102mm (4in) Mk V guns (mount P Mk.I); 2 × QF 40mm (2-pounder) Mk II 'pom-pom' or 1 × QF 76mm (3in) 20 cwt (mount HA Mk.II); 6 (2x3) tubes for 533mm (21in) torpedoes
Complement:	110

Below: HMS Walker served during the final six months of World War I, acting as a mine layer.

Performance
As with all the ships of its class, *Walker* was a fast vessel, with a maximum speed of 63km/h (34 knots; 39mph) from its two steam turbines.

Armament
The heaviest firepower available to HMS *Walker* was its QF 102mm (4in)- Mk V gun, which could perform both anti-aircraft and low-angle fire.

Admiralty W Class
HMS *Walker* was specifically of the Admiralty W class. These were largely of the Admiralty V-class design, but with triple torpedo tube mountings.

HEAVY SEAS
Here HMS *Walker* labours in heavy seas during convoy escort duties. In total, British shipyards built 67 V- and W-class destroyers, making them among the most prolific Royal Navy warship types of the conflict.

D-DAY SERVICE
HMS *Walker* performed regular, arduous convoy escort duties during World War II, guiding merchant ships through the Western Approaches or making the perilous run through Arctic waters to northern Russia. During the Normandy landings of June 1944, however, the warship was tasked with escorting troopships to the invasion beaches, as well as supporting logistics vessels once the beachhead had been established.

HMS *Hood* (1920)

TYPE • *Battleship* **COUNTRY** • *United Kingdom*

At the time of its launch in 1918, HMS *Hood* was the Royal Navy's largest warship, intended as the first of five vessels, bigger and more heavily gunned than the German Mackensen class (begun, but never completed).

SPECIFICATIONS

Dimensions:	Length: 262m (859ft 7in); Beam: 31.8m (104ft 4in); Draught: 9.8m (32ft 2in)
Displacement:	41,859 tonnes (46,128 US tons) standard
Propulsion:	24 × Yarrow small-tube boilers, 4 Brown-Curtis geared turbines, 4 screws, developing 107,381kW (144,000shp)
Speed:	57.4km/h (31 knots; 35.9mph)
Range:	9260km (5000 nm; 5750 miles) at 33.3km/h (18 knots; 20.8mph)
Armament:	8 × 381mm (15in) guns; 12 × 140mm (5.5in) guns; 4 × 102mm (4in) AA guns; 6 × 533mm (21in) torpedo tubes
Armour:	Belt: 152–305mm (6–12in); Forecastle deck: 44–50mm (1.75–2in); Main deck: 19–76mm (0.75–3in); Upper deck: 19–76mm (0.75–3in); Lower deck: 25–76mm (1–3in); Barbettes: 127–305mm (5–12in); Turrets: 279–381mm (11–15in)
Complement:	1433

Left: In American waters, c.June–July 1924. Few modifications were made in the Hood's lifetime. A major refit had been planned, but was shelved with the advent of war in 1939.

Boilers
Hood was the first British capital ship to be equipped with small-tube boilers. It had 24 Yarrow three-drum boilers, operating at a pressure of 16.5kg/cm² (235psi).

Superstructure
Hood had a more substantial superstructure than earlier ships to accommodate a wider range of control equipment. Fire-control directors were positioned above the conning tower and on the foremast, with a transmission station and an emergency steering position located in the conning tower.

Propellers
The turbines were housed in three compartments, with the forward set driving both outer propellers, and the middle and aft sets driving the port and starboard propellers, respectively.

ARMOUR
Given that *Hood* was destroyed by shellfire from *Bismarck* and *Prinz Eugen* on 24 May 1941, much focus has been on the ship's armour. The armour had already been increased during construction. The side armour was graded in four bands, from 305mm (12in) at the waterline to 127mm (5in) at the forecastle deck. Anti-torpedo bulges extended up to the top of the 305mm (12in) belt. Protection accounted for 33 per cent of the displacement.

HMS *HOOD*, 1921
HMS *Hood* seen in 1921, a year in which she conducted long-range voyages between the Mediterranean and South America. The terrible end to this noble ship was caused by a massive explosion in the aft magazine, triggered by an armour-piercing shell from one of the German ships.

Nagato (1920)

TYPE • *Battleship* **COUNTRY** • *Japan*

SPECIFICATIONS (Pre-1935)

Dimensions:	Length: 215.8m (708ft); Beam: 29m (95ft 3in); Draught: 9.1m (29ft 9in)
Displacement:	32,720 tonnes (36,045 US tons) standard
Propulsion:	21 boilers (15 oil, 6 coal), 4 Gihon turbines, 4 screws, developing 59,656kW (80,000shp)
Speed:	49.6km/h (26.75 knots; 31mph)
Range:	10,550km (5700 nm; 6560 miles) at 29.6km/h (16 knots; 18.4mph)
Armament:	8 × 406mm (16in) guns; 20 × 140mm (5.5in) guns; 4 × 76mm (3in) AA guns; 8 × 533mm (21in) torpedo tubes
Armour:	Belt: 102–305mm (4–12in); Deck: Upper 25–44mm (1–1.7in), Lower 50–75mm (2–2.9in); Barbettes: 300mm (11.8in); Turrets: 356mm (14in); Conning tower: Forward 371mm (14.6in), Aft 97mm (3.8in)
Complement:	1333

With the commission of the super-dreadnought *Nagato* in 1920, the Imperial Japanese Navy (IJN) introduced the 406mm (16in) gun. The ship was designed by Yuzuru Hiraga, who aimed to make the IJN a formidable rival to the US Navy (USN).

Left: During sea trials in the 1920s, Nagato *reached 49.4km/h (26.7 knots; 30.7mph), making it faster than any US Navy capital ship at the time.*

Curved funnel
The curved fore funnel was a distinctive feature of the *Nagato* before the ship's 1925 reconstruction.

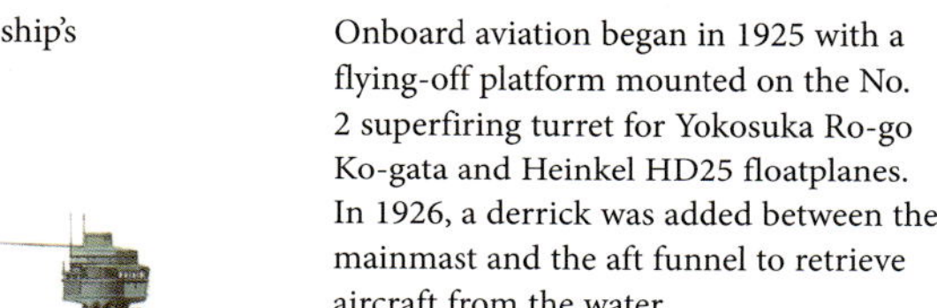

Aircraft
Onboard aviation began in 1925 with a flying-off platform mounted on the No. 2 superfiring turret for Yokosuka Ro-go Ko-gata and Heinkel HD25 floatplanes. In 1926, a derrick was added between the mainmast and the aft funnel to retrieve aircraft from the water.

Propulsion
The propulsion system included 21 Kampon water-tube boilers (15 oil-fired and six coal-fired) powering four Gihon turbines.

INITIAL DESIGN
Heavily revised after the Battle of Jutland, Hiraga's design adopted the 'all or nothing' armour concept, with three armoured decks protecting the machinery and magazines, the main deck being 100mm (4in) thick. The ship also featured significant side protection, including torpedo bulges that extended outside and below the armour belt, which were enlarged in 1936 and used partly for additional oil storage.

CREW WELCOME DIGNITARIES
The *Nagato* underwent several reconstructions, resulting in its final configuration, which included transforming the foremast into a multi-platform tower, removing the curved fore funnel in 1925, installing 10 new Kampon boilers and fitting new turbines.

V-boats (1924)

TYPE • *Submarine* **COUNTRY** • *United States*

Known initially by the designation V + numeral before they were named in 1931, the V-boats were pivotal in the development of subsequent submarine classes for the US Navy. A total of nine were built between 1921 and 1934.

SPECIFICATIONS

Dimensions:	Length: 113m (37ft 9in); Beam: 10.14m (33ft 3in); Draught: 5.16m (16ft 11in)
Displacement:	2770 tonnes (3053 US tons) surfaced; 4000 tonnes (4410 US tons) submerged
Propulsion:	2 direct-drive diesels producing 1750kW (2350shp), 2 auxiliary 300kW (400shp) charging diesels, 2 600kW (800shp) electric motors
Speed:	26km/h (14 knots; 16mph) surfaced; 12km/h (6.5 knots; 7.5mph) submerged
Range:	17,372km (9380nm; 10,794 miles) surfaced; 166.7km (90nm; 103.6 miles) submerged
Armament:	6 × 533mm (21in) torpedo tubes; 24 torpedoes; 2 × 152mm (6in) 53cal Mk XII Mod2 wet-type deck guns
Complement:	89

Below: V-4, Argonaut *(SM-1), commissioned in April 1928, was the first US submarine of partially welded construction, though riveting was used for the pressure hull and all vital areas.*

Internal layout
The 1941 modifications also included internal rearrangement for conveyance of special mission troops and supplies.

Deck guns
The deck guns were designed for the secondary battery of Lexington-class battle cruisers and South Dakota-class battleships, but were only installed in Omaha-class cruisers.

V-6 Nautilus Refit
In July 1941, a refit provided new radio equipment, two external torpedo tubes at bow and stern, air conditioning and new GM-Winton diesel engines.

US TORPEDOES

The Mk XIV torpedo, dating from 1931, was the standard for US submarines at the start of the war. Despite the remonstrations of submarine crews, its serious defects, chiefly in failing to detonate or under-running the target, were not fully remedied until September 1943. From 1944, a wakeless, electric-powered Mk18 torpedo was available, modelled on the German G7e, and widely used.

NAUTILUS
V-6, *Nautilus* (SS-168), commissioned in 1930, was based on the 'submarine cruiser' concept – large, well-armed, intended for long-range patrols.

HMS *Eagle* (1924)

TYPE • *Aircraft carrier* **COUNTRY** • *United Kingdom*

SPECIFICATIONS	
DIMENSIONS:	Length: 203.5m (667ft 6in); Beam: 35.1m (115ft); Draught (max): 8.1m (26ft 8in)
DISPLACEMENT:	22,200 tonnes (24,469 US tons)
PROPULSION:	32 Yarrow boilers, 4 geared turbines, 37,000kW (50,000shp)
SPEED:	44km/h (24 knots; 28mph)
RANGE:	8,900km (4800nm; 500 miles) at 29.6km/h (16 knots; 18.4mph)
ARMAMENT:	9 x 152mm (6in) guns; 5 x 102mm (4in) AA guns
AIRCRAFT:	24
COMPLEMENT:	791

Like all the first-generation carriers, *Eagle* was not originally intended for the role, and retained much of its battleship appearance even after conversion to an aircraft carrier. Eagle was the first carrier to have an island structure on the flight deck.

Left: HMS Eagle *was originally laid down in 1913 for Chile, as a battleship, purchased in 1918 and converted into an aircarft-carrier in the succeeding years.*

ENGINE ROOM
The engine room instruments were ordered prior to purchase by the British. Uniquely for a British warship, they were calibrated in metric units and labelled in Spanish.

ISLAND
Eagle was the ship that confirmed the starboard placement of the island, although its island, with a huge tripod mast, was larger than most.

TORPEDO BLISTERS
Eagle was fitted with torpedo blisters intended to be capable of absorbing a charge of 52kg/cm² (750psi).

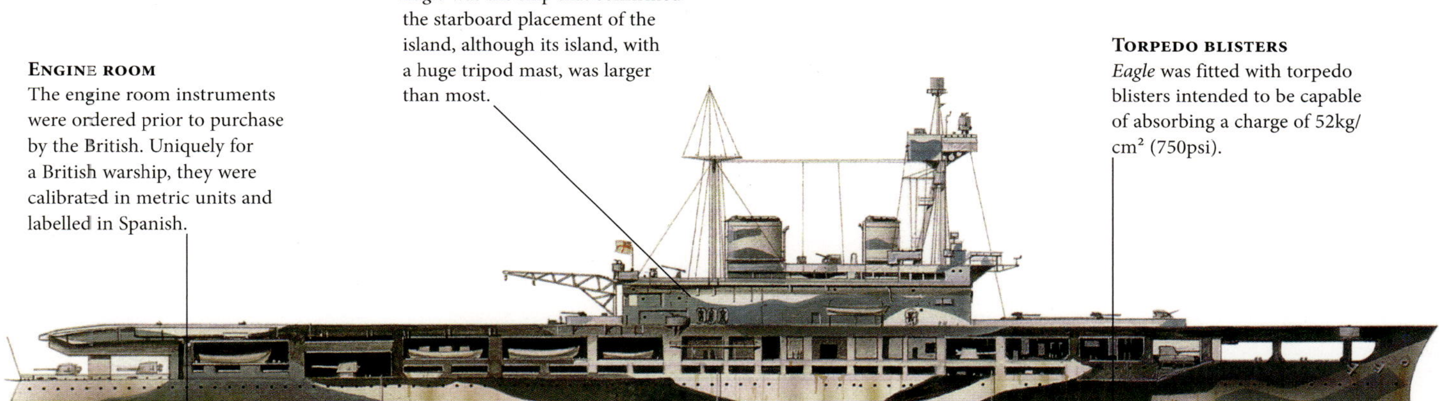

AIRCRAFT
Two aircraft lifts were fitted, one just forward of the island, the other at the stern. *Eagle*'s battleship-type hull restricted it to carry a maximum of 24 aircraft, usually only 20–21. On its final mission, it was carrying 20 Sea Hurricanes; at earlier stages in World War II, it flew Fairey Swordfish, Fairey Flycatchers, Gloster Sea Gladiators and Fairey Fulmars.

FLIGHT DECK
Eagle in the 1930s. While the forward end of the flight deck conformed to the hull shape, at the stern it was canted out to provide a broader landing area.

Akagi (1927)

TYPE • *Aircraft carrier* COUNTRY • *Japan*

SPECIFICATIONS

Dimensions:	Length: 260.6m (855ft); Beam: 31.4m (103ft); Draught: 8.8m (29ft)
Displacement:	37,084 tonnes (40,872 US tons); 41,961 tonnes (46,246 US tons) full load
Propulsion:	19 Kampon boilers, 4 turbines, 4 shafts, 41,013kW (55,000shp)
Speed:	57.3km/h (31 knots; 35.6mph)
Range:	18,520km (10,000nm; 11,510 miles) at 25.9km/h (14 knots; 16.1mph)
Aircraft:	91
Armament:	6 × 354mm (8in) guns; 12 × 120mm (4.7in) guns; 14 × twin 25mm (1in) AA guns
Complement:	1630

Flagship of Japan's Pearl Harbor naval attack fleet, and flagship again at the start of the Battle of Midway in 1942, the aircraft carrier *Akagi* participated in every major action in the early stages of the Pacific War.

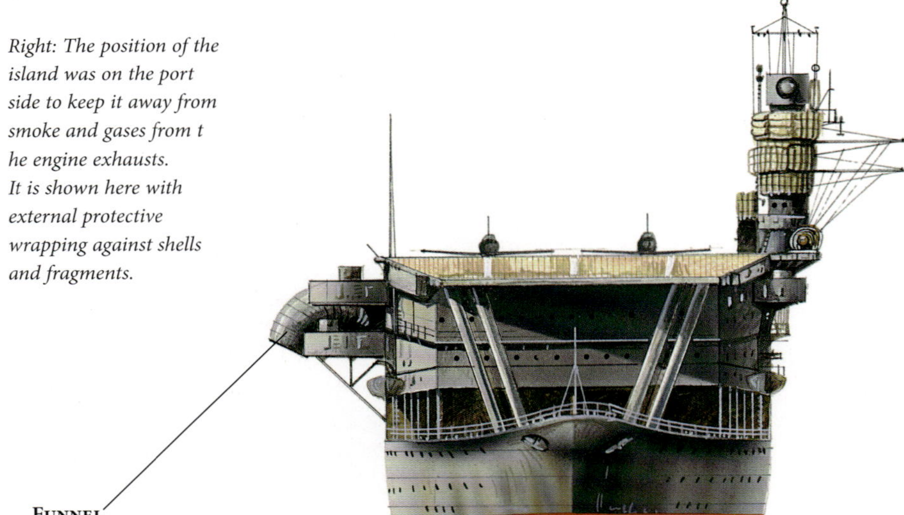

Right: The position of the island was on the port side to keep it away from smoke and gases from t he engine exhausts. It is shown here with external protective wrapping against shells and fragments.

FUNNEL
The funnel had a large vent on the starboard side. Water could be sprayed into the smoke as it left the funnel, making it heavier so that it would not roll up and over the flight deck and interfere with flight operations.

FLIGHT DECK
From 1938, the flight deck was 249.2m (817ft 6in) long. The flight decks of Japanese carriers were wood-laid, with the planks running longitudinally rather than transversely as in US carriers.

HANGAR DECKS
The hangar decks were fully enclosed – a feature that contributed to the ship's destruction when accumulated gas and vapour exploded in the unventilated space.

PEARL HARBOR

On 7 December 1941, *Akagi* launched two waves of aircraft, the first including 15 dive-bombers, 12 torpedo planes and 10 fighter planes; the second formed of eight dive-bombers and nine fighters. The Japanese carriers lost 29 aircraft in the attack, while, apart from the loss of five battleships and damage to numerous other warships, the US lost 239 aircraft in simultaneous raids on the airfields. *Akagi*'s torpedo bombers were responsible for the destruction of USS *Oklahoma* and *West Virginia*. It was a shattering display of naval air power.

AIRCRAFT LAUNCH
Akagi prepares to launch two aircraft from its deck. In 1938, a nine-wire Type 1 hydraulic arrester gear system, developed at Kure, was fitted to the carrier to provide quicker and safer recovery of aircraft using arrester hooks.

HMS *Rodney* (1927)

TYPE • *Battleship* **COUNTRY** • *United Kingdom*

SPECIFICATIONS

Dimensions:	Length: 216.8m (710ft); Beam: 32.4m (106ft); Draught: 9.1m (30ft)
Displacement:	34,493 tonnes (38,019 US tons)
Propulsion:	8 three-drum boilers with superheaters, Brown-Curtis geared turbines, 33,556kW (45,000shp), 2 screws
Armament:	9 × 406mm (16in) guns; 12 × 152mm (6in) guns; 6 × 119mm (4.7in) AA guns; 8 × 2-pounder pom-poms; 2 × 622mm (24.5in) underwater torpedo tubes
Armour:	Belt: 356mm (14in); Barbettes: 381mm (15in); Turret faces: 406mm (16in); Deck: 158mm (6.25in) max
Range:	26,500km (14,300nm; 16,466 miles) at 22.2km/h (12 knots; 13.8mph)
Speed:	42.6km/h (23 knots; 26.5mph)
Complement:	1314

With all its big guns mounted forward, Rodney's design was an unusual departure for the Royal Navy. It represented the compromises necessary to make a big-gun battleship that displaced no more than 36,000 tonnes (39,283 US tons) as specified by the 1922 Washington Treaty.

Left: A 406mm (16in) shell is brought aboard Rodney. *The Mk1 406mm (16in) guns were of wire-wound, built-up type, and 45 calibre (i.e. the barrel length was 45 times the bore).*

Triple turrets
Set in triple turrets, each of the main guns could be aimed individually. Weighing 109.7 tonnes (108 US tons), they could elevate to 40°.

Long forward
Although its armour was substantial, including a deck 158mm (6.25in) thick over the magazine and a maximum of 356mm (14in) on the belt, efforts to keep the weight down resulted in weaknesses that required strengthening of the long forward part of the hull.

Boilers
Rodney and *Nelson* were among the first large warships fitted with three-drum Admiralty boilers.

MODIFICATIONS
Few modifications were made in the ship's career, the advent of war preventing a planned major refit. A catapult was fitted to the aft turret in 1934 and a collapsible aircraft crane was added in 1937. A Fairey Swordfish torpedo bomber was replaced by a Supermarine Walrus amphibian plane. *Rodney* was the first RN battleship to acquire a radar set, a Type 79Y early warning prototype. By 1944, it had a full set of early warning, air- and surface-search and gunnery control radars.

BATTLE FLEET
Rodney presents a formidable sight as it steams in the line of battle. *Rodney*'s most dramatic war action came with participation in the sinking of *Bismarck* in May 1941. In reserve from 1945, it was broken up in 1948–49.

Oberon and Odin classes (1927)

TYPE • *Submarine* **COUNTRY** • *United Kingdom*

HMS *Oberon* signified the start of a new generation of British submarines developed after World War I. Completed in 1927, *Oberon* was advanced for her time, featuring up-to-date instrumentation.

SPECIFICATIONS

Dimensions:	Length: 82m (269ft); Beam: 8.5m (27ft 11in); Draught: 4.6m (15ft 1in)
Displacement:	1332 tonnes (1469 US tons) surfaced; 1922 tonnes (2119 US tons) submerged
Propulsion:	2 Vickers diesels producing 1099kW (1475hp), 2 × 260kW (350shp) electric motors, 2 screws
Speed:	27.8km/h (15 knots; 17.3mph) surfaced; 17km/h (9 knots; 10mph) submerged
Range:	9260km (5000nm; 5755 miles) surfaced; 111km (60nm; 69 miles) submerged
Armament:	8 × 533mm (21in) torpedo tubes; 16 torpedoes; 1 × QF 102mm (4in) deck gun; 2 × 7.7mm (0.303in) Lewis guns
Complement:	56

Above: HMS Odin. Odin, Orpheus *and* Oswald *were sunk by Italian destroyers, while* Olympus *struck a mine off Malta.*

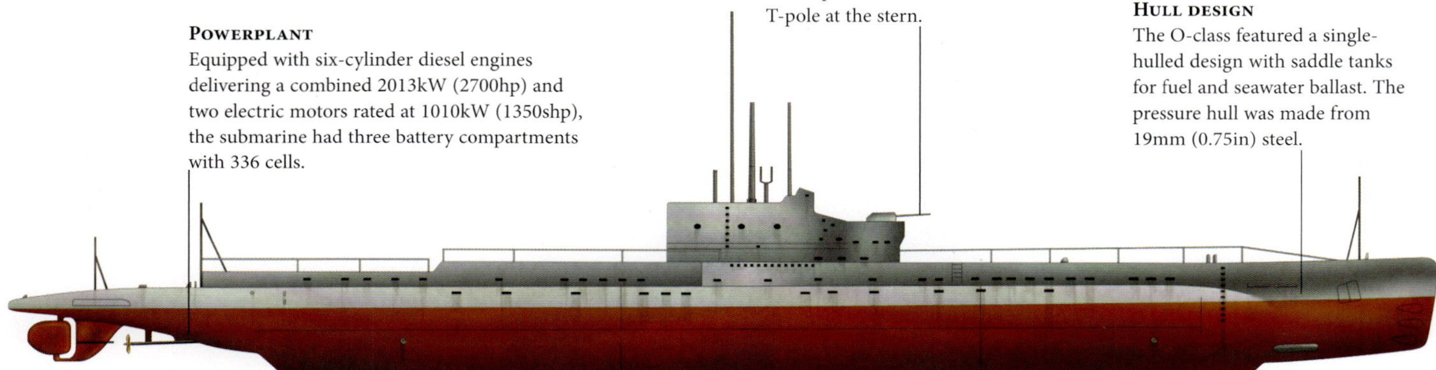

HMS *Oberon*
The substantial tower housed a 102mm (4in) gun on a platform forward of the bridge, with a tall telescopic radio mast linked to a low T-pole at the stern.

Powerplant
Equipped with six-cylinder diesel engines delivering a combined 2013kW (2700hp) and two electric motors rated at 1010kW (1350shp), the submarine had three battery compartments with 336 cells.

Hull design
The O-class featured a single-hulled design with saddle tanks for fuel and seawater ballast. The pressure hull was made from 19mm (0.75in) steel.

CLASS VARIATIONS

While she is often regarded as the lead vessel of the O-class, *Oberon* had substantial differences from her successors. The O-class is more accurately named after HMS *Odin*, which was longer, heavier and more powerful than *Oberon*. There was also the related Parthian class, similar to the Odin class and also designed for long-range patrols in the Far East. They featured a more bulbous bow, were slightly longer and had diesels uprated to 3430kW (4600hp).

HMS *OBERON*
The crew of HMS *Oberon* perform regular maintenance duties at anchor. Placed in reserve from 1937 to 1939, she was used primarily for training during World War II and decommissioned in July 1944.

Chervona Ukraina (1927)

TYPE • *Destroyer* **COUNTRY** • *Soviet Union*

SPECIFICATIONS

Dimensions:	Length: 166.7m (546ft 11in); Beam: 15.7m (51ft 6in); Draught: 6.2m (20ft 4in)
Displacement:	8400 tonnes (9260 US tons)
Propulsion:	14 Yarrow boilers, 4 geared steam turbines, 41,000kW (55,000shp), 4 shafts
Armament:	15 × 130mm (5.1in)/55 B7 Pattern 1913 guns; 3 × 100mm (3.9in)/47 Minizini AA guns; 4 × 45mm (1.8in) 21-K AA guns; 2 × 457mm (18in) triple torpedo tubes; 60–100 mines
Armour:	Upper and lower armoured decks: 20mm (0.79in) each; Gun shields: 25mm (0.98in); Lower armour belt: 76mm (3.0in); Upper armour belt: 25mm (0.98in)
Range:	6900km (3700nm; 4300 miles)
Speed:	54.6km/h (29.5 knots; 33.9mph)
Complement:	830

***Chervona Ukraina*'s wartime service came to an abrupt end in November 1941 when it was sunk off Sevastopol by German dive-bombers. The ship was nevertheless raised in 1947 and thereafter used as a training hulk.**

Left: Chervona Ukraina, *1927–1930 (visible MU-1 / Avro 504 floatplane with initial form of crane, 75mm (2.95in) Meller AA guns).*

Crew
As designed, the warship had a complement of 630 officers and men, but by the time it reached service the actual figure had swelled to more than 800.

Power
The ship's power came from 14 Yarrow water-tube boilers. Four of these were coal-fired while the rest were mixed-firing, using both coal and oil.

Main armament
Chervona Ukraina's main armament consisted of 15 55-calibre 130mm (5.1in) B7 Pattern 1913 guns, all of which were set in single mounts.

SHIP CLASS
The *Chervona Ukraina* belonged to the Admiral Nakhimov class of light cruisers. Four were intended, but only two actually proceeded to the shipyards. These were laid down between 1913 and 1932, but as with many pre-World War I Russian ship types, the Russian Revolution interrupted their construction and they did not enter service until the 1920s and 1930s.

COMMISSIONING
Chervona Ukraina was laid down in October 1913, originally as the *Admiral Nakhimov*, but was commissioned into service under her final name in March 1927.

USS *Lexington* (1927)

TYPE • *Aircraft carrier* **COUNTRY** • *United States*

Laid down first as a battlecruiser, *Lexington* (CV-2) was redesigned as a carrier and taught the US Navy much about sea flying in the 1930s. In 1942, it played a key part in the Battle of the Coral Sea before succumbing to fire after heavy attacks.

SPECIFICATIONS

Dimensions:	Length: 270.66m (888ft); Beam: 32.12m (105ft 5in); Draught: 10.15m (33ft 4in)
Displacement:	38,284 tonnes (42,184 US tons); 43,744 tonnes (48,213 US tons) full load
Propulsion:	16 water-tube boilers, turboelectric drive, 134,226kW (180,000shp), 4 shafts
Speed:	61.5km/h (33.25 knots; 38mph)
Range:	19,456km (10,500nm; 12,075 miles) at 27.7km/h (15 knots; 17.2mph)
Armament:	8 × 203mm (8in) guns; 12 × 127mm (5in) guns
Aircraft:	63
Complement:	2791

Below: Lexington*'s massive funnel structure, separate from the island, gave it a unique and easily recognizable profile.*

Catapult
Until 1936, the ship carried a flywheel-powered F Mk II catapult on the starboard bow, intended to launch seaplanes.

Hangar deck
The hangar deck was enclosed; the explosion of gasoline vapour in the confined space resulted in uncontrollable fire on 8 May 1942, a major factor in the ship's loss.

Armament
Original armament was eight 203mm (8in) guns in quadruple turrets, 12 127mm (5in) and 48 28mm (1.1in) guns. The guns could be depressed to −5° and elevated to +41°.

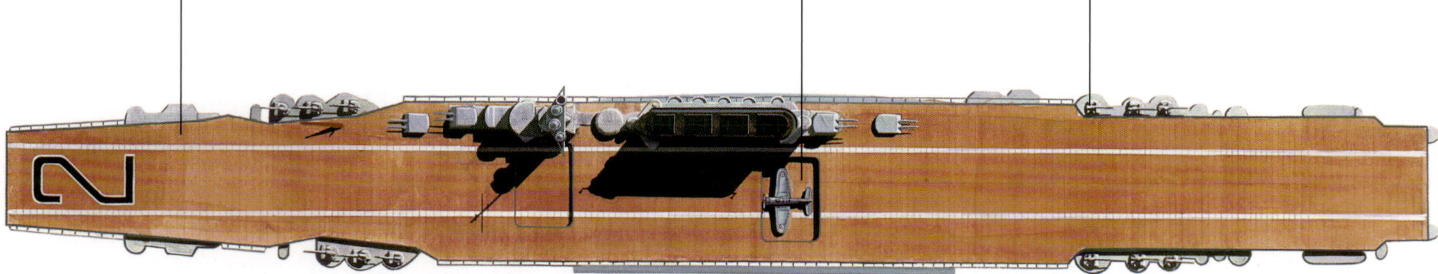

DESTRUCTION

On 8 May 1942, during the Battle of the Coral Sea, *Lexington* was hit by two aerial torpedoes on the port side near the bow as well as three bombs, and it caught fire. At first, the fires appeared to have been extinguished, but leaking vapour from ruptured fuel tanks built up and exploded at 12.47, causing a series of further explosions. The ship developed a heavy list to port, and its captain gave the order to abandon at 17.00. There were 216 fatalities and 2770 survivors. Its orphan aircraft were redeployed to *Yorktown*.

NAVAL BASE
USS *Lexington* with many other American warships at Hawaii during the 1930s. There had been a naval station at Pearl Harbor since 1908, but it was much enlarged in the 1930s as the base of the US Pacific Fleet.

Dekabrist class (1928)

TYPE • *Submarine* **COUNTRY** • *Soviet Union*

SPECIFICATIONS

Dimensions:	Length: 76m (249ft 4in); Beam: 6.5m (21ft); Draught: 3.8m (12ft 6in)
Displacement:	933 tonnes (1028 US tons) surfaced; 1354 tonnes (1492 US tons) submerged
Propulsion	2 shafts with three-bladed propellers, 2 x 809kW (1100hp) MAN/ Kolomna diesels, 2 x 391kW (525hp) PG-20 electric motors, 2 electric creeping motors of 37kW (50hp)
Speed:	26km/h (14 knots; 16mph) surfaced; 17km/h (9 knots; 10mph) submerged
Range:	13,900km (7500nm; 8633 miles) surfaced; 244km (132nm; 152 miles) submerged
Armament:	8 × 533mm (21in) torpedo tubes (6 bow, 2 stern); 14 torpedoes carried; 1 × 100mm (3.9in) 51cal main deck gun; 1 × 45mm (1.8in) 46cal K-21 AA gun; 1 × 7.62mm (0.3in) MG
Complement:	53

The Dekabrist class were the Soviet Navy's first post-World War I class of submarines. Six were built between 1927 and 1929. They were double-hulled, with electric creep motors and a test depth of 90m (295ft).

Left: A Soviet postage stamp from the 1970s shows the D-class submarine D-3 Krasnogvardeyets.

DEKABRIST
Here we see the lead ship of the class, *D-1*. It was launched on 3 November 1928 and lost in a training accident on 13 November 1940 in Motovsky Gulf near Murmansk.

ANCHOR
The Dekabrist submarines were fitted with anchors for submerged use, although this feature was rarely used as it was prone to cause accidents.

TORPEDO TUBES
As well as six torpedo tubes at the bow of the submarine, it had two at the stern.

WARTIME FATES
In total, six Dekabrist-class vessels were launched between November 1928 and November 1930. All saw service in World War II, but only two would survive the conflict. *D-1* was lost in an accident in 1940, while *D-3* and *D-4* were sunk in 1942 and 1943 respectively, likely due to hitting mines. *D-6* was scuttled by her own crew at the Sevastopol dockyard in December 1941 to prevent capture by the Germans.

D-3 KRASNOGVARDEYETS, 1929
The six Dekabrist submarines were deployed to both the Baltic and the Black Sea Fleets. The Black Sea Fleet submarines were used to support Red Army operations during the siege of Odessa (1941) and the Battle of Sevastopol (1941–42).

Pisani and Mameli classes (1928)

TYPE • *Submarine* **COUNTRY** • *Italy*

SPECIFICATIONS
(*Giovanni Bausan*)

DIMENSIONS:	Length: 68.2m (223ft 9in); Beam: 6m (19ft 8in); Draught: 4.9m (16ft 1in)
DISPLACEMENT:	894 tonnes (985 US tons) surfaced; 1075 tonnes (1185 US tons) submerged
PROPULSION:	2 diesel engines 1118.5kW (1500hp), 2 410kW (550hp) electric motors, 2 screws
SPEED:	27.8km/h (15 knots; 17.3mph) surfaced; 5.2km/h (8.2 knots; 9.4mph) submerged
RANGE:	9260km (5000 nm; 5755 miles) at 14.8km/h (8 knots; 9.2mph) surfaced; 113km (61nm; 70 miles) at 7.4km/h (4 knots; 4.6mph) submerged
ARMAMENT:	6 × 533mm (21in) torpedo tubes; 9 torpedoes; 1 × 102mm (4in) deck gun; 2 × single 13.2mm (0.5in) MGs
COMPLEMENT:	49

Unlike most other navies, the Regia Marina had a large and relatively modern submarine force by 1939. These two closely related classes, although designed by different studios, established the standard for future submarine development.

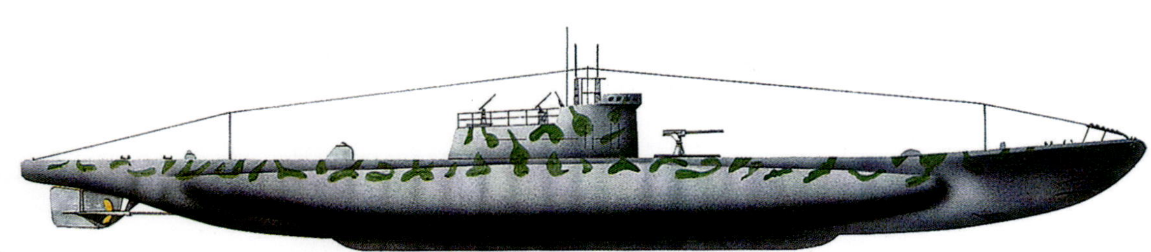

Above: Despite its age and obsolescence, Giovanni da Procida *was on active service until January 1942 and was stricken only in 1948.*

GIOVANNI BAUSAN
Of the Pisani class, *Des Geneys* served as a battery-charging hulk, and *Marcantonio Colonna* was scrapped in 1943. Only *Vettor Pisani* survived the war. *Giovanni Bausan* (show) was converted into an oil barge in the spring of 1942.

STABILITY
The Pisani class had stability issues, partly resolved by adding bulges to the bows. Due to these issues and their outdated design, they saw limited use in World War II.

FUEL CAPACITY
The Pisani class, built at the Triestino yard, had a greater fuel capacity than the Mameli, providing a surface range of 9260km (5000nm; 5755 miles) at 14.8km/h (8 knots.)

DESIGN MODEL

During the 1920s and 1930s, the Italian Navy was in an experimental phase, building only small classes with long construction times, often starting a new version before the previous one was launched. The double hull design, which began in Italy, was a feature of both classes. A typical characteristic was the large tower, which remained on Italian submarines despite making them a more visible target and causing instability on the surface and increased resistance underwater.

SS GOFREDO MAMELI, 1944
The primary external difference of the Mameli class from the Pisani class was that the Mameli boats' 102mm (4in) gun was mounted on a low breakwater platform. Built at the Tosi yard in Taranto, this class was powered by two Franco Tosi four-stroke S8 eight-cylinder diesels producing 1156kW (1550hp).

Kaga (1928)

TYPE • *Aircraft carrier* **COUNTRY** • *Japan*

SPECIFICATIONS

Dimensions:	Length: 247.5m (812ft); Beam: 32.6m (107ft); Draught: 9.45m (31ft)
Displacement:	38,811 tonnes (42,792 US tons); 43,222 tonnes (47,641 US tons) full load
Propulsion:	8 Kampon boilers, 4 Kampon geared turbines, 4 shafts, 95,002kW (127,400shp)
Speed:	52km/h (28 knots; 32mph)
Range:	18,500km (10,000nm; 11,500 miles) at 29.6km/h (16 knots; 18.4mph)
Armament	10 × 203mm (8in) guns; 16 × 127mm (5in) guns; 22 × 25mm AA guns
Aircraft:	90
Complement:	1,708

Planned as a battleship, the Japanese aircraft carrier *Kaga* was part of the Japanese fleet that attacked Pearl Harbor. It went on to engage in other operations in the Pacific before being sunk in the Battle of Midway in 1941.

Above: Japanese carriers could have six arrester wires. Where only three were fitted, hooking on to the second wire was the ideal, and pilots who achieved this were given a pay bonus of 5 yen.

Armament
The ship was heavily armed with 10 203mm (8in) guns and 16 120mm (4.7in) guns, a cruiser-type armament again similar to that of the two American fleet carriers.

Funnels
Japanese carrier designers showed concern for smoke and hot gas turbulence on the flight deck. When they finally followed the British and American practice of installing tall funnels, these were canted outwards.

Island
The profile shows the ship in post-1934 modernized form, with the lower flight decks removed. The small island, essentially a conning tower, was added at that time.

RECONSTRUCTION
A thorough reconstruction of the upperworks was made in 1934–35. *Kaga* emerged with a lengthened hull, a single flight deck laid with longitudinal wood planking above a thin steel base, and an increased displacement. A third aircraft lift was installed and the exits from the boiler uptakes were replaced by a single midships funnel to starboard, canted outwards and downwards to keep the flight deck clear. Removal of the lower take-off decks enabled the hangars to be enlarged and gave the ship capacity to hold 90 aircraft.

FLIGHT OPERATIONS
May 1937, and carrier biplanes stack up for launch from the *Kaga* during operations against China. There was no launch catapult fitted to the carrier, and in fact, no Japanese carriers of the 1920s and 1930s actually carried a catapult.

Köln (1929)

TYPE • *Cruiser* **COUNTRY** • *Germany*

The Kriegsmarine's three K-class cruisers were the public face of the resurgent German Navy during the 1930s. They were a bold new design that used modern techniques such as electric welding in their construction.

SPECIFICATIONS

Dimensions:	Length: 174m (571ft); Beam: 15.29m (50ft 2in); Draught: 5.56m (18ft 3in)
Displacement:	6500 tonnes (7165 US tons)
Propulsion:	6 navy boilers, 2 double-acting 4-stroke 10-cylinder MAN diesel engines, 1300kW (1800shp) diesel power, 48,470kW (65,000shp) turbine power, 2 screws
Speed:	59km/h (32 knots; 37mph)
Range:	10,600km (5700 m; 6600 miles) at 35km/h (19 knots; 22mph)
Armament:	9 × 152mm (6in) main guns; 4 × 88mm guns; 8 × 37mm guns; 8 × 20mm AA guns; 8 × 500mm (19.7in) torpedo tubes; 2 aircraft
Armour:	Belt: 50–70mm (2–2.75in); Torpedo bulkhead: 12mm (0.5in); Turrets: 31mm (1.25in)
Complement:	850

Right: The German cruiser Köln *lies damaged at Wilhelmshaven on 9 May 1945, a British officer inspecting one of its main gun turrets.*

POWERPLANT
A combination of steam and diesel powerplants was fitted, though the two could only function separately. This still allowed for a diesel cruising speed of 19km/h (10 knots; 11.5mph).

MAIN TURRETS
The nine 152mm (6in) main guns were fitted in three triple turrets, one fore and one aft.

REAR TURRETS
The two rear turrets were positioned offset to the centreline and could fire at 40° elevation in all directions.

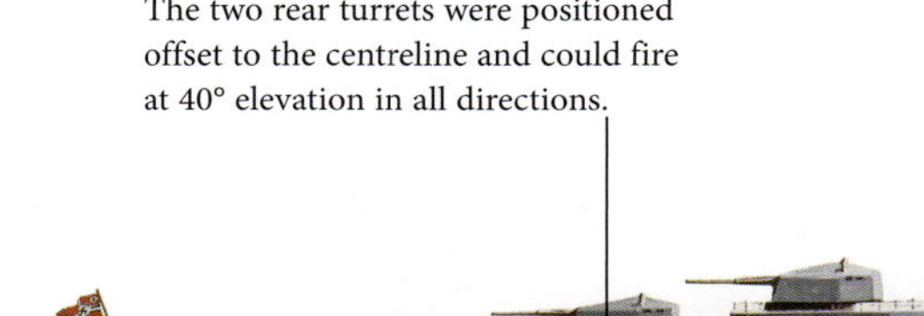

BATTLE OF NORWAY

Once the war had started, it was no longer plain sailing for the K-class. Both *Königsberg* and *Karlsruhe* were diverted from mine-laying duties in the Atlantic to participate in the invasion of Norway, as part of the ill-fated Task Forces 3 and 4. Both were so badly damaged – on 10 and 9 April 1940 respectively – that they were put out of action for the rest of the war. *Köln* had joined *Königsberg* as part of Task Force 3 but managed to escape the devastation wrought among the German ships.

AFT VIEW OF *KÖLN*

From 1940 until 1943, *Köln* remained within the Baltic Sea or in Norway, along with the bulk of Germany's remaining surface navy, part of Hitler's misguided 'force in waiting'. In 1944, she became a training ship, still in the Baltic, and escorted convoys to and from Norway. On 3 March 1945, she was caught undergoing work at the Wilhelmshaven shipyards by an RAF bombing raid and was sunk at the dockside.

HMS *Glorious* (1930)

TYPE • *Aircraft carrier* **COUNTRY** • *United Kingdom*

Converted from a battlecruiser to an aircraft carrier in the 1920s, *Glorious* became one of the few carriers to be sunk by gunfire from a surface ship, rather than by aircraft or submarines, in an encounter with *Scharnhorst* that remains controversial.

SPECIFICATIONS

DIMENSIONS:	Length: 239.8m (786ft 9in); Beam: 27.6m (90ft 6in); Draught: 8.5m (27ft 9in)
DISPLACEMENT:	25,370 tonnes (27,966 US tons); 27,859 tonnes (30,709 US tons) full load
PROPULSION:	18 Yarrow boilers, 4 geared turbines, 4 shafts, 67,113kW (90,000shp)
SPEED:	55.5km/h (30 knots; 34.5mph)
RANGE:	11,000km (6,000nm; 6900 miles) at 37km/h (20 knots; 23mph)
ARMAMENT:	16 x 120mm (4.7in) DP guns
AIRCRAFT:	48
COMPLEMENT:	1283

Left: HMS Glorious*, as seen in Gibraltar in 1931.* Glorious *underwent carrier conversion between 1924 and 1930 at the RN Dockyards of Rosyth and Devonport, completed at the latter yard on 24 February 1930.*

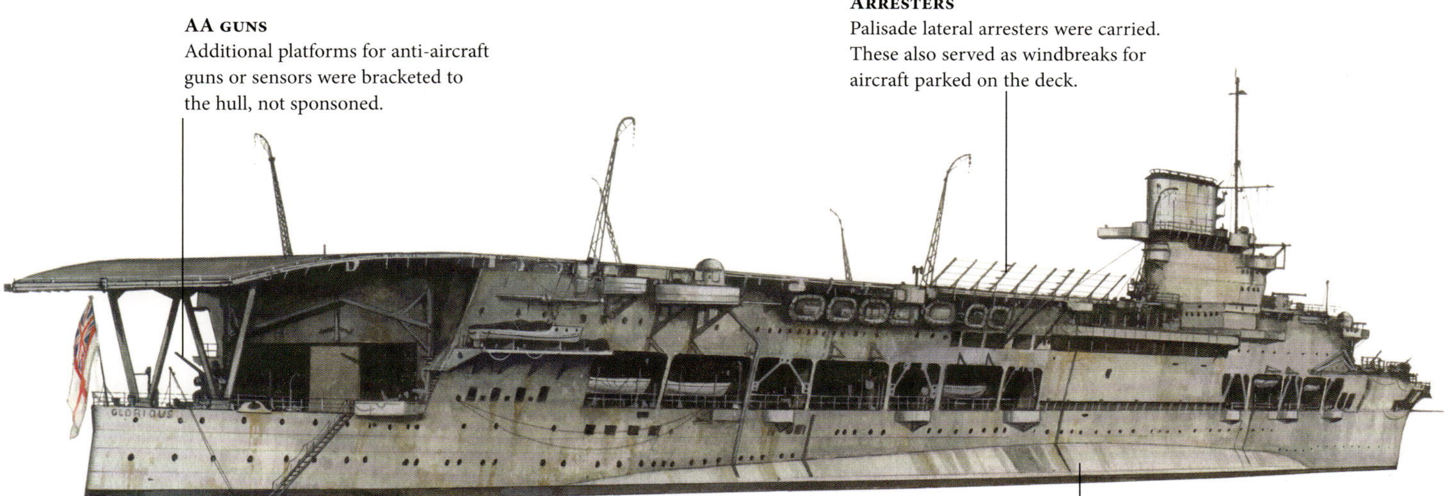

AA GUNS
Additional platforms for anti-aircraft guns or sensors were bracketed to the hull, not sponsoned.

ARRESTERS
Palisade lateral arresters were carried. These also served as windbreaks for aircraft parked on the deck.

TORPEDO BULGE
A torpedo bulge was fitted, but the upper sides had insufficient protection to withstand 280mm (11in) shells.

FUEL LIMITATIONS

Under heavy demand, the 18 boilers on *Glorious* could consume from 610 to 711 tonnes (672 to 783 US tons) of oil a day, setting strict limits to the carrier's time at sea unless it was accompanied by a fleet oiler that could replenish the bunkers. As a result, *Glorious* had to make return trips from the Norwegian Sea to Scapa Flow every five or six days, taking it off station and requiring escort protection.

CARRIER CONVERSION

During the conversion process, everything above the main deck was removed and the hull sides raised by 9.7m (32ft) to provide two hangar decks 167.6m (550ft) long. The upper hangar deck initially opened on to a fly-off deck built above the forecastle, enabling planes to take off and land at the same time.

USS *Pensacola* (1930)

TYPE • *Submarine* **COUNTRY** • *United States*

The two heavy cruisers of the Pensacola class were the first to be laid down in the United States in the US as 'treaty cruisers', a reference to the 10,000-ton limitation placed on such warships by the 1922 Washington Treaty.

SPECIFICATIONS

DIMENSIONS:	Length: 178.46m (585ft 8in) overall; Beam: 19.89m (65ft 3in); Draught: 6.7m (21ft 11in) max
DISPLACEMENT:	9246 tonnes (10,191 US tons)
PROPULSION:	4 × Parsons reduction steam turbines, 80,000kW (107,000shp), 12 × White-Forster boilers, 4 screws
SPEED:	60.6km/h (32.7 knots; 37.6mph)
RANGE:	19,000km (10,000nm; 12,000 miles) at 28km/h (15 knots; 17mph)
ARMAMENT:	10 × 203mm (8in) guns; 8 × 127mm (5in) AA guns; 2 × 47mm (1.9in) 3pdr saluting guns; 6 × 533mm (21in) torpedo tubes
ARMOUR:	Belt: 64–102mm (2.5–4in); Deck: 25–44mm (1–1.75in); Barbettes: 19mm (0.75in); Turrets: 19–64mm (0.75–2.5in)
COMPLEMENT:	530

Below: The USS Pensacola *was laid down on 27 October 1926, launched on 25 April 1929 and commissioned on 6 February 1930.*

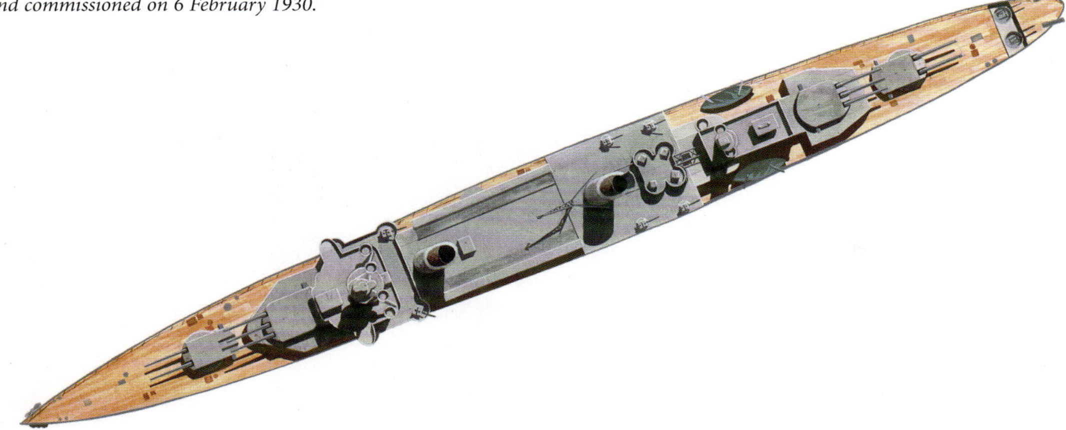

FLOATPLANES
Pensacola could carry four floatplanes for patrol and reconnaissance purposes, with two launch catapults fitted amidships.

LAYOUT
Some security from the ship's lack of heavy armour came from the layout of the fire and engine rooms, which alternated through the ship, and thus were more likely to survive single shell or torpedo hits.

ARMAMENT
The USS *Pensacola* was geared towards firepower and armed with 203mm (8in) guns when most rival cruisers had only 152mm (6in) guns.

BATTLE OF MIDWAY
By February 1942, *Pensacola* was operating as part of Task Force 11 with the carrier *Lexington*. She provided AA protection for the *Lexington* against waves of Japanese bombers during the fighting off Bougainville, in the Solomons. *Pensacola* continued duty as a carrier escort in the Coral Sea, New Caledonia, and at the Battle of Midway. At Midway, she escorted *Enterprise* and defended the stricken carrier *Yorktown*, preventing her from being attacked by Japanese torpedo bombers.

HAWAIIAN MANOEUVRES
Here we see the USS *Pensacola* underway in Hawaiian waters during battle practice with other units of the Pacific Fleet, in early August 1942, shortly before she deployed to the South Pacific.

S-class (1931)

TYPE • *Submarine* **COUNTRY** • *United Kingdom*

SPECIFICATIONS (Group III)

Dimensions:	Length: 66.1m (217ft); Beam: 7.2m (23ft 7in); Draught: 4.5m (14ft 9in)
Displacement:	879 tonnes (969 US tons) surfaced; 1010 tonnes (1113 US tons) submerged
Propulsion:	2 diesels producing 700kW (950bhp), 2 435kW (650hp) electric motors, 2 screws
Speed:	28km/h (15 knots; 17mph) surfaced; 19km/h (10 knots; 12mph) submerged
Range:	11,112km (6000nm; 6905 miles) surfaced; 220km (120 nm; 140 miles) submerged
Armament:	7 × 533mm (21in) torpedo tubes; 12 torpedoes; 1 × 76mm (3in) deck gun; 1 × 20mm (0.79in) AA gun
Complement:	48

The S-class became the Royal Navy's largest group of submarines, with 62 built in total. In terms of design, appearance and production, they are divided into three groups: two sets commissioned in the 1930s and the largest group of 50 between 1940 and 1945.

Below: Commissioned in November 1932, Swordfish *was among the first of the S-class and underwent several modifications throughout the 1930s, which were incorporated into later boats of the class.*

Deck gun
Little could be done to protect the deck gun crew, as the expectation was that it would only be used against unarmed vessels. Air attacks were not anticipated.

HMS *Storm*
Storm was commissioned in July 1943. These were the first British submarines equipped with radar for both surface and air search.

Extra fuel
Storm operated in eastern waters, with a ballast tank converted for fuel storage to accommodate long patrols.

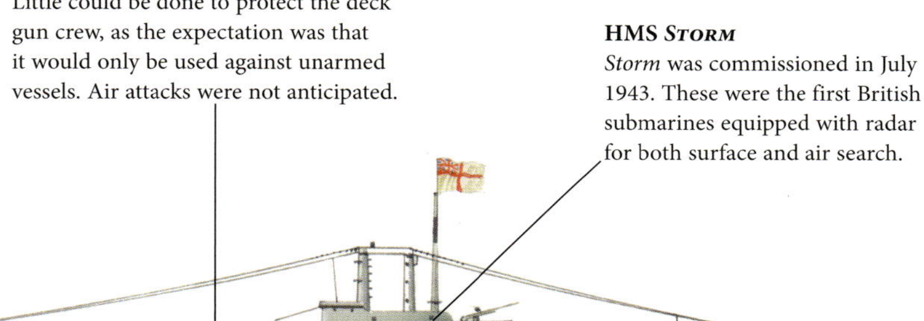

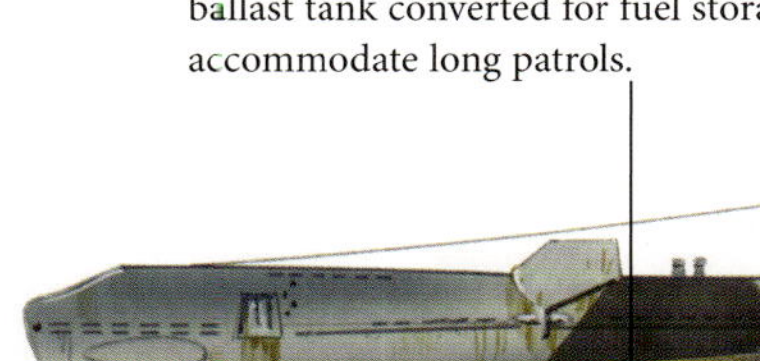

ORIGINAL DESIGN
The original design was limited by the terms of the 1930 naval agreement, and the designers struggled to keep the displacement low. The tower was elliptical in shape, small and relatively low. On the first eight submarines, the bridge was enclosed, but during wartime service, it was converted to an open bridge. There was no bow net-cutter, but a heavy wire cable stretched from the stem over the periscope columns to the stern. The forward diving planes could be folded to rise like a pair of ears above deck level.

HMS *SEA DEVIL*
HMS *Sea Devil* was a Group III S-class vessel, of which 50 were launched between 1940 and 1945. In the final 18 boats, the stern torpedo tube was removed (likely to balance the addition of a snorkel), and the 76mm (3in) deck gun was replaced by a 102mm (4in) gun.

Akatsuki class (1931)

TYPE • *Destroyer* **COUNTRY** • *Japan*

Generally regarded as a sub-class of the Fubuki-class destroyers, the four Akatsuki-class vessels were highly advanced warships when they emerged in the 1930s, although they wrestled with some stability problems at sea.

SPECIFICATIONS

Dimensions:	Length: 118.41m (388ft 5in) overall; Beam: 10.4m (34ft 1in); Draught: 3.2m (10ft 6in)
Displacement:	1780 tonnes (1930 US tons) standard
Propulsion:	4 Kampon type boilers, 2 Kampon Type Ro geared turbines, 2 shafts at 37,000kW (50,000ihp)
Speed:	70km/h (38 knots; 44mph)
Range:	9300km (5000nm; 5780 miles) at 26km/h (14 knots; 16mph)
Armament:	6 × 127mm (5in) Type 3 naval guns; up to 28 × 25mm (1in) Type 96 AT/AA guns; up to 10 × 13.2mm (0.52in) Type 93 AA guns; 9 × 610mm (24in) torpedo tubes for Type 93 torpedoes; 36 depth charges
Complement:	219

Right: The Akatsuki *destroyer sails near Kiska Island in the Aleutians, during the summer of 1942. At this time Kiska was under Japanese occupation.*

Hibiki
Hibiki was the second of the class to be completed, launched in 1931 and entering service in 1933. It was also the only of the class to survive the war intact.

Main guns
The main armament used by the class were Type 3 127mm (5in) 50-calibre naval guns, each turret featuring a pair of the weapons.

Stability
The heavy amount of armament combined with a small hull displacement initially rendered the Akatsuki class unstable, rectified in a major reconstruction in the 1930s.

INAZUMA
Here the fourth vessel of the Akatsuki class, the *Inazuma*, makes high speed. Having fought in many Pacific battles, the ship was ultimately torpedoed west of Celebes on 14 May 1944, sinking with the loss of 161 of its crew.

FATE OF THE *AKATSUKI*
The *Akatsuki* fought in both the Second Sino-Japanese War and World War II. For much of 1942, the ship had been in operation around the Solomon Islands, and by the autumn was engaged in action around Guadalcanal. On 12–13 November, she fought in the major night battle with US Navy warships, known informally as the 'The Night of the Big Guns'. *Akatsuki* was hit repeatedly by heavy naval gunfire and sank; only 18 of her crew survived.

HMS *Exeter* (1931)

TYPE • *Cruiser* **COUNTRY** • *United Kingdom*

SPECIFICATIONS

Dimensions:	Length: 175.26m (575ft) overall; Beam: 17.68m (58ft); Draught: 6.17m (20ft 3in)
Displacement:	8390 tonnes (9245 US tons) standard
Propulsion:	8 x Admiralty boilers driving four-shaft Parsons geared turbines, developing 59,656kW (80,000hp)
Speed:	59km/h (32 knots; 37mph)
Range:	19,000km (10,000 nm; 12,000 miles) at 28km/h (15 knots; 17mph)
Armament:	6 × 203mm (8in) main guns; 4 × 102mm (4in) quick-firing guns (later 8); 2 × 2pdr AA guns; 6 × 533mm (21in) torpedo tubes
Armour:	Box protection for ammunition storage: 102–25mm (4–1in); Side armour: 76mm (3in)
Complement:	630

HMS *Exeter* was the sole ship of her class, a cruiser that followed the lead set by the earlier York, Norfolk and London classes. As such, she was a small, lightly armoured vessel fitted with 203mm (8in) main guns.

Above: An aerial photograph of HMS Exeter, *taken c.1929.*

Boiler room damage
In the Battle of the Java Sea, in February/March 1942, *Exeter* was hit by a Japanese 203mm (8in) shell, which damaged the aft boiler room and cut her cruising speed to 30km/h (16 knots; 18.4mph).

Gun elevation
As fitted, *Exeter*'s guns could not be elevated beyond 50°, but upgrades in 1940 raised the elevation to 70°.

Above: A front view of Exeter; *she had a beam of 17.68m (58ft).*

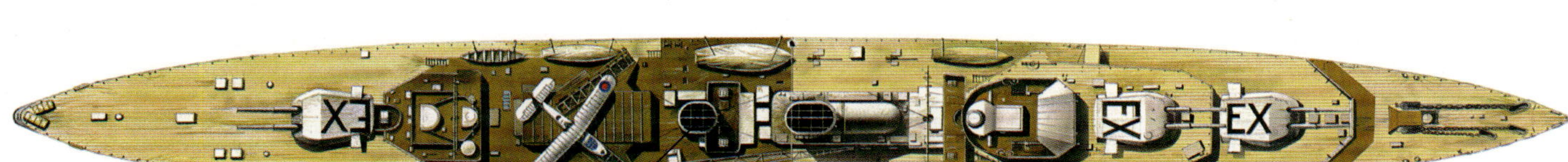

GRAF SPEE
Together with HMS *Achilles* and HMS *Ajax*, *Exeter* was part of the British cruiser squadron commanded by Commodore (later Admiral) H. H. Harwood that was involved in the famous action against the *Graf Spee* at the River Plate in December 1939. After engaging *Graf Spee* alone, *Exeter* was hit by seven 280mm (11in) shells from the German cruiser, and fragments from other near-misses. She was badly damaged, with all of her own 203mm (8in) guns knocked out.

Powerplant
The ship had four Parsons geared steam turbine sets, each driving one shaft, the drive by eight Admiralty three-drum boilers.

FLOATPLANES
As this aerial view of *Exeter* shows, taken in 1934, the ship was capable of carrying two floatplanes on positions amidships. The aircraft were the Fairey Aviation Company's Fairey III.

Alberto di Giussano class (1931)

TYPE • *Cruiser* **COUNTRY** • *Italy*

SPECIFICATIONS

DIMENSIONS:	Length: 169.29m (555ft 5in) overall; Beam: 15.49m (50ft 10in); Draught: 5.4m (17ft 9in)
DISPLACEMENT:	5130 tonnes (5656 US tons) standard
PROPULSION:	6 × Yarrow boilers driving two-shaft Belluzzo geared turbines, developing 95,584kW (128,200hp)
SPEED:	56km/h (30 knots; 34.5mph)
RANGE:	9300km (5000nm; 5800 miles)
ARMAMENT:	8 × 152mm (6in) main guns; 6 × 102mm (4in) AA guns; 8 × 37mm AA guns; 8 × 13.2mm AA guns; 4 × 533mm (21in) torpedo tubes; plus 2 aircraft
ARMOUR:	Belt: 178–240mm (7–9.4in); Deck: 200mm (7.9in); Bulkheads: 200mm (7.9in); Main turrets: 229mm (9in)
COMPLEMENT:	507

One of four ships built in response to the powerful French Lion-class destroyers, *Alberto di Giussano* was a large and well-armed vessel, though lightly armoured. In total, four ships were built in her class.

Right: The light cruiser Alberto di Giussano *at her launch in Genoa, 1930.*

ARMAMENT
As built, the class were respectably armed, with a total of 24 guns mounted and four torpedo tubes.

ALBERTO DI GIUSSANO
Alberto di Giussano was laid down in April 1928, launched in August 1930 and finally completed for service with the Regia Marina in June 1941.

SPEED
The class was very fast – *Bartolomeo Colleoni* achieved a speed of 77.8km/h (42 knots; 46mph) during trials.

FOUR-SHIP CLASS
The Alberto di Giussano class of light cruisers were part of the Condottieri class within the Regia Marina. There were four ships in the class: *Alberto di Giussano*, *Bartolomeo Colleoni*, *Alberico da Barbiano* and *Giovanni delle Bande Nere*. All four of the vessels were destroyed by war's end. Two of them – *Alberto di Giussano* and *Alberico da Barbiano* – were sunk in the Battle of Cape Bon off Tunisia on 13 December 1941.

AT ANCHOR IN VENICE
Alberto di Giussano is here seen at anchor in Venice during the 1930s. Prior to World War II, the ship did gain some operational experience during the Spanish Civil War of 1936–39.

Leander class (1931)

TYPE • *Cruiser* **COUNTRY** • *United Kingdom*

SPECIFICATIONS

DIMENSIONS:	Length: 169.1m (554ft 9in); Beam: 17.1m (56ft); Draught: 5.8m (19ft 1in)
DISPLACEMENT:	7390 tonnes (8146 US tons) standard
PROPULSION:	6 × Admiralty 3-drum boilers or 4 × Admiralty 3-drum boilers, 4 geared steam turbines, 4 shafts, 54,000kW (72,000shp)
SPEED:	60.2km/h (32.5 knots; 37.4mph)
RANGE:	10,610km (5730nm; 6590 miles) at 24km/h (13 knots; 15mph)
ARMAMENT:	4 × twin BL 152mm (6in) guns; 4 × single QF 102mm (4in) guns; 3 × quadruple 12.7mm (0.5in) AA machine guns; 2 × quadruple 533mm (21in) torpedo tubes
ARMOUR:	Magazine: 76mm (3in) box; Deck: 25mm (1in); Gun turrets: 25mm (1in)
COMPLEMENT:	570

Named after a series of figures from mythology, the Leander-class light cruisers were intended to provide heavy and fast protection for merchant shipping in contested waters. Eight vessels of the class were built, with three lost in action.

Left: Many of the Leander class were sold or transferred to the Royal Australian Navy or Royal New Zealand Navy in the late 1930s or early 1940s.

SECONDARY ARMAMENT
In addition to the main guns, the class had four high-angle QF 4 102mm (4in) Mk V naval guns, which were later replaced by twin mountings for eight guns (the later high angle QF 102mm Mk XVI naval gun).

LEANDER
The class had four geared steam turbines driving the four shafts at the rear with a total power output of 54,000kW (72,000shp).

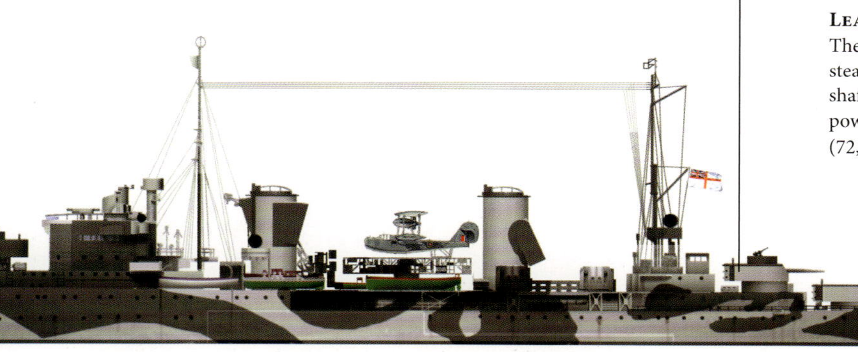

ARMOUR
The heaviest armour applied to the ship surrounded its magazine. This armoured box had a total thickness of 76mm (3in).

RIVER PLATE
Two of the Leander class warships – HMS *Achilles* and HMS *Ajax* – fought in the famous Battle of the River Plate in the South Atlantic on 13 December 1939. Along with the heavy cruiser HMS *Exeter*, they fought the powerful German pocket battleship *Graf Spee*, both sustaining battle damage in the process. *Graf Spee* was also damaged and docked in the port of Montevideo, Uruguay, with *Ajax* and *Achilles* waiting offshore. The final showdown was avoided when the *Graf Spee* was scuttled on the orders of its captain.

FIREPOWER
The principal main gun of the Leander class was officially termed the 50-calibre BL 6-inch gun Mark XXII. They had a maximum firing range of 23,300m (25,480yd).

Leninets class, Series XIII (1931)

TYPE • *Submarine* **COUNTRY** • *Soviet Union*

The conditions of the Baltic and Black seas made mines a significant concern for the Soviet Navy (Russia's *Krab* of 1912 was the first submarine minelayer), and the large L-class was developed throughout the 1930s as a minelayer that also functioned as an attack submarine.

SPECIFICATIONS (Series III)

DIMENSIONS:	Length: 81m (265ft 9in); Beam: 7.5m (24ft 7in); Draught: 4.8m (15ft 9in)
DISPLACEMENT:	1219 tonnes (1344 US tons) surfaced; 1573 tonnes (1733 US tons) submerged
PROPULSION:	2 diesel engines, 2 electric motors, 2 screws
SPEED:	27.8km/h (15 knots; 17.3mph) surfaced; 16.7km/h (9 knots; 10.4mph) submerged
RANGE:	11,112km (6000 nm; 6096 miles) surfaced; 285km (154 nm; 177 miles) submerged
ARMAMENT:	5 × 533mm (21in) torpedo tubes; 12 torpedoes; 20 mines; 1 × 100mm (3.9in) gun, 1 × 45mm (1.75in) gun
COMPLEMENT:	53

Above: An L-class submarine in 1942, with a good view of the 45mm (1.75in) deck gun.

POWER
The first group of L-class vessels, launched in 1931–32, with three submarines operating in the Black Sea and three in the Baltic, were considered underpowered, equipped with diesel engines totalling 1600kW (2200hp) and electric motors of 1080kW (1450hp).

DIVE SPEED
Boats *L1* to *L6* encountered several issues, including a very slow dive speed of approximately three minutes, which was addressed in later builds.

STERN TORPEDOES
The first three groups, totalling 19 submarines, lacked stern torpedo tubes but had mines in two stern galleries.

BALTIC WARFARE

Germany's declaration of war on the Soviet Union in June 1941 led to Russia joining the Allied war effort on its western fronts (the Soviet Union did not declare war on Japan until August 1945). For the navy, this meant operations in the Baltic, Barents and Black seas. Submarine warfare in the Baltic Sea was heavily influenced by extensive minefields and large nets, often stretching many miles, laid by the Germans and Finns, which Soviet submarines had to navigate around. Until the end of 1944, German ships dominated the surface.

COLD WAR SUBS
These Series III L-class submarines were actually Cold War vessels, photographed in the Baltic Sea in 1957. L-class submarines remained in Soviet service until the early 1970s.

Giovanni delle Bande Nere (1931)

TYPE • *Cruiser* **COUNTRY** • *Italy*

SPECIFICATIONS

Dimensions:	Length: 169.29m (555ft 5in) overall; Beam: 15.49m (50ft 10in); Draught 5.4m (17ft 9in)
Displacement:	5130 tonnes (5656 US tons) standard
Propulsion:	6 × Yarrow boilers driving two-shaft Belluzzo geared turbines, developing 95,584kW (128,200hp)
Speed:	56km/h (30 knots; 34.5mph)
Range:	9300km (5000nm; 5800 miles)
Armament:	8 × 152mm (6in) main guns; 6 × 102mm (4in) AA guns; 8 × 37mm AA guns; 8 × 13.2mm AA; 4 × 533mm (21in) torpedo tubes; plus 2 aircraft
Armour:	Belt: 178–240mm (7–9.4in); Deck: 200mm (7.9in); Bulkheads: 200mm (7.9in); Main turrets: 229mm (9in)
Complement:	520

The Giussano class were the first cruisers to be built in Italy after World War I. They were part of the major 1927–28 expansion programme and were conceived as fast scout cruisers, intended to hunt and sink smaller enemy ships, such as destroyers.

Right: The Giovanni delle Bande Nere *in harbour, c.1933. Italy's naval designers showed flair in developing modern fighting ships to expand the navy in the late 1930s.*

Performance
During her own sea trials, she attained a maximum of 70.7km/h (33.2 knots; 44mph), but regular sea speed was 56km/h (30 knots; 34.5mph).

Launch catapult
All of the ships were equipped for minelaying, and a catapult was located on the forecastle of the ship, from which it could launch its two seaplanes.

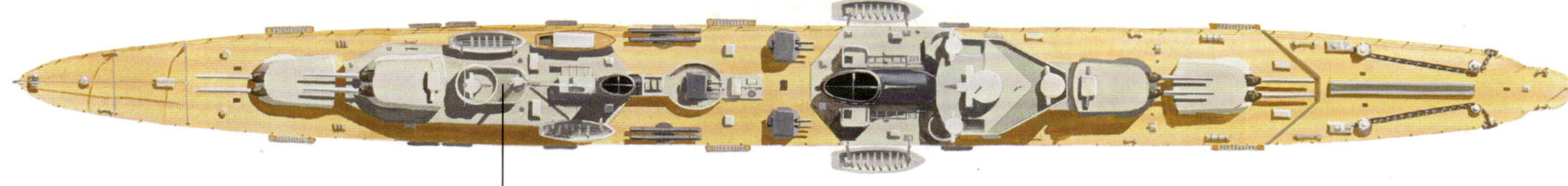

Final ship in class
Giovanni delle Bande Nere was the fourth and final ship in the class. She was laid down on 31 October 1928, launched on 27 April 1930 and completed in April 1931.

DESIGN ISSUES

Unfortunately for the Giussano class, too much was sacrificed for the sake of speed, and they were very lightly armoured. So poor was their basic protection that a typical destroyer would be capable of inflicting serious damage once within range. Built for the easy conditions of the Mediterranean, the class was rather unstable and lacking in endurance. Crews also disliked the cramped conditions inside.

ANTI-AIRCRAFT GUN
Here the gun crew of one of the ship's 102mm (4in) AA guns conduct a gunnery exercise. Note the style of the crew's helmets and life belts slung over the rail on the platform. Also note the apparent wicker padding for splinter protection.

Krasny Kavkaz (1932)

TYPE • *Cruiser* **COUNTRY** • *Soviet Union*

The *Krasny Kavkaz* was a Russian, then Soviet, cruiser that was laid down in October 1913, launched in 1916, but not completed to a commissioned state until 1932. The vessel thereafter served the Soviet Navy until the early 1950s.

SPECIFICATIONS

Dimensions:	Length: 159.5m (523ft 4in); Beam: 15.7m (51ft 6in); Draught: 6.6m (21ft 8in)
Displacement:	7560 tonnes (8333 US tons) standard
Propulsion:	10 × Yarrow boilers, 4 shafts, 4 geared steam turbines, developing 41,000kW (55,000shp)
Speed:	54km/h (29 knots; 33mph)
Range:	6500km (3500 nm; 4000 miles) at 28km/h (15 knots; 17mph)
Armament:	4 × 180mm (7.1in) guns; 8 × 100mm (3.9in) AA guns; 2 × 76mm AA guns; 4 × 45mm (1.8in) AA guns; 12 × 533mm (21in) torpedo tubes; 60–120 mines
Armour:	Upper and lower armoured decks: 20mm (0.79in) each; Turrets: 76mm (3.0in); Lower armour belt: 76mm (3.0in); Upper armour belt: 25mm (0.98in)
Complement:	878

Above: Krasny Kavkaz's *journey from an incomplete Russian cruiser to a modernized warship illustrates the challenges faced by Soviet shipbuilding across a period of intensive political and technological change.*

AA guns
Prior to the German invasion of the USSR in 1941, *Krasny Kavkaz* received significant anti-aircraft upgrades, replacing its original 76.2mm (3in) guns with more advanced 100mm (3.9in) Minizini twin mounts and additional smaller-calibre AA guns to bolster its air defence.

Armament
Initially intended to carry heavier 203mm (8in) guns, *Krasny Kavkaz* was instead outfitted with 180mm (7.1in) MK-1-180 guns due to hull constraints. The ship's superstructure was heavily modified to accommodate these turrets.

Torpedoes and mines
The cruiser was equipped with four triple 533mm (21in) torpedo mounts on each side and could carry up to 120 mines. These features were added as part of the extensive post-World War I modifications.

NAVAL SUPPORT

The Soviet Navy during World War II fought few ship versus ship engagments, as most of the conflict was fought on the land. Ships such as the *Krasny Kavkaz*, however, were often called upon to deliver offshore fire support to army operations, land troops on contested shores or perform evaucation duties. *Krasny Kavkaz* served in all these capacities, particularly around the Black Sea and Crimea.

EVOLVING DESIGN

Initially the *Krasny Kavkaz* was launched as *Admiral Lazarev*, but the ship's completion was delayed by revolution until it was completed for Soviet service in the 1930s. The vessel was modified from its original design, particularly in its armament and layout, to better suit the needs of the new Soviet Navy.

600 and 630 series (1932)

TYPE • *Submarine* **COUNTRY** • *France*

SPECIFICATIONS (*Argonaute*)

Dimensions:	Length: 63.4m (208ft); Beam: 6.4m (21ft); Draught: 4.24m (13ft 11in)
Displacement:	630 tonnes (694 US tons) surfaced; 798 tonnes (380 US tons) submerged
Propulsion:	2 Schneider-Carel diesels producing 485kW (650hp), 2 × 373kW (500hp) electric motors, 2 screws
Speed:	26km/h (14 knots; 16mph) surfaced; 17km/h (9 knots; 10mph) submerged
Range:	7408km (4000nm; 4603 miles) surfaced; 152km (82 nm; 34.4 miles) submerged
Armament:	6 × 550mm (21.45in) torpedo tubes; 13 torpedoes; 2 × 400mm (15.7in) torpedo tubes; 9 torpedoes; 1 × 76mm (3in) 35cal deck gun; 1 × 8mm (0.3in) MG
Complement:	41

French naval policy required an effective fleet of coastal submarines, particularly in the Mediterranean Sea, where Italy was considered a potential enemy. This resulted in two main classes of broadly similar type, defined by their displacement tonnage.

Below: Although classified as coastal submarines, the 600 series were designed for service in the Mediterranean.

Argonaute
Argonaute was a 600 series Schneider-Laubeuf design. Assigned to the Mediterranean squadron, it was sunk by British ships at Oran in November 1942.

Deck gun
Both series carried a light single gun on the foredeck: in the case of *Argonaute* a 76mm (3in) 35-cal Schneider M1928, though boats of the 600 class had older models.

Armament
Torpedo armament in the 600 class consisted of six 550mm (21.45in) tubes, three forward (two external), two aft (both external) and two midships in a twin traversing mount.

TWIN SERIES
The basic specification was given by the navy but design features varied according to the builder. The 600 class, built between 1923 and 1927, numbered 12, completed by 1930. The 630 tonne class was formed of four distinct groups. All were double-hulled, with a sharply raked stem, some with a pronounced downwards-sloping foredeck. The tower was oblong, with varying profiles, but all had the bridge forward and a space behind for machine guns.

***ARIANE*, 1932**
Ariane, seen here at Cherbourg, was lead boat of a sub-class of four 600-type vessels built at the Augustin-Normand yard. It was scuttled at Oran on 9 November 1942.

USS *Indianapolis* (1932)

TYPE • *Cruiser* **COUNTRY** • *United States*

SPECIFICATIONS

Dimensions:	Length: 185.92m (610ft) overall; Beam: 20.1m (66ft); Draught: 6.4m (21ft)
Displacement:	10,258 tonnes (11,310 US tons) standard
Propulsion:	8 × Yarrow boilers driving 4-shaft Parsons turbines, developing 79,814kW (107,000hp)
Speed:	60.2km/h (32.5 knots; 37.5mph)
Range:	19,000km (10,000 nm; 12,000 miles) at 28km/h (15 knots; 17mph)
Armament:	9 × 203mm (8in) main guns; 8 × 127mm (5in) secondary guns; 40mm (1.5in) and 20mm (0.79in) AA guns; 8 × 12.7mm (0.5in) machine guns; plus 4 aircraft
Armour:	Belt: 57–146mm (2.25–5.57in)

Few ships hold such a place in naval history as the USS *Indianapolis* (CA-35), or such a controversial one. She was the second and last of the Portland-class cruisers to be built, from an intended total of five. The subsequent ships were revised to offer better armour.

Left: Indianapolis *served as the flagship of the US Navy's Fifth Fleet, but she entered the public consciousness through the 1975 film* Jaws, *after the scene where the shark hunter Quint (played by Robert Shaw) tells of the night she was lost and the fate of her crew.*

AA guns
The ship was fitted with anti-aircraft guns of multiple calibres, particularly automatic 40mm (1.5in) and 20mm (0.79in) cannon.

Main guns
The cruiser had nine 203mm (8in) /55 calibre Mark 9 guns in three triple-mount turrets, a superfiring pair fore and one pair aft.

Boilers
The ship was powered by eight Yarrow boilers driving four-shaft Parsons turbines, giving a top speed of 60.2km/h (32.5 knots; 37.5mph).

SINKING
Indianapolis was the last major US ship to be sunk in World War II. She carried the first atomic bomb from the United States to the island of Tinian, but on 30 July 1945, was sunk by a Japanese submarine. Of the 1196 crew on board, about 900 made it into the water. Deaths by shark attacks, drowning and exposure followed over the next four days until rescue came. Of the 900 initial survivors, only 317 were rescued.

OVERHAUL AND REPAIR
The USS *Indianapolis* is seen here off the Mare Island Navy Yard, California, on 10 July 1945, after her final overhaul and repair of combat damage sustained in Pacific operations.

Shch class (1932)

TYPE • *Submarine* COUNTRY • *Soviet Union*

SPECIFICATIONS (Series X)

DIMENSIONS:	Length: 58.5m (192ft); Beam: 6.2m (20ft 4in); Draught: 4.2m (13ft 9in)
DISPLACEMENT:	595 tonnes (656 US tons) surfaced; 713 tonnes (786 US tons) submerged
PROPULSION:	2 diesels producing 510kW (635hp), 2 × 300kW (400hp) electric motors, 2 screws
SPEED:	23.2km/h (12.5 knots; 14.4mph) surfaced; 11.7km/h (6.3 knots; 7.2mph) submerged
RANGE:	11,112km (6000nm; 6905 miles) surfaced; 194.5km (105 nm; 121 miles) submerged
ARMAMENT:	6 × 553mm (21in) torpedo tubes; 10 torpedoes; 2 × 45mm (1.75in) guns
COMPLEMENT:	38

Eight-strong (though 200 were planned), the Shch or Shchuka ('Pike') class were coastal submarines, and as so often is the case, multiple variants appeared even before a new and improved type followed.

Left: An S-class vessel readies itself to head out to sea. Many of the submarines operated in the Baltic. For most of World War II, the Baltic was a German pond (with Finnish help), with the Soviet fleet hemmed in at Kronstadt and Leningrad, where Submarine Brigades 1 and 2 were based.

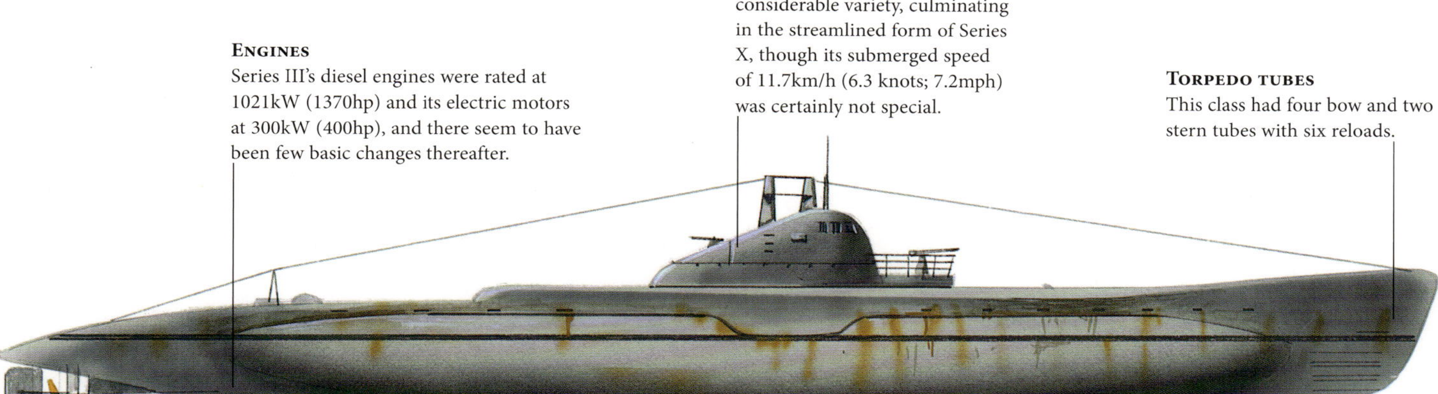

ENGINES
Series III's diesel engines were rated at 1021kW (1370hp) and its electric motors at 300kW (400hp), and there seem to have been few basic changes thereafter.

TOWERS
The towers of the S-class showed considerable variety, culminating in the streamlined form of Series X, though its submerged speed of 11.7km/h (6.3 knots; 7.2mph) was certainly not special.

TORPEDO TUBES
This class had four bow and two stern tubes with six reloads.

PRODUCTION YARDS

This class of 12 ocean-going boats was built from 1935 into the 1940s. Only basic technical details are available of a class that operated from ice-bound to almost subtropical waters, but no doubt there were differences between boats of the same series built at seven yards from Leningrad to Vladivostok. Some were built inland, at Mykolaiv, Ukraine, for example, and sent by river to the Black Sea.

UNOFFICIAL NICKNAME
Aerial view of a Soviet S-class submarine. The Soviet Navy classified the first prototypes as IX, with two following versions as IX-bis and IX-bis2. Their nickname of 'Stalinets' was unofficial.

Pola (Zara class) (1932)

TYPE • *Cruiser* **COUNTRY** • *Italy*

The Italian Zara-class cruisers followed a different path from contemporary Italian designs, opting for armour rather than speed. It proved impossible to keep the desired 203mm (8in) guns and armour within the limits of the Washington Treaty, so the limits were quietly ignored.

SPECIFICATIONS

Dimensions:	Length: 169.8m (557ft 2in); Beam: 19.15m (62ft 10in); Draught: 6.68m (21ft 11in)
Displacement:	11,545 tonnes (12,732 US tons) standard; 14,330 tonnes (15,796 US tons) deep load
Machinery:	8 Thornycroft (Yarrow in Fiume) boilers, two-shaft Parsons geared turbines, 70,836kW (95,000hp)
Speed:	59.3km/h (32 knots; 36.8mph)
Armour:	Belt: 150–120mm (5.9–4.7in); Decks: 70–20mm (2.75–0.78in); Bulkheads: 119–89mm (4.7–3.5in); Main turrets: 150–119mm (5.9–4.7in)
Armament:	8 × 203mm (8in) main guns; 16 × 102mm (4in) AA guns (later reduced to 14); 6 × 40mm AA guns; 8 × 37mm AA guns; 8 × 13.2mm AA guns (later increased to 16)
Complement:	841

Above: Pola *underway. On 29 March 1941, at the Battle of Cape Matapan,* Pola *suffered heavy damage from an air-launched torpedo and was finally sunk by a British destroyer.*

Pola
Pola was different to the other ships, being fitted with an enlarged bridge structure and lacking the distinctive flutes that ran along the forecastle sideplating on the other Zaras.

Weight
Some attempt was made to stay within the 10,000-ton restriction, by fitting lightweight machinery and less armour in specific areas, but the ships were still significantly overweight.

Length
The warship had an overall length of 169.8m (557ft 2in).

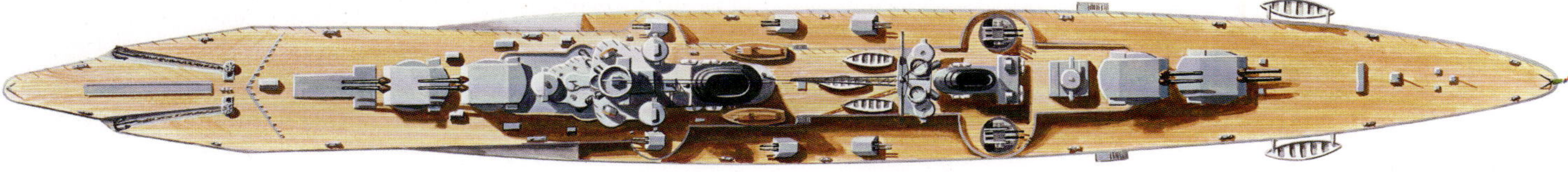

ZARA CLASS

The four Zara-class cruisers were built in two batches, with the *Pola* coming in the second. The ships were originally classified as light cruisers, then armoured cruisers (to distinguish them from other less well-protected ships) and finally as heavy cruisers. Despite their weight the cruisers were still fast, with a maximum speed of 65km/h (35 knots; 40mph) being achieved in special trials.

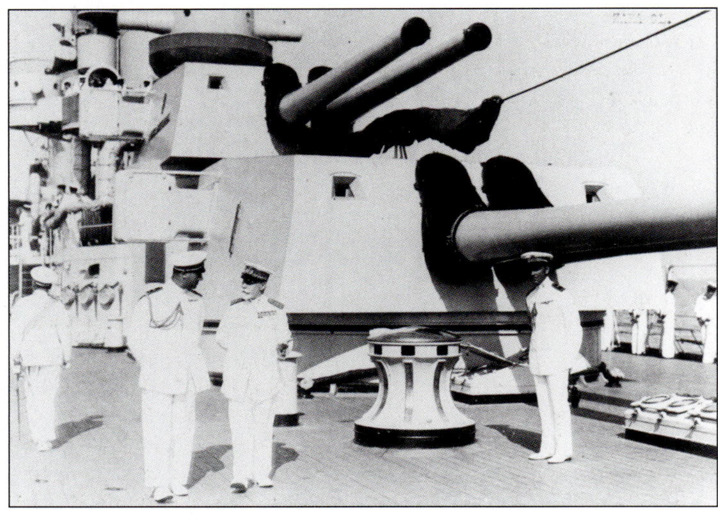

***POLA* MAIN GUNS**
Officers on the deck of *Pola* stand in front of her twin-mounted 203mm (8in) main guns. During the late 1930s, the cruisers were modified to carry additional small calibre AA guns, replacing other larger guns, and more were steadily added as the war progressed.

Deutschland / *Lützow* (1933)

TYPE • *Cruiser* **COUNTRY** • *Germany*

SPECIFICATIONS

DIMENSIONS:	Length: 186m (610ft 3in); Beam: 20.6m (67ft 7in); Draught: 7.2m (23ft 7in)
DISPLACEMENT:	10,659 tonnes (11,750 US tons)
PROPULSION:	4 x 9-cylinder double-acting 2-stroke MAN diesel engines, 40,268kW (54,000hp), Vulcan gearboxes, 2 screws
SPEED:	52km/h (28 knots; 32mph)
RANGE:	16,110km (8700nm; 10,010 miles) at 35km/h (19 knots; 22mph)
ARMAMENT:	6 x 280mm (11in) guns; 8 x 150mm (5.9in) guns; 3 x 88mm (3.5in) guns; 8 x 500mm (19.7in) torpedo tubes
ARMOUR:	Bel: 80–60mm (3.1–2.4in); Deck: 45–40mm (1.8–1.6in); Barbettes: 150–50mm (5.9–2in); Turrets: 140–85mm (5.5–3.3in)
COMPLEMENT:	619

In 1927, the concept of a fast Panzerschiff (armoured ship) began to crystallize: faster than a battleship, with thicker armour and heavier guns than a cruiser. It became the 'pocket battleship', the first major warship powered by diesel engines.

Left: On commissioning, Deutschland *became the flagship of the German Navy, until 1936. Its name was changed to* Lützow *on 15 November 1939.*

REFITTING
In 1935, a mainmast was attached abaft the funnel, AA gun control was fitted, an aircraft catapult installed between the bridge tower and funnel, and twin-mount 88mm (3.5in) AA guns replaced the original singles.

TORPEDO TUBES
Eight 500mm (19.7in) torpedo tubes were fitted in two sets of four on the upper deck, with armoured covers; later, 533mm (21in) tubes were fitted.

SIDE ARMOUR
Deutschland's side armour was intended to withstand fire from cruisers. It was not expected to engage heavy-gun battleships.

BATTLE DAMAGE

On 11 April 1940, the British submarine *Spearfish* hit *Deutschland* with a torpedo off Norway, and it was towed back to Kiel. On 13 July 1941, attempting an entry to the Atlantic, it was again badly damaged by a torpedo from an RAF Beaufort and returned to Kiel for repairs until January 1942. From October 1943, it remained at Gotenhafen (Gdynia). A bomb attack on 15 April 1945 left the ship disabled and it was scuttled by its crew on 4 May.

LIGHTWEIGHT WARSHIP

Deutschland was laid down at the Deutsche Werke, Kiel, on 5 February 1929, launched on 19 March 1931 and completed on 1 April 1933. Every effort was made to save weight, with electric welding resulting in a hull weight 15 per cent less than if riveting had been used.

Algérie (1934)

TYPE • *Cruiser* **COUNTRY** • *France*

SPECIFICATIONS

DIMENSIONS:	Length: 186.2m (611ft); Beam: 20m (66ft); Draught: 6.15m (20ft 2in)
DISPLACEMENT:	10,000 tonnes (11,023 US tons) standard
PROPULSION:	4 shafts, direct geared SR turbines Rateau-Bretagne, 6 Indret boilers, 62,628kW (84,000hp)
SPEED:	57km/h (31 knots; 35mph)
RANGE:	16,110km (8,700nm; 10,006 miles)
ARMAMENT:	8 x 203mm (8in)/55 guns (Mod. 1931); 12 x 100mm (3.9in) DP guns (6 x 2); 8 x 37mm (1.5in) AA guns (4 x 2); 16 x 13.2mm (0.5in) AA HMGs (4 x 4); 2 x triple 550mm (21.7in) torpedo tubes
ARMOUR:	Belt: 120mm (4.7in); Armoured bulkheads: 70mm (2.8in); Deck: 80mm (3.1in); Turrets: 95mm (3.7in); Conning tower: 95mm (3.7in)
COMPLEMENT:	748

***Algérie* was a fine French heavy cruiser, designed to meet the requirements of the 1922 Washington Naval Treaty. It managed to find a good balance between the design trinity of armament, speed and armour.**

Left: Here we see Algérie *at harbour in Brest on 27 May 1937, after conducting an offshore naval review with the battleship* Dunkerque.

IMPROVEMENTS
In 1941 the *Algérie* was given a better AA battery (16 x 37mm and 36 x 13.2mm) and in 1942 a radar, of early French design.

DESIGN
The *Algérie* had a distinctive flush deck, giving her a very 'straight' appearance. This design helped to acheive significant weight savings.

ARMOUR
The warship was heavily armoured, including a 120mm (4.7in) main belt, 70 mm (2.8in) transverse bulkheads and 40mm (1.6in) longitudinal bulkheads.

SCUTTLED
As with all vessels of the French Navy, *Algérie* faced an uncertain future following the defeat of France by Germany in June 1940. Like many French vessels, she remained with the navy of the Vichy fleet, based at Toulon in the south of the country, where she received significant upgrades. But on 27 November 1942, along with 77 other ships, she was scuttled by her crew to prevent the ship falling into German hands.

DESIGN
The *Algérie* had particularly fine lines, with a sleek and slender profile that hinted at speed. At full pace, the warship could achieve a speed of 57km/h (31 knots; 35mph).

River class (1934)

TYPE • *Submarine* **COUNTRY** • *United Kingdom*

This small class of three was the Royal Navy's final attempt at a fleet submarine. In the context of the RN's need to be a global force, a submarine of sufficient size, speed and endurance to accompany a battle fleet seemed to be desirable.

SPECIFICATIONS (HMS *Thames*)

Dimensions:	Length: 105m (344ft 6in); Beam: 8.61m (28ft 3in); Draught: 4.85m (15ft 11in)
Displacement:	2199.6 tonnes (2425 US tons) surfaced; 2723 tonnes (3001 US tons) submerged
Propulsion:	2 supercharged diesels producing 3750kW (5000hp), 2 × 950kW (1250hp) electric motors, 2 screws
Speed:	41km/h (22 knots; 25mph) surfaced; 19km/h (10 knots; 11.5mph) submerged
Range:	22,224km (12,000nm; 13,809 miles) surfaced; 218.5km (118 nm; 136 miles) submerged
Armament:	6 × 533mm (21in) torpedo tubes; 12 torpedoes; 1 × 102mm (4in) QF gun
Complement:	61

Left: HMS Thames *flies its colours. This was the era when streamlining became an essential aspect of fast-moving machines, and the Rivers presented an elegantly rounded form of superstructure, with minimal encumbrances on the long deck and the gun, set on a forward extension of the tower, shielded in a trainable turret.*

Weaponry
The torpedo armament consisted of six 533mm (21in) bow tubes. A 119mm (4.7in) gun was originally fitted, but in keeping with submarine policy of the period was changed, after completion, to a 102mm (4in) QF gun with 120 rounds of ammunition.

HMS *Thames*
To achieve a surface speed of 41km/h (22 knots) – a record at the time – two vertical four-stroke blast injection 10-cylinder diesels of Admiralty design, developing a total power of 5965kW (8000bhp) at 400rpm, were installed.

Hull plating
Stern torpedo tubes were dropped in order to save weight, and the pressure hull plating was 1.75kg/cm² (25psi), allowing for an operational depth of 60m (200ft) and a maximum depth of 91m (300ft).

DRIVE SYSTEMS

Apart from the U/V class, RN submarines in World War II had direct drive: each diesel engine was linked by a drive shaft via a clutch to a double armature electric motor. A shaft from this, via another clutch ('tail clutch') turned the propeller shaft. By disengaging the diesel engine from the drive shaft, the boat could run on the electric motors only. With the tail clutch disengaged, the diesels could be used to charge the batteries. With diesel-electric drive, the diesel engines act as electricity generators, to power electric motors that turn the propeller shafts.

HMS *SEVERN*
The main difference between *Severn* and *Thames* was an increase in length of the motor room due to a change from the 330-volt battery grouping in *Thames* to a 220-volt power grouping.

Type IA (1935)

The two Type IA submarines paved the way for the Kriegsmarine's wartime ocean-going flotillas, especially the Type IX. Their limitations, as well as their strengths, indicated the future direction of German submarine design.

SPECIFICATIONS

Dimensions:	Length: 72.39m (237ft 6in); Beam: 6.21m (20ft 5in); Draught: 4.3m (14ft 1in)
Displacement:	Surface: 875.8 tonnes (965 US tons); Submerged: 998.7 tonnes (1101 US tons)
Propulsion:	2 diesel engines producing 1044kW (1400hp), 2 double electric motors rated at 373kW (500hp) each, 2 screws
Speed:	Surface: 32.8km/h (17.75 knots; 20.4mph); Submerged: 15.35km/h (8.3 knots; 9.54mph)
Range:	Surface: 12,395km (6700 nm; 7712 miles); Submerged: 144km (78 nm; 90 miles)
Armament:	6 × 533mm (21in) torpedo tubes; 14 torpedoes; 1 × 105mm (4.1in) SKC/36 gun; 1 × 20mm (0.79in) Flak/30 AA gun
Complement:	43

Left: U-25 *and* U-26 *were valuable as training vessels, but by 1939, they were barely battle-worthy. However, both participated in active service, sinking several merchant ships and small warships before being lost in minefields in 1940.*

Tower
The tower had a basic bathtub shape, consistent with U-boats up to Type XXI, with a narrower aft extension. A 105mm (4.1in) gun was placed forward of the tower, and a 20mm (0.79in) AA gun was mounted at bridge level at the rear.

Torpedo tubes
Four bow and two stern 533mm (21in) torpedo tubes were installed, capable of launching either G7e (electric) or G7v (compressed air) torpedoes, depending on availability.

Stability
The surface stability was poor, causing significant rolling and pitching, and the rudder and propeller setup limited manoeuvrability.

CONSTRUCTION

Construction of Type IA began in 1934 at the Deschimag A.G. Weser yard in Bremen. The design featured a double hull, with the outer hull extending down to the keel. Ballast tanks and fuel bunkers were located between the hulls. These submarines were among the first to have electrically welded hulls, but the rolled carbon steel used limited diving depth to 100m (330ft). A serrated cable cutter was permanently mounted on the bow, which was typical for most early-war submarines.

U-25
U-25 could carry 14 torpedoes or, alternatively, four torpedoes plus mines of both TMA and TMB types, with a maximum of 28 TMA or 42 TMB mines if no torpedoes were loaded.

Type II (1935)

TYPE • *Submarine* **COUNTRY** • *Germany*

SPECIFICATIONS (*U-137*, Type IID)

DIMENSIONS:	Length: 44m (144ft 5in); Beam: 5m (16ft 5in); Draught: 3.9m (12ft 10in)
DISPLACEMENT:	Surface: 319.1 tonnes (352 US tons); Submerged: 370 tonnes (408 US tons)
PROPULSION:	2 MWM 6-cylinder diesels producing 261kW (350hp), 2 SSW electric motors rated at 153kW (205hp), 2 screws
SPEED:	Surface: 25.5km/h (12.7 knots; 14.6mph); Submerged: 13.7km/h (7.4 knots; 8.5mph)
RANGE:	Surface: 5926km (3200 nm; 3683 miles); Submerged: 104km (56 nm; 64.5 miles)
ARMAMENT:	3 x 533mm (21in) torpedo tubes; 1 × 20mm (0.79in) Flak twin AA gun
COMPLEMENT:	25

Fifty German Type II submarines in four variations, from IIA to IID, were built. Their design lineage traces back to the UF class of World War I and the Finnish-built prototype *Vesikko* (1933). The first of the series, *U-1*, was launched at Deutsche Werke, Kiel, in 1935.

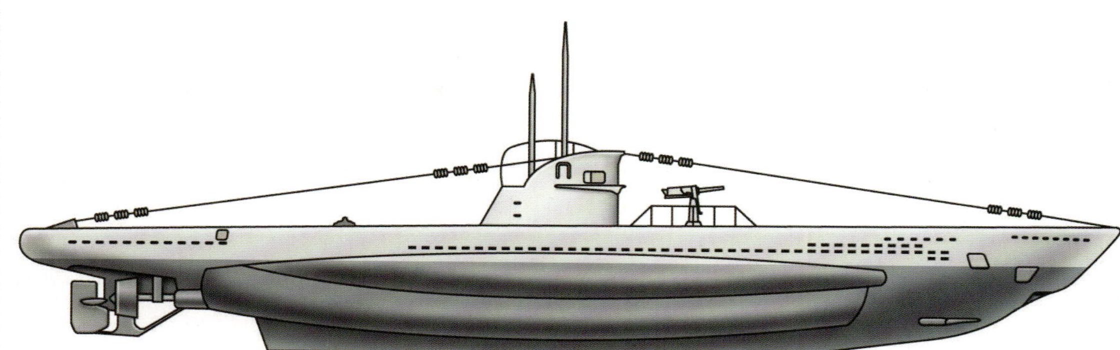

Above: The Type IID had blister tanks fitted to the hull to increase fuel capacity and therefore range. 'Kort nozzle' ducted propellers were added for quieter running.

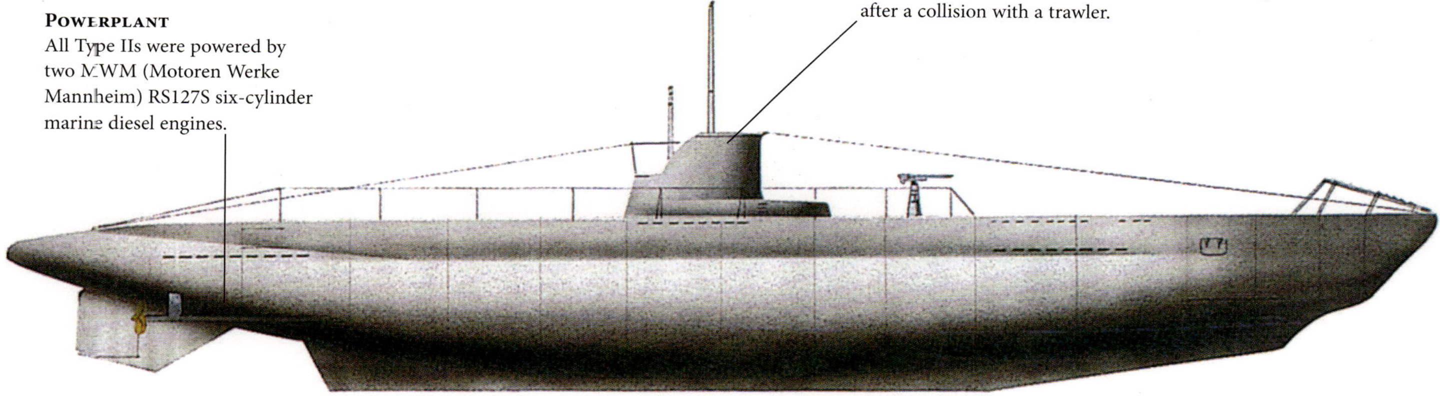

POWERPLANT
All Type IIs were powered by two MWM (Motoren Werke Mannheim) RS127S six-cylinder marine diesel engines.

***U-2* (TYPE IIA)**
Although not a large boat, *U-2* was quickly built: laid down in February 1935 and commissioned on 25 July 1935 at Deutsche Werke, Kiel. It served entirely as a training vessel under 10 different commanders and sank on 8 April 1944 after a collision with a trawler.

VARIANTS
The different sub-types mainly varied in length and displacement to accommodate increased fuel capacity and extended operational range. The Type II remained compact, known as *Einbaum* ('dugout') by its crews, designed primarily for coastal operations. It was single-hulled with welded construction and initially intended as a training submarine. However, the outbreak of war in September 1939 saw many pressed into active service.

U-4 & U-6
The small size of the Type II is evident here with the humans for scale. Accommodation for the 25-man crew was cramped, with 15 bunks plus the skipper's cubicle.

Town class (1936)

TYPE • *Cruiser* **COUNTRY** • *United Kingdom*

SPECIFICATIONS

Dimensions:	Length: 186.99m (613ft 6in); Beam: 19.3m (63ft 4in; Draught: 5.56m (18ft 3in) forward
Displacement:	11,550 tonnes (12,738 US tons)
Propulsion:	4 Admiralty oil-fired 3-drum boilers, 4 Parsons single-reduction geared steam turbines, 60,000kW (80,000shp)
Speed:	59km/h (32 knots; 37mph)
Range:	16,050km (8664nm; 9970 miles)
Armament:	12 × 152mm (6in) Mk XXIII guns; 12 × 102mm (4in) Mk XVI dual-purpose guns; 16 × 40mm (2-pounder) AA guns; 6 × 533mm (21in) torpedo tubes (2×3)
Armour:	Main belt: 114mm (4.5in); Main turrets: Up to 102mm (4in); Decks over magazines: 76mm (3in); Decks over machinery: 51mm (2in); Bulkheads: 63.5mm (2.5in)
Complement:	781–881

The Town-class light cruisers were built under the limitations of the London Naval Treaty, agreed between the United Kingdom, Japan, France, Italy and the United States in April 1930. The class of 10 ships saw much service during World War II.

Below: HMS Birmingham *survived the war and had a long post-war career until she was paid off in 1959.*

HMS *Birmingham* (C19)
Although classed as 'light' cruisers, the armament of the Town class was substantial, with three 152mm (6in) guns in each triple turret.

Aircraft
The cruisers could also transport two Supermarine Walrus amphibious biplanes. When not in use these were stored in forward hangars.

Armour
The Town class had decent armour, with a main belt 114mm (4.5in) thick and 102mm (4in) over the turrets.

Performance
With the screws driven by four Parsons steam turbines, the Town-class ships could attain a maximum speed of 59km/h (32 knots; 37mph).

TOWN CLASS IN WAR

The Town-class cruisers were commissioned between March 1937 and July 1939, which meant that all 10 were in service when war broke out in September 1939. Four of the class – *Southampton*, *Manchester*, *Gloucester* and *Edinburgh* – did not survive the war, sunk or scuttled by German air attack or from U-boat torpedoes. The other six survived the war and served into the 1950s and 1960s. The most famous survivor is HMS *Belfast*, today a landmark museum ship on the Thames in London.

HMS *GLOUCESTER*
HMS *Gloucester* was commissioned on 31 January 1939. With the outbreak of war, the ship was sent to the China Station and subsequently the Indian Ocean and off South Africa. Her fate, however, was sealed in the Mediterranean, when she was sunk by German dive-bombers during the battle of Crete on 22 May 1941.

HMS *Penelope* (1936)

TYPE • *Cruiser* **COUNTRY** • *United Kingdom*

SPECIFICATIONS

Dimensions:	Length: 154.23m (506ft) overall; Beam: 15.54m (51ft); Draught: 5.03m (16ft 6in)
Displacement:	5270 tonnes (5806 US tons) standard
Propulsion:	4 x Admiralty 3-drum boilers, driving 4-shaft Parsons geared turbines, developing 47,735kW (64,000hp)
Speed:	59.8km/h (32.3 knots; 37.2mph)
Range:	9817km (5301nm; 6100 miles) at 28km/h (15 knots; 17.3mph)
Armament:	6 x 152mm (6in) main guns; 8 x 102mm (4in) quick-firing guns; 6 x 533mm (21in) torpedo tubes; and 1 aircraft
Armour:	Box protection to ammunition storage: 25–76mm (1–3in); Belt: 57mm (2.25in); Turrets: 25mm (1in)
Complement:	500

With the Arethusa class, to which HMS *Penelope* belonged, the Royal Navy tried to build the smallest possible useful cruiser. It was similar in design to the cruisers of the Perth class but had only three turrets instead of four.

Left: This photograph of HMS Penelope *shows her with her hull rendered in one of the many variants of dazzle camouflage, intended to break up the silhouette of the ship against the seascape.*

Gun magazines
One unfortunate element of the design was that the magazines for the secondary 102mm (4in) guns were not near the guns themselves, which proved a serious problem in combat.

Catapults
The four Arethusas were initially fitted with catapults and aircraft, but these were removed during major overhauls of the class between 1940 and 1941.

Launch
HMS *Penelope* was the third of her class to be built. She was laid down on 30 May 1934, launched on 15 October 1935 and completed on 13 November 1936.

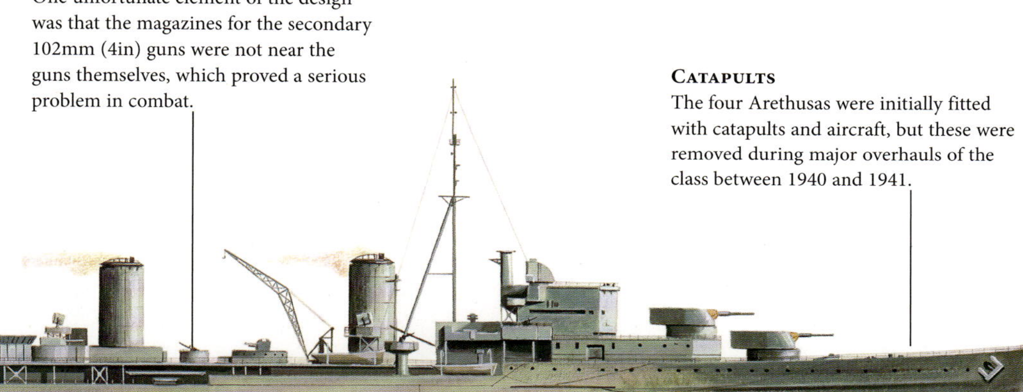

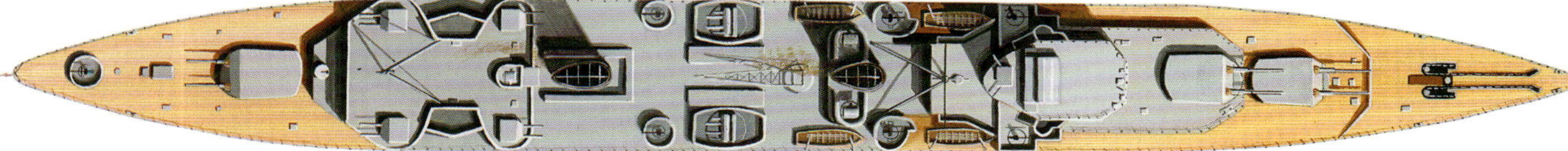

MALTA CONVOY
HMS *Penelope* distinguished herself as one of the escorts involved in the infamous Force H convoy to Malta in 1942. With the island about to succumb to Axis air attacks, a last-ditch effort was made to force supplies through the German and Italian blockade. After intense air and sea battles, only one merchant vessel made it to Malta, the US tanker *Ohio*, which was by then barely afloat. Her arrival was enough to keep Malta fighting.

***PENELOPE*'S FATE**
Penelope continued to serve with the Mediterranean and Home Fleets until 1944, when she was sunk on 18 February by the *U-410*. While steaming at 48.1km/h (26 knots; 29.9mph), *Penelope* was hit by first one and then a second torpedo and sank straightaway.

HMS *Porpoise* and Grampus class (1936)

TYPE • *Submarine* **COUNTRY** • *United Kingdom*

SPECIFICATIONS (HMS *Porpoise*)

Dimensions:	Length: 88m (288ft 9in); Beam: 9.09m (29ft 10in); Draught: 4.83m (15ft 10in)
Displacement:	Surfaced: 796 tonnes (1980 US tons); Submerged: 2067 tonnes (2279 US tons)
Propulsion:	2 diesels of 1250kW (1650hp), 2 electric motors of 610kW (815hp), 2 screws
Speed:	Surfaced: 28.7km/h (15.5 knots; 17.8mph); Submerged: 16.2km/h (8.75 knots; 10mph)
Range:	11,667km (6300nm, 7251 miles) surfaced; 118km (64nm, 73.6 miles) submerged
Armament:	6 × 533mm (21in) torpedo tubes; 12 torpedoes; 50 mines; 1 × 102mm (4in) deck gun; 2 × 7.7mm (0.303in) Lewis guns
Complement:	59

This class was specifically designed as a minelayer. Minelaying from submarines could be done secretly, provided the submarine was not seen. The immediate precursor was HMS *Porpoise* (1932), but the five Grampus-class boats had notable differences.

Below: Subsequent orders for this class were cancelled once mines deployable via torpedo tubes became available. The minelayers then served as supply boats, particularly in the Mediterranean, conducting supply runs to Malta with the mine deck repurposed for cargo.

Mines
The Grampus boats carried 50 Mk XVI mines in a casing above the pressure hull, which moved the mines to stern discharge vents using a chain-and-rack system.

Deck gun
Porpoise was initially armed with a 119mm (4.7in) deck gun, later replaced with a 102mm (4in) gun on the Grampus class.

HMS *Porpoise*
Three battery sets with 112 cells each, weighing 141 tonnes (155 US tons), allowed for a submerged endurance of 122km (66 nm; 76 miles) at 7.4km/h (4 knots; 4.6 mph).

Propulsion
All six submarines were powered by Admiralty-type vertical four-stroke blast-injection six-cylinder diesel engines, collectively producing 2461kW (3300bhp), and two electric motors on each shaft, developing 1215kW (1630bhp).

HMS *PORPOISE*'S FATE
Porpoise, seen below, differed from its class members with external fuel tanks ending about 18m (60ft) before the bow structure. These boats served in various locations, including the West Indies, the Mediterranean and the China Station. Five were lost during World War II, including *Porpoise*, which was sunk by Japanese aircraft in the Malacca Straits on 19 January 1945.

DIFFERENCES
Porpoise featured welded saddle tanks, with a hull design based on the P-class, while the Grampus boats utilized a double-hulled design based on the T-class, with some streamlining. Unlike *Porpoise*, which stored fuel in the saddle tanks, Grampus boats had internal fuel bunkers within the pressure hull, with capacities ranging from 120 to 149 tonnes (132 to 164 US tons).

Duca degli Abruzzi class (1936)

TYPE • *Cruiser* **COUNTRY** • *Italy*

SPECIFICATIONS

Dimensions:	Length: 171.1–187m (561–614ft); Beam: 18.9m (62ft); Draught: 6.9m (23ft)
Displacement:	11,350 tonnes (12,515 US tons) standard
Propulsion:	6 boilers, 2 shafts, 75,000kW (100,000hp)
Speed:	63km/h (34 knots; 39mph)
Range:	7640km (4125nm; 4747 miles)
Armament:	10 × 152mm (6in) guns; 8 × 100mm (4in) guns; 8 × 37mm (1.5in) guns; 12 × 20mm (1in); 6 × 533mm (21in) torpedo tubes; 2 × anti-submarine mortars
Armour:	Outer belt: 30mm (1.2in); Inner belt: 100mm (3.9in); Main deck: 40mm (1.6in); Upper deck: 10–15mm (0.39–0.59in); Turrets: 135mm (5.3in); Barbettes: 30–100mm (1.2–3.9in)
Complement:	640

The Duca degli Abruzzi class of light cruisers were actually one of five sub-classes of the Italian Condottieri class. Of the five, the Duca degli Abruzzi was the last to be developed, and consequently had the heaviest armour and armament.

Below: There were two ships in the Duca degli Abruzzi class, the Luigi di Savoia Duca degli Abruzzi, *the lead ship (seen below), and the* Giuseppe Garibaldi.

Firepower
Unlike the preceding Condottieri-class vessels, the two Duca degli Abruzzi cruisers received triple-gun turrets in the 'A' and 'Y' positions, rather than twin guns.

Aircraft
Mounted amidships was an IMAM Ro.43 floatplane. This aircraft was used for observation duties, providing over-the-horizon reconnaissance.

Duca degli Abruzzi
Here we see the lead ship of the class as she appeared in 1939, with diagonal camouflage applied to the superstructure.

Propulsion
The vessels of this class were driven by two screws, the power coming from six boilers with a total power output of 75,000kW (100,000hp).

LUIGI DI SAVOIA DUCA DEGLI ABRUZZI
This profile view of the *Luigi di Savoia Duca degli Abruzzi* shows the slender lines and fairly low silhouette of the class. This photograph was taken in Naples just prior to the outbreak of war, hence the ship does not have any dazzle camouflage applied.

POST-WAR SERVICE
The lead ship of the class, *Luigi di Savoia Duca degli Abruzzi* was commissioned in December 1937. She fought in several major engagements in 1940 and 1941, but was later interned by the Allies following the Italian armistice in 1943. After the war, however, the vessel served in the Italian Navy until 1961, her armament and search radar being upgraded to bring her into the modern age.

Zuiho (1936)

TYPE • *Aircraft carrier* **COUNTRY** • *Japan*

SPECIFICATIONS

Dimensions:	Length 204.8m (671ft 11in); Beam 18.2m (59ft 9in); Draught 6.68m (21ft 9in)
Displacement:	11,262 tonnes (12,414 US tons) standard; 13,730 tonnes (15,134 US tons) full load
Propulsion:	4 Kampon boilers, 2-shaft geared turbines, 38,800kW (52,000shp)
Speed:	52km/h (28 knots; 32mph)
Range:	14,448km (7800nm; 8977 miles) at 33km/h (18 knots; 20.7mph)
Armament:	8 x 127mm (5in) Type 89 dual-purpose guns; 8 x twin 25mm (1in) Type 96 AA guns
Aircraft:	30
Complement:	785

***Zuiho* had a long combat career, starting the war with the East Indies invasions of 1942. She went on to see action in the Guadalcanal and Marianas campaigns, during December 1942 and June 1943, but was finally sunk during the Leyte Gulf battles in October 1944.**

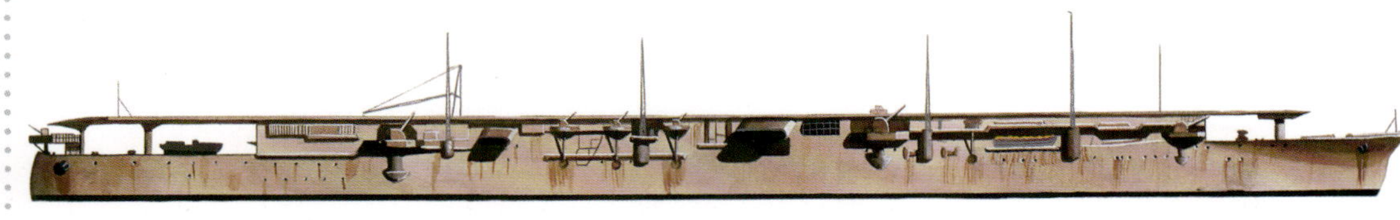

Above: The top view of the Zuiho *shows the two aircraft elevators for taking the aircraft to and from the flight deck.*

Aircraft
In total, the *Zuiho* could carry 30 combat aircraft. They were stored in a single hangar that measured 120m (406ft 10in) long and 18m (59ft) wide.

Conversion
In the conversion from depot ship, two lifts were added to the flight deck, no island was built and the smokestack curved down to one side, in the standard Japanese fashion.

Flight deck
The carrier's flight deck was 180m (590ft 6in) long and had a maximum width of 23m (75ft 6in).

DEPOT SHIP

As part of a shadow shipbuilding programme to get around Washington Treaty restrictions, Japan built two submarine depot ships, named *Takasaki* and *Tsurugisaki*, which could be converted to fleet oilers or small aircraft carriers in time of war. In the event *Tsurugisaki* (the first to be laid down) was built as a depot ship, but *Takasagi* was modified to carrier status while still in the yard. At that point she was renamed *Zuiho*. Her sister ship did not follow this route, becoming the carrier *Shoho*.

UNDER ATTACK
Japanese aircraft carrier *Zuiho* under attack by planes from USS *Enterprise* during the Battle off Cape Engano, 25 October 1944. Aircraft from the US Navy's Task Force 38 scored a succession of torpedo and bomb hits to sink the Japanese carrier.

Salmon class (1937)

TYPE • *Submarine* **COUNTRY** • *United States*

SPECIFICATIONS

Dimensions:	Length: 93.9m (308ft 3in); Beam: 7.9m (26ft); Draught: 4.78m (15ft 8in)
Displacement:	Surfaced: 1458 tonnes (1607 US tons); Submerged: 2233 tonnes (2462 US tons)
Propulsion:	4 HOR 9-cylinder diesels of 1145kW (1535hp), 4 496kW (665hp) geared electric motors, 2 screws
Speed:	39km/h (21 knots; 24mph) surfaced; 17km/h (9 knots; 10.3mph) submerged
Range:	20,372km (11,000nm; 12,659 miles) surfaced; 178km (96nm; 110 miles) submerged
Armament:	8 × 533mm (21in) torpedo tubes; 24 × torpedoes; 1 × 76mm (3in) deck gun; 4 × machine guns
Crew:	59

USS *Salmon* (SS-182) was the lead boat of 16, built at Electric Boat, Groton, and the Portsmouth and Mare Island Navy Yards. They were partially double-hulled, and with the preceding P-class, were the first all-welded US submarines.

Above: USS Salmon *(SS-182) off the Mare Island Navy Yard, California, 10 August 1944. The United States' oceanic coasts and the remoteness of any likely aggressor ensured that the US Navy kept a keen interest in developing long-range submarines capable of maintaining surface speed with a battle fleet.*

Armament
Salmon boats carried eight internal torpedo tubes, four bow and four stern, with a warload of 24 torpedoes. A 76mm (3in) 50cal aft-facing deck gun was first installed, later supplemented by four 20mm (0.79in) machine guns.

Propeller shafts
The propeller shafts led aft from each of the reduction gears. Two high-speed Elliott-geared electric motors were mounted outboard of each shaft, connected directly to the reduction gears.

TESTING
The class was tested to a depth of 76m (250ft). Within the basic configuration, differences between the EB and Navy builds separated *Salmon*, *Seal* (SS-183) and *Skipjack* (SS-184) from *Snapper*, *Stingray* and *Sturgeon* (SS-185–187), including tower design (although the 'sail' type of tower was reduced in height on all in the course of the war). On all, the stern was designed to hold two 533mm (21in) torpedo tubes. Four spare torpedoes were initially held in wells in the casing, but this was discontinued in wartime.

Diesel power
There were two diesel engine rooms plus a motor room. Two engines in the forward engine room drove generators.

OVERHAUL
USS *Salmon* at the Mare Island Navy Yard, California, 23 March 1943, following completion of an overhaul. The circles on the image mark recent alterations to the ship.

Hiryu (1937)

TYPE • *Aircraft carrier* **COUNTRY** • *Japan*

SPECIFICATIONS

DIMENSIONS:	Length 227.4m (746ft 1in); Beam 22.3m (73ft 2in); Draught 7.9m (26ft)
DISPLACEMENT:	17,577 tonnes (19,375 US tons) standard; 22,403 tonnes (24,696 US tons) full load
PROPULSION:	8 Kampon Ro boilers, 4 geared turbines, 4 shafts, 114,000kW (153,000shp)
SPEED:	63.5km/h (34.3 knots; 39.5mph)
RANGE:	19,130km (10,330nm; 11,890 miles) at 33.3km/h (18 knots; 20.7mph)
ARMAMENT:	12 × 127mm (5in) guns; 31 × 25mm AA guns
AIRCRAFT:	73
COMPLEMENT:	1,100

The Imperial Japanese Navy was building up its carrier force in the late 1930s, with *Soryu* and *Hiryu* as fast carriers added to the fleet in 1937 and 1939. Both were to become victims of the Battle of Midway.

Above: Hiryu *making speed during its sea trials in April 1939. Both it and* Soryu *were fast ships, capable of 63km/h (34 knots; 39mph) or more.*

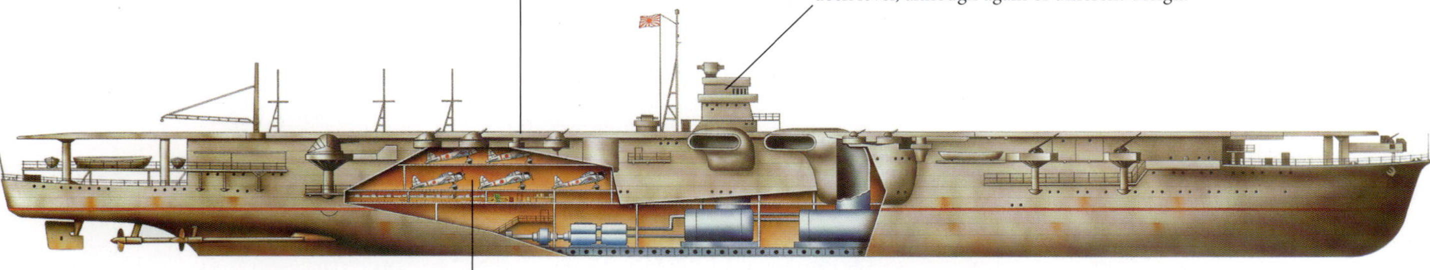

RISING SUN
A large *Hinomaru* (rising sun) was painted on *Hiryu*'s flight deck, ironically providing a 'bullseye' target for US dive-bombers.

ISLAND
Both *Soryu* and *Hiryu* had similar tower-type islands, although differently located, and *Hiryu*'s had an additional deck level. Both had masts rising from flight-deck level, although again of different design.

HANGARS
Soryu and *Hiryu* retained the two-level enclosed hangar design of earlier carriers like *Kaga*. The height of the lower hangar at 4.3m (14ft) restricted the type of plane that could be carried.

SISTER SHIPS

Hiryu and *Soryu* were sister ships, both often referred to as Soryu class, although *Hiryu* was sufficiently different in details to the earlier ship as to really form a separate or sub-class. *Soryu* (whose name means Blue Dragon) was laid down at the Kaigun Kosho Yard at Kure on 20 November 1934, launched on 23 December 1935 and commissioned on 29 January 1937. Although designed from the start as a carrier, the ship had a conventional bow with the forward part of the flight deck extended over it on stanchions; the stern was treated in a similar way.

***HIRYU* BURNING**
The burning Japanese aircraft carrier *Hiryu*, photographed by an aircraft from the carrier *Hosho* shortly after sunrise on 5 June 1942. *Hiryu* sank a few hours later. Note the collapsed flight deck over the forward hangar.

Dunkerque (1937)

TYPE • *Battleship* **COUNTRY** • *France*

SPECIFICATIONS

Dimensions:	Length: 214.5m (704ft); Beam: 31.1m (102ft); Draught: 8.7m (29ft)
Displacement:	26,925 tonnes (29,677 US tons) standard; 36,070 tonnes (39,756 US tons) full load
Propulsion:	6 Indret boilers, 4 sets of Parsons geared turbines, 4 screws, 80,200kW (107,500shp)
Armament:	8 × 330mm (13in) guns; 16 × 130mm (5.1in) guns; 8 × 37mm (1.5in) guns; 32 × 13.2mm (0.5in) AA guns
Armour:	Belt: 225mm (8.9in); Main deck: 115mm (4.5in); Barbettes: 310mm (12.2in); Turrets: 345–310mm (13.6–12.2in); Conning tower: 270mm (10.6in)
Range:	14,540km (7350nm; 9038 miles)
Speed:	57.5km/h (31 knots; 35.7mph)
Complement:	1432

Laid down at Brest on 24 December 1932, *Dunkerque* was not liable to the same Treaty regulations as German ships. Its larger guns and greater speed were a response to the powerful Deutschland class.

Left: Dunkerque*'s superstructure followed the form established with HMS* Rodney, *a tower-cum-mast rising behind the armoured conning tower, which was topped by the navigation bridge.*

Fire control
Fire control and optics, placed in three stations on the tower, were largely French-made, from OPL (Optique et Précision de Levallois-Perret).

Catapult
A 22m (72ft) compressed-air catapult and a crane were fitted on the after deck, aft of a two-level hangar, with lift, and three Loire 130 seaplanes were carried.

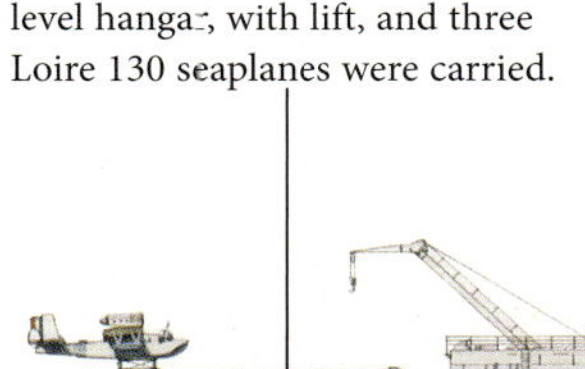

Side armour
The side armour covered about 60 per cent of the hull, with bow and stern unprotected. A 60mm (2.4in) layer of teak wood backed the outer plating.

FLAGSHIP
In World War II, *Dunkerque* was the proud flagship of the French Atlantic fleet at Brest before it was transferred to the Mediterranean in 1940. It was damaged in the controversial British naval attack on Mers-el-Kebir on 3 and 6 July that year. Moored facing the land, it could not return fire. Transferred to Toulon, it was scuttled by its crew in November 1944.

MAIN TURRETS
The main turrets of *Dunkerque*, built by St-Chamond, each weighed 1497 tonnes (1650 US tons). Elevating to a maximum 35°, the guns had a muzzle velocity of 870m/s (2854ft/s) and a range of 41,500m (45,385yd).

HMS *Cossack* (1937)

TYPE • *Destroyer* **COUNTRY** • *United Kingdom*

SPECIFICATIONS

DIMENSIONS:	Length: 111.5m (364ft 8in); Beam: 11.13m (36ft 6in); Draught: 4m (13ft)
DISPLACEMENT:	1696 tonnes (1870 US tons)
PROPULSION:	2 shaft Parsons geared turbines, 33,131kW (44,000shp)
SPEED:	66.7km/h (36 knots; 41.4mph)
ARMAMENT:	8 × 120mm (4.7in) twin turrets; 1 × quadruple 0.9kg (2lb) anti-aircraft guns; 2 × quadruple 12.7mm (0.5in) calibre MGs; 1 × quadruple torpedo tubes (533mm [21in] Mk IX torpedoes); 2 × depth charge throwers; 1 × depth charge rail
COMPLEMENT:	190

Among the finest destroyers ever built for the Royal Navy, the 16 Tribal-class vessels, including *Cossack*, were developed as a counter to potential enemies' destroyers rather than to fulfil a specific, clearly defined role within the fleet.

Right: The Tribal-class destroyer HMS Cossack *underway on completion. The 'Tribals' were quite different from previous designs, featuring a sharply raked stem. This added 3m (10ft) to the length of the forecastle deck.*

FIREPOWER
The Tribal class were built to a concept that differed from other Royal Navy destroyers built up to the time, with more emphasis on guns than torpedoes.

HULL
By any standards, the Tribal-class ships were magnificent to look at, with their pleasingly balanced profile in harmony with the high freeboard hull, introduced to improve their fighting qualities in poor weather.

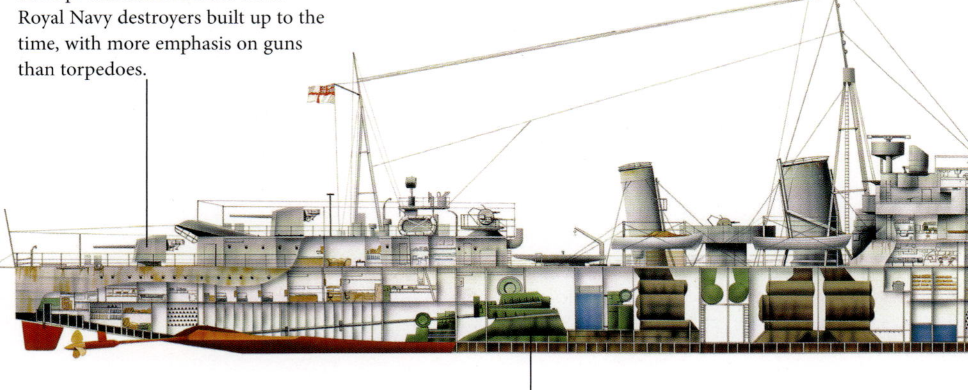

MACHINERY
The Tribal-class destroyers were powered by two sets of Parsons geared turbines, producing 33,131kW (44,000shp) and giving a maximum speed of 36 knots.

TRIBAL-CLASS SHIPS

Of 27 ships built, only four of the original 16 'Tribals' remained afloat by the end of 1942. *Afridi* and *Gurkha*, for example, were bombed off Norway and *Maori* off Malta; *Mohawk* was torpedoed off Cape Bon; *Zulu* was bombed at Tobruk; *Mashona* was bombed south-west of Ireland; *Matabele* was sunk by *U-454* in the Barents Sea; *Punjabi* was lost in a collision with the *King George V*; *Sikh* was sunk by shore batteries at Tobruk; and *Somali* was torpedoed by *U-703* south of Iceland.

RETURN IN VICTORY
HMS *Cossack* returns to Leith on 17 February 1940, after rescuing the British prisoners held in Graf Spee's supply ship *Altmark*. Taking place during the so-called 'Phoney War' period, the incident was to generate huge publicity worldwide.

U-class (1937)

TYPE • *Submarine* COUNTRY • *United Kingdom*

SPECIFICATIONS

DIMENSIONS:	Length: 59.8m (196ft 2in); Beam: 4.8m (15ft 9in); Draught: 4.8m (15ft 9in)
DISPLACEMENT:	640 tonnes (705 US tons) surfaced; 741.7 tonnes (817.5 US tons) submerged
PROPULSION:	Diesel-electric: 2 × diesels of 298kW (400hp), 2 × 307kW (412hp) electric motors, 2 screws
SPEED:	20.8km/h (11.25 knots; 12.9mph) surfaced; 16.7km/h (9 knots; 10.3mph) submerged
RANGE:	7500km (4050nm; 4661 miles) surfaced; 42.6km (23nm; 26.5 miles) submerged
ARMAMENT:	4 × 533mm (21in) bow torpedo tubes; 1 × 76mm (3in) deck gun; 3 × 0.78mm (0.303in) machine guns
CREW:	27

Planned in 1936, originally as unarmed training boats, the U-class was the Royal Navy's first diesel-electric submarine. The first three, *Undine*, *Unity* and *Ursula*, were modified during construction, adding six internal and two external bow tubes.

Left: HMS Unrivalled *(P45). Altogether, 49 U-class boats were commissioned into the Royal Navy. A further 21 served in other navies. Most U-class submarines were attached to the 10th flotilla at Malta, and 16 were lost in the Mediterranean.*

PERISCOPES
Search and attack periscopes, 200mm (8in) bifocal and 150mm (6in) low power respectively, were extendable only to 3.7m (12ft 2in).

HMS *UNDINE*
A single deck gun was fitted close to the tower, as the design omitted an ammunition hatch: a QF 12-pdr (76mm) in the earliest boats, later a 76mm (3in) gun.

HULL CONSTRUCTION
All were of riveted single-hull construction, of a maximum 0.78mm (0.5in) thickness, with all fuel and ballast tanks fitted inside, giving very cramped space.

TORPEDOES
The primary torpedo used by Royal Navy submarines was the Mark VIII** variant (asterisks indicating third modification), though shortages led to some submarines using the older Mark IV in the early stages. Its range was 4570m (5000yd) at 45.5km/h (24.5 knots; 28.3mph) or 6400m (7000yd) at 41km/h (22 knots; 25.5mph). Its hit rate during the war, reckoned at 1040 definite hits for 5421 torpedoes fired, was remarkable.

HMS *UNITED* (P44)
Undine, *Unity* and *Ursula* were modified during construction, with six internal and two external bow tubes. They were completed in 1938, with another 12 in 1940–41. A second group of 28 (including P44 seen here) followed between 1940 and 1943, of very similar displacement but with 1.78m (5ft 10in) longer sterns, and with four internal tubes only.

USS *Yorktown* (CV-5) (1937)

TYPE • *Aircraft carrier* **COUNTRY** • *United States*

The first of the US Navy's large purpose-built carriers, *Yorktown* (CV-5) saw fierce action in the Pacific War. Fatally crippled in the Battle of Midway in 1942, it was eventually abandoned and subsequently torpedoed.

SPECIFICATIONS

DIMENSIONS:	Length: 251.4m (824ft 9in); Beam: 33.4m (109ft 6in); Draught: 7.9m (25ft 11in)
DISPLACEMENT:	20,100 tonnes (22,165 US tons)
PROPULSION:	9 B&W boilers, 4 Parsons turbines, 89,000kW (120,000shp)
SPEED:	60.2km/h (32.5 knots; 37.4mph)
RANGE:	23,200km (12,500nm; 14,400 miles) at 27.7km/h (15 knots; 17.2mph)
ARMAMENT:	8 × 127mm (5in) 38 cal guns; 4 × quad 28mm (1.1in) 75 cal guns; 24 × .50 cal machine guns
AIRCRAFT:	90
COMPLEMENT:	2217

Right: The USS Yorktown *seen here in 1943 is actually CV-10, an Essex-class carrier that bore the same name as her sunk predecessor. Planes on deck include F6F Hellcat fighters and SB2C Helldiver scout-bombers. Note this carrier's unique longitudinal black flight deck stripe.*

INTERNAL LAYOUT
Internal hull arrangements were worked out specifically for carriers, with three transverse bulkheads and partial longitudinal bulkheads protecting the engine rooms, fuel tanks and ammunition magazines.

ARMOUR
External armour of 82mm (3.25in) was provided below fourth deck level, protecting the fuel tanks and ammunition, and 70mm (2.75in) for the engine space, forming an armoured box.

FLIGHT DECK
The flight deck was formed of Douglas fir planks, 7.6cm (3in) thick and 15.2cm (6in) wide, laid over steel sheet 2.5mm (0.1in) thick.

LAUNCH CATAPULTS
Yorktown was the first US carrier to use hydraulic catapults, in which hydraulic fluid under high pressure was released into a cylinder containing a piston. Catapults on through-deck carriers were not at first considered essential as the aircraft in use were lightweight and had slow take-off speeds. As planes became heavier and bigger payloads were needed, catapults became an important part of the carrier's equipment.

BOMB DAMAGE
The scene on board USS *Yorktown* (CV-5), shortly after she was hit by three Japanese bombs on 4 June 1942. Dense smoke is from fires in her uptakes, caused by a bomb that punctured them and knocked out her boilers. The man with the hammer at right is probably covering a bomb entry hole in the forward elevator.

Adua class (1937)

TYPE • *Submarine* **COUNTRY** • *Italy*

SPECIFICATIONS (*Dagabur*)

Dimensions:	Length: 60.28m (197ft 9in); Beam: 6.45m (21ft 2in); Draught: 4.64m (15ft 3in)
Displacement:	697.2 tonnes (686 US tons) surfaced; 856.4 tonnes (843 US tons) submerged
Propulsion:	2 diesel engines producing 500 W (700hp), 2 electric motors producing 300kW (400hp), 2 screws
Speed:	26km/h (14 knots; 16mph) surfaced; 13.9km/h (7.5 knots; 8.6mph) submerged
Range:	5889 km (3180nm; 3659 miles) surfaced; 137 km (74 nm; 85 miles) submerged
Armament:	6 × 533mm (21in) torpedo tubes; 12 torpedoes; 1 × 100mm (3.9in) deck gun; 2 × 13.2mm (0.5in) MGs
Crew:	44

The 17 Adua-class submarines were quickly built and commissioned, with the lead submarine laid down in January 1936 and completed by November the same year. By October 1938, all boats were in service, constructed at three different shipyards.

Above: The Adua-class submarine Dagabur *was active in the Mediterranean until it was detected by HMS* Wolverine's *Type 271 radar on 12 August 1942. Without surface radar capabilities,* Dagabur *was rammed and sunk by the destroyer.*

Adua
The conning towers of most boats in the class were modified in 1942–43 to allow periscope retraction and accommodate additional anti-aircraft mounts.

Deck masts
Most of the Adua-class submarines were equipped with detachable T-shaped deck masts for supporting radio antennas and net-cutting cables, and many featured serrated, angled bow net-cutters.

Engines
Italian submarines generally had less powerful engines compared to their German or British counterparts, which made them slower, but they were otherwise effective as attack boats.

TORPEDOES
Italy entered the war with stocks of both 533mm (21in) and 450mm (18in) torpedoes, with some submarines equipped with adapters to launch the smaller torpedoes from 533mm tubes. All torpedoes were of the wet-heater type, and their performance was generally superior to those of other European navies. The Type W 4x7.2 Veloce torpedo weighed 1700kg (3784lb), was 7.2m (23ft 7in) long, carried a 270kg (595lb) explosive warhead and could operate up to 12,000m (13,100yd).

ADUA CLASS IN DOCK
These submarines followed the proven '600' type design initiated with the Argonauta class, characterized as single-hulled with midship ballast tanks inside the hull and side blisters. Each shipyard introduced minor differences in appearance and used machinery sourced from their own facilities or suppliers.

Type KD6 and KD7 (1937)

TYPE • *Submarine* **COUNTRY** • *Japan*

The line of KD (*Kaidai*) submarines began in 1925 with KD1. The KD6 series consisted of eight submarines built between 1931 and 1934. All went on to serve in World War II and almost all achieved kills, including assisting in the sinking of US carriers and escort carriers.

SPECIFICATIONS (KD7)

Dimensions:	Length: 105.5m (346ft 5in); Beam: 8.25m (27ft 1in); Draught: 4.6m (15ft 1in)
Displacement:	1,656 tonnes (1,826 US tons) surfaced; 2,644 tonnes (2,915 US tons) submerged
Propulsion:	2 × diesels of 2983kW (4000hp), 2 × 671kW (900hp) electric motors, 2 screws
Speed:	42.8km/h (23.1 knots; 26.6mph) surfaced; 14.8km/h (8 knots; 9.2mph) submerged
Range:	14,816km (8,000nm; 9,206 miles) at 16 knots surfaced; 93km (50nm; 107 miles) at 5 knots submerged
Armament:	6 × 533mm (21in) torpedo tubes; 12 torpedoes; 1 × 120mm (4.7in) L/40 deck gun; 2 × Type 96 25mm (1in) AA guns
Crew:	86

Right: I-168*, a KD6a-class boat, sank the destroyer USS* Hammann *(DD-412) and finished off the crippled carrier USS* Yorktown *(CV-5), both at the Battle of Midway in June 1942.*

I-73
I-73 of Type KD6a was torpedoed on the surface and sunk by USS *Gudgeon* (SS-211) on 27 January 1942.

Armament
This class of submarines had six 533mm (21in) torpedo tubes as their main armament, with a 120mm (4.7in) L/40 deck gun for surface defence and attack.

Performance
The KD6 submarines had a surface speed of 42.8km/h (23.1 knots; 26.6mph) surfaced, which was faster than most submarines of their day in the mid 1930s.

KD7 SUBMARINES

The KD7 (I-176) class of 10 boats was the final specification, and unlike its immediate predecessors, had only medium-range endurance, though still classed as an ocean-going attack boat. It did not handle well when submerged and after 1942 three were converted to transports. As transports they normally carried a small landing craft to ferry supplies ashore. The six torpedo tubes were all forward-facing.

_I-174_ ON PATROL

All the Japanese KD6 submarines were eventually destroyed during World War II, by either surface-ship actions or anti-ship aircraft. *I-174* seen here was sunk by a United States Navy B-24 Liberator patrol aircraft near Truk on 12 April 1944.

HMS *Eskimo* (1938)

TYPE • *Destroyer* **COUNTRY** • *United Kingdom*

SPECIFICATIONS

DIMENSIONS:	Length: 111.5m (364ft 8in); Beam: 11.13m (36ft 6in); Draught: 4m (13ft)
DISPLACEMENT:	1696 tonnes (1870 US tons)
PROPULSION:	2 shaft Parsons geared turbines, 33,131kW (44,000shp)
SPEED	66.7km/h (36 knots; 41.4mph)
ARMAMENT:	8 × 120mm (4.7in) twin turrets; 1 × quadruple 0.9kg (2lb) anti-aircraft guns; 2 × quadruple 12.7mm (0.5in) calibre MGs; 1 × quadruple torpedo tubes (533mm [21in] Mk IX torpedoes); 2 × depth charge throwers; 1 × depth charge rail
COMPLEMENT:	190

HMS *Eskimo* was the Tribal-class sister ship of HMS *Cossack*. Unlike many others of her class, *Eskimo* survived the war, despite seeing plenty of combat, although her ultimate fate was to be used as a target ship in 1949.

Right: HMS Eskimo *is here seen on duty in an Arctic convoy. The explosion of a German bomb is seen amidst the Allied ships.*

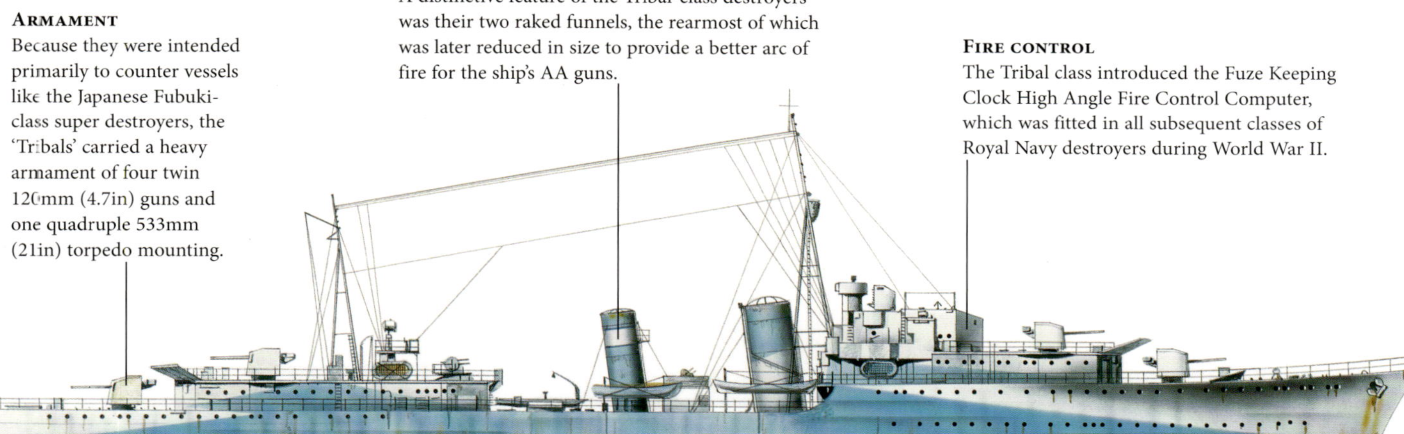

ARMAMENT
Because they were intended primarily to counter vessels like the Japanese Fubuki-class super destroyers, the 'Tribals' carried a heavy armament of four twin 120mm (4.7in) guns and one quadruple 533mm (21in) torpedo mounting.

FUNNELS
A distinctive feature of the Tribal-class destroyers was their two raked funnels, the rearmost of which was later reduced in size to provide a better arc of fire for the ship's AA guns.

FIRE CONTROL
The Tribal class introduced the Fuze Keeping Clock High Angle Fire Control Computer, which was fitted in all subsequent classes of Royal Navy destroyers during World War II.

WAR DAMAGE
Although *Eskimo* would survive the war years, she took some particularly hard knocks along the way. During the Second Battle of Narvik in April 1940, she was hit by a torpedo fired from the German destroyer *Z2 Georg Thiele*. The explosion ripped off her entire bow. Temporary repairs were effected by the shipwrights of the fleet repair ship *Vindictive* at Skjelfjorden in Norway, enabling her return to the Vickers-Armstrong works at Newcastle for rebuilding.

UNDER SAIL
The British Royal Navy destroyer HMS *Eskimo* (F75) under sail in wartime camouflage. This class was admired by both their crews and the public, often becoming symbols of prestige while in service.

USS *Enterprise* (CV-6) (1938)

TYPE • *Aircraft carrier* **COUNTRY** • *United States*

SPECIFICATIONS

Dimensions:	Length: 251.4m (824ft 9in); Beam: 34.9m (114ft 5in); Draught: 7.9m (25ft 11in)
Displacement:	21,336 tonnes (23,517 US tons); 32,573 tonnes (35,909 US tons) full load
Propulsion:	9 B&W boilers, 4 Parsons geared turbines, 4 shafts, 89,484kW (120,000shp)
Speed:	60.2km/h (32.5 knots; 37.4mph)
Range:	23,200km (12,000nm; 14,400 miles) at 27.7km/h (15 knots; 17.2mph)
Armament:	8 × 127mm (5in) 38 cal guns; 8 twin and 6 quad 40mm Bofors guns; 50 × 20mm Oerlikon guns
Aircraft:	90
Complement:	2217

The seventh US ship to carry the name, the 'Big E' played a prominent part in all the great Pacific campaigns of World War II, surviving bombs and kamikaze attacks to gain both battle scars and stars as the most decorated US ship of the war.

Left: Torpedo Squadron Six (VT-6) TBD-1 aircraft are prepared for launching on USS Enterprise *(CV-6) at about 0730–0740hrs, 4 June 1942.*

Deck tractors
Deck tractors and trolleys speeded up the loading of torpedoes and bombs. This was done on the flight deck, whereas Japanese practice was to send up ready-loaded planes from the hangars.

Island
Aft of the pilot house and navigation bridge, the island also held a flag officer's suite and operations room as well as the captain's sea cabin.

Elevators
Three elevators were fitted, plus two flight deck catapults and a single hangar deck catapult.

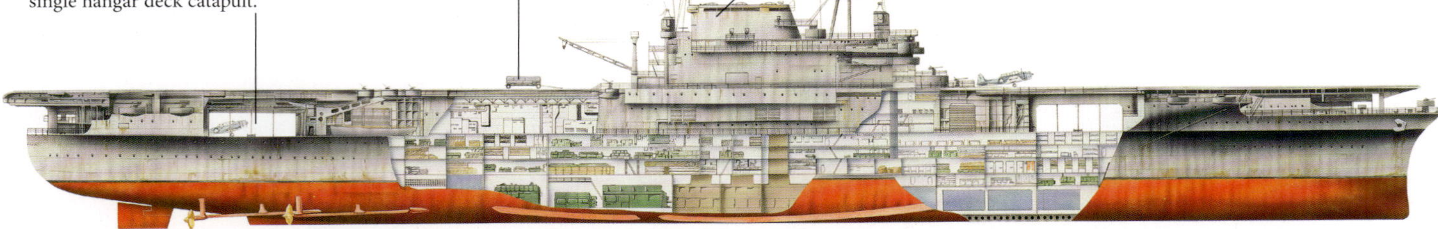

DEVELOPMENT

With USS *Yorktown*, *Enterprise* (CV-6) formed a class of two, built side by side at Newport News Shipbuilding & Dry Dock Co. *Enterprise* was laid down on 16 July 1934, launched on 3 October 1936 and commissioned on 12 May 1938. The Yorktown class followed USS *Ranger* (CV-4, 1934) in being designed as carriers from the start, and so able to carry more aircraft and function more effectively. *Enterprise* carried as many aircraft as *Lexington* but had only half the older ship's displacement.

CELEBRATIONS
USS *Enterprise* steams towards the Panama Canal on 10 October 1945, en route to New York to participate in Navy Day celebrations. *Enterprise* was one of the ships used in late 1945–46 for Operation *Magic Carpet*, the hangars fitted with thousands of temporary berths, making four voyages to bring US troops back from Pearl Harbor and Europe.

Gneisenau (1938)

TYPE • *Battleship* COUNTRY • *Germany*

SPECIFICATIONS

DIMENSIONS:	Length: 229.8m (753ft 11in); Beam: 30m (98ft 5in); Draught: 9.9m (32ft 6in)
DISPLACEMENT:	32,100 tonnes (35,400 US tons) standard
PROPULSION:	3 Germania geared steam turbines, developing 122,040kW (163,660shp)
SPEED:	57km/h (31 knots; 36mph)
RANGE:	11,500km (6200nm; 7100 miles)
ARMAMENT:	9 x 280mm (11in) guns; 12 x 150mm (5.9in) guns; 14 x 105mm (4.1in) guns; 16 x 37mm (1.5in) guns; 10 (later 16) x 20mm (0.79in) AA guns; 6 x 533mm (21in) torpedo tubes
ARMOUR:	Belt: 350mm (13.8in); Deck: 50–105mm (2–4.1in); Turrets: 200–360mm (7.9–14.2in); Conning tower: 350mm (13.8in)
COMPLEMENT:	1669

Gneisenau *ranked among mighty vessels such as* Bismarck *and* Tirpitz *in terms of naval firepower. This great battlecruiser was launched in December 1936 and commissioned in July 1942. Her might, however, failed to protect her adequately from air power.*

Left: A view of the Gneisenau *from the port side from astern, 1938. Note the seaplanes on catapults: a Heinkel HE 114 on the forward catapult and an Arado AR 95 on the catapult atop #3 turret.*

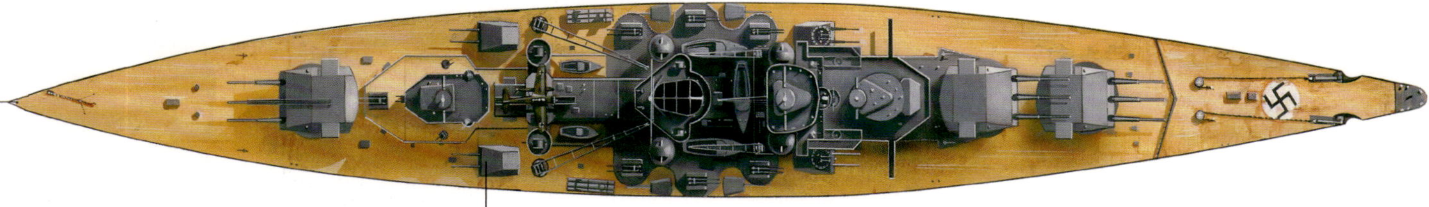

POWERPLANT
Diesel propulsion had been originally intended for both ships, but no diesel engines could produce the necessary power output per shaft, and 12 Wagner extra-high-pressure boilers drove the turbines.

OUTLINE
A general resemblance of outline between *Scharnhorst*, *Gneisenau*, *Bismarck* and *Tirpitz* was deliberately planned in order to confuse their identities.

DECK PLAN
The 150mm (5.9in) secondary guns are clearly visible from this perspective, as are the many smaller 37mm (1.5in) and 20mm (0.79in) AA guns.

COMMERCE RAIDING

Gneisenau and its companion *Scharnhorst* had their bows lengthened in 1939, improving their seaworthiness and performance. In World War II, they attacked British commerce in the North Atlantic and also participated in the sinking of the British aircraft carrier *Glorious* on 8 June 1940. Rendered unusable by RAF bombs in 1942, *Gneisenau* was broken up between 1947 and 1951.

HEAVY GUNS
Gneisenau's main armament was a battery of nine 28cm (11.1in) L/54.5 guns, set in three triple gun turrets: two forward and one aft. From stern to bow the guns were known as Anton, Bruno and Caesar.

Richelieu class (1938)

TYPE • *Cruiser* **COUNTRY** • *France*

SPECIFICATIONS
(Richelieu)

Dimensions:	Length: 247.9m (813ft); Beam: 33m (108ft); Draught: 9.7m (32ft)
Displacement:	43,987 tonnes (48,487 US tons) standard
Propulsion:	6 Indret superheated boilers, 4 Parsons geared turbines, 4 screws, 111,855kW (150,000shp)
Speed:	56km/h (30 knots; 35mph)
Range:	18,240km (9,850nm; 11,340 miles)
Armament:	8 × 380mm (15in) guns in quadruple mounts; 9 × 152mm (6in) guns; 12 × 100mm (3.9in) AA guns; 14 × 37mm (1.5in) AA guns
Armour:	Belt: 343–250mm (13.5–9.8in); Upper deck: 170–130mm (6.7–5.1in); Lower deck: 100–40mm (3.9–1.6in); Barbettes: 405mm (16in); Turrets: 430–195mm (16.9–7.7in)
Complement:	1550

The Richelieu class of fast battleships had the honour of being the last battleships built for the French Navy. Two of the class were built between 1935 and 1955, with two intended upgraded variants never laid down.

Right: Here we see Jean Bart, *a Richelieu-class battleship in a British Admiralty Standard paint scheme.*

Aircraft
The ship's hangar could hold two SNCAC NC.420 floatplanes, with a third on the ship's rear catapult.

Gascogne
Gascogne was a significant revision of the class, with the superfiring forward turret now moved to the aft of the ship. It was never laid down, however.

Armour
The ship's belt armour had to be lengthened to accommodate the new gun layouts. There was a slight reduction in the number of secondary guns.

CONSTRUCTION

Richelieu was laid down in Brest in 1935. During construction, numerous changes were made to the original design, which had the funnel placed between the main and aft towers. The funnel and aft tower were merged into a single structure, with the funnel angled sharply towards the stern. Despite the ever-increasing size and displacement of capital ships, designers were always looking for possible ways to save weight, if only to reuse it elsewhere, and this was one solution.

BATTLESHIP *RICHELIEU*
The *Richelieu* cuts through heavy seas in the Indian Ocean in 1944, her quad 380mm (15in) gun turrets standing proud of the water. From 1943, *Richelieu*, as France's largest battleship, was a powerful symbol of Free France while the country lay under German occupation.

Type IX (1938)

TYPE • *Submarine* **COUNTRY** • *Germany*

SPECIFICATIONS

Dimensions:	Length: 76.5m (251ft); Beam: 6.5m (21ft 4in); Draught: 4.7m (15ft 5in)
Displacement	1048.5 tonnes (1155 US tons) surfaced; 1587.5 tonnes (1750 US tons) submerged
Propulsion:	2 1640.5kW (2200hp) diesels, 6-cylinder 4-stroke RS34.5S outputting 432.5kW (580hp)
Speed	33.7km/h (18.2 knots; 21mph) surfaced; 14.3km/h (7.7 knots; 8.9mph) submerged
Range:	43,892km (23,700nm; 27,273 miles) at 22.2km/h (12 knots; 13.8mph)
Armament:	4 × bow, 2 × stern 533mm (21in) torpedo tubes; 22 torpedoes; 1 × 37mm (1.4in) gun; twin 20mm (0.79in) AA guns
Crew:	48

Building on the lessons of Type IA, this was the Kriegsmarine's prime ocean-going attack submarine. Type IX was a great advance on IA, double-hulled, with a streamlined outer shell and an internal pressure hull formed of 18mm (0.7in) steel.

Above: Although a part of 2. Flottille, U-107 *took part in the attack on convoy HG 76. While unsuccessful in this operation,* U-107 *did sink 37 ships over the course of 14 patrols, making her one of the most successful U-boats of the war.*

Snorkel pipe
The snorkel pipe angled down into a horizontal recess on the forward starboard side of the tower. Fitting of a snorkel required removal of the forward deck gun. Previously this might have been a 105mm (4.1in) SK C/32 or a 37mm (1.5) single flak gun.

Extra torpedoes
Up to 24 torpedoes were carried, including four stored in upper deck containers, below the aft flak platform.

***U-156*, Type IXD/2**
Type IXD/2 was 11.1m (36.4ft) longer than Type IXA, with a surface displacement of 1642 tonnes (1809 US tons) compared to 1048.5 tonnes (1155 US tons).

TYPE OVERVIEW

There were eight versions of Type IX, but the first four, IXA to IXC/40, had very similar vital statistics. All were powered by 1640.5kW (2200hp) MAN diesel engines, two SSW 373kW (500hp) electric motors and two 62-cell battery sets. Bunker capacity increased slightly in each revision with a consequent increase in surface range. Wartime modifications and repairs resulted in a variety of tower configurations. The foredeck gun was also removed in many cases.

TYPE IX, NORWAY
A German Type IX submarine docks at Tromso, Norway, cutting through evidently icy waters. The tower was set aft of midships, with a long foredeck that helped in rapid emergency diving.

Brooklyn class (1938)

TYPE • *Cruiser* **COUNTRY** • *United States*

SPECIFICATIONS

DIMENSIONS:	Length: 185.42m (608ft 4in); Beam: 18.77m (61ft 7in); Draught :7.3m (24ft)
DISPLACEMENT:	9924 tonnes (10,939 US tons) standard
PROPULSION:	8 steam boilers, 4 geared turbines, 4 screws, 75,000 kW (100,000shp)
SPEED:	60.2 km/h (32.5 knots; 37.4 mph)
RANGE:	18,520 km (10,000nm; 11,510 miles)
ARMAMENT:	15 × 152mm (6in) 47-calibre guns (5 × 3); 8 × 127mm (5in) 25-calibre guns (8 × 1)
ARMOUR:	Belt: 83–127mm (3.25–5in); Deck: 51mm (2in); Barbettes: 150mm (6in); Turrets: 32–152mm (1.25–6in); Conning tower: 57–127mm (2.25–5in)
COMPLEMENT:	868

During the early 1930s, the US Navy upgraded the Brooklyn-class cruiser design in response to the new Japanese Mogami-class cruisers. Good protection was provided by weight saved in the hull. There were nine vessels in the new class, and all served during World War II.

Above: A port profile view of USS Brooklyn *under way, clearly showing her superfiring turret layout.*

ARMAMENT
The main guns of the Brooklyn class were 15 152mm (6in) 47-calibre Mark 16 naval guns, which had an effective firing range of more than 18,000m (19,685yd).

FIRE CONTROL
As built, the ship's main armament was linked to the Mark 34 director and, later, the Mark 3 radar; these were later upgraded to the Mark 8 and the Mark 13 radar.

CATAPULT
The rear of the ship featured a steam catapult for launching floatplanes, four of which were carried aboard.

WAR SERVICE
While many US Navy destroyers spent at least some of the war in the Pacific, USS *Brooklyn* spent her war service in more westerly waters. In early 1942 she was first deployed to the Caribbean, but from April 1942 she performed Atlantic convoy escort duties. From November 1942 to 1944, however, *Brooklyn* served principally in the MTO, often providing fire support for US ground operations around North Africa and Italy.

USS *BROOKLYN* (CL-40)
From late 1944 until May 1945, *Brooklyn* underwent a substantial overhaul in the United States. She served in a reserve status during the late 1940s, but from 1951 was transferred to the Chilean Navy, in which she served for four decades.

HMS *Ark Royal* (1938)

TYPE • *Aircraft carrier* **COUNTRY** • *United Kingdom*

SPECIFICATIONS

DIMENSIONS:	Length: 208m (682ft); Beam: 28.9m (94ft 10in); Draught: 8.73m (27ft 10in)
DISPLACEMENT:	22,352 tonnes (24,644 US tons); 28,163 tonnes (31,042 US tons) full load
PROPULSION:	6 Admiralty boilers, 3 Parsons geared turbines, 76,807kW (103,000shp)
SPEED:	57km/h (31 knots; 36mph)
RANGE:	14,100km (7600nm; 8700 miles) at 37km/h (20 knots; 23mph)
ARMAMENT:	16 × 110mm (4.5in) DP guns; 32 × 2-pdr 40mm (1.57in) pom-pom guns; 12.7mm (32.5in) AA machine guns
AIRCRAFT:	60
COMPLEMENT:	1580

The third *Ark Royal*, albeit the first aircraft carrier to bear the illustrious name, saw intensive action in the early part of World War II in the Atlantic, the Norwegian Sea and finally in the Mediterranean theatre, where it was sunk by a U-boat on 13–14 November 1941.

Left: A forward profile, with a Fairey Swordfish torpedo bomber poised on the bow.

MAST
A hinged telescopic mast was placed in the centre of the flight deck to carry navigation guidance lights.

AIRCRAFT
Almost from the start, naval aircraft were made with folding wings to fit lifts and maximize use of hangar space. The first naval aircraft with folding wings was the British Short Folder seaplane in 1913.

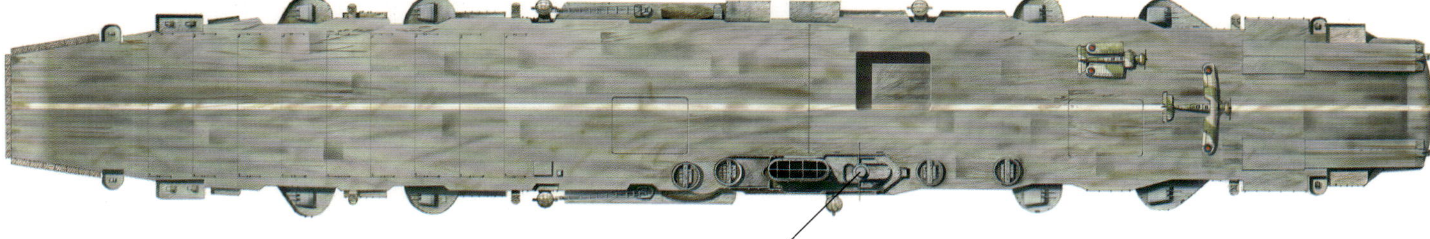

LAYOUT
Though massive in appearance from the starboard side, the minimal space occupied by *Ark Royal*'s island is clearly seen from the plan view: it is hardly wider than the ship's funnel.

THE FLEET AIR ARM
After World War I it was intended that the Navy would provide carriers and the RAF would supply the aircraft, flying crews and maintenance teams. This was a most unworkable decision. Despite the increasingly obvious problems of managing naval aviation through two separate services, it was 1937 before the Fleet Air Arm once again became an integral part of the Royal Navy.

FUTURE LESSONS
Ark Royal had been a model for the Illustrious class, and the failure of its torpedo protection caused rapid design changes in new carriers along with improved damage control systems and practice, and the provision of diesel generators to provide electric power in the event of a mechanical failure.

Kirov class (1938)

TYPE • *Cruiser* COUNTRY • *Soviet Union*

The six Kirov-class cruisers were the first large naval vessels to be entirely built in Soviet shipyards after the Russian Revolution. The design was based on that of the Italian Navy's Raimondo Montecuccoli-class cruisers.

SPECIFICATIONS

Dimensions:	Length: 191.3m (627ft 7in); Beam: 17.66m (57ft 11in); Draught: 6.15m (20ft 2in)
Displacement:	7890 tonnes (8697 US tons) standard
Propulsion:	Steam turbines totalling 84,600kW (113,500hp)
Speed:	66.56km/h (35.94 knots; 41mph)
Range:	6940km (3750nm; 4312 miles)
Armament:	9 x 180mm (7.1in); 6 x 100mm (3.9in) (AA); 6 x 45mm (1.77in); 4 x 12.7mm (0.5in); 6 x 533mm (21in) torpedo tubes; Mines 96–164; Depth charges 50
Armour:	50mm (2in) belt, deck, turrets and barbettes; 150mm (5.9in) conning tower
Aircraft:	2
Complement:	872

Right: A forward view of the main gun armament of a Soviet Kirov-class heavy cruiser during World War II. The barrels of two single light anti-aircraft guns appear in the extreme left foreground.

Catapult
The ship was equipped with a Heinkel K-12 aviation catapult, which was used to deploy the ship's two Beriev Be-2 floatplanes.

Armament
The class suffered from an attempt to pack in too much armament on a limited displacement. Their triple 180mm (7.1in) turrets gave constant trouble.

Armour
While the conning tower had the thickest armour on the ship, the rest of the ship had a general covering of about 50mm (2in), certainly not enough to withstand a heavy shell impact.

FIRST ACTION

Kirov first saw action against Finnish coastal batteries during the Winter War. She acted as the flagship for the evacuation of Tallinn in August 1941, before taking refuge in Kronstadt. She gave gunfire support during the siege of Leningrad and bombarded Finnish positions in mid-1944 during the Vyborg–Petrozavodsk offensive, but played no further part in the war. *Kirov* was reclassified as a training cruiser in 1961 and scrapped in 1974.

KIROV IN PROFILE

The first two pairs of ships (*Kirov*, *Voroshilov*, *Maxim Gorky* and *Molotov*) were deployed on shore bombardment and supply missions with the Baltic and Black Sea Fleets throughout the war, while the last pair (*Kaganovich* and *Kalinin*) were still under construction for the Pacific Fleet at the Amur Shipbuilding Plant and saw no combat.

Leonardo da Vinci (Marconi class) (1939)

TYPE • *Submarine* **COUNTRY** • *Italy*

SPECIFICATIONS

Dimensions:	Length: 76.5m (251ft); Beam: 6.81m (22ft 5in); Draught :4.72m (15ft 6in)
Displacement:	1194 tonnes (1175 US tons) surface; 1489 tonnes (1465 US tons) submerged
Propulsion:	2 diesels of 1342.5kW (1800hp), 2 556kW (750hp) electric motors, 2 screws
Speed:	33km/h (17.8 knots; 20.5mph) surface; 15.2km/h (8.2 knots; 9.4mph) submerged
Range:	16,898km (9124nm; 10,500 miles) surface; 177km (95.6nm; 110 miles) submerged
Armament:	8 x 533mm (21in) torpedo tubes; 12 torpedoes; 1 x 100mm (4in) 47cal deck gun; 4 x 13.2mm (0.5in) machine guns
Crew:	57

Six-strong, the Marconis were the Regia Marina's most successful class. A wider operating range of 19,446km (10,500nm; 12,083 miles) was the main difference between the Marconi-class boats and the preceding Marcellos.

Below: Built at Monfalcone, this boat made some of the longest patrols of any World War II submarine, operating into the South Atlantic for up to 135 days.

Leonardo da Vinci
Leonardo da Vinci as fitted for the planned New York attack, with the CA-2 in place of the deck gun. The tall fairing around the periscopes was removed to reduce the boat's silhouette. As with many other submarine classes, the Marconi boats showed tower-shape variations as the war went on.

Towers
The original towers, with a tall narrow periscope casing rising above the oblong base, were cut back in 1941–42, in reaction to Atlantic weather and fighting conditions.

Propulsion
Power came from the same CRDA diesels of a combined 2684.5kW (3600hp) as the Marcellos, but the two Marelli electric motors were uprated to a combined 1118.5kW (1500hp).

Armament
A warload of 16 torpedoes was carried. The type mounted a single 100mm (4in) 47cal gun, on the foredeck, and for AA defence two twin 13.2mm (0.5in) guns were mounted in the tower.

NEW YORK ATTACK

In the summer of 1942, *Leonardo da Vinci* was temporarily modified to carry a CA-2 midget submarine on the foredeck, which could be launched underwater. The aim was a stealth attack on New York harbour, which was cancelled. The fittings were later removed, and the deck gun was restored. Planned conversion to a transport submarine in 1943 was forestalled by its sinking on 23 May that year.

GUGLIELMO MARCONI
The class leader, *Guglielmo Marconi*, launched at Monfalcone on 27 July 1939. It disappeared in the Atlantic at the end of October 1941.

Yukikaze (Kagero class) (1939)

TYPE • *Destroyer* **COUNTRY** • *Japan*

SPECIFICATIONS

Dimensions:	Length: 118.49m (388ft 9in); Beam: 10.79m (35ft 5in); Draught: 3.76m (12ft 4in)
Displacement:	2033 tonnes (2241 US tons) standard; 2450 tonnes (2700 US tons) trial
Propulsion:	3 boilers, 2-shaft geared turbines, 38,811kW (52,000hp)
Speed:	65km/h (35 knots; 40.3mph)
Armour:	None
Armament:	6 × 127mm (5in) main guns; 4 × 25mm AA guns; 8 × 609mm (24in) torpedo tubes; 16 depth charges
Complement:	240

The Kagero-class destroyers were the most modern of their type available to the Japanese Navy when war broke out in Europe. They were similar to the earlier Asashio class, but could take advantage of a refined design that had been well and truly 'wrung out'.

Left: A post-war Yukikaze *as seen in Tokyo on 26 May 1947. The destroyer had been repatriating Japanese nationals from overseas, hence was stripped of her armament.* Yukikaze *later became the Republic of China Navy's destroyer* Tan Yang.

Yukikaze
Yukikaze was the sixth Kagero destroyer and was launched at the Sasebo naval yard on 24 March 1939.

Powerplant
The destroyer was powered by three boilers connected to two-shaft geared turbines, generating a total power output of 38,811kW (52,000hp).

Armament
The Kageros were designed with three twin 5in (127mm) gun turrets but the centre X turret was deleted from the remaining ships between 1943 and 1944 to make way for more AA armament.

SURVIVOR
One of the Kagero class, *Hamakaze*, made a small contribution to Japanese naval history by becoming the first Japanese destroyer to be fitted with radar. The smaller combat vessels of the Japanese fleet were virtually wiped out by the US Navy and the Kagero class was no exception, although it was virtually the only Japanese destroyer class not to have every member sunk by 1945. Of the 18 ships built, only *Yukikaze* survived the war, one of half a dozen destroyers to survive from a total force of over 100 vessels.

***Yukikaze*, Tokyo 1947**
A view of the ship's deck, looking aft from her bow. The ship at this time was being exhibited to representatives of the leading Allied powers. To the right we can see the escort ship *Shisaka*.

Katori class (1939)

TYPE • *Destroyer* COUNTRY • *Japan*

SPECIFICATIONS

Dimensions:	Length: 129.77m (425ft 9in); Beam: 15.95m (52ft 4in); Draught: 5.75m (18ft 10in)
Displacement:	5985 tonnes (6598 US tons) normal
Propulsion:	2-shaft geared turbines plus diesel motors, 3 Kampon boilers, 6000kW (8000shp)
Speed:	33km/h (18 knots; 21mph)
Range:	17,000km (9,000nm; 10,563 miles) at 19km/h (10 knots; 12mph)
Armament:	4 x 140mm (5.5in)/50 cal guns (2 x 2); 2 x 127mm (5in)/40 cal AA guns (1 x 2); 4 x Type 96 AA guns (later increased to 30); 8 x 13.2mm (0.52in) AA guns; 4 x 533mm (21in) torpedo tubes (2 x 2)
Armour:	Gun turrets: 10mm (0.4in); Conning tower: 10mm (0.4in)
Complement:	315 + 275 midshipmen

The Katori-class cruisers were originally conceived as training vessels for the Imperial Japanese Navy in the late 1930s and the 1940s. The outbreak of the Pacific War in December 1941, however, meant that they were soon repurposed for active combat.

Left: A Japanese Katori-class cruiser photographed off the coast of the atoll of Kwajalein in the Marshall Islands in 1944.

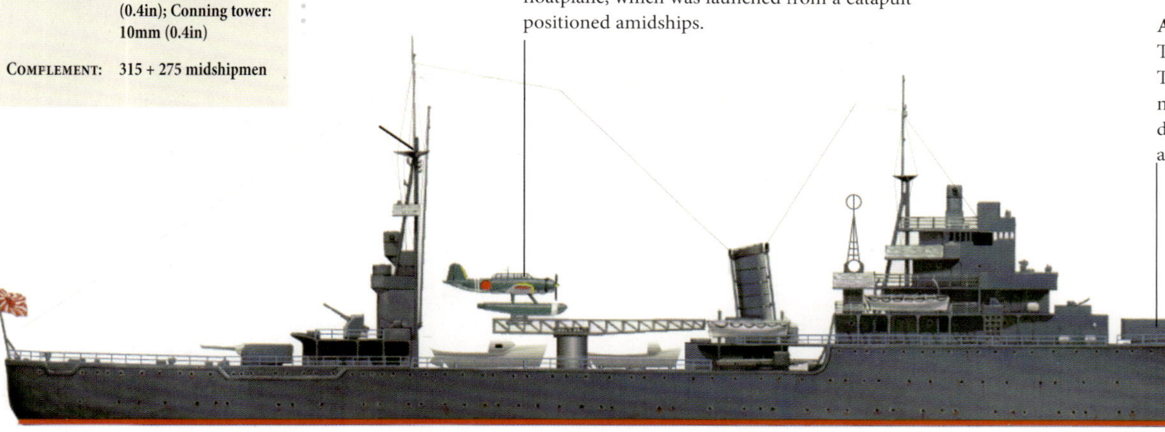

Aircraft
The ship was capable of deploying a single floatplane, which was launched from a catapult positioned amidships.

AA armament
The class as-built had just four Type 96 AA guns, but this number was later increased to 30 due to the elevated threat of air attack in the Pacific theatre.

Displacement
The Katori class had a normal displacement of 5985 tonnes (6598 US tons) and a full-load displacement of 6279 tonnes (6921 US tons).

KATORI
The lead ship of the class was commissioned on 20 April 1940. During the war, *Katori* was seriously damaged by US dive-bombers and torpedo-bombers in February 1942, but was repaired and returned to service. On 17–18 February 1944, off Truk, she was again damaged by a US air attack, but was subsequently finished off by heavy gunfire from the US battleships *Iowa* (BB-61) and *New Jersey* (BB-62).

AERIAL PHOTOGRAPH
This Japanese Katori-class cruiser was photographed by a British reconnaissance aircraft over the Pacific. Of the four ships intended for the class, two were sunk in action, one survived the war and one was laid down but not completed.

Karl Galster (Z20) (1939)

TYPE • *Destroyer* **COUNTRY** • *Germany*

SPECIFICATIONS

Dimensions:	Length: 125m (410ft 1in); Beam: 11.78m (38ft 5in); Draught: 3.98m (13ft 1in)
Displacement:	1811 tonnes (1996 US tons) standard; 3415 tonnes (3766 US tons) full load
Machinery:	6 Wagner boilers, driving 2-shaft Wagner geared turbines, developing 52,199kW (70,000shp)
Speed:	40 knots (74km/h; 46mph)
Armament:	5 × 127mm (5in) main guns; 4 × 37mm (1.45in) AA guns; 7 × 20mm (0.79in) AA guns; 8 × 533mm (21in) torpedo tubes
Armour:	None
Complement:	315

When Germany declared war, the German Navy had only a small force of 21 destroyers. *Karl Galster* was one of the six 1936-type destroyers laid down between 1936 and 1937. She was launched on 15 June 1938.

Right: A large-diameter signalling light was mounted above the bridge. A powerful searchlight for surface or air defence was mounted behind the aft funnel.

AA and anti-submarine

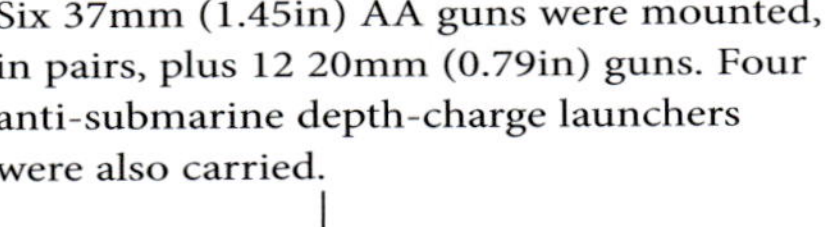

Six 37mm (1.45in) AA guns were mounted, in pairs, plus 12 20mm (0.79in) guns. Four anti-submarine depth-charge launchers were also carried.

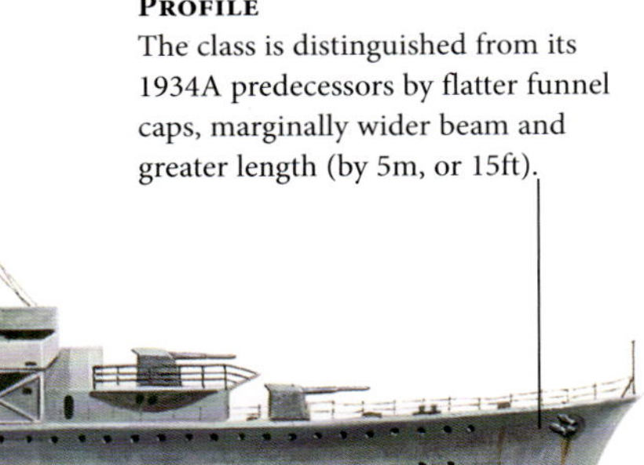

Profile

The class is distinguished from its 1934A predecessors by flatter funnel caps, marginally wider beam and greater length (by 5m, or 15ft).

Machinery

The high-pressure boilers and turbines, with a substantial power output of 55,554kW (74,500shp), were more reliable than in previous classes.

SERVICE

By April 1940, the German destroyer force had been cut in half with the sinking of 10 destroyers by British forces in the Norwegian campaign. *Karl Galster* was the only one of its class to survive the war; the other five were sunk either at Narvik or in Rombaksfjord. In 1946 the *Karl Galster* was handed over to the Soviet Navy as part of Germany's war reparations to the Soviet Union. She served in the Baltic fleet as the *Protshnyi* into the 1950s.

***KARL GALSTER* (Z20), 1939**

The 1934-type ships were well-built and cleverly engineered but they were over-sophisticated, particularly in their powerplants, and technical troubles prevented them attaining their full design performance.

HMS *Kelly* (1939)

TYPE • *Destroyer* **COUNTRY** • *United Kingdom*

SPECIFICATIONS

Dimensions:	Length: 108.66m (356ft 6in); Beam: 10.87m (35ft 8in); Draught: 4.22m (13ft 10in)
Displacement:	2330 tonnes (2570 US tons) standard; 2540 tonnes (2800 US tons) full load
Machinery:	2 Admiralty 3-drum boilers, driving 2-shaft Parsons geared turbines, developing 29,828kW (40,000shp)
Speed:	67km/h (36 knots; 41mph)
Armament:	6 × 119mm (4.7in) main guns; 4 × 2-pounder 'pom-pom' AA guns; 10 × 533mm (21in) torpedo tubes; 45 depth charges
Armour:	None
Complement:	183–218

HMS *Kelly* was the lead ship of the K class, which was built alongside the J- and N-class destroyers laid down between 1937 and 1938. *Kelly* herself was launched on 25 October 1938 and was destined for an ill-fated war service.

Above: HMS Kelly, *photographed from the nearby HMS* Kipling, *is here seen on her return to service after repairs, once more taking her place as Fifth Destroyer Flotilla Leader.*

Speed
The two-shaft Parsons geared turbines could take the *Kelly* to an impressive maximum speed of 67km/h (36 knots; 41mph).

Armour
As with many British destroyers, the *Kelly* was unarmoured, relying principally on its speed and manoeuvrability for its survival.

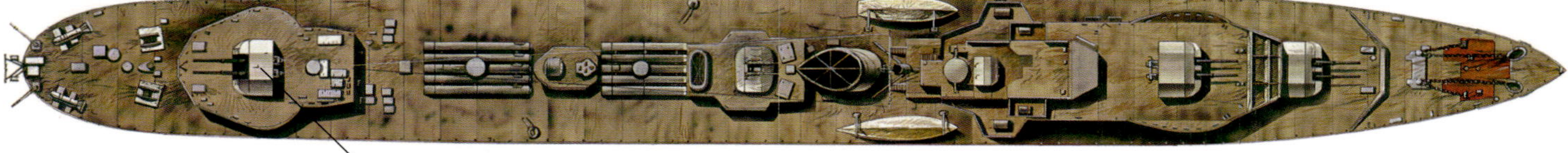

Armament
The K class featured the same 119mm (4.7in) guns as the Tribal destroyers, and were also armed with torpedoes and depth charges.

K-CLASS AT WAR

In all, eight K-class destroyers were built between 1938 and 1939. Of these, four were lost to enemy action and one was destroyed by an accidental internal explosion. On 20 May 1941 off Crete, the *Kelly* and her unit came under persistent Stuka attack. While making speed and turning hard to port, the vessel suffered severe bomb damage. Still moving fast, *Kelly* rolled over and capsized, sinking in half an hour.

MESSAGE TRANSFER
HMS *Kelly* transfers a message to another K-class destroyer, HMS *Kelvin*, by line. *Kelly* was famed as the flagship of Lord Louis Mountbatten's flotilla; Mountbatten survived the ship's sinking in 1941.

HMS *Audacity* (1939)

TYPE • *Aircraft carrier* COUNTRY • *United Kingdom*

SPECIFICATIONS

DIMENSIONS:	Length: 142.4m (467ft 3in); Beam: 17.15m (56ft 3in); Draught: 8.4m (27ft 6in)
DISPLACEMENT:	10,230 tonnes (10,068 US tons); 12,192 tonnes (12,000 US tons) full load
PROPULSION:	7-cylinder MAN diesel, single shaft, 3900kW (5200bhp)
SPEED:	28km/h (15 knots; 17mph)
RANGE:	Not known
ARMAMENT:	1 × 102mm (4in) gun; 4 × 2-pdr AA guns; 4 × 20mm (0.787in) AA guns
AIRCRAFT:	6
COMPLEMENT:	480

There was a touch of audacity in the action of converting the German merchant ship *Hannover*, seized in the Atlantic in March 1940, into the first British escort carrier. Its brief career as a warship clearly showed the value of such ships.

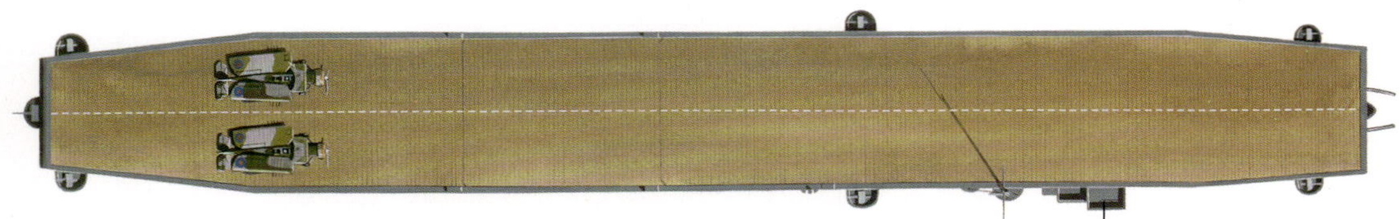

Above: Audacity *was a complete 'flat-top' with no island, only an open conning post at flight deck level. There was no hangar deck and the aircraft were parked and refuelled on the open flight deck.*

ISLAND
A minimal island unit, placed forward, was added to *Audacity* some time after completion, in order to provide better shelter for flight control and navigation.

AIRCRAFT
A Fairey Swordfish is shown on deck. *Audacity* was the first British carrier to operate Grumman Martlet Mk II fighters. The F4F Wildcat was renamed Martlet by its British users, but from March 1944 the Royal Navy also used the Wildcat name.

DECK CONSTRUCTION
The flight deck was wood-surfaced, unlike standard RN carriers, in the interest of rapid construction, saving of steel and reducing top weight. In action it was painted in camouflage colours.

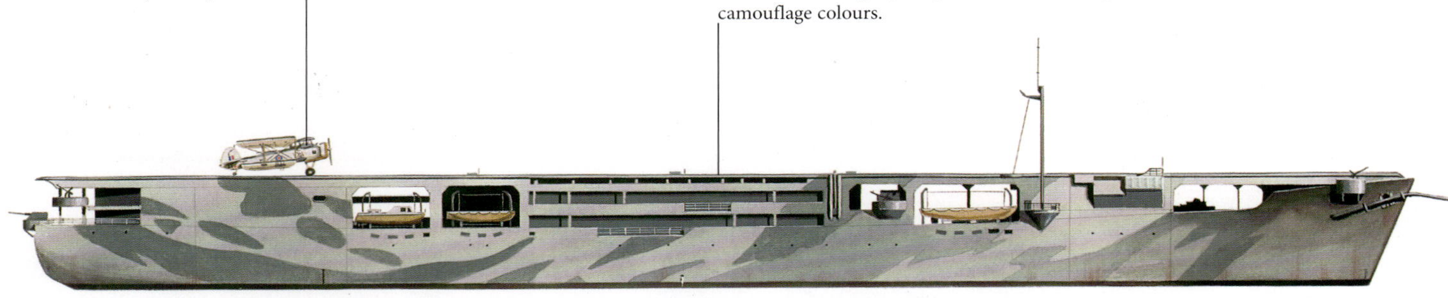

RN CARRIERS
Between August 1942 and June 1943, 18 purpose-built escort carriers were manufactured in the USA and supplied both to the US Navy and the Royal Navy. The RN had eight, supplied on Lend-Lease terms to Britain. Based on a cargo ship hull design adapted to form a light carrier with hangar deck and lifts, they could hold 24 aircraft. A further 24 were built in 1943–44, almost all transferred to the Royal Navy. During the war, they functioned as transport, escort and attack carriers.

***AUDACITY*'S FATE**
Audacity was sunk by a German U-boat on 21 December 1941, while performing escort duties off the coast of Portugal. It foundered at 22.10, with the loss of 73 crew members, most of them drowned.

USS *Sangamon* (1939)

TYPE • *Aircraft carrier* **COUNTRY** • *United States*

SPECIFICATIONS

DIMENSIONS:	Length: 169m (553ft); Beam: 23m (75ft); Draught: 9.8m (32ft)
DISPLACEMENT:	11,582 tonnes (12,768 US tons); 24,663 tonnes (27,194 US tons) full load
PROPULSION:	4 boilers, 2 steam turbines, 2 shafts, 10,067kW (13,500shp)
SPEED:	33km/h (18 knots; 21mph)
RANGE:	43,000km (23,920nm; 26,783 miles) at 27.7km/h (15 knots; 17.2mph)
ARMAMENT (ORIGINAL):	2 × 127mm (5in) 38 cal guns; 2 quad; 7 twin 40mm 56 cal and 21 single 20mm 70 cal AA guns
AIRCRAFT:	32
COMPLEMENT:	1080

***Sangamon* had a dual career with the US Navy, first as a fleet oiler, then as the Navy's first escort carrier. It was first of a class of escort carriers that would play essential supporting roles in achieving the US Navy's dominance in the Pacific.**

Above: The side openings show the level of the main deck, or fuel deck as the crew called it. Sangamon *was fitted for at-sea refuelling and the pumps were housed on this deck.*

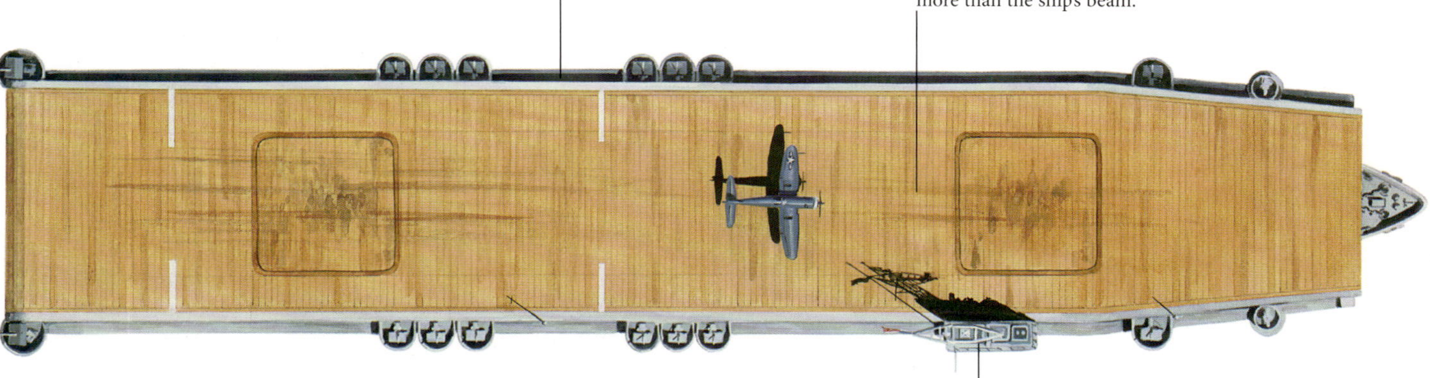

CATWALKS
As on most carriers, 'catwalks' for the crew were positioned all round the flight deck, partly outboard and supported by struts, to enable safe passage while take-offs and landings were happening.

FLIGHT DECK
This extended well beyond the hull to port and starboard, with a maximum width of 12m (39ft) more than the ship's beam.

ISLAND
Despite its small size, the island incorporated an admiral's bridge below the captain's bridge, which was open and on the same level as the primary flight control station, one to port and one to starboard.

DEVELOPMENT

Laid down on 13 March 1939 at the Federal Shipbuilding & Drydock Co., Kearny, New Jersey, for Standard Oil's fleet as *Esso Trenton*, the ship was launched on 4 November the same year. The Navy purchased it on 22 October 1940, giving it the designation AO28 and changing the name to *Sangamon* on 12 April 1941. From December 1941 there was a search under way for ships or hulls suitable for rapid conversion to carriers. *Sangamon* was picked and commissioned as a carrier in August 1942.

WORKHORSE CARRIERS
Nautical historians consider the Sangamon class as equal to the purpose-built CVL light carriers that succeeded them, and perhaps in some ways superior in all respects save speed. They could not keep up with fast Task Groups, but that still left a wide range of potential duties.

Scharnhorst (1939)

TYPE • *Battleship* • **COUNTRY** • *Germany*

Often referred to as the first German battleship to be constructed since World War I, *Scharnhorst* was actually laid down and commissioned after *Gneisenau*. Despite being sister ships, there were numerous minor differences between them.

SPECIFICATIONS

Dimensions:	Length: 235m (772ft); Beam: 30m (98ft 5in); Draught: 9.7m (31ft 9in)
Displacement:	29,121 tonnes (32,100 tons); 34,564 tonnes (38,100 tons) full load
Propulsion:	12 Wagner HP boilers, 3 Brown-Boveri geared turbines developing 119,312kW (160,000hp)
Speed:	57km/h (31 knots; 35.4mph)
Range:	16,298km (8800nm; 10,127 miles) at 35km/h (19 knots; 22mph)
Armament:	9 x 280mm (11in) guns; 12 x 150mm (5.9in) guns; 14 x 105mm (4.1in) guns; 16 x 37mm (1.5in) and 10 x 20mm (0.79in) AA guns; 6 x 533mm (21in) torpedo tubes
Armour:	Belt: 350–200mm (13.8–7.9in); Bulkheads: 200–150mm (7.9–5.9in); Deck: 50–20mm (2–0.79in); Barbettes: 350–200mm (13.8–7.9in); Turrets: 350–200mm (13.8–7.9in); Conning tower: 350–100mm (13.8–3.9in)
Complement:	1968

Below: Deck plan: the 150mm (5.9in) secondary guns are clearly visible from this perspective, as are the many smaller 37mm (1.5in) and 20mm (0.79in) AA guns.

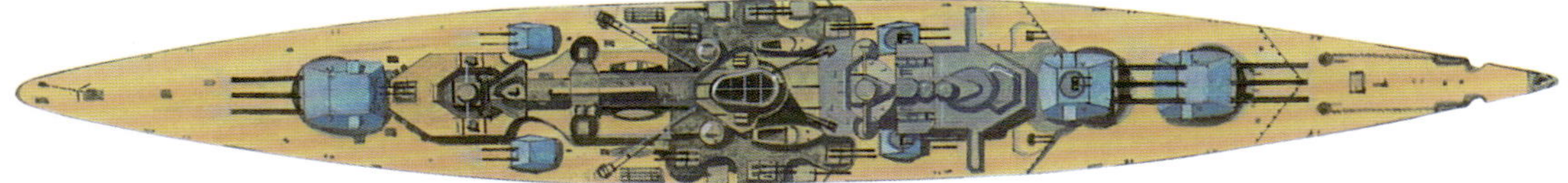

Boats
Three picket boats, two motor yawls, five cutters, one motor pinnace and one motor launch were carried.

Outline
A general resemblance of outline between *Scharnhorst*, *Gneisenau*, *Bismarck* and *Tirpitz* was deliberately planned in order to confuse their identities.

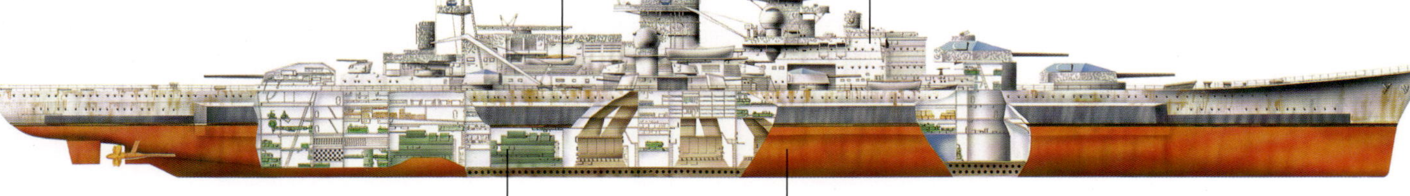

Propulsion
Diesel propulsion had been originally intended for both ships, but no diesel engines could produce the necessary power output per shaft, and 12 Wagner extra-high-pressure boilers drove the turbines.

Fuel Capacity
Maximum fuel capacity was 5624 tonnes (5535) tons of oil, giving a range of 8800nm (16,298km; 10,127 miles) at 19 knots (35km/h; 22mph).

CONVOY ACTION

By the end of 1943, *Scharnhorst* was the Reich's only operational capital ship. With a force of five destroyers under Rear Admiral Bey, it was sent on 25 December to attack Convoy JW55B en route for Murmansk, and came under fire from the guns of the battleship *Duke of York*, with four escorting destroyers. A combination of torpedoes and shell fire finally destroyed *Scharnhorst*. It sank at 19.44 on 26 December, in 290m (950ft) of water, with the loss of 1803 men.

OCEAN GOING
Captain Otto Ciliax (front left), of the battleship *Scharnhorst*, carries out an inspection of the crew, c.1939.

USS *Wasp* (1940)

TYPE • *Aircraft carrier* **COUNTRY** • *United States*

The last of the 'treaty carriers' whose size was restricted by the 1922 Washington Naval Treaty, and the last US carrier to be commissioned before America entered World War II, *Wasp* was the only ship of its class.

SPECIFICATIONS

Dimensions:	Length: 230m (754ft 7in); Beam: 29.2m (95ft 10in); Draught: 8.8m (29ft)
Displacement:	23,368 tonnes (25,763 US tons); 30,206 tonnes (33,297 US tons) full load
Propulsion:	6 boilers, Parsons geared turbines, 3 shafts, 83,000kW (111,000shp)
Speed	56km/h (30.5 knots; 35mph)
Range:	20,000km (11,000nm; 13,000 miles) at 25.9km/h (14 knots; 16.1mph)
Armament:	16 × 110mm (4.5in) guns; 48 × 2-pdr and 10 × 20mm AA guns
Aircraft:	48
Complement:	1600

Above: Wasp's *profile shows that its design continued the practice of building the flight deck as a superstructure above the hull.*

Offset
Wasp was not parallel-sided and an outward cant to port balanced the weight of the island and the internal funnel trunking.

Catapults
Two catapults were fitted on the flight deck and two on the hangar deck, all hydraulically operated.

Deck-edge elevator
The deck-edge elevator was fitted as an experiment but was quickly recognized as great help in flight deck and hangar operations.

REQUIREMENTS

Intended as a replacement for the US Navy's first carrier, *Langley*, and designated CV-7, *Wasp* was laid down on 1 April 1936, launched on 4 April 1939 and commissioned on 25 April 1940. In October 1940, after further trials and training, it joined the fleet. Its dimensions and capacity were governed by the 1922 Naval Treaty. The new carrier was to be only about three-quarters the displacement of *Enterprise*, and its cost was $20 million.

SAILORS WATCH USS *WASP*
With the loss of *Lexington* and *Yorktown* in May–June 1942 seriously weakening the US Navy's carrier force in the Pacific, *Wasp* was directed to that ocean in June 1942, embarking F4F Wildcat fighters, SBD-3 Dauntless dive-bombers and TBF Avenger torpedo bombers at San Diego.

Vittorio Veneto (1940)

TYPE • *Battleship* **COUNTRY** • *Italy*

SPECIFICATIONS

Dimensions:	Length: 237.8m (778ft 9in); Beam: 32.9m (107ft 9in); Draught: 9.6m (31ft 5in)
Displacement:	42,040 tonnes (41,377 US tons)
Propulsion:	Quadruple shafts, 8 Yarrow boilers, 4 Belluzzo geared turbines, 100,383kW (134,616shp)
Speed:	58.2km/h (31.4 knots; 36.1mph)
Armament:	9 × 381mm (15in) guns; 12 × 152mm (6in) guns; 4 × 120mm (4.7in) guns; 12 × 90mm (3.5in) AA guns; 20 × 37mm (1.5in) AA guns; 16 × 20mm (0.79in) AA guns
Armour:	Belt :350–60mm (13.8–2.4in); Barbettes: 350mm (13.8in); Turrets: 350–100mm (13.8–3.9in); Deck: 205–35mm (8.1–1.4in)
Complement:	1861

Classified officially as *corazzate* (literally 'armour-clads'), Italy's last battleship class was to be formed of four ships, but only three were completed, of which two saw active service. *Vittorio Veneto* was launched on 25 July 1937 and completed on 28 April 1940.

Above: The lengthy construction time of the Vittorio Veneto *reflects difficulties in the provision of materials and equipment, and much of the build quality was poor. However, the general appearance was both warlike and elegant.*

Main guns
With a maximum elevation of 35°, the main guns had a range of 42,260m (46,210yd) and fired both AP (armour-piercing) shells of 885kg (1950lb) and HE shells of 774kg (1710lb). They fired a round every 45 seconds.

Design
Vittorio Veneto and *Littorio* were launched with slightly raking stems, giving a waterline length of 236m (774ft 3in). After trials, they were given straight stems down to the waterline, resulting in an increase of 1.8m (4ft 6in).

Torpedo defences
Against torpedoes it had the Pugliese system: a lateral space between the torpedo bulkhead and the inner hull bulkhead, holding a long empty cylinder, maximum diameter 12ft 6in (3.8m), suspended in oil, and intended to absorb explosive energy.

CONVOY RAIDER

Assigned to the 9th Division of the 1st Squadron, from 31 August to the end of 1940, *Vittorio Veneto* was frequently in action against British convoys to Malta. For example, it was the Italian flagship in the Battle of Cape Matapan, on 27 March 1941, when it was hit by a torpedo launched by a bomber from HMS *Formidable*. Taking on around 4000 tonnes (4409 US tons) of water, it struggled back to Taranto. The ship was torpedoed again the following August, but also survived.

DECOMMISSIONING

On 8 September 1943, Italy's fleet was surrendered to the Allies. *Vittorio Veneto* was moved first to Malta, then to the Great Bitter Lake in the Suez Canal, for internment. It was returned to Italy in February 1946 and allocated to Great Britain as reparation. Decommissioned on 1 February 1948, it was scrapped at La Spezia between then and 1950.

Prinz Eugen (1940)

TYPE • *Battleship* **COUNTRY** • *Germany*

SPECIFICATIONS

Dimensions:	Length: 207.25m (679ft 11.5in); Beam: 21.48m (70ft 6in); Draught: 7.2m (23ft 7.5in)
Displacement:	16,974 tonnes (18,717 US tons)
Propulsion:	9 Wagner (La Mont) boilers, 3-shaft Deschimag geared turbines, 98,441kW (132,000hp)
Speed:	60.2km/h (32.5 knots; 37.4mph)
Armament:	8 × 203mm (8in) main guns; 12 × 105mm (4.1in) secondary guns; 12 × 37mm (1.45in) AA guns; 8 × 20mm (0.79in) AA guns; 12 × 533mm (21in) torpedo
Armour:	Belt: 89–38mm (3.5–1.5in); Deck: 38–31mm (1.5–1.25in); Main turrets: 158–57mm (6.25–2.25in)
Complement:	1600

Twelve 533mm (21in) torpedo tubes and three aircraft added to the capabilities of this Admiral Hipper-class ship, commissioned in 1940. It accompanied *Bismarck*, then *Scharnhorst* and *Gneisenau*, on their Atlantic sorties.

Right: An Italian admiral inspects the crew of the Prinz Eugen *on the foredeck in 1942. The ship was ceded to the USA after the Potsdam Conference of 1945, and was used as a target ship in the Crossroads atomic tests at Bikini Atoll in July 1946.*

Steam propulsion

The five Hipper-class cruisers had a sophisticated high-pressure steam propulsion system that demanded a very high level of training and operator expertise.

Displacement

Standard displacement was 16,974 tonnes (18,717 US tons), but the ship's deep-load displacement was 19,042 tonnes (21,000 US tons).

Powerplant

Prinz Eugen had no fewer than nine Wagner (La Mont) boilers, providing the power to three-shaft Deschimag geared turbines and generating 98,441kW (132,000hp) of energy.

Aircraft

The ship could carry a maximum of three floatplane aircraft for reconnaissance purposes. The aircraft type was the Arado Ar 196 low-wing monoplane.

EVASION

Prinz Eugen was laid down on 23 April 1936, launched on 22 August 1938 and commissioned on 1 August 1940. Together with the *Bismarck*, *Prinz Eugen* undertook the infamous 'channel dash' that took the two out into the North Atlantic. When *Bismarck* was sunk not long afterwards, *Prinz Eugen* managed to evade the British fleet and find refuge in St Nazaire.

***PRINZ EUGEN* IN DRYDOCK**

Prinz Eugen is seen here in a floating drydock, probably at Bremen, soon after VE Day. *Prinz Eugen* was the first of the second batch of three Hipper-class cruisers to be laid down. However, the other two ships – *Seydlitz* and *Lützow* – were never completed as planned.

Littorio (1940)

TYPE • *Battleship* **COUNTRY** • *Italy*

SPECIFICATIONS

Dimensions:	Length: 237.74m (780ft); Beam: 32.18m (105ft 7in); Draught: 9.6m (31ft 5in)
Displacement:	40,724 tonnes (44,902 US tons)
Machinery:	8 Yarrow boilers, driving 4-shaft Belluzzo turbines, developing 95,565kW (128,200hp)
Max speed:	30 knots (55.6km/h; 34.5mph)
Armour:	Belt: 280–70mm (11–2.65in); Deck: 162–45mm (6.37–1.75in); Main turrets: 350–200mm (13.78–7.87in)
Armament:	9 × 381mm (15in) main guns; 12 × 152mm (6in) secondary guns; 4 × 119mm (4.7in) guns; 12 × 89mm (3.5in) AA guns; 36 × 37mm (1.45in) or 20mm (0.79in) AA guns
Complement:	1830–1950

The Littorio class consisted of two batches each of two ships, laid down in 1934 and 1938 respectively. *Littorio* and her sister ship *Vittorio Veneto* were laid down on the same day and the names of both ships have been used interchangeably to identify the class.

Left: Littorio *was armed with high-velocity 381mm (15in) guns, which was the largest calibre that could be reliably built in Italy at the time.*

Littorio class
The two Littorio-class battleships included de-capping armour plates, enhanced anti-torpedo protection, auxiliary rudders and an exceptional arc of salvo fire.

Rear turret
The rear main turret was mounted higher than normal to allow blast clearance for the ship's aircraft, typically a Reggiane Re 2000 fighter, which was carried unhangared.

TORPEDO PROTECTION
Vittorio Veneto and *Littorio* both incorporated Pugliese's torpedo protection system, formed of longitudinal cylinders within the ship's side, packed with tubes, intended to absorb the shock of a torpedo hit. On their inner side a longitudinal watertight bulkhead was intended to protect the machinery and magazines. It avoided the torpedo bulges that reduced the maximum speed of other battleships, but was criticized for the weakness of the inner bulkhead.

Secondary turrets
Flanking the three main turrets were the secondary 152mm (6in) guns, mounted in four triple turrets.

GUNNERY EXERCISES
Here the *Littorio* was photographed during the summer of 1940 while on gunnery exercises. On 30 July 1943, five days after Mussolini's overthrow, *Littorio* was renamed *Italia*.

***Bismarck* (1940)**

TYPE • *Battleship* **COUNTRY** • *Germany*

SPECIFICATIONS

Dimensions:	Length: 251m (793ft); Beam: 36m (118ft); Draught: 9.3m (31ft)
Displacement:	44,905 tonnes (49,500 US tons)
Propulsion:	12 Wagner HP boilers, 3 Brown-Boveri geared turbines developing 111,982kW (150,170hp)
Speed:	53.7km/h (29 knots; 33.3mph)
Range:	16,430km (8,870nm; 10,210 miles) at 35km/h (19 knots; 22mph)
Armament:	8 × 380mm (15in) guns; 12 × 150mm (5.9in) guns; 16 × 105mm (4.1in) guns; 16 × 37mm (1.5in) guns; 12 × 20mm (0.79in) AA guns
Armour:	Belt: 320–80mm (12.6–3.1in); Bulkheads: 220–45mm (8.6–1.7in); Deck: 120–80mm (4.3–1.7in); Barbettes: 340–220mm (13.4–8.6in); Turrets: 360–180mm (14.2–7in)
Complement:	2291

***Bismarck* and *Tirpitz* represented the peak of German battleship design in terms of size, armament, speed and staying power. However, *Bismarck*'s first combat mission, although including a major success, was also its last.**

Above: A cutaway side profile of Bismarck. German practice was to name the main turrets A, B, C, D from front to back as Anton, Bruno, Cäsar and Dora.

Engine
Initial plans for propulsion – later dropped – featured turbo-electric drive, in a compact arrangement with boilers on each side, the generator in the middle and an electric motor for each shaft.

Radar equipment
Bismarck carried FuMO radar equipment on the forward and aft rangefinders and the foretop, although blast concussion disabled it. It also had hydrophone detectors.

Bow anchors
Three bow anchors were carried, two on the port side and one stern anchor (also port side). Each anchor weighed 9500kg (20,944lb).

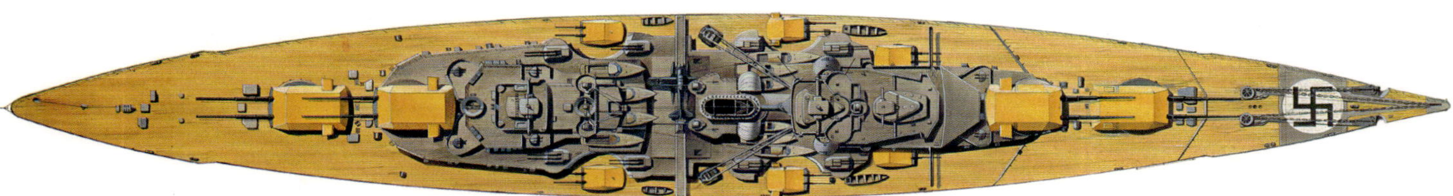

HUNTING BISMARCK
On 24 May 1941, the battlecruiser HMS *Hood* was sunk by *Bismarck*'s fifth salvo in the Atlantic. A huge Allied pursuit followed, and *Bismarck* was hit by Swordfish torpedo bombers from HMS *Ark Royal* on 26 May, jamming the port rudder. On 27 May, the battleships HMS *Rodney* and *King George V* opened fire. By around 10.00, all *Bismarck*'s guns were disabled and the order was given to scuttle. Hit by British torpedoes, it sank with 1977 men lost.

INSPECTION
Adolf Hitler inspects the almost completed *Bismarck* at the Gotenhafen (Gdynia) naval base on 5 May 1940. Although *Bismarck* was powerful, Hitler lost interest and belief in naval surface warfare.

HMS *Howe* (1940)

TYPE • *Battleship* **COUNTRY** • *United Kingdom*

HMS *Howe* was one of the King George V-class battleships built between 1937 and 1940, the others being HMS *King George V* (commissioned 1940), HMS *Prince of Wales* (1941), HMS *Duke of York* (1941) and HMS *Anson* (1942).

SPECIFICATIONS

Dimensions:	Length: 227.1m (744ft 11.5in); Beam: 31.4m (103ft); Draught: 9m (29ft 6in)
Displacement:	39,780 tonnes (43,313 US tons) standard
Propulsion:	8 Admiralty 3-drum small-tube boilers, 4 sets of Parsons geared turbines, 82,000kW (110,000shp)
Speed:	52.4km/h (28.3 knots; 32.6mph)
Range:	28,900km (15,600nm; 18,000 miles)
Armament:	10 × 356mm (14in) BL Mark VII guns; 16 × 133mm (5.25in) QF Mk. I guns; 48 × 40mm (1.575in) QF 2-pounder Mk.VIII guns; 18 × 20mm (0.8in) Oerlikon AA guns
Armour:	Main belt: 370mm (14.7in); Lower belt: 140mm (5.4in); Deck: 127–152mm (5–6in); Main turrets: 324mm (12.75in); Barbettes: 324mm (12.75in); Bulkheads: 254–305mm (10–12in)
Complement:	1422

Left: HMS Howe *participates in trials after its launch in February 1940.*

George V-class design
Britain opted for 356mm (14in) guns but with armour capable of resisting 406mm (16in) shells.

Armour
Much effort was spent on designing and developing the ships' armour, and the five battleships of the class had extensive armour belts and internal bulkheads.

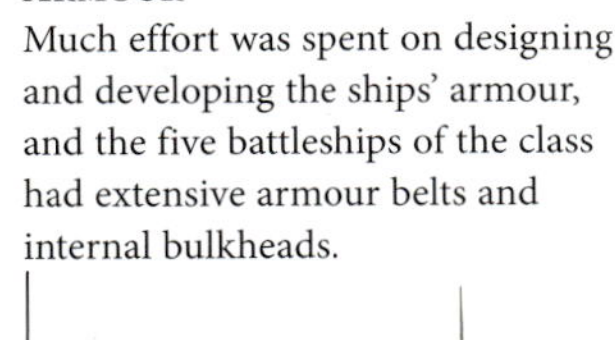

Submarine protection
Submarine protection proved to be less than satisfactory. The only member of the class to be lost during World War II – HMS *Prince of Wales* – was sunk by a small and outdated German torpedo.

KING GEORGE V CLASS
The final King George V design was ready by 1936. HMS *Howe* (formerly HMS *Beatty*) was laid down on 1 June 1937, launched on 9 April 1940 and completed on 29 August 1942. The other King George Vs were involved in several major actions, but *Howe* fought a solid war away from the front pages. Along with HMS *King George V*, HMS *Duke of York* and HMS *Anson*, *Howe* outlasted the war and remained in front-line service alongside her sisters into the 1950s.

B turret
It had originally been intended to fit 12 main guns, but to increase the level of armour protection two guns were deleted on the forward 'B' turret.

SUEZ CANAL
Howe passes through the Suez Canal, en route to join the British Eastern Fleet in the Indian Ocean, c.1944. *Howe* supported invasion forces in Sicily and Italy, and in 1945 was the British flagship in the Pacific. Placed in reserve in 1951, it was broken up in 1957.

HMS *Jervis Bay* (1940)

TYPE • *Merchant cruiser* **COUNTRY** • *United Kingdom*

SPECIFICATIONS

Dimensions:	Length: 167m (549ft); Beam: 21m (68ft); Draught: 10m (33ft)
Displacement:	14,160 tonnes (15,609 US tons)
Propulsion:	Unavailable
Speed:	28km/h (15 knots; 17 mph)
Range:	Not specified
Armament:	7 × 152mm (6in) Mk. VII guns; 2 × 76mm (3in) AA guns
Armour:	None
Complement:	254

Built for the Australian emigrant trade in 1922, *Jervis Bay* was fitted out as an armed merchant cruiser with eight 152mm (6in) guns. In November 1939, its convoy was intercepted by the German battleship *Admiral Scheer*. *Jervis Bay* attacked and was sunk with heavy loss of life.

Above: HMS Jervis Bay *was a 1922-vintage ship of 14,160 tonnes (15,608 US tons) and a former passenger liner.*

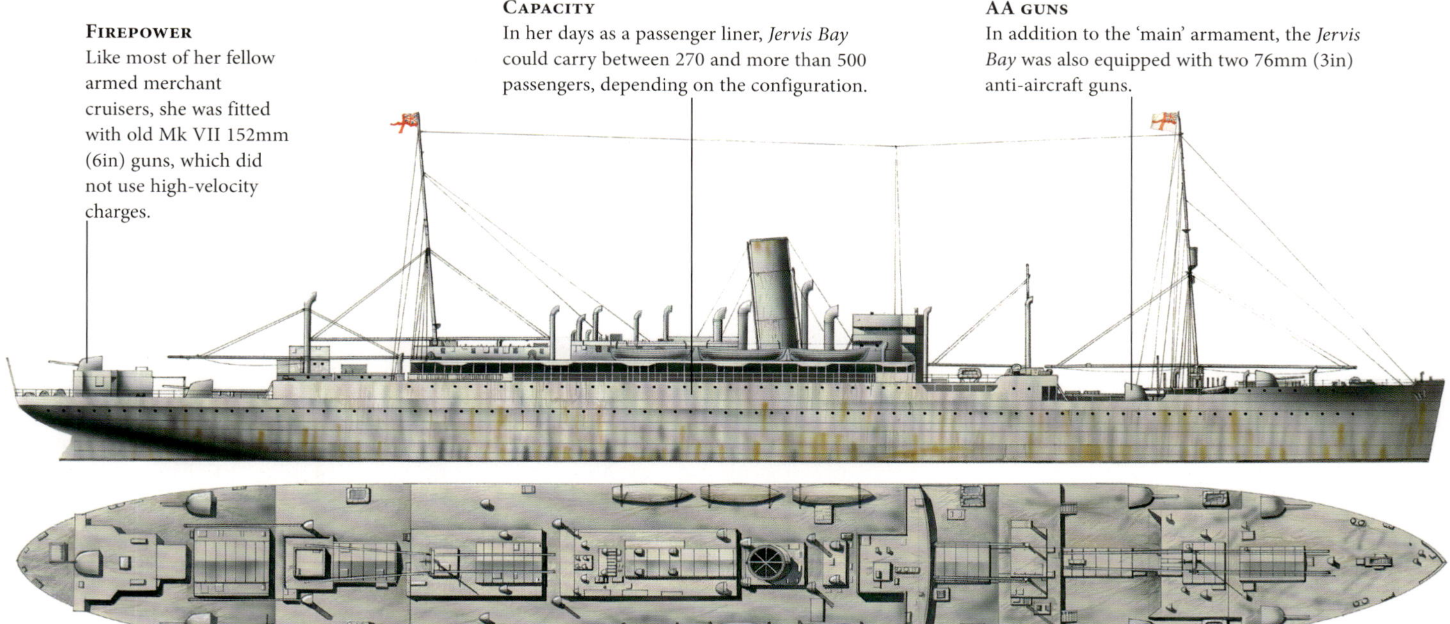

Firepower
Like most of her fellow armed merchant cruisers, she was fitted with old Mk VII 152mm (6in) guns, which did not use high-velocity charges.

Capacity
In her days as a passenger liner, *Jervis Bay* could carry between 270 and more than 500 passengers, depending on the configuration.

AA guns
In addition to the 'main' armament, the *Jervis Bay* was also equipped with two 76mm (3in) anti-aircraft guns.

ARMED MERCHANTS

Atlantic convoys were tempting targets for German submarines or surface raiders, and there simply were not enough naval escorts available. To provide a modicum of protection, chiefly against U-boats running on the surface, Britain adapted commercial shipping to serve as armed merchant cruisers. HMS *Jervis Bay* was one of over 50 such vessels commissioned.

***JERVIS BAY*, 1940**
Jervis Bay is here seen in Dakar in 1940. As the war in Europe worsened this year, Britain became totally dependent on the Atlantic convoys to bring essential supplies from the United States.

Tashkent class (1940)

TYPE • *Destroyer* **COUNTRY** • *Soviet Union*

SPECIFICATIONS

Dimensions:	Length: 139.7m (458ft 4in); Beam: 13.7m (44ft 11in); Draught: 3.7m (12ft 2in)
Displacement:	2890 tonnes (3130 US tons)
Propulsion:	2 Yarrow boilers, 2 shafts, 2 geared steam turbines, 75,000kW (100,000shp)
Speed:	78.7km/h (42.5 knots; 48.9mph)
Range:	9320km (5030nm; 5790 miles)
Armament:	3 × twin 130mm (5.1in) guns; 1 × twin 76mm (3in) AA guns; 6 × single 37mm (1.5in) AA guns; 6 × single 12.7mm (0.5in) machine guns; 3 × triple 533mm (21in) torpedo tubes; 76 mines; 24 depth charges; 2 depth charge throwers; 1 rack
Complement:	250

A total of 11 Tashkent-class vessels were planned for construction in the Soviet Union from the late 1930s, but only four actually went on the order books and only one of those – the lead ship *Taskhkent* – was actually completed.

Left: This photograph of Tashkent *was taken in the late 1930s, likely during sea trials. The class was actually designed in Italy.*

Performance
Driven by two geared steam turbines, the *Tashkent* could reach a maximum speed of 78.7km/h (42.5 knots; 48.9mph).

AA guns
In 1941 the vessel's 45mm (1.77in) AA guns were replaced by fully automatic 37mm (1.5 in) 70-K AA guns, which gave a faster rate of fire.

Main guns
The main weapons on the *Tashkent* were 130mm (5.1in) 50-calibre B13 Pattern 1936 guns, which were standard on Soviet destroyers through to the 1950s.

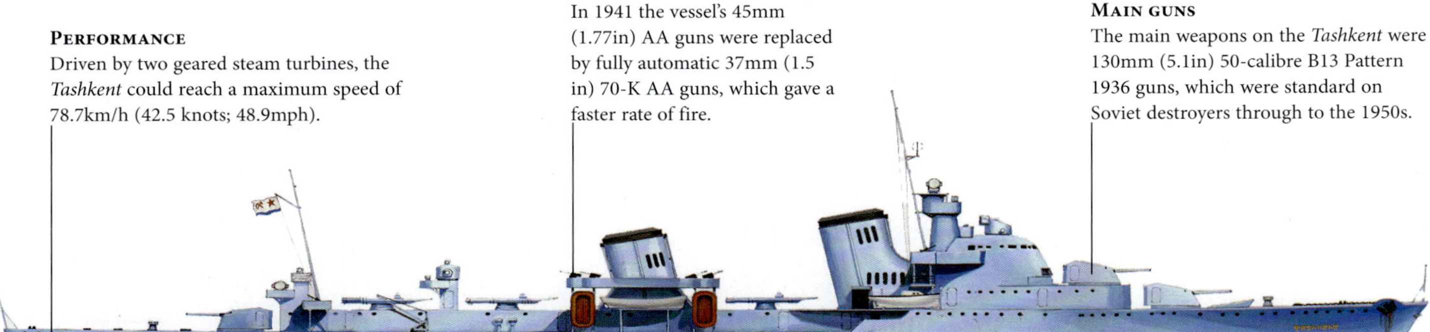

TASHKENT AT WAR

Tashkent was laid down in January 1937, completed in October 1939 and assigned to the Black Sea Fleet in October 1940. With the German invasion of the Soviet Union in June 1941, *Tashkent* found herself in heavy combat on the southern fringes of the Eastern Front, especially around Sevastopol. It was on the Black Sea on 2 July 1942 that she was bombed to destruction by German aircraft.

TASHKENT GUNNERY

This grainy image shows the forward guns of *Tashkent* in action. Apart from convoy escort, evacuation duties and logistics, a key role of *Tashkent* was to provide offshore naval gunnery support to Red Army troops.

HMS *Prince of Wales* (1940)

TYPE • *Battleship* **COUNTRY** • *United Kingdom*

SPECIFICATIONS

Dimensions:	Length: 227m (745ft 1in); Beam: 31.4m (103ft 2in); Draught: 10.5m (34ft 4in)
Displacement:	38,610 tonnes (42,560 US tons)
Propulsion:	8 Admiralty 3-drum boilers, 4 Parsons geared turbines, 4 screws, 82,000kW (110,000shp)
Armament:	10 × 356mm (14in) guns; 16 × 133mm (5.25in) guns; 32 × 40mm (1.5in) AA guns; 80 UP projectors
Armour:	Belt: 381–114mm (15-4.5in); Bulkheads: 381mm (15in); Deck: 152-127mm (6-5in); Barbettes: 330-280mm (13–11in); Turrets: 330–152mm (13–6in)
Range:	28,900km (15,600nm; 17,957 miles)
Speed:	28.3 knots (52.4km/h; 32.74mph)
Complement:	1612

All five of the King George V class were laid down in 1937, the *Prince of Wales* at Cammell Laird's yard in Birkenhead in January. The second of the class, *Prince of Wales* had a brief career: it was the first battleship sunk by aircraft on the open sea.

Left: Prince of Wales *shows the elevation capability of her forward main arsenal.*

Design
The design was a balanced and handsome one, with two widely spaced funnels, the fore-funnel marginally taller than the aft one, between two tall tripod masts, and the now standard tower structure rising directly behind the forward turrets, with a high-set enclosed navigation bridge.

Quadruple turrets
The King George V-class were the first British battleships to have quadruple main turrets; they were to carry 12 356mm (14in) guns in three quadruple turrets.

Armour
Protection was on the 'all or nothing' principle, and armour amounted to 40 per cent of design displacement, based on the realistic awareness that it would have to face 406mm (16in) guns in combat.

EARLY LOSS

On 10 December 1941, *Prince of Wales* was off the east Malayan coast as flagship of Force 'Z' with the battlecruiser *Repulse* and four destroyers when they were attacked by waves of Japanese naval aircraft. The ships opened intensive AA fire, increased speed and began zig-zagging, but control of *Prince of Wales*'s port propellers was lost and its manoeuvrability was restricted. After many bomb and torpedo hits, both battleships were sunk. The escorting destroyers rescued 1285 men from *Prince of Wales*.

AIRCRAFT LAUNCH
Prince of Wales photographed in 1941, sometime prior to her 24 May 1941 engagement with the German battleship *Bismarck*. She is in the process of lowering a Supermarine Walrus amphibian aircraft over the side of the hull.

HMS *Indomitable* (1940)

TYPE • *Aircraft carrier* **COUNTRY** • *United Kingdom*

SPECIFICATIONS

DIMENSIONS:	Length: 230m (754ft 7in); Beam: 29.2m (95ft 10in); Draught: 8.8m (29ft)
DISPLACEMENT:	23,368 tonnes (25,763 US tons); 30,206 tonnes (33,297 US tons) full load
PROPULSION:	6 boilers, Parsons geared turbines, 3 shafts, 83,000kW (111,000shp)
SPEED:	56km/h (30.5 knots; 35mph)
RANGE:	20,000km (11,000nm; 13,000 miles) at 25.9km/h (14 knots; 16.1mph)
ARMAMENT:	16 × 110mm (4.5in) guns; 48 × 2-pdr and 10 × 20mm AA guns
AIRCRAFT:	48
COMPLEMENT:	1600

***Indomitable* was commissioned in 1941. A ruggedly built and well-equipped fleet carrier, she was the fourth member of a class that gained a distinguished service record through World War II and endured into the 1950s.**

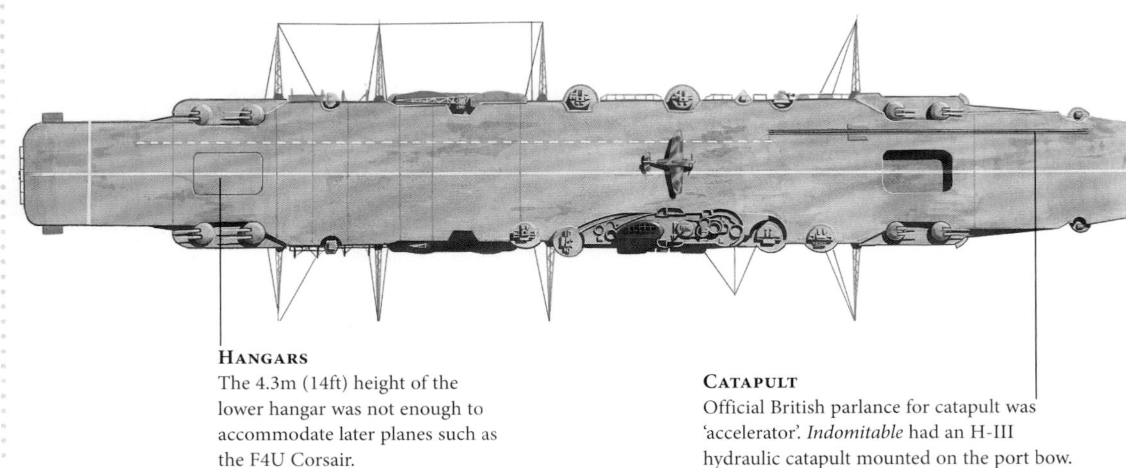

HANGARS
The 4.3m (14ft) height of the lower hangar was not enough to accommodate later planes such as the F4U Corsair.

CATAPULT
Official British parlance for catapult was 'accelerator'. *Indomitable* had an H-III hydraulic catapult mounted on the port bow.

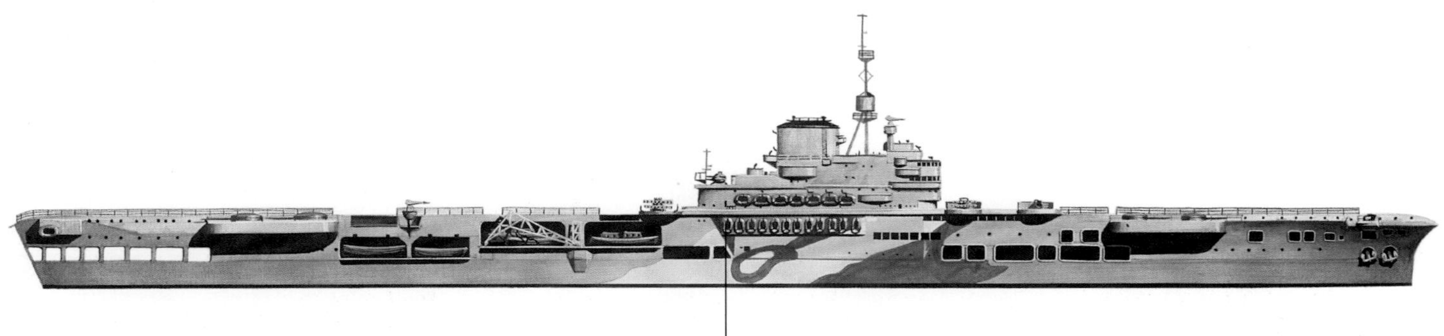

CARLEY FLOATS
Multiple Carley floats were carried in addition to the boats because in combat conditions it might be carrying survivors from other ships.

STRIKE POWER
Indomitable in effect formed an interim design between the Illustrious and Implacable classes. *Implacable* (in service from 1944 to 1955) was slightly larger and faster, also with two hangar decks, but with hangar-side armour of 51mm (2in). It had more powerful engines, with eight boilers and four shafts, and made a faster speed. Most importantly, it could carry up to 81 aircraft, giving it considerably greater strike power.

POST-WAR CARRIER
Indomitable served on into the 1950s. An explosion on board on 3 February 1953, caused by a leak of aviation fuel and resulting in nine deaths, meant *Indomitable* was struck from the Navy list in 1955, and scrapped in October that year.

Type VIIC (1940)

TYPE • *Submarine* **COUNTRY** • *Germany*

SPECIFICATIONS

Dimensions:	Length: 67.1m (220ft 1in); Beam: 6.2m (20ft 4in); Draught: 4.8m (15ft 9in)
Displacement:	773.1 tonnes (761 US tons) surfaced; 878.8 tonnes (865 US tons) submerged
Propulsion:	2 2087kW (2800hp) diesels, 2 559kW (750hp) electric motors, 2 screws
Speed:	31.8km/h (17.2 knots; 19.8mph) surfaced; 14km/h (7.6 knots; 8.7mph) submerged
Range:	12,038km (6500nm; 7481 miles) at 22.2km/h (12 knots; 13.8mph) surfaced; 148km (80nm; 92 miles) at 7.4km/h (4 knots; 4.6mph) submerged
Armament:	5 x 533mm (21in) torpedo tubes; 14 torpedoes or 26 TMA/39TMB mines; 1 x 88mm (3.4in) gun; 1 x 20mm (0.79in) gun
Complement:	44

An effective hunter-killer in the first years of the war, the Type VII eventually fell victim to intensive anti-submarine warfare both from the surface and the air. In production from 1935 to 1945, this was the most numerous submarine type ever built, with a total of 709 completed.

Above: U-320 *was a Type VIIC/41, which had a stronger pressure hull enabling it to dive operationally to 120m (394ft). Ninety were built in this form.*

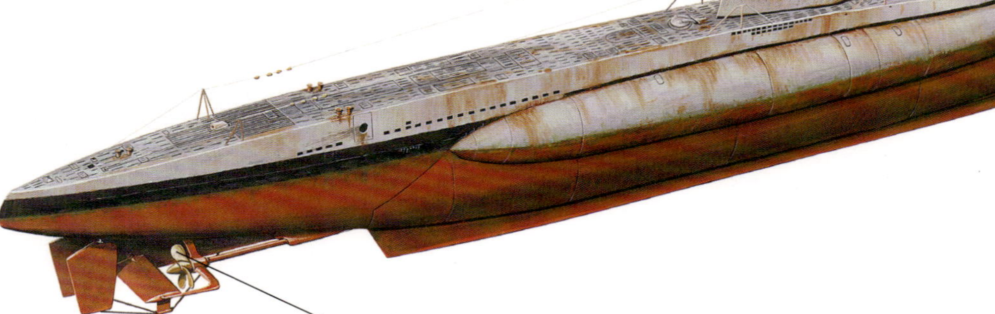

U-210
U-210 was a typical Type VIIC U-boat. Almost all U-boats carried their own emblem, painted on the tower. *U-210*'s was a lobster, with claws extended in attacking mode.

Wake reduction
During 1940, anti-vibration wires were added to the tops of periscopes to help reduce the wake left by a raised periscope. All the VIICs had this feature.

Anchor chain
The boat was fitted with a Hall stockless type anchor and chain 150m (492ft) in length. The anchor weighed 400kg (880lb) and chain weight was 1676kg (3694lb).

Propellers
The standard U-boat propellers were three-bladed, with a diameter of 1,620mm (5ft 3in).

VIIC ADVANCES

The Type VIIC numbered 577 boats, with 17 shipyards sharing the building. The hull was further lengthened to allow for an active S-Gerät sonar installation, which in the event was not ready in time. The tower was slightly widened and made 30cm (11.7in) longer. Fuel capacity was increased to 115 tonnes (113 US tons), allowing an operating range of 16,020km (8650nm; 9954 miles) at 22km/h (12 knots; 14mph).

TYPE VIIC MAINTENANCE

The crew of a VIIC submarine conduct routine maintenance. Some Type VIIC had both electric and diesel air compressors. With so many boats, builders and repairers, the range of detail variations across the VIIC Type is enormous, especially in armament and tower design.

Type C (1940)

TYPE • *Submarine* **COUNTRY** • *Japan*

SPECIFICATIONS	
Dimensions:	Length: 109.3m (358ft 6in); Beam: 9.1m (29ft 10in); Draught :7.8m (25ft 7in)
Displacement:	2219 tonnes (2184 US tons) surfaced; 3618 tonnes (3561 US tons) submerged
Propulsion:	2 diesels of 4623kW (6200bhp), 2 745kW (1000hp) electric motors, 2 screws
Speed:	43.7km/h (23.6 knots; 27mph) surfaced; 14.8km/h (8 knots; 9.2mph) submerged
Range:	25,928km (14,000nm; 16,111 miles) surfaced; 110km (60nm; 69 miles) submerged
Armament:	8 × 533mm (21in) torpedo tubes; 20 torpedoes; 1 × 140mm (5.5in) deck gun; 2 × Type 96 25mm (1in) AA guns
Complement:	95

As with other navies, Japanese warship design was incremental, with successive classes building on the experience and performance of their predecessors. The Japanese Type C submarines were themselves divided into three classes, under which 12 submarines were constructed.

Above: The Japanese Type C I-51-class submarine I-55 *was renamed* I-155 *in 1942.*

Type C-1 class
The five C-1 class, double-hulled, numbered *I-16, 18, 20, 22* and *24*, did not carry an aircraft: instead, they were fitted with cradles to hold midget submarines (A Type) and carried support equipment.

Torpedo tubes
The eight torpedo tubes were all forward, in two torpedo rooms, one above the other. Twenty torpedoes were carried. A 140mm (5.5in)/50cal deck gun and two Type 96 25mm (1in) AA guns were fitted.

Performance
Powerful Kampon Mk2 Model 10 diesel engines and two electric motors enabled a surface speed of 43.7km/h (23.6 knots; 27mph) and 15km/h (8 knots; 9mph) submerged.

Operating depth
Maximum operating depth for the submarine was 100m (330ft), a depth at which the submarine was very vulnerable to depth-charge explosions.

JAPANESE IDENTIFIERS

The designations *I*, *Ro*, and *Ha* of submarine types began as generic, denoting ocean-going, medium-range/coastal and small or midget submarines respectively, each including a range of types. Individual classes and types have their own identifiers, either a combination of letters and numbers, such as *K-6*, or simply a number, as in *I-201*. From May 1942, all submarine types were given the prefix number 1. For example, *K-6* became *K-16*.

I-52
A 140mm (5.5in)/50cal deck gun and two Type 96 25mm (1in) AA guns were fitted as standard to the Type C submarines.

Yamato (1941)

TYPE • *Battleship* COUNTRY • *Japan*

SPECIFICATIONS

Dimensions:	Length: 263m (862ft 9in); Beam: 36.9m (121ft 1in); Draught: 10.39m (34ft 1in)
Displacement:	61,698 tonnes (68,010 US tons); 65,008 tonnes (71,659 US tons) full load
Propulsion:	12 Kampon HP boilers, 4 Kampon turbines developing 111,855kW (150,000hp), 4 screws
Speed:	50km/h (27 knots; 31mph)
Range:	13,330km (7,200nm; 8,280 miles) at 29.6km/h (16 knots; 18.4mph)
Armament:	9 × 460mm (18.1in) guns, 12 × 155mm (6.1in) guns, 12 × 127mm (5in) guns, 24 × 25mm (0.98in) AA guns, 4 × 13.2mm (0.52in) AA guns
Armour:	Belt: 410mm (16in); Deck: 230–200mm (9.1–7.9in); Barbettes: 546–50mm (21.5–2in); Turrets: 650–193mm (19.7–11.8in)
Complement:	2500

The Japanese Yamato class were to be 'super-battleships': bigger, more heavily armed and better protected than anything else afloat. Intended to enforce Japan's mastery of the Pacific, they made a minimal contribution to the country's war effort.

Left: Here we see Yamato *in the late stages of construction alongside the large fitting out pontoon at the Kure Naval Base, Japan, on 20 September 1941. Note* Yamato*'s 460mm (18.1in) main battery gun turret and superfiring 155mm (6.1in) secondary battery gun turret.*

Hull
The hull shape was carefully worked out to bear the huge stresses. The stem design was estimated to reduce water resistance by 8.2 per cent; the overall design gave a power saving of 11,797kW (15,820hp).

Turret
The turret was formed of two concentric armoured cylinders, the inner one of 1.5m (4ft 10in) containing a hoist for four men.

Design
The deck plan reveals the distinctive hull shape, reaching maximum beam towards the stern. The 'wings' carried Type 96 25mm AA guns in triple mounts.

FATE OF THE *YAMATO*
Despite their evident power, both the *Yamato* and her equally impressive sister ship *Musashi* would not survive the war. *Yamato*'s last sortie was a one-way suicide mission against US invasion forces around Okinawa. Detected before her guns could have an impact, the great ship was destroyed in a relentless attack by US carrier aircraft on 7 April 1945.

***YAMATO* TRIALS, OCTOBER 1941**
Yamato is shown at speed during sea trials in October 1941. Striking aspects of the ship's appearance included the typical Japanese tall tower, more compact than on converted older ships, and a single large backwards-tilted funnel.

Tirpitz (1941)

TYPE • *Battleship* **COUNTRY** • *Germany*

SPECIFICATIONS

Dimensions:	Length: 251m (823ft 6in); Beam: 36m (118ft 1in); Draught: 9.3m (30ft 6in)
Displacement:	38,283 tonnes (42,200 US tons)
Propulsion:	12 Wagner superheated boilers, 3 Brown-Boveri geared turbines, 102,906kW (138,000hp)
Speed:	56km/h (30 knots; 34.8mph)
Range:	16,430km (8870nm; 10,210 miles) at 35km/h (19 knots; 22mph)
Armament:	8 × 380mm (15in) guns; 12 × 150mm (5.9in) guns; 16 × 105mm (4.1in) guns; 16 × 37mm (1.5in) AA guns; 12 × 20mm (0.79in) AA guns
Armour:	Belt: 320–80mm (12.6–3.1in); Bulkheads: 220–45mm (8.6–1.7in); Deck: 120–80mm (4.3–1.7in); Barbettes: 340–220mm (13.4–8.6in); Turrets: 360–180mm (14.2–7in)
Complement:	2065

Sister ship to *Bismarck*, *Tirpitz* had similar qualities of power and resistance. Although its active service was very limited, the fact of its presence tied up substantial British resources until its ultimate destruction.

Above: Tirpitz *anchored in the Alta Fjord, in northern Norway, in 1943–44. She is protected from submarine attack by anti-torpedo nets.*

Funnel
At first black, the funnel cowling was painted silver or light grey from 1942. The catwalk from the funnel platform to the tower was added in 1942.

Deck plan
The deck plan was essentially the same as that of *Bismarck*.

Superstructure
The open fore part of the superstructure, hardly higher than 'B' turret, was rimmed out to deflect blast from gunfire.

Paint scheme
Tirpitz is depicted here in 'Paint Scheme K', which it carried between March and July 1944. The camouflage style was frequently changed to confuse aerial observers.

DESTRUCTION

On 12 November 1944, 32 RAF Lancaster bombers converged on Tirpitz from 09.35, when she was at anchor in Norway. The ship's main guns opened up on them, but there was no aerial opposition from the Luftwaffe. The Lancasters scored at least two direct hits and four near misses with 'Tallboy' 5080kg (11,199lb) bombs carrying around 3000kg (6614lb) of high explosive. The most destructive hit was between the aircraft catapult and funnel, which blew a massive hole in the side armour.

***TIRPITZ* IN NORWAY**

Tirpitz spent much of her wartime career in Norwegian waters. The ship did not have a 'glorious' career, but its influence on the Arctic war was important.

HMS *Anchusa* (Flower class) (1941)

TYPE • *Corvette* **COUNTRY** • *United Kingdom*

SPECIFICATIONS

DIMENSIONS:	Length: 62m (205ft); Beam: 10.11m (33ft 2in); Draught: 4.8m (15ft 9in)
DISPLACEMENT:	1190 tonnes (1170 long tons); 1410 tonnes (1390 long tons) full load
PROPULSION:	2 boilers driving 1 VTE engine generating 2051kW (2750hp)
SPEED:	30.6km/h (16.5 knots; 19mph)
ARMAMENT:	1 × 102mm (4in) BL Mk IX gun; 40 depth charges; 72 Hedgehog rockets
ARMOUR:	None
COMPLEMENT:	85–109

The bulk of convoy escort duties were handled by corvettes from the Royal Navy and the Royal Canadian Navy. In turn, the bulk of the corvettes were the Flower-class or modified Flower-class ships, which played one of the most important and unsung roles of the entire war at sea.

Above: A side view of Anchusa. *The Flower class were diminutive vessels, with a displacement of just 1190 tonnes (1170 long tons).*

ARMAMENT
By the end of the war the weapons fit on most of the Flowers had changed at least once, though most ships kept the 102mm (4in) main gun.

HEDGEHOG
Their chief weapon was the Hedgehog anti-submarine mortar. Hedgehog consisted of high-explosive rockets fired in groups which would (hopefully) straddle the target U-boat and force it to the surface.

PROPULSION
The ship was powered by two boilers driving one VTE engine generating 2051kW (2750hp).

FLOWER CLASS
Over 200 Flower-class ships were built. The class was based on a pre-war whaler design drawn up by Smith's Docks, which was lengthened and fitted out with military equipment. They were built in 30 different ship yards in the UK and Canada, with the highest number being produced by Belfast's Harland & Wolff. HMS *Anchusa* was one of the 34 Flower-class ships built in Northern Ireland, launched between 1940 and 1942.

ANCHUSA IN LIVERPOOL, 1943
A total of 34 Flower-class ships were lost during the course of the war, but *Anchusa* survived the conflict. The role of the corvette was to escort merchant shipping in convoy and, if possible, to find and attack enemy submarines.

Fairmile Type C (1941)

TYPE • *Motor torpedo boat* **COUNTRY** • *United Kingdom*

The Fairmile series of motor torpedo boats (MTBs) were developed from the earlier Type A and Type B motor launches/minelayers, which led to the Type C and larger Type D MTBs. The first Type C was launched in 1941 and, of the 23 built, five were lost during the war.

SPECIFICATIONS

Dimensions:	Length: 35.66m (117ft); Beam: 5.3m (17ft 5in); Draught: 1.73m (5ft 8in)
Displacement:	69 tonnes (76 US tons); 75 tonnes (83 US tons) deep load
Machinery:	3-shaft Hall-Scott petrol engines, developing 2013kW (2700hp)
Speed:	50km/h (27 knots; 31mph)
Range:	930km (500nm; 580 miles)
Armour:	None
Armament:	Two 2-pounder 'pom-pom' AA guns; 4 12.5mm (0.5in) machine guns; 4 7.6mm (3in) machine guns (later 6 20mm (0.79in) and 4 7.6mm (0.3in) guns)
Complement:	16

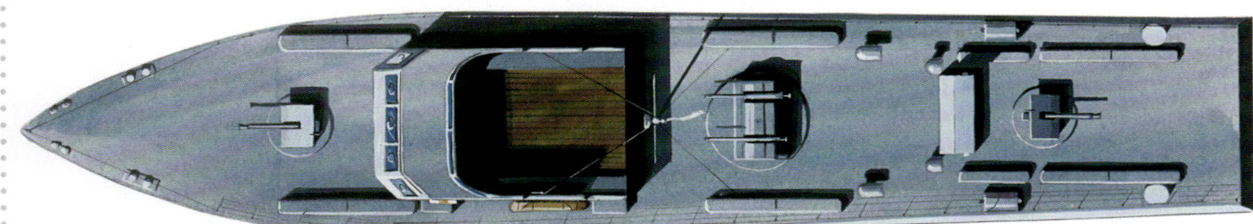

Above: The Type C was made with prefabricated double diagonal mahogany hulls over plywood frames.

Performance
The Type C could achieve speeds of 50km/h (27 knots; 31mph), and its shallow draught meant it could sail close to the shoreline.

Armament
The Type C had only light firepower, but plenty of it for its size, the heaviest weapons being two 2-pounder automatic AA guns, which could also be used against surface targets.

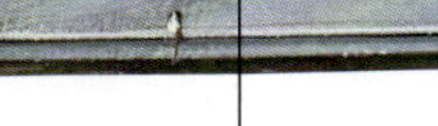

Type C
This vessel is a Type C MTB, known individually by their pennant numbers (*MGB 312–335*).

Complement
The vessel had an overall length of 35.66m (117ft) and was operated by a crew of two officers and 14 enlisted men.

MTB ROLES

Britain developed a range of motor torpedo boats (MTBs), motor gun boats (MGBs) and motor anti-submarine boats (MA/SBs) to serve with the coastal forces. All eventually became grouped under the MTB classification. Their role was to harry enemy shipping and guard against intruders. They were also tasked with specialist roles such as inserting commando teams, minelaying/minesweeping and providing fast targets for other units.

US NAVY FAIRMILE
This World War II photograph shows a British Fairmile-type MTB in US Navy service. MTBs were built in large numbers by a range of shipyards such as Vosper, Whites, Camper & Nicholson, British Power Boats and Thornycroft, and to a range of different designs.

Ariete class (1941)

TYPE • *Destroyer* **COUNTRY** • *Italy*

Built at Trieste, *Ariete* was the lead ship of Italy's final class of World War II destroyers, and the only one of the class to be commissioned before the surrender of Italy in 1943. After the war, it was transferred to Yugoslavia, and served as *Durmitor* until 1963.

SPECIFICATIONS

Dimensions:	Length: 83.5m (273ft 11in); Beam: 8.62m (28ft 3in); Draught: 3.15m (10ft 4in)
Displacement:	757 tonnes (833 US tons); 1118 tonnes (1232 US tons) full load
Machinery:	2 boilers, 2-shaft geared steam turbines, developing 16,400kW (22,000hp)
Speed:	58.3km/h (31.5 knots; 36.2mph)
Armour:	None
Armament:	2 × 100mm (4in) dual-purpose guns; 10 × 20mm (0.79in) AA guns; 6 × 450mm (18in) torpedo tubes (2 triple mounts); 20 mines
Complement:	158

Below: Ariete *is here seen in a fractured camouflage pattern, good for breaking up the ship's profile against a grey seascape.*

Ariete
Ariete was constructed by the famous Ansaldo shipbuilders in Genoa, laid down in July 1942 and completed in August 1943.

Torpedo launchers
The Ariete class put a heavier focus on torpedo armament than the previous Spica class of torpedo boats, with six tubes mounted on the centreline.

Powerplant
The ship was propelled by two-shaft geared steam turbines, developing a total of 16,400kW (22,000hp).

TA47 *BALESTRA*
Seen here off the coast of Yugoslavia is the ex-German TA47 *Balestra*, an Ariete-class torpedo boat. In Yugoslav Navy service from 1949, it was known as *Učka*.

FAILED PRODUCTION
The Ariete class had a particularly troubled production history. In total, 42 of the vessels were planned for development, but in the early 1940s only 16 were ultimately laid for construction, owing to supply problems caused by the war. Of these 16, only one was actually completed, the rest taken into the hands of the Germans and completed for Kriegsmarine service.

CAM and MAC ships (1941)

TYPE • *Escort carrier* **COUNTRY** • *United Kingdom*

Pressed into action as convoy protection vessels, the CAM and MAC ships had an important role in the Battle of the Atlantic, where warfare was conducted on three levels – sea surface, undersea and in the air.

SPECIFICATIONS

DIMENSIONS:	Length: 142m (465ft); Beam: 18m (59ft); Draught: 8.4m (27ft 6in)
DISPLACEMENT:	8145 tonnes (8979 US tons); 16,256 tonnes (17,917 US tons) full load
PROPULSION:	Diesel engine, single shaft, 2610kW (3500bhp)
SPEED:	24km/h (13 knots; 15mph)
RANGE:	18,520km (10,000nm; 11,510 miles)
ARMAMENT:	1 × 100mm (4in) gun; 8 × 20mm (0.787in) AA guns
AIRCRAFT:	3
COMPLEMENT:	100

Above: The 19 'Empire'-named MAC ships flew Swordfish Mk I and Mk II torpedo bombers whose biplane construction allowed take-off at lower speeds than Sea Hurricanes.

STRUCTURE
The island, like the rest of the carrier structure, was made as much as possible of prefabricated parts. CAM ships had a larger crew than normal merchantmen and carried additional rescue boats in the form of Carley floats.

ROCKET CATAPULT
The rocket catapult was 22.8m (75ft) long, sited on the port side of the ship's forecastle and extending to the foremast.

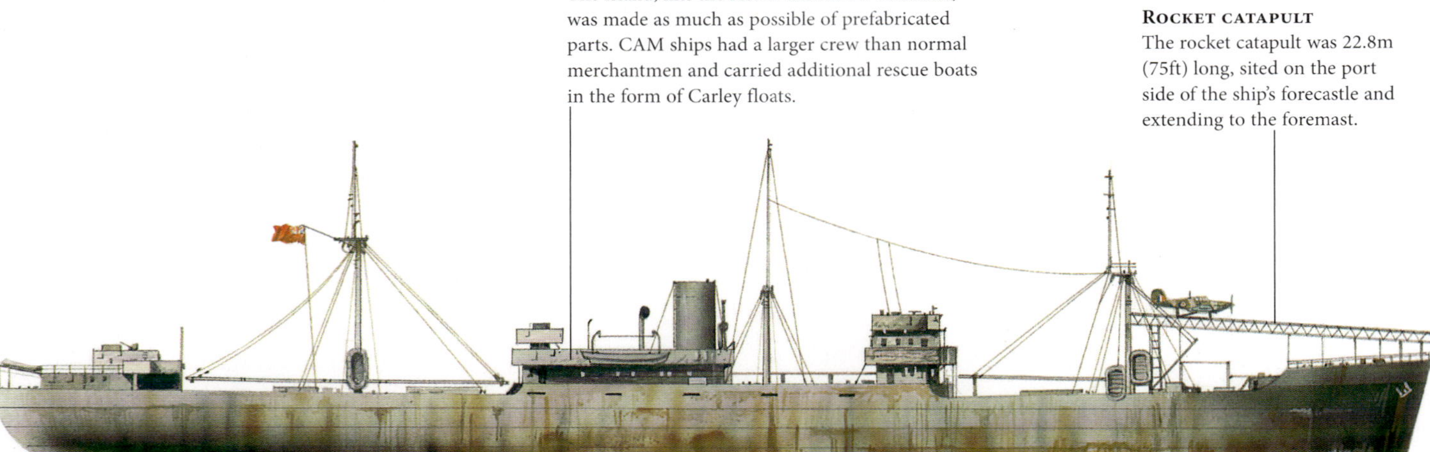

CAM SHIPS
In 1941 the Royal Navy had no carriers to spare to mount Atlantic patrols. Instead, the idea of the CAM or Catapult Aircraft Merchant ship was developed. Ships were already available: what was needed was a system mounted on the forecastle to launch a fighter plane defence against air attack. Altogether 35 merchant ships were fitted with bow catapults that used a cordite-powered rocket to drive a launch trolley.

MAC SHIPS
MAC (Merchant Aircraft Carrier) ships were a more highly developed form of the CAM ship. As converted bulk carriers, mostly originally built as grain ships and oil tankers, they were both cargo carriers and capable of launching and landing assault planes.

Type XIV (1941)

TYPE • *Submarine* COUNTRY • *Germany*

SPECIFICATIONS

DIMENSIONS:	Length: 67.10m (220ft 1in); Beam: 9.35m (30ft 8in); Draught: 6.51m (21ft 4in)
DISPLACEMENT:	1688 tonnes (1661 US tons) surfaced; 1932 tonnes (1901 US tons) submerged
PROPULSION:	2 1640.5kW (2200hp) diesels; 2 373kW (500hp) electric motors, 2 screws
SPEED:	27.6km/h (14.9 knots; 17.1mph) surfaced; 11.5km/h (6.2 knots; 7.1mph) submerged
RANGE:	22,872km (12,350nm; 14,212 miles) at 18.5km/h (10 knots) surfaced; 102km (55nm; 63 miles) at 7.4km/h (4 knots) submerged
ARMAMENT:	2 × 37mm (1.4in) guns; 1 × 20mm (0.79in) AA gun
COMPLEMENT:	53

Known to the German submariners as *Milchkühe* (Milk Cows), this was a class of 10 supply boats intended to refuel and restock U-boats on ocean patrol. Consideration of a 'submarine' tanker went back to the 1930s, though specifications for the Type XIV were not drawn up until 1940.

Above: The Type XIV submarine U-461*. The concept of the U-boat feeder, able to avoid detection until it reached a meeting point, was effective until the German radio codes were broken and their missions ceased to be secret. The system then had to be abandoned.*

AIR DEFENCE
For air defence, the 10 boats of the class originally had two quick-firing 37mm (1.4in) cannon, one forward and one aft of the bridge, and a 20mm (0.79in) AA gun on a raised platform attached to the tower.

STORAGE
Inside the pressure hull was a double-deck layout, with cargo storage compartments where up to 20 tonnes (19.7 US tons) of supplies could be held on pallets, ready for transfer.

ENGINES
Its engines were the same as used in Types VII and IX, 1640.5kW (2200hp) MAN diesel engines, two SSW 373kW (500hp) electric motors and two 62-cell battery sets.

ACOUSTIC PROTECTION
Alberich was the code name of the anechoic acoustic protection system developed from 1940. Synthetic rubber tiles were applied to the outer hull surface, muffling the submarine's sonar signature. The tiles were 4mm (0.2in) thick and there was great difficulty in finding a binding adhesive. Tested on *U-67* (IXC), more than half of its coating disappeared on its first voyage. It was 1944 before an adequate adhesive was found and used with considerable success on *U-480* (VIIC) until its sinking on 24 February 1945. But it never went into general use.

'MILK COW'
Deep in the Atlantic Ocean, the German Type XIV *U-459* prepares to refuel two hunter-killer U-boats. The transfer operation, in anything other than a flat calm, was a tricky business.

Shokaku (1941)

TYPE • *Aircraft carrier* **COUNTRY** • *Japan*

The large carriers *Shokaku* and *Zuikaku* were key elements in Japan's Pacific war plan. With long-range and high-endurance capacity, and able to hold 84 aircraft, they were considered to be battle-winners for the Imperial Navy.

SPECIFICATIONS

Dimensions:	Length: 257.5m (844ft 10in); Beam: 29m (95ft 2in); Draught: 9.3m (30ft 7in)
Displacement:	26,086 tonnes (28,758 US tons); 32,619 tonnes (35,944 US tons) full load
Propulsion:	8 boilers, 4 Kampon geared turbines, 4 shafts, 120,000kW (160,000shp)
Speed:	64km/h (34.5 knots; 39.7mph)
Range:	18,000km (9700nm; 11,200 miles) at 33.3km/h (18 knots; 20.7mph)
Armament (original):	8 × Type 89 127mm (5in) 40-cal twin HA guns; 12 × Type 96 triple 25mm machine guns
Aircraft:	84
Complement:	1660

Above: Shokaku *in 1941. The very long, low profiles of* Shokaku *and* Zuikaku *were not deliberately planned to minimize radar detection, but they certainly helped. In daylight combat, they presented a substantial target area.*

Stern-mounted boats
In total, 12 boats were carried on the stern, with four-tonne folding cranes to unship and retrieve them.

Radio masts
The radio masts along the aft part of the flight deck were lowered when landing and take-offs were in progress.

Aircraft windbreak
A recessable windbreak, raised when aircraft were on the flight deck, was set in the flight deck just forward of the island.

Forefoot
A bulbous forefoot was fitted below the bow, both to improve forward buoyancy and to reduce drag.

VAPOUR EXPLOSIONS

Aviation fuel tanks in Japanese carriers were not independently installed and protected by water-filled spaces but integral with the hull and far more prone to shocks and leakage. Following the loss of *Kaga* at Midway, concrete protection was applied to the fuel tanks on *Shokaku* and *Zuikaku*, although this was of limited value against leaking vapour. Historians have pointed out that *Shokaku*, *Taiyo* and *Hiyo* all suffered similar vapour-induced explosions after torpedo attacks.

UNDER ATTACK
The Japanese aircraft carrier *Shokaku* under attack by planes from USS *Yorktown*, during the morning of 8 May 1942. Splashes from dive bombers' near misses are visible off the ship's starboard side as she makes a sharp turn to the right.

USS *Indiana* (1942)

TYPE • *Battleship* **COUNTRY** • *United States*

SPECIFICATIONS	
DIMENSIONS:	Length: 210m (680ft); Beam: 32.9m (107ft 8in); Draught: 8.9m (29ft 3in)
DISPLACEMENT:	34,446 tonnes (37,970 US tons)
PROPULSION:	8 Foster Wheeler boilers, 4 Westinghouse geared turbines, developing 96,941kW (130,000hp)
SPEED:	50km/h (27 knots; 31mph)
RANGE:	27,750km (15,000nm; 17,245 miles) at 27.7km/h (15 knots; 17.2mph)
ARMAMENT:	9 × 406mm (16in) guns; 20 × 127mm (5in) guns; 24 × 40mm (1.6in) AA guns; 50 × 20mm (0.79in) AA guns
ARMOUR:	Belt: 310–22mm (12.2–0.87in); Bulkheads: 279mm (11in); Barbettes: 439–287mm (17.3–11.3in); Turrets: 457–184mm (18–7.25in); Deck: 152–146mm (6–5.75in)
COMPLEMENT:	1793

***Indiana* was the second of the four South Dakota class ships. Its 127mm (5in) guns were on two levels amidships, and the single funnel was faired into the rear of the bridge. In World War II, it was deployed mostly for carrier protection and shore bombardment.**

Left: USS Indiana *(BB-58) off Norfolk, Virginia, September 1942. Decommissioned in 1947, it was scrapped in 1963.*

CRANES
The heavy boat cranes by the aft superstructure were carried only on the USS *Indiana* and the USS *Massachusetts.*

AIRCRAFT
A Vought OS 2 U-1 Kingfisher is on the catapult. Two of these aircraft were carried on board the ship.

AA GUNS
A 40mm (1.6in) four-barrelled anti-aircraft gun was placed on 'B' turret in 1944 to enhance forward AA fire.

LAYOUT

These were the first American ships to be given inclined internal side armour, reaching from the armoured deck to the inner bottom and 310mm (12.2in) thick, tapering to 25mm (1in). This layout gave the ships a long indented inward-angled stretch of the central hull, just below the flush deck, rather reminiscent of the old casemate structure. Torpedo bulges were not fitted to this class, but a splinter protection deck placed 0.8cm (2ft 7in) below the main armour deck was a new feature.

USS *INDIANA*, UNDERWAY IN 1944
The South Dakota class was relatively compact in form – 210m (680ft) long compared to the preceding North Carolina's 222.1m (728ft 8in) – but of almost the same beam, and capable of considerably greater speed.

HMS *Jamaica* (1942)

TYPE • *Cruiser* **COUNTRY** • *United Kingdom*

The Fiji-class cruisers to which HMS *Jamaica* belonged were considered to be the best available to the Royal Navy in the early years of the war. All 11 ships were named after British possessions or overseas territories.

SPECIFICATIONS (Fiji class)

Dimensions:	Length: 169.32m (555ft 6in) overall; 164m (538ft) p/p; Beam: 19m (62ft); Draught: 5.03m (16ft 6in)
Displacement:	8670 tonnes (9554 US tons) standard
Propulsion:	4 Admiralty 3-drum boilers, 4 shafts, 4 geared steam turbines, 54,100kW (72,500shp)
Speed:	58.3km/h (31.5 knots; 36.2mph)
Range:	18,700km (10,100nm; 11,600 miles)
Armament:	9 × 152mm (6in) Mark XXIII guns; 8 × 102mm (4in) Mark XVI guns; 8 × 40mm (2-pdr) Mark VIII 'pom-pom' guns; 2 × triple 533mm (21in) torpedo tubes for Mark IX torpedoes
Armour:	Belt: 89–83mm (3.5–3.25in); Bulkheads: 51–38mm (2–1.5in); Turrets: 51–25mm (2–1in); Ring bulkheads: 25mm (1in) max
Complement:	730; 920 wartime

Right: HMS Jamaica *at anchor on 18 September 1943; note how effective the dazzle camouflage is amidships.*

Displacement
Following later modifications to the class, the full load displacement rose to 11,270 tonnes (12,423 US tons).

Firepower
The Fiji-class vessels were mostly armed with 12 152mm (6in) guns, although some had a reduced armament and carried only nine.

Armour
Jamaica's thickest concentration of armour was over the engine and boiler rooms, with a depth of 83mm (3.25in).

WAR SERVICE

HMS *Jamaica* is best known for her clashes with larger German warships. While serving as part of Convoy 51B to Murmansk, *Jamaica* encountered the German raiders *Lützow* and *Admiral Hipper*. The *Jamaica* scored direct hits on the *Hipper*, causing damage to her boiler room before contact was broken. Later, *Jamaica* participated in the sinking of the *Scharnhorst* on 26 December 1943.

HMS *JAMAICA*
HMS *Jamaica* was the sixth ship of the class to be laid down, on 28 April 1939. She was launched on 16 November 1940 and completed on 29 June 1942. By then several of her sister ships had seen considerable action, and HMS *Fiji* herself had been sunk.

USS *Independence* (1941)

TYPE • *Aircraft carrier* **COUNTRY** • *United States*

SPECIFICATIONS

Dimensions:	Length: 190m (623ft); Beam: 21.8m (71ft 6in); Draught: 7.4m (24ft 4in)
Displacement:	10,833 tonnes (11,942 US tons); 14,987 tonnes (16,515 US tons) full load
Propulsion:	4 boilers, GE turbines, 4 shafts, 75,470kW (100,000shp)
Speed:	57km/h (31 knots; 35.6mph)
Range:	24,000km (13,000nm; 14,963 miles) at 27.7km/h (15 knots; 17.2mph)
Armament:	24 x 40mm AA guns; 16 x 20mm AA guns
Aircraft:	34
Complement:	1569

Leader of a class of light carriers, during World War II the USS *Independence* fought with fast carrier battle groups and operated as the first night carrier, but ultimately became a target for post-war atom bomb testing.

Left: This stern view of Independence *taken on 30 April 1943 shows the unusual tumble-home hull form of the class.*

Armour
Independence had no side armour, apart from a 51mm (2in) section protecting the forward magazine. The armoured deck had 51mm (2in) of plate and the bulkheads ranged between 63mm and 127mm (2.5–5in).

Antennas
By mid-1944 the antennas mounted on the mast included a YE radio beacon, on top, with an SG surface search radar just below.

Flight deck
The flight deck, narrowed towards the bow, was 186m (610ft) long. It did not extend over the finely tapered bow, and a 127mm (5in) 38-cal gun was mounted right on the bows (this was removed early on).

ATOM BOMB TESTS

In 1946 *Independence* was selected as one of the test vessels to be used in the Operation *Crossroads* atomic bomb tests of Bikini Atoll. The hull survived two explosions without sinking. Despite being highly radioactive, it was towed first to Kwajalein, then to Pearl Harbor and finally to San Francisco for examination. It was ultimately scuttled in the Pacific on 29 January 1951.

SAN FRANCISCO BAY
USS *Independence* in San Francisco Bay in July 1943, on its way to join the Pacific Fleet. Leaving on 14 July, it was redesignated as a light carrier, CVL-22, on the 15th.

USS *Bogue* (1942)

TYPE • *Aircraft carrier* **COUNTRY** • *United States*

SPECIFICATIONS

Dimensions:	Length: 151.08m (495ft 8in); Beam: 25m (82ft); Draught: 7.9m (26ft)
Displacement:	8524 tonnes (9400 US tons) standard
Propulsion:	2 Foster-Wheeler 285 psi (1970 kPa) boilers, 1 Allis-Chalmers steam turbine, developing 8500shp (6300kW)
Speed:	33km/h (18 knots; 21mph)
Range:	48,700km (26,300nm; 30,300 miles)
Armament:	2 × 127mm (5in)/38-cal dual-purpose guns; 8 × twin 40mm (1.57in) Bofors anti-aircraft guns; 20 × 20mm (0.79in) Oerlikon anti-aircraft cannons
Aircraft:	19–24
Complement:	890

USS *Bogue* (CVE-9) was commissioned on 26 September 1942. It was the lead ship of the Bogue class of escort carrier, known in the British Navy as the Attacker class. The vessel survived service in the Atlantic and Pacific and remained on reserve until 1959.

Left: USS Bogue *served in both the Atlantic and Pacific theatres. In the Atlantic, the ship's aircraft destroyed or damaged multiple German U-boats, and they repeated their successes against Japanese submarines in the Pacific.*

Armament
Bogue's armament was focused principally on fast-firing automatic AA guns to defend herself against air attack.

Classification
Bogue was originally classified as AVG-9, but this was changed to ACV-9 in August 1942, CVE-9 in July 1943 and CVHE-9 in 1955.

Aircraft
Bogue could carry up to 24 aircraft, typically a mixture of Grumman F4F Wildcat fighters and Grumman TBF Avenger torpedo bombers.

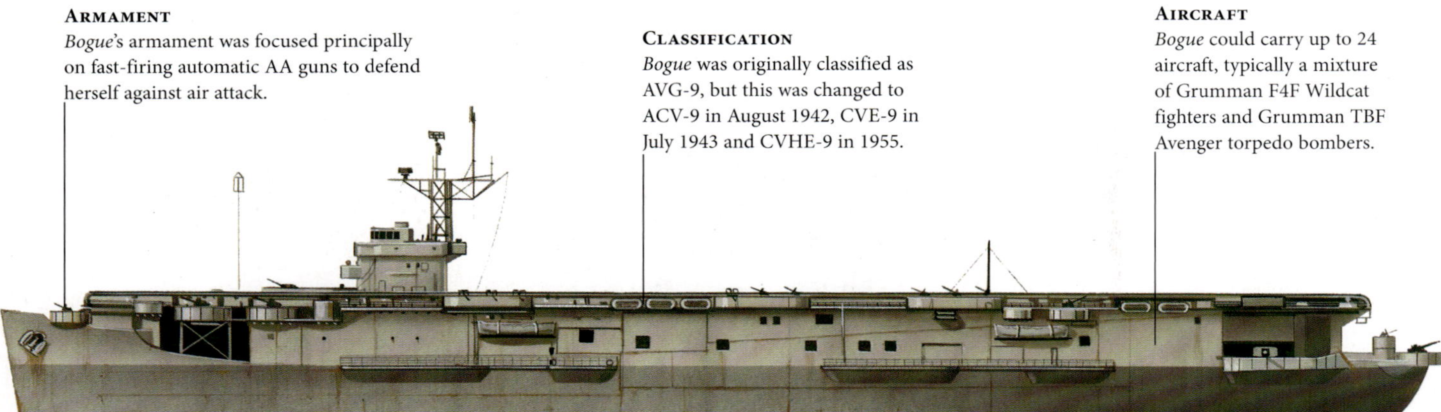

ESCORT CARRIERS

Escort carriers were a distinct category of aircraft carrier during World War II. They were smaller and lighter than the large fleet carriers – they were about half the length and a third the displacement – thus they carried far fewer aircraft, about 24–36. But because they were built on modified merchant ship hulls, they were fast to produce and served in significant numbers: 122 escort carriers were produced during World War II.

USS *BOGUE* AT ANCHOR
USS *Bogue* (CVE-9) at anchor at Bermuda with a pair of TBM Avengers visible on deck. *Bogue* is painted in Camouflage Measure 32 Design 4A.

USS *Piper* (Balao class) (1942)

TYPE • *Submarine* **COUNTRY** • *United States*

SPECIFICATIONS

Dimensions:	Length: 95m (311ft 9in); Beam: 8.3m (27ft 3in); Draught: 5.1m (16ft 9in)
Displacement:	1550 tonnes (1708 US tons) surfaced; 2440 tonnes (2689 US tons) submerged
Propulsion:	4 F-M diesel generator engines of a combined 4026kW (5400hp), 2 511kW (685hp) Elliott geared electric motors, 2 screws
Speed:	39km/h (21 knots; 24mph) surfaced; 16.6km/h (9 knots; 10mph) submerged
Range:	20,372km (11,000nm; 12,659 miles) surfaced; 176km (95nm; 109 miles) submerged
Armament:	10 × 533mm (21in) torpedo tubes; 24 torpedoes; 1 × 127mm (5in) 25cal deck gun; 1 × 40mm (1.5in) Bofors; 1 × twin 20mm (0.79in) Oerlikon AA gun
Complement:	80

The Balao was the largest class of submarine in the US Navy. The design was so similar to the later Gato class that USS *Balao* (SS-285) and others of its class were being laid down even as the last of the Gato boats were nearing completion.

Left: Here we see USS Piper *(SS-409) and* Threadfin *(SS-410) double launching at the Portsmouth Navy Yard, Kittery, Maine on 26 June 1944.*

USS *Piper* (SS-409)
The two tapering and robust periscopes were the main visual definer between the 121 Balaos and the Gatos, the latter with thinner scopes and supporting ribs. Supporting brackets were mounted two-thirds of the way up and at the top of the shears and were extended back to the SJ surface radar mast and the base part of the telescopic air search SD mast.

Armament
Some Balao-class submarines acquired a second Mk 17 127mm (5in) deck gun from late 1943, as torpedo-worthy targets were becoming scarce.

Watertight trunk
A useful feature of all the class was a watertight trunk from the deck to the control room, allowing gun crews to reach position without going through the packed conning tower.

DIVE DEPTH

The US Navy was aware that Japanese depth charges were effective to 90m (295ft) and that the Gato class's operating depth was down to only 91.4m (300ft). Greater depth ability was needed. By changing the pressure hull cover to high tensile steel (HTS) 20mm (0.79in) thick, a maximum diving depth of 198m (650ft) could be achieved. In the interest of safety, the test depth of the Balao design was finally fixed at 123m (400ft). The Gato plans were modified to incorporate the thicker pressure hull.

USS *PIPER*
USS *Piper* (SS-409) arrives at the US Naval Submarine Base, New London, Connecticut, on 15 October 1945. Though American fleet submarines did serve as fleet escorts and scouts, especially to carrier groups, they also had a 'hunter-killer' role in seeking out and destroying Japanese naval craft.

X-class (1942)

TYPE • *Midget submarine* **COUNTRY** • *United Kingdom*

SPECIFICATIONS (HMS *X-5*)

Dimensions:	Length: 15.6m (51ft 2in); Beam: 1.75m (5ft 9in); Draught: 1.6m (5ft 3in)
Displacement:	27.4 tonnes (30.2 US tons) surfaced; 30.48 tonnes (33.6 US tons) submerged
Propulsion:	1 diesel of 31.3kW (42hp), 1 22.3kW (30hp) electric motor, single screw
Speed:	12km/h (6.5 knots; 7.5mph) surfaced; 9.2km/h (5 knots; 5.1mph) submerged
Range:	2444km (1320nm; 1519 miles) surfaced; 148km (80nm; 92 miles) submerged
Armament:	2 x 2000kg (4400lb) detachable charges
Complement:	4

The Italians, Japanese and British all made extensive use of very small submarines for secret penetration of protected anchorages and bases. The Royal Navy's versions were known as X-craft, developed under tight security from Varley Marine and built for river work.

Right: Habitability was at the bottom of the scale even given the expectation that missions would be relatively short.

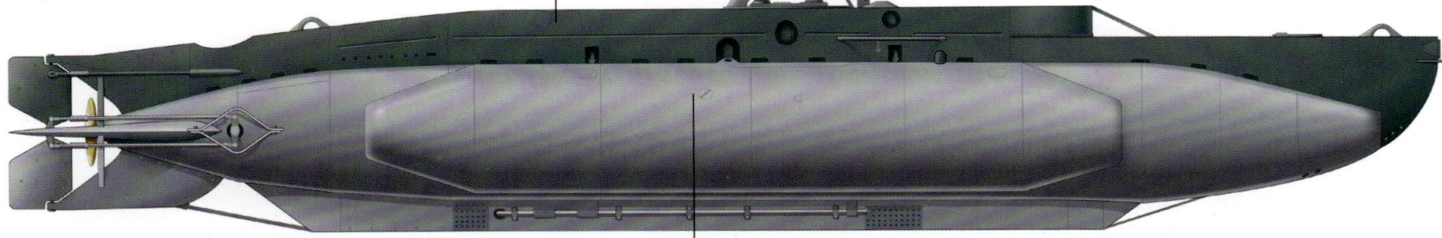

Hull
The hull, formed of welded 0.703kg (1.5lb) 'S' type steel, was formed of three sections, bolted together. It had a 'wet and dry' airlock hatch for a diver in addition to a surface hatch.

***X-5* equipment**
Equipment consisted of gyro (Browns A) and magnetic (ACO MkXX) compasses, an AFV 6A/602 direction indicator, a Type 159 target indicator, a specially developed hydrophone, Browns auto-helmsman, and a night and an attack periscope.

Explosives
Bolted on each side were its mine-type warloads: cased amatol explosive charges, each of two tons, to be released from inside and deposited beneath a target vessel.

PAINTWORK
The standard scheme for RN submarines was grey sides and black upper surfaces, and this continued through the war for Home Fleet boats. During World War II, the camouflage scheme for submarines operating in the Mediterranean was light and dark green, but dark blue appears also to have been used, and some were even painted pink (a shade favoured by the future Admiral Lord Mountbatten). In the Far East, dark olive green was the standard colour.

SINGLE HATCH
The X-craft had only a single exit hatch, creating huge operational risks for the crew. The first operational type was *X-3* (1942). *X-5* was built by Vickers at Barrow in the winter of 1942–43. It had all the key features of a full-size submarine incorporated in a hull 15.5m (51ft) long.

Landing Ship, Tank (LST) (1942)

TYPE • *Landing craft* **COUNTRY** • *United States*

SPECIFICATIONS (Maracaibo class)

DIMENSIONS:	Length: 116m (382ft); Beam: 19.5m (64ft); Draught fully laden: 4.6m (15ft) aft, 1.2m (4ft) forward
TONNAGE:	4877 tonnes (4800 long tons)
RAMPS:	Double hinged ramp, effective length 30m (100ft)
PROPULSION:	Reciprocating steam engine, 2 shafts, 2237kW (3000shp)
CAPACITY:	18 × 30-ton tanks or 22 × 25-ton tanks or 33 × 3-ton trucks
TROOPS	Berths for 217 troops
ARMAMENT:	1 × twin 40mm (1.5in) gun; 6 × 20mm (0.79in) guns; 3 × Lewis guns; 2 × 100mm (4in) smoke mortars
COMPLEMENT:	98 combined operations personnel

The standard US tank landing craft (LST), which has now become an almost timeless design, grew from a British requirement for a tank carrier capable of transporting new tanks from US factories directly to Europe.

Below: The hull design proved to be highly versatile and LSTs were converted to serve as MTB tenders, aircraft engine repair ships, salvage craft tenders, battle-damage repair ships and auxiliaries.

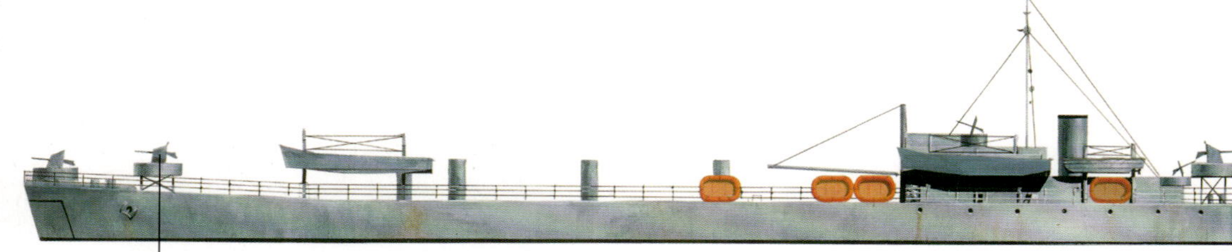

VARIATIONS
Differences between individual LSTs could be substantial, with several davit configurations and a wide range of armament fits.

ARMAMENT
By the end of the war, most US LSTs were fitted with seven 40mm (1.5in) and 12 20mm (0.79in) AA guns, but there were many exceptions to this rule.

CAPACITY
Alongside the tanks, the LSTs could carry more than 200 troops (depending on the class), enabling them to land infantry and armour in a single pass.

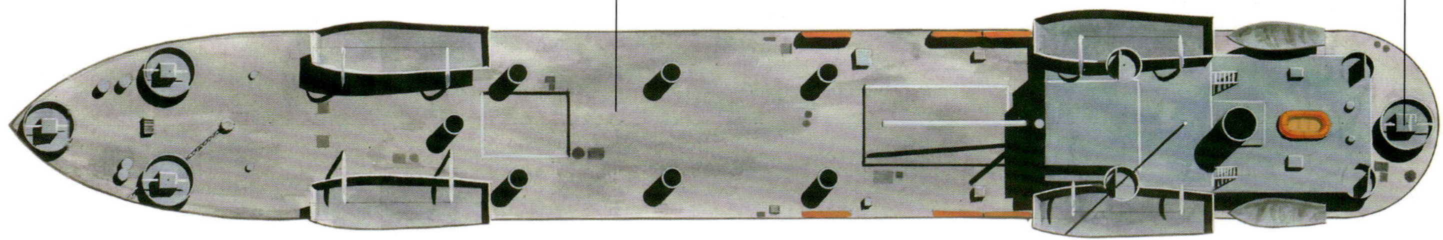

CAPABILITY
What emerged as the LST had to be able to carry about 20 tanks, or equivalent vehicles, which could be driven straight off the ship via a ramp in the bow. Some tanks could be carried on the weather deck, above the main hold, and so the early LSTs had a lift between the two decks (this was later replaced by a ramp). The LSTs were also required to carry at least one tank landing craft (LCT) to allow operations in waters where the larger LST could not make it to the beach.

LCT-401
LCT-401 is launched at Norfolk Navy Yard, Norfolk, Virginia, on 3 January 1943. The LSTs were designed to have great range, up to and beyond 9260km (5000nm; 5940 miles). They were also very slow and could manage only about 10 knots when loaded and underway.

Landing Craft, Infantry Large (LCI(L)) (1943)

TYPE • *Landing craft* **COUNTRY** • *United States*

The Landing Craft, Infantry Large, abbreviated to LCI(L), was a useful Allied vessel designed to deliver more than 200 troops to enemy shores, being able to make open-water journeys of up to 48 hours in duration.

SPECIFICATIONS

DIMENSIONS:	Length: 48.31m (158ft 6in); Beam: 7.09m (23ft 3in); Draught: 1.63m (5ft 4in) forward, 1.80m (5ft 11in) aft
DISPLACEMENT:	238 tonnes (234 long tons) standard
PROPULSION:	2 banks GM/Detroit diesel 6051 quad-71 engines, 2 shafts (4 engines per shaft), developing 1193kW (1600bhp)
SPEED:	30km/h (16 knots; 18mph)
RANGE:	7400km (4000nm; 2485 miles) at 12 knots, carrying extra fuel instead of troops and cargo
TROOPS:	180, later increased to 210
ARMAMENT:	4 x 20mm Oerlikon cannons (one forward, one amidships, two aft)
ARMOUR:	5cm (2in) plastic armour for splinter protection of gunners and pilot house
COMPLEMENT:	24

Right: A flotilla of LCI(L)s are here seen underway. They could be distinguished from the other LCIs by the vessel's short conning tower.

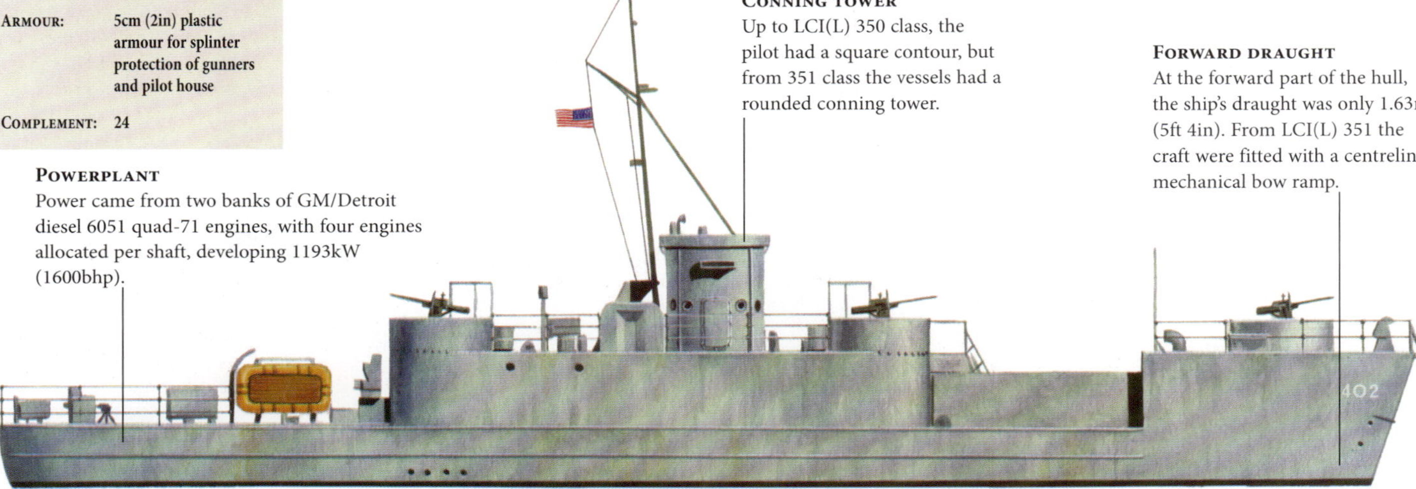

CONNING TOWER
Up to LCI(L) 350 class, the pilot had a square contour, but from 351 class the vessels had a rounded conning tower.

FORWARD DRAUGHT
At the forward part of the hull, the ship's draught was only 1.63m (5ft 4in). From LCI(L) 351 the craft were fitted with a centreline mechanical bow ramp.

POWERPLANT
Power came from two banks of GM/Detroit diesel 6051 quad-71 engines, with four engines allocated per shaft, developing 1193kW (1600bhp).

SHALLOW DRAUGHT

One of the most dangerous moments of an amphibious landing was when assaulting infantry, heavily laden with arms and equipment, had to wade ashore from the landing craft under the enemy guns. If the landing vessels were too far out, troops could only move slowly, exposing them to fire, and they risked drowning. The LCIs were developed with a shallow draught and gangways on each bow, so the infantry could be deposited right at the water's edge.

RETURNING LCIS
Here various LCI(L)s are seen returning to the United States from Europe after combat service in that theatre. The type was heavily used in the D-Day landings in Normandy on 6 June 1944.

Type XXI (1943)

TYPE • *Submarine* **COUNTRY** • *Germany*

SPECIFICATIONS

Dimensions:	Length: 76.7m (251ft 10in); Beam: 8m (26ft 3in); Draught: 6.32m (20ft 9in)
Displacement:	1621 tonnes (1787 US tons) surfaced; 1819 tonnes (2006 US tons) submerged
Propulsion:	2 1640.5kW (2200hp) diesels; 2 1864kW (500hp) electric motors; 2 241kW (323hp) creep motors, 2 screws
Speed:	28.9km/h (15.6 knots; 18mph) surfaced; 31.9km/h (17.2 knots; 19.8mph) submerged
Range:	20,650km (11,150nm; 12,831 miles) surfaced; 528km (285nm; 328 miles) submerged
Armament:	6 × 533mm (21in) torpedo tubes; 2 × twin 20mm (0.79in) Flak mountings
Complement:	57

German scientists and naval architects, led by Dr Helmuth Walter, were working on a 'true' submarine design that could run submerged for days rather than hours and would be virtually undetectable. But that was still a good way off. The Type XXI was intended to fill the gap.

Below: Type XXI's smooth lines made existing submarines look antique: everything – guns, aerials, bollards – was retractable (including the bow diving planes) to ensure minimum drag in the water.

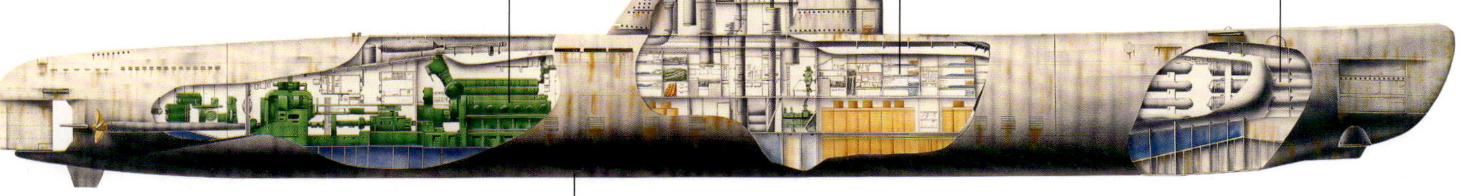

Engines
Walter's ultimate aim was for an air-independent main engine, but he had to compromise with two MAN M6V409/46KBB supercharged six-cylinder diesels delivering 2900kW (3900hp).

Limited accommodation
The amount of technical equipment packed into the hull meant that only 47 berths were available for a crew of 57. Hammock hooks were provided.

Torpedoes
Six torpedo tubes, all forward-facing, were fitted, and 17 reload torpedoes were carried. Alternatively, the Type XXI could hold 14 torpedoes and 12 TMC mines.

Passive/active sonar
In the Type XXI an improved Gruppenhorchgerät (GHG) passive sonar system fitted beneath the keel, and a new active system, Unterwasser-Ortungsgerät Nibelung, enabled detection and attack of enemy shipping without optical contact – another revolutionary feature.

EVASION TACTICS

Though the Type XXI would attack at slow speed, with the listening gear unaffected by its own propeller noise, it would use high speed to evade escort hunts. Its manoeuvrability (despite a large submerged turning circle of 450m (1500ft)) would pose difficulties for a single escort trying to hold contact, and several escort vessels might be needed to hem it in. Depth charge attacks would be wholly ineffective if the U-boat got any warning of the attack.

TYPE XXI IN PORT

The speed of design and production for the Type XXI meant that many modifications had to be made, often requiring retrofitting. One major change was the incorporation of a snorkel.

Matsu class (1943)

TYPE • *Destroyer* **COUNTRY** • *Japan*

The Matsu class of destroyers were built from 1943 onwards, by which time the war in the Pacific had irrevocably turned against the Japanese. Rapid losses in naval shipping compelled the Japanese to design the class for rapid construction.

SPECIFICATIONS (April 1944)

DIMENSIONS:	Length: 100.0m (328ft 1in) overall; Beam: 9.35m (30ft 8in); Draught: 3.30m (10ft 10in)
DISPLACEMENT:	1260 tonnes (1389 US tons) standard
PROPULSION:	2 Kampon water-tube boilers, 2 Kampon impulse geared turbines, developing 14MW (19,000shp), 2 shafts
SPEED:	51.5km/h (27.8 knots; 32mph)
RANGE:	6500km (3500nm; 4039 miles)
ARMAMENT:	3 × 127mm (5.0in) L/40 Type 89 AA guns; 24 × 25mm (1in) Type 96 AA guns; 4 × 610mm (24in) Type 92 torpedo tubes; 4 × Type 93 torpedoes; 4 depth charge throwers; 36 × Type 2 depth charges
COMPLEMENT:	211

Above: Momi *(5489) was sunk on 5 January 1945 by US Navy torpedo bombers off Manila, with all hands lost.*

FUNNELS
The two widely spaced funnels were a distinguishing feature of the class, and they also made the boats look bigger than they actually were.

MAIN GUN
The main gun on the forward deck was a 127mm (5in) Type 89 dual-purpose gun, the 'dual-purpose' meaning it could engage surface and air targets.

PERFORMANCE
Despite being underpowered compared to many other Japanese destroyer types, the Matsu class could still achieve 51.5km/h (27.8 knots; 32mph).

CONSTRUCTION

The Matsu class of destroyers, also known as the D-class, were designed from the outset for rapid construction and fitting out. Compared to previous destroyer types, economies were made in every area, including dimensions, armament and armour, and a powerplant producing only about a third of the output of a fleet destroyer. Nevertheless, the vessels were serviceable and effective, and they were further streamlined for production in the modular Tachibana sub-class.

TYPE C ESCORT SHIP
The Type C was an even smaller class of escort vessel produced by Japan in the late war years. Although many were sunk by US air attacks, large numbers survived and some served in civilian capacities well into the 1950s.

USS *The Sullivans* (Fletcher class) (1943)

TYPE • *Destroyer* **COUNTRY** • *United States*

SPECIFICATIONS

DIMENSIONS:	Length: 114.7m (376ft 6in); Beam: 12.1m (39ft 8in); Draught: 5.4m (17ft 9in)
DISPLACEMENT:	1859 tonnes (2050 US tons)
PROPULSION:	2 General Electric steam turbines, developing 45MW (60,000shp), 2 screws
SPEED:	70.4km/h (38 knots; 44mph)
RANGE:	12,000km (6500nm; 7456 miles) at 28km/h (15 knots; 17mph)
ARMAMENT:	5 × 127mm (5in) guns; 10 × 40mm (1.57in) AA guns; 7 × 20mm (0.79in) AA guns; 10 × 533mm (21in) torpedo tubes; 6 depth charge projectors and tracks
ARMOUR:	Not available
COMPLEMENT:	208

The Fletcher-class destroyer *The Sullivans* was named in honour of the five Sullivan brothers, who lost their lives when *Juneau* was sunk by a Japanese submarine off Guadalcanal in November 1942. It was the greatest combat loss suffered by any one American family in World War II.

Left: USS The Sullivans *(DD-537) underway on 29 October 1962. Post-war, the vessel would eventually become a museum ship.*

SUPERSTRUCTURE
The US Navy ordered the Fletcher class to be built with a simplified superstructure to hasten production. A new bridge design also increased the overhead view available to the captain.

MACHINERY
The Fletcher-class boats were powered by two General Electric turbines, producing 45MW (60,000shp) and giving a maximum speed of 70.4km/h (38 knots; 44mph).

HULL
The flush deck hull of the Fletcher class added strength but reduced internal hull volume, so conditions on board were somewhat cramped.

FLETCHER CLASS

A total of 175 Fletcher-class destroyers were completed between 1941 and 1945. Although the vessels in the Fletcher class were generally rushed out to the Pacific on completion, those built on the Atlantic seaboard saw some service in that ocean. The *Fletcher* herself served on convoy-protection duty in the western Atlantic before her deployment to the Pacific in time for the naval actions off Guadalcanal. All the ships of this class were named after US Navy personnel or civilians who had rendered outstanding service.

***THE SULLIVANS* (DD-537)**
Though the extensive Benson class achieved the aim of putting the US destroyer-building industry onto a war footing, the design had limitations for a Pacific war, both in terms of endurance and in its curtailed weapons fit. The Fletcher class would remedy these deficiencies.

USS *Johnston* (Fletcher class) (1943)

TYPE • *Destroyer* **COUNTRY** • *United States*

SPECIFICATIONS

DIMENSIONS:	Length: 114.7m (376ft 6in); Beam: 12.1m (39ft 8in); Draught: 5.4m (17ft 9in)
DISPLACEMENT:	1859 tonnes (2050 US tons)
PROPULSION:	2 General Electric steam turbines, developing 45MW (60,000shp), 2 screws
SPEED:	70.4km/h (38 knots; 44mph)
RANGE:	12,000km (6500nm; 7456 miles) at 28km/h (15 knots; 17mph)
ARMAMENT:	5 × 127mm (5in) guns; 10 × 40mm (1.57in) AA guns; 7 × 20mm (0.79in) AA guns; 10 × 533mm (21in) torpedo tubes; 6 depth charge projectors and tracks
ARMOUR:	Not available
COMPLEMENT:	208

In October 2019, the wreck of the USS *Johnston* (DD-557) was discovered more than 6100m (20,000ft) below the surface in the Philippine Sea. The ship had been sunk following the thunderous naval engagement now known as the Battle off Samar.

Left: USS Johnston *is here seen in the United States (off Seattle or Tacoma, Washington) on 27 October 1943.*

DEPTH CHARGE RACKS
The Fletcher-class ships were fitted with two racks, each holding eight 270kg (600lb) depth charges, and adjacent to them were two storage racks with five depth charges each.

COMPLEMENT
The usual complement of the Fletcher class was 208 and, despite the rather congested conditions below decks, veteran US Navy destroyer men claimed that the boats were the best of their era.

AA ARMAMENT
The destroyer's AA weaponry was progressively increased as the Pacific War went on, additional firepower being added as the threat of Japanese air attacks increased.

BATTLE OFF SAMAR

The Battle off Samar was part of the Battle of Leyte Gulf, a vast clash of Japanese and US surface vessels and carrier aircraft off the coast of the Philippines in October 1944. At one point in the battle, *Johnston* made a valiant torpedo charge against a superior Japanese force that included the battleship *Yamato* and three other battleships. The valiant destroyer was eventually sunk by heavy shellfire, with 186 lives lost.

SHIP LAUNCH
USS *Johnston* slips down the building ways at the Seattle-Tacoma Shipbuilding Corporation shipyard, Seattle, Washington, 25 March 1943.

River class (1943)

TYPE • *Frigate* **COUNTRY** • *United Kingdom*

SPECIFICATIONS

DIMENSIONS:	Length: 91.8m (301.25ft) o/a; Beam: 11.1m (36ft 6in; Draught: 2.7m (9ft) standard
DISPLACEMENT:	1392 tonnes (1534 US tons) standard
PROPULSION:	2 × Admiralty 3-drum boilers, 2 shafts, reciprocating vertical triple expansion engines, developing 4100kW (5500hp)
SPEED:	37km/h (20 knots; 23 mph); 20.5 knots for turbine ships (38.0km/h; 23.6mph)
RANGE:	13,300km (7200nm; 8300 miles)
ARMAMENT:	2 × QF 102mm (4in)/40 Mk.XIX guns; single mounts CP Mk.XXIII; up to 10 × QF 20mm (0.79in) Oerlikon AA on twin mounts Mk.V and single mounts Mk.III; 1 × Hedgehog 24 spigot A/S projector; 8 × depth charge throwers; 2 × rails; up to 150 depth charges
COMPLEMENT:	107

The River class were a major part of the Royal Navy's surface fleet during World War II, with a total of 151 of the frigates (although initially classified as corvettes) built and launched between 1941 and 1944.

Left: HMAS Condamine *was a River-class frigate of the Royal Australian Navy (RAN). Although it had been launched in November 1944, it was not commissioned until February 1946.*

FORECASTLE
The River-class ships had a distinctive raised forecastle fitted with a single 102mm (4in) gun.

MACHINERY
The River class achieved an improved performance over the Flowers class by doubling the size of the powerplant and using more efficient water-tube boilers.

HULL
To speed up production, the River class used merchant-shipping models in the hull design.

SERVICE

The River-class frigates served extensively during World War II, and not only with the Royal Navy (RN). Other users of this class included the Royal Australian Navy, the Royal Canadian Navy (the next most prolific user after the RN), the Free French Naval Forces, the Royal Netherlands Navy and the South African Navy. Two were even used by the US Navy: USS *Asheville* and USS *Natchez*.

DUTCH RIVER CLASS
Initially built as HMS *Ripple*, HNLMS *Johan Maurits van Nassau* (F802) was a River-class frigate transferred to the Royal Netherlands Navy (RNN) during its construction in 1943.

Unryu (1943)

TYPE • *Aircraft carrier* **COUNTRY** • *Japan*

SPECIFICATIONS

Dimensions:	Length: 227.35m (745ft 11in); Beam: 22m (72ft 2in); Draught: 8.73m (28ft 8in)
Displacement:	20,450 tonnes (22,550 US tons)
Propulsion:	8 Kampon water-tube boilers, 4 shafts, 4 geared steam turbine sets, 113,000kW (152,000shp)
Speed:	63km/h (34 knots; 39mph)
Range:	15,000km (8000nm; 9200 miles)
Armament:	6 × twin 12.7cm (5in) DP guns; 16 × triple and 3 × single 25mm (1in) AA guns; 6 × 28-tube 12cm (4.7in) AA rocket launchers
Armour:	Belt: 46–140mm (1.8–5.5in); Deck: 25–56mm (0.98–2.20in)
Aircraft:	48 (up to 65)
Complement:	1595

A strike carrier, for use against convoys, *Unryu* was one of only three to be completed out of a planned class of 17. With the island sponsoned out, it had a wide flight deck, served by two lifts. *Unryu* was sunk by the US submarine *Redfish* in December 1944, before it saw any action.

Above: Unryu *was sunk on her maiden sea voyage, at a time when US submarines were killing both merchant and naval vessels at record rates.*

Sensors
As built, the *Unryu* was fitted with two Type 21 radars on top of the island and flight deck and a Type 13 radar mast.

Aircraft
The standard aircraft carried aboard the *Unryu* were the Mitsubishi A6M fighter, Aichi D3A dive-bomber and Nakajima B5N torpedo-bomber

Powerplant
The ship had eight water-tube boilers linked to Kampon geared turbines, in total generating 113,000kW (152,000shp) of propulsive energy.

Island
Although the Unryu class was based on the carrier *Hiryu*, the island was placed on the starboard side instead of the port side.

TORPEDOED

Unryu arrived late in the war, not being commissioned until August 1944. Her service history lasted a mere five months. On 19 December 1944, while heading to the island of Luzon to reinforce Japanese operations, *Unryu* was torpedoed by the submarine USS *Redfish*, causing major explosions on board. A total of 1238 people went down with the ship.

UNRYU CLASS
In total three aircraft carriers of the Unryu class were completed – *Unryu*, *Amagi* and *Katsuragi* (pictured here) – while three others of the class were unfinished by war's end.

USS *Intrepid* (CV-11) (1943)

TYPE • *Aircraft carrier* **COUNTRY** • *United States*

SPECIFICATIONS

DIMENSIONS:	Length: 250m (820ft); Beam: 28m (93ft); Draught: 10.41m (34ft 2in)
DISPLACEMENT:	27,534 tonnes (30,340 US tons)
PROPULSION:	8 boilers, 4 Westinghouse geared turbines, 4 shafts, 110,000kW (150,000shp)
SPEED:	61km/h (33 knots; 38mph)
RANGE:	28,564km (15,440nm; 17,756 miles)
ARMAMENT:	12 × 127mm (5in) 38-cal guns (4 twin, 4 single); 8 × quad 40mm (1.5in) 56-cal AA guns; 46 × 20mm 78-cal AA guns
AIRCRAFT:	110
COMPLEMENT:	2600

Despite being the most frequently hit US carrier in World War II, *Intrepid* served in the US Navy for more than 30 years on missions from Pacific battles to spacecraft recovery, and remains today one of the four surviving Essex-class carriers.

Above: In the 1960s and 1970s, Intrepid *had three deployments in the Vietnam War as an attack carrier, each operating with different aircraft groups.*

AIRCRAFT
The *Intrepid* carried 110 aircraft of various types, including Hellcats and Helldivers.

RADIO ANTENNAS
On completion there were four lattice masts holding radio antennas, and these could be hinged horizontally outwards during flight operations. A similar arrangement was made on most other carriers.

ELEVATORS
Like other Essex-class carriers, *Intrepid* had three aircraft elevators, originally wooden-planked like the flight deck, two on the centreline and one on the port side of the flight deck.

TWO-OCEAN NAVY

On 10 July 1940, President Franklin D. Roosevelt signed the 'Two-Ocean Navy' Act, affirming the USA's aim to have a powerful naval presence in both the Atlantic and Pacific zones, and authorizing funding for three more fleet carriers of the Essex class: *Yorktown*, *Intrepid* and *Hornet*. As American involvement in the war grew more likely, a further seven fleet carriers were approved in the same month.

ON OPERATIONS

Hull CV-11 was laid down at Newport News, Virginia, on 1 December 1941, a few days before the Pearl Harbor attack, launched as USS *Intrepid* on 26 April 1943 and commissioned on 16 August that year.

USS *Princeton* (1943)

TYPE • *Aircraft carrier* **COUNTRY** • *United States*

The fourth US Navy ship to bear the name, the USS *Princeton* (CV-23) was originally intended to be a light cruiser, but the need for more carriers saw it converted to an Independence-class aircraft carrier.

SPECIFICATIONS

Dimensions:	Length: 189.7m (622ft 6in); Beam: 21.8m (71ft 6in); Draught: 7.9m (26ft)
Displacement:	11,176 tonnes (11,000 tons) standard
Propulsion:	GE geared turbines, 2 shafts, 74,570kW (100,000shp)
Speed:	58.5km/h (31.6 knots; 36.4mph)
Range:	12,500nm (23,125km; 14,375 miles)
Armament:	24 40mm (1.5in) and 22 20mm (0.79in) AA guns
Aircraft:	34
Complement:	1569

Left: Princeton *was sunk by air attack at the Battle of Leyte Gulf in October 1944. Here the battleship* Birmingham *tries vainly to help with firefighting.*

Island
The small island was almost completely clear of the flight deck, which because of the relatively narrow cruiser-form hull needed all possible space.

Aircraft wing
The planned aircraft wing was formed of 30 planes – 12 fighters, nine dive-bombers and nine torpedo bombers – although the Independence class normally carried around 28.

Gun tubs
The gun emplacements were known as gun tubs. They were not sponsoned but bracketed out in balcony style.

Measure 21 camouflage
Princeton's paint scheme, here its original dark grey, went through different camouflage types. Measure 21, all-over sea-blue, was frequently used on the large surface areas of carriers. When sunk it was painted in Measure 33/Design 7A.

DEVELOPMENT

The future *Princeton* had been ordered as a light cruiser in July 1940. To be named *Tallahassee*, it was laid down at the New York Shipbuilding Corporation yard, Camden, New Jersey, on 2 June 1941. On 6 February 1942 the change of plan was made, by which time the hull was complete up to the main deck level. As a carrier it was launched on 18 October 1942 and commissioned at the Philadelphia Navy Yard on 25 February 1943 as USS *Princeton* (CV-23). In July 1943 the designation was modified to CVL to indicate its 'light' status.

SHAKEDOWN CRUISE
Here USS *Princeton* is underway during her shakedown cruise in 1943. (A 'shakedown' cruise is performed to test the function of a new ship's systems and its performance at sea.) The carrier was classified as CVL-23 later that year.

Taiho (1943)

TYPE • *Aircraft carrier* COUNTRY • *Japan*

SPECIFICATIONS

DIMENSIONS:	Length: 260.6m (855ft); Beam: 27.4m (89ft 11in); Draught: 9.6m (31ft 6in)
DISPLACEMENT:	29,769 tonnes (29,300 tons); 33,243 tonnes (32,720 tons) full load
PROPULSION:	8 Kampon boilers, 4 Kampon geared turbines, 4 shafts, 120,000kW (160,000shp)
SPEED:	61.7km/h (33.3 knots; 38.3mph)
RANGE:	19,000km (10,000nm; 12,000 miles) at 18 knots (33.3km/h; 20.7mph)
ARMAMENT:	6 × twin 100mm (3.9in) 65-cal Type 98 guns; 17 × triple 25mm (1in) AA cannon
AIRCRAFT:	84
COMPLEMENT:	1751

Marking an advance in Japanese carrier construction and considered unsinkable, *Taiho* was a powerful and formidably armed ship, but its fighting life was destined to last for only three months as the Japanese lost grip of the Pacific waters.

Above: A profile of Taiho. *The carrier was torpedoed and sunk by a US submarine on 19 June 1944.*

ELEVATORS
The lifts could raise an aircraft from the lower hangar in 15 seconds. They were larger than those on British and American carriers as Japanese naval aircraft did not have wholly folding wings (wing-tips only).

ARRESTER WIRES
Taiho mounted 14 arrester wires, six forward and eight aft, with electrically operated deceleration gear. Two crash barriers were placed aft of the island and a third to forward.

ARMAMENT
The 100mm (3.9in) guns were controlled by two Type 89 Mod 1 directors, with 4.5m (14ft 9in) Type 94 rangefinders, one mounted forward of the island, the other amidships on the port side below the flight deck.

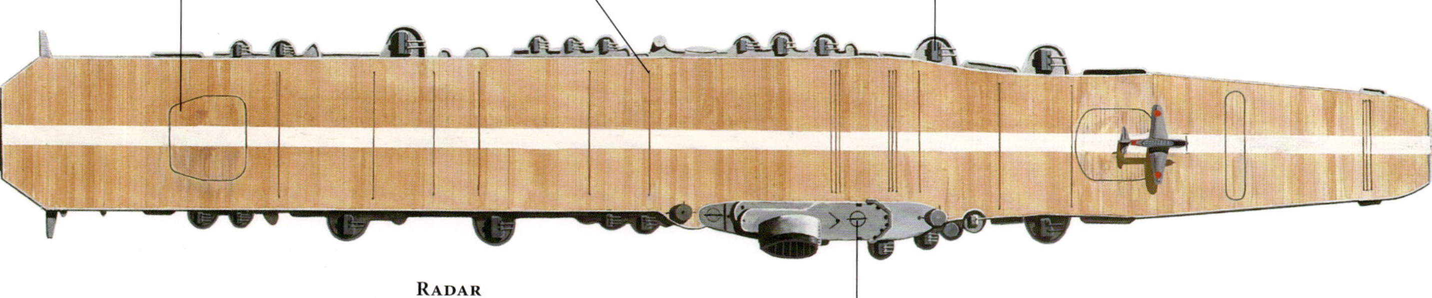

RADAR
Two sets of Type 21 Mod 3 radars, one in front of the bridge, the other abaft the funnel, gave 360° coverage, with a maximum 150km (92 miles) in the air and 20km (12.5 miles) on the surface.

AVIATION ADVANTAGES

Japanese aircraft carriers never employed catapult launchers, so aircraft had to rely on their own speed and windspeed to launch their aircraft. They were also helped by their planes' relatively light weight. This also gave the Japanese planes a somewhat greater range, and thus a tactical advantage, especially in reconnaissance and long-range strikes. On the negative side, it meant a lesser degree of protection for the aircrew and greater liability in the airframe to break up under attack.

FLAGSHIP
Battle of the Philippine Sea, 19 June 1944: a shot-up Japanese plane crashes into the sea close to a Japanese light carrier. *Taiho* was Admiral Ozawa's flagship in the battle.

Type I-400 (1943)

TYPE • *Submarine* **COUNTRY** • *Japan*

SPECIFICATIONS

Dimensions:	Length: 122m (400ft); Beam: 12m (39ft 4in); Draught: 7m (23ft)
Displacement:	5307 tonnes (5848 US tons) surfaced; 6760 tonnes (7449 US tons) submerged
Propulsion:	4 diesels of 1680kW (2250hp), 2 1600kW (2100hp) electric motors, 2 screws
Speed:	34.6km/h (18.7 knots; 21.5mph) surfaced; 12km/h (6.5 knots; 7.5mph) submerged
Range:	68,524km (37,000nm; 42,579 miles) surfaced; 111km (60nm; 69 miles) submerged
Armament:	8 × 533mm (21in) torpedo tubes; 12 × torpedoes; 1 × Type 11 140mm (5.5in) gun; 3 × waterproofed Type 96 triple and 1 × single AA guns
Complement:	157 including aircrew

In 1942, under the Fifth Fleet Replenishment Programme, a total of 18 super-submarines, designated Sen-Toku (special class), were included. Work commenced immediately, and *I-400* was laid down at Kure on 18 January 1943.

Above: Great ingenuity went into the folding and collapsible equipment, including a retrieval crane.

Operational depth
Operational depth was 100m (330ft), less than the boat's own length. The best diving time was 58 seconds, almost twice that of a US Balao-class boat.

Deck layout
The upper section with the bridge deck was canted out on the port side, with the pressurized conning tower alongside. The AA placings were to starboard and port of the centreline.

Aircraft
This I-400 mounts an Aichi M6A1 'Seiran' floatplane. The Seirans were launched from a 26m (85ft) Type 4 No. 2 Model 10 compressed-air catapult, rising at a shallow angle from the hangar door.

Endurance
Despite the consumption needs of four engines, the I-400 could carry enough fuel to cruise for 68,524km (37,000nm; 42,579 miles) at 26km/h (14 knots; 16mph) and maintain a patrol for 90 days.

COVERT PROPERTIES

The boat was given a coating of anechoic material formed from gum, asbestos and adhesive, to reduce its detectability, and also fitted with demagnetizing cables. A snorkel of fixed rather than retractable type was installed during a refit in May 1945. Day and night periscopes of German design were included along with a telescopic radar mast on the tower. At times a dummy funnel was placed behind the bridge to hide the boat's identity.

I-400 CARGO LOADING
Japanese crew form a line to take cargo aboard an I-400. Only two I-400s were commissioned into service in early 1945. Special sea-air missions were intended, including an attempt to block the Panama Canal (the US Navy's most vital artery). Both were sunk as targets in 1946.

HMS *Vagabond* (V-class) (1944)

TYPE • *Submarine* **COUNTRY** • *United Kingdom*

SPECIFICATIONS

Dimensions:	Length: 62m (203ft 1in); Beam: 4.8m (15ft 9in); Draught: 4.8m (15ft 9in)
Displacement:	681 tonnes (750 US tons) surfaced; 752 tonnes (829 US tons) submerged
Propulsion:	Diesel-electric: 2 × diesels of 298kW (400hp), 2 × 307kW (412hp) electric motors, 2 screws
Speed:	20.84km/h (11.25 knots; 12.95mph) surfaced; 19km/h (10 knots; 12mph) submerged
Range:	8704km (4700nm; 5410 miles) surfaced; 55.5km (30nm; 34.5 miles) submerged
Armament:	4 × 533mm (21in) torpedo tubes; 8 torpedoes; 1 × 76mm (3in) 50cal deck gun; 3 × 0.78mm (0.303in) machine guns
Complement:	33

A highly successful type, V-class attack submarines that survived the war served several navies into the 1950s. The V-class was a modification of the U-class, designed in 1941 to be built faster and with greater diving strength than its predecessors.

Left: A V-class submarine control room. HMS Venturer, *with Lieutenant James Launders in command, used its Type 129 ASDIC for an hour, in hydrophone effect mode, while it stalked German U-boat Type IXD2 U-864 off Norway on 9 February 1945, before becoming the first and only submarine so far to sink another submarine while both were below the surface.*

Pressure hull
Resemblance to the U-class was close, but the V-class had a sharper bow design, were 2.4m (8ft) longer, and most importantly the pressure hulls were of 19mm (0.75in) steel rather than 12.7mm (0.5in).

Propulsion
As with the U-class, all V-class submarines had diesel-electric propulsion.

Armament
Armament was four bow-mounted 533mm (21in) torpedo tubes, with 8–10 torpedoes, and a single 76mm (3in) deck gun.

HMS *Vagabond*
Commissioned on 19 September 1944, *Vagabond* was powered by two six-cylinder Davey-Paxman engines generating 298kW (400hp) compared to the original U-class's 229kW (307hp) Admiralty diesels.

ASBESTOS

Asbestos, prized for its fire-resistant qualities, was widely used in submarine building and running, sometimes in unexpected ways. Palladized asbestos was incorporated in the catalytic scrubbers that reduced hydrogen in the V-class's battery exhaust. Asbestos was one of the substances used in anechoic coating of submarine hulls, and also in internal fireproofing.

HMS *VORACIOUS* (P78)
Here the V-class submarine HMS *Voracious* (P78) pulls into an Australian harbour on 8 November 1945. The official designation of these vessels was 'V-class long hull'.

Type XXIII (1944)

TYPE • *Submarine* **COUNTRY** • *Germany*

SPECIFICATIONS (U-2326)

Dimensions:	Length: 34.68m (113ft 9in); Beam: 3.02m (9ft 11in); Draught: 3.66m (12ft)
Displacement:	237.7 tonnes (262 US tons) surfaced; 262 tonnes (289 US tons) submerged
Propulsion:	469.8kW (630hp) diesel, 426.5kW (572hp) electric motor, creep motor of 26kW (35hp), single screw
Speed:	18km/h (9.7 knots; 11mph) surfaced; 23km/h (12.5 knots; 14.4mph) submerged
Range:	4815km (2600nm; 2992 miles) surfaced; 359km (194nm; 223 miles) submerged
Armament:	2 × bow torpedo tubes
Complement:	14

This urgently needed coastal patrol submarine shared many characteristics of the Type XXI. *U-2321*, the class leader, was laid down on 10 March 1944 and commissioned on 12 June that year, – an indication of high priority.

Below: The small Type XXIII boat had a short range and was lightly armed, but its high underwater speed made it a potentially deadly opponent in coastal waters. U-2326 *survived the war, surrendering at Dundee on 14 May 1945.*

Tower
The tower was teardrop-shaped, tapering to a point, as was the stern. A single periscope, contained inside the tower casing with the snorkel, was fitted at the back of the tiny open bridge.

Countermeasures
Radar countermeasures began in August 1942 with the cumbersome FuMB-1 (Funkmessbeobachtungsgerät), using a makeshift antenna.

Hull
The streamlined hull formation was designed for submerged speed and silence. In cross-section, the forward part of the hull was of expanded figure-of-eight form, with the tubes above and the battery compartment in a narrower lower section.

Machinery
The machinery had to be as compact as possible: a single MWM RS-348 469.8kW (630hp) diesel and an AEG GU 4463/8 426.5kW (572hp) electric motor.

NO GUNS

The Type XXIII carried no guns and presumably relied on its nine-second crash-diving ability to avoid aerial attack – it could go down to 180m (590ft). The operational Type XXIIIs were appreciated by crews for their manoeuvrability both on the surface and submerged. While the surface speed was moderate, the submerged speed of 22km/h (12.5 knots; 13.8mph) could get them out of depth charge attacks, assuming the boat was detected.

U-2321
U-2321, a Type XXIII submarine, is here seen (right) in a floating drydock at the Deutsche Werft AG, Hamburg, Finkenwerder, prior to the end of World War II.

USS *Tench* (Tench class) (1944)

TYPE • *Submarine* **COUNTRY** • *United States*

SPECIFICATIONS
USS Tench (SS-417)

Dimensions:	Length: 95m (311ft 8in); Beam: 8.33m (27ft 3in); Draught: 5.18m (17ft)
Displacement:	1800 tonnes (1984 US tons) surfaced; 2455 tonnes (2706 US tons) submerged
Propulsion:	4 diesel generator engines of a combined 4026kW (5400hp), 4 511kW (685hp) electric motors, two screws
Speed:	39km/h (21 knots; 24mph) surfaced; 16.6km/h (9 knots; 10mph) submerged
Range:	20,372km (11,000nm; 12,659 miles) surfaced; 176km (95nm; 109 miles) submerged
Armament:	10 × 533mm (21in) torpedo tubes; 28 torpedoes; 1 × 127mm (5in) deck gun; 1 × Bofors 40mm (1.5in) and 1 × twin Oerlikon 20mm (0.79in) AA gun
Complement:	81

The US Navy's final submarine class of the war served in modernized form for another 30 years. Ten Tench-class were completed in time for war service. They were almost identical in externals to the Balao boats, though the fairwater was even shorter.

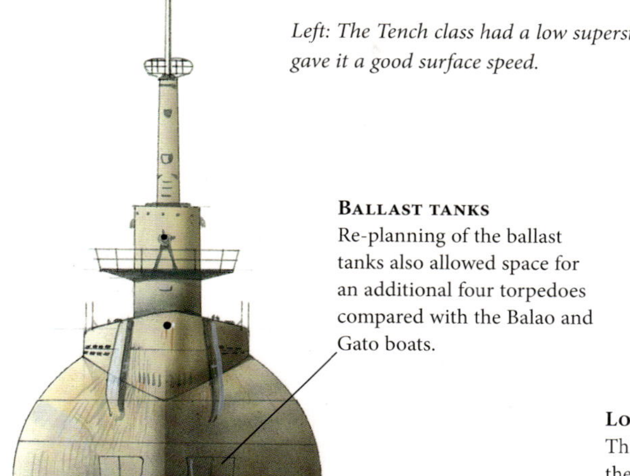

Left: The Tench class had a low superstructure and hull profile, as well as streamlined lines that gave it a good surface speed.

Ballast tanks
Re-planning of the ballast tanks also allowed space for an additional four torpedoes compared with the Balao and Gato boats.

Loop antenna
This was mounted between the periscopes, although later Tench-class boats had it mounted on a bracket aft of the SJ mast.

USS *Tench* (SS-417)
Forward-diving planes were stowed ready-tilted in dive position so that when extended they would immediately force the bow down. Diving to periscope depth could be achieved in 30–40 seconds.

DECK ARMAMENT
As designed, the *Tench* boats carried a single 127mm (5in) 25-cal gun aft of the tower and two 40mm (1.5in) AA guns on the fairwater platforms. Spindle mounts for portable .50-cal machine guns were mounted on the bridge and alongside the fairwater.

ACCOMMODATION
From stem to stern, the compartments consisted of a forward torpedo room with escape trunk; officers' quarters (above the forward battery); control room, with pump room, stores and access hatch to conning tower above; crew's mess and crew's quarters, with aft battery below; forward engine room; aft engine room; machine room with manoeuvring room above; aft torpedo room. Crew accommodation was the best of all wartime submarines.

Landing Ship Tank, Mk III (1943)

TYPE • *Landing craft* **COUNTRY** • *United States/Canada/United Kingdom*

SPECIFICATIONS

Dimensions:	Length: 105.8m (347ft 6in); Beam: 16.84m (55ft 3in); Draught: 3.78m (12ft 5in)
Displacement:	2300 tonnes (2535 US tons) standard; 4980 tonnes (5490 US tons) deep load
Propulsion:	2 Admiralty 3-drum boilers with 2-shaft VTE, developing 4101kW (5500hp)
Speed:	25km/h (13.5 knots; 15.5mph)
Armour:	None
Armament:	4 × 40mm Bofors AA guns; 6 × 20mm AA guns (or 10 × 20mm AA guns)
Complement:	118 to 190

The LST(2) proved to be a successful design but there were simply not enough of them available to meet British and US demands in the later years of the war. To remedy this the UK developed another class of LST, the LST Mk III or LST(3).

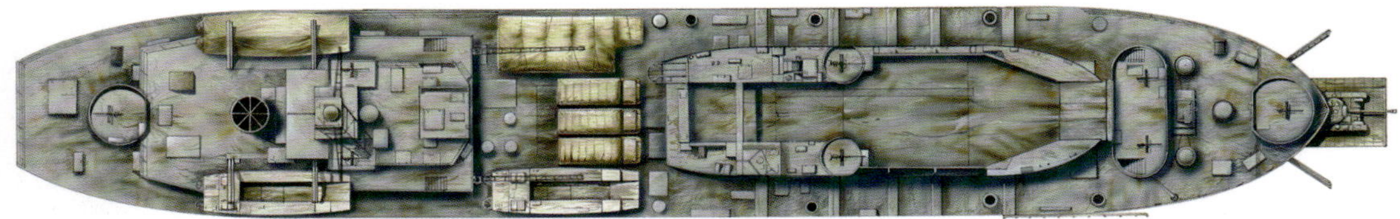

Above: A deck plan of the LST(3). The LST(3)s proved to be remarkably versatile and after the war most remained in service even into the 1970s.

LCA transporter
As well as the tanks, vehicles and infantry, the LST(3) could carry five Landing Craft Assault (LCA), or similar craft, and one LCT (5) or LCT (6) on the upper deck.

Capacity
The LST(3)s were true maritime heavy lifters. The ships could carry 15 40-ton tanks or 20 25-ton tanks, plus 14 three-ton trucks and up to 170 troops.

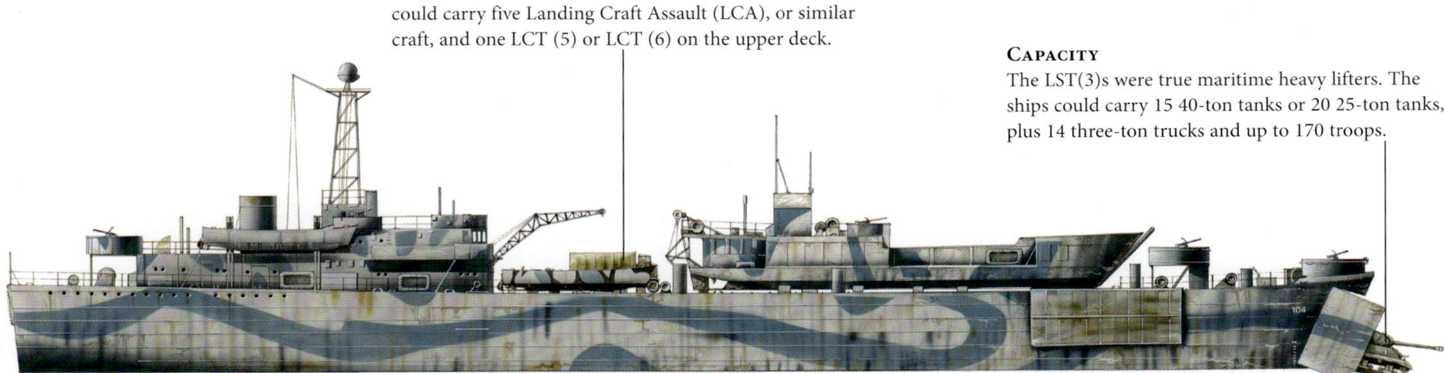

LST-3043
The LST(3)s were all launched between 1944 and 1945. A total of 62 were built in US and Canadian yards. More were ordered but some hulls were diverted to become merchant ships and others were cancelled at the end of the war.

PREDECESSORS

Britain built its own range of specialist amphibious warfare ships, large and small, including tank landing ships (LSTs). US-built LSTs were known as LST Mk IIs or LST(2)s. However, all LSTs had British design roots which could be traced back to the LST Mk I or LST(1). The LST(2) was a compromise between the sea-going qualities of the first British-designed tank landing ships and the simplicity and ease of construction that came with the larger landing craft then being built.

Landing Ship Medium (Rocket) (1944)

TYPE • *Landing craft* **COUNTRY** • *United States*

SPECIFICATIONS

Dimensions:	Length: 62.03m (203ft 6in); Beam: 10m (34ft); Draught: 1.63m (5ft 4in) light
Displacement:	1194 tonnes (1316 US tons) fully loaded
Propulsion:	2 General Motors Cleveland diesels, 2088kW (2800shp), 2 screws
Speed:	24.4km/h (13.2 knots; 15.2mph)
Range:	9300km (5000nm; 5800 miles)
Armament:	1 × 127mm (5in)/38-cal gun; 2 × Bofors 40mm (1.5in) guns; 3 × Oerlikon 20mm (0.79) cannon; 75 × 4-rail Mark 36 automatic rocket launchers on topside rocket deck; 30 × 6-rail Mark 30 launchers mounted along gunwales (removed early April 1945)
Complement:	81

The Landing Ship Medium (Rocket) was a curious vessel designed purposely to bombard the shorelines of landing beaches with ripples of '3 inch' rockets. The ship was used by both the Americans and the British.

Right: USS LCS-6 photographed from LSM(R)-509 in Lock 41 on the Ohio River, October 1945. Landing Craft, Support (LCS) vessels could be adapted for a range of purposes, and were armed with three guns and 10 rocket launchers.

Rocket launchers
The ship was armed with 75 four-rail Mark 36 automatic rocket launchers on the topside rocket deck and 30 six-rail Mark 30 launchers mounted along the gunwales.

Trajectory
The rocket racks were set to send the unguided rockets on a high arcing trajectory, the intention being to drop the rockets down behind enemy forward defences.

AA defence
For air defence, the LSM(R)vessels carried a mix of Bofors and Oerlikon automatic cannon.

Main gun
In addition to its rockets, the ship was fitted with a single 127mm (5in) naval gun.

ROCKET BARRAGE

The 3-inch rockets fired from the LSM(R) and larger LCT(R) vessels each carried a 27kg (60lb) warhead and could reach ranges of up to about 1600m (1750yd). Individually, the weapons were quite inaccurate, but when fired en masse the area effects compensated for that imprecision. In the Pacific where the LSM(R)s served, however, sometimes barrages did little more than erase sand and coral or churn the water.

Right: USS Blackstone River, *LSMR-403, was laid down on 6 January 1945 at Charleston, SC, launched on 26 January 1945 and commissioned on 25 April 1945. It did not see combat in World War II, but it did during the Korean War (1950–53).*

USS *Missouri* (Iowa class) (1944)

TYPE • *Battleship* **COUNTRY** • *United States*

SPECIFICATIONS

Dimensions:	Length: 270.4m (887ft 3in); Beam: 33m (108ft 2in); Draught: 11.5m (37ft 9in)
Displacement:	52,834 tonnes (52,000 tons); 58,372 tonnes (57,540 tons) full load
Propulsion:	8 Babcock & Wilcox boilers, 4 General Electric steam turbines, 4 screws, 158,088kW (212,000shp)
Armament:	9 × 406mm (16in) guns; 20 × 127mm (5in) guns; 60 × 40mm (1.6in) 4-barreled AA guns
Armour:	Belt: 310mm (12.2in); Barbettes: 440–287mm (17.3–11.3in); Turret faces: 500mm (19.7in); Deck: 152mm (6in)
Range:	28,000km (15,000nm; 17,400 miles) at 28km/h (15 knots; 17mph)
Speed:	33 knots (61.2km/h; 38mph)
Complement:	1921

The USS *Missouri* (BB-63) was the last of the Iowa class to be completed, being commissioned on 11 June 1944 at the New York Navy Yard. In profile and general detail, the ships were very much alike.

Left: A commercial tug escorts the battleship USS Missouri *(BB-63) as the ship prepares to dock at Naval Air Station, North Island.*

Engines
The engines were reliable: *Missouri* is recorded as steaming continuously for 58 days with no mechanical problems.

Main guns
As with the other ships in the class, the main armament was nine Mk 7 406mm (16in) guns in three turrets. Each gun could be aimed and fired independently.

Hull design
One unwelcome feature of the widening hull design was that the ship's 'shoulders' pushed out waves that broke against the sea waves and caused heavy spray to break over the bridge.

Rudders
Two rudders were fitted, each with a protected area of 31.6sq m (340sq ft). Despite their great length, the class was regarded as easily manoeuvrable.

LATER SERVICE

Missouri is famous as the site of Japan's formal surrender on 31 August 1945. However, between periods in reserve, it was put back in service in 1950–55 and 1984–91, including during the Korean War and Gulf War. In the 1950s a nuclear-capped shell was made specifically for the 406mm (16in) guns. Weighing 862kg (1900lb), its estimated yield was between 15 and 20 kilotons of TNT. Information on whether these shells were actually carried on the ships remains classified.

MUSEUM SHIP

Missouri was finally decommissioned on 1 March 1992. As a museum ship, the battleship today stands moored to a pier at Naval Station Pearl Harbor, Hawaii.

USS *Guam* (1944)

TYPE • *Battleship* **COUNTRY** • *United States*

The last battlecruisers to be built, the two-ship Alaska class was supposed to be an answer to the German Navy's *Scharnhorst* and *Gneisenau*. By the time *Guam* was launched in 1944, the answer was no longer required.

SPECIFICATIONS

Dimensions:	Length: 264.4m (808ft); Beam: 27.8m (91ft 1in); Draught: 9.7m (31ft 10in)
Displacement:	30,257 tonnes (29,779 tons); 34,803 tonnes (34,253 tons) full load
Propulsion:	8 Babcock & Wilcox boilers, 4 General Electric geared turbines, 4 screws, 114,092kW (153,000shp)
Armament:	9 × 305mm (12in) guns; 12 × 127mm (5in) AA guns; 56 × 40mm (1.6in) guns; 34 × 20mm (0.8in) AA guns
Armour:	Belt: 229–127mm (9–5in); Turrets: 325mm (12.8in); Deck: 102mm (4in)
Range:	22,094km (12,000nm; 13,700 miles) at 15 knots (27.6km/h; 17.26mph)
Speed:	33 knots (61.1km/h; 38mph)
Complement:	1517

Right: The flag is raised over Guam *for the first time during her commissioning ceremony at the Philadelphia Navy Yard, 17 September 1944.*

Elevation
The 127mm (5in) guns could elevate to 85° for AA fire (their number was increased to 68 in 1945) and the 20mm to 90°.

Engine rooms
Each engine room had two GE turbogenerators, rated at 1000kW, 450 volt AC, and there were two diesel-powered generators of similar capacity, one at each end of the machinery space.

Armour
The Alaska class was armoured only against 305mm (12in) shells. Total thickness of the three armoured decks over the magazines was 169mm (6.65in).

Boilers
Steam was raised by eight Babcock & Wilcox express boilers. Fitted with superheaters of the same type as the Iowa-class ships, they worked at a maximum pressure of 44.6kg/sq cm (634psi).

FIREPOWER

Nine Mk 8 305mm (12in) guns were carried. The three-gun turret, with each gun elevating independently up to 40°, was preferred for its compactness. Shell weight was 57kg (1140lb) and the muzzle velocity of 762m/s (2500ft/s) gave a maximum range of 35,271m (38,573yd). Magazine capacity was 1500 rounds. The Mk 8 was generally regarded as an excellent gun, capable of penetrating deck armour 121mm (4.75in) thick at a range of 25,055m (27,400yd).

GUNNERY PRACTICE
Guam tests out her main guns at distant targets. She entered service in early 1945 and operated with *Alaska* in supporting carrier raids on the Japanese mainland and patrols in the China Sea. Both ships went into reserve after only three years' service. In 1961 they were sold for scrapping.

Shinano (1944)

The *Shinano* was to have been another mighty Yamato-class battleship, but changing needs brought conversion to the largest carrier yet built. However, it was sunk even before it went into operational service.

SPECIFICATIONS

Dimensions:	Length: 265.8m (872ft 1in); Beam: 36.3m (119ft 1in); Draught: 10.3m (33ft 10in)
Displacement:	65,800 tonnes (64,800 tons); 73,000 tonnes (72,000 tons) full load
Propulsion:	12 Kampon boilers, 4 geared turbines, 4 shafts, 110,000kW (150,000shp)
Speed:	50km/h (27 knots; 31mph)
Range:	19,000km (10,000nm; 12,000 miles)
Armament:	8 x twin 127mm (5in) Type 89 guns; 35 x triple 25mm Type 96 guns; 12 x 28-barrel 127mm rocket launchers
Aircraft:	139
Complement:	2400

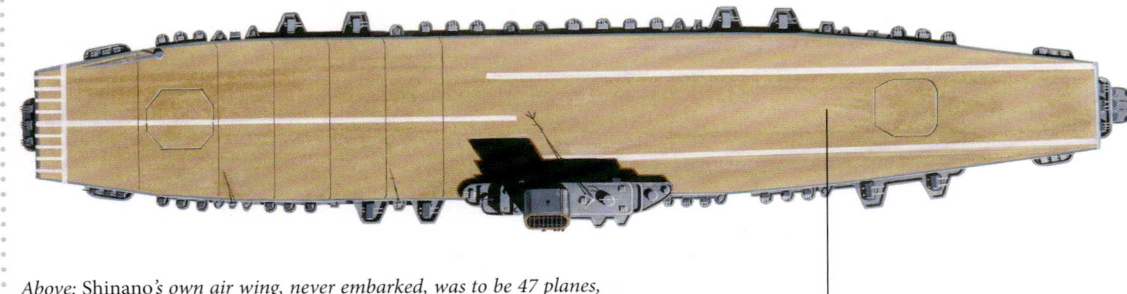

Above: Shinano*'s own air wing, never embarked, was to be 47 planes, intended to provide combat air cover in the event of aerial attack.*

Flight deck
The flight deck itself was 256m (839ft 11in) long and 40m (131ft 3in) wide and was partly armoured. Like other Japanese carriers, multiple arrester wires were fitted, 10 towards the stern and five towards the bow, to allow for forward landings.

Hangar area
The hangar area, 163.4m by 33.8m (536ft by 111ft) had unarmoured sides and much of it was open-sided – the enclosed hangar sides of earlier carriers had contributed to their destruction – although with a series of fire curtains to close off sections.

Island
The island was placed slightly forward of midships and sponsoned well out to give the maximum flight deck and plane parking area. The funnel was integrated with the island.

Armour
The Yamato-class had 400mm (15.7in) belt armour, reduced on *Shinano* to 205mm (8in), and lateral anti-torpedo bulges were fitted, backed up internally by armoured and watertight bulkheads, making a double hull below the waterline and a triple bottom.

OHKA ROCKET PLANES

Shinano was transporting 30 Ohka MXY-7 rocket-powered attack aircraft when it was sunk. These were kamikaze craft, essentially human-guided flying bombs, with a 1200kg (2650lb) high-explosive bomb forming the nose of the craft. Normally transported beneath Mitsubishi G4M2e 'Betty' bombers, they would be released and glide towards the target vessel. The pilot would then fire the solid-fuel rocket motors and crash-dive his plane on to the target.

***SHINANO*'S FATE**
Shinano was sunk on 29 November 1944 off the coast of Japan, hit by four torpedoes from the US Navy submarine *Archerfish*. A total of 1435 lives were lost.

Type I-201 (1945)

TYPE • *Submarine* **COUNTRY** • *Japan*

SPECIFICATIONS

Dimensions:	Length: 79m (259ft); Beam: 5.8m (19ft); Draught: 7m (23ft)
Displacement:	1312 tonnes (1446 US tons) surfaced; 1470 tonnes (1620 US tons) submerged
Propulsion:	2 diesels of 1025kW (1375hp), 4 × 932kW (1250hp) electric motors, 2 screws
Speed:	29.2km/h (15.75 knots; 18mph) surfaced; 35km/h (19 knots; 21.8mph) submerged
Range:	27,780km (15,000nm; 17,262 miles) surfaced; 250km (135nm; 155 miles) submerged
Armament:	4 × 533mm (21in) torpedo tubes; 10 × torpedoes; 2 × Type 96 25mm (1in) AA guns
Crew:	50

By late 1943 the Imperial Japanese Navy (IJN) command had to accept that its existing submarines were simply incapable of defending themselves against the range of US anti-submarine technologies. The powerful Type 201 was Japan's belated hope to stem the US seaborne

Below: In the planning and formulation of this design, there is some evidence of cooperation and exchange of information between Japan and Germany, and it is probable that some elements of the late German designs were incorporated in I-201.

Weaponry
As with previous IJN classes, the four torpedo tubes were all in the bow, with six reloads. The two deck-mounted 25mm Type 96 AA guns, forward and aft of the tower, were retractable to reduce underwater resistance.

Hull construction
Electric welding was used as much as possible in the hull construction, with the complete hull assembled from prefabricated sections transported to the launch slip.

Electric motors
Four electric motors, two in tandem on each shaft and linked by a tail clutch, developed 3728.5kW (5000shp) for submerged power.

AERIAL VIEW
As this aerial view shows, the beam of the Type I-201 was unusually narrow for the boat's length, with retractable forward dive planes in order to reduce underwater resistance, though low-set broad horizontal stern fins increased it to 9.2m (30ft).

HISTORY

Although Japan had built a small experimental high-speed submarine in 1938, this had not been followed up and the boat had been scrapped in 1940. It was not until October 1943 that the formal request was made for an attack submarine that would have high submerged speed and silent running. Using the 1938 design as a basis, planning was rapid and the first of the new Sen-Taka class, *I-201*, was laid down at Kure Naval Arsenal in March 1944, launched in July and commissioned after trials in February 1945. Only two more were completed.

Index

Picture Credits

Alamy: 16 bottom (The Picture Art Collection), 19 (World History Archive), 24 (Pictorial Press), 33 (De Luan), 54 top (World History Archive), 54 bottom (The Print Collector), 70 (De Luan), 121 bottom (Granger Historical Picture Archive), 141 top (Shawshots), 149 (JuistLand), 162 (Prestor Pictures), 172 top (Viktor Karasev), 172 bottom (Pukhov Konstantin), 174 (BNA Photographic), 177 top (Interfoto), 177 bottom (Oleg Konin), 187 top (Interfoto), 188 (Associated Press), 233 (BTEU/NEDMIL), 235 (Claude Thibault), 258 (Jimlop collection), 265 (Panzermeister), 271 (Paul Grove), 272 top (Zoonar), 292 (Interfoto), 297 bottom (Nikolay Mukhorin), 298 bottom (Michael Cremin), 314 top (Interfoto), 326 (Trinity Mirror/Mirrorpix), 335 top (Hilary Morgan), 336 (Pictorial Press), 343 (mccool), 344 top (piemags), 344 bottom (The Picture Art Collection), 345 top (Vintage Mechanics), 350 top (colaimages), 360 bottom (dpa picture alliance), 364 & 365 bottom (Hilary Morgan), 371 bottom & 372 top (dpa picture alliance), 372 bottom & 377 top (Trinity Mirror/Mirrorpix), 398 top (Associated Press), 414 bottom (Old Paper Studios)

Alamy/Chronicle: 49 bottom, 51 top, 81, 93, 112, 118, 130, 329 bottom, 371 top, 399 top

Alamy/Piemags: 180, 195, 232, 276 bottom both, 290 top, 331, 365 top, 366, 377 bottom, 389 both, 407 both, 414 top

Alamy/Sueddeutsche Zeitung: 43, 122, 154, 160, 163, 173, 281 bottom, 287-289 all, 316 bottom, 362 both

Amber Books: 13, 15, 17, 25-31 all, 35, 39, 40 both, 45, 50 both, 53, 59, 60, 65 top, 66, 68, 69 both, 71, 75, 76, 82-84 all, 86, 88, 90-92 all, 94-99 all, 103, 104 top right, 105, 110, 113, 117, 126, 127 bottom, 128, 129, 133, 134, 136, 138, 152, 156, 157, 159, 161 bottom, 164-167 all, 169, 170, 178, 185, 190, 192, 193, 196 bottom, 198,199, 201, 208, 210 bottom, 212, 216, 217, 221, 223, 224, 225 top, 228, 234, 238, 241, 244, 251, 252, 254, 255, 260, 264, 270, 272 bottom, 273, 286, 290 bottom, 291 bottom, 297 top, 304 top both, 306 top, 313 bottom, 337 top, 380 bottom, 383, 392, 394 bottom, 397, 401 top, 403

ASL Photos: 14, 20 top, 21, 23, 34, 37, 44, 55-57 all, 63, 64, 67, 72, 73 both, 78-80 all, 85, 87, 89, 101, 102, 104 top left & bottom, 111 both, 116, 120 both, 121 top, 123 both, 124, 131, 135, 137, 139, 142,145-148 all, 150 both, 153, 155 both, 158, 171 top, 176, 179 both, 181, 183, 184, 189, 194, 196 top, 197 both, 202, 203, 204 top, 209, 214, 215, 220, 222, 227, 231, 239, 240, 245, 247, 249, 250, 253, 257, 261-263 all, 267 both, 274, 276 top, 277, 279 both, 280 top, 281 top, 282 both, 283, 284 bottom, 285 bottom, 291 top, 293, 294 bottom, 298 top, 299 both, 300 top, 301, 304 bottom, 305 top, 306 bottom, 307 top, 308, 310, 311, 313 top, 314 bottom, 315 both, 317, 318, 320, 335 bottom, 340, 341 bottom, 345 bottom, 347, 352 both, 355, 357 bottom, 361 both, 373 both, 376 both, 380 top, 388, 391, 393, 404 bottom, 409-411 all , 412 bottom, 415 top, 418 both, 421, 427 top, 428 top, 431 both

Nik Cornish/STAVKA: 168 both, 171 bottom, 191, 242

Creative Commons Attribution-Share Alike 3.0 Unported License: 278

DAF: 175

Dreamstime: 319 (Mikhail Blajenov), 321 bottom (Elliott Cowand Jr)

Getty Images: 12 (Royal Air Force Museum), 22 (Photo 12), 36 (ullstein bild), 38 (Hulton), 41 (Sovfoto), 48 (Historical), 51 bottom (Keystone), 62 (ullstein bild), 119 (Fox Photos), 161 top (AFP), 186 & 187 bottom (IWM), 204 bottom (Corbis), 207 (ullstein bild), 210 top (Hulton Archive), 211 (Royal Air Force Museum), 219 (Horace Abrahams), 225 bottom (Keystone), 229 (IWM), 230 (Express), 237 (ullstein bild), 243 (SovFoto), 246 both (Keystone), 256 & 259 (Fred Ramage), 266 (ullstein bild), 268 (Photo 12), 300 bottom (PhotoQuest), 316 top (ullstein bild), 337 bottom (Central Press), 342 (Corbis), 385 (De Agostini), 402 (Charles E. Brown/Royal Air Force Museum)

Allan C Green/State Library of Victoria: 332 bottom, 425 top

Nationaal Archief, The Hague: 425 bottom

National Archives & Records Administration: 107, 109, 284 top, 285 top, 328 bottom, 413 top, 429

Naval History & Heritage Command: 10, 32, 42, 46 bottom, 47 both, 52, 61, 74, 77, 108, 114, 115, 127 top, 205 top, 322-325 all, 327 bottom, 328 top, 330 bottom, 332 top, 333 both, 338, 346, 348 top, 349 both, 350 bottom, 351 both, 353 bottom, 356 both, 358-359 all, 367-370 all, 374 both, 378-379 all, 381, 382 both, 384 both, 386-387 all, 390, 394 top, 395-396 all, 398 bottom, 400 bottom, 401 bottom, 404 top, 405-406 all, 408, 413 bottom, 415 bottom, 416 both, 419, 420 both, 424 both, 426 bottom, 427 bottom, 428 bottom, 430, 432-435 all, 437 both

Public Domain: 16 top, 18, 20 bottom, 49 top, 58 both, 65 bottom, 106 both, 140, 144, 151, 182, 200, 206, 218, 236, 280 bottom, 294 top, 296, 303, 307 bottom, 309, 329 top, 330 top, 339 both, 341 top, 348 bottom, 353 top, 354 both, 357 top, 360 top, 363, 375, 399 bottom, 400 top, 412 top, 422 both, 426 top, 438, 439

Shutterstock: 321 top (Pixiaomo)

Ukrainian State Archive: 213, 248, 295, 305 bottom

U.S. Air Force: 125

U.S. Department of Defense: 269, 436 both

U.S. Marine Corps: 205 bottom

U.S. Navy: 46 top,141 bottom, 327 top, 334, 417 both, 423 both

ARTWORK CREDITS:

All artworks courtesy Amber Books Ltd, except the following:

Edward Jackson/artbyedo: 13 (both), 40, 43 (lower), 44 (lower), 45 (both), 57 (both), 63, 78 (top), 88 (both), 106

David Bocquelet/Tank Encyclopedia: 149 (all), 160 (all), 162 (all), 174 (all), 176 (lower), 200, 202 (all), 203 (lower), 204, 205, 208 (all), 210, 218 (lower), 221 (lower), 224, 225, 226 (top and middle), 232 (all), 233, 244–245 (all), 249 (all), 252 (all), 256, 267, 268 (top), 270, 273 (all), 285, 302 (top), 305, 311 (all), 312 (lower), 317 (all), 339, 351, 354, 364, 367, 382, 387, 400, 422

Oliver Missing (www.o5m6.de): 146 (all), 147 (all), 156 (all), 167 (all), 172, 178 (top), 191 (all), 192 (top), 198 (lower), 213 (all), 215 (all), 240–243 (all), 247–248 (all), 261 (all), 271, 272, 280, 292–293 (all), 295 (top), 296–297 (all), 302 (top), 308 (all), 319 (top)

Rolando Ugolini: 35 (all), 29 (lower), 41 (both), 107 (lower), 108 (both)

Teasel Studios: 12 (lower), 20, 47, 68 (lower), 70 (lower), 102 (both)